Environmental Economics

An Introduction

Environmental Economics

An Introduction   Seventh Edition

Barry C. Field
Department of Resource Economics
University of Massachusetts Amherst

Martha K. Field
Department of Business and
Information Technology
Greenfield Community College

Mc
Graw
Hill
Education

ENVIRONMENTAL ECONOMICS: AN INTRODUCTION, SEVENTH EDITION
Published by McGraw-Hill, a business unit of The McGraw-Hill Companies, Inc., 1221 Avenue of
the Americas, New York, NY 10020. Copyright © 2017 by The McGraw-Hill Companies, Inc. All
rights reserved. Printed in the United States of America. Previous editions © 2013, 2009, and 2006.
No part of this publication may be reproduced or distributed in any form or by any means, or
stored in a database or retrieval system, without the prior written consent of The McGraw-Hill
Companies, Inc., including, but not limited to, in any network or other electronic storage or
transmission, or broadcast for distance learning.

Some ancillaries, including electronic and print components, may not be available
to customers outside the United States.

This book is printed on acid-free paper.

2 3 4 5 6 7 8 9 DOC 21 20 19 18 17 16

ISBN 978-0-07-802189-3
MHID 0-07-802189-8

Senior Vice President, Products & Markets: *Kurt L. Strand*
Vice President, General Manager, Products & Markets: *Marty Lange*
Vice President, Content Design & Delivery: *Kimberly Meriwether David*
Managing Director: *James Heine*
Senior Brand Manager: *Katie Hoenicke*
Director, Product Development: *Rose Koos*
Senior Product Developer: *Christina Kouvelis*
Product Developer: *Sarah Otterness*
Marketing Manager: *Virgil Lloyd*
Director, Content Design & Delivery: *Linda Aveharius*
Program Manager: *Faye M. Herrig*
Content Project Managers: *Jeni L. McAtee, Karen Jozefowicz*
Buyer: *Susan K. Culbertson*
Content Licensing Specialist: *Shannon Manderscheid*
Cover Image: *Design Pics / Natural Selection Craig Tuttle*
Compositor: *MPS Limited*
Printer: *R. R. Donnelley*

Cover image: *View of a mountain meadow of purple lupines (Lupinus sp.) in bloom, Paradise Valley,
Mount Rainier National Park, Washington state, USA.*

All credits appearing on page or at the end of the book are considered to be an extension of the
copyright page.

Library of Congress Cataloging-in-Publication Data

Field, Barry C., | Field, Martha K., author.
    Environmental economics : an introduction/Barry C. Field, Department of Resource
    Economics, University of Massachusetts/Amherst, Martha K. Field, Department of Business
    and Information Technology, Greenfield Community College.
    Seventh Edition. | Dubuque : McGraw-Hill Education, 2016. | The mcgraw-hill series | Revised
    edition of the authors' Environmental economics, 2013.
    LCCN 2015047833 | ISBN 9780078021893 (alk. paper)
    LCSH: Environmental economics. | Economic development—Environmental aspects.
    LCC HC79.E5 F47 2016 | DDC 333.7—dc23
    LC record available at http://lccn.loc.gov/2015047833

mheducation.com/highered

To Leslie, Sidney, and Tory

About the Authors

Barry C. Field is Professor Emeritus of Resource Economics at the University of Massachusetts Amherst. Previously he taught at the University of Miami and The George Washington University. He received his B.S. and M.S. degrees from Cornell University and his Ph.D. from the University of California at Berkeley.

At the University of Massachusetts he has devoted many years to teaching environmental economics to students at all levels and has worked to develop an undergraduate major in environmental and resource economics.

Martha K. Field is Professor of Economics at Greenfield Community College, where she has taught environmental economics for many years. She has taught at the University of Massachusetts, Mount Holyoke College, Westfield State College, Holyoke Community College, and the Consumer Cooperative at Gomel, Belarus. She received a B.S. and M.S. from the University of Massachusetts and holds a Ph.D. from the University of Connecticut.

They reside in Leverett, Massachusetts.

Contents in Brief

Contents

Preface

When our descendants look back at the last part of the 20th century, and now at the beginning of the 21st, we want them to be able to say: "That's when they began to take the degradation of the natural environment, with its threats to human life and the life of the planet, seriously." Furthermore, we would like them to be able to see that around this time we took serious steps to halt and reverse this process. This book is an introduction to environmental economics, one way of approaching the steps that need to be taken. It's about the way human decisions affect the quality of the environment, how human values and institutions shape our demands for improvement in the quality of that environment, and, most especially, about how to design effective public policies to bring about these improvements.

Problems of environmental quality are not something new; in fact, history is filled with bleak examples of environmental degradation, from deforestation by ancient peoples to mountains of horse manure in urban areas in the days before automobiles. But today's world is different. For one thing, many people in economically developed countries, having reached high levels of material well-being, are beginning to ask questions: What good is great material wealth if it comes at the cost of large-scale disruptions of the ecosystem by which we are nourished? More fundamental, perhaps, is the fact that with contemporary economic, demographic, and technological developments around the world, the associated environmental repercussions are becoming much more widespread and lethal. What once were localized environmental impacts, easily rectified, have now become widespread effects that may very well turn out to be irreversible. Indeed some of our most worrisome concerns today are about global environmental impacts.

It is no wonder, then, that the quality of the natural environment has become a major focus of public concern. As we would expect, people have responded in many ways. Environmental interest groups and advocates have become vocal at every political level, especially in those countries with open political systems. Politicians have taken environmental issues into their agendas; some have sought to become environmental statespersons. Environmental law has burgeoned, becoming a specialty in many law schools. Thousands of environmental agencies have appeared in the public sector, from local conservation commissions to environmental agencies at the United Nations. At the scientific level, environmental problems have become a focus for chemists, biologists, engineers, and many others. And within economics there has developed *environmental economics*, the subject of this book.

Environmental economics focuses on all the different facets of the connection between environmental quality and the economic behavior of individuals and groups of people. There is the fundamental question of how the economic system shapes economic incentives in ways that lead to environmental degradation as well as improvement. There are major problems in measuring the benefits and costs of environmental quality changes, especially intangible ones. There is a set of complicated macroeconomic questions: for example, the connection between economic growth and environmental impacts and the feedback effects of environmental laws on growth. And there are the critical issues of designing environmental policies that are both effective and equitable.

The strength of environmental economics lies in the fact that it is analytical and deals with concepts such as efficiency, trade-offs, costs, and benefits. Many believe strongly that the times call for more direct political action, more consciousness-raising, more political-organizing, and, especially, more representation and influence of environmental interests on the political scene. Nobody can doubt this. We live in a complicated world, however, where human problems abound; domestically we have health care, drugs, education, violence, and other critical issues, all competing for attention and public resources. Throughout the world, vast numbers of people struggle to alter their political and economic institutions, develop their economies, and raise their material standards of living and well-being.

In these settings, just raising the political heat for environmental issues is necessary but not sufficient. We have to get hard scientific results on how people value environmental quality and how they are hurt when this quality is degraded. We also have to put together environmental policy initiatives that get the maximum impact for the economic and political resources spent. This is where environmental economics comes in. It is a way of examining the difficult trade-off types of questions that all environmental issues entail; it is also a valuable means of inquiring why people behave as they do toward the natural environment, and how we might restructure the current system to rectify harmful practices and inspire favorable behavior.

In fact, the subject is important enough to deserve to be widely available to the nonspecialist. Economics is a discipline that has developed a sophisticated body of theory and applied knowledge. Courses in economics now follow a hierarchy of introductory- and intermediate-level principles that are designed to lead students along and prepare them for the more advanced applications courses. But these run the risk of closing off the subject, making it inaccessible to those who do not want to become specialists. This book is intended, instead, for people who have not necessarily had any economics courses, at least not yet. It was written on the assumption that it's possible to present the major principles of economics in a fairly commonsensical, although rigorous, way and then apply them to questions of environmental quality.

This book is an introduction to the basic principles of environmental economics as they have been developed in the past and as they continue to evolve. The real world, certainly the real world of environmental policy, is much more complicated than these principles would often seem to imply. The examples discussed represent only a sample of the full range of issues that actually exists. If and when you confront that real world of environmental politics and policy, you will find it necessary to adapt these principles to all the details and nuances of reality. Unfortunately, there is not enough space in one book to look at all the ways that environmental economists have found to make the basic concepts and models more specific and relevant to concrete environmental issues. So we stick to the basic ideas and hope they excite your interest enough to make you want to pursue the refinements and adaptations of these ideas as they relate to a subject of growing relevance and importance.

When the first edition was published, there was no way of knowing how many others might be teaching a course similar to the one from which the book sprang: a course in environmental economics for people who have not necessarily had a course in economics. The reception that the previous editions have had, therefore, is gratifying. The comments received, sometimes directly and sometimes via the grapevine, have in general been quite positive. We hope the seventh edition will be as well received.

The basic structure and sequence of chapters in this edition are unchanged although we have reorganized and updated the last section on global issues. The first section of the book is an introduction, beginning with a chapter on what environmental economics is about, followed by one on the basic relationships between the economy and the environment. The next section is devoted to studying the "tools" of analysis, the principles of demand and cost, and the elements of economic efficiency both in market and nonmarket activities. These chapters are not meant to be completely thorough treatments of these theoretical topics; however, given the objective of the book, the introductory chapters are essential. Even those who have had a course in microeconomic principles might find them valuable for purposes of review. Section 2 also contains a chapter in which these economic principles are applied to a simple model of environmental pollution control. In these chapters, as well as the others, we have tried to leaven the presentation with examples taken from current sources, such as in the news media.

Section 3 is on environmental analysis. Here we look closely at some of the techniques that have been developed by environmental economists to answer some of the fundamental value questions that underlie environmental decision making. We focus especially on the principles of benefit–cost analysis. After this we move to Section 4, on the principles of environmental policy design. It begins with a short chapter dealing with the criteria we might use to evaluate policies, then moves on to chapters on the main approaches to environmental quality management.

Sections 5 and 6 contain policy chapters, where we examine current developments in environmental policy with the analytical tools developed earlier. Section 5 is devoted to environmental policy in the United States, covering federal policy on water, air, and toxic materials. It also contains a chapter on environmental issues at the state and local levels, including recycling. Finally, the last section looks at international environmental issues: global climate change, the economics of international environmental agreements, globalization, and economic development and the environment.

The seventh edition contains much new material, including new exhibits and updated figures and tables. It also contains new materials on:

- Carbon taxes — Chapters 1 and 12
- Pollution and GDP in India — Chapter 1
- Oil spills from pipelines and trains — Chapter 2
- Regulatory flexibility — Chapter 9
- European emissions taxes — Chapter 12
- Offset trading — Chapter 13
- Emission rate trading — Chapter 13
- Carbon market in California — Chapter 13
- Controlling greenhouse gas emissions — Chapter 15
- Energy-efficiency gap — Chapter 15
- Burden of proof in toxic testing — Chapter 15
- Social cost of carbon — Chapter 18
- Globalization and the environment — Chapter 18
- Clean Air Act updates — Chapter 5

A collection of relevant web links and additional sources is available on the Web site. Also available is a tutorial for working with graphs. For instructors, the Web site offers an Instructor's Manual available for easy download. To access the Web site associated with this book, please see **www.mhhe.com/field7e.**

Acknowledgments

This text is the result of teaching the subject for many years in the classroom, so first we want to thank all those students through the years who have listened, asked questions, and provided the feedback that shaped the book. Many people have helped review and shape previous editions of the book. Thanks to John Stranlund, University of Massachusetts Amherst; Stephen Holland, University of North Carolina at Greensboro; Jacqueline Geoghegan, Clark University; Roger H. von Haefen, North Carolina State University; Andrew A. Wilson, University of Virginia; Juliette K. Roddy, University of Michigan—Dearborn; John Peter Tiemstra, Calvin College; Mustafa Sawani, Truman State University; Jennifer Peterson, Doane College; Forrest Stephen Trimby, Worcester State College; Hui Li, Eastern Illinois University; Paul C. Huszar, Colorado State University; John R. Stoll, University of Wisconsin—Green Bay; Richard Claycombe, McDaniel College; and Ellen T. Fitzpatrick, State University of New York, Plattsburgh.

Special thanks to Christina Kouvelis, Sarah Otterness, Jeni McAtee and the other folks at McGraw-Hill who continue to represent the book so strongly.

And finally, thanks to Tory, Sidney, and Leslie for your support, love, and insightful comments.

Barry C. Field

Martha K. Field

Section 1

Introduction

This first section contains two introductory chapters. The first is a brief, nontechnical review of some of the main topics and ideas of environmental economics. The second contains a general discussion of the interactions that exist between the economy and the environment, and introduces some fundamental concepts and definitions that are used throughout the book.

Chapter 1

What Is Environmental Economics?

Economics is the study of how and why individuals and groups make decisions about the use and distribution of valuable human and nonhuman resources. It is not solely the study of profit-making businesses making decisions in a capitalist economy. It is much broader than this; it provides a set of analytical tools that can be used to study any situation in which the scarcity of means requires the balancing of competing objectives. It includes, for example, important questions in the behavior of nonprofit organizations, government agencies, and consumers.

Environmental economics is the application of the principles of economics to the study of how environmental resources are managed. Economics is divided into **microeconomics,** the study of the behavior of individuals and small groups, and **macroeconomics,** the study of the economic performance of economies as a whole. Environmental economics draws from both sides, although more from microeconomics than from macroeconomics. It focuses primarily on how and why people make decisions that have consequences for the natural environment. It is concerned also with how economic institutions and policies can be changed to bring these environmental impacts more into balance with human desires and the needs of the ecosystem itself.

One of our first jobs, therefore, is to become acquainted with some of the basic ideas and analytical tools of microeconomics. To do this at the very beginning, however, would risk giving the impression that the tools are more important than their uses. The tools of analysis are not interesting in themselves, but for the understanding, they can give us about why the natural environment becomes degraded, what the consequences of this are, and what can be done effectively to reduce this degradation. For this reason, the first chapter is devoted to sketching out, in commonsense terms, the kinds of questions environmental economists ask and the kinds of answers they seek. After a brief discussion of some general issues, we look at a series of examples of some of the problems addressed in environmental economics.

Economic Analysis

To study economics is to study the way an economy and its institutions are set up, and how individuals and groups make decisions about transforming and managing scarce resources to increase human wealth, in its broadest sense. Environmental economics focuses on a society's natural and environmental resources, and examines the way people make decisions that lead to environmental destruction and environmental improvements.

Environmental economics is an **analytical subject.** We want not only to describe the state of the environment and changes in it, but also to understand why these conditions exist and how we might bring about improvements in environmental quality. This means we will have to introduce a specialized set of concepts and vocabulary. We will also have to use specialized means of expressing connections between important factors that are involved in the environmental quality issues we explore. To do this, economists use what are called **analytical models.** A model is a simplified representation of reality, in the sense that it isolates and focuses on the most important elements of a situation and neglects the others. The models we will use are graphical in nature, and they will be quite simple.[1]

It is important to distinguish between **positive economics** and **normative economics.** Positive economics is the study of what is; normative economics is the study of what ought to be. Positive economics seeks to understand how an economic system actually operates by looking at the way people make decisions in different types of circumstances. A study to show how the housing market reacts to changes in interest rates is an exercise in positive economics. A study to estimate how electric utilities would respond to a new tax on sulfur emissions is also an example of positive economics. However, a study to determine what kind of regulation we ought to adopt for a particular environmental problem is a case of normative economics because it involves more than just knowing how things work; it also involves value judgments. We make use of this distinction repeatedly throughout the book.

The economic approach to environmental issues is to be contrasted with what might be called the **moral approach.** According to the latter, environmental degradation is the result of human behavior that is unethical or immoral. Thus, for example, the reason people pollute is because they lack the moral and ethical strength to refrain from the type of behavior that causes environmental degradation. If this is true, then the way to get people to stop polluting is somehow to increase the general level of environmental morality in the society. In fact, the environmental movement has led a great many people to focus on questions of environmental ethics, exploring the moral dimensions of human impacts on the natural

---

[1] The Web page associated with the book contains a section on working with graphs. See **www .mhhe.com/economics/field7e.**

environment. These moral questions are obviously of fundamental concern to any civilized society. Certainly one of the main reasons environmental issues have been put on the front burner of social concern is the sense of moral responsibility that has led people to take their concerns into the political arena.

But there are practical difficulties with relying on moral reawakening as the main approach to combatting pollution. People don't necessarily have readily available moral buttons to push, and environmental problems are too important to wait for a long process of moral rebuilding. Nor does a sense of moral outrage, by itself, help us make decisions about all the other social goals that also have ethical dimensions: housing, health care, education, crime, and so on. In a world of competing objectives we have to worry about very practical questions: Are we targeting the right environmental objectives, can we really enforce certain policies, are we getting the most impact for the money, and so on. But the biggest problem with basing our approach to pollution control strictly on the moral argument is the basic assumption that people pollute because they are somehow morally underdeveloped. It is not moral underdevelopment that leads to environmental destruction; rather, it is the way the economic system, within which people make decisions about how to conduct their lives, has been arranged.

The Importance of Incentives

People pollute because it is the cheapest way they have of solving a certain, very practical problem. That problem is the disposal of the waste products remaining after consumers have finished using something, or after business firms have finished producing something. People make these decisions on production, consumption, and disposal within a certain set of economic and social institutions[2]; these institutions structure the **incentives** that lead people to make decisions in one direction rather than another. What needs to be studied is how this incentive process works and, especially, how it may be restructured so that people will be led to make decisions and develop lifestyles that have more benign environmental implications.

One simplistic incentive-type statement that one often hears is that pollution is a result of the **profit motive.** According to this view, in private enterprise economies such as the Western industrialized nations, people are rewarded for maximizing profits, the difference between the value of what is produced and the value of what is used up in the production process. Furthermore, the thinking goes, the profits that entrepreneurs try to maximize are strictly monetary profits. In this headlong pursuit of monetary profits, entrepreneurs give no thought to the environmental impacts of their actions

[2] By "institutions" we mean the fundamental set of public and private organizations, laws, and practices that a society uses to structure its economic activity. Markets are an economic institution, for example, as are corporations, a body of commercial law, public agencies, and so on.

because it "does not pay." Thus, in this uncontrolled striving for monetary profits, the only way to reduce environmental pollution is to weaken the strength of the profit motive.

There is substantial truth in this proposition, but also a degree of misunderstanding. It is certainly the case that if operators of private firms make decisions without taking environmental costs into account, excess pollution will result. But this is true of anybody: private firms, individuals, and public agencies. When individuals pour paint thinner down the sink drain or let their cars get seriously out of tune, they are making decisions without putting adequate weight on environmental consequences. Because individuals don't keep profit-and-loss statements, it can't be profits per se that lead people to pollute. The same can be said of government agencies, which have sometimes been serious polluters even though they are not profit motivated. But the most persuasive argument against the view that the search for profits causes pollution comes from looking at the history of Eastern Europe and the former USSR. With the collapse of these ex-Communist regimes, we became aware of the enormous environmental destruction that occurred in some of these regions—heavily polluted air and water resources in many areas, which have a major impact on human health and ecological systems. China is currently experiencing the same problem: headlong emphasis on economic development (by both public and private firms) with insufficient regard for the environmental consequences of this process. These examples show that it is not the profit motive itself that causes pollution, but any resource-using and waste-producing decisions that are made without exercising appropriate control over their environmental consequences.

In the sections and chapters that follow, we will place great stress on the importance of incentives in the functioning of an economic system. *Any* system will produce destructive environmental impacts if the incentives within the system are not structured to avoid them. We have to look more deeply into any economic system to understand how its incentive systems work and how they may be changed so that we can have a reasonably progressive economy without disastrous environmental effects.

Incentives: A Household Example

An incentive is something that attracts or repels people and leads them to modify their behavior in some way. An *economic incentive* is something in the economic world that leads people to channel their efforts at economic production and consumption in certain directions. We often think of economic incentives as consisting of payoffs in terms of material wealth; people have an incentive to behave in ways that provide them with increased wealth. But there are also nonmaterial incentives that lead people to modify their economic behavior; for example, self-esteem, the desire to preserve a beautiful visual environment, or the desire to set a good example for others.

Worcester Reduces Trash and Increases Recycling

EXHIBIT **1.1**

"Pay-as-you-throw" (PAYT) works by putting a price on an activity that has an environmental cost: the disposal of household trash. Many cities and towns in the U.S. have adopted PAYT systems over the last few decades. One of the most successful has been the program in Worcester, Massachusetts. That program was started in 1993, as a result of a municipal budget crisis that forced the Department of Public Works to look for new ways of generating revenues. There was massive opposition to the idea at first. Why should people have to pay for a municipal service that had traditionally been free? But the system was installed over this opposition: $1.50 for a large, 30-gallon trash bag and $0.75 for a smaller, 15-gallon bag.

The data collected to monitor the program showed that within the first week the recycling rate was up from a meager 2% to 38%; so that Worcester residents throw out about 400 pounds of trash per capita per year compared to a national average of 900 pounds. The data show that over 400,000 pounds of trash that would have ended up in Worcester landfills was recycled instead. The program has saved Worcester an estimated $10 to $20 million over the last twenty years. Revenues from sales of the bags are primarily used to support a curbside recycling program and bulky waste collection. Worcester City Council Kathleen Toomey says, "While no one likes to pay for trash bags, it has truly made an enormous difference in the amount of recycling over the past two plus decades. People are more cognizant about what goes into their trash bags and make an effort to increase their recycling."

For added information see: Go Local Worcester, *Worcester's Pay-As-You-Throw Trash Removal Saves City $10 – 20M*, April 2014, http://www.golocalworcester.com/news/worcesters-pay-as-you-throw-trash-removal-saves-city-10-20-M.

For a simple first look at the importance of changing incentives to get improvements in environmental quality, consider the story shown in Exhibit 1.1. It is about the new ways of paying for trash disposal, focusing on the experience of Worcester, Massachusetts. Before the program, people in the city paid a flat annual fee to have their trash collected. This is a common practice in most communities. The problem with this approach is that there is simply no incentive for any individual family to limit its trash production, because the family will pay the same annual trash-collection fee no matter how much, or little, it produces. This might not be a problem if there were ample landfill space and if there were no danger that the landfill would contaminate the surrounding environment, such as a nearby groundwater system. But for most communities these conditions don't hold any more, if they ever did. Residents of Worcester were confronted by rapidly escalating trash-collection costs. They faced the problem of how to get a significant reduction in the quantity of solid waste handled by the city.

The response in this case was to introduce a system that gives people an incentive to search for ways to reduce the amount of solid waste they produce. This was done by charging people for each bag of trash they put on the curb. What this does is to give families the incentive to reduce the number of bags of trash they set out. They can do this by recycling, by switching to products that have less waste, by putting food scraps in a compost pile, and so on. These have led, according to the story, to a large increase in the amount of trash recycled and a reduction in the total amount of trash. There are many other communities around the country where this system has been adopted. Of course, no system is perfect. Increases in illegal dumping and difficulties with applying the plan to apartment houses are problems. Nevertheless, the new approach does illustrate in a very clear way the effects of a shift from a system where there were no incentives for people to reduce their solid waste to one where there are such incentives. The technical name for this approach is **unit pricing.**

Incentives and Global Warming

Municipal solid waste and other trash have traditionally been local problems, both because the possible environmental impacts are usually local, and because, policy-wise, local governments have had the primary responsibilities for dealing with them. Obviously, not all environmental problems are local: traditional air pollution is usually a regional or national issue, and sometimes it is an international problem because it crosses country borders. And some environmental problems are truly global in that they have causes and impacts that involve everyone around the world, though not necessarily in equal intensity.

Of course, the global issue that is thrusting itself into the world's consciousness is the greenhouse effect, the buildup of heat-trapping gases in the earth's atmosphere that is producing long-run changes in global climate. We will have much more to say about this issue in later chapters. A major focus of environmental economists is to try to identify the most effective policy approaches to combat the emissions of substances causing the greenhouse effect, especially carbon dioxide (CO_2), but also including many other gases, such as methane (CH_4).

One way to approach this is with conventional "command-and-control" policies. This relies on laws and regulations that directly or indirectly specify pollution-control technologies or practices that polluters should use. Then standard enforcement procedures are used (inspections, monitoring, fines, etc.) to produce acceptably high degrees of compliance. Although this approach still characterizes much of the environmental policy arena, there has been a lot of attention recently given to incentive-based policies. There are two basic types of incentive policies: emission charges or taxes, analogous to the trash-collection fees discussed in the previous section; and market-based trading programs. We

Carbon Taxes Around the World		EXHIBIT **1.2**
Country/Region	Year Started	Currency Rate/ton CO_2e
British Columbia	2012	CAD 30
Chile	2018	USD 5
Denmark	2014	USD 31
Finland	2013	EUR 35
France	2014	EUR 7
Iceland	2014	USD 10
Ireland	2013	EUR 20
Japan	2014	USD 2
Mexico	2014	MEX 10-50
Norway	2014	USD 4-69
South Africa	2016	R 120
Sweden	2014	USD 168
Switzerland	2014	USD 68
United Kingdom (U.K.)	2014	USD 15.75

Source: OECD, *Climate and Carbon-Aligning Prices and Policies*, Environmental Policy Paper No. 01, 2013.

will discuss each of these at length; trading programs in Chapter 13 and emission charges in Chapter 12.

Emission charges work essentially by putting a price on emissions. Many people have argued that this would be the most effective approach to getting reductions in greenhouse gas emissions. In many countries, such charges have been introduced. Exhibit 1.2 lists some of the charges currently in effect; they have become popular especially in Europe. They are generally charges per ton of CO_2e, that is, equivalent tons of CO_2.

The Design of Environmental Policy

Environmental economics has a major role to play in the design of **public policies** for environmental quality improvement. There are an enormous range and variety of public programs and policies devoted to environmental matters, at all levels of government: local, state, regional, federal, and international. They vary greatly in their efficiency and effectiveness. Some have been well designed and will no doubt have beneficial impacts. Others are not well designed. Not being cost-effective, they will end up achieving much less environmental improvement than they would have if they had been designed better.

The problem of designing efficient environmental policies is often not given the emphasis it deserves. It is easy to fall into the trap of thinking that any programs or policies that flow out of the rough and tumble of the environmental political process are likely to be of some help, or that they certainly will be better than nothing. But history is full of cases where policymakers and public administrators have pursued policies that don't work; the public is frequently led to believe a policy will be effective even when any reasonable analysis could predict that it will not. All of this means that it is critically important to study how to design environmental policies that are effective and efficient.

In 2005, pollution control expenditures (including both capital and operating costs) amounted to about 1 percent of GDP, or about $130 billion. These are very large amounts of money, even though we could probably agree that they ought to be higher. A question of great importance, however, is whether we are getting the most improvement possible in environmental quality for the money spent. Former EPA director William Reilly is quoted as saying that "at this level of expenditure, there's a very large obligation to get it right." By "getting it right," he means having programs that get the maximum improvement in environmental quality for the resources spent. Everybody has an interest in this: environmentalists, for obvious reasons; public regulators, because they are tapping a limited supply of taxpayer resources and consumer tolerance; and the regulated polluters themselves, because matters of efficiency are critical to business success.

"Getting it right" means paying attention to the factors that affect the cost-effectiveness of environmental regulations, and especially to the way they create incentives for actions taken by polluters. An important problem in environmental policy is that of **perverse incentives**—that is, incentives created by a policy that actually work against the overall objectives of that policy. Environmental policies often created perverse incentives, because environmental policymakers have too often tried to legislate results directly, rather than establish the types of regulations that harness the self-interest of polluters to move toward efficient emission reductions. Exhibit 1.3 discusses perverse incentives in the federal program to control power plan emissions, specifically the incentive inherent in the decision to switch from old, highly polluting technology to newer, cleaner plants.

Issues related to the design of environmental policy are a major part of environmental economics. It is important to know how alternative policy approaches measure up in terms of cost-effectiveness, getting the most pollution reduction for the money spent, and, in terms of efficiency, appropriately balancing the benefits and costs of environmental improvements.

Macroeconomic Questions: Environment and Growth

The incentive issues discussed in the previous section are microeconomic problems; they deal with the behavior of individuals or small groups of consumers, polluting firms, and firms in the pollution-control industry. The macroeconomy, on the other hand, refers to the economic structure and

---

Incentive Aspects of New Source Review

EXHIBIT 1.3

The Clean Air Act, as amended, distinguishes between existing sources of air pollutants and new or modified sources. Pollution control requirements for the latter are much more stringent than those on the former. The thinking behind this is that building pollution control into new plants is normally much less costly than retrofitting older plants. Thus, as older plants are retired in favor of new technologies, the extent of overall industry emissions would decline. But this approach actually involves incentive problems. If new or upgraded plants would be required to have expensive emission controls, the incentive would be to hold onto the old plants for as long as possible, making whatever repairs and minor changes would be required to keep them in reasonable operating shape. To counter the incentive, the EPA put into effect a procedure called New Source review (NSR),

essentially an evaluation of individual plants to make sure that any changes may have changed its classification for existing to "new," thereby requiring better pollution control. But this made the problem worse: now plant operators had an incentive to keep operating the old plants with few or no changes, for fear of triggering an NSR if they did too much. In effect, the way the CAA was written, which seemed to foster a gradual cleaning up of the power industry as old plants were retired and newer, cleaner plants were built, actually created incentives that produced a slowing of the rate at which the industry converted to new pollution control technologies.

For further information see: Sarah K. Adair, D.C. Hoppock, and J.J. Monast, "New Source Review and Coal Efficiency Gains: How New and Forthcoming Air Regulations Affect Outcomes," *Energy Policy*, 70, July 2014, pp. 183–192.

---

performance of an entire country taken as a single unit. When we study topics such as changes in GDP, rates of inflation, and the unemployment rate, we are focusing on the performance of the country as a whole; that is to say, we are doing **macroeconomics.**

There are a number of important questions about the relationship between environmental issues and the behavior of the macroeconomy:

- What overall preferences do citizens have with respect to the balance between environmental protection and economic growth?
- Historically, have measures to protect the environment led to lower economic growth rates?
- How might environmental regulations be designed to minimize their impacts on growth?
- When the perspective is broadened from growth to human welfare, how do environmental protection measures stack up?

From a political standpoint, perhaps the most sensitive question is whether stricter environmental policies will tend to retard economic growth. There is little evidence that from the perspective of the total economy, environmental protection costs have been a significant economic burden. As mentioned, pollution-control costs today are probably about 1 to 2 percent of GDP in the country. Costs of this magnitude are unlikely to be large enough to cause large-scale layoffs and reduced economic growth. Nevertheless, this question continues to be politically sensitive.

Environmental regulations have also been blamed for reducing employment in industries subject to the regulations. But environmental regulations also provide the incentive for growth in the envirotech industries, with the added employment this implies. Exhibit 1.4 discusses some of these issues in the context of reducing atmospheric emissions that are causing global warming.

The Macroeconomic Cost of Reducing CO_2 Emissions: It Depends on How It's Done   EXHIBIT **1.4**

Global warming is the process by which the buildup of certain gases in the earth's atmosphere increases its heat-trapping capacity sufficiently to produce an increase in mean global surface temperatures. A small increase in this could have major meteorological repercussions, with huge economic and social impacts around the world. Scientists have almost unanimously concluded that the only way of effectively forestalling global warming in the long run is to reduce the emissions of greenhouse gases, chief among which is carbon dioxide (CO_2). Emissions of CO_2 stem largely from the burning of fossil fuels, which is ubiquitous in the industrial, transportation, and domestic sectors of modern economies. But how much to try to reduce these emissions is highly controversial. Many in the environmental community believe that vigorous action is required. One of the controversial aspects of this is how much it will cost. Macroeconomic studies appear to indicate that the minimum costs of limiting U.S. carbon emissions to their 1990 level would be 1 or 2 percent of GDP. This is a relatively small number in percentage terms but a larger one in terms of dollars (1 percent of the U.S. GDP in 2010 was about $145 billion).

But this is a minimum, achievable only if greenhouse gas policies are cost-effective, and likely to be much higher if they are not. Cost-effectiveness means that the policies get the biggest "bang for the buck," in this case the biggest emission reduction for the resources spent. The fact is that the cost of reducing greenhouse gases differs a lot among industries (coal-fired power generation versus automobile manufacturing, for example) and even among firms in the same industry. For a pollution-control policy to be cost-effective, it has to take these costs differences into account. Basically, it should bring about proportionally greater emission reductions from sources with lower emission-reduction costs. How to get this result will be a major topic of this book.

Source: Joseph E. Aldy, Alan J. Krupnick, Richard G. Newell, Ian W.H. Parry, and William A. Pizer, "Designing Climate Mitigation Policy," Resources for the Future, Discussion Paper 08-16, Washington, D.C., May 2009.

The Relationship of Environmental Regulation, Economic Growth, and Human Welfare in India EXHIBIT 1.5

In many countries, especially those of the developing world, economic growth and improved environmental quality are both of critical importance. In countries such as India, it is important for researchers to understand the nature of the tradeoff between these two objectives, and how the tradeoffs could be altered with appropriate public policies. The World Bank recently completed a study on the connection between growth and the environment in India. Their conclusion: a low-emission greening of the economy should be possible with a very low cost in terms of GDP growth; the cost of a more vigorous pollution control effort would directly add more net benefits.

Among their conclusions are the following:

- Reducing emissions of particulates by 10% could be expected to reduce GDP by about $46 billion by 2030. While this may sound like a lot, it would represent about 0.3% of total GDP in that year.

- Reducing particulate emissions by 30% would reduce GDP by about 0.7%.

- In both cases significant improvements in health would occur: by about $24 billion in the first case and by $105 billion in the more aggressive case.

In each case the main benefits come from reduction in particulate air pollution, one of the most dangerous pollutants in terms of health impact. In addition there would be a substantial reduction in greenhouse gases, especially CO_2.

In India, then, tradeoff scenarios between economics and the environment would appear to call for much more aggressive pollution control efforts, especially air pollution control.

Source: World Bank, *India: Green Growth-Overcoming Environmental Challenges to Promote Development*, March 2014, **http://www.worldbank.org/en/news/feature/2014/03/06/greengrowth-overcoming-india-environment-challenges-promote-development.**

Another macroeconomic question concerns the impacts of economic growth on environmental quality. Do higher rates of growth, that is, increases in our traditional measures such as GDP, imply greater environmental degradation, or might the opposite be true? Or, is economic growth sustainable? Two economists who studied this problem recently concluded: "Some pollution increases during the early stages of a country's development and then begins to diminish as countries gain adequate resources to tackle pollution problems."[3] This happens because at low incomes, people tend to value development over environmental quality, but as they achieve greater wealth, they are willing to devote greater resources to environmental quality improvements. This is clearly a matter of great importance for developing countries, and we come back to it in Chapter 21. Exhibit 1.5 discusses the particular problem in India. In

[3] Alan B. Kreuger and Gene Grossman, "Economic Growth and the Environment," *Quarterly Journal of Economics*, 110(2), May 1995, pp. 353–377.

developed countries also, macroeconomic problems—growth, recession, inflation, unemployment—are constant topics of national concern. So it's important
to pursue studies of the relationships between these phenomena and questions
of environmental quality.

Benefit–Cost Analysis

Effective decision making requires that there be adequate information about the
consequences of the decisions. This is as important in the **public sector,** where
the issue is effective **public policy,** as it is in the **private sector,** where the main
concern is with the bottom line of the profit-and-loss statement. The primary
type of public-sector analysis in environmental policy questions is **benefit–cost
analysis.** Policies or projects are studied in terms of the environmental benefits
they would produce, and these are compared with the costs that are entailed.
It was first used in this country early in the 20th century to evaluate water development projects undertaken by federal agencies. Today it is used by many
government agencies to help make rational policy decisions.

Benefit–cost analysis is such an important and widely used approach that we
devote several chapters to it later in the book (Chapters 6, 7, and 8). In this type
of analysis, as the name implies, the benefits of some proposed action are estimated and compared with the total costs that society would bear if that action
were undertaken. If it is a proposal for a public park, for example, the benefits
in terms of recreational experiences provided by the park are compared with
the expected costs of building the park and of using the land in this way rather
than some other way. Or a proposal to build a solid-waste incinerator would
compare the costs of building and operating the incinerator, including the costs
of disposing of the remaining ash and the costs of possible airborne emissions,
with benefits, such as reducing the use of landfills for the solid waste. Exhibit 1.6
shows some results of a recent study to estimate the benefits and costs of reducing nitrogen oxide (NO_x) emissions in a group of Eastern U.S. states.

The benefit–cost approach implies that we need to consider both the benefits
and the costs of environmental programs and policies. This often puts benefit–
cost studies squarely in the middle of political controversy on many environmental issues. In the political struggles that characterize many environmental
problems, groups on one side consist of people whose major concern is with the
benefits, whereas groups on the other side are primarily concerned with costs.
Environmental groups typically stress the benefits; business groups usually focus on the costs.

Valuing the Environment

To complete a benefit–cost analysis of an environmental program or regulation successfully, it's necessary to estimate both the benefits and the costs of
the actions. One factor that complicates this type of analysis is that the benefits

Benefits and Costs of Reducing Nitrogen Oxide (NO$_x$) Emissions EXHIBIT **1.6**

Nitrogen oxide (NO$_x$) emissions are produced from a variety of industrial and transportation sectors, as a consequence of the burning of fossil fuels. NO$_x$ reacts with volatile organic compounds in the presence of sunlight and produces ground-level ozone, ambient concentrations of which produce a range of health damages. NO$_x$ emissions are also precursors of particulate matter (PM), which is fine soot or dust that can be composed of a number of substances and have deleterious effects on human health. Thus, reducing NO$_x$ emissions has been a major objective of the EPA and many state environmental agencies. To support these efforts, numerous economic studies have been done to estimate the benefits and the costs of reducing NO$_x$ emissions. To do this, researchers examine the various types and location of sources of NO$_x$ emissions (e.g., power plants, industrial boilers) and what it would cost these sources to reduce these emissions by a given amount. On the other side, they must estimate the effect of these reductions on ambient ozone levels, and the benefits of these reductions for people living and working in these ambient conditions.

Recently, a group of economists conducted a benefit–cost analysis of NO$_x$ emission reductions in 19 Eastern U.S. states and regions.[1] They asked the question: What would be the benefits and costs of a 20 percent reduction in NO$_x$ emissions from 925 large electric utility boilers in these states? To estimate the costs, they looked at the different technical options available to reduce emissions and identified the least costly alternative for meeting the emission reductions. To estimate the benefits, they used a model showing the relationship between emission reductions and changes in ambient ozone and PM, and another model to estimate the health effects of these ambient changes.

Some of these results are as follows:

NO$_x$ reduction (tons/day)	987
Benefits ($1,000/day)	
Ozone reduction	$238
PM reduction	$1,541
Total benefits	$1,779
Costs ($1,000/day)	$914
Net benefits ($1,000/day)	$865

Note that the health benefits of PM reduction are about six times higher than those of ozone reduction. Note also that there are substantial net benefits (total benefits minus total costs). These amount to $864,000 per day, which translates into about $315 million per year. Results of benefit–cost analyses of this type can help buttress the case for tightening air-pollution-control standards under the Clean Air Act.

[1] Michelle S. Bergin, Jhih-Shyang Shih, Alan J. Krupnick, James W. Boylan, James G. Wilkinson, M. Talat Odman, and Armistead G. Russell, "Regional Air Quality: Local and Interstate Impacts of NO$_x$ and SO$_2$ Emissions on Ozone and Fine Particulate Matter in the Eastern United States," *Environmental Science and Technology*, 41(13), 2007.

of environmental improvements are usually **nonmarket** in nature. If we were trying to assess the benefits to society of a program to support potato farmers, we could get a good idea of the value of potatoes by looking at how much people are willing to pay for them when they buy them at the supermarket. But suppose we have a program of air-pollution reduction that will, among other things, lower the risk that people in a certain region will have of contracting chronic bronchitis. How might we estimate the social value of this result? It cannot be done by looking directly at market behavior, as in the case of potatoes, because there is no market where people buy and sell directly the changes in health risk produced by the environmental program. Environmental economists have developed a series of **nonmarket valuation techniques** that are used to estimate these types of environmental outcomes. We will discuss some of these techniques in Chapter 7.

Environment and Development

Countries of the world are sometimes, perhaps misleadingly, divided into two categories: developed and developing. The latter comprises all those countries whose private and public wealth per capita are relatively low and who seek the means of developing their economies to levels comparable with the more developed world. Most developing countries have environmental issues, and many have put into place laws and regulations to deal with cases of pollution and resource degradation. Although many have embraced command-and-control policy approaches, there has also been heavy reliance on voluntary pollution-control plans.[4] The trend in the developed countries toward incentive-based (IB) programs has suggested to some that countries in the developing world also be well advised to adopt them, as their cost-effectiveness would be especially valuable in resource-scarce situations. Others have stressed that IB plans might be too complex for the special institutional characteristics of developing countries. Exhibit 1.7 sheds some light on this question.

International Issues

Many environmental problems are local or regional, in the sense that the causal factors and resulting damages lie within the same country. But many others are international in scope. Some are **international** simply because there is a national border between the pollution source and the resulting impacts. Airborne emissions that are carried from one country upwind to another downwind are a case in point, as is water pollution of a river that traverses several countries. There is another class of problems that are **global** in nature because they impact the global environment. One of these is the destruction of the earth's protective layer of **stratospheric ozone** by chemicals devised by humans for a number of industrial purposes. Another is the problem of **global warming,** the possible rise in surface temperatures of the earth stemming from the accumulation of carbon dioxide (CO_2) in the atmosphere. The 1997 Kyoto conference

[4] See, for example, Allen Blackman, *Alternative Pollution Control Policies in Developing Countries,* Resources for the Future, Discussion Paper EFD DP 09-14, Washington, D.C., June 2009.

Incentive-Based Pollution Control in the Developing World   EXHIBIT 1.7

Incentive-based (IB) approaches to pollution control have become fairly common in the developed world, although there is still scope for their wider use. This includes emission trading in its various forms, and direct emission charges. Some people have argued that countries of the developing world would be well advised to adopt these types of programs, because they achieve, at least theoretically, cost-effective pollution control. But others have argued that the "institutional machinery" present in the developing world is often inadequate for the sophisticated monitoring and implementing that IB plans require. Weak public regulatory agencies, inadequate public laws, and substantial corruption are often the lot of developing countries, though not all of them.

In Latin America, there have been the following recent attempts to implement IB programs:

Chile: This was an emission trading program for air pollutants, primarily particulate matter, starting in 1993. A new public agency was created to implement the program.

Columbia: This was a plan to institute a fee for the discharge of Biochemical Oxygen Demand (BOD) and Total Suspended Solids (TSS) from a variety of point sources of these pollutants. This was begun in 1997, and included a plan for redistributing the revenues obtained from the charges.

Costa Rica: This was a program for charging a fee for the discharge of TSS and BOD. The fee was based on the concentration of these substances in the discharge stream and was meant to complement the existing program of emission standards. The program started in 2008; it also incorporated a plan for redistributing the resulting revenues.

How have these IB programs worked in these countries? The general conclusion appears to be that it is difficult to get them up and running effectively because the necessary administrative/regulatory systems are not yet in place. This means that the technical aspects of new IB programs are difficult to clarify and implement. Without effective administrative institutions, the programs are often ensnared and hindered by political pushing and shoving among politically connected participants. What this tells us is that effective environmental policies depend on both the design of the policies and the presence of the administrative institutions that can implement them.

Source: Marcelo Caffera, "The Use of Economic Instruments for Pollution Control in Latin America: Lessons for Future Policy Design," *Environment and Economic Development* 16, Cambridge University Press, 2010, pp. 247–273.

featured an attempt by developed countries to agree on future cutbacks of CO_2 emissions. Cost-effective CO_2 emission reductions and the design of equitable international agreements are two topics among many on which environmental economists have worked.

The Kyoto Protocol expired in 2012, and there is hope that the countries of the world will negotiate a new and better agreement to reduce emissions of greenhouse gases. How this plays out will depend on the negotiating skills of the parties, and on the incentives that the countries have to take part

TABLE 1.1   GDP and CO_2 Emissions per Capita, Selected Countries

Country	GDP ($ billions, 2013)	CO_2 Emissions per Capita (metric tons, 2010)	Share of Global Emissions (%, 2010)
Australia	1,560.3	16.9	1.1
Brazil	2,146.1	2.2	1.3
Chile	277.2	4.2	0.2
China	9,240.3	6.2	24.7
Columbia	378.4	1.6	0.2
France	2,806.4	5.6	1.1
India	1,875.1	1.7	6.0
Indonesia	868.3	1.8	1.3
Iraq	229.3	3.7	0.3
Kuwait	175.8	31.3	0.3
Nepal	19.3	0.1	<0.1
Norway	512.6	11.7	0.2
Russia	2,096.8	12.2	5.2
United Kingdom	2,678.5	7.9	1.5
United States	16,768.1	17.6	16.2

Source: GDP: The World Bank, Data, 2015, **http://www.worldbank.org/indicator;** Emissions: EDGAR, European Commission, Netherlands Environmental Assessment Agency, 2012; United Nations Statistical Division, Millennium Development Goal Indicators, Table 7.2, July 2013, **http://www.mdgs.org/unsd/mdg.**

in an effective agreement. What complicates this is the fact that different countries are likely to be differently affected by global warming, so they come to the bargaining table with different incentives for entering into a meaningful agreement.

To get an idea of the magnitude of this situation, Table 1.1 shows some data for 2010 CO_2 emissions, per capita, for a small group of countries. Note the enormous differences, from 31.3 tons in Kuwait to 0.1 in Nepal. Even among countries of the "developed" world, there is great variation, for example, 17.6 tons in the United States and 5.6 tons in France. A topic of increasing interest is how differences such as this affect the willingness of countries to enter into international environmental agreements, and how the terms of these agreements might be shaped so as to motivate widespread participation. We will take up these matters in Chapter 19.

Globalization and the Environment

There is another sense in which global environmental problems have recently taken on greater urgency. These are the environmental implications of globalization. **Globalization** is a term used to refer to the perceived changes that are taking place in the world economy, including the rapid growth of **trade** among nations, **privatization** of economic institutions, massive international flows of

financial capital, and growth in the numbers and sizes of **multinational firms.** Advocates of a more integrated world economy point to its potential for stimulating economic growth and increasing wealth in the developing world. But many people also have pointed to the potential downside of globalization, one part of which may be the degradation of natural environments in developing countries.

Globalization has become a politically charged concept; it is sometimes hard to cut through the rhetoric and identify the substantive issues that are involved. One part of globalization is the substantial increase that has occurred in the volume of trade among nations. This has led to a concern about the implications of the increasing volume of trade on environmental impacts in both developed and developing countries. International trade in goods and services has been touted as an engine of growth for the countries involved. Some people take the view that the long-run environmental implications of this are positive. Many others feel that unrestricted trade will have severe environmental consequences. We will take up this topic at greater length in Chapter 20.

Another aspect of globalization is the growth of multinational firms and the relocation of industrial firms from developed to developing countries. Environmental regulations are often less stringent in the latter than in the former. The fear is that some developing countries could become **pollution havens,** places to which firms move in order to have to spend less on pollution control measures. We will look more closely at this phenomenon in Chapter 20.

Economics and Politics

Finally, we need to discuss briefly the question of how to achieve effective environmental policy in a highly **political policy environment.** Environmental policies not only affect the natural environment, but also affect people. This means that environmental policy decisions come out of the political process, a process where, at least in democratic systems, people and groups come together and contend for influence and control, where interests collide, coalitions shift, and biases intrude. Policies that come out of a process like this may bear little relationship to what we might think of as efficient approaches to particular environmental problems. Many people have questioned the very idea that a democratic political process could or should strive to produce policies that are efficient in some technical economic sense.

So where does that leave the environmental economist? Why spend so much time and energy on questions of efficiency and cost-effectiveness when the political process most likely is going to override these considerations and go its own way? Why worry about economic incentives and economic efficiency when "everything is political," as the saying goes? The answer is that although we know that the real world is one of compromise and power, the best way for scientists and economists to serve that process is to produce studies that are as clear and as objective as possible. It is the politician's job to compromise or seek advantage; it is the scientist's job to provide the best information he or she can.

For economists, in fact, this means studies in which economic efficiency is a central role, but it means more than this. Because the policy process is one where "who gets what" is a dominant theme, environmental economics also must deal with the distribution question, on how environmental problems and policies affect different groups within society. It is also the role of scientists and economists to provide information to policymakers on alternative courses of action. Although we will focus in later chapters on what appear to be "the" most efficient policies or "the" least-cost courses of action, it has to be recognized that in the give-and-take of the political world in which policy is actually made, choosing among alternatives is always the order of the day.

But economists have no right these days to complain about their role in the environmental policy process. If anything, these are the days of the rising influence of economists. Benefit–cost procedures and results have become more widely accepted, in public policy arenas and in law courts hearing environmental cases. New pollution-control initiatives incorporating economic incentive principles are being adopted at both federal and state levels in the United States. All the more reason, then, to study and understand the basic economics of environmental analysis and policy.

Summary

The purpose of this brief chapter was to whet your appetite for the subject of environmental economics by indicating some of the main topics that the field encompasses, showing very briefly the approach that economists take in studying them. It's also to give you something to remember. When we get involved in some of the conceptual and theoretical issues that underlie the topic, it is easy to lose sight of what we are trying to accomplish. We are trying to develop these principles so that we can actually use them to address real-world problems such as those discussed in this chapter. Although the principles may appear abstract and odd at first, remember the objective: to achieve a cleaner, healthier, and more beautiful natural environment.

For additional readings and Web sites pertaining to material in this chapter, see **http://www.mhhe.com/field7e.**

Chapter 2

The Economy and the Environment

The **economy** is a collection of technological, legal, and social arrangements through which individuals in society seek to increase their material and spiritual well-being. The two elementary economic functions pursued by society are **production** and **distribution.** Production refers to all those activities that determine the quantities of goods and services that are produced and the technological and managerial means by which this production is carried out. Distribution refers to the way in which goods and services are divided up, or distributed, among the individuals and groups that make up society. Distribution puts goods and services in the hands of individuals, households, and organizations; the final utilization of these goods and services is termed **consumption.**

Any economic system exists within, and is encompassed by, the natural world. Its processes and changes are of course governed by the **laws of nature.** In addition, economies make use directly of **natural assets** of all types. One role the natural world plays is that of provider of raw materials and energy inputs, without which production and consumption would be impossible. Thus, one type of impact that an economic system has on nature is by drawing upon raw materials to keep the system functioning. Production and consumption activities also produce leftover waste products, called "residuals," and sooner or later these must find their way back into the natural world. Depending on how they are handled, these residuals may lead to pollution or the degradation of the natural environment. We can illustrate these fundamental relationships with a simple schematic:

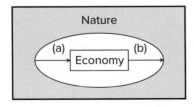

The link marked (a) represents raw materials flowing into production and consumption. The study of nature in its role as provider of raw materials is called **natural resource economics.** The link labeled (b) shows the impact of economic activity on the quality of the natural environment. The study of this residuals flow and its resultant impacts in the natural world comes under the heading of **environmental economics.** Although pollution control is the major topic within environmental economics, it is not the only one. Human beings have an impact on the environment in many ways that are not related to pollution in the traditional sense. Habitat disruption from housing developments and scenic degradation from any number of human activities are examples of environmental impacts that are not related to the discharge of specific pollutants.

The topic of this book is environmental economics. We will study the management of waste flows and the impacts of human activity on the quality of environmental assets. But in a real sense, many of these problems originate in the earlier, raw-material phase of the nature–economy interaction. So before proceeding, we consider briefly the major dimensions of natural resource economics.

Natural Resource Economics

In modern industrial/urban societies, it is sometimes easy to overlook the fact that a large part of total economic activity still relies on the extraction and utilization of natural resources. **Natural resource economics** is the application of economic principles to the study of these activities. To get a general impression of what this discipline includes, the following is a list of its major subdivisions and examples of questions pursued in each one.[1]

Mineral economics: What is the appropriate rate at which to extract ore from a mine? How do exploration and the addition to reserves respond to mineral prices?

Forest economics: What is the appropriate rate at which to harvest timber? How do government policies affect the harvest rates pursued by timber companies?

Marine economics: What kinds of rules need to be established for managing fisheries? How do different harvest rates affect the stocks of fish?

Land economics: How do people in the private sector (builders, home purchasers) make decisions about the use of land? How do the laws of property rights and public land-use regulations affect the way space is devoted to different uses?

Energy economics: What are the appropriate rates for extracting underground petroleum deposits? How sensitive is energy use to changes in energy prices?

---

[1] Natural resource economics is the subject of a companion book written by one of the authors. See Barry C. Field, *Natural Resource Economics, an Introduction*, 3rd ed., Waveland Press, 2016.

Water economics: How do different water laws affect the way water is utilized by different people? What kinds of regulations should govern the reallocation of water from, for example, agriculture to urban users?

Agricultural economics: How do farmers make decisions about using conservation practices in cultivating their land? How do government programs affect the choices farmers make regarding what crops to produce and how to produce them?

A fundamental distinction in natural resource economics is that of **renewable** and **nonrenewable** resources. The living resources, such as fisheries and timber, are renewable; they grow in time according to biological processes. Some nonliving resources are also renewable—the classic example being the sun's energy that reaches the earth. Nonrenewable resources are those for which there are no processes of replenishment—once used they are gone forever. Classic examples are petroleum reservoirs and nonenergy mineral deposits. Certain resources, such as many groundwater aquifers, have replenishment rates that are so low that they are in effect nonrenewable.

It is easy to see that the use of nonrenewable resources is a problem with a strong **intertemporal** dimension; it involves trade-offs between the present and the future. If more oil is pumped out of an underground deposit this year, less will be available to extract in future years. Establishing today's correct pumping rate, therefore, requires a comparison of the value of oil now with the anticipated value of oil in the future.

But complicated intertemporal trade-offs also exist with renewable resources. What should today's codfish harvesting rate be, considering that the size of the remaining stock will affect its future growth and availability? Should this timber be cut today, or does its expected rate of growth warrant holding off harvesting until some time in the future? Biological and ecological processes create connections between the rates of resource use in the present and the quantity and quality of resources available to future generations. It is these connections that are the focus of what has come to be called **sustainability.**

A resource-use rate that is sustainable is one that can be maintained over the long run without impairing the fundamental ability of the natural resource base to support future generations. Sustainability does not mean that resources must remain untouched; rather, it means that their rates of use must be chosen so as not to jeopardize future generations. In the case of nonrenewable resources, this implies using the extracted resource in such a way that it contributes to the long-run economic and social health of the population. For renewable resources, it means establishing rates of use that are coordinated with the natural productivity rates affecting the way the resources grow and decline.

Many environmental problems also have strong intertemporal dimensions, that is, important trade-offs between today and the future. For example, many pollutants tend to accumulate in the environment rather than dissipate and disappear. Heavy metals, for example, can accumulate in water and soil. Carbon dioxide emissions over many decades have accumulated in the earth's atmosphere. What is in fact being depleted here is the earth's **assimilative capacity,** the ability of the natural system to accept certain pollutants and render them benign or inoffensive. Some of the theoretical ideas about the depletion of natural resources are also useful in understanding environmental pollution. In this sense, assimilative capacity is a natural resource akin to traditional resources such as oil deposits and forests.

A resource that resides not in any one substance but in a collection of elements is **biological diversity.** Biologists estimate that there may be as many as 30 million different species of living organisms in the world today. These represent a vast and important source of genetic information that is useful for the development of medicines, natural pesticides, resistant varieties of plants and animals, and so on. Human activities have substantially increased the rate of species extinctions, so habitat conservation and species preservation have become important contemporary resource problems.

One feature of the modern world is that the dividing line between natural resources and environmental resources is blurring in many cases. Many resource extraction processes, such as timber cutting and strip mining, have direct repercussions on environmental quality. In addition, there are many instances where environmental pollution or disruption has an impact on resource extraction processes. Estuarine water pollution that interferes with the replenishment of fish stocks is an example, as is air pollution that reduces agricultural yields. Furthermore, certain things, such as wildlife, may be considered both natural resources and attributes of the environment.

Despite the very close connections, however, the distinction that economists have made between these two services of the natural world—as raw materials and as environment—is sufficiently strong and well developed that it makes sense for us to proceed with a book that focuses primarily on the latter. We begin by considering a somewhat more complicated version of the simple diagram depicted at the beginning of the chapter.

The Fundamental Balance

In this book you will find a lot of simple analytical models of situations that in reality are somewhat complex. A model is a way of trying to show the essential structure and relationships in something, without going into all of its details, much as a caricature of a person accentuates distinguishing features at the cost of all the details.

Figure 2.1 is a more complex rendering of the relationships shown at the beginning of the chapter. The elements within the circle are parts of the economic system, the whole of which is basically encapsulated within the natural environment. The economy has been divided into two broad segments, **producers** and **consumers.**

- The producers category includes all private firms that take inputs and convert them to outputs; it also includes units such as public agencies; nonprofit organizations; and firms producing services, such as transportation.

FIGURE 2.1 The Environment and the Economy

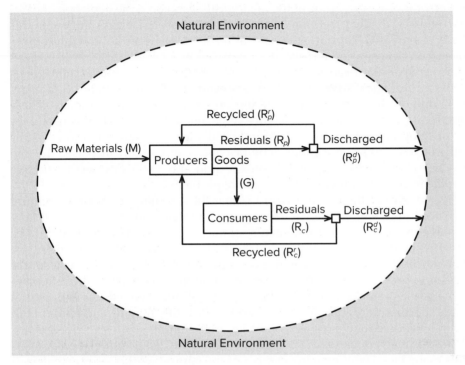

The primary inputs from the natural environment to the producing sector are materials, in the form of fuels, nonfuel minerals, and wood; fluids (e.g., water and petroleum); and gases of various types (e.g., natural gas and oxygen). All goods and services are derived from materials with the application of energy inputs.

- The consumers category includes all of the private households to whom the vast collections of final goods and services are distributed. One could argue that consumers sometimes use inputs directly from nature, like producers; many households, for example, get their water supplies directly from groundwater aquifers rather than water distribution companies. In the interest of keeping the model simple, however, we have not drawn this type of relationship.

It needs to be kept in mind that producers and consumers actually consist of the same people in different capacities. The "us-versus-them" quality that characterizes many environmental disputes is really an internal disagreement within a single group. Society as a whole is essentially in the same position as a single household that pumps water from its own well and discharges wastes into its own septic system, which happens to be near the well.

Production and consumption create **residuals,** which is another way of saying leftovers. They include all types of material residuals that may be emitted into the air or water or disposed of on land. The list is incredibly long: sulfur dioxide, volatile organic compounds, toxic solvents, animal manure, pesticides, particulate matter of all types, waste-building materials, heavy metals, and so on. Waste energy in the form of heat and noise, and radioactivity, which has characteristics of both material and energy, are also important production residuals. Consumers are also responsible for enormous quantities of residuals, chief among which are domestic sewage and automobile emissions. All materials in consumer goods must eventually end up as leftovers, even though they may be recycled along the way. These are the source of large quantities of solid waste as well as hazardous materials such as toxic chemicals and used oil.

Let us first consider the question of production and consumption residuals from a strictly physical standpoint. Figure 2.1 shows raw materials and energy being extracted from the natural environment (M) and residuals being discharged back into the environment.

In the early days of environmental concern, the main focus was on the end flows of discharged residuals by producers (R_p^d) and by consumers (R_c^d). By treating these residuals and otherwise changing the time and place of discharge, their impacts on humans and the environment could be substantially changed. Although this is still an important locus of activity, recent years have seen a broadening of perspective to what is called **environmental management.**

To appreciate this broadening of focus, let us consider the flows of Figure 2.1 in greater detail. From physics, the law of the conservation of matter assures us that, in the long run, these two flows must be equal. In terms of the symbols of Figure 2.1[2]:

$$M = R_p^d + R_c^d$$

We must say "in the long run" for several reasons. If the system is growing, it can retain some proportion of the natural inputs, which go toward increasing the size of the system through a growing population, the accumulation of capital equipment, and so on. These would be disposed of if and when the system ceases to grow. Also, recycling can obviously delay the disposal of residuals. But recycling can never be perfect; each cycle must lose some proportion of the recycled material. Thus, the fundamental **materials/energy balance** equation must hold in the long run. This shows us something very fundamental: To reduce the mass of residuals disposed of in the natural environment, it is necessary to reduce the quantity of raw materials taken into the system.[3] To look more closely at the various options for doing this, substitute for M. According to the flow diagram,

$$R_p^d + R_c^d = M = G + R_p - R_p^r - R_c^r$$

which says that the quantity of raw materials (M) is equal to output of goods and services (G) plus production residuals (R_p), minus the amounts that are recycled

[2] To make these direct comparisons, all flows must be expressed in terms of mass.

[3] Note that $G = R_c$; that is, everything that flows to the consumption sector eventually ends up as a residual from that sector.

from producers (R_p^r) and consumers (R_c^r). There are essentially three ways of reducing M and, therefore, residuals discharged into the natural environment.

Reduce G Assuming the other flows stay the same, we can reduce residuals discharged by reducing the quantity of goods and services produced in the economy. Some people have fastened on this as the best long-run answer to environmental degradation; reducing output, or at least stopping its rate of growth, would allow a similar change in the quantity of residuals discharged. Some have sought to reach this goal by advocating "zero population growth."[4] A slowly growing or stationary population can make it easier to control environmental impacts, but for two reasons, it does not in any way ensure this control. First, a stationary population can grow economically, thus increasing its demand for raw materials. Second, environmental impacts can be long run and cumulative, so that even a stationary population can gradually degrade the environment in which it finds itself. It is certainly true, however, that population growth will often exacerbate the environmental impacts of a particular economy. In the U.S. economy, for example, although the emissions of pollutants per car have dramatically decreased over the last few decades through better emissions-control technology, the sheer growth in the number of cars on the highways has led to an increase in the total quantity of automobile emissions in many regions.

Reduce R_p Another way of reducing M, and therefore residuals discharged, is to reduce R_p. Assuming the other flows are held constant, this means essentially changing the amounts of production residuals produced for a given quantity of output produced. There are basically only two ways of doing this:

- Reduce the **residuals' intensity of production** in all sectors of the economy by inventing and adopting new production technologies and practices that leave smaller amounts of residuals per unit of output produced. For example, in later discussions of carbon dioxide (CO_2) emissions and atmospheric warming, we will see that there is much that can be done to reduce the CO_2 output per unit of output produced, especially by shifting to different fuels, and by reducing (actually by continuing to reduce) the quantities of energy required to produce a unit of final output. This approach has come to be called **pollution prevention** or **source reduction.**

- Shift the composition of final output; that is, reduce those sectors that have relatively high residuals per unit of output and expand those sectors that produce relatively few residuals per unit of output. The shift from primarily a manufacturing economy toward services is a step in this direction. This is called a **sectoral shift** because it changes the relative shares of the different economic sectors in the aggregate economy. The rise of the so-called information sectors is another example. It is not that these new sectors produce no significant residuals; indeed, some of them may produce harsher

---

[4] For example, see Herman E. Daly, *Steady State Economics, Second Edition with New Essays,* Island Press, Washington, D.C., 1991.

leftovers than we have known before. The computer industry, for example, uses a variety of chemical solvents for cleaning purposes. But on the whole these sectors probably have a smaller waste-disposal problem than the traditional industries they have replaced.

Increase $(R_p^r + R_c^r)$ The third possibility is to increase recycling. Instead of discharging production and consumption residuals into the environment, they can be recycled back into the production process. What this shows is that the central role of recycling is to replace a portion of the original flow of virgin materials (M). By substituting recycled materials for virgin materials, the quantity of residuals discharged can be reduced while maintaining the rate of output of goods and services (G). In modern economies, recycling offers great opportunities to reduce waste flows. But we have to remember that recycling can never be perfect, even if enormous resources were devoted to the task. Production processes usually transform the physical structure of materials inputs, making them difficult to use again. The process of energy conversion changes the chemical structure of energy materials so thoroughly that recycling is impossible. In addition, recycling processes themselves can create residuals. But materials research will continue to progress and discover new ways of recycling. For a long time, automobile tires could not be recycled because the original production process changed the physical structure of the rubber. Now with new technology, vast quantities of used tires, instead of blighting the landscape, can be incorporated into park benches, roads, and other products.

These fundamental relationships are very important. We must remember, however, that our ultimate goal is to reduce the damages caused by the discharge of production and consumption residuals. Reducing the total quantity of these residuals is one major way of doing this, and the relationships discussed indicate the basic ways this may be done. But damages also can be reduced by working directly on the stream of residuals, a fact that must be kept in mind in our later discussions.

The Environment as an Economic and Social Asset

One good way of thinking about the environment is as an asset that produces important services for humans and nonhuman organisms. But the ability of the environment to produce these services can be degraded. In recent years, the concept of sustainability has become popular as a criterion for evaluating decisions that have environmental implications. Sustainability is a matter of making decisions in the short run that do not have serious negative impacts in the long run.

A way of thinking about this is in terms of a **trade-off** between conventional economic output (conventional goods and services such as cars, loaves of bread, insurance policies, etc.) and environmental quality. A trade-off of this type is depicted in Figure 2.2. Consider first panel (a). This shows a **production possibility curve** (PPC), which is simply a curve showing the

FIGURE 2.2   **Production Possibility Curves for Current and Future Generations**

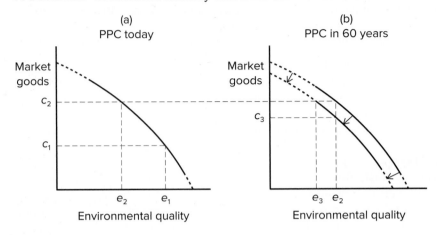

different combinations of two things a society may produce at any time, given its resources and technological capabilities. The vertical axis has an index of the aggregate output of an economy, that is, the total market value of conventional economic goods traded in the economy in a year. The horizontal axis has an index of environmental quality, derived from data on different dimensions of the ambient environment, for example, airborne sulfur dioxide (SO_2) concentrations, urban noise levels, and water-quality data. The curved relationship shows the different combinations of these two outcomes—marketed output and environmental quality—that are available to a group of people who have a fixed endowment of resources and technology with which to work.[5]

The exact shape and location of the PPC are determined by the **technical capacities** in the economy, together with the ecological facts—meteorology, hydrology, and so on—of the natural system in which the society is situated. It says, for example, that if the current level of economic output is c_1, an increase to c_2 can be obtained only at the cost of a decrease in environmental quality from e_1 to e_2. One major objective of any society, of course, is to change the PPC so that the underlying trade-off is more favorable—in other words, so that a given economic output is consistent with higher levels of environmental quality.

Although the PPC itself is a technical constraint, where a society chooses to locate itself on its PPC is a matter of **social choice.** This depends on the values that people in that society place on conventional economic output as opposed to environmental quality. Where values come from is an open question, but it is clear that values differ from one person to another and even for the same person at different points in time. The study of the values that people place on environmental factors is a major part of environmental economics and will be discussed in more detail in Chapters 7 and 8.

[5] The extremes of the PPC perhaps should be drawn with dashed lines. It's not clear what an outcome would be with "zero" environmental quality, or with "zero" economic output. Thus, these extreme points are essentially undefined, and we focus on points in the interior of the diagram.

If a society puts too much stress on increasing its measured output, it may end up at a point like (c_2, e_2) in Figure 2.2, panel (a), even though true social welfare may be higher at a point like (c_1, e_1).

Production possibility curves can also be used to elucidate other aspects of social choice about the environment. One of the fundamental distinctions that can be made in environmental analysis and the development of environmental policy is that between the **short run** and the **long run.** Short-run decisions are those made on the basis of consequences that happen in the near term or of impacts as they are felt by the present generation. Long-run decisions are those in which attention is paid to consequences that occur well into the future or to future generations. There is a widespread feeling that economic decisions today are being made primarily through short-run considerations, whereas environmental policy needs to be made with long-run considerations in mind. A good way of thinking about this is through the use of PPCs, introduced earlier.

Consider again Figure 2.2. The two panels actually show PPCs for two time periods. Panel (a) shows the trade-offs facing the current generation. Panel (b) shows the PPCs for people in, say, 60 to 80 years, the generation consisting of your great-grandchildren. According to panel (a), the present generation could choose combinations (c_1, e_1), (c_2, e_2), or any others on the curve. But the future is not independent of the choice made today. It is conceivable, for example, that degrading the environment too much today will affect future possibilities—by depleting certain important resources, by pollution that is so high it causes irreversible damage, or simply by a pollutant that is very long lived and affects future generations. In effect, this could shift the future PPC back from where it otherwise would be. This is depicted in panel (b) of the diagram. Your grandchildren will be confronted with a reduced set of possibilities as compared to the choices we face today. The future generation, finding itself on the inner PPC, can still have the same level of marketed output we have today (c_2), but only at a lower level of environmental quality (e_3) than we have today. Alternatively, it could enjoy the same level of environmental quality, but only with a reduced level of marketed output (c_3).

It needs to be recognized, of course, that the influence of today's decisions on future production possibilities is much more complicated than this discussion might suggest. It's not only environmental degradation that affects future conditions, but also technical developments and changes in human capacities. Thus, today's decisions could shift the future PPC either in or out, depending on many dynamic factors that are hard to predict. But we need to be particularly alert to avoid decisions today that would have the effect of shifting the future PPC to the left. This is the essence of recent discussions about sustainability. Sustainability means that future PPCs are not adversely affected by what is done today. It does not mean that we must maximize environmental quality today, because that implies zero output of goods and services. It means simply that environmental impacts need to be reduced enough today to avoid shifting future PPCs back in comparison to today's production possibilities. We will meet the idea of sustainability at several points throughout this book.

Basic Terminology

Throughout the chapters that follow we use the following terms:

- **Ambient quality:** *Ambient* refers to the surrounding environment, so *ambient quality* refers to the quantity of pollutants in the environment, for example, the concentration of SO_2 in the air over a city or the concentration of a particular chemical in the waters of a lake.

- **Environmental quality:** A term used to refer broadly to the state of the natural environment. This includes the notion of ambient quality and such things as the visual and aesthetic quality of the environment.

- **Residuals:** Material that is left over after something has been produced. A plant, for example, takes in a variety of raw materials and converts these into some product. Materials and energy left after the product has been produced are *production residuals. Consumption residuals* are whatever is left over after consumers have finished using the products that contained or otherwise used these materials.

- **Emissions:** The portion of production or consumption residuals that is placed in the environment, sometimes directly, sometimes after treatment.

- **Recycling:** The process of returning some or all of the production or consumption residuals to be used again in production or consumption.

- **Pollutant:** A substance, energy form, or action that, when introduced into the natural environment, results in a lowering of the ambient quality level. We want to think of this as including not only the traditional things, such as oil spilled into oceans or chemicals placed in the air, but also activities, such as certain building developments, that result in "visual pollution."

- **Effluent:** Sometimes *effluent* is used to talk about water pollutants, and *emissions* to refer to air pollutants, but in this book these two words are used interchangeably.

- **Pollution:** *Pollution* is actually a tricky word to define. Some people might say that pollution results when any amount, no matter how small, of a residual has been introduced into the environment. Others hold that pollution is something that happens only when the ambient quality of the environment has been degraded enough to cause some damage.

- **Damages:** The negative impacts produced by environmental pollution on people in the form of health effects, visual degradation, and so on, and on elements of the ecosystem through disruption of ecological linkages, species extinctions, and so forth.

- **Environmental medium:** Broad dimensions of the natural world that collectively constitute the environment, usually classified as land, water, and air.

- **Source:** The location at which emissions occur, such as a factory, an automobile, or a leaking landfill.

Emissions, Ambient Quality, and Damages

Let us now focus on what happens at the end of those two discharge arrows at the right side of Figure 2.1. Very simply, **emissions** produce changes in ambient levels of environmental quality, which in turn cause damages to humans and nonhumans. Figure 2.3 shows one way of sketching out this relationship. It shows n sources of emissions[6]; they might be private firms, government agencies, or consumers. Sources take in various inputs and use different types of technologies in production and consumption. In the process they produce residuals. How these residuals are handled then has a critical effect on subsequent stages. Some may be recovered and recycled back into production or consumption. Many can be put through treatment processes (residuals handling) that can render them more benign when emitted. Some of these processes are strictly physical (mufflers on cars and trucks, settling ponds at wastewater treatment plants, catalytic converters); others involve chemical transformations of various types (advanced treatment of domestic wastewater).

All emissions must necessarily go into one or more of the different **environmental media** (land, air, water), and there is an important relationship among them. For a given quantity of total residuals, if the amounts going into one medium are reduced, the amounts going into the others must necessarily increase. When SO_2 is removed from the stack gases of power plants, for example, the sulfur compounds have not been destroyed. Instead, we end up with a sulfurous sludge that must be disposed of some other way, perhaps by land burial. If this material is incinerated, airborne emissions result, but there will still be certain quantities of solid residuals that must be disposed of elsewhere.

In a situation involving multiple sources, emissions will often become mixed into a single flow. In the real world this mixing may be complete; for example, the effluent from two pulp mills located at the same point on a river may mix so thoroughly that a few miles downstream it is impossible to differentiate one source's effluent from the other's. When there are a million or so cars moving about an urban area, the emissions from all become uniformly mixed together. In other cases the mixing is less than complete. If one power plant is just outside the city and another is 20 miles upwind, the closer plant will normally bear a greater responsibility for deteriorating air quality in the city than the other.

This mixing of emissions is a more significant problem than might first appear. With just a single source, the line of responsibility is clear, and to get an improvement in ambient quality, we know exactly whose emissions have to be controlled. But with multiple sources, responsibilities become less clear. We may know how much we want to cut back total emissions, but the problem of distributing this total reduction among the different sources still exists. Each source then has an incentive to get the others to bear a larger share

---

[6] In economic writing, the letter n is often used to designate an unspecified number of items, the exact value of which will vary from one situation to another.

FIGURE 2.3   Emissions, Ambient Quality, and Damages

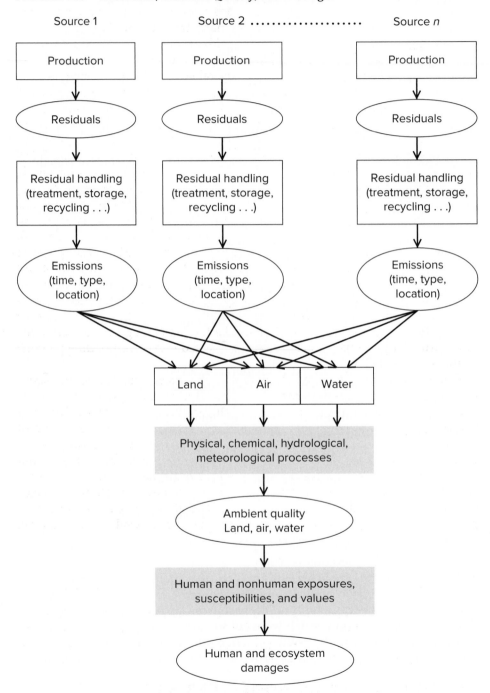

Source: *Inspired by John B. Braden and Kathleen Segerson,* "Information Problems in the Design of Nonpoint Source Pollution Policy," in *The Management of Nonpoint Source Pollution,* Association of Environmental and Resource Economics (AERE) Workshop Papers Lexington, June 6–7, 1991.

of the burden of reducing emissions. With every source thinking along the same lines, pollution-control programs face a real problem of design and enforcement. We will run into this problem many times in the chapters to come.

Once a given quantity and quality of residuals have been introduced into a particular environmental medium, it is the physical, chemical, biological, meteorological, and so on, processes of the natural system that determine how the residuals translate into particular **ambient quality levels.** For example, wind and temperature conditions will affect whether and how residuals emitted into the air affect nearby neighborhoods, as well as people living farther downwind. In addition, because these meteorological conditions vary from day to day, the same level of emissions can produce different ambient quality levels at different times. Acid rain is produced through chemical processes acting primarily on sulfur dioxide emissions emitted far upwind; smog is also the result of complex chemical reactions involving sunlight and quantities of various pollutants. Underground hydrological processes affect the transportation of materials disposed of in landfills. And so on. Thus, to know how particular emissions will affect ambient quality levels, we must have a good understanding of the physical and chemical workings of the environment itself. This is where the natural and physical sciences come in—to study the full range of environmental phenomena, from small, localized models of groundwater flow in a particular aquifer, to complex models of large lakes and river basins, to studies of interregional wind patterns, to global climate models. The fundamental goal is to determine how particular patterns of emissions are translated into corresponding patterns of ambient quality levels.

Finally, there are damages. A given set of ambient conditions translates into particular exposure patterns for living and nonliving systems. Of course, these exposures are a function not only of the physical processes involved, but also of the human choices that are made about where and how to live, and of the susceptibilities of living and nonliving systems to varying environmental conditions. Last, damages are related to human values. Human beings do not have amorphous preferences over all possible outcomes of the economical/ environmental interaction; they prefer some outcomes over others. A major part of environmental economics is trying to determine the relative values that people place on these different environmental outcomes, a subject to which we will turn in later chapters on benefit–cost analysis.

Types of Pollutants

Physically, the residuals identified in Figure 2.3 consist of a vast assortment of materials and energy flowing into the three environmental media. It is helpful to distinguish among broad types of emissions according to factors that critically affect their economic characteristics.

Cumulative Versus Noncumulative Pollutants

One simple and important dimension of environmental pollutants is whether they accumulate over time or tend to dissipate soon after being emitted.

The classic case of a **noncumulative pollutant** is noise; as long as the source operates, noise is emitted into the surrounding air, but as soon as the source is shut down, the noise stops. At the other end of the spectrum there are pollutants that cumulate in the environment in nearly the same amounts as they are emitted. Radioactive waste, for example, decays over time but at such a slow rate in relation to human life spans that for all intents and purposes it will be with us permanently; it is a strictly cumulative type of pollutant. Another **cumulative pollutant** is plastics. The search for a degradable plastic has been going on for decades, but so far plastic is a substance that decays very slowly by human standards; thus, what we dispose of will be in the environment permanently. Many chemicals are cumulative pollutants; once emitted they are basically with us forever.

Between these two ends of the spectrum there are many types of effluent that are to some extent, but not completely, cumulative. The classic case is organic matter emitted into water bodies—for example, the wastes, treated or not, emitted from municipal waste treatment plants. Once emitted, the wastes are subject to natural chemical processes that tend to break down the organic materials into their constituent elements, thus rendering them much more benign. The water, in other words, has a natural assimilative capacity that allows it to accept organic substances and render them less harmful. As long as this assimilative capacity has not been exceeded in any particular case, the effluent source can be shut off, and in a few days, weeks, or months, the water quality will return to normal. Once emissions exceed this assimilative capacity, however, the process becomes cumulative.

Whether a pollutant is cumulative or noncumulative, the basic problem is essentially the same: trying to figure out the environmental damages and relating these back to the costs of reducing emissions. But this job is much more difficult for cumulative than for noncumulative pollutants. With noncumulative emissions, ambient concentrations are strictly a function of current emissions—reducing these emissions to zero would lead to zero ambient concentrations. But with cumulative pollutants the relationship is more complex. The fact that a pollutant cumulates over time in the environment has the effect of breaking the direct connection between current emissions and current damages. This has a number of implications. For one thing it makes the science more difficult. The cause-and-effect relationships become harder to isolate when there is a lot of time intervening between them. It also may make it more difficult to get people to focus on damages from today's emissions, again because there may only be a weak connection between today's emissions and today's ambient quality levels. Furthermore, cumulative pollutants by definition lead to future damages, and human beings have shown a depressing readiness to discount future events and avoid coming to grips with them in the present.

Local Versus Regional and Global Pollutants

Some emissions have an impact only in restricted, localized regions, whereas others have an impact over wider regions, perhaps on the global environment. Noise pollution and the degradation of the visual environment are local in their impacts; the damages from any particular source are usually limited to relatively small groups of people in a circumscribed region. Note that this is a statement about how widespread the effects are from any particular pollution source, not about how important the overall problem is throughout a country or the world. Many pollutants, on the other hand, have widespread impacts, over a large region or perhaps over the global environment. Acid rain is a regional problem; emissions in one region of the United States (and of Europe) affect people in other parts of the country or region. The ozone-depleting effects of chlorofluorocarbon emissions from various countries work through chemical changes in the earth's stratosphere, which means that the impacts are truly global.

Other things being equal, local environmental problems ought to be easier to deal with than regional or national problems, which in turn ought to be easier to manage than global problems. If I smoke out my neighbor with my wood stove, we may be able to arrange a solution among ourselves, or we can call on local political institutions to do it. But if my behavior causes more distant pollution, solutions may be more difficult. If we are within the same political system, we can call on these institutions to arrange solutions. For a growing number of international and global environmental issues, we are far from having effective means of responding, both because the exact nature of the physical impacts is difficult to describe and because the requisite international political institutions are only beginning to appear.

Point-Source Versus Nonpoint-Source Pollutants

Pollution sources differ in terms of the ease with which actual points of discharge may be identified. The points at which sulfur dioxide emissions leave a large power plant are easy to identify; they come out the end of the smokestacks associated with each plant. Municipal waste treatment plants normally have a single outfall from which all of the wastewater is discharged. These are called **point-source pollutants.** There are many pollutants for which there are no well-defined points of discharge. Agricultural chemicals, for example, usually run off the land in a dispersed or diffused pattern, and even though they may pollute specific streams or underground aquifers, there is no single pipe or stack from which these chemicals are emitted. This is a **nonpoint-source** type of pollutant. Urban storm water runoff is also an important nonpoint-source problem.

As one would expect, point-source pollutants are likely to be easier to come to grips with than nonpoint-source pollutants. They will probably be easier to measure and monitor and easier to study in terms of the connections between emissions and impacts. This means that it will ordinarily be easier to develop and administer control policies for point-source pollutants. As we will see, not all pollutants fit neatly into one or another of these categories.

Continuous Versus Episodic Emissions

Emissions from electric power plants or municipal waste treatment plants are more or less continuous. The plants are designed to be in operation continuously, although the operating rate may vary somewhat over the day, week, or season. Thus, the emissions from these operations are more or less continuous, and the policy problem is to manage the rate of these discharges. Immediate comparisons can be made between control programs and rates of emissions. The fact that emissions are continuous does not mean that damages are also continuous, however. Meteorological and hydrological events can turn continuous emissions into uncertain damages. But control programs are often easier to carry out when emissions are not subject to large-scale fluctuations.

Many pollutants are emitted on an episodic basis, however. The classic example is accidental oil or chemical spills. The policy problem here is to design and manage a system so that the probability of accidental discharges is reduced. Yet, with an episodic effluent there may be nothing to measure, at least in the short run. Even though there have been no large-scale radiation releases from U.S. nuclear power plants, for example, there is still a "pollution" problem if they are being managed in such a way as to increase the **probability** of an accidental release in the future. To measure the probabilities of episodic emissions, it is necessary to have data on actual occurrences over a long time period or to estimate them from engineering data and similar information. We then have to determine how much insurance we wish to have against these episodic events. Exhibit 2.1 discusses the case of a common episodic pollutant: pipeline spills.

Managing Episodic Sources of Pollution

EXHIBIT **2.1**

Episodic, largely accidental, releases of environmental pollutants are relatively common in today's world. A source that has recently gained prominence in the United States is railroad tank cars. The surge in oil production has been accompanied by a large increase in petroleum shipments via long trains of tank cars. Periodic derailments have led to spills, with accompanying fires and contamination of land and water resources.

Another source of episodic spills is through pipeline breaches. The United States, like many countries, is crisscrossed with thousands of miles of underground pipelines. Breakages and spills, small and large, result from a variety of human and technical factors.

A prime element in dealing with these kinds of spills is the concept of **risk**. Risk refers to the likelihood of accidents such as these, and the benefits and costs of changing these likelihoods.

Risk can be reduced by all kinds of technical and behavioral factors: more frequent inspections, stronger pipes and tank cars, changes in operating procedures, better clean-up technology, etc.

Risky situations make it more difficult to know underlying cause and effect relationships. If we change operating procedures, how do we know that we are changing the likelihood and severity of accidents? We can try to analyze it through uncertain engineering predictions, or collect accident data over a period of time and see if probabilities have changed. Either way we are dealing with uncertainty. The other part of the equation is how people in general value reductions in risk. How much is it worth to people to reduce the chances of tank-car accidents from say one in a hundred trains, to one in two hundred trains? Or to reduce pipeline leaks from one every 1,000 pipe miles to one every 1,500 pipe miles?

Environmental Damages Not Related to Emissions

So far the discussion has focused on the characteristics of different types of environmental pollutants as they relate to the discharge of residual materials or energy, but there are many important instances of deteriorating environmental quality that are not traceable to residuals discharges. The conversion of land to housing and commercial areas destroys the environmental value of that land, whether it be its ecosystem value, such as habitat or wetland, or its scenic value. Other land uses, such as logging or strip mining, also can have important impacts. In cases such as these, the policy problem is still to understand the incentives of people whose decisions create these impacts and to change these incentives when appropriate. Although there are no physical emissions to monitor and control, there are nevertheless outcomes that can be described, evaluated, and managed with appropriate policies.

Summary

The purpose of this chapter was to explore some basic linkages between the economy and the environment. We differentiated between the role of the natural system as a supplier of raw material inputs for the economy and as a receptor for production and consumption residuals. The first of these is normally called natural resource economics and the second environmental economics. After a very brief review of natural resource economics, we introduced the fundamental balance phenomenon, which says that in the long run all materials taken by human beings out of the natural system must eventually end up back in that system. This means that to reduce residuals flows into the environment, we must reduce materials taken from the ecosystem, and we discussed the three fundamental ways that this can be done. This led into a discussion of the inherent trade-off that exists between conventional economic goods and environmental quality and between current and future generations.

We then focused more directly on the flow of residuals back into the environment, making a distinction among emissions, ambient environmental quality, and damages. The environmental damages from a given quantity of emissions can be very substantially altered by handling these emissions in different ways. Our next step was to provide a brief catalog of the different types of emissions and pollutants, as well as nonpollution types of environmental impacts such as aesthetic effects.

Questions for Further Discussion

1. Economies grow by investing in new sources of productivity, new plants and equipment, infrastructure such as roads, and so on. How does this type of investment affect the flows depicted in Figure 2.1?

2. What is the difference between a residual and a pollutant? Illustrate this in the context of a common airborne emission such as sulfur dioxide (SO_2); with noise; with junked automobiles; with an unsightly building.

3. Why are long-lived, cumulative pollutants so much harder to manage than short-lived, noncumulative pollutants?

4. As depicted in Figure 2.3, most emissions from individual sources get mixed in with those of other sources, to produce the general level of ambient quality. What problems does this present in adopting emission-control policies to get a cleaner environment?

5. Consider the production and use of single-use, plastic shopping bags, and examine their flows along all parts of Figure 2.1. Do the same for paper shopping bags.

6. What considerations come into play when considering whether a country or any other political entity is spending the right amount for environmental quality improvements?

7. Suppose there is a technological change that allows firms to produce goods and services with less pollution. How would this affect the production possibilities curves of Figure 2.2, and where might society choose to locate itself on this curve?

For additional readings and Web sites pertaining to the material in this chapter, see **www.mhhe.com/field7e.**

Section 2

Analytical Tools

Scientific analysis consists of giving coherent explanations of relevant events and of showing how other outcomes might have occurred if conditions had been different. It is to show connections among variables and to detail the ways in which they are interrelated. To do this, a science must develop a specialized vocabulary and conceptual structure with which to focus on its chosen subject matter. In this section, we cover some of the basic ideas of economics and their application to environmental problems. Those of you who have already been introduced to microeconomics can treat the next few chapters as a review. For those who are seeing this material for the first time, remember that the purpose is to develop a set of analytical tools that can be used to focus on issues of environmental quality.

Chapter 3

Benefits and Costs, Supply and Demand

This and the next chapter contain discussions of certain basic tools of **microeconomics.** The objective is to provide an understanding of fundamental concepts so that they can be used later in analyzing environmental impacts and policies. The current chapter is about benefits and costs. The juxtaposition of these two words indicates that we are going to approach things in a **trade-off,** or **balancing,** mode. Economic actions, including environmental actions, have two sides: On the one side they create value and on the other side they encounter costs. Thus, we must have basic concepts that deal with these two parts of the problem. We look first at the question of value, later at costs.

It needs to be mentioned at the very outset that microeconomic theory is **abstract.** This means that it normally proceeds with simplified models that try to capture the essence of a problem without all the details that one observes in the real world. The reason for this is that we want to reveal basic connections and relationships among the important elements of a problem, relationships that are difficult to see if we just observe the surface richness of the real world. There are dangers in this, of course; one can inadvertently overlook details that do have an important impact in reality. For example, in the past, many environmental models have been developed without considering the costs of actually enforcing environmental laws. But in the real world, **enforcement costs** are more than a detail; they can have a great impact on the outcomes of environmental regulations. Thus, we need to be careful that our abstractions truly serve to reveal basic connections and do not cover up important dimensions of problems we are trying to understand.

Willingness to Pay

The value side of the analysis is based on the fundamental notion that individuals have **preferences** for goods and services; given a choice, they can express preferences for one good over another or one bundle of goods over another bundle. How to make visible this abstract notion of preference? We need to simplify the discussion; in a modern economy there are thousands of different goods and services available, so let us focus on just one of them. We now can present the following fundamental concept: The value of this good to a person is what the person is willing and able to sacrifice for it. Sacrifice what? In a barter economy, the willingness to sacrifice for one thing would be expressed in terms of some other thing. In a market economy, it makes most sense to talk about sacrificing generalized purchasing power. Thus, the fundamental idea of value is tied to **willingness to pay;** the value of a good to somebody is what that person is *willing to pay* for it.[1]

What determines how much a person is willing to pay to obtain some good or service or some environmental asset? It's partly a question of **individual values.** Some people are willing to sacrifice a lot to visit the Grand Canyon; others are not. Some people are willing to pay a lot for a quiet living environment; others are not. Some people place a high value on trying to preserve the habitat of unique animal and plant species; others do not. It is obvious also that a person's **wealth** affects the willingness to sacrifice; the wealthier a person is, the better that person can afford to pay for various goods and services. Willingness to pay, in other words, also reflects **ability to pay.**

It is easy to misunderstand the implications of using willingness to pay as a measure of value of an outcome. It does not imply, for example, that the only thing that counts is money payments in a market. Many people speak of and genuinely feel spiritual qualities associated with nature and the natural environment. For a person holding these values, it is simply to say that they would be willing to sacrifice to attain these ends.

Let us build a graphic picture of a person's willingness to pay for pounds of organic potatoes per week. We go through the following steps:

1. Assuming he or she has no organic potatoes at present, how much would he or she be willing to pay for one pound? Suppose the answer is $3.80.
2. Assuming he or she presently possesses one pound, how much is he or she willing to pay for the second pound? Assume he or she answers $2.60.
3. Assuming he or she possesses two pounds, how much would he or she be willing to pay for a third pound? Assume he or she answers $1.70.
4. How much is he or she willing to pay for additional potatoes? Assume he or she answers $1.40 for the fourth, 90¢ for the fifth, 60¢ for the sixth, and nothing for the seventh.

These willingness-to-pay numbers are shown in Figure 3.1. These numbers depict a fundamental relationship of economics: the notion of diminishing willingness to pay. As the number of units consumed increases, the willingness to pay for additional units of that good normally goes down.

---

[1] It may sound as though we are limiting the analysis only to physical goods and services, but this is not true. The concept of willingness to pay is quite general, and in Chapter 5 we will apply it to differing levels of environmental quality.

FIGURE 3.1 **The Concept of Willingness to Pay**

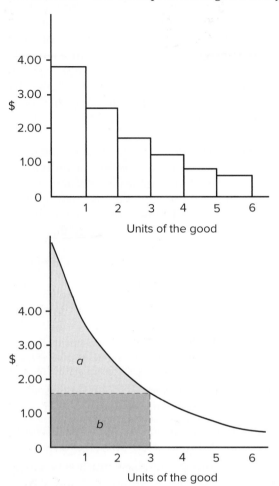

It is not very convenient to work with diagrams that are step-shaped as in the top of Figure 3.1. So we now change things a bit by assuming that people can consume fractions of items in addition to integer values. What this does is produce a smoothly shaped willingness-to-pay curve, such as the one pictured in the bottom of Figure 3.1. On this smooth function we have singled out one quantity for illustrative purposes. It shows that the willingness to pay for the third unit is $1.70.

The next step is to distinguish between total and marginal willingness to pay. Suppose a person is already consuming two units of this good; according to the willingness-to-pay curve, that person would be willing to pay $1.70 for a third unit. This is the **marginal willingness to pay**—in this case, for the third unit. *Marginal* is thus a word that describes the *additional* willingness to pay of a person for one more unit. So the height of the rectangles in the top of Figure 3.1 and the height of the curve in the bottom graph show the marginal willingness to pay for this good.

The **total willingness to pay** for a given consumption level is the total amount a person would be willing to pay to attain that consumption level rather than go without the good entirely. Suppose the person is consuming at a level of three units, his or her total willingness to pay for consuming this quantity is $8.10, which is in fact the sum of the heights of the demand rectangles between the origin and the consumption level in question ($3.80 for the first plus $2.60 for the second plus $1.70 for the third). This corresponds, in the smooth version of the willingness-to-pay function, to the whole area under the willingness-to-pay curve from the origin up to the quantity in question. For three units of consumption, the total willingness to pay is equal to an amount represented by the combined areas *a* and *b*.

Demand

There is another way of looking at these marginal willingness-to-pay relationships. They are more familiarly known as **demand curves.** An individual demand curve shows the quantity of a good or service that the individual in question would demand (i.e., purchase and consume) at any particular price. For example, suppose a person whose marginal willingness-to-pay/demand curve is shown in the bottom part of Figure 3.1 is able to purchase this item at a unit price of $1.70. The quantity he or she would demand at this price is three units. The reason is that his or her marginal willingness to pay for each of the first three units exceeds the purchase price. He or she would not push his or her consumption higher than this because his or her marginal willingness to pay for additional quantities would be less than the purchase price.

An individual's demand/marginal willingness-to-pay curve for a good or service is a way of summarizing his or her personal consumption attitudes and capabilities for that good. Thus, we would normally expect these relationships to differ somewhat among individuals, because individual tastes and preferences vary. Figure 3.2 displays several different demand curves. Panel (a) shows two demand curves, one steeper than the other. The steeper one shows a situation in which marginal willingness to pay drops off fairly rapidly as the quantity consumed increases; the flatter one shows marginal willingness to pay that, although lower to begin with, goes down less rapidly as quantity increases. These two demand curves could represent the case of one consumer and two different goods or services, or the case of two different consumers and the same good or service.

FIGURE 3.2 **Typical Demand/Marginal Willingness-to-Pay Curves**

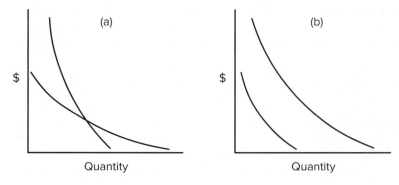

Panel (b) of Figure 3.2 also has two demand curves; they have the same general shape, but one is situated well to the right of the other. The demand curve above and to the right shows a good for which the marginal willingness to pay is substantially higher than it is for the same quantity of the other good. Several factors could account for the difference. They might be:

- demand curves of two different people, with different tastes and preferences;
- demand curves for the same person, the one on the right being after an income rise; or
- demand curves for the same person, before and after that person receives more information about the good (for example, the possible presence of pesticide residues in a food item).

Note that the demand curves are in fact curvilinear, rather than straight lines. A straight-line demand relationship would imply a uniform change in the quantity demanded as its price changes. For most goods, however, this is unlikely to be true. At low prices and high rates of consumption, studies have shown that relatively small increases in price will lead to substantial reductions in quantity demanded. At high prices and low quantity demanded, however, price increases have a much smaller effect: they produce much smaller reductions in quantity demanded. This gives us a demand relationship that is convex to the origin (i.e., relatively flat at low prices and steep at higher prices). (See Example 3.1.)

The Demand for Water   EXAMPLE 3.1

Researchers have investigated the demand for water by households. Many might think that the amount of water a household uses would be related only to such things as the size of the family rather than the price of the water. This is not the case, however. In general, as the price people pay for water increases, the amount of water they use declines.

This demand is somewhat complicated. Water is used for a number of household purposes—for example, inside the house for sanitation and food preparation and outside the house for car washing, lawn sprinkling, and so forth. At higher prices, consumers will curtail unessential water uses substantially, but their water use for essential purposes will not decline as much in relative terms.

This means that the demand curve for water is shaped as in the diagram.

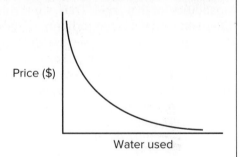

At low and moderate prices, increased prices will lead to a substantial drop in household water use as people cut back on unessential uses. Thus, the demand curve is relatively flat in this range. But, at higher prices where most of the water is going to essential purposes, further price increases will lead to relatively smaller drops in consumption, and hence a steeper demand curve.

Economics is sometimes misunderstood as assuming that people are driven only by thoughts of their own welfare, that they are complete egoists. Because these are individual demand curves, they do indeed summarize the attitudes of single individuals, but this does not imply that individuals make decisions with only themselves in mind. Some people may indeed act this way, but for most there are many other powerful motives that affect their demands for different goods, including altruism toward friends and relatives, feelings of civic virtue toward their communities, a sense of social responsibility toward fellow citizens, and so on. Individual tastes and preferences spring from these factors as well as from more narrow considerations of personal likes and dislikes.

Aggregate Demand/Willingness to Pay

In examining real-world issues of environmental quality and pollution-control policy, we normally focus our attention on the behavior of groups of people rather than single individuals. Our interest is in the total, or aggregate, demand/marginal willingness to pay of defined groups of people.

An **aggregate demand curve** is the summation of a number of individual demand curves.[2] What individuals are involved depends on which particular aggregation we want to look at: the demand of people living in the city of New York for brussels sprouts; the demand of people living in New Orleans for clean water in the Mississippi River; the demand of people living in the entire country for public parks; and so on.

Figure 3.3 depicts a very simple aggregate demand curve, one in which the group consists of only three people. The aggregate demand curve is found by summing together, at each price, the quantities that are demanded by the three individuals, as in the following tabulation.

FIGURE 3.3   **Aggregate Demand/Marginal Willingness-to-Pay Curves**

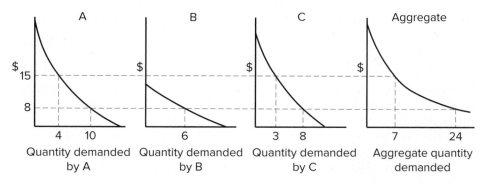

---

[2] The term *aggregate demand* is also used in macroeconomics to refer to the total of goods and services produced in the entire economy during a given year. We are using it in a more restricted sense, to refer to the combined demand of a defined group of people, sometimes, but not always, smaller than the national total.

	Individual Quantities Demanded			Aggregate Quantity Demanded
Price ($)	A	B	C	
8	10	6	8	24
11	6	2	5	13
15	4	0	3	7

Looked at in the other direction, we note that when Person A is consuming ten units, his or her marginal willingness to pay is $8, whereas when Persons B and C consume, respectively, at six units and eight units, their marginal willingness to pay is also $8. Therefore, on the aggregate level, the marginal willingness to pay is $8. If one more unit is made available to this aggregate, it must be distributed to Person A, Person B, or Person C, each of whom has a marginal willingness to pay of $8; thus, the aggregate marginal willingness to pay is also $8.

Benefits

We now come to the idea of **benefits**. *Benefit* is one of those ordinary words to which economists have given a technical meaning. When the environment is cleaned up, people obtain benefits; when the environment is allowed to deteriorate in quality, benefits are taken away from them—they are, in fact, being damaged. We need some way of conceptualizing and measuring this notion of benefits.

The word *benefits* clearly implies being made better off. If individuals are benefited by something, their position is improved—they are better off. Conversely, if they are worse off, it must be because benefits were somehow taken away from them. How do we confer benefits on people? We do this by giving them something they value. How do we know that they value something? We know by the fact that they are willing to sacrifice, or willing to pay, for it. According to this logic, then, the benefits that people get from something are equal to the amount they are willing to pay for it.

The logic behind this definition of *benefits* is quite strong. It means we can use ordinary demand curves to determine the benefits of making various things available to people. For example, Figure 3.4 shows two demand curves, and on the horizontal axis two quantity levels are indicated. Suppose we wish to estimate the total benefits of increasing the availability of this item from quantity q_1 to quantity q_2. According to our previous thinking, benefits are measured by willingness to pay, and we know that total willingness to pay is measured by areas under the demand curve; in this case, the area under the demand curves between quantity q_1 and quantity q_2. So for the lower demand curve, the benefits of such an increase in availability are equal to an amount shown by area b, whereas benefits in the case of the higher demand curve are equal to the total area $a + b$.

FIGURE 3.4   **Willingness to Pay and Benefits**

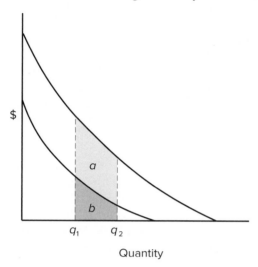

The logic of this seems reasonable. The people with the higher demand curve must place a greater value on this item; whatever it is, they are willing to pay more for it than the people whose demand curve is the lower function. This is in agreement with common sense. The more people value something, the more they are benefited by having more of that something made available, or, to say the same thing, you can't damage people by taking away from them something that they don't value.

This is the fundamental logic underlying much of environmental economics. It underlies, for example, questions of measuring the damage done to people when the natural environment surrounding them is degraded. It underlies the question of evaluating the impacts of environmental programs and policies undertaken by local, state, and federal governments. This is the strength of the economic approach, the fact that it is based on a clear notion of the value that people place on different things.

But the idea also has shortcomings. For one thing, demand and therefore benefits are often very hard to measure when it concerns environmental questions, as we will see in later chapters. For another, we have to remember that demand curves are critically affected by the ability to pay for something as well as preferences. In Figure 3.4, for example, the lower demand curve could represent a group of people with lower incomes than those with the higher demand curve. The logic of the argument would lead to the conclusion that the increase in quantity of q_2-q_1 would produce fewer benefits among lower-income people than among higher-income people. This may not be a very equitable conclusion, depending on the circumstances. Thus, although the logic of the concept is clear, we have to be careful in using it, especially when we are dealing with groups of people with diverse income levels. The main step in doing this is to find out as clearly as possible how the various environmental policies and programs, present or proposed, affect people at different income levels.

One other possible problem exists in using conventional demand curves to measure benefits. An individual's demand for something is clearly affected by how much he or she knows about it; a person would not be willing to pay for a good if, for example, he or she was ignorant of its very existence. In Figure 3.4, the higher demand curve might be the demand for a good before it is found out that it contains a carcinogenic substance, and the lower demand curve shows demand after this fact becomes known. There is nothing especially surprising about this; people, after all, do become more knowledgeable about things over time as a matter of course. But in today's world, this could be a complication, especially with regard to the environment. We don't fully understand many of the effects of environmental degradation; furthermore, people's views about the importance of many of these effects are blown back and forth almost from day to day, by the media, by the scientific press, and so on. Care must be exercised in taking people's demand curves of the moment, influenced as they are by all kinds of real and imagined factors, as true expressions of the benefits of environmental actions.

Cost

We now switch to the other side of the picture and consider costs. Although some things in life are free—an idea, for example—it is generally true that goods and services cannot be produced out of thin air; they require the expenditure of productive resources, or inputs, in the process. The more of something that is desired, the more resources we will have to devote to its production. What is needed is a way of describing and talking about the costs of producing useful things, whether these are normal consumer goods, such as cars or hot-water bottles, or services, such as transportation or insurance, or environmental quality through the treatment of waste residuals, recycling, or land-use controls.

Imagine a simple production process. Suppose, for example, we are producing a certain line of cardboard boxes. To produce boxes, many types of productive inputs are required: labor, machinery of various descriptions, energy, raw materials, waste-handling equipment, and so on. The first thing needed is a way of valuing these productive resources. If we are a private firm operating in a market economy, we would have little problem: We would value them according to what they cost to procure in the markets. Our profit-and-loss statement at the end of the year would reflect the monetary out-of-pocket costs of the inputs used in the production operation. But our concept of cost will be broader than this. From this wider perspective the costs of these cardboard boxes are what could have been produced with these productive inputs had they not been used in box production. The name for this is *opportunity cost*.

Opportunity Cost

The **opportunity cost** of producing something consists of the maximum value of other outputs we could and would have produced had we not used the resources to produce the item in question. The word *maximum* is used for a reason. The productive inputs used to produce the cardboard boxes could have been used to produce a variety of other things, perhaps automobiles, books, or pollution-control equipment. The opportunity cost of the boxes consists of the maximum value of the alternative output that could have been obtained had we used these resources differently.

Opportunity costs include out-of-pocket costs but are wider than this. Some inputs that are actually used in production may not get registered as cash costs. For example, the spouse of the cardboard box plant operator works as an unpaid assistant in the front office. This may not register as an out-of-pocket cost, but he certainly has an opportunity cost because he could have been working somewhere else if he was not working here. Even more important for our purposes, the cardboard box manufacturing process may produce waste products that are pumped into a nearby stream. Downstream these production residuals produce environmental damage, which are real opportunity costs of producing cardboard boxes, even though they do not show up as costs in the plant's profit-and-loss statement.

The opportunity cost idea is relevant in any situation in which a decision must be made about using productive resources for one purpose rather than another. For a public agency with a given budget, the opportunity costs of a particular policy are the value of alternative policies it might have pursued. For a consumer, the opportunity cost of spending time searching for a particular item is the value of the next most valuable thing to which the consumer could have devoted time.

How is opportunity cost measured? It is not very useful to measure it in terms of the number of other physical items that could have been produced. Nor is there enough information in most cases to be able to measure the value of the next best output that was forgone. In practice, therefore, opportunity costs are measured by the market value of inputs used up in production. For this to work, we have to take care that the inputs have been correctly valued. The office labor must be valued at the going rate even though it is not paid in practice. The effects on downstream water quality must be evaluated and included. Once all inputs have been accounted for, their total value may be taken as the true opportunity costs of production.

Private and Social Costs

Another important distinction is that between **private costs** and **social costs.** The private costs of an action are the costs experienced by the party making the decisions leading to that action. The social costs of an action are *all* of the costs of the action, no matter who experiences them. Social costs include private costs, but also may include much more in certain situations.

Consider the action of driving a car. The private costs of this include the fuel and oil, maintenance, depreciation, and even the driving time experienced by the operator of the car. The social costs include all these private costs and also the costs experienced by people other than the operator who are exposed to the congestion and air pollution resulting from use of the car. This distinction between private and social costs will be very important in later sections where we begin to analyze environmental problems with these tools.

Cost Curves

To summarize cost information, we use cost curves, which are geometric representations of the costs of producing something. And, just as in the case of willingness to pay, we differentiate between **marginal costs** and **total costs.** Consider the cost curves in Figure 3.5. They are meant to apply to a single producing organization, a firm, or perhaps a public agency that is producing some good or service. The graph is laid out, the same as in previous graphs, with quantity on the horizontal axis and a monetary index on the vertical axis. The quantity relates to some period of time, such as a year. The top panel shows marginal costs in terms of a step-shaped relationship. It shows that it costs $5 to produce the first unit of output. If the firm wants to increase output to two units, it must spend an added $7. The addition of a third unit would add $10 to total costs, and so on. Marginal cost is the added costs, the amount by which total costs increase, when output is increased by one unit. It is also the cost savings if production were to decrease by one unit. Thus, the reduction in output from four units to three units would reduce total costs by $15, the marginal cost of the fourth unit.

It is inconvenient to work with step-shaped curves, so we make the assumption that the firm can produce intermediate quantities as well as integer values. This gives a smooth marginal cost curve, as shown in the bottom panel of Figure 3.5. This curve now shows the marginal cost—the added cost of one more unit of output—for any level of output. For example, at an output level of 4.5 units, marginal cost is $19.

Marginal cost curves can be used to determine **total production costs.** On the stepped marinal cost curve of Figure 3.5, suppose we want to know the total cost of producing five units of this item. This is equal to the cost of the first unit ($5), plus that of the second ($7), plus that of the third ($10), and so on. This total is $60; geometrically, this is equal to the total area of the rectangles above the first five units of output. Analogously, in the smoothly shaped marginal cost function in the bottom of the diagram, the total cost of producing a given quantity is the dollar amount equal to the area under the marginal cost curve between the origin and the quantity in question. The total cost of producing 4.5 units of output is thus given by the area marked *a* in the figure.

The Shapes of Cost Curves

The height and shape of the marginal cost curve for any production process will differ from one situation to another, based on several underlying factors. A key

FIGURE 3.5 **The Concept of Marginal Cost**

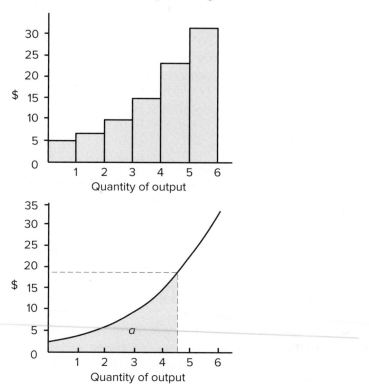

determining factor is the technology utilized in production, and we will discuss this concept later. The price of inputs is also an important factor influencing the heights of marginal cost curves. In general, if input prices increase to a firm or group of firms, their marginal cost curves will shift upward. Another important element is *time,* specifically, the amount of time that a firm has to adjust to changes in its rate of output. These factors may be better understood by looking at some actual marginal cost curves.

Figure 3.6 shows several marginal cost curves. Panel (a) shows a very typical marginal cost curve; initially it declines as output increases but then it increases as output gets larger. The initial decline comes about because of basic efficiencies achievable with larger quantities at this level. Suppose our "output" refers to the quantity of wastewater handled in a municipal treatment plant. At very low levels of output, the plant is not being fully utilized; thus, output increases in this range are accompanied by less-than-proportionate increases in production cost, giving marginal costs that diminish. But as output increases, the capacity of the plant is approached. Machinery must be worked longer, additional people must be hired, and so on. Thus, marginal cost begins to increase.

FIGURE 3.6 Typical Marginal Cost Curves

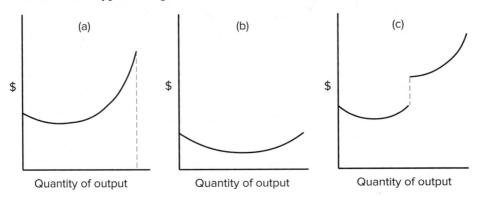

As the capacity of the operation is neared, these problems become more acute. A point may come at which it becomes almost impossible to increase output further, which is the same as saying that the marginal costs of production at this point increase without limit. This limit is indicated by the vertical dashed line in panel (a) of Figure 3.6.

This marginal cost curve depicts an important generic characteristic of all marginal cost curves, namely, that although they may initially decline, they will always increase, eventually, as output becomes large enough. These increases are related to certain underlying factors, such as increased plant utilization, the need to reach farther away for raw materials, and the inevitable higher management costs that accompany larger operations. Virtually all economic studies of particular operations and industries demonstrate increasing marginal production costs, and this fact will be an important shaping element in our later discussions specifically related to environmental quality management. (See Example 3.2.)

Panel (b) of Figure 3.6 shows a marginal cost curve similar in general shape to the one in panel (a), but with less pronounced curvature. In the short run, our wastewater treatment plant had a certain capacity that was basically fixed; but in the long run, there is time to build a larger treatment plant with higher capacities. For larger outputs, the marginal costs of this larger plant will be lower than those of the smaller plant. Yet, even in these long-run situations marginal costs will eventually increase, as is depicted in panel (b). *In our subsequent discussions we will assume that we are working with long-run marginal cost curves, unless specified otherwise.*

Panel (c) of Figure 3.6 represents a more complicated case where there is a discontinuity in the marginal cost curve. After a short downward section, the marginal costs generally trend upward, and at one point they jump upward by some amount. This might represent a "lumpy" investment in new types of technology at a certain point as output increases.

The Marginal Costs of a Firm Producing Organic Apples

EXAMPLE 3.2

Suppose a local orchard produces organic apples, and we consider what the marginal cost curve would look like for this operation. At the very beginning of production (going from none to a small positive amount), we might expect marginal costs to be initially relatively high, because any production at all requires a certain minimum set of inputs. At slightly higher, but still low, rates of production, added output might be obtainable with relatively modest increases in cost because the existing equipment and labor force may be used more intensively and a little extra fuel and apple-picking labor may be all that would be needed. In other words, at low levels of production we might expect marginal costs of producing organic apples to be modest, or even declining. But at somewhat higher levels of output marginal costs will undoubtedly increase. Machinery must be used more intensively, resulting in added maintenance and upgrading costs. At this point we are talking about short-run marginal costs, that is, the marginal costs of increasing production with an apple orchard of given size.

Clearly, when all available steps have been taken, the short-run marginal cost curve would rise rapidly, as the maximum biological capacity of the trees to produce apples is reached.

But if we consider what could happen in the longer run, we would recognize that the orchard, for a cost, could be expanded by buying more land and planting more trees. Of course, additional labor inputs would be necessary. But even in the long run like this, we would expect marginal costs to be increasing. Additional land would have to be bid away from other uses, and it would probably be more difficult to coordinate and carry out decisions over an ever-increasing size of operation.

Thus, the conventional thinking among economists is that all types of production processes would display increasing marginal costs, as pictured in the accompanying diagram. How fast marginal cost rises with output would depend on the technological options available as well as the amount of time allowed for the adjustment. In later chapters, we will apply this thinking to the costs of pollution control.

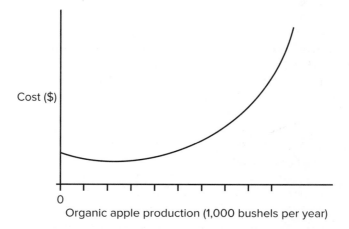

Cost ($)

0

Organic apple production (1,000 bushels per year)

Technology

The most important factor affecting the shapes of marginal cost functions is the **technology** of the production process. By technology we mean the inherent productive capabilities of the methods and machines being employed. Any modern production requires capital goods (machinery and equipment) of various types and capacities, labor inputs, operating procedures, raw materials, and so on. The quantity of output a firm can get from a given set of inputs depends on the technical and human capabilities inherent in these inputs. The marginal cost curves pictured in Figure 3.6 could relate to different industries because the marginal cost curves are so different. But even within the same industry marginal cost curves can differ among firms. Some firms will be older than others; they may be working with older equipment that has different cost characteristics. Even firms of the same age may have different production techniques; past managerial decisions may have put them in different positions in terms of the marginal production costs they experience today.

This concept of technology is vitally important in environmental economics because **technological change** can provide ways to produce goods and services with fewer environmental side effects and also better ways of handling the quantities of production residuals that remain. In our simple cost model, technical advancement has the effect of shifting marginal cost curves downward. Technological progress makes it possible to produce a given increase in output at a lower marginal cost. It also reduces total production cost. Consider Figure 3.7. MC_1 is the firm's marginal cost curve before a technical improvement; MC_2 is the

FIGURE 3.7   **Technological Improvement**

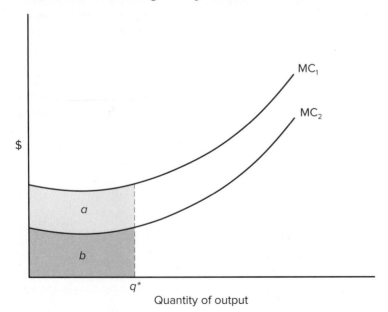

marginal cost curve after some technical improvement has been put into effect. The technical change, in other words, shifts the marginal cost curve downward. We also can determine how much total production costs are reduced as a result of the technological change. Consider output level q^*. With MC_1, the total annual cost of producing output q^* is represented by the area $a + b$, whereas after the reduction in the marginal cost curve to MC_2, the total annual cost of producing q^* is equal to area b. Thus, the reduction in total cost made possible by the technological change is equal to area a.

Technological change does not normally happen without effort; it normally requires research and development (R&D). R&D in environmental industries is obviously an important activity to promote, and one of the criteria we will want to use to evaluate environmental policies is whether the policies create incentives for individuals, firms, and industries to engage in vigorous R&D programs. In very simple terms, the incentive to engage in R&D is the cost savings that result from the new techniques, materials, procedures, and so on, that are discovered in the effort. The cost savings shown in Figure 3.7 (area a) show part of this incentive. This is the cost savings that would result each year, and the accumulation of these annual cost savings represents the full R&D incentive.

The Equimarginal Principle

We come now to the discussion of a simple but important economic principle, one that is used repeatedly in chapters to come. It is called the **equimarginal principle.** To understand it, take the case of a firm producing a certain product and assume that the firm's operation is divided between two different plants. For example, suppose there is a single power company that owns two different generating plants. Each plant produces the same item, so that the total output of the firm is the sum of what it produces in the two plants. Assume that the plants were built at different times and make use of different technology. The old one, Plant A in Figure 3.8, has older technology; it has a marginal cost curve that starts relatively low but rises steeply as production increases. The new plant, Plant B in Figure 3.8, uses newer technology; it has a higher marginal cost at low output levels, but marginal costs do not rise as steeply as production increases.

Consider now a situation in which this two-plant firm wants to produce a total output of, say, 100 units. How many units should it produce in each plant in order to produce the 100 units at the *least total cost?* Would it be best to produce 50 units in each plant? This is depicted in Figure 3.8; at an output of 50, Plant A has a marginal cost of $12, whereas Plant B has a marginal cost of $8. Total production costs are the sum of total costs at each plant, or $(a + b + c) + d$. Here is the important point: The total cost of the 100 units can be lowered by reallocating production. Reduce production in Plant A by one unit and costs will fall by $12. Then increase the production in Plant B by one unit and costs there will rise by $8. Total output is still 100 units, but there has been a cost savings of $12 − $8 = $4. Thus, total cost, the sum of the costs in the two plants, has gone down.

FIGURE 3.8 The Equimarginal Principle

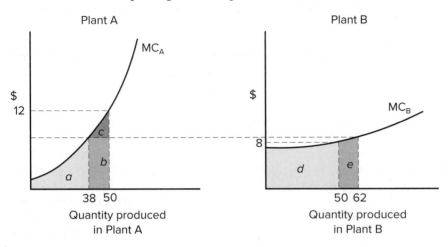

As long as the marginal costs in the two plants differ from one another, we can continue to reallocate production—away from the high-marginal-cost plant and toward the low-marginal-cost plant—and get a reduction in total cost. In fact, the total costs of producing the 100 units in the two plants will be at a minimum only when the marginal costs of the two plants are equal, hence the "equimarginal principle." In the figure, this happens when the output in Plant A is 38 units and the output in Plant B is 62 units. Total costs in geometric terms are now $a + (d + e)$.

The equimarginal principle therefore says the following: If you have multiple sources to produce a given product or achieve a given goal, and you want to minimize the total cost of producing a given quantity of that output, distribute production in such a way as to equalize the marginal costs between the production sources. There is another way of saying it that may look different but actually is not: If you have a given amount of resources and you want to maximize the total amount produced, distribute total production among the sources in such a way as to equalize marginal costs. This principle will be very valuable when we take up the issue of getting maximum emissions reductions from given amounts of resources.

Marginal Cost and Supply

A critical question in the analysis of any economic system is whether private profit-seeking firms (as well as public, politically minded agencies) will produce the correct quantities of output from the standpoint of society as a whole, not only for conventional items such as cardboard boxes, but also for less conventional items such as the amounts of environmental quality. To address this question, one must understand how firms normally determine the quantities they will produce. The marginal cost of production is a key factor in determining the **supply** behavior of firms in competitive circumstances. In fact, the marginal cost curve of a firm acts essentially as a **supply curve,** showing the quantity of the good the firm would supply at different prices. Consider Figure 3.9. Assume that the firm with the indicated marginal cost curve is able to sell its output at a price of p^*. The firm will maximize its profits by producing that quantity of output where marginal cost is equal to p^*; that level is designated q^*. At any output level less than this, MC $< p^*$, so a firm could increase its profits by increasing output. At any output level above this, $p^* <$ MC, so a firm is actually producing items for which the marginal cost is higher than price; in this case, the firm should reduce output if it wishes to maximize its profits.

We are often interested in the supply performance of industries composed of many firms. The aggregate supply curve of a group of firms is the sum of the individual supply curves of all the firms in the group. This is depicted in Figure 3.10. There are three firms, A, B, and C, with marginal cost curves as depicted in the first three panels of the figure. At a common price, say $4, Firm A supplies ten units, Firm B supplies eight units, and Firm C supplies six units. Thus, the aggregate supply at that price is 24 units, as depicted in the far right panel of Figure 3.10. At other possible prices, the quantities supplied by the three firms would be determined by their respective individual supply curves, and the horizontal summations of these would trace out the aggregate supply curves.

FIGURE 3.9   Marginal Cost and Supply

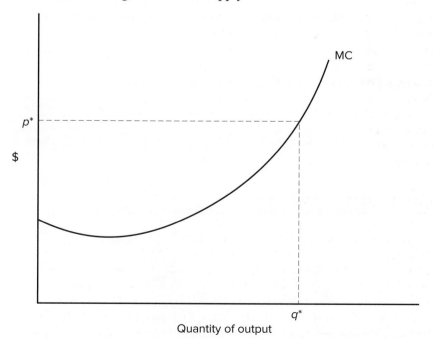

FIGURE 3.10   **Derivation of Aggregate (Market) Supply from Individual Firm Supply Curves**

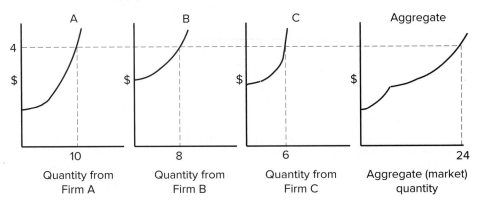

Summary

In this chapter, we covered briefly some of the basic tools of microeconomics. Later chapters will rely heavily on these ideas, especially on the equimarginal principle and on graphs, where we will want to jump back and forth between marginal and total measures. When we begin to look at real-world problems of environmental analysis and policy design, it is easy to get pulled so far into the countless details that basic economic ideas get lost. It is the fundamental economic building blocks, such as those in this chapter, that allow us to identify the primary economic characteristics of these problems and proceed to develop solutions to them.

Questions for Further Discussion

1. Use the logic of willingness to pay to interpret the statement "I like clean air more than you do."
2. Below is the marginal willingness to pay of a consumer for organic apples.

Consumption Level (apples per week, lbs.)	Marginal Willingness to Pay
0	5.00
1	4.00
2	3.20
3	2.60
4	2.20
5	1.80
6	1.50

a. What is this individual's total willingness to pay at a consumption level of 4 apples?

b. If the price of organic apples is $2.40, how many apples would this person consume?

3. Below are the marginal willingness-to-pay schedules for organic apples for two individuals.

Consumption Level (apples per week, lbs.)	Marginal WTP	
	Jill	John
0	5.00	6.40
1	4.00	5.20
2	3.20	4.00
3	2.60	3.00
4	2.20	2.10
5	1.80	1.30
6	1.50	.60
7	1.30	.30
8	1.20	.00

Construct the aggregate marginal willingness-to-pay (the demand) curve for this group of two people.

4. What are the advantages and disadvantages of using willingness to pay as a measure of value? What are some alternatives?

5. Figure 3.10 illustrates the derivation of an industry supply curve under competitive conditions where each firm receives the same price for its output. What is the relationship of this procedure to the equimarginal principle discussed earlier in the chapter?

6. Consider the marginal cost curve associated with cleaning your dorm room. Label the vertical axis "time" and the horizontal axis "percent clean." What would this marginal cost curve look like?

7. Somebody invents a small machine that electrostatically is able to remove dust from rooms very quickly. What does this do to the marginal cost curve depicted in question 6?

For additional readings and Web sites pertaining to the material in this chapter, see **www.mhhe.com/field7e.**

Chapter 4

Markets, Externalities, and Public Goods

This chapter has several objectives.

1. Develop the notion of **economic efficiency** as an index of examining how an economy functions and as a criterion for judging whether it is performing as well as it might.
2. Address the question of whether an unregulated **market system** can produce results that are socially efficient.

Economic efficiency is a simple idea and one that has much to recommend it as a criterion for evaluating the performance of an economic system or a part of that system, but it has to be used with care. A single firm or group of firms may be judged very efficient in their own limited way as long as they are keeping costs low and making a profit. Yet, to evaluate the *social* performance of these firms, we must use the idea of economic efficiency in a wider sense. In this case, it must include all the social values and consequences of economic decisions—in particular, environmental consequences. It is important also to discuss the relationship between **economic efficiency** and **economic equity.**

Market systems work by allowing individuals, both buyers and sellers, to seek out exchanges that are individually beneficial. People in the United States and in most of the world live in a market economy. We will see that there are a number of circumstances in which a system of private markets will not normally be able to bring about results that are efficient in this wider sense. This leads into the next chapter, where we will examine the following policy question: If the economy is not operating the way we want it to, especially in matters of environmental quality, what kind of public policy might be used to correct the situation?

Economic efficiency is a criterion that can be applied at several levels: to input usage and to the determination of output levels. We are going to concentrate in this chapter on the second of these because ultimately we want to apply the concept to the "output" of environmental quality. There are two questions of interest: (1) What quantity ought to be produced and (2) what quantity is produced in fact? The first question deals with the notion of efficiency, the second with the way markets normally function.

Economic Efficiency

In the preceding chapter we introduced two relationships, that between the quantity of output and willingness to pay, and that between output and marginal production costs. Neither of these two relationships, by itself, can tell us what the most desirable level of output is from society's standpoint. To identify this output level, it is necessary to bring these two elements together. The central idea of **economic efficiency** is that there should be a balance between the value of what is produced and the value of what is used up to produce it. In our terminology, there should be a balance between willingness to pay and the marginal costs of production.

Efficiency is a notion that has to have a reference point. It is critical to ask: efficient from the standpoint of whom? What is efficient for one person, in the sense of balancing costs and benefits, may not be efficient for somebody else. We want to have a concept of efficiency that is applicable to the economy as a whole. This means that when referring to marginal costs, *all* of the costs of producing the particular item in question must be included, no matter to whom they accrue. When dealing with marginal willingness to pay, we must insist that this represents accurately *all* of the value that people in the society place on the item. This does not necessarily mean that all people will place the same value on all goods; it means only that we do not leave out any missing sources of value.

How do we identify the rate of output that is socially efficient? Suppose we focus on a particular type of output; in practice it could be refrigerators, automobiles, a college education, or a certain type of pollution-control equipment. Suppose that our item is currently being produced at a particular rate, and we wish to know whether it would benefit society to have this output level increased by a small amount. To answer this requires comparing the marginal willingness to pay for that extra output with the marginal opportunity costs of the output. If the former exceeds the latter, we would presumably want the extra output to be produced; otherwise, we would not.

This can be analyzed graphically by bringing together the two relationships discussed in the last chapter. Figure 4.1 shows the aggregate marginal willingness-to-pay curve (labeled MWTP) and the aggregate marginal cost curve (MC) for the good in question. The efficient level of production for this item is the quantity identified by the intersection of the two curves, labeled q^e in the figure. At this output level the costs of producing one more unit of this good are just exactly equal to the marginal value of it, as expressed by the marginal willingness-to-pay curve. This common value is p^e.

The equality of the marginal willingness to pay and the marginal production cost is the test for determining if output is at the socially efficient level. There is another way of looking at this notion of efficiency. When a rate of output is at the socially efficient level, the net value, defined as **total willingness to pay** minus **total costs,** is as large as possible. In fact, we can measure this net value on the diagram. At q^e we know that the total willingness to pay is equal

FIGURE 4.1 **The Socially Efficient Rate of Output**

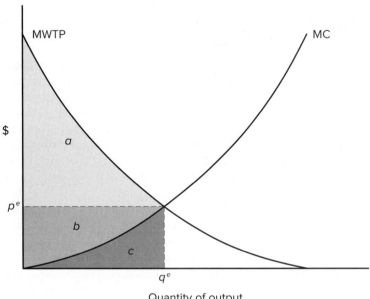

to an amount corresponding to the area under the marginal willingness-to-pay curve from the origin up to q^e; this area consists of the sum of the three subareas: $a + b + c$. Total cost, however, consists of the area under the marginal cost curve, or area c. Thus, the surplus is $(a + b + c) - c = a + b$, which is the triangular area enclosed by the marginal willingness-to-pay curve and the marginal cost curve. At any other quantity, the corresponding value of total willingness to pay minus total production costs will be less than this area $a + b$.

Let's be clear on what this graph is saying. We noted previously that the marginal willingness-to-pay curve is assumed to represent accurately all the benefits that people in our economy actually experience when the good becomes available. The marginal production cost curve is assumed to contain all the true opportunity costs that are required to produce this good—no hidden or overlooked costs have been left out. Thus, the quantity q^e is **efficient** because it produces a balance between the two sides—between the marginal worth of a good, as indicated by consumers' willingness to pay for it, and what it costs society to produce it, as measured by marginal costs.[1]

---

[1] The graphs discussed in this and the preceding chapter show the production and consumption of some good or service that has positive value. In later chapters, we will adapt them to explore the production of what we might call a "bad" value, namely, environmental pollution. Then the units along the horizontal axis would be quantities of some pollutant. The marginal cost curve would show the increasing costs, or damages, to society from increasing quantities of pollutants. The demand curve, on the other hand, would show the diminishing marginal savings to polluting firms from being able to emit more pollution into the environment. We will discuss this in much greater detail in Chapter 5.

Efficiency and Equity

From the standpoint of society at large, production is at an efficient level when marginal benefits equal marginal production costs, that is, when net benefits are maximized, *no matter to whom those net benefits accrue.* Efficiency doesn't distinguish among people. A dollar of net benefits to one person is considered to be worth a dollar to anybody else. One hundred dollars of benefits to one person is considered to be worth the same as one dollar of benefits to each of 100 people. In the real world, an outcome that benefits very rich people at the expense of poor people would be regarded by most people as inequitable. This is simply another way of saying that an outcome that is efficient in this sense need not necessarily be equitable.

Equity is tied closely to the distribution of income and wealth in a society. If this distribution is regarded as essentially fair, then judgments about alternative output levels may justifiably be made using only the efficiency criterion. But if wealth is distributed unfairly, the efficiency criterion by itself may be too narrow. Having said this, however, we have to recognize that in the assessment of economic outcomes, the relative emphasis to be put on efficiency and equity is a matter of controversy. It is controversial in the political arena; it is controversial among economists themselves.

We will have much to say about distributional issues and equity throughout this book. Chapter 6 contains terminology for describing the distributional impacts of environmental policies. Chapter 9 contains a discussion of the role of economic equity as a criterion for evaluating environmental policies.

Markets

Having specified what economic efficiency means, we next ask whether a market system, a system in which the major economic decisions about how much to produce are made by the more or less unhindered interaction of buyers and sellers, gives results that are socially efficient. In other words, if we rely entirely on the market to determine how much of this item gets produced, will it settle on q^e?

Why worry about this question? Why not simply jump to the question of public policy? Doesn't this question imply that, at bottom, we are committed to the market system, and isn't this the system that, from an environmental point of view, has gotten us into trouble in the first place? If the market doesn't do the job, maybe we should just ignore whatever the market does and proceed through political/administrative means to bring about the desired rate of output.

The short answer to this is that as a nation we are in fact committed to a market-based economy. For all its faults, a market system will normally produce better economic results overall than any other system. Those who doubt this need only look at the environmental horror stories uncovered in the countries of Eastern Europe following the Communist era. Of course, it needs to be remembered that although our system is "market based," we do not necessarily have to accept whatever results it yields. The results are acceptable only if they are reasonably efficient and equitable. We will find that in the case of environmental quality, market institutions are not likely to give us results that are socially efficient.

The slightly longer answer to the question is that the market system contains within it certain incentive structures that in many cases can be harnessed toward the objective of improved environmental quality. One of these is the cost-minimizing incentive that stems from the competitive process. Another is the incentive provided through the rewards that may be reaped through initiative in finding better, that is, less expensive, technical and organizational means of production. It will be far more effective in many cases to take advantage of these incentives than to try to do away with them. By altering them so that they take environmental values into account, the market system will yield more effective results than if we tried to jettison the whole system and adopt a different set of institutions.

A **market** is an institution in which buyers and sellers of goods and services, carry out mutually agreed-upon exchanges. When they buy or sell in a market, people naturally look for the best terms they can get. Presumably buyers would like to pay a low price, whereas sellers would prefer high prices. What brings all these conflicting objectives into balance is the adjustment of prices on the market.

Figure 4.2 shows a simple market model. Buyers' desires are represented by the **demand curve,** labeled D; it shows the quantity of the good that buyers would buy at different prices. It has the typical downward slope; the higher

FIGURE 4.2 **The Market Model**

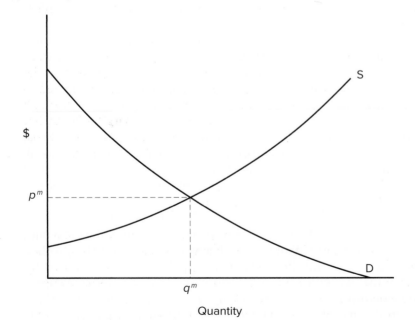

the price, the lower the quantity demanded, and vice versa. Underlying the demand curve are such factors as consumer tastes and preferences, the number of potential consumers in the market, and consumer income levels.

The curve labeled S is the **supply curve,** which shows the quantity of the good that suppliers would willingly make available at different prices. It is upward sloping; higher prices represent greater incentives for suppliers, and therefore larger quantities are supplied, and vice versa. The main factors affecting the height and shape of the supply curve are production costs. These, in turn, are related to the prices of inputs used in the production of this item and the level of technology inherent in the production process.

It is important to keep in mind that the demand and supply curves represent possibilities, or alternatives. During any particular time, only one quantity of a good can change hands, and sellers and buyers can be on only one point of their supply and demand curves, respectively. It is easy to see that there is only one price at which the quantity demanded by buyers is consistent with the quantity that sellers will make available. That is the price where the two curves intersect, marked p^m. Similarly, the total quantity that buyers and sellers will exchange at this price is labeled q^m.

For the market to work effectively, there must be competition among sellers and among buyers. None can be large enough that its own performance affects market prices or powerful enough that it can control how the market performs. Price must be allowed to adjust freely so that it can "discover" the quantities that bring buyers and sellers into balance. At prices higher than p^m, sellers will attempt to supply more than buyers want. In a surplus situation such as this, competition among sellers forces prices downward. If prices are temporarily lower than p^m, a shortage develops and competition among buyers will force the price to adjust upward. At the equilibrium, quantity demanded equals quantity supplied.

It is important to look at it also from the other direction. At the quantity q^m there is an equality between the marginal willingness to pay by consumers for an additional unit of the item and the marginal costs of producing the item. These are equal at the value of p^m. If price and quantity are allowed to adjust freely and competition does in fact exist, an equality will arise through the normal interaction of buyers and sellers, between the marginal valuation that consumers have for a good (their marginal willingness to pay) and the cost of making available another unit of the good (the marginal cost of production).

Markets and Social Efficiency

The next question is whether markets ordinarily produce results that are efficient from the standpoint of society. Compare Figures 4.1 and 4.2. They look the same, but there is actually a big difference. The first shows a socially efficient rate of output for a particular item; the second shows the rate of output and price that would prevail on a competitive market for that item. Are these two rates of output, labeled q^e and q^m, likely to be the same in the real world?

The answer is yes *if,* and it is a big *if,* the market demand and supply curves, as pictured in Figure 4.2, are the same as the marginal cost and willingness-to-pay curves shown in Figure 4.1. Here is the nub of the problem: When environmental values are concerned, there are likely to be very substantial differences between market values and social values. This is called **market failure,** and it will often call for public intervention, either to override the markets directly or to rearrange things so that they will work more effectively.

In the rest of this chapter, we will discuss the performance of markets when matters of environmental quality are involved. There are two phenomena to account for, one on the supply side and the other on the demand side. Environmental effects can drive a wedge between normal market supply curves and true marginal social cost curves. On the other side of the market, environmental effects can create a difference between market demands and true social marginal willingness to pay. On the supply side the problem is *external costs,* whereas on the demand side the problem is *external benefits.*

External Costs

When entrepreneurs in a market economy make decisions about what and how much to produce, they normally take into account the price of what they will produce and the cost of items for which they will have to pay: labor, raw materials, machinery, energy, and so on. We call these the **private costs** of the firm; they are the costs that show up in the profit-and-loss statement at the end of the year. Any firm, assuming it has the objective of maximizing its profits, will try to keep its production costs as low as possible. This is a worthwhile outcome for both the firm and society because inputs always have opportunity costs; they could have been used to produce something else. Furthermore, firms will be alert to ways of reducing costs when the relative prices of inputs change. For example, we know that during the U.S. energy "crisis" of the 1970s, when energy inputs became much more expensive, firms found ways of reducing energy inputs by using more energy-efficient machinery, changing operating procedures, and so on.

In many production operations, however, there is another type of cost that, although representing a true cost to society, does not show up in the firm's profit-and-loss statement. These are called **external costs.** They are external because, although they are real costs to some members of society, firms do not normally take them into account when they go about making their decisions about output rates. Another way of saying this is that these are costs that are external to firms but internal to society as a whole.[2]

One of the major types of external cost is the cost inflicted on people through environmental degradation. An example is the easiest way to see this. Suppose

[2] External costs are sometimes called third-party costs. The first two parties are, respectively, the producer and the consumer. So a third-party cost is one that is inflicted on people who are not directly involved in the economic transactions between buyers and sellers. It is also sometimes called a **spillover effect.**

a paper mill is located somewhere on the upstream reaches of a river and that, in the course of its operation, it discharges a large amount of wastewater into the river. The wastewater is full of organic matter that arises from the process of converting wood to paper. This waste material gradually is converted to more benign materials by the natural assimilative capacity of the river water, but, before that happens, a number of people downstream are affected by the lower quality of water in the river. Perhaps the waterborne residuals reduce the number of fish in the river, affecting downstream fishers. The river also may be less attractive to look at, affecting people who would like to swim or boat on it. Worse, the river water perhaps is used downstream as a source of water for a public water supply system, and the degraded water quality means that the town has to engage in more costly treatment processes before the water can be sent through the water mains. All of these downstream costs are real costs associated with producing paper, just as much as the raw materials, labor, energy, and so on, used internally by the plant. But from the mill's standpoint, these downstream costs are *external costs*. They are costs that are borne by someone other than the people who make decisions about operating the paper mill. At the end of the year the profit-and-loss statement of the paper mill will contain no reference to these real downstream external costs.

If rates of output are to be socially efficient, decisions about resource use must take into account both types of costs: the private costs of producing paper plus whatever external costs arise from adverse environmental impacts. In terms of full social cost accounting:

Social costs = Private costs + External (environmental) costs

This is pictured in Figure 4.3. The top panel shows the relationship between the rate of paper production and the occurrence of these downstream external costs. It shows that the marginal external costs increase as paper production increases. The bottom panel shows several things. It shows the demand curve for paper and the marginal private costs of producing paper. The intersection of these occurs at a price of p^m and a quantity of q^m. This is the price and quantity that would arise in a competitive market where producers pay no attention to external costs. But marginal social costs are in fact higher, as shown, because they contain both the marginal private costs and the marginal external costs.[3] Thus, the full socially efficient rate of output is q^* and the associated price is p^*.

Compare the two rates of output and the two prices. The market output is too high compared to the socially efficient rate of output ($q^m > q^*$). In addition, the market price is too low compared to the socially efficient price ($p^m < p^*$). It's not hard to understand the reason for this. In considering just its private costs, the firm is essentially using a productive input it is not paying for. What is this unpaid input? The unpaid input is the services of the river, which provides the firm with a cheap way to dispose of its production residuals. Although it may be cheap for the firm to do this, it may not be cheap to society; in fact, in this case we have costs being

---

[3] Note that MEC is zero below a certain quantity. The graph is drawn under the assumption that a threshold exists: a quantity of paper production below which there are no external costs.

FIGURE 4.3 **External Costs and Market Outcomes**

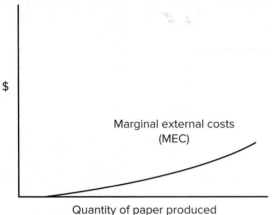

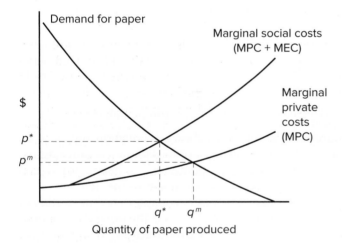

Quantity of paper produced

inflicted on downstream users that are being overlooked by the paper mill. So the private market system in this case produces too much paper at too low of a price compared to socially efficient results.

Most of the cases of environmental destruction are related to external costs of one type or another. Many external costs stem from industrial activity. Producing electricity, especially with fossil fuels, results in downwind air pollution, and greenhouse gases, that cause a variety of health and ecosystem damages. A recent report of the U.S. National Research Council indicates, for example, that for every dollar of conventional production costs of coal-fired power plants, there are an additional 70¢ of external costs from air pollution.[4]

---

[4] National Research Council, *Hidden Costs of Energy*, The National Academies Press, Washington, D.C., 2010, p. 149.

External Costs Associated with Driving Automobiles

EXAMPLE **4.1**

Source of Cost	Cents/Gallon[1]	Cents/Mile[1]
Greenhouse gas emissions	6	0.3
Local air pollution	42	2.0
Congestion	105	5.0
Accidents	63	3.0
Oil dependency	12	0.6
Total	228	10.9

[1] Costs converted assuming fuel economy of 21 miles/gallon.

Source: Ian W.H. Parry, Margaret Walls, and Winston Harrington, "Automobile Externalities and Policies," *Journal of Economic Literature*, XLV(2), June 2007, p. 384.

There are many other types of external costs. Users of chemicals emit toxic fumes that affect people living in the vicinity, developers build on land without taking into account the degradation of the visual environment of local inhabitants, and so on. Nor are businesses the only ones responsible for external environmental costs. External costs arise from individual actions, an important example of which is driving cars and trucks. Example 4.1 shows estimates of external costs in the United States from driving automobiles. Note that the largest of these cost items relates to costs of congestion and accidents. The largest conventional environmental costs are for local air pollution, which are about seven times the external costs related to global warming.

Most, but not all, environmental externalities are expressed through physical linkages among parties involved—that is, polluter and people damaged. The simplest is where there are just two parties involved: one polluter and one person suffering damages. An upstream pulp mill and a downstream firm that uses the river water in its production operations provide an example. There are cases of single polluters and multiple damaged parties, such as a power plant that emits sulfur dioxide (SO_2) affecting a group of community residents living downwind. Other cases involve multiple polluters but only one damaged party, such as the runoff from many farms that affects a local water supply system. Finally, there are many cases where both polluters and parties damaged are many in number. An example of this is urban air pollution stemming from automobile emissions: Each driver is both a producer and a recipient of the externality. The same is true of global phenomena, such as climate change.

Some externalities do not involve physical linkages. Degradation of the scenic environment through thoughtless land development is an example. In addition, some externalities involve neither physical linkages nor close proximity. People in one part of a country, for example, may feel loss when those in another region cause damage to an important environmental resource, such as a unique species of animal or plant.

This brings up a problem that we will state but not solve. What is the limit, if any, to be placed on external damage that people may legitimately claim? I suffer damages when someone in my vicinity plays her music too loudly, but can I legitimately claim that I suffer damages if, for example, she adopts a life-style with which I don't agree? If people in Boston pollute the waters of Boston Harbor, may residents in California claim that they have been damaged? If residents of New Jersey thin out the suburban deer population in order to save their flower gardens, may people in Chicago justifiably claim that they have been damaged?

The answer to these questions hinges on the notion of willingness to pay. In this approach, whether someone has or has not been affected by another action hinges on his or her willingness to pay to have that action changed. If people in New York are willing to pay to preserve clean air in Tokyo, then this is evidence that air quality in Tokyo affects the welfare of people in New York. If people in Chicago are not willing to pay anything to clean up the Ohio River, we conclude that the water quality of that river has no effect on the welfare of people in Chicago. The presence or absence of willingness to pay, in other words, is the economic index of whether an action may be said to affect somebody.

Open-Access Resources

One source of external costs has been widely studied by environmental econ-omists (as well as natural resource economists): open-access resources. An **open-access resource** is a resource or facility that is open to uncontrolled access by individuals who wish to use the resource. A classic example is an ocean fishery in which anyone willing to buy a boat and take up fishing is free to do so. Other examples are a pasture that is open to anyone to graze animals, a forest where anyone may go and cut wood, or a public park open to free access.

In these situations we have, in effect, problems in property rights—their defi-nition, distribution, and/or enforcement. If someone owns a pasture or a forest, he or she will presumably keep out encroachers, or perhaps charge them for use of the resource or otherwise control their rate of access. But when a resource or facility is open to unrestricted access, there is no way of ensuring that its rate of use is kept to the level that will maximize its overall value.[5]

To understand this, consider the following example. Suppose there are four similar firms situated on a lake. The firms use the water of the lake in producing their output and discharge emissions back into the lake. Because of the emis-sions, each firm must treat the water taken from the lake before it uses the water in production. The treatment costs of each firm depend on the ambient quality of the lake, which of course depends on the total emissions of the four firms. Suppose that the cost of intake water treatment is currently $40,000 per year for

[5] This is what is involved in the "tragedy of the commons," as it was popularly termed by Garrett Hardin in "Tragedy of the Commons," *Science,* 162, December 13, 1968, pp. 1243–1248. His example was an open-access pasture on which all farmers had the right to pasture their sheep.

each firm. A new firm is contemplating starting operations on the lake. If it adds its untreated emissions to those of the current four, it will make ambient water quality worse and drive the cost of water treatment for each firm up to $60,000 per year. When the fifth firm makes its location and production decisions, it will take into account its various operating costs, which will include the $60,000 per year of water treatment costs. But the total social water-related costs of the firm's decisions are higher. There are also external costs inflicted on the other four firms, amounting to $20,000 each of added water treatment costs if the fifth firm locates on the lake. The social marginal costs of water supply when the new firm locates on the lake are $140,000, consisting of $60,000 of internal costs of the new firm plus $80,000 ($20,000 × 4) of external costs inflicted on firms already on the lake. These are often called open-access externalities because they result from the fact that the firms have uncontrolled access to the lake.

We have focused on the externalities flowing from the fifth firm's decisions, but everything is symmetrical in the sense that we could say exactly the same thing about each of the other firms. Each firm will make its decisions without regard to the external costs inflicted on other firms. It is this reciprocal nature of these externalities that distinguishes them from the type we talked about before (e.g., the pulp mill upstream inflicting external costs on people downstream), but the effect is the same: externalities that lead to rates of output that are too high compared to socially efficient rates.

As another example of an open-access problem, consider a road that is open to access by anyone desiring to use it. A road is not a natural resource but a person-made facility. But the essence of the uncontrolled access problem is identical, and perhaps it is easier to understand with this particular example. It uses very simplifying assumptions in order to highlight the basic issues. There is a road connecting two cities—City A and City B. The figures in Table 4.1 show the average travel time it takes to get from City A to City B along this road, as a function of the number of motorists using the road. Thus, for example, if there are just 10 travelers on the road, it takes 10 minutes to get from A to B (we assume a speed limit that is enforced). Likewise, when there are

TABLE 4.1 Travel Times Related to the Number of Cars on the Road

Number of Cars	Average Travel Time Between A and B
10	10
20	10
30	10
40	11
50	12
60	14
70	18
80	24

either 20 or 30 motorists on the road, the average travel time is still 10 minutes, but when the traffic increases to 40 travelers, the average travel time increases to 11 minutes. This is because of congestion; cars begin to get in each other's way and average speeds drop. As the number of motorists continues to increase, the congestion increases, thus driving up travel times even more.

Now suppose you are considering using this road to go from A to B and that there are already 50 cars using it. Suppose, furthermore, that you have an alternative route that will take you 18 minutes. Assume that you know the state of the traffic and the resulting travel times. Because taking the given road will save you 4 minutes over the alternative, your individual decision would be to use the road. But from the standpoint of "society," in this case consisting of you plus all the other motorists on the road, this is not efficient. When you enter the highway on which there are already 50 cars, the added congestion causes an increase in average travel times of 2 minutes to the people already using the road. Thus, your 4-minute individual savings is offset by added travel costs of 100 minutes (50 cars times 2 minutes per car) on the part of the other motorists, meaning that if all minutes are treated as equally valuable, there is a net social loss of 96 minutes when you decide to use the road. The advent of global positioning system (GPS) units used by drivers, either in their car or on their phone, has increased the availability of traffic information. Thus, the decision process of selecting a driving route, based on congestion and travel time, has become more efficient for society.

The problem arises because there is uncontrolled access to the road, and in using it people may inflict external costs on others in the form of added congestion and higher travel times. The same kind of effect holds when a fisher enters a fishery; in catching a portion of the stock, he leaves fewer to be caught by other fishers. When one farmer puts animals on a common pasture, he or she reduces the forage available to other herds on that pasture. When one person cuts wood from a communal forest, she leaves fewer trees for other users and makes it more difficult for them to supply themselves with wood. We can see that this is related to the notion of external costs. The added costs that one user of a common-property resource inflicts on other users of that resource are in fact costs that are external to that user but internal to the whole group of users. When a single individual is making a decision about whether and how much to utilize a common-property resource, she takes into account the costs and benefits that impinge directly on her. Some people might also altruistically take into account the common-property externalities they inflict on others, but most will not. The result will be, as it was with the road example, a rate of use that is higher than what is called for on grounds of social efficiency.

Thus, when external costs are present, private markets will not normally produce quantities of output that are socially efficient. This market failure may justify public policy to help move the economy toward efficiency. This may be done sometimes by changing rules, such as property rights rules, so that the market will function efficiently. Other cases may call for more direct public intervention. We will take up these matters again in Section 4. We must now move to the demand side of the market and consider another important source of market failure, that of external benefits.

External Benefits

An **external benefit** is a benefit that accrues to somebody who is outside, or external to, the decision about consuming or producing the good or resource that causes the externality. When the use of an item leads to an external benefit, the market willingness to pay for that item will understate the social willingness to pay. Suppose a quieter lawn mower would provide $50 a year of extra benefits to me if I were to buy it. This is therefore the maximum that I would be willing to pay for this machine. But suppose my use of the new lawn mower would create $20 of added benefits to my neighbor because of reduced noise levels in the course of the year. These $20 of benefits to the neighbor are external benefits for me. I make my purchasing decision on the basis of benefits accruing only to me. Thus, my marginal willingness to pay for a quieter lawn mower is $50, whereas the social marginal benefits (where "society" in this case includes just me and my neighbor) is $70 (my $50 and her $20).

As another example of an external benefit, consider a farmer whose land is on the outskirts of an urban area. The farmer cultivates the land and sells his produce to people in the city. Of course, the farmer's main concern is the income he can derive from the operation, and he makes decisions about inputs and outputs according to their effect on that income. But the land kept in agriculture produces several other benefits, including a habitat for birds and other small animals and scenic values for passers-by. These benefits, although internal from the standpoint of society, are external from the standpoint of the farmer. They don't appear anywhere in his profit-and-loss position; they are external benefits of his farming decisions. In this case, the agricultural value of the land to the farmer understates the social willingness to pay to have the land in agriculture.

Many goods do not involve external benefits. Indeed, when economists discuss the rudiments of supply and demand, the examples used are normally simple goods that do not create this complication. Farmers produce and supply so many thousand cantaloupes; individual and market demand curves for cantaloupes are easy to comprehend. If we want to know the total number of cantaloupes bought, we can simply add up the number bought by each person in the market. Each person's consumption affects no one else. In this case, the market demand curve will represent accurately the aggregate marginal willingness to pay of consumers for cantaloupes. But in cases involving external benefits, this no longer holds. We can perhaps best see this by considering a type of good that inherently involves large-scale external benefits, what economists have come to call "public goods."

Public Goods

Consider a lighthouse. This is a service provided to mariners at sea so that they can locate themselves and avoid running aground at night. But the lighthouse has an interesting technical characteristic: If its services are made available to one mariner at sea, they immediately become available to all others in the vicinity. Once the services are made available to one person, others cannot be excluded from making use of the same services. This is the distinguishing characteristic of a **public good.** It is a good that, if made available to one person, automatically becomes available to others.

Another example of a public good is a radio signal. Once a radio station broadcasts a signal, it is available to anybody who has a receiver. Each individual can listen to the broadcast without diminishing its availability to all other people within range of the station. Note carefully that it is not the ownership of the supplying organization that makes a public good public. Lighthouses are usually publicly owned, but radio stations, at least in the United States, are typically privately owned. A public good is distinguished by the technical nature of the good, not by the type of organization making it available.

We are interested in public goods because environmental quality is essentially a public good. If the air is cleaned up for one person in an urban area, it is automatically cleaned up for everybody else in that community. The benefits, in other words, accrue to everyone in the community. Private markets are likely to undersupply public goods, relative to efficient levels. To see why, let's look at another very simple example: a small freshwater lake, the shores of which have three occupied homes. The people living in the houses use the lake for recreational purposes, but, unfortunately, the water quality of the lake has been contaminated by an old industrial plant that has since closed. The contaminant is measured in parts per million (ppm). At present the lake contains 5 ppm of this contaminant. It is possible to clean the water by using a fairly expensive treatment process. Each of the surrounding homeowners is willing to pay a certain amount to have the water quality improved. Table 4.2 shows these individual marginal willingnesses to pay for integer values of water quality. It also shows the aggregate marginal willingness to pay, which is the sum of the individual values.

The table also shows the marginal cost of cleaning up the lake, again just for integer values of water quality. Note that marginal cost is increasing; as the lake becomes cleaner, the marginal cost of continued improvement increases. Marginal cost and aggregate marginal willingness to pay are equal at a water quality of 2 ppm. At levels less than this (higher ppm), aggregate marginal willingness to pay for a cleaner lake exceeds the marginal cost of achieving it. Hence, from the standpoint of these three homeowners together, improved water quality is desirable,

TABLE 4.2 Individual and Aggregate Demand for Lowering Lake Pollution

Level of Contaminant (ppm)	Marginal Willingness to Pay ($ per year)			Aggregate MWP	Marginal Cost of Cleanup
	Home-owner A	Home-owner B	Home-owner C		
4	110	60	30	200	50
3	85	35	20	140	65
2	70	10	15	95	95
1	55	0	10	65	150
0	45	0	5	50	240

FIGURE 4.4   Aggregate Willingness to Pay for a Public Good

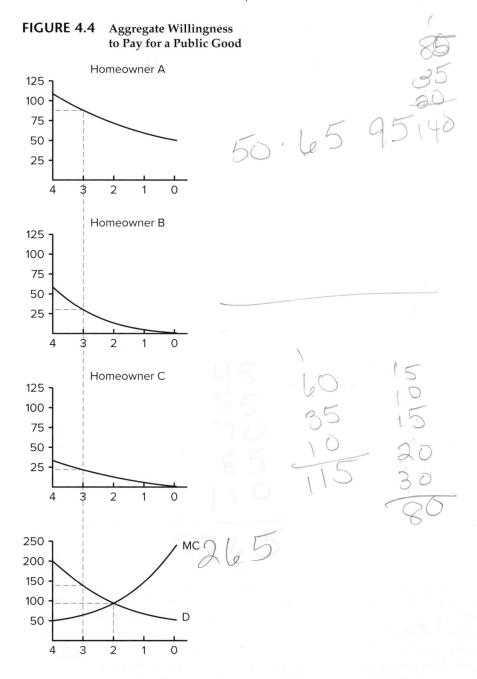

but at quality levels better than 2 ppm, total willingness to pay falls below marginal costs. Thus, 2 ppm is the socially efficient level of water quality in the lake.

This is depicted graphically in Figure 4.4. The top three panels show the marginal willingness to pay by each of the three homeowners. When summing individual demand curves for private goods, we could add together the individual quantities demanded at each price to get the aggregate quantity demanded. But with a public good people are, in effect, consuming the same units, so we must add together the individual marginal willingness to pay at each quantity to get the aggregate demand function, as shown in Figure 4.4. At a water-quality level of 3 ppm, for example, the marginal willingnesses to pay are, respectively, $85, $35, and $20 for individuals A, B, and C. Thus, the aggregate marginal willingness to pay at this level of water quality is $140. The bottom panel of the graph shows the aggregate marginal willingness-to-pay/demand function labeled D, the marginal cost function (MC), and the efficient level of water quality.

Having identified the efficient level of water quality, could we rely on a competitive market system, where entrepreneurs are on the alert for new profit opportunities, to get the contaminant in the lake reduced to that level? Suppose a private firm attempts to sell its services to the three homeowners. The firm goes to person A and tries to collect an amount equal to that person's true willingness to pay. But that person will presumably realize that once the lake is cleaned up, it is cleaned up for everybody, no matter how much each homeowner actually contributed. So A may have the incentive to underpay, relative to his true willingness to pay, in the hopes that the other homeowners will contribute enough to cover the costs of the cleanup. Of course, the others may react in the same way. When a public good is involved, each person may have an incentive to **free ride** on the efforts of others. A free rider is a person who pays less for a good than her or his true marginal willingness to pay, that is, a person who underpays relative to the benefits she or he receives.

Free riding is a ubiquitous phenomenon in the world of public goods, or in fact for any good for which its consumption produces external benefits. Because of the free-riding impulse, private, profit-motivated firms will have difficulty covering their costs if they go into the business of supplying public goods.[6] Because of these reduced revenues, private firms will normally *undersupply* goods and services of this type. Environmental quality improvements are essentially public goods. Because we cannot rely on the market system to provide efficient quantities of goods of this type, we must fall back on some type of nonmarket institution involving collective action of one type or another. In the lake example, the homeowners may be able to act together **privately,** perhaps through a homeowners' association, to secure contributions for cleaning up the lake. Of course, the free-rider problem will still exist even for the homeowners' association, but if there are not too many of them, personal acquaintance and the operation of moral pressure may be strong enough to overcome the problem. When there are many more people involved (thousands, or perhaps millions, as there are in many large urban areas), the free-rider problem can be addressed effectively only with more direct governmental action. This opens up the huge topic of **public policy** for environmental quality, a topic we will spend much more time discussing throughout the rest of the book.

---

[6] This sentence emphasizes the point made earlier: It is the technical nature of the good that makes it a public or private good, not whether the organization providing it is public or private. A lighthouse (a public good) might be built and operated by a private firm; insurance (a private good) might be provided by a public agency.

Summary

The main goal in this chapter was to discuss the operation of private markets and then apply the market model to situations in which environmental quality is an issue. Markets are places where buyers and sellers interact over the quantities and prices of particular goods or services. Buyers' desires are represented by the aggregate demand curve, which shows the quantities demanded at alternative prices. Sellers' supply capabilities are represented by supply curves, which ultimately are based on underlying production costs and show quantities that would be made available at alternative prices. The intersection of the supply and demand curves shows the unique quantity and price that can simultaneously satisfy both buyers and sellers. For many types of goods and services, market outcomes (output and price levels) also may be the outcomes that are socially efficient. Outcomes that are socially efficient are those in which the aggregate marginal willingness to pay in society is equal to the aggregate marginal social costs of production. When market results are not socially efficient, we speak of market failures.

We then discussed two main situations where market failures may result. The primary reason, on a conceptual level, is the existence of external costs and external benefits. In matters of the environment, external costs are the damages that people experience from environmental impacts that are not taken into account by the firms, public agencies, or consumers whose decisions produce them. A classic case is water pollution from an upstream pulp mill that damages people using the water downstream. Another important case is the external costs that users of an open-access resource inflict upon one another through uncontrolled use of the resource. External benefits are benefits accruing to people other than the direct buyers or recipients of a good. The classic case of external benefits concerns what are called public goods; these are goods or services that, when they are made available to one person, automatically become available to others.

Faced with external costs and benefits, public goods, and common-property resources, markets cannot be relied upon to supply efficient levels of environmental quality. Some type of nonmarket actions by private or public groups may be called upon to rectify these situations.

Questions for Further Discussion

1. Suppose that the following discrete numbers show the integer values of MWTP and MC as depicted in Figure 4.1. Determine the socially efficient rate of output. Show that at any other output level, the net benefits to society will be lower than they are at the efficient level. (Remember, the marginal cost of increasing output from 4 to 5 units is $9, which is also the amount by which cost decreases in going from 5 to 4 units.)

Output	1	2	3	4	5	6	7	8	9	10
MWTP	20	18	16	14	12	10	8	6	4	2
MC	5	6	7	8	9	11	15	21	30	40

2. Go back to question 2 in Chapter 3. Suppose the marginal cost of producing this item is constant at $5 per item. What is the socially efficient rate of output?

3. Following are portions of the demand curves of three individuals for the water quality in a small pond. The water quality is expressed in terms of the parts per million (ppm) of dissolved oxygen (DO). Water quality improves at higher DO levels. The demand curves show the marginal willingness to pay of each individual (A, B, C).

   a. Complete the table. Find the aggregate marginal willingness-to-pay curve of these three people at each DO level.

   b. If the actual marginal cost of increasing DO is $12, what is the socially efficient level of DO in the lake, assuming these three people are the only ones involved?

DO Level	Marginal WTP			Aggregate
(ppm)	A	B	C	MWTP
0	$10	$10	$12	
1	6	8	10	
2	4	6	8	
3	2	4	6	
4	0	2	4	
5	0	0	2	
6	0	0	0	

4. Considering the definition of public goods introduced in the chapter, is a bus a public good? Is an automatic teller machine (ATM)? Is a public park? Is a library?

5. Consider the example of the three homeowners around the lake (the ones depicted in Table 4.2). Suppose the lake was cleaned up to the efficient level of 2 ppm and that the total costs of the cleanup were shared equally among the homeowners (stick to integer values here). Will all three homeowners be better off? What problems does this bring up about sharing the costs of public goods?

For additional readings and Web sites pertaining to the material in this chapter, see **www.mhhe.com/field7e.**

Chapter 5

The Economics of Environmental Quality

In the preceding chapter we concluded that the market system, left to itself, is likely to malfunction when matters of environmental pollution are involved. That is to say, it will not normally produce results that are socially efficient. This brings us to the **policy question:** If we do not like the way things are currently turning out, what steps should be undertaken to change the situation?[1]

The policy problem includes a number of closely related issues:

- Identifying the most appropriate level of environmental quality we ought to try to achieve
- Dividing the task and costs of meeting environmental quality goals
- Distributing benefits and costs across society appropriately

In this chapter we take up these issues on a conceptual basis; in subsequent chapters we will look at specific policy alternatives.

Before developing a simple policy model, we need to stress again that effective public policy depends on good information on how economic and environmental systems actually work. This might be called the scientific basis of environmental policy—that is, the study of how firms and consumers normally make decisions in the market economy, how residuals are emitted into the natural environment, and the ways in which these residuals behave in that environment to produce human and nonhuman damages. Thousands of scientists have worked and continue to work on these issues to clarify these diverse linkages. Great effort will continue to be needed to expand the scientific base on which to develop environmental policy.

---

[1] This goes back to the distinction made earlier between positive and normative economics (see chapter 1). Explaining why there is a certain amount of sulfur dioxide (SO_2) in the air at any particular time is a question of positive economics; deciding what best to do about it is a case of normative economics.

Pollution Control—A General Model

Diverse types of environmental pollutants obviously call for diverse types of public policy, but in order to build up the required policy analyses, it is better to start with one very simple model that lays out the fundamentals of the policy situation. The essence of the model consists of a simple **trade-off** situation that characterizes all pollution-control activities. On the one hand, reducing emissions reduces the damages that people suffer from environmental pollution; on the other hand, reducing emissions takes resources that could have been used in some other way.

To depict this trade-off, consider a simple situation where a firm (e.g., a pulp mill) is emitting production residuals into a river. As these residuals are carried downstream, they tend to be transformed into less damaging chemical constituents, but before that process is completed the river passes by a large metropolitan area. The people of the area use the waters of the river for various purposes, including recreation (boating, fishing) and as a source for the municipal water supply system. When the river becomes polluted with industrial waste, the people downstream are damaged by the disruption of these and other services provided by the river. One side of the trade-off, then, is the **damages** that people experience when the environment is degraded.

Upstream, the offending pulp mill could reduce the amount of effluent put in the river by treating its wastes before discharge, as well as by recycling certain materials that currently just run out of the discharge pipe. This act of reducing, or abating, some portion of its wastes will require resources of some amount, the costs of which will affect the price of the paper it produces.[2] These **abatement costs** are the other side of the basic pollution-control trade-off.

Pollution Damages

By *damages* we mean all the negative impacts that users of the environment experience as a result of the degradation of that environment. These negative impacts are of many types and, of course, will vary from one environmental asset to another. In the river pollution example, damages were to recreators, who could no longer use the river or who suffered a higher chance of picking up waterborne diseases, and to all the city dwellers who had to pay more to treat the water before they could put it into the public water mains.

Air pollution produces damage through its impacts on human health. Excess deaths from diseases such as lung cancer, chronic bronchitis, and asthma are related to elevated levels of various pollutants, such as particulate matter, asbestos fibers, and radon emissions. Air pollution can cause

---

[2] The word *resources* has a double meaning in economics. On the one hand, it is a shorthand way of referring to natural resources. On the other hand, it is more generally used to refer to the inputs that are utilized to produce outputs.

TABLE 5.1   Estimated Primary Annual Benefits (Reduced Damages) from CAA Reductions from PM* and Ozone

Benefit Category	Annual Monetized Benefits (million 2006$) by target year		
	2000	**2010**	**2020**
Health Effects			
PM Mortality	$710,000	$1,200,000	$1,270,000
PM Morbidity	$27,000	$46,000	$68,000
Ozone Mortality	$10,000	$33,000	$55,000
Ozone Morbidity	$420	$1,300	$2,100
Subtotal Health Effects	$750,000	$1,300,000	$1,900,000
Visibility			
Recreational	$3,300	$8,600	$19,000
Residential	$11,000	$25,000	$48,000
Recreational visibility only includes benefits in the regions analyzed (California, the Southwest and the Southeast).			
Subtotal Visibility	$14,000	$34,000	$67,000
Agricultural and Forest Productivity	$1,000	$5,500	$11,000
Materials Damage	$58	$93	$110
Ecological	$6.9	$7.5	$8.2
Reduced lake acidification benefits to recreational fishing.			
Total: all categories	$770,000	$1,300,000	$2,000,000

*PM is particulate matter.

Source: U.S. EPA, *The Benefits and Costs of the Clean Air Act from 1990 to 2020 Final Report*, April 2011.

damages through the degradation of materials (all of the important outdoor sculpture from Renaissance Florence has had to be put inside to protect it from air pollution) and the deterioration of the visual environment. Table 5.1 shows the range of estimated **damages reduced** (i.e., benefits) in the United States for a major part of the Clean Air Act. It includes projection of benefits to the year 2020.

Besides damage to human beings, environmental destruction can have important impacts on various elements of the nonhuman ecosystem. Some of these, such as the destruction of genetic information in plant and animal species driven to extinction, will ultimately have important implications for humans. Estimating environmental damages is one of the primary tasks facing environmental scientists and economists, and we will devote Chapter 7 to a discussion of this problem.

Damage Functions

In general, the greater the pollution, the greater the damages it produces. To describe the relationship between pollution and damage, we will use the idea of a **damage function.** A damage function shows the relationship between the quantity of a residual and the damage that residual causes. There are two types of damage functions:

- **Emission damage functions:** These show the connection between the quantity of a residual emitted from a source or group of sources and the resulting damage.
- **Ambient damage functions:** These show the relationship between the concentration of particular pollutants in the ambient environment and the resulting damages.

Damage functions can be expressed in a variety of ways, but our primary model will make use of **marginal damage functions.** A marginal damage function shows the **change** in damages stemming from a unit change in emissions or ambient concentration. When necessary, we also can use these relationships to discuss total damages because we know that, graphically, the areas under marginal damage functions correspond to total damages.

The height and shape of a damage function depends on the pollutant and circumstances involved. Several marginal damage functions are depicted in Figure 5.1. The top two are marginal emission damage functions; the horizontal axes measure the quantity of an effluent emitted into the environment during some specified period of time. The exact units (pounds, tons, etc.) in any particular case depend on the specific pollutant involved. The vertical axes measure environmental damages. In physical terms, environmental damage can include many types of impacts: miles of coastline polluted, numbers of people contracting lung disease, numbers of animals wiped out, quantities of water contaminated, and so on. Every case of environmental pollution normally involves multiple types of impacts, the nature of which will depend on the pollutant involved and the time and place it is emitted. To consider these impacts comprehensively, we need to be able to aggregate them into a single dimension. For this purpose, we use a monetary scale. It is sometimes easy to express damage in monetary units—for example, the "defensive" expenditures that people make to protect themselves against pollution (e.g., heavier insulation to protect against noise or more robust railroad tank cars). Usually, however, it is very difficult, as we will see.

The marginal emission damage function in panel (a) of Figure 5.1 shows marginal damages increasing only modestly at the beginning but more rapidly as emissions get larger and larger. Work by environmental scientists and economists seems to suggest that this is a typical shape for many types of pollutants, although probably not for all of them. At low levels of emissions, marginal damages may be comparatively small; ambient concentrations are so modest that only the most sensitive people in the population are affected. But when emission levels go higher, damages mount, and at still higher levels of emissions,

FIGURE 5.1   **Representative Marginal Damage Functions**

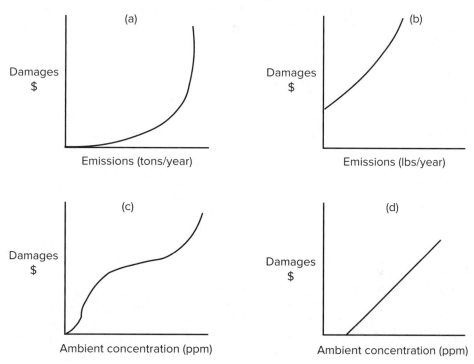

marginal damages become very elevated as environmental impacts become widespread and intense.

Panel (b) shows a marginal (emission) damage function that has the same general shape as panel (a) (i.e., it shows increasing marginal damage), but it begins much higher on the vertical axis and rises more sharply. It might represent a toxic substance that has a deadly effect even at very low levels of emission.

Panel (c) and panel (d) are marginal ambient damage functions. Whereas the vertical axes have a monetary index of damages, the horizontal axes have an index of ambient concentration, such as parts per million (ppm). Panel (c) shows a complicated function that increases at low concentrations, then tends to level off until much higher concentrations are reached, after which damages increase rapidly. This might apply, for example, to an air pollutant that causes marked damages among particularly sensitive members of society at relatively low concentrations, and among all people at very high concentrations, whereas in the middle ranges marginal damages do not increase rapidly. Panel (d) demonstrates an ambient marginal damage function that begins to the right of the origin and then increases linearly with ambient concentration.

Panels (a) and (d) illustrate a characteristic that is in fact quite controversial. They have **thresholds;** that is, they have values of emissions or ambient concentrations below which marginal damages are zero. Thus, the pollutant can increase to these threshold levels without causing any increase in damages. As will be seen in chapters to come, the assumed existence or nonexistence of a threshold in the damage functions for particular pollutants has had important impacts on real-world environmental control policies. There have been long, vigorous arguments about whether the damage functions of certain types of pollutants do or do not have thresholds.

Marginal Damage Functions

We need to look more deeply into the concept of the damage function because it will be used later to express and analyze a variety of different types of pollution problems and public policy approaches. Accordingly, Figure 5.2 shows two marginal emissions damage functions.[3] It is important to remember that, like the demand and supply curves discussed earlier, these are time specific; they show the emissions and the marginal damages for a particular period of time. There are a couple of ways of thinking about this. One is to assume, for purposes of simplicity, that the graph refers to a strictly noncumulative pollutant. Thus, all damages occur in the same period as emissions. A somewhat more complicated assumption is that for a pollutant that cumulates over time, the damage function shows the total value that people place on current and future damages. In Chapter 6 we will discuss this concept more fully.

Consider first just one of the marginal damage functions, the lower one labeled MD_1. In previous chapters we discussed the relationship between marginal and total quantities, for example, the relationship between marginal and total costs. We have the same relationship here. The height of the marginal damage curve shows how much total damages would change with a small change in the quantity of emissions. When the effluent level is at the point

---

[3] The marginal damage function goes up to the right because the quantity on the *x*-axis is emissions, which start at zero and increase to the right. Reducing pollution is thus going to be a move to the left, and the benefits this produces are shown by the reduction in marginal damages in a leftward move. In some models, however, what is indexed on the horizontal axis is *reductions* from current emission levels. Then a move to the right corresponds to a reduction in pollution, and the marginal damage function appears as a standard marginal benefit function, pictured here.

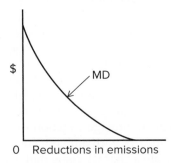

Of course either approach allows the same analysis. We chose the former (pollution upward to the right) because it means the origin corresponds to no pollution. In our models, the rising marginal damage function might suggest to you a rising marginal cost curve. In essence it is, though in this case the marginal cost refers to the marginal cost to society of increasing pollution.

marked e_1, for example, marginal damages are \$12. That is to say, if emissions were to increase by 1 ton from point e_1, the damages experienced by people exposed to those emissions would increase by \$12. By the same token, if emissions decreased by a small amount at point e_1, total damages would be reduced by \$12. Because the height of the curve, as measured on the y-axis, shows marginal damages, the area under the curve between the point where it is zero and some other point, such as the one labeled e_1, shows the total damages associated with that level of emissions. In the case of marginal damage function MD_1 and point e_1, total damages are equal to the monetary amount expressed by the triangular area bounded by the x-axis, the curve MD_1, and the effluent quantity e_1. That is area b in Figure 5.2.

What factors might account for the difference between MD_1 and MD_2 in Figure 5.2? Let us assume that they apply to the same pollutant. For any given level of emissions, marginal damages are higher for MD_2 than for MD_1. At emission level e_1, for example, a small increase in effluent would increase damages by \$12 if the marginal damage function were MD_1, but it would increase damages by \$28 if it were MD_2. Remember that any damage function shows the impacts of emitting a particular effluent in a particular time and place, so one possible explanation might be that MD_2 refers to a situation in which many people are affected by a pollutant, such as a large urban area, whereas MD_1

FIGURE 5.2   **Anatomy of a Marginal Damage Function**

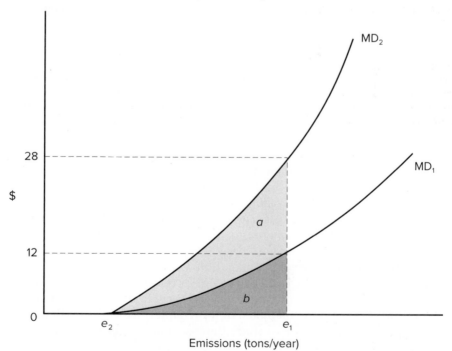

refers to a more sparsely populated rural area—fewer people, smaller damage. Some factors that move damage functions upward are:

a. Differences in population exposed, such as more people.

b. Different time periods, such as a temperature inversion that traps the pollutant over the city and produces relatively high ambient concentrations. MD_1 would be the damage function, however, when normal wind patterns prevail so that most of the effluent is blown downwind and out of the area. Thus, the same emission levels at two different times could yield substantially different damage levels due to the workings of the natural environment.

c. New scientific estimates of increased pollution impact. Because MD_2 is above MD_1, it corresponds not only to higher marginal damages, but also to higher total damages. At emission level e_1, total damages are equal to area b when the damage function is MD_1, but to area $(a + b)$ when the damage function is MD_2.

Damages and Uncertainty

The damage functions just drawn give the appearance of being very clear and unambiguous. In the real world, however, they hardly ever are. Usually there is a lot of uncertainty about the connections between pollution emissions and various types of damage: health impacts on humans, ecosystem damages, and so on. When we say "uncertain," we are not implying that pollution actually causes less damage than we might have thought, but rather that the exact amount of damage caused by different levels of pollution is difficult to measure with certainty. Uncertainty in nature affects the relationship between emissions and ambient environmental conditions, and uncertainty in human reaction affects the damages that result. This is exacerbated by the fact that much of the damage can be expected to occur well off in the future, making it difficult to predict with accuracy.

Another factor of importance is the implicit assumption we are making that damage functions are **reversible.** If emissions increase, damages increase; and if emissions decrease, damages will go back to their previous level. This may fit many pollutants: more ozone, more asthma; less ozone, and cases of asthma go back down. But for many pollutants this may not be true. The buildup of global greenhouse gases could perhaps initiate global changes that are essentially irreversible. Even some local changes may be of this type; higher levels of pollution lead to ecosystem changes that take us to new situations from which there is no easy return. For example, once a groundwater aquifer is contaminated, it may never be the same again.

Environmental economists, in cooperation with environmental scientists, epidemiologists, and the like, have worked to develop means by which damage functions can be measured with greater accuracy. In the next few chapters, we will look at some of these methods. In this chapter, we will simply use the concept of the damage function to study the essential choices that face society in pollution-control decisions.

Damages and Time

Another important factor we need to recognize in the case of pollution damage functions is time. Many pollutants are persistent; once emitted they remain in the environment for many years, potentially causing damage far off into the future. For example, the emission of greenhouse gases today will contribute to a buildup in the atmosphere that will have repercussions in the future, some of which will be in the very distant future. In addition, health and ecological impacts may result from long-term exposure to pollutants, so this can create a potentially long time gap between emissions and their damages. Obviously this creates problems in estimating damage functions: being able with reasonable accuracy to predict what future damages will be from current emissions. It also brings up the problem of how we should compare future damages to current damages. We will have much more to say about this problem in the next several chapters.

Having considered the concept of damages, it is now necessary to look at the other side of the trade-off relationship mentioned previously. It is tempting not to do this, to conclude instead that the damage functions themselves give us all the information needed to make decisions about pollution control. One might be tempted to say, for example, that society ought to strive for emission levels around point e_2 where marginal damages are zero, or perhaps even the origin, corresponding to a point at which emissions are zero. There may be certain pollutants and situations where the efficient level of emissions is indeed zero. But to determine this we have to look at the other side of the problem: abatement costs. We consider abatement costs in the next section.

Abatement Costs

Abatement costs are the costs of reducing the quantity of residuals being emitted into the environment, or of lowering ambient concentrations. Think of the pulp mill located upstream. In its normal course of operation it produces a large quantity of organic wastes. On the assumption that it has free access to the river, the cheapest way to get rid of these wastes is simply to pump them into the river, but the firm normally has technological and managerial means to reduce these emissions. The costs of engaging in these activities are called "abatement costs" because they are the costs of abating, or reducing, the quantity of residuals put into the river.[4] By spending resources on this activity, the pulp mill can abate its emissions; in general, the greater the abatement, the greater the cost.

Abatement costs normally will differ from one source to another, depending on a variety of factors. The costs of reducing emissions of SO_2 from electric power plants obviously will be different from the costs of reducing, say, toxic fumes from chemical plants. Even for sources producing the same type of effluent, the costs of abatement are likely to be different because of differences

---

[4] In Chapter 2, this would be reducing R_p^d in Figure 2.1.

in the technological features of the operation. One source may be relatively new, using modern production technology, whereas another may be an old one using more highly polluting technology. In the discussion that follows, keep in mind that *abatement* is used with the widest possible connotation and includes all the many ways there are of reducing emissions: changes in production technology, input switching, residuals recycling, treatment, abandonment of a site, and so forth.

Abatement Cost Functions

We represent this idea graphically using the concept of the **marginal abatement cost** function. The units on the axes are the same as before: quantities of pollutants on the horizontal axis and monetary value on the vertical axis. Marginal emission abatement costs show the added costs of achieving a one-unit decrease in emission level, or alternatively the costs saved if emissions are increased by a unit. On the horizontal axis, marginal abatement cost curves originate at the uncontrolled emission levels, that is, emission levels prior to undertaking any abatement activities. From this origin point, marginal abatement costs show the marginal costs of producing reductions in emissions. Thus, these marginal cost curves rise from right to left, depicting rising marginal costs of reducing emissions.[5] Exhibit 5.1 shows data pertaining to the abatement cost function for cleaning up the water of Boston Harbor.

Figure 5.3 shows three alternative marginal abatement cost functions.

Panel (a) depicts marginal abatement costs rising very modestly as emissions are first reduced, but then rising very rapidly as emissions become relatively small.

Panel (b) shows marginal abatement costs that rise rapidly from the beginning.

Panel (c) shows a marginal abatement cost curve that has an initial declining phase, followed by increasing values; this might characterize a situation in

FIGURE 5.3   **Representative Marginal Abatement Cost Functions**

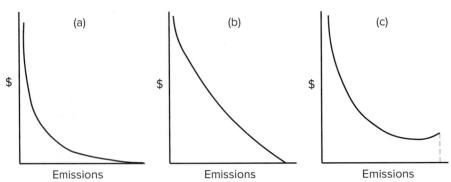

---

[5] In Chapter 3, we showed marginal cost curves sloping upward to the right. The graph goes in the opposite direction because here we are producing *reductions* in emissions.

The Abatement Cost Function for Cleaning Up Boston Harbor[1]   EXHIBIT 5.1

Cost/ Household/ Year	What You Get	Effects on the Community and the Environment	Legality
$0.00	No running water; no sewage pipes to remove sewage from houses.	City life impossible; unsafe drinking water leads to disease; local ponds and rivers drained for water; water shortages; sewage in streets causes epidemics; local ponds and rivers destroyed by sewage; major changes in animal life and urban ecology.	($0) Illegal: Federal Clean Water Act (CWA) and others violated.
$125.00	Running water in your house; clean, safe drinking water; no sewage removed from your house.	City life miserable due to raw sewage in the streets; epidemics caused by raw sewage; rivers, lakes, and harbor polluted with bacteria; destruction of local ponds and rivers by sewage; major changes in animal life and urban ecology; no safe swimming; coastal seafood contaminated.	($125) Illegal: Federal CWA and others violated.
$175.00	Running water in your house; clean, safe drinking water; sewage piped to harbor—no treatment.	Harbor unswimmable and smelly; health risk presented by raw sewage; harbor polluted by sewage and excess nutrients; shellfish contaminated; no safe ocean swimming; rats feed on fish killed by low oxygen levels.	($175) Illegal: Federal CWA and others violated.
$225.00	Running water in your house; clean, safe drinking water; sewage removed from house; primary treatment under typical conditions; frequent releases of raw sewage through combined sewer outfalls.	Boston Harbor polluted with bacteria and toxins; health risk presented by raw sewage in harbor; fish growth limited by low oxygen in the summer; all harbor seafood (except lobster) contaminated; beaches closed frequently in summer.	($225) Illegal: Federal CWA and others violated.

(Continued)

EXHIBIT **5.1** (Continued)

Cost/ Household/ Year	What You Get	Effects on the Community and the Environment	Legality
$725.00	Running water in your house; clean, safe drinking water; sewage removed from house; primary treatment under typical conditions; secondary treatment under typical conditions; many releases of raw sewage through CSOs per year.	Improvement in harbor from present; bacterial pollution and low oxygen levels caused by combined sewer outfall (CSO) releases; all harbor seafood (except lobster) contaminated; beaches closed frequently in summer.	($725) Legal: Under typical conditions. ($725) Illegal: Federal CWA violated during heavy rain storms.
$800.00	Running water in your house; clean, safe drinking water; sewage removed from house; primary treatment; secondary treatment and sludge recycling; long outfall; storage for CSO water; infrequent releases of raw sewage through CSOs.	Improvement in harbor from present; seafood caught in harbor is edible; few or no beaches closed during summer; harbor swimmable under good conditions.	($800) Legal: Federal CWA requirements met.
$1,200.00	Running water in your house; clean, safe drinking water; sewage removed from house; primary treatment; secondary treatment and sludge recycling; tertiary treatment; long outfall; containment of CSO water.	Sewage has no effect on harbor; healthy marine environment in harbor; harbor swimmable.	($1,200) Legal: Federal CWA requirements exceeded.

[1] These abatement costs are in terms of dollars per household per year. They are not, strictly speaking, marginal abatement costs, but you can determine what these are by looking at the differences in costs between the various levels.

Source: Exhibit material displayed at the New England Aquarium, Boston, MA, Spring 2000. Thanks to Stephen Costa for finding this material.

which small reductions can be handled only by technical means that require a substantial initial investment.

For somewhat larger reductions, the marginal costs actually may decline as it becomes possible to utilize these techniques more fully. Ultimately, however, marginal abatement costs increase. We have to keep in mind that in dealing with abatement costs we are dealing with a cost concept similar to that discussed in Chapter 3. The level of costs encountered when carrying out any particular task depends on the technology available to do the task and also on the managerial skills that are applied to the job. It is quite possible to suffer extremely high abatement costs if the wrong technology is used or if what is available is used incorrectly. In other words, the marginal abatement cost functions pictured are to be understood as the **minimum** costs of achieving reductions in emissions.

To investigate more deeply the concept of marginal abatement cost, consider Figure 5.4, which shows two marginal abatement cost curves. For the moment we focus on the higher one, labeled MAC_2. It begins at an effluent level marked $\bar{e}$, the uncontrolled emission level. From there it slopes upward to the left. Beginning at the uncontrolled level, the first units of emission reduction can be achieved with a relatively low marginal cost. Think again of the pulp mill. This first small decrease might be obtained with the addition of a modest settling pond, but as emission levels are reduced further, the marginal cost of achieving additional reductions increases. For example, to get a 30 to 40 percent reduction, the pulp mill may have to invest in new technology that

FIGURE 5.4   **Anatomy of a Marginal Abatement Cost Curve**

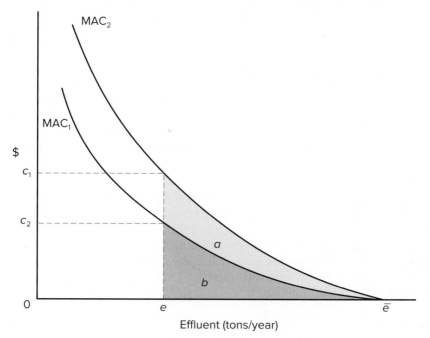

is more efficient in terms of water use. A 60 to 70 percent reduction in efflu-ent might require substantial new treatment technology in addition to all the steps taken previously (such as screens and filters), whereas a 90 to 95 percent reduction might take very costly equipment for recycling virtually all of the production residuals produced in the plant. Thus, the larger the reduction in emissions, the greater the marginal costs of producing further reductions. This yields a marginal abatement cost function that gets steeper in slope as emis-sions are reduced.[6]

Of course, there is an upper limit on these abatement costs. The extreme option for a single plant or pollution source is to cease operations, thereby achieving a zero level of emissions. The costs of doing this depend on circum-stances. If the source is just one small plant within a large industry consisting of many such plants, the costs of closing it down may not be that great. In fact, it may have very little impact on, say, the price to consumers of whatever is being produced (e.g., paper in the pulp mill), although the local impact on jobs and community welfare may be substantial. But if we are talking about the marginal abatement costs for an entire industry—electric power production in the midwestern United States, for example—the shutdown option, as a way of achieving zero emissions, would have enormous costs.

The marginal abatement cost function can express **actual** marginal costs of a source or group of sources or the **lowest possible** marginal abatement costs. Actual costs, of course, are determined by the technologies and procedures that firms have adopted in the past to reduce emissions. These could have been affected by a variety of factors, including managerial shortsightedness or public pollution-control regulations. To use the model for studying ques-tions of social efficiency and cost-effectiveness, however, we don't want ac-tual costs but the lowest possible abatement costs. In this case, we have to assume that sources have adopted whatever technological and managerial means are available to achieve emission reductions at the lowest possible costs. We have to assume, in other words, that sources are acting in a **cost-effective** manner.

As with any marginal graph, we can depict not only marginal but also total values. If emissions are currently at e tons per year, the value on the vertical axis shows the marginal cost of achieving one more unit of emission reduction. The area under the marginal abatement cost curve, between its origin at point $\bar{e}$ and any particular emission level, is equal to the **total costs** of abating emissions to that level. For example, with the curve labeled MAC_2, the total abatement cost of achieving an emission level of e tons per year is equal to the area under the curve between e and $\bar{e}$, the area $(a + b)$; remember that we are reading the graph from right to left.

---

[6] Remember that the quantity indexed on the horizontal axis is the quantity of emissions, starting at zero on the left. Thus, the marginal abatement costs of reducing emissions increase as you move to the left, that is, as you decrease emissions. In Chapter 3, we introduced marginal cost curves that had the conventional shape of increasing to the right as output increased. If we indexed the *quantity of emissions reduced* starting at zero, then the MAC curve would indeed increase to the right. We think it more intuitive, however, to have the origin correspond to zero actual emissions.

Consider now the other marginal abatement cost curve shown in Figure 5.4, labeled MAC_1. Its main feature is that it lies below MAC_2, meaning that it corresponds to a situation where the marginal abatement costs for any level of emissions are lower than those of MAC_2. At e tons per year of emissions, for example, the marginal costs of abating an extra ton are only c_2 in the case of MAC_1, which are substantially lower than the marginal abatement costs of MAC_2 at this point. What could account for the difference? Let us assume that we are dealing with the same pollutant in each case. One possibility is that these apply to different sources—for example, a plant that was built many years ago and another that was built more recently and uses different production technology. The newer plant lends itself to less costly emissions reduction, MAC_1.

Another possibility is that MAC_1 and MAC_2 relate to the same pollutant and the same source, but at different times. The lower one represents the situation after a new pollution-control technology has been developed, whereas the upper one applies before the change. Technological change, in other words, results in a lowering of the marginal abatement cost curve for a given pollutant. It is possible to represent graphically the annual cost that this source would save, assuming the emission rate is e before and after the change. Before the firm adopted the new technology, its total abatement cost of achieving effluent level e was equal to $(a + b)$ per year, whereas after the change, the total abatement costs are b per year. The annual cost savings from the technological change are thus a.[7] This type of analysis will be important when we examine different types of pollution-control policies because one of the criteria we will want to use to evaluate these policies is how much cost-saving incentive they offer to firms to engage in research and development to produce new pollution-control technologies.

Aggregate Marginal Abatement Costs

The discussion of the last few pages has treated the marginal abatement cost function as something applying to a single firm, such as a single pulp mill on a river. Suppose, however, we want to talk about the marginal abatement cost of a group of firms, perhaps a group of firms in the same industry or a group of firms all located in the same region. Most environmental policies, especially at state or federal levels, are aimed at controlling emissions from groups of pollution sources, not just single polluters. Suppose, furthermore, that the individual marginal abatement cost functions differ among the various firms. To control organic pollutants in Boston Harbor or San Francisco Bay, for example, would require controlling emissions from a large variety of different sources in different industries with different production technologies, and therefore with very different individual marginal abatement cost functions. In this case, we would have to construct the overall, or **aggregate, marginal abatement cost function** for the collection of firms by adding together the individual marginal abatement cost curves.

---

[7] Note that up-front capital costs are spread over the lifetime of the technology.

Although this sounds simple, and it basically is, it nevertheless leads into one of the more important concepts underlying the design of effective environmental policy. It is critical to keep in mind the central idea of the abatement cost function. It is a function that shows the *least costly* way of achieving reductions in emissions for an individual firm if we are looking at an individual marginal abatement cost function, or for a group of polluting sources if we are considering the aggregate marginal abatement cost function.

Figure 5.5 shows, on the left, two individual marginal abatement cost functions, labeled Source A and Source B. Note that they are not the same (although remember that the scales are the same; that is, we are dealing with the same pollutant). MAC_A starts at 20 tons/week and rises rather rapidly as emissions are reduced. MAC_B also begins at the uncontrolled discharge level of 20 tons/week, but rises much less rapidly. Why the difference? Perhaps Source B is a newer plant with more flexible technological alternatives for pollution control. Or perhaps the two sources, although producing the same type of effluent, are manufacturing different consumer goods and using different production techniques. For whatever reason, they have different marginal abatement cost curves.

The aggregate marginal abatement cost curve is a summation, or aggregation, of these two individual relationships. But because the individual curves are different, it makes a great deal of difference how they are added together. The problem is that when there are two (or any other number greater than one) sources with different abatement costs, the total cost will depend on how the total emissions are allocated among the different sources. The principle to follow is to add together the two individual functions in such a way as to yield the lowest possible aggregate marginal abatement costs. The way to do this is to add them horizontally. Select a particular level of marginal abatement cost— for example, the one marked w in Figure 5.5. This level of marginal abatement cost is associated with an effluent level of 10 tons/week from Source A and an

FIGURE 5.5 **Aggregate Abatement Costs**

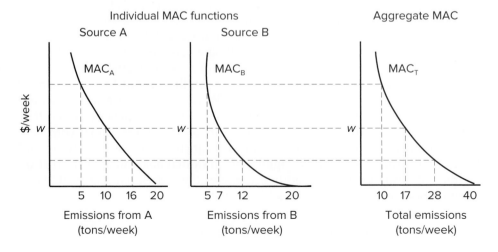

Individual MAC functions

Source A — Source B — Aggregate MAC

Emissions from A (tons/week) — Emissions from B (tons/week) — Total emissions (tons/week)

effluent level of about 7 tons/week from Source B. On the aggregate curve, thus, a marginal abatement cost of w would be associated with an effluent level of 10 tons + 7 tons = 17 tons/week. All the other points on the aggregate marginal abatement cost curve are found the same way, by summing across horizontally on the individual marginal abatement cost curves.

In effect, what we have done here is to invoke the important **equimarginal principle,** an idea that was introduced earlier in Chapter 4. To get the minimum aggregate marginal abatement cost curve, the aggregate level of emissions must be distributed among the different sources in such a way that they all have the same marginal abatement costs. Start at the 10 tons/week point on the aggregate curve. Obviously, this 10-ton total could be distributed among the two sources in any number of ways: five tons from each source, or eight tons from one and two from the other, and so on. Only one allocation, however, will give the lowest aggregate marginal abatement costs; this is the allocation that leads the different sources to the point at which they have exactly the same marginal abatement costs. At the end of this chapter, we will come back to this equimarginal principle, illustrating it with a simple numerical example.

The Socially Efficient Level of Emissions

We have considered separately the marginal damage function and the marginal abatement cost function related to a particular pollutant being released at a particular place and time; it is now time to bring these two relationships together. This we do in Figure 5.6, which depicts a set of conventionally shaped

FIGURE 5.6   **The Efficient Level of Emissions**

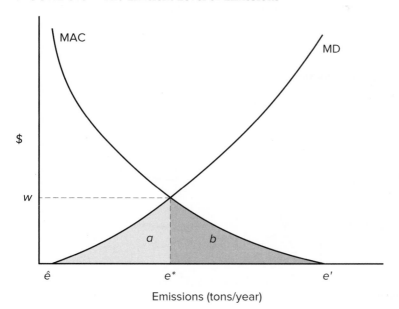

marginal damage and marginal abatement cost curves labeled, respectively, MD and MAC. Marginal damages have a threshold at emission level ê, whereas the uncontrolled emission level is é.

The efficient level of emissions is defined as that level at which marginal damages are equal to marginal abatement costs. What is the justification for this? Note the trade-off that is inherent in the pollution phenomenon: higher emissions expose society, or some part of it, to greater costs stemming from environmental damages. Lower emissions involve society in greater costs in the form of resources devoted to abatement activities. The efficient level of emissions is thus the level at which these two types of costs exactly offset one another—that is, where **marginal abatement costs equal marginal damage costs.** This is emission level e^* in Figure 5.6. Marginal damages and marginal abatement costs are equal to each other and to the value w at this level of emissions.

We also can look at this outcome in terms of total values because we know that the totals are the areas under the marginal curves. Thus, the triangular area marked a (bounded by points $\hat{e}$ and e^* and the marginal damage function) depicts the total damages existing when emissions are at level e^*, whereas the triangular area b shows the total abatement costs at this level of emissions. The sum of these two areas $(a + b)$ is a measure of the total social costs from e^* tons per year of this particular pollutant. The point e^* is the unique point at which this sum is minimized. Note that the size of area a need not equal the size of area b.

You might get the impression, on the basis of where point e^* is located on the x-axis, that this analysis has led us to the conclusion that the efficient level of emissions is always one that involves a relatively large quantity of emissions and substantial environmental damages. This is not the case. What we are developing, rather, is a conceptual way of looking at a trade-off. In the real world every pollution problem is different. This analysis gives us a generalized way of framing the problem that obviously has to be adapted to the specifics of any particular case of environmental pollution. Figure 5.7, for example,

FIGURE 5.7 **Efficient Emission Levels for Different Pollutants**

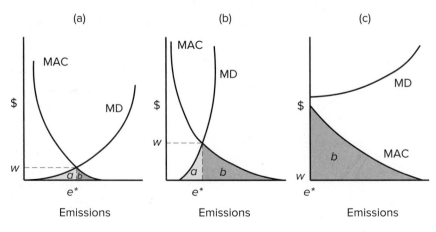

depicts three different situations that might characterize particular environmental pollutants. In each case, e^* depicts the efficient level of emissions and w shows marginal damages and marginal abatement costs at that quantity of emissions. Panel (a) shows a pollutant for which e^* is well to the right of zero (of course, because the horizontal axis has no units, it's not clear exactly what "well to the right" actually means here). Marginal damages at this point are quite small; so are total damages and abatement costs, as shown by the small size of the triangles corresponding to these values. The reason is that this is a pollutant where both marginal abatement costs and marginal damages increase at first only very slowly.

Panel (b) shows a situation where the marginal abatement function rises moderately, then rapidly, whereas the marginal damage function rises very rapidly from the beginning. In this case, e^* is well to the right of zero, and w lies well above what it was in the first diagram (assuming the vertical axes of these diagrams all have the same scale). Note, however, that at e^* total abatement costs are substantially higher than total damages, as is indicated by the relative sizes of the triangles that measure these total values (*a* and *b*). What this emphasizes is that it is not the equality of total abatement costs and total damages that defines the efficient level of effluent, but the equality of the **marginal abatement costs** and **marginal damages.**

In panel (c) of Figure 5.7 the efficient level of emissions is zero. There is no point of intersection of the two functions in the graph; area *a* does not even appear on the graph. The only way we could conceivably get them to intersect is if we could somehow extend them to the left of the vertical axis, but this would imply that emissions could actually be negative, which is an oddity that we will avoid. What makes $e^* = 0$ is that the marginal damage function doesn't begin at zero, but rather well up on the *y*-axis, implying that even the first small amount of this pollutant placed in the environment causes great damage (perhaps this diagram applies to some extremely toxic material). Relative to this, the marginal costs of abatement are low, giving an efficient emission level of zero.

Changes in the Efficient Level of Emissions

The real world is a dynamic place, and this is especially true of environmental pollution control. For our purposes this implies, for example, that the level of emissions that was efficient last year, or last decade, is not necessarily the level that is efficient today or that is likely to be in the future. When any of the factors that lie behind the marginal damage and marginal abatement cost functions change, the functions themselves will shift and e^*, the efficient level of emissions, also will change.

Before taking a look at this, we need to remind ourselves of what we are doing. Remember the distinction made earlier between positive and normative economics, between the **economics of *what is*** and the **economics of *what ought to be.*** The idea of the efficient level of emissions comes firmly under normative economics, under the idea of what ought to be. We are presenting emission level e^*, the level that balances abatement costs and damage costs, as a desirable target for public policy. Do not get this confused with the actual level of emissions. If the world worked so that the actual level of emissions was always equal to, or close to, the efficient level, we presumably would have no need to worry about intervening with environmental policy of one type or another. Of course it does not, which is why we must turn to public policy.

Figure 5.8 shows several ways in which e^* might change when underlying factors change. Panel (a) shows the results of a shift upward in the marginal damage function, from MD_1 to MD_2. One of the ways this could happen is through population growth. MD_1 might apply to a municipality in 2005 and MD_2 to the same municipality in 2015 after its population has grown. More people means that a given amount of effluent will cause more damage.[8] This leads to a conclusion that is intuitively straightforward: The efficient level of emissions drops from e^*_1 to e^*_2. With a higher marginal damage function, the logic of the efficiency trade-off would lead us to devote more resources to pollution control.

Panel (b) of Figure 5.8 shows the case of a shift in the marginal abatement cost function, from MAC_1 to MAC_2. What could have caused this? The most obvious, perhaps, is a change in the technology of pollution control. As stressed earlier, abatement costs depend critically on the technology available for reducing effluent streams: treatment technology, recycling technology, alternative fuel technology, and so forth. New techniques normally arise because resources, talents, and energy have been devoted to research and development. So the shift downward in marginal abatement costs depicted in Figure 5.8 might be

FIGURE 5.8 **Changes in e^*, the Efficient Level of Emissions**

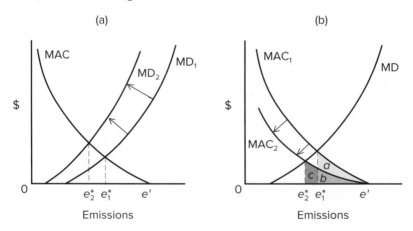

[8] This diagram also could apply, of course, to a different situation. MD_1 could be the damage function pertaining to a relatively sparsely settled rural region; MD_2 could be the marginal damage function pertaining to a more populous urban area. Everything we say about the relationship between e^*_1 and e^*_2 applies also to cases like this where we are comparing two different places at the same time, in addition to the previous comparison of the same place at two different times.

the result of the development of new treatment or recycling technologies that make it less costly to reduce the effluent stream of this particular pollutant. It should not be too surprising that this leads to a reduction in the efficient level of emissions, as indicated by the change from e^*_1 to e^*_2. We might note that this could lead to either an increase or a decrease in the total cost of abating emissions. Before the change, total abatement costs were an amount equal to the area $(a + b)$, that is, the area under MAC_1 between the uncontrolled level e' and the amount e^*_1. After the change, total abatement costs are equal to area $(b + c)$, and the question of whether total abatement costs at the efficient level of emissions have increased or decreased hinges on the relative sizes of the two areas a and c. This in turn depends on the shapes of the curves and the extent to which the marginal abatement cost curve has shifted; the more it has shifted, the more likely it is that the efficient level of total abatement costs after the change will exceed the costs before the change.[9]

Enforcement Costs

So far the analysis has considered only the private costs of reducing emissions, but emission reductions do not happen unless resources are devoted to enforcement. To include all sources of cost we need to add **enforcement costs** to the analysis. Some of these are private, such as added recordkeeping by polluters, but the bulk are public costs related to various regulatory aspects of the enforcement process.

Figure 5.9 shows a simple model of pollution control with enforcement costs added. To the normal marginal abatement cost function has been added the marginal costs of enforcement, giving a total marginal cost function labeled MAC + E. The vertical distance between the two marginal cost curves equals marginal enforcement costs. The assumption drawn into the graph is that marginal enforcement costs, the added costs of enforcement that it takes to get emissions reduced by a unit, increase as emissions decrease. In other words, the more polluters cut back emissions, the more costly it is to enforce further cutbacks.

In effect, the addition of enforcement costs moves the efficient level of emissions to the right of where it would be if they were zero. This shows the vital importance of having good enforcement technology because lower marginal enforcement costs would move MAC + E closer to MAC, decreasing the efficient emission level. In fact, **technical change in enforcement** has exactly the same effect on the efficient level of emissions as technical change in emissions abatement. We will have more to say about enforcement in later chapters, especially Chapter 11.

---

[9] These diagrams also can be used to examine some of the implications of making mistakes. For example, suppose the public control authorities think that the real marginal abatement cost was MAC_1, but, in fact, because there is a cheaper way of reducing this effluent that they do not know about, marginal abatement costs are actually MAC_2. Then we would conclude that the efficient level of effluent is e^*_1, whereas it is actually e^*_2. We might be shooting at a target that involves excessive emissions.

FIGURE 5.9 Enforcement Costs

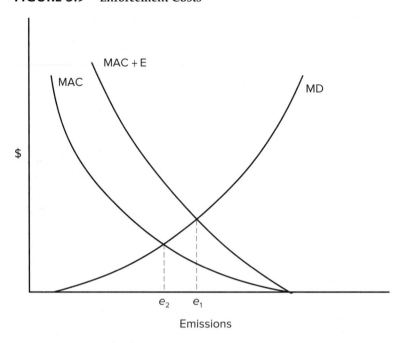

The Equimarginal Principle Applied to Emission Reductions

Before going on, we will take a last, very explicit look at the equimarginal principle. In the present context, the application of the equimarginal principle says the following: If there are **multiple sources** of a particular type of pollutant with **differing marginal abatement costs,** and if it is desired to reduce aggregate emissions at the **least possible cost** (or, alternatively, get the greatest reduction in emissions for a given cost), then emissions from the various sources must be reduced in accordance with the **equimarginal principle.**

To illustrate this, look at the numbers in Table 5.2. This shows explicitly the marginal abatement costs of each of two firms emitting a particular residual into the environment. If neither source makes any effort to control emissions, they will each emit 12 tons/week. If Source A reduces its emissions by 1 ton, to 11 tons/week, it will cost $1,000/week; if it reduces effluent further to 10 tons/week, its abatement costs will increase by $2,000/week, and so on. Note that the marginal abatement cost relationships of the two sources are different: that of Source B increases faster than that of Source A.

Suppose that initially each plant is emitting at the uncontrolled level; total emissions would then be 24 tons/week. Now assume that we want to reduce overall emissions to half the present level, or a total of 12 tons/week. One way to do this would be to have **equiproportionate** cutbacks. Because we

TABLE 5.2   The Equimarginal Principal

Emissions (tons/week)	12	11	10	9	8	7	6	5	4	3	2	1	0
Marginal Abatement Costs:													
Source A ($1,000/week)	0	1	2	3	4	5	6	8	10	14	24	38	70
Source B ($1,000/week)	0	2	4	6	10	14	20	25	31	38	58	94	160

want a total reduction of 50 percent, each source is required to reduce by 50 percent. If Source A were cut 50 percent to 6 tons/week, its marginal abatement costs at this level would be $6,000/week, whereas at this level of emissions the marginal abatement costs of Source B would be $20,000/week. Total abatement costs of the 12-ton total can be found by adding up the marginal abatement costs:

Source A: $21,000 ($1,000 + $2,000 + $3,000 + $4,000 + $5,000 + $6,000)

Source B: $56,000 ($2,000 + $4,000 + $6,000 + $10,000 + $14,000 + $20,000)

Total $77,000/week.

The overall reduction to 12 tons/week, however, can be achieved with a substantially lower total cost. We know this because the equiproportionate reduction violates the equimarginal principle; marginal abatement costs are not equalized when each source reduces its effluent to 6 tons/week. What is required is different emission rates for the two sources, where, simultaneously, they will emit no more than 12 tons of effluent and have the same marginal abatement costs. This condition is satisfied if Source A emits four tons and Source B emits eight tons. These rates add up to 12 tons total and give each source a marginal abatement cost of $10,000/week. Calculating total abatement costs at these emission levels gives:

Source A: $39,000 ($1,000 + $2,000 + $3,000 + $4,000 + $5,000 + $6,000 + $8,000 + $10,000)

Source B: $22,000 ($2,000 + $4,000 + $6,000 + $10,000)

Total $61,000/week.

By following the equimarginal principle, the desired reduction in total emissions has been obtained, but with a savings of $16,000/week over the case of an equiproportionate reduction.

Thus, we see that an emission reduction plan that follows the equimarginal rule gives emission reduction at minimum cost. Another way of saying this is that for any particular amount of money devoted to effluent reduction, the maximum quantitative reduction in total effluent can only be obtained by following the equimarginal principle. The importance of this principle cannot be overstated. When defining the efficient level of emissions, we were going on the assumption that we were working with the lowest possible marginal abatement cost function. The only way of achieving this is by controlling individual sources in accordance with the equimarginal rule. If we are designing public policy under the rule of equiproportionate reductions at the various sources, the marginal abatement cost function will be higher than it should be. And the extra cost spent on this pollution problem could have been spent to clean up another pollution problem. One of the results of this is that the efficient emission level will be higher than it should be, or, to say the same thing, we will seek smaller reductions in emissions than are socially efficient.

Summary

In this chapter, we have looked at a simple model of pollution control. It is based on the notion of a trade-off between environmental damages and pollution abatement costs. We introduced the notion of a **marginal damage function,** showing the marginal social damages resulting from varying levels of residual emissions or ambient pollutant levels. Then we looked at **marginal abatement cost** relationships, first for an individual pollution source and then for a group of such sources. By bringing together these two types of relationships, we then defined an **efficient level of emissions:** that level at which marginal damages and marginal abatement costs are equal. At this level of emissions, total social costs, the total of abatement costs and damages, are minimized.

The efficient level of emissions is subject to change as underlying factors shift. Population growth and the results of scientific studies can shift marginal damage functions; technological changes can cause marginal abatement cost functions to shift. We illustrated one case in which the efficient level of a particular pollutant is zero. Finally, we reviewed the equimarginal principle as it applies to pollution control. That principle states that when multiple sources have different marginal abatement costs, equalizing these costs will be the least-cost way of achieving a reduction in total emissions.

A word of caution is appropriate. The model presented in this chapter is very general and risks giving an overly simplistic impression of pollution problems in the real world. In fact, there are very few actual instances of environmental pollution where the marginal damage and marginal abatement functions are known with certainty. The natural world is too complex, and human and nonhuman responses are too difficult to identify with complete clarity. Furthermore, polluters come in all types and sizes and economic circumstances, and it takes enormous resources to learn even simple things about the costs of pollution abatement in concrete instances. Pollution-control technology is changing rapidly, so what is efficient today will not necessarily be so tomorrow. Nevertheless, the simple model is useful for thinking about the basic problem of pollution control, and it will be useful in our later chapters on the various approaches to environmental policy.

Questions for Further Discussion

1. Prove (graphically) that the point labeled e^* in Figure 5.6 is indeed the point that minimizes total social costs, the sum of abatement and damage costs. (Do this by showing that at any other point, this total cost will be higher.)

2. Suppose there is a river on which are located several micro breweries, each of which discharges pollutants into the water. Suppose somebody invents a new technology for treating this waste stream that, if adopted by the breweries, could substantially diminish emissions. What are the impacts of this invention on (*a*) the actual level of emissions and (*b*) the efficient level of emissions?

3. Suppose there is a suburban community where domestic septic tanks are responsible for contaminating a local lake. What is the effect on actual and efficient levels of water quality in the lake of an increase in the number of homes in the community?

4. Following are the marginal abatement costs of three firms, related to the quantity of emissions. Each firm is now emitting 10 tons/week, so total emissions are 30 tons/week. Suppose we wish to reduce total emissions by 50 percent, to 15 tons per week. Compare the total costs of doing this: (*a*) with an equiproportionate decrease in emissions and (*b*) with a decrease that meets the equimarginal principle.

Emissions (tons/week)	10	9	8	7	6	5	4	3	2	1	0
Marginal Abatement Costs:											
Firm 1 ($/ton)	0	4	8	12	16	20	24	28	36	46	58
Firm 2 ($/ton)	0	1	2	4	6	8	12	20	24	28	36
Firm 3 ($/ton)	0	1	2	3	4	5	6	7	8	9	10

5. Suppose a new law is put into effect requiring oil tankers to use certain types of navigation rules in coastal waters of the United States. Suppose that the very next year there is a large tanker accident and oil spill in these waters. Does this mean that the law has had no effect?

For additional readings and Web sites pertaining to the material in this chapter, see **www.mhhe.com/field7e.**

Section 3

Environmental Analysis

In the last few chapters we have used the concepts of abatement costs and damages without worrying too much about how the actual magnitudes of these concepts might be measured in particular situations. In the next three chapters this is rectified. Several types of analysis have been developed over the years to provide environmental, economic, and social valuations that can be used to inform the policy process. In the next chapter we deal with these at the framework level. From the standpoint of economics, benefit–cost analysis is the primary analytical tool, so much of the chapter will be devoted to a discussion of its major elements. Then, in the following two chapters, we look more closely at the methods available for estimating benefits and costs of environmental policy decisions.

Chapter 6

Frameworks of Analysis

Policy decisions require information, and although the availability of good information doesn't automatically mean that decisions also will be good, its *un*availability will almost always contribute to bad decisions. There are a variety of alternative frameworks for generating and presenting information useful to policymakers, calling for different skills and research procedures. We briefly review the most important of these, before focusing on benefit–cost analysis.

Impact Analysis

Impact is a very general word, meaning the effects of any actual or proposed policy. Because there are many types of effects, there are many different types of impact analysis.

Environmental Impact Analysis

An environmental impact analysis (EIA) is essentially an identification and study of all significant environmental repercussions stemming from a course of action. For the most part, these focus on impacts that are expected to flow from a proposed decision, although retrospective EIAs are of great value also, especially when they are done to see if earlier predictions were accurate. EIAs can be carried out for any social action, public or private, industrial or domestic, local or national. They are largely the work of natural scientists, who focus on tracing out and describing the physical impacts of projects or programs, following through the complex linkages that spread these impacts through the ecosystem. They do not directly address the issue of placing social values on these impacts.

Many countries have laws requiring environmental impact studies when substantial public programs and projects are under consideration, as well as private projects in some cases. In the United States, environmental impact analyses are mandated by the **National Environmental Policy Act of 1970** (NEPA).

The resulting environmental impact statements (EIS's) are primarily the work of natural scientists, yet economists have a distinct role to play. It is not only ecological linkages through which environmental impacts spread; they also spread through economic linkages. Suppose, for example, it is proposed to build a dam that will flood a certain river valley while providing new flat-water recreation possibilities. A substantial part of the environmental impact will stem from the inundation itself and the resulting losses in animals and plants, wild-river recreation, farmland, and so on. But much also could come from changes in patterns of behavior among people affected by the project. Recreators traveling into and out of the region could affect air pollution and traffic congestion. New housing or commercial development spurred by the recreation opportunities could have negative environmental effects. Thus, to study the full range of environmental impacts from the dam, it is necessary to include not just the physical effects of the dam and its water impoundment, but also the ways in which people will react and adapt to this new facility.

Economic Impact Analysis

When interest centers on how some action—a new law, a new technological breakthrough, a new source of imports, and so forth—will affect an economic system, in whole or in terms of its various parts, we can speak of **economic impact analysis**. In most countries, especially developing ones, there is usually wide interest in the impact of environmental regulations on economic growth rates. Sometimes the focus will be on tracing out the ramifications of a public program for certain economic variables that are considered particularly important. One might be especially interested, for example, in the impact of an environmental regulation on employment, the impact of import restrictions on the rate of technological change in an industry, the effects of an environmental law on the growth of the pollution-control industry, the response of the food industry to new packaging regulations, and so on.

Economic impact analyses can be focused at any level. Local environmental groups might be interested in the impact of a wetlands law on the rate of population growth and tax base in their community. Regional groups might be interested in the impacts of a national regulation on their particular economic circumstances. At the global level, an important question is how efforts to control carbon dioxide (CO_2) emissions might impact the relative growth rates of rich and poor countries. Whatever the level, economic impact analysis requires a basic understanding of how economies function and how their various parts fit together.

Regulatory Impact Analysis

Regulatory agencies and others are concerned with the array of possible impacts that might result from any actual or proposed regulation. What has developed over time, therefore, is the concept of **regulatory impact analysis** (RIA), which is supposed to systematically and comprehensively identify and estimate the impacts flowing from regulations. Many countries have requirements for doing these types of studies, and they differ somewhat in terms of what kinds of impacts they focus on and some of the procedures for carrying them out.[1] In the United States, RIAs essentially involve full **benefit–cost analyses** of regulatory options. We will discuss benefit–cost analysis later in this chapter.

Cost-Effectiveness Analysis

Suppose a community determined that its current water supply was contaminated with some chemical and that it had to switch to some alternative supply. Suppose it had several possibilities: It could drill new wells into an uncontaminated aquifer, it could build a connector to the water-supply system of a neighboring town, or it could build its own surface reservoir. A **cost-effectiveness analysis** would estimate the costs of these different alternatives with the aim of showing how they compared in terms of, say, the costs per million gallons of delivered water into the town system. Cost-effectiveness analysis, in other words, takes the objective as given, then costs out various alternative ways of attaining that objective.

Table 6.1 shows some cost-effectiveness data for reducing methane emissions in natural gas production and transmission. Methane is a potent greenhouse gas, and quantities of it escape at various points of the natural gas production and transmission cycle. Note that there is a substantial difference among the different technologies for reducing methane: the most cost-effective is only 41 cents per thousand cubic feet of methane reduction, while the least cost-effective is over $7.00 per thousand cubic feet.

Cost-effectiveness is desirable in and of itself. Being cost-effective means getting the biggest "bang for the buck." But cost-effectiveness also underlies the idea of efficiency. For a policy to be efficient, it must at the very least be cost-effective.

TABLE 6.1   **Cost-Effectiveness of Alternative Means of Reducing Methane Leaks in Natural Gas Operations**

Technique	Costs per Thousand Cubic Feet
Upgrading pneumatic control devices	1.99
Upgrading compressor pumps	6.89
Installing new systems for liquid extraction	5.03
Replacing pneumatic with solar pumps	4.86
Change venting procedures	0.41
Leak detection and repair at wells	7.60
Leak detection and repair in transmission	2.15

Source: ICF International, *Economic Analysis of Methane Emission Reduction Opportunities in the U.S. Onshore Oil and Natural Gas Industries*, Proposal for Environmental Defense Fund, March 2014.

[1] See, for example, Organization for Economic Cooperation and Development, *Sustainability in Impact Assessment: A review of Impact Assessment Systems in Selected OECD Countries and the European Commission*, Paris, 2012.

Damage Assessment

In 1980, the Comprehensive Environmental Response, Compensation and Liability Act was enacted.[2] This law allows federal, state, and local governments to act as trustees for publicly owned natural resources and to sue people who are responsible for the release of harmful materials that damage these resources. This has led to a type of study called **damage assessment**, the objective of which is to estimate the value of the damages to an injured resource so that these amounts can be recovered from those held liable by the courts. The U.S. Department of Interior (DOI) was assigned the job of determining how damages are to be measured in these cases.

The conclusions of the DOI were that damages should be equal to the lesser of (1) the **lost value of the resource** or (2) the **value of restoring the resource** to its former state. Consider the following figures, which represent resource values and restoration values for several cases.

	A	B
Lost resource value	$1.2 million	$1.6 million
Restoration cost	0.6 million	3.8 million

For case A, the resource value lost from an oil or hazardous waste release is $1.2 million, but the cost of restoring the resource to its former state is only $0.6 million, so the latter is taken as the true measure of damages. In case B, the lost resource value at $1.6 million is substantially less than restoration costs of $3.8 million; therefore, the former would be used to assess damages.

The lost economic values associated with a reduction in the quality of a natural resource can stem from many sources: for example, on-site recreation such as camping, hiking, or snow mobiling; extractive uses of natural resources, such as energy production and mining; uses of stream flows for irrigation, municipal, and industrial water supplies; and transportation services. The task of measuring these values is very similar to the steps undertaken in standard benefit–cost studies of natural and environmental resource use, which we discuss next.

Currently, restoration costs are the preferred measure of damages. Restoration costs are defined to include restoration, rehabilitation, replacement, and/or the acquisition of equivalent resources. Exhibit 6.1 discusses one such case. Some of the difficulties in estimating restoration costs are:

- The determination of what the original or baseline resource quality actually was.
- The choice among alternative ways of restoring a resource in a cost-effective way.
- The determination of what is meant by a natural or environmental resource of equivalent value to a resource that was lost.

---

[2] This law will be studied in more detail in Chapter 16.

$4.485 Million Settlement for Natural Resource Injuries at the Superfund Site in South Plainfield, NJ   EXHIBIT 6.1

March 2015—On February 24, 2015, the United States entered into a settlement agreement with the owner of the property where an electronics manufacturing facility operated in New Jersey. The $22 million settlement includes $4.485 million to compensate for injuries to natural resources in Bound Brook and its associated wetlands and floodplains including lost use of the recreational fishery since 1997, when the New Jersey Department of Environmental Protection (NJDEP) issued a ban on consumption of all species of fish in Bound Brook due to Polychlorinated biphenyl (PCB) contamination.

The firm manufactured electronic parts and components and tested transformer oils at their facility in South Plainfield, NJ, from 1936 to 1952 and disposed of PCB-contaminated material directly into an unnamed stream that flows half a mile into Bound Brook, a tributary of the Raritan River.

Hundreds of acres of wetlands and stream bottom were contaminated with PCBs and other contaminants. Funds available from this and other settlements of natural resource injury related to releases from this Superfund Site will be used to restore natural resources. NOAA and our co-Trustees, the U.S. Fish and Wildlife Service and the NJDEP, are evaluating opportunities for natural resource restoration in the Raritan River watershed and will seek public input during restoration planning.

Source: Damage Assessment, Remediation, & Restoration Program, National Oceanic and Atmospheric Administration, May 7, 2015.

It is apparent that it is impossible to discuss restoration in physical terms without considering its monetary costs.

Green GDP

In recent years, interest has grown in having an aggregate measure of a country's environmental health analogous to gross domestic product (GDP), which is a measure of the economic status of a country. GDP is a measure of the total annual output of goods and services. The concept, and methods for driving it, were developed in the 1930s, when policymakers in those economically depressed years realized they were blind about whether the economy was growing, declining, or standing still. The concept of GDP was invented to provide this information. It has been a hugely successful index and has made it possible to fashion increasingly successful macroeconomic policies with which to manage the economy.

Over the years, GDP has come to be regarded as a measure of the overall material well-being of the people of a nation. In practice, however, it is only an approximation, because it omits activities that do not trade in markets at observed prices, such as "black market" goods and the home production of goods and services for the family.

GDP also omits services of the environment. The services of clean air or water are not directly included, nor are the costs of dirty air or water, except in so far as they might lead to the purchase of goods that protect against pollution, such as air or water filters. It also does not include the value of unique "services" of features of the natural world, such as the value of a preserved species, for example, bald eagles, or of a collection of species, as in biological diversity preservation.

GDP becomes Net Domestic Product when it is adjusted for the value of capital assets that are used up in production. But no adjustment is made for the using up of natural assets. When an oil pump is depreciated, its value is deducted from GDP; however, when the oil itself is pumped out and used (thereby reducing the deposit of a natural resources), no adjustment is made. As a result, measured GDP may substantially misrepresent fundamental shifts in human welfare.

The concept of **Green GDP** is based on the idea of making reasonable comprehensive adjustments to standard GDP measures to adjust for changes in the value of the natural resources and services produced from them. Exhibit 6.2 discusses a report recommending this idea. The difficulties of developing valuation estimates of resource and environmental assets should not be underestimated. In the next chapter, we will discuss some of the ways this might be done.

Benefit–Cost Analysis

Benefit–cost analysis is for the public sector what a profit-and-loss analysis is for a business firm or a budget is for a household. If an automobile company was contemplating introducing a new car, it would want to get some idea of how its profitability would be affected. On the one hand, it would estimate costs of production and distribution: labor, raw materials, energy, emission-control equipment, transportation, and so forth.[3] On the other hand, it would estimate revenues through market analysis. Then it would compare expected revenues with anticipated costs. Benefit–cost analysis is an analogous exercise for programs in the public sector. This means there are two critical differences between benefit–cost analysis and the car example: It is a tool for helping to make **public decisions**, done from the standpoint of society in general rather than from that of a single profit-making firm, and it usually is done for policies and programs that have **unmarketed types of outputs**, such as improvements in environmental quality.

Benefit–cost analysis has led two intertwined lives. The first is among its practitioners: economists inside and outside public agencies who have developed the techniques, tried to produce better data, and extended the scope of the analysis. The second is among the politicians and administrators who have set the rules and procedures governing the use of benefit–cost analysis for public decision making. In the United States, benefit–cost analysis was first used in conjunction with the United States Flood Control Act of 1936. That act specified

---

[3] Of course, it probably would not factor in the costs of air-pollution damage inflicted on people breathing the emissions of the new cars; if everyone did this without being required to, we probably wouldn't be here studying this topic.

Green GDP

EXHIBIT 6.2

Over the last 80 years, our nation has moved from crude, limited measures of economic activity to an incredibly sophisticated system of national accounts. In the 1930s, if you wanted to know the state of the U.S. economy, you would have had to count boxcars traveling between New York City and Chicago or the number of unemployed you could see in the streets. All we had was impressions of the economy, not measures that allowed for diagnosis, prediction, and cure.

We are at a similar moment today with respect to our natural economy—the environmental goods and services we don't pay for but that make all other economic activity possible. We know the natural economy is under stress and clearly in decline in some areas.

GDP allows us to see the market economy it measures. Green accounts will do the same thing. Without it, we are doomed to surprises, an inability to experiment and learn, and poor public accountability. Accounting systems exist because of a simple human truth: complexity is overwhelming, whether you're a household, business, or nation. Accounting embraces that complexity but ultimately simplifies it into a clear message.

What we need is an environmental analog to GDP—a scientific, consistent, apolitical way to measure the health of our natural economy. Integrated accounts will allow us to pinpoint the most important adverse environmental trends and intervene accordingly.

An economic account requires two things. First, clear definitions are needed of the goods and services to be counted. In order to avoid double-counting, GDP counts only final goods and services, not all the other inputs used to create them (though indices for inputs are also part of our national accounts). An environmental index should have the same property: namely, we should count only *final* environmental goods and services.

Consider a salmon population that is commercially or recreationally harvested. The salmon population is a final good, but the food chain on which the salmon depends is not.

Other final environmental goods and services include commodities such as water supplies, timber, and open space. These commodities should be measured as place- and time-specific amounts, because their value depends on where and when they are available. Air, water, and soil quality are final environmental goods as well. We should also measure environmental services such as reduced flood, fire, and disease risks because these too are valuable.

Second, we need weights to attach to those final goods and services so that differences in the value of goods and services are reflected in the index. Because the goal of an environmental index is to evaluate the contributions of public goods, we must find a substitute for market prices.

Source: Excerpted from James Boyd, "A Plea for Environmental Accounts," in *Issues of the Day,* Ian W. H. Perry and Felicia Day, eds., Resources for the Future Press, Washington, D.C., 2010.

that federal participation in projects to control flooding on major rivers of the country would be justifiable *"if the benefits to whomever they accrue are in excess of the estimated costs."* In order to determine if this criterion was satisfied for any proposed flood-control dam or large levee project, procedures had to be developed to measure these benefits and costs.

These procedures have been altered from time to time as benefit–cost analysis has evolved and matured. The status and role of benefit–cost analysis in public natural resource and environmental decision making have been the subject of continuing discussions as well as political and administrative conflicts.

In 1981, President Reagan issued an executive order requiring that benefit–cost analysis be done for all major government regulations. In the early 1990s, President Clinton renewed this requirement, in slightly revised form. Congress has enacted several laws requiring benefit–cost analysis of federal programs: the Regulatory Right to Know Act, the Congressional Review Act, and the Unfunded Mandates Reform Act. Supporters of these laws argue that such legislation is a way to ensure that costs are given appropriate weight in public regulation. Opponents say that, because many benefits are hard to measure, such requirements will make it more difficult to pursue socially beneficial public regulation.[4]

The Basic Framework

As the name implies, a benefit–cost analysis involves measuring, adding up, and comparing all of the benefits and all of the costs of a particular public project or program. There are essentially four steps in a benefit–cost analysis:

1. Specify clearly the project or program.
2. Describe quantitatively the inputs and outputs of the program.
3. Estimate the social costs and benefits of these inputs and outputs.
4. Compare these benefits and costs.

Each of these steps incorporates a number of component steps. In doing a benefit–cost analysis, the very first step is to decide on the **perspective** from which the study is to be done. Benefit–cost analysis is a tool of public analysis, but there are actually many publics. If we were doing a benefit–cost study for a national agency, the public typically would be all the people living in the particular country. But if we were employed by a city or regional planning agency to do a benefit–cost analysis of a local environmental program, we would undoubtedly focus on benefits and costs accruing to people living in those areas. At the other extreme, the rise of global environmental issues has forced us to undertake some benefit–cost analyses from a worldwide perspective.

Step 1 also includes a **complete specification of the main elements of the project or program:** location, timing, groups involved, connections with other programs, and so on. There are two primary types of public environmental programs for which benefit–cost analyses are done:

1. *Physical projects* that involve direct public production: public waste treatment plants, beach restoration projects, hazardous-waste incinerators, habitat improvement projects, land purchase for preservation, and so on.

---

[4] For a discussion of these and other examples of the use of benefit–cost analysis in environmental policymaking, see Winston Harrington, Lisa Heinzerling and Richard D. Morgenstern, eds., *Reforming Regulatory Impact Analysis*, Resources for the Future Press, Washington, D.C., 2009.

2. *Regulatory programs* that are aimed at enforcing environmental laws and regulations, such as pollution-control standards, technological choices, waste-disposal practices, restrictions on land development, and so on.

After the basic project or program has been specified, the next step is to determine the full range of **consequences** that flow from it. For physical projects this amounts to specifying the inputs and outputs the project will entail. For some projects this is reasonably easy. In planning a wastewater treatment facility, the engineering staff will be able to provide a full physical specification of the plant, together with the inputs required to build it and keep it running. For an incinerator, one would need to estimate both the conventional costs of running the plant and any environmental costs stemming from whatever emissions the plant might produce.

For regulatory programs, estimating the full set of important consequences can be difficult. It involves predicting how members of the regulated community (power plants, oil refineries, car owners, building contractors, etc.) will respond to the new regulations in terms of altering both their behavior patterns and the technologies they might adopt for pollution-control purposes. Moreover, secondary impacts—that is, impacts in other sectors that have connections with the one being regulated—should also be considered. It is in this step that we first have to recognize the great importance of time. Environmentally related projects or programs do not usually last for a single year but are spread out over long periods of time. So the job of specifying consequences involves predictions of future events, often quite remote in time. This puts a premium on having a good understanding of issues such as future growth patterns, future rates of technological change, and possible changes in consumers' preferences.

The next step is to place values on the consequences—that is, to estimate benefits and costs in comparable terms. We could do this in any units we wish, but typically this implies measuring benefits and costs in monetary terms. This does not mean in market-value terms because in many cases we will be dealing with effects, especially on the benefit side, that are not directly registered on markets. Nor does it imply in some fundamental manner that only monetary values count. It means that we need a single metric into which to translate all of the impacts of a project or program in order to make them comparable among themselves as well as with other types of public activities. Ultimately, certain environmental impacts of a program may be irreducible to monetary terms because we cannot find a way of measuring how much people value these impacts. In this case, it is important to supplement the monetary results of the benefit–cost analysis with estimates of these intangible impacts.

Finally, we must **compare benefits and costs**. To understand what is involved in very general terms, consider the numbers in Exhibit 6.3. These show the primary benefits and costs of tighter standards applied to operations of coal-fired power plants for handling the huge generation of coal-combustion residues. For the most part, these have been handled by placing the material in large impoundments (ponds for storing sludge or residue), but the failure of

Benefits and Costs of New Regulations Requiring Coal-Fired Power Plants to Improve Their Handling of Coal Combustion Residues (CCR)

EXHIBIT 6.3

In response to a major industrial accident, the EPA has initiated steps to bring the control of coal combustion residues (CCR) under the regulatory structure of the Resource Conservation and Recovery Act of 1976. Its efforts included doing a series of benefit–cost studies of different technological requirements for handling this type of waste. One alternative was to require composite liners on CCR impoundments (ponds for storing sludge or residue) for all new impoundments and liners within five years for all existing impoundments. The estimated benefits and costs of this option were as follows:

	$ Millions, 2009 prices 7% discount rate, 50-year life	
Benefits:		
Value of human cancer risks avoided	37	
Groundwater remediation costs avoided	34	
Cleanup costs avoided	670	
Induced future CCR beneficial use*	6,122	
Total		6,863
Costs:		
Engineering controls	491	
Ancillary regulatory requirements	107	
Conversion to dry CCR disposal	876	
Total		1,474
Net Benefits		5,389

*The assumption is that by increasing the cost of handling CCR, firms would be more creative in finding markets for CCR for beneficial use by other industries.

Source: U.S. EPA, Office of Resource Conservation and Recovery, *Regulatory Impact Analysis for EPA's Proposal RCCA Regulation of* *Coal Combustion Residues (CCR) Generated by the Electric Utility Industry*, Washington, D.C., April 30, 2010.

one of these in 2008 led to efforts to bring them under stricter regulatory control. The results are shown in Exhibit 6.3.

Benefits and costs can be compared in several ways: **net benefits** are simply total benefits minus cost. In the example they are $6,863 million – $1,474 million = $5,389 million. Another criterion sometimes used is the **benefit–cost ratio**, which is simply the ratio of benefits to costs, or the amount of benefits produced per dollar of costs. In the example this ratio is $6,863 ÷ $1,474 = 4.66.

FIGURE 6.1 **Establishing the Size of a Public Program**

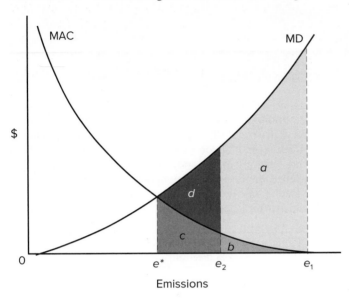

Scope of the Program

One important problem in benefit–cost analysis is deciding on the **scope** of the project or program. A benefit–cost analysis must be specified completely in terms of its size or scope. In reality, however, it is always possible to make a project or program larger or smaller by some amount. How can we be sure that the program we are evaluating is of the appropriate scope?

To explore this issue, consider Figure 6.1. It shows the standard emission-control model as developed in the last chapter, with marginal damage (MD) and marginal abatement cost (MAC) functions. Assume that the current level of emissions is e_1; that is, emissions are essentially uncontrolled. A control program is proposed that would lower emissions to e_2. For this program, total benefits (total damages reduced) are equal to $(a + b)$, whereas total abatement costs are equal to b. Net benefits are therefore equal to area a.

For an emission-reduction program to give maximum net benefits, however, it would have to reduce emissions to e^*, the level at which MD = MAC. Here, net benefits would equal $(d + a)$. The problem is that when we do a benefit–cost analysis of a specific proposal, how can we be sure that we are dealing with one such as e^* in the figure and not one such as e_2?

The general procedure here is to carry out **sensitivity analyses** on these results. This means recalculating benefits and costs for programs somewhat larger and somewhat smaller than the one shown in the example. We would analyze a program that has somewhat more restrictive emission reductions, with appropriate enforcement resources, and one that is somewhat less restrictive. If the chosen program is indeed appropriately scaled, each of the variations will produce lower net benefits.

The benefit–cost ratio is often used in public debates in describing environmental projects or programs, but the efficient program size is not the one that gives the maximum benefit–cost ratio. At emission level e^*, the benefit–cost ratio is equal to $(a + b + c + d) + (b + c)$. At emission level e_2, the benefit–cost ratio is $(a + b) + b$, which is higher than that at e^*. The benefit–cost ratio may be used to make sure that, at the very least, benefits exceed cost, but beyond this it is a misleading indicator in planning the appropriate scope of public programs.

Under some circumstances, there may be grounds for sizing programs at less than that which maximizes net benefits. Suppose there is a regional public agency in charge of enforcing air-pollution laws in two medium-sized urban areas. Suppose further that it has a fixed and predetermined budget of $1 million to spend. There are two possibilities: (1) Put it all in one enforcement program in one of the cities or (2) divide it between two programs, one in each city. Suppose the numbers are as follows:

	Costs	Benefits	Net Benefits	Benefit–Cost Ratio
One-city program	$1,000,000	$2,000,000	$1,000,000	2.0
Two-city program				
City A	500,000	1,200,000	700,000	2.4
City B	500,000	1,200,000	700,000	2.4

In this case, the agency can do better with its fixed budget by putting it into two half-sized programs rather than just one. In this case, the correct approach is to allocate resources so that the net benefits produced by the total budget are maximized.

Discounting

We turn now to the important problem of how to compare costs and benefits that occur at very different points in time. In a pollution-control program, for example, how do we compare the high initial-year capital costs of abatement equipment with the long-run costs of maintaining it? In the global warming problem, how do we compare the very high costs today of controlling CO_2 emissions with the benefits that won't really start accruing for several decades? Suppose there are two programs, one with relatively high net benefits that materialize well into the future and another with smaller net benefits that occur in the near future. How do we compare these two options? The standard way to address problems such as these is through **discounting**, a technique employed to add and compare costs and benefits that occur at different points in time. Discounting has two facets: first, the mechanics of doing it; then, the reasoning behind the choice of discount rates to be used in specific cases. We take these up in turn.

A cost that will occur 10 years from now does not have the same significance as a cost that occurs today. Suppose, for example, that I have incurred a bill of $1,000 that I must pay today. To do that I must have $1,000 in the bank, or my pocket, with which to pay the obligation. Suppose, however, that I have a $1,000 bill to pay, not today, but 10 years from now. If the rate of interest I can get in a bank is 5 percent, and I expect it to stay at that level, I can deposit $613.90 in the bank today and it will compound up to $1,000 in 10 years, exactly when I need it. The formula for compounding this sum is

$$\$613.90 \ (1 + .05)^{10} = \$1,000$$

Now turn this around and ask: What is the **present value** to me of this $1,000 obligation 10 years from now? Its present value is what I would have to put in the bank today to have exactly what I need in 10 years, and we get this by rearranging the above expression:

$$\text{Present value} = \frac{\$1,000}{(1 + .05)^{10}} = \$613.90$$

The present value is found by discounting the future cost back over the 10-year period at the interest rate, now called the discount rate, of 5 percent.[5] If it were higher—say, 8 percent—the present value would be lower—$463.20. The higher the discount rate, the lower the present value of any future dollar amount.

The same goes for a benefit. Suppose you expect someone to give you a gift of $100, but only at the end of six years. This would not have the same value to you today (i.e., the same present value) as $100 given to you today. If the applicable discount rate is 4 percent, the present value of that future gift would be

$$\frac{\$100}{(1 + .04)^6} = \$79.03$$

Discounting is used extensively in benefit–cost analyses. Its main role is to help in aggregating a series of costs or benefits that are strung out over the life of a project or program. Consider the following illustrative numbers, showing benefits for two different programs over their short lives:

	Benefits ($) in Year:				
	1	2	3	4	Total net benefits
Project A	20	20	20	20	80
Project B	50	10	10	10	80

If we simply add these benefits across the four years for each project, they have the same total: $80. But Project A has a series of equal annual benefits, whereas

---

[5] In general, the discount formula is PV = $m/(1 + r)^t$, where m is the future value, r is the discount rate, and t is the number of years involved.

B has substantial benefits in the first period and lower annual benefits thereafter. To compare the total benefits of the two projects, we must calculate the **present value** of total benefits for each program. For illustrative purposes we use a discount rate of 6 percent.

$$PV_A = \$20 + \frac{\$20}{1 + .06} + \frac{\$20}{(1 + .06)^2} + \frac{\$20}{(1 + .06)^3} = \$73.45$$

$$PV_B = \$50 + \frac{\$10}{1 + .06} + \frac{\$10}{(1 + .06)^2} + \frac{\$10}{(1 + .06)^3} = \$76.73$$

Note first that both present values are less than the undiscounted sums of benefits. This will always be true when a portion of a program's benefits accrues in future years. Note also that the present value of benefits for B exceeds that of A, because more of B's benefits are concentrated early in the life of the program. That is to say, the time profile of B's benefits is more heavily concentrated in earlier years than the time profile of A's benefits.

Similar calculations are made for costs in order to find the present value of the stream of annual costs of a program. And the same reasoning applies: discounting reduces the present value of a dollar of cost more the farther in the future that cost will be incurred. The present value of the stream of benefits minus the present value of costs gives the present value of net benefits. Alternatively, we could calculate for each year in the life of a project its *net benefits*, then calculate the present value of this stream of net benefits in the same way, by summing their discounted values.

Choice of Discount Rate

Because discounting is a way of aggregating a series of future net benefits into an estimate of present value, the outcome depends importantly on which particular discount rate is used. A low rate implies that a dollar in one year is very similar in value to a dollar in any other year. A high rate implies that a dollar in the near term is much more valuable than one later on. Thus, the higher the discount rate, the more we would be encouraged to put our resources into programs that have relatively high payoffs (i.e., high benefits and/or low costs) in the short run. The lower the discount rate, on the contrary, the more we would be led to select programs that have high net benefits in the more distant future.

The choice of a discount rate has been a controversial topic through the years, and we can only summarize some of the arguments here. First, it is important to keep in mind the difference between **real** and **nominal** interest rates. Nominal rates are the rates one actually sees on the market. If you take a nominal rate and adjust it for inflation, you get a real interest rate. Suppose you deposit $100 in a bank at an interest rate of 8 percent. In 10 years your deposit would have grown to $216, but this is in monetary terms. Suppose over that 10-year period prices increase 3 percent per year on average. Then the real value of your accumulated deposit would be less; in fact, the real interest rate at which your deposit would accumulate would only be 5 percent (8 percent minus 3 percent), so in real terms your deposit would be worth only $161 after the 10 years.[6] So we have to be careful about the interest rate we use for discounting. If the cost estimates are expected real costs, that is, adjusted for expected inflation, we want to use a real interest rate for discounting purposes. If our cost estimates are nominal figures, then we use a nominal interest rate in the discounting analysis.

The discount rate reflects the current generation's views about the relative weight to be given to benefits and costs occurring in different years. One way of thinking about this is to say that the discount rate should reflect the way people themselves think about time. Any person normally will prefer a dollar today to a dollar in 10 years; in the language of economics, they have a positive rate of **time preference.** We see people making savings decisions by putting money in bank accounts that pay certain rates of interest. These savings account rates show what interest the banks have to offer in order to get people to forgo current consumption. We might therefore take the average bank savings account rate as reflecting the average person's rate of time preference.

The problem with this is that there are other ways of determining people's rates of time preference, and they don't necessarily give the same answer. Economists at Resources for the Future[7] completed a large survey in which they asked individuals to choose between receiving $10,000 today and larger amounts in five or ten years. The responses yielded implied rates of discount of 20 percent for a five-year time horizon and 10 percent for a 10-year horizon. These were substantially higher than bank savings rates at the time of the survey.

Another approach in thinking about the discount rate is based on the notion of the marginal productivity of investment. When investments are made in productive enterprises, people anticipate that the value of future returns will offset today's investment costs; otherwise, these investments would not be made. The thinking here is that when resources are used in the public sector for natural resource and environmental programs, they ought to yield, on average, rates of return to society equivalent to what they could have earned in the private sector. Private-sector productivity is reflected in the rates of interest banks charge their business borrowers. Thus, by this reasoning, we should use as our discount rate a rate reflecting the interest rates that private firms pay when they borrow money for investment purposes. These are typically higher than savings account interest rates.

Discounting and Future Generations

The logic of a discount rate, even a very small one, is inexorable (see the numbers in Exhibit 6.4). A thousand dollars, discounted back over a century at 5 percent, has a present value of only slightly over $7.60. The present generation,

---

[6] These are slight approximations. The deposit would actually be worth $160.64, and the real rate of accumulation would be 4.89 percent.

[7] Resources for the Future (RFF) is a well-known Washington organization that specializes in natural resource and environmental economics research. It publishes a quarterly newsletter discussing its work. This information comes from RFF, *Resources*, 108, Summer 1992, p. 3.

The Effects of Discounting   EXHIBIT 6.4

Discounting is a process that expresses the value to people today of benefits and costs that will materialize at some future time. As the time increases between today and the point where these benefits or costs actually occur, their present value diminishes. The following figure shows how much the present value of $100 of benefits, discounted at 3 percent, diminishes as the time when it will be received recedes into the future.

Similarly, for a given time period, the present value will diminish as the discount rate increases. The following figure shows how the present value of a $100 benefit, to be received 100 years from now, diminishes as the discount rate increases.

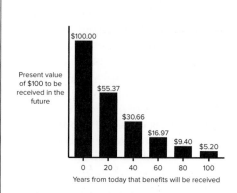

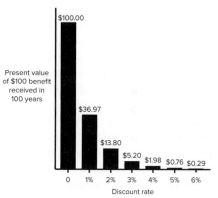

considering the length of its own expected life, may not be interested in programs having very high but long-run payoffs such as this.

The logic is even more compelling if we consider a future cost. One of the reasons that environmentalists have looked askance at discounting is that it can have the effect of downgrading future damages that result from today's economic activity. Suppose today's generation is considering a course of action that has certain short-run benefits of $10,000 per year for 50 years, but that, starting 50 years from now, will cost $1 million a year *forever*. This may not be too unlike the choice faced by current generations on nuclear power or on global warming. To people alive today, the present value of that perpetual stream of future cost discounted at 10 percent is only $85,000. These costs may not weigh particularly heavily on decisions made by the current generation. The present value of the benefits ($10,000 a year for 50 years at 10 percent, or $99,148) exceeds the present value of the future costs. From the standpoint of today, therefore, this might look like a good choice, despite the perpetual cost burden placed on all future generations.

But when future generations are involved, the question of what discount to use is more controversial. Most, but not all, economists and policymakers probably would agree that some positive rate of discount is appropriate. Probably most also agree that it ought to be fairly low (1 percent, 2 percent?), but beyond that there is no alternative that is widely agreed upon. We will have more to say about this in later chapters, especially in connection with the long-run impacts of global warming.

Distributional Issues

The relation of total benefits and total costs is a question of economic efficiency. Distribution is a matter of who gets the benefits and who pays the costs. In public-sector programs, distributional matters must be considered along with efficiency issues, which implies that benefit–cost analyses must incorporate studies of how net benefits are distributed among different groups in society.

The distribution of benefits and costs is primarily a matter of equity, or fairness. There are two main types of equity: horizontal and vertical. **Horizontal equity** is a case of treating similarly situated people the same way. An environmental program that has the same impact on an urban dweller with $20,000 of income as on a rural dweller with the same income is horizontally equitable. Consider the following numbers, which illustrate in a simple way the annual values of a particular program accruing to three different individuals who, we assume, all have the same income. Abatement costs show the costs of the program to each individual; these may be higher prices on some products, more time spent on recycling matters, higher taxes, or other factors. The reduced damages are measures of the value of the improvements in environmental quality accruing to each person.

	Person A	Person B	Person C
Reduced environmental damages ($/year)	60	80	120
Abatement costs ($/year)	40	60	80
Difference	20	20	40

Costs and reduced damages are different for individuals A and B, but the difference between them ($20/year) is the same; hence, the difference as a proportion of their income is the same. With respect to these two people, therefore, the program is horizontally equitable. It is not, however, for individual C, because this person experiences a net difference of $40/year. Because Person C is assumed to have the same income as the other two people, they are clearly better off as a result of this program; horizontal equity in this case has not been achieved.

Vertical equity refers to how a policy impinges on people who are in different circumstances, in particular on people who have different income levels. Consider the numbers in Table 6.2. These show the impacts, expressed in monetary values, of three different environmental quality programs on three people with, respectively, a low income, a medium income, and a high income.

TABLE 6.2   Vertical Equity*

	Person A		Person B		Person C	
Income	5,000		20,000		50,000	
Program 1						
Reduced damages	150	(3.0)	300	(1.5)	600	(1.2)
Abatement costs	100	(2.0)	100	(0.5)	100	(0.2)
Difference	50	(1.0)	200	(1.0)	500	(1.0)
Program 2						
Reduced damages	150	(3.0)	1,400	(7.0)	5,500	(11.0)
Abatement costs	100	(2.0)	800	(4.0)	3,000	(6.0)
Difference	50	(1.0)	600	(3.0)	2,500	(5.0)
Program 3						
Reduced damages	700	(14.0)	2,200	(11.0)	3,000	(6.0)
Abatement costs	200	(4.0)	1,000	(5.0)	1,500	(3.0)
Difference	500	(10.0)	1,200	(6.0)	1,500	(3.0)

*Figures in this table show annual monetary values. Numbers in parentheses show the percentage of income these numbers represent.

In parentheses next to each number is shown the percentage that number is of the person's income level. Note, for example, the "difference" row of Program 1; it shows the difference between how much the person benefits from the program (in terms of reduced environmental damages impinging on him) and how much it will cost him (in terms of the extent to which he will bear a part of the abatement costs of the program). Note that this net difference represents 1 percent of the income of each person. This is a *proportional impact*; that is, it affects the people of each income level in the same proportion.

Program 2, on the other hand, is *regressive*; it provides higher proportional net benefits to high-income people than to low-income people. Program 3 has a *progressive* impact because net benefits represent a higher proportion of the low-income person's income than they do of the wealthy person's income. Thus, an environmental program (or any program for that matter) is proportional, progressive, or regressive, according to whether the net effect of that policy has proportionally the same, greater, or less effect on low-income people as on high-income people.

It is to be noted that although the net effects of a program may be distributed in one way, the individual components need not be distributed in the same way. For example, although the overall effects of Program 2 are regressive, the abatement costs of that program are in fact distributed progressively (i.e., the cost burden is proportionately greater for high-income people). In this case damage reduction is distributed so regressively that the overall program is regressive. This is the same in Program 3; although the overall program is progressive, abatement costs are distributed regressively.

These definitions of distributional impacts can be misleading. A program that is technically regressive could actually distribute the bulk of its net benefits to low-income people. Suppose a policy raised the net income of one rich person by 10 percent, but raised each of the net incomes of 1,000 low-income people by 5 percent. This policy is technically regressive, although more than likely the majority of its aggregate net benefits go to low-income people.

It is usually hard to estimate the distributional impacts of environmental programs, individually or in total. To do so requires very specific data showing impacts by income groups, race/ethnicity, or other factors. In recent years, epidemiologists have collected much better environmental and health data broken down by income, race, and other socioeconomic variables. We still lack good estimates of how program costs are distributed among these groups because these depend on complex factors related to tax collections, consumption patterns, the availability of alternatives, and so on. Despite the difficulties, however, benefit–cost analyses should try to look as closely as possible at the way in which the aggregates are distributed through the population.

Although distributional aspects of local pollution-control programs are important to understand, issues of global equity are critical in considering such problems as global warming, and the steps that might be undertaken to combat it. Global warming will affect countries in different ways. Most of the developed countries have economies that are heavily dependent on manufacturing and services, and these are not closely related to weather and climate. Things like insurance, health care, banking, and entertainment can be done most anywhere, and they can move around fairly easily. Likewise, most manufacturing is not weather dependent, although of course it is subject to short-run disruptions if it is forced to relocate. On the other hand, economies that are heavily dependent on agriculture, forestry, and fisheries are likely to be much more heavily impacted, because these activities are weather dependent. But these are the sectors that are so important in many less developed countries, which are also the countries having relatively higher numbers of people at lower levels of income and wealth. All of this means that global warming is likely to have a strongly regressive impact in the world, hurting poorer people much greater than it does richer ones.

Risk Analysis

The future can never be known with certainty. Uncertainty about future benefits and costs can arise from many sources. It is difficult to predict exactly the preferences of future generations, who may feel differently than we do about matters of environmental quality. The complexities of world meteorological systems make predicting future global environmental factors very uncertain. Uncertain advancements in pollution-control technologies could markedly shift future abatement costs. New chemicals, and even many that have been around for years, can have damage effects that are very uncertain.

Because of the high levels of uncertainty in environmental factors, policy analysts have sought to develop modes of analysis specifically directed at the risk factor in environmental decisions. **Risk analysis** involves essentially three actions:

- **Risk assessment:** The study of where risk comes from and how people normally respond to it.
- **Risk valuation:** The study of what values, in terms of concepts such as willingness to pay, people place on risk reduction.
- **Risk management:** The study of how different policies affect levels of environmental risk to which people are exposed.

Risk Assessment

Suppose there is a landfill into which a hazardous chemical has been dumped for a number of years. Suppose also that the residents of a nearby community rely on a local groundwater aquifer for their water supply. Risk assessment in this case means estimating the extent of the risk that the dump site poses for the community. It consists of several steps:

1. **Exposure analysis:** Engineers, hydrologists, and others must determine the likelihood that the chemical will migrate to the aquifer, and how much the citizens of the community will be exposed to it if it does. It could be that other pathways of exposure also might have to be considered.
2. **Dose–response analysis:** Scientists must determine the relationship between exposure levels to the chemical and impacts such as incidences of cancer. Relationships like this are sought by laboratory scientists and by epidemiologists.
3. **Risk characterization:** Combining steps (1) and (2) makes it possible to estimate the specific risks faced by members of the community in terms of, for example, the number of premature deaths they could expect.

Risk Valuation

Although the work of risk assessment is the province of physical and health scientists, risk valuation falls primarily to economists. If the dump site is cleaned up, thereby leading to a reduced level of health risk to the nearby people, how much is this actually worth to them?

In order to answer questions like this, special concepts are needed with which they may be described. One of these is **expected value**. When future events are probabilistic, we may be able to estimate the most likely or expected values of their occurrence. Consider the problem of predicting the number of excess cancer deaths caused by the hazardous waste dump site. Suppose we are told by scientists that the probabilities in any year of getting cancer deaths from this source are as shown in Table 6.3. These show a **probability distribution** of excess cancer deaths. For example, the probability of having no deaths is 0.80, of one death is 0.14, of two deaths is 0.05, and so on.[8] The

---

[8] These are illustrative numbers only.

TABLE 6.3 Calculating the Annual Expected Value of Cancer Deaths from Hazardous Chemicals at Landfill

Number of Deaths	Probability	Expected Value of Deaths
0	0.80	$0 \times 0.80 = 0.00$
1	0.14	$1 \times 0.14 = 0.14$
2	0.05	$2 \times 0.05 = 0.10$
3	0.01	$3 \times 0.01 = 0.03$
4	0.00	$4 \times 0.00 = 0.00$
		Expected value: 0.27

probability of getting four or more deaths is so low that we can treat it as zero. The expected value of cancer deaths is found by essentially taking a weighted average, where each number of deaths in the distribution is weighted by its probability of occurrence. According to this calculation, the expected number of deaths per year is 0.27.

We now can deal with the **valuation** question. Suppose it's estimated that cleaning up the hazardous waste site will lower the expected number of premature deaths from 0.27 to 0.04. How much is this worth to the people of the community? Experience has shown that the scientific results of relative risks stemming from different sources may not agree very well with how people actually feel about different types of risk. For example, people may be willing to pay substantial sums to have a chemical taken out of their water supply even though the health risk is relatively low, whereas they may not be willing to pay much for improved seat belts, which would reduce their overall risk by a great deal.

One way of looking at how people value risky situations is to look at how they react to cases that have similar expected values but quite different profiles of risk.

Consider the following numbers:

Program A		Program B	
Net Benefits	**Probability**	**Net Benefits**	**Probability**
$500,000	0.475	$500,000	0.99
$300,000	0.525	−$10,000,000	0.01
Expected value:	$395,000	Expected value:	$395,000

These two programs have exactly the same expected value. Suppose we have only a one-time choice between the two, which perhaps relates to the choice of a nuclear versus a conventional power plant to generate electricity. With Program A the net benefits are uncertain, but the outcomes are not extremely different and the probabilities are similar—it is very nearly a 50–50 proposition. Program B, however, has a very different profile. The probability is very high that the net benefits will be $500,000, but there is a small probability of a disaster in which there would be large negative net benefits. If we were making decisions strictly on the basis of expected values, we would treat these projects as the same; we could flip a coin to decide which one to choose. If we did this, we would be displaying **risk-neutral** behavior—making decisions strictly on the basis of expected values. But if this is a one-shot decision, we might decide that the low probability of a large loss in the case of Program B represents a risk to which we do not wish to expose ourselves. In this case, we might be **risk averse**, preferring Program A over B.

There are many cases in environmental pollution control where risk aversion is undoubtedly the best policy. The rise of planetary-scale atmospheric change opens up the possibility of catastrophic human dislocations in the future. The potential scale of these impacts argues for a conservative, risk-averse approach to current decisions. Risk-averse decisions also are called for in the case of species extinction; a series of incremental and seemingly small decisions today may bring about a catastrophic decline in genetic resources in the future, with potentially drastic impacts on human welfare. Global issues are not the only ones for which it may be prudent to avoid low risks of outcomes that would have large negative net benefits. The contamination of an important groundwater aquifer is a possibility faced by many local communities. In addition, in any activity in which risk to human life is involved, the average person is likely to be risk averse.

Risk Management

Once policymakers know how people value risk and the degree of risk inherent in situations of environmental damages, they are in the position to consider policies and regulations designed to manage those risks. This may incorporate **risk–benefit analysis**.

Suppose an administrative agency, such as the Environmental Protection Agency (EPA), is considering whether a particular pesticide should be allowed on the market. It might do a study comparing the benefits farmers and consumers would gain, in the form of production cost savings, when the pesticide is used, as well as of the increased health risks to farm workers, who must handle it, and possibly to consumers if there are pesticide residues on the market crop. In essence, this is a benefit–cost analysis in which the cost side is treated more explicitly in terms of risk.

Another type of analysis is **comparative-risk analysis**, which focuses on looking at different policy options and the levels of risk they entail. For example, in the landfill example the authorities may look at the different ways of managing the landfill and water-supply system (capping the landfills, looking for an alternative water supply) in terms of the levels of risk to which each alternative exposes people in the affected communities.

Summary

In previous chapters we put the issue of environmental improvement in a trade-off type of format with willingness to pay (benefits) on one side and abatement costs on the other. In this chapter we started to focus on the problem of measuring these benefits and costs. To do this measurement, researchers have to use some underlying analytical framework to account for these benefits and costs. We considered several types of frameworks (impact analysis and cost-effectiveness analysis), then settled on the primary approach used in resource and environmental economics: benefit–cost analysis. The rest of the chapter was devoted to a discussion of the main conceptual issues involved in benefit–cost analysis. These are

- The basic analytical steps involved.
- Determining the appropriate size of a project or program.
- The difference between net benefits and the benefit–cost ratio as a decision criterion.
- Discounting.
- Distributional issues.
- Risk analysis.

Having discussed the basic structure of benefit–cost analysis, we turn in the next two chapters to a discussion of the problems of actually measuring the benefits and costs of specific environmental programs.

Questions for Further Discussion

1. Air-pollution-control authorities in southern California propose to control mobile-source emissions by requiring that a certain percentage of all new cars sold in the region be electric. Contrast the different perspectives that would be involved in analyzing this proposal with (*a*) economic impact analysis, (*b*) cost-effectiveness analysis, and (*c*) benefit–cost analysis.

2. Suppose we are comparing two ways of protecting ourselves against mobile-source air pollution: putting additional controls on the internal combustion engine or developing an entirely different type of engine that is cleaner. How would changes in the discount rate be likely to affect the comparison among these two options?

3. Following are some illustrative numbers for benefits and costs arising from a program to restrict emissions of a pollutant. Current emissions are 10 tons per month. Identify the emission level at which net benefits would be maximized. Show that this is not the same as the emission level that gives the highest benefit–cost ratio. Explain the discrepancy.

Emissions (tons/month)	10	9	8	7	6	5	4	3	2	1	0
Benefits ($ mil)	0	4	8	18	32	44	54	62	68	72	74
Costs ($ mil)	0	2	4	6	9	14	21	36	48	64	86

4. Suppose the costs of an environmental pollution-control program are expected to be equal to $80 per year, and that benefits will be $50 per year for 50 years, then $150 per year thereafter. At a discount rate of 4 percent, what are the net benefits of this program? What would the net benefits be at a discount rate of 2 percent? Comment on the difference.

5. When setting public policy on environmental risks, should we base it on the levels of risk to which people think they are exposed or on the risk levels as scientists have determined them to be in fact?

For additional readings and Web sites pertaining to the material in this chapter, see **www.mhhe.com/field7e.**

Chapter 7

Benefit–Cost Analysis: Benefits

Remembering the provisos about the distribution of income and the availability of information, we already have made the connection between benefits and willingness to pay. We see that the benefits of something are equal to what people are willing to pay for it. The question is: how is willingness to pay to be estimated in specific cases? For goods and services sold on markets it may be relatively easy to estimate willingness to pay. To estimate people's willingness to pay for potatoes, for example, we can observe them buying potatoes—so many potatoes at certain prices—and develop a good idea of the value people place on this item. This will not work, however, when valuing changes in environmental quality. There are no markets where people buy and sell units of environmental quality. Instead, we have to fall back on indirect means. As one environmental economist put it: "Benefit estimation often involves a kind of detective work for piecing together the clues about the values individuals place on [environmental services] as they respond to other economic signals."[1]

The measurement of benefits is an activity pursued on many levels. For an analyst working in an environmental agency, it can turn into a plug-in-the-numbers exercise. So many acres of clam bed destroyed (information provided by a marine biologist) times the going price of clams (provided by a quick trip to the local fish market) equals damages of water pollution in the "X" estuary. At the other extreme, for an environmental economist whose interest is in extending the technique, it can be an excursion into sophisticated means of squeezing subtle information from new sets of data. Our path in this chapter lies between these extremes. We review the main techniques environmental economists have developed to measure the benefits of improvements in environmental quality. The objective is to understand the economic logic behind these techniques, without getting bogged down in the theoretical and statistical details.

---

[1] A. Myrick Freeman III, "Benefits of Pollution Control," in U.S. Environmental Protection Agency, *Critical Review of Estimating Benefits of Air and Water Pollution Control*, Washington, D.C., EPA 600/5-78-014, 1978, pp. 11–16.

The Damage Function: Physical Aspects

When environmental degradation occurs, it produces damages; the emissions control model of Chapter 5 is based in part on the relationship between emissions and marginal damages. Thus, the **benefits** of environmental quality improvements stem from the reduced damages this would produce. To measure an emissions damage function, it's necessary to go through the following steps:

1. Measure **emissions.**
2. Determine the resulting levels of ambient quality through the use of **diffusion models.**
3. Estimate the resulting **human exposure** that these ambient levels would produce.
4. Estimate the **physical impacts** of these exposure levels.
5. Determine the **values** associated with these physical impacts.

The primary work of environmental economists is in step 5, and we will devote most of the chapter to this activity. Let us begin, however, with some brief comments on the first four steps.

Some of the most important damages caused by environmental pollution are those related to human health. Air pollution, especially, has long been thought to increase mortality and morbidity[2] among people exposed to it, certainly in the episodic releases of toxic pollutants, but also from long-run exposure to such pollutants as sulfur dioxide (SO_2) and particulate matter. Diseases such as bronchitis, emphysema, lung cancer, and asthma are thought to be traceable in part to polluted air. Water pollution also produces health damages, primarily through contaminated drinking water supplies. So the measurement of the human health damages of environmental pollution is a critical task for environmental economists.

Many factors affect human health—lifestyles, diet, genetic factors, age, and so on—besides ambient pollution levels. To separate the effects of pollution, one has to account for all the other factors or else run the risk of attributing effects to pollution that are actually caused by something else (e.g., smoking). This calls for large amounts of accurate data on health factors, as well as the numerous suspected causal factors. The major work here is that of **epidemiologists,** who derive statistical results from large data sets to derive relationships between ambient pollution exposure and adverse health effects. One of the first such studies of air pollution and human health in the United States was done by Lave and Seskin in the 1970s.[3] The data were for 1969 and refer to published information on standard metropolitan statistical areas (SMSAs). They concluded that, in general, a 1 percent reduction in air pollution produces a

---

[2] Morbidity refers to the incidence of ill health and can be expressed in many ways: for example, days missed from work, days spent in the hospital, and the duration of particular symptoms.

[3] Lester B. Lave and Eugene P. Seskin, *Air Pollution and Human Health,* Johns Hopkins Press, Baltimore, MD, 1977.

0.12 percent reduction in death rates. In the last few decades, literally thousands of additional studies have been done to investigate the linkage between pollution and human health, in terms of both premature mortality and morbidity. A study sponsored by the California Air Resources Board (CARB) showed clear relationships in children between exposure to air pollutants and reduced lung function.[4] A study by Ritz and colleagues showed a relationship between birth defects and the exposure of pregnant women to air pollutants.[5] Bell and colleagues studied national data and showed a pronounced relationship between ozone levels and increased risk of death.[6] Many summary and review papers are available.[7] The next step, where environmental economics comes into play in a major way, is to value these outcomes so that the information can be used in classic benefit–cost type studies.

Measuring Damage Costs Directly

There are a number of situations where it would appear possible to measure directly the monetary costs of health and other types of outcomes.

Health Costs

The greatest concern about diminished air and water quality is the impacts these have on human health. One approach to assessing damages in this case is to estimate the increased medical and other costs associated with particular pollution-related illnesses. This is called the **cost of illness** (COI) approach. For example, Table 7.1 shows data from a recent study of this type on asthma, a disease that has increased rapidly in recent years and that researchers believe may be related to air pollution. The estimates are divided into direct and indirect costs. Direct costs are the costs of medical visits to hospitals or doctors' offices, together with the costs of medications used to fight asthma. Indirect costs are related to the opportunity costs of lost work time for people who become ill, lost school days, and lost economic productivity of people who die prematurely from asthma.

With the COI perspective, the benefits of pollution control are the reduced health-related costs they produce. This could be regarded as a minimum, or lower-bound, assessment of these benefits, because the improved health also produces a better quality of life for those who are impacted. Many researchers in the health area have sought to create health indices that capture the

[4] California Air Resources Board, *The Children's Health Study*, CARB, Sacramento, 2002.

[5] Beate Ritz et al., "Ambient Air Pollution and Risk of Birth Defects in Southern California," *American Journal of Epidemiology*, 155(1), January 2002, pp. 17–25.

[6] Michelle L. Bell et al., "Ozone and Short-Term Mortality in 95 U.S. Urban Communities, 1987–2000," *Journal of the American Medical Association*, 292(19), November 2004, pp. 2372–2378.

[7] H. Chen, M.S. Goldberg, and P.J. Villeneuve, "A Systematic Review of the Relation between Long-Term Exposure to Ambient Pollution and Chronic Diseases," *Review of Environmental Health*, 23, 2008, pp. 243–296; World Health Organization, *Ambient and Household Air Pollution and Health*, 2014; OECD, *The Cost of Air Pollution: Health Impacts of Road Transport*, May 2014.

TABLE 7.1 Estimated Cost of Asthma in the United States

	Billion $
Direct Costs	
Prescriptions	13.62
Inpatient care	15.33
Outpatient care	1.34
Office visits	7.32
Home health	4.54
Emergency room	1.14
Other	0.29
Indirect Costs	
Work related	13.70
Total	57.28

Source: Harvey Rappaport and Vijayveer Bonthapally, "The Direct Expenditures and Indirect Costs of Treating Asthma in the United States," *Journal of Allergy and Therapy*, 3(118), 2012.

improvements in physical health parameters that less environmental pollution would produce. This involves assigning numeric values to various health states, both mortality and morbidity, to develop aggregate measures of health outcomes. These indices are sometimes "monetized" to develop estimates of values of health outcomes that can be compared with the monetary costs of pollution control. They do not rely, however, on the basic concept of willingness to sacrifice as a measure of value. We will take this up later in this chapter.

The Effects of Pollution on Production Costs

Air pollution can reduce yields of exposed crops; it also can reduce the growth rates of commercially valuable timber. Water pollution can adversely affect firms and municipalities that use the water for production purposes or for domestic use. Diminished water quality also can have a negative impact on commercial fishing industries. Soil contamination can have serious impacts on agricultural production. Pollution in the workplace can reduce the effectiveness of workers and often can increase the rate at which machinery and buildings deteriorate. In these cases, the effects of pollution are felt on the production of goods and services. The damage caused by the pollution comes about because it interferes in some way with these production processes, in effect making it more costly to produce these outputs than it would be in a less polluted world.

How we actually measure production-related benefits of reducing pollution depends on circumstances. Suppose we are looking at a small group of agricultural producers living in a certain region who will be affected by reduced airborne emissions coming from an upwind factory. Pollutants from the factory have depressed yields, so reducing emissions will cause yields to increase. The crop being produced is sold in a national market, and its price will be unaffected by the output changes in this one region. This situation is depicted in

FIGURE 7.1 **Benefits from Reduced Production Costs**

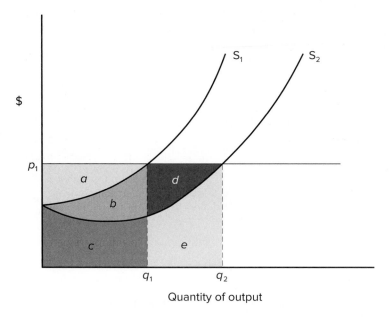

Quantity of output

Figure 7.1. In this diagram, S_1 is the supply curve for this group of farms before the improved air quality; S_2 is the supply curve after the improvement. The price of the output is p_1. Before the change, these farmers produce at an output level of q_1, whereas after the improvement their output increases to q_2.

One way of approximating the benefits of this environmental improvement is to measure the value of increased output produced by this group of farms. This is the increased output, $q_2 - q_1$, multiplied by the price of the crop. This gives an estimate corresponding to the area $(d + e)$ in Figure 7.1.

Numerous studies have been done along these lines.[8] Murphy et al.[9] studied the effects on agriculture of eliminating ozone precursor emissions from motor vehicles in the United States. They estimated that the benefits to the agricultural sector of this change would amount to between $3.5 and $6.1 billion annually. Another study was done by Page et al.[10] to measure crop-related air pollution losses in a six-state area. They estimated annual losses in

---

[8] These are reviewed in Gardner M. Brown Jr. and Mark L. Plummer, "Market Measures of User Benefits," in *Acid Deposition: State of Science and Technology*, Report 27, Methods for Valuing Acidic Deposition and Air Pollution Effects, National Acid Precipitation Assessment Program, Washington, D.C., U.S. Superintendent of Documents, 1990, pp. 27–73.

[9] James Murphy, Mark Delucchi, Donald McCubbin, and H. J. Kim, *The Cost of Crop Damage Caused by Ozone Air Pollution from Motor Vehicles*. Institute of Transportation Studies. Paper UCD-ITS-REP-99-03, April 1, 1999, **http://repositories.cdlib.org/itsdavis/UCD-ITS-REP-99-03**.

[10] W.P. Page, G. Abogast, R. Fabian, and J. Ciecka, "Estimation of Economic Losses to the Agricultural Sector from Airborne Residuals in the Ohio River Basin," *Journal of Air Pollution Control Association*, 32(2), February 1982, pp. 151–154.

the production of soybeans, wheat, and corn and then aggregated these to see what the present value of total losses would be during the period 1976–2000. They came up with an estimate of about $7 billion. Another example of this approach is in estimating the benefits of forestalling climate change (at least in part) by estimating the reduction in lost future output that current reductions in greenhouse gases will produce.

A more refined approach to this problem is possible. The problem with taking just the value of the increased output is that production costs also may have changed. When air pollution diminishes, farmers actually may increase their use of certain inputs and farm this land more intensively. How do we account for this possibility? We can analyze the full change by using the net incomes of the farmers (total value of output minus total production costs).

The situation before the change:

$$\text{Total value of output: } a + b + c$$
$$\text{Total costs: } b + c$$
$$\text{Net income: } a$$

The situation after the change:

$$\text{Total value of output: } a + b + c + d + e$$
$$\text{Total costs: } c + e$$
$$\text{Net income: } a + b + d$$

Thus, the improvement in net incomes is $(a + b + d) - a$, or an amount equal to area $b + d$ in Figure 7.1.

How we measure this amount depends on how much information we are able to get. If we have studied these farms and know their supply curves before and after the change, we can measure the increased net income directly. If the supply curves are not known, we might look at the increased values of agricultural land in the area. In many cases, added net incomes of this type will get capitalized into land values, and we can use the **increased land values** to estimate the benefits of the environmental improvements.

Materials Damage

Air pollutants cause damage to exposed surfaces, metal surfaces of machinery, stone surfaces of buildings and statuary, and painted surfaces of all types of items. The most heavily implicated pollutants are the sulfur compounds, particulate matter, oxidants, and nitrogen oxides. For the most part, the damage is from increased deterioration that must be offset by increased maintenance and earlier replacement. In the case of outdoor sculpture, the damage is to the aesthetic qualities of the objects.

In this case the dose–response relationship shows the extent of deterioration associated with exposure to varying amounts of air pollutants. The basic physical relationships may be investigated in the laboratory, but in application to any particular area, one must have data on the various amounts of exposed materials that actually exist in the study region. Then it is possible to estimate the total amount of materials deterioration that would occur in an average year of exposure to the air of the region with its "normal" loading of various pollutants. One must then put a value on this deterioration. Taking a strict damage-function approach, we could estimate the increased cost of maintenance (labor, paint, etc.) made necessary by this deterioration, but this would be an underestimate of the true damages from a willingness-to-pay (WTP) perspective. Part of the damages would be aesthetic—the reduced visual values of less-sightly buildings and painted surfaces. We might arrive at these values through contingent valuation methods, discussed later. In addition, the maintenance cost approach would not be complete if pollution causes builders to switch to other materials to reduce damages.

Problems with Direct Damage Approaches

The basic problem with direct damage estimates is that they are almost always seriously incomplete. Consider the case of measuring health damages by lost productivity and medical expenditures. We note, first, that these tend to be market measures. They measure the value of marketed goods and services a person might, on average, produce. So the many nonmarket contributions people make, both inside and outside the home, sometimes don't get counted. This method also would assign a zero value to a person with disabilities unable to work or to a retiree. There are also numerous monetary, as well as psychic, benefits received by others—friends and relatives, for example—that the productivity measure does not account for. Nor does it account for the pain and suffering of illness. Similar conclusions may be drawn about using medical expenditures to estimate damages from reduced environmental quality. Suppose we estimate the damages to you of getting a head cold. We come up with an estimate of $1.27, the cost of the aspirin you consume to reduce the discomfort. This probably would be a serious understatement of the true damages of the cold. If you were asked how much you would be willing to pay to avoid the cold, the answer is likely to be substantially more than the cost of the aspirin. This is perhaps an unfair example because major medical expenditures for a person suffering from air pollution-induced lung cancer are much more significant than a bottle of aspirin. But the principle is valid.

Another major problem with attempts to measure damage functions directly is that people and markets normally will change and adjust to environmental pollution, and a full accounting of the damages of pollution must take these adjustments into account. Farmers raising crops affected by pollution may shift to other crops, while the prices of the damaged crops may change, affecting consumers. People often will change their behavior when faced with polluted air or water, engaging in what is called **averting behavior,** or making major changes in lifestyle. These effects are difficult to measure when using a direct approach to damage measurement. For this reason, we must turn back to our fundamental concept for determining value: willingness to pay.

Willingness to Pay: Estimating Methods

There are essentially three ways of trying to find out how much people are willing to pay for improvements in environmental quality. We can illustrate them by considering a case of noise pollution. One feature of the modern world is high-speed roadways (expressways, freeways, and turnpikes), and a major characteristic of these roads is that the traffic on them creates noise. Thus, the people who live nearby suffer damages from this traffic noise. Suppose our job is to estimate the willingness to pay of people living near expressways to reduce traffic noise. How might we do this?

1. The homeowners themselves may have made expenditures to reduce the noise levels inside their homes. For example, they may have installed additional insulation in the walls of their homes or put double-thick glass in the windows. When people make expenditures such as these, they reveal something about their willingness to pay for a quieter environment. In general, then, if we can find cases where market goods are purchased in order to affect a consumer's exposure to the ambient environment, we may be able to analyze these purchases for what they say about the value people place on changes in that ambient environment. The technical term for this is the study of **averting costs.**

2. The noise in the vicinity of the road may have affected the prices that nearby residents may have paid for their houses. If two houses have exactly the same characteristics in all respects except the level of exterior noise, we would expect the one in the noisier environment to be less valuable to prospective buyers than the one in the quieter environment. If the housing market is competitive, the price of the noisier house would be lower than the price of the other one. Thus, by looking at the difference in house prices, we can estimate the value people place on reduced noise pollution. In general, therefore, any time the price of some good or service varies in accordance with its environmental characteristics, we may be able to analyze these price variations to determine people's willingness to pay for these characteristics.

3. The third way is deceptively simple. It is to conduct a survey among homeowners and ask them how much they would be willing to pay for reductions in noise levels around and inside their homes. This direct-survey approach has received a lot of attention from environmental economists in recent years, primarily because of its flexibility. The primary method in this survey-type approach is called **contingent valuation.** Virtually any feature of the natural environment that can be described accurately to people can be studied by this method.

The first two of these methods involve the study of individuals' choices so as to uncover the implied values that have led them to make these decisions. For this reason they are often called **revealed preference** methods, as individuals are essentially revealing their underlying values. The third method involves asking people directly what their willingnesses to pay are, and are therefore called **stated preference** approaches. In the remainder of the chapter we will examine some of the ways these methods have been applied to estimate the benefits of improvements in environmental quality.

Willingness to Pay: Revealed Preference Methods

The thought behind these indirect approaches is that when people make market choices among certain items that have different characteristics related to the environment, they reveal the value they place on these environmental factors. Perhaps the most important is what they reveal about the values of health and human life.

Using willingness to pay to measure health benefits has the virtue of being consistent with other types of economic-demand studies, and it recognizes that even with something as important as health care, it is people's evaluations of its worth that should count. But the concept must be used with care. In any real-world situation, willingness to pay implies ability to pay; one cannot express a willingness to pay for something if one lacks the necessary income or wealth. So we must be sensitive to the income levels of people whose demand we are trying to measure. If the analysis includes a substantial number of people with low incomes, the measured willingness to pay may be lower than what might be justified. We may not want to lower the estimated health benefits of an environmental program simply because the target population has lower-than-average incomes.

Another feature about health care as a normal economic good is that people may be willing to pay for the health of others. I do not care if my daughter eats meat; her own willingness to pay is a good expression of her demand for meat. I do care about her health, however, and, to her own willingness to pay for good health, I would be willing to add a substantial sum of my own. Thus, strictly individualistic measures of willingness to pay for health improvements may underestimate the true benefits of programs that increase health.

The Value of Human Health as Expressed in Averting Costs

Air and water pollution can produce a variety of adverse health conditions, ranging from slight chest discomfort or headaches all the way to acute episodes requiring hospital care. People often make expenditures to try to avoid, or avert, these conditions, and these averting costs are an expression of their willingness to pay to avoid them. A number of studies have been done in which these averting expenditures have been analyzed for what they tell about willingness to pay.[11] One study was done of a sample of people in the Los Angeles area in 1986 and looked at expenditures they made to avoid a variety of respiratory symptoms.

---

[11] These are reviewed in Maureen L. Cropper and A. Myrick Freeman III, "Environmental Health Effects," in John B. Braden and Charles D. Kolstad (eds.), *Measuring the Demand for Environmental Quality*, North-Holland, Amsterdam, 1991, pp. 200–202.

Expenditures included such things as cooking with electricity rather than gas, operating a home air conditioner, and driving an air-conditioned car. Their estimates of the willingness to pay to avoid various respiratory symptoms ranged from $0.97 for shortness of breath to $23.87 for chest tightness.

One place where averting-cost analysis has been done is to value water quality, because of the usually ready availability of alternatives to water of dubious quality, such as water filtration devices and bottled water. At the other extreme, averting behavior has been studied to deduce the value of a statistical life, a concept discussed more fully in the next section.[12]

The Value of Human Life as Expressed in Wage Rates

Diminished air quality and contaminated water can lead to deteriorated health and death. How are these impacts to be valued? It is tempting to say that "human life is beyond measure," but that is not the way people behave in the real world. We can see by casual observation that individuals do not, in fact, behave as if prolonged life, or the warding off of disease, is in some sense an ultimate end to which all their resources must be devoted. We see people engaging in risky activity, in some sense trading off risk for the benefits received. Almost everybody drives a car, some people smoke, some rock climb, many strive to get tans, and so on. We also see people allocating portions of their income to reducing risk: buying locks, installing smoke alarms, staying away from dark places at night. In addition, we observe people making differential judgments of their own worth: parents with children buying more life insurance than single people, and so on. All of this suggests that people treat the risk of death in a reasonably rational manner, and that we could use willingness to pay as a way of evaluating the benefits of reducing the risk of death or illness.

But we must be clear on exactly what is involved. There is a joke about the stingy millionaire, walking down a street, who gets held up. The robber points a gun at her and says, "Your money or your life," and the victim replies: "Ah, let me think about that." Estimating the WTP value of a human life does not involve this kind of situation. People are not asked for their willingness to pay to save their own lives. Under some circumstances a person presumably will be willing to give everything he or she owns, but these are not the kinds of situations people normally face. When I express a willingness to pay for reducing air pollution, the relevant concept is the **value of a statistical life** (VSL), not the life of some particular individual. This does not imply that people are assumed to care only about the average, or random, person and not about specific people. People obviously feel closer to their relatives, friends, and neighbors than to strangers. What is involved is the value people place on rearranging the living conditions of a large group of people by, for example, reducing their exposure to environmental pollutants in order to lower the probability that some **randomly determined individual** from the group will suffer illness or premature death. Suppose, for example, that the average person in a group of 100,000

[12] Glenn C. Blomquist, "Self Protection and Averting Behavior, Values of Statistical Lives, and Benefit Cost Analysis of Environmental Policy," *Review of Economics of the Household*, 2(1), 2004, pp. 89–110.

people would be willing to pay $20 to lower the probability of a random death among members of that group from 7 in 100,000 to 6 in 100,000. Then the total willingness to pay is $20(100,000) = $2,000,000, which is the VSL based on willingness to pay.

The most fully developed revealed preference approach to measuring the willingness to pay for reducing risk to life is through **industrial wage rate studies.** Suppose there are two jobs similar in all respects except that in one, because of the type of machinery used, the risk of death is somewhat higher than in the other. Suppose that initially the wage rates in the two industries were the same. In this case, it would obviously be preferable to work in the safer industry—same wage, lower risk. Workers would then seek to move from the dangerous industry to the safer industry. This would tend to drive down the wage in the safer industry and increase the wage in the other, as firms sought to keep workers from leaving that industry. Thus, a wage differential would evolve between the two industries; the amount of that differential would show how workers valued the differences between them in terms of risk of death. The wage differential, in other words, represents an implicit valuation of a statistical life. By analyzing wage differences such as this, we can get a measure of the benefits people would get from reducing pollution-related premature deaths.

Table 7.2 summarizes some of the recent results of wage-rate studies aimed at estimating the VSL in the United States. Note that the estimates range from $1.5 million to over $10 million. What accounts for these differences? Different data and statistical techniques probably account for most of them. These studies are difficult because there are many other factors that have to be taken into account and because it is hard to get exactly the right data. For example, most worker accident and wage data apply to industry groupings, and within these groups there may be substantial variation among individual firms, not only because of technological differences among them, but also because some firms may have done a lot more than others to make the workplace safer. It is also

TABLE 7.2 Implied Value of a Statistical Life as Estimated in Labor Market Studies

A Statistical Study	Estimated Value of Statistical Life ($ million)
Moore and Viscusi (1990)	20.8
Kniesner, et al. (2012)	4.0–10.0
Leigh (1995)	8.1–16.8
Rose (2014)	3.2
Lott and Manning (2000)	1.5, 3.0

Sources: J. P. Leigh, "Compensating Wages, Value of a Statistical Life, and Inter-Industry Differentials," *Journal of Environmental Economics and Management*, 28(1), 1995, pp. 83–97; J.R. Lott and R.L. Manning, "Have Changing Liability Rules Compensated Workers Twice for Occupational Hazards? Earnings Premiums and Cancer Risks," *Journal of Legal Studies*, 29, 2000, pp. 99–130; M.J. Moore and W. Kip Viscusi, "Models for Estimating Discount Rates for Long-Term Health Risks Using Labor Market Data," *Journal of Risk and Uncertainty*, Vol. 3, 1990, pp. 381–401; J. Rose, "Official Estimates for the Value of Statistical Life for Road Accidents in Selected Countries," *Transport Economics*, posted July 24, 2014, **http://utopiayouarestandinginit.com/;** T.J. Kniesner, W. Kip Viscusi, C. Woock, and J.P. Ziliak, "The Value of a Statistical Life, Evidence from Panel Data," *Review of Economics and Statistics*, 94(1), 2012, pp. 74–87.

the case that wage-rate studies such as these are predicated on the reasonably efficient working of the labor market, and this may not be the case in some industries. Union agreements, collusion among firm managers, and lack of information can upset the competitive wage-making process in some industries. These problems do not mean that these studies are not useful, only that we have not yet reached a point where they are giving us a consistent story.[13]

Valuing Children's Health

Most WTP studies in the health area are focused on the valuations of adults. But a large percentage of the people impacted by environmental pollution are children, and it is not clear that the WTP estimates of adults are applicable also to children. Children may be more heavily impacted than adults by given concentrations of pollutants in the air and water. And children themselves are in no position to offer WTP information on their health. Thus, what we need are WTP estimates of adults for reducing health risks to children, and these may be quite different than their WTP to reduce health risks to themselves. For example, Liu and colleagues found that a mother's WTP for her child's health was greater than the WTP for her own health.[14] Blomquist and colleagues gathered data on the use of seat belts and found that they implied a VSL of $3.7 million for the average child under five years of age, and $2.8 million for adults.[15]

The Value of Environmental Quality as Expressed in House Prices

The wage-rate studies we just looked at estimate the willingness to pay to be exposed to a lower risk of death, which is a specific consequence of being exposed to lower levels of environmental pollution. But there are wider benefits to a cleaner environment than simply health benefits. A more inclusive approach is to examine people's willingness to pay to live in a less polluted environment. This would include the health effects but also other dimensions such as aesthetic impacts.

Suppose you had two houses that were exactly the same in terms of all of their physical characteristics—number of rooms, floor area, age, and so on—as well as in locational factors—distance to neighbors, distance to shopping facilities, and so forth. Assume, however, that one house is located in an area of substantial air pollution, whereas the other is located in an area with relatively clean air. We would expect the market prices of these two houses to differ because of the air quality difference. This conclusion generalizes to a large housing market involving many properties. The surrounding air quality is essentially a

[13] Trudy Ann Cameron, "Valuing Morbidity in Environmental Benefit Cost Analysis," *Annual Review of Resource Economics*, 6, 2014, pp. 249–272; W. Kip Viscusi, "What's to Know? Puzzles in the Literature on the Value of Statistical Life," *Journal of Economic Surveys*, 26(5), 2011, pp. 763–768.

[14] J.-T. Liu, J.K. Hammitt, J.-D. Wang, and J.-L. Liu, "Mother's Willingness to Pay for Her Own and Her Child's Health: A Contingent Valuation Study in Taiwan," *Health Economics*, 9, 2000, pp. 319–326.

[15] Glenn C. Blomquist, Ted R. Miller, and David T. Levy, "Values of Risk Reduction Implied by Motorist Use of Protection Equipment: New Evidence from Different Populations," *Journal of Transport Economics and Policy*, 30, 1996, pp. 55–66.

FIGURE 7.2   **Relationship of Ambient SO₂ Concentration and House Prices**

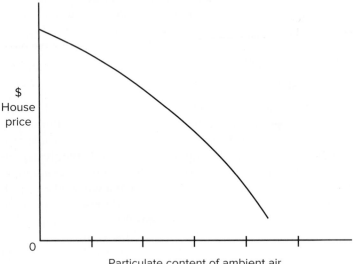

Particulate content of ambient air

feature of the location of a house so, as houses are bought and sold in the house market, these air quality differences would tend to get "capitalized" into the market prices of the houses. Of course, homes differ in many respects, not just in terms of air quality. So it is necessary to collect large amounts of data on many properties and then use statistical techniques to identify the role played by air pollution, as well as other factors.[16]

Assuming we had collected enough data and conducted the appropriate statistical analyses, we might end up with a relationship such as that shown in Figure 7.2. This shows that as the particulate content of the surrounding air increases, house prices decrease, everything else held equal. Information of this type can then be used to estimate homeowners' marginal willingness to pay (benefits) for small decreases in particulate exposure. Smith and Huang reviewed a number of studies of this type. They found that, in general, the marginal willingness to pay for a one-unit decrease in exposure to total suspended particulate matter (TSP) was in the range of $100 to $300 for most studies.[17] Another study of house prices by Chattopadhyay estimated that people are willing to pay on average about $310 for a one-unit decrease in exposure to PM10.[18]

---

[16] The technical name for this type of approach is "hedonic" analysis. When the price of something is related to the many characteristics it possesses, we can study patterns of price differences to deduce the value people place on one of those characteristics.

[17] TSP is expressed in terms of micrograms per cubic meter. See V. Kerry Smith and Ju-Chin Huang, "Can Markets Value Air Quality? A Meta Analysis of Hedonic Property Value Models," *Journal of Political Economy*, 103(1), 1995, pp. 209–227.

[18] PM10 refers to the concentration of particulate matter composed of particles less than 10 microns in diameter. See S. Chattopadhyay, "Estimating the Demand for Air Quality: New Evidence Based on the Chicago Housing Market," *Land Economics*, 75(1), February 1999, pp. 22–38.

The same kind of approach might be used with some cases of water pollution. In Chapter 4 we used lake pollution to introduce the concept of a public good. Suppose a lake is surrounded by a number of residences. The market price of these homes will be affected by many things: their age, size, condition, and so on. They also will be affected by the water quality of the lake. If this water quality degrades over time, we would expect the market values of the surrounding properties to go down. The deteriorating water quality means that homeowners will obtain less utility from living in that vicinity, other things remaining equal, and this will get capitalized into the values of the houses. One approach to measuring the benefits of cleaning up the lake is to estimate the overall increase in property values among the homes in the vicinity of the lake. We have to remember, however, that this is likely to be only a partial estimate of total benefits. If nonresidents have access to the lake or park, they also would be gaining benefits, but these would not show up in property value changes. Property value changes to measure benefits from pollution reduction also can be used in other situations: for example, in valuing the damage from noise around airports and major highways and in measuring the benefits flowing from urban parks.

House price studies can also be used to estimate VSLs. Houses near superfund sites, for example, expose residents to higher degrees of risk, and the extent to which these house prices are lower than others can give an implied VSL. In one study the researchers found that this gave a VSL of $4.7 million.[19]

The Value of Environmental Quality and Intercity Wage Differentials

We talked about using wage-rate differences among jobs to measure the value of reducing health risks from pollution. Wage-rate studies also have been used to estimate the value of living in a cleaner environment. Suppose there were two cities, alike in every respect, but one has higher air pollution than the other. Suppose that initially wage rates in the two cities were equal. Because everything else is exactly the same, it would be more desirable to work in the less polluted city—same wages but less air pollution. Workers would therefore migrate to the cleaner city. To keep a labor force in the dirty city, one of two things must happen: the air must be cleaned up or a higher wage must be offered to offset the damages of living in more polluted air. So we could study wage-rate differentials among cities with different degrees of air pollution to measure the value that people place on cleaner air. This would give us a way of estimating the benefits of cleaning up the air in the more polluted cities.

The Value of Environmental Quality as Expressed in Travel Costs

One of the first approaches that environmental economists ever used to estimate the demand for environmental amenities is a method that takes travel

[19] Ted Gayer, James T. Hamilton, and W. Kip Viscusi, "Private Values of Risk Trade-offs at Superfund Sites: Housing Market Evidence on Learning About Risk," *Review of Economics and Statistics*, 82, 2000, pp. 439–451.

costs as a proxy for price. Although we don't observe people buying units of environmental quality directly, we do observe them traveling to enjoy, for example, recreational experiences in national and state parks, swimming and fishing experiences in lakes and streams, and so on. Travel is costly; it takes time as well as out-of-pocket travel expenses. By treating these travel costs as a price that people must pay to experience the environmental amenity, we can estimate, under some circumstances, a demand function for those amenities.

By getting travel cost data for a large number of people, we can build up estimates of the aggregate willingness to pay for particular environmental amenities. Of course, information must be obtained on more than just their travel costs. Families will differ in terms of many factors, not just in terms of their travel costs to this park. They will have different income levels, they will differ in terms of the presence of alternative parks and other recreational experiences available to them, and so on. So surveys have to collect large amounts of data on many visitors to be able to statistically sort out all these various influences on park visitation rates.

This approach may be used to estimate the benefits of improving the quality of the environment at the visitation site, for example, by improving the water quality at a recreation lake so that fishing is better. To do this we must collect information not only on the travel costs of recreators to a single recreation site but also on the travel costs to many different sites with differing natural characteristics. Then we can parse out the effects on visitation of various qualitative aspects of different sites. From this we can then determine their willingness to pay for improvements in these qualitative changes.

Willingness to Pay: Stated Preference Methods

We come now to what might seem as a more direct way of assessing willingness to pay. This is a **stated preference** approach, because it involves asking people directly to indicate their willingness to pay for some environmental feature, or some outcome that is closely connected to the state of the environment.

The best known stated preference method is a technique called **contingent valuation** (CV). In this method individuals are asked to make WTP responses when placed in contingent situations. If we were interested in measuring people's willingness to pay for something like potatoes, we could station ourselves at stores and see them choosing in real situations. But when there are no real markets for something, such as an environmental quality characteristic, we can only ask them to tell us how they would choose *if* they were faced with a market for these characteristics.

Contingent valuation methods have been utilized in two different types of situations: (1) to estimate valuations for specific features of the environment, for example, the value of view-related amenities, the recreational quality of beaches, preservation of wildlife species, congestion in wilderness areas, hunting and fishing experiences, toxic waste disposal, preservation of wild rivers, and others [20]; and (2) to estimate the valuations people place on outcomes that are related to environmental quality. A major justification for more stringent environmental regulations has always been the improvements in human health that these would produce. What is important here are the valuations that people place on such things as reduced risk of premature mortality, decreased risk of chronic lung disease, decreased risk of asthma, and so on.

In fact, the use of contingent valuation methods has also spread into nonenvironmental areas, such as estimating the value of programs for reducing the risks of heart attacks, the value of supermarket price information, and the value of a seniors companion program. Over time, the method has been developed and refined to give what many regard as reasonably reliable measures of the benefits of a variety of public goods, especially environmental quality.

The basic steps in a CV analysis are the following:

1. Identification and description of the environmental quality characteristic or health outcome to be evaluated
2. Identification of respondents to be approached, including sampling procedures used to select respondents
3. Design and application of a survey questionnaire, interview, or focus group
4. Analysis of results and aggregation of individual responses to estimate values for the group affected by the environmental change

The nature of CV analysis can best be understood by looking more closely at the questionnaire design phase.

Valuing an Environmental Amenity

In this case the questionnaire is designed to elicit from respondents their willingness to pay for some feature of the environment. The questionnaire would normally have three components:

1. A clear statement of exactly what the environmental feature or amenity is that people are being asked to evaluate
2. A set of questions that will describe the respondent in economically relevant ways, such as income, residential location, age, and use of related goods
3. A question, or set of questions, designed to elicit WTP responses from the respondent

The central purpose of the questionnaire is to elicit from respondents their estimate of what the environmental feature is worth to them. In economic terms, this means getting them to reveal the maximum amount they would be

---

[20] For the classic discussions of CV analysis, see Robert Cameron Mitchell and Richard T. Carson, *Using Surveys to Value Public Goods: The Contingent Valuation Method*, Resources for the Future, Washington, D.C., 1989; and Ronald G. Cummings, David S. Brookshire, and William D. Schulze, *Valuing Environmental Goods: An Assessment of the Contingent Valuation Method*, Rowland and Allanheld Publishers, Totowa, NJ, 1986.

willing to pay rather than go without the amenity in question. Numerous techniques have been used to get at this response. The most obvious is to ask people outright to provide the number with no prompting or probing on the part of the interviewer. Other approaches include using a bidding game, where the interviewer starts with a bid at a low level and progressively increases the value until the user indicates that the limit has been reached. Alternatively, the interviewer could start with a high figure and lower it to find where the respondent's threshold value is located. Another method is to give the respondents a selection of a range of values, and then ask the respondents to check off their maximum willingness to pay.

One great advantage of contingent valuation is that it is flexible and applicable to a wide range of environmental amenities, not just those that can somehow be measured in conjunction with some marketable good. Virtually anything that can be made comprehensible to respondents can be studied with this technique.

- CV was first used in 1963 by Bob Davis to estimate the benefits of outdoor recreation opportunities in the Maine backwoods. He found that the modal willingness to pay per family for the use of a wilderness recreation area was between $1.00 and $2.00 per day.[21]
- A contingent valuation study of bird hunting in Delaware found that the average willingness to pay for a bagged duck was $82.17; this value was influenced by, among other things, the amount of congestion in the hunting area.[22]
- J. Loomis and colleagues found that the average respondent in their CV survey would be willing to pay $21 per month for improved water quality in the Platte River.[23]
- Banzhaf and colleagues found that residents in the Adirondack region of New York would be willing to pay between $48 and $107 for ecological improvements in air and water that might flow from currently proposed environmental regulations.[24]
- Holmes et al., using a contingent valuation approach, found that riparian landowners along the Little Tennessee River would be willing to pay $89.50 per foot along the river for restoration activities.[25]

[21] Robert K. Davis, "The Value of Big Game Hunting in a Private Forest," in *Transactions of the Twenty-ninth North American Wildlife Conference*, Wildlife Management Institute, Washington, D.C., 1964.

[22] John MacKenzie, "A Comparison of Contingent Preference Models," *American Journal of Agricultural Economics*, 75, August 1993, pp. 593–603.

[23] John Loomis, Paula Kent, Liz Strange, Kurt Fausch, and Alan Covich, "Measuring the Total Economic Value of Restoring Ecosystem Services in an Impaired River Basin: Results from a Contingent Value Survey," *Ecological Economics*, 33(1), 2000, pp. 103–117.

[24] H. Spencer Banzhaf, Dallas Burtraw, David Evans, and Alan J. Krupnick, *Valuation of Natural Resource Improvements in the Adirondacks*, paper presented at National Center for Environmental Economics, Environmental Protection Agency workshop, October 26–27, 2004.

[25] Thomas P. Holmes, John C. Bergstrom, Eric Huszar, Susan B. Kask, and Fritz Orr III, "Contingent Valuation, Net Marginal Benefits, and the Scale of Riparian Ecosystem Restoration," *Ecological Economics*, 49(1), May 2004, pp. 19–30.

- Brookshire and Coursey did a CV study to determine people's willingness to pay for a change in tree density in an urban park from 200 to 250 trees per acre. The median willingness to pay among their respondents was $9.30. In eliciting these responses, researchers showed respondents pictures of the park with different tree densities.[26]

- Stevens et al. used CV to estimate the benefits people would receive from reducing damages due to air pollution from power plants in the White Mountains of New Hampshire. These were amenity damages from reduced visibility at scenic vistas. Respondents were shown a series of computer-generated photos of a view showing varying degrees of visibility corresponding to different levels of pollution control. For moderate levels of improved visibility, willingness to pay ranged from $3 to $12.[27]

Economists in many other countries have worked at estimating respondents' willingness to pay for environmental improvements and amenities. Some are noted in Table 7.3.

Valuing Health Outcomes

A major justification for many environmental regulations is to reduce the damages to human health caused by pollution. Epidemiological studies have drawn links between the presence of pollutants in air and water and a variety of adverse health impacts. Contingent valuation studies have been done to value these outcomes, or their avoidance, in terms of willingness to pay.

The studies have been of two general types: those estimating respondents' willingness to pay to avoid premature mortality, and those estimating willingness to pay to achieve certain reductions in morbidity. The latter can be further subdivided into studies of chronic diseases, such as bronchitis and asthma, and temporary but acute health conditions.[28]

In the mortality studies the outcomes have been expressed probabilistically, that is, the willingness to pay for a reduction of a certain amount in the probability of premature death. We discussed earlier how responses can be used to estimate the value of a statistical life (VSL). Studies of chronic illnesses have also usually been aimed at probabilistic measures, for example, willingness to pay to lower the probability of having chronic bronchitis. Acute health conditions have usually been valued as though they were certain to be avoided, for example, willingness to pay to avoid a common cold, or a visit to the emergency room of a hospital.

[26] David S. Brookshire and Don L. Coursey, "Measuring the Value of Public Goods: An Empirical Comparison of Elicitation Procedures," *American Economic Review*, 77(4), September 1987, pp. 554–566.

[27] John Halstrad, T.H. Stevens, Wendy Harper, and L. Bruce Hill, "Electricity Deregulation and the Value of Visibility Loss in Wilderness Areas: A Research Note," *Journal of Regional Analysis and Policy*, 30(1), 2004, pp. 85–95.

[28] For a discussion of these matters, see Alan J. Krupnick, *Valuing Health Outcomes: Policy Choices and Technical Issues*, Resources for the Future, Washington, D.C., 2004.

TABLE 7.3 **Examples of Benefit Estimation Studies Carried Out by Environmental Economists in Other Countries**

Country and Study	Results
Australia[a]	
Contingent valuation (CV) study to measure willingness of people to pay (WTP) to develop biological means of fly control	$13.40/person/yr
Finland[b]	
WTP for grouse hunting, as a function of the grouse population (CV method)	
Grouse population at current level	604 FIM/person/yr
Grouse population half of current level	462 FIM/person/yr
Grouse population two times current level	786 FIM/person/yr
France[c]	
WTP to maintain more nearly constant water level in a flood control reservoir to benefit recreationists (CV method)	47 FF/person/yr
Germany[d]	
WTP to have an improvement in air quality (CV method)	75–190 DM/person/month
Israel[e]	
WTP for a 50 percent reduction in air pollution in Haifa	
Indirect means (hedonic)	$66.2/household/yr
Direct means (CV)	$25.1/household/yr
Netherlands[f]	
WTP to prevent further deterioration of the Dutch forests and heath (CV method)	22.83 DFL/person/month
Norway[g]	
WTP for improved water quality in the inner Oslo fjord (CV method)	
Users	942 NOK/household/yr
Nonusers	522 NOK/household/yr
Sweden[h]	
WTP for a reduction in the risk of getting lung cancer from radon exposure (CV method)	4,300 SEK/household
United Kingdom[i]	
WTP for an improvement in river water quality (CV method)	£12.08/person/year

[a] B. Johnston, "External Benefits in Rural Research and the Question of Who Should Pay," presented to 26th Annual Conference of the Australian Agricultural Economic Society, February 9–11, 1982, University of Melbourne.
[b] V. Owaskainen, H. Savolainen, and T. Sievanen, "The Benefits of Managing Forests for Grouse Habitat: A Contingent Valuation Experiment," paper presented at Biennien Meeting of the Scandinavian Society of Forest Economics, April 10–13, 1991, Gausdal, Norway.
[c] B. Desaigues and V. Lesgards, *La Valorisation des Actifs Naturels un Example d'Application de la Method d'Evaluation Contingente*, Université de Bordeaux, working paper, 1991.
[d] K. Holm-Müller, H. Hansen, M. Klockman, and P. Luther, "Die Nachfrage nach Umweltqualität in der Bundesrepublik Deutschland" (The Demand for Environmental Quality in the Federal Republic of Germany), *Berichte des Umweltbundesamtes* 4/91, Erich Schmidt Verlag, Berlin, 1991, p. 346.
[e] M. Shechter and M. Kim, "Valuation of Pollution Abatement Benefits: Direct and Indirect Measurement," *Journal of Urban Economics*, Vol. 30, 1991, pp. 133–151.
[f] J.W. van der Linden and F.H. Oosterhuis, *De maatschappelijke waardering voor de vitaliteit van bos en heide* (The Social Valuation of the Vitality of Forests and Heath), in Dutch, English summary, Publication by the Ministry of Public Housing, Physical Planning and Environmental Management, VROM 80115/3, Leidschendam, 1987, p. 46.
[g] A. Heiberg and K.-G. Him, "Use of Formal Methods in Evaluating Countermeasures of Coastal Water Pollution," In H.M. Seip and A. Heiberg (eds.), *Risk Management of Chemicals in the Environment*, Plenum Press, London, 1989.
[h] J. Aakerman, *Economic Valuation of Risk Reduction: The Case of Indoor Radiation*, Stockholm School of Economics, Stockholm, Sweden, 1988, p. 65.
[i] C.H. Green and S. Tunstall, "The Evaluation of River Water Quality Improvements by the Contingent Valuation Method," *Applied Economics*, 1991, p. 23.

TABLE 7.4 Benefits and Costs of a Proposal for Controlling Power Plant Emissions in Order to Reduce Interstate Air Pollution

Benefits	Millions (2007 U.S. dollars)
Premature mortality	$270,000
Chronic bronchitis	$4,200
Nonfatal heart attacks	$1,700
Hospital admissions	$130
Other health	$50
Recreational visibility	$4,100
Other nonhealth	$1,500
Total	*$281,680*
Costs	$810

Sources: U.S. EPA, Office of Air and Radiation, *Regulatory Impact Analysis for the Federal Implementation Plan to Reduce Interstate Transport of Fine Particulate Matter and Ozone in 27 States*; Correction of SIP Approvals for 22 States, June 2011.

Table 7.4 shows some recent results on health-related benefits produced by a plan proposed by the Environmental Protection Agency (EPA) to reduce the interstate flow of air pollution from power plants. These estimates are primarily based on WTP studies of health outcomes. Note that the greatest source of health-related benefits is the reduction in premature deaths from air pollution.

Problems of CV Analysis

The most problematic aspect of contingent valuation is its hypothetical character. When people buy potatoes, to go back to our example, they have to "put their money where their mouth is," as the saying goes. It is a real situation, and if the wrong choices are made, people suffer real consequences. In a CV questionnaire, however, the same real-world implications are not present. People face a hypothetical situation to which they may give hypothetical responses not governed by the discipline of a real marketplace. In thinking about this, two types of questions come up: First, will people know enough about their real preferences to be able to give valid responses, and, second, even if they know their preferences, will they have incentives to misrepresent them to the investigator?

Everyone develops experience buying some things, but not others, on the market. In 17th-century New England, people were used to buying and selling pews in the church. In some countries official papers from public officials require standard monetary bribes. In contemporary society there are going prices for cantaloupes and blood. When people face market prices for a good or service over a period of time, they have time to learn about their values, adjust their purchases, and settle on a willingness to pay that accurately represents their preferences. But when asked to place a monetary value on something that does not normally carry a price, it may be much more difficult to state one's true willingness to pay. What would you be willing to pay for 10 more beautiful sunsets per year? People also develop ideas over time about the appropriate extent of the market in allocating certain goods and services; when asked to put a value on something that is currently beyond the market, their answers may reflect not just the value of a particular item, but something about what kind of an economic system they want to live in, which is a much broader question.

The other question is whether respondents could normally be expected to have incentives to misstate their true willingness to pay. Environmental quality characteristics are public goods, as we saw in Chapter 4. People can be expected to understate their preferences for these kinds of goods when they expect that their answers will be used to establish payment schedules for the goods. Yet, in CV studies, there is no threat that responses could be used, for example, to set taxes to pay for the item being evaluated. So, perhaps, this source of bias is unlikely. The opposite bias may be more likely. People may be led to give an inflated estimate of their willingness to pay hoping, perhaps, that others will do the same thing, realizing that their share of the cost of making the item available will, in any case, be very small.

There have been hundreds of contingent valuation studies carried out to estimate people's willingness to pay for environmental quality. Despite the difficulties, CV analysis offers great flexibility and a chance of estimating many values that no other technique can match. The technique is still evolving, however, and we can expect it over time to produce increasingly reliable estimates of the value people place on environmental assets of all types.

Problems in Benefit Estimation

Many problems remain in estimating the benefits of improved environmental quality. Good data are always hard to come by. Better techniques are always useful to separate out the effects of other factors and isolate the true environmental impacts. More thought has to be given to the conceptual problems that remain. We will indicate very briefly some of the latter.

Discounting

One of the most important is the matter of **discounting.** Should we discount future benefits, as we talked about in the last chapter, and, if so, what discount rate is appropriate? When we discount the future value of something, we reduce its present value, and the longer in the future these benefits will be realized, the lower their present value. So discounting tends to decrease the relative value of programs that produce benefits far in the future and increase those that produce benefits in the next few years. This might make sense with certain types of benefits. People today presumably would put more value on reducing environmentally related premature deaths next year than they would on premature deaths 50 years from now. But there are some significant environmental issues, such as global warming, where substantial impacts are expected to occur in the distant future, and in this case discounting tends to reduce substantially the importance of programs addressing this problem.

There is no easy answer to this problem. We cannot simply reject discounting altogether; even future generations would be unlikely to agree with that if they could make their wishes known. In ordinary affairs, however, the present generation is undoubtedly too oriented to the short run; too much reliance is placed on recent history and not enough on future possibilities. For society as a whole, a longer-run perspective is appropriate. As mentioned in the last chapter, perhaps the best approach is to combine discounting with the idea of sustainability. Discounting is appropriate as long as it does not lead to a reduction in the long-run environmental capital of the society.

Willingness to Pay Versus Willingness to Accept

An alternative way of approaching the problem of valuing environmental improvements is to ask people how much they would be **willing to accept** to give up some environmental amenity. To value better air quality we could ask either how much people would be willing to pay for a small improvement or how much they would have to receive to compensate them for a small reduction in air quality. Suppose public authorities are contemplating locating a hazardous waste incinerator in a particular community. As a measure of the damages suffered by the community, we could take the amount of money required to get the community members willingly to accept the incinerator (rather than, in other words, the amount they would be willing to pay to keep it out).

Clearly, willingness to accept is not constrained by one's income, as is willingness to pay. So it may be no surprise that when people are asked willingness-to-accept questions, their answers are usually higher than their WTP responses for the same item. To some extent it may depend on what they are asked. For a small change we would expect the two measures to be close. Suppose what is involved is a single cantaloupe. If I am willing to pay $1.99 for one more cantaloupe, that is also probably close to what it would take to compensate for my loss of a single cantaloupe, but for large changes (what are called nonmarginal changes) this may not be the case. If we are talking, for example, of large changes in air pollution in my neighborhood that will substantially change my welfare, the two measures may be quite different.

Economists have taken several approaches to resolving this problem. One is to look closely at the questionnaire and the way questions are asked of respondents. Experience has shown that responses will differ according to how questions are phrased; therefore, one possibility is that the differences between willingness to pay and willingness to accept are traceable primarily to the way questions are being framed. The other approach is to replace the standard economic principles, which imply that there should be no difference between these two measures, with new concepts that can explain the difference.

Nonuse Values

When people buy potatoes, we assume that they do so because they expect to eat them; the value of potatoes to people lies in their *use* value. This reasoning extends also to environmental assets, but in this case there may be more. When people voluntarily donate money for the preservation of unique environmental assets that they may never even see, except perhaps in photographs, something other than use value must be involved. People's willingness to pay for these environmental characteristics also must involve certain **nonuse values.** One possibility is that although perhaps not currently in a position to experience directly a particular environmental asset, people often want to preserve the option to do so in the future. **Option value** is the amount a person would be willing to pay to preserve the option of being able to experience a particular environmental amenity in the future. People may even be willing to pay to preserve something they in all likelihood will never see—African wildlife, for example. In this case, what is involved is **existence value,** a willingness to pay simply to help preserve the existence of some environmental amenity. Such altruistic values may be focused to some extent on future generations, in which case they might be called **bequest values.** Last, we might add a **stewardship value,** which is a value not related necessarily to human use of the environment, but rather to maintaining the health of the environment for the continued use of all living organisms. One of the reasons contingent valuation studies have become more common is that questions can be phrased so as to get at these nonuse values.

Summary

Benefit measurement is a major focus of study within environmental economics. New techniques are being developed to uncover values that previously were hidden from view. From legislatures and courts a brisk demand has arisen for benefits information on which to base laws and legal settlements. Public environmental agencies have devoted considerable time and effort to generating benefits estimates in order to justify their policy rulings. After reviewing briefly what we mean by *benefits*, we discussed some of the main techniques environmental economists use to measure these benefits. Health impacts, previously assessed by direct damage estimation, are now more frequently pursued through WTP procedures, especially wage-rate studies showing how people value risks to health. We also covered house-price studies, production cost studies, and travel cost studies. Finally, we reviewed the technique of contingent valuation. This technique allows benefits to be measured over a much wider range of environmental phenomena than other techniques permit. Indeed, contingent valuation techniques allow analysts to push beyond traditional use values and explore some of the less tangible, but no less real, sources of environmental benefits, such as option value, existence value, and stewardship value.

Questions for Further Discussion

1. Suppose you were hired by the homeowners located around a lake to determine the benefits of improving the water quality in the lake. How might you go about doing it?

2. The Chinese government has elected to close high polluting power plants and some factories. Compare and contrast how the Chinese government would evaluate the benefits versus how an individual Chinese worker would evaluate the benefits.

3. Suppose you want to determine the aggregate willingness to pay among students at your school for increasing recycling at the school. How might you do this?

4. What is the usual meaning that economists give to the expression "the value of a human life"? What are the different ways of estimating this value?

5. Design some contingent valuation-type questions for evaluating the value to people of improving the air quality in the Grand Canyon.

6. Survey 10 other students, asking them how much they would be willing to pay for one visit to their favorite beach. What qualifying questions did your respondents ask you before they could assign a dollar value? What are some factors influencing people's willingness-to-pay value?

For additional readings and Web sites pertaining to the material in this chapter, see **www.mhhe.com/field7e**.

Chapter 8

Benefit–Cost Analysis: Costs

In this chapter we look at the cost side of benefit–cost analysis. The importance of accurate cost measurement often has been underestimated. The results of a benefit–cost analysis can be affected as easily by overestimating costs as by underestimating benefits. In developing countries, where people place a high priority on economic growth, it is critically important to know how environmental programs will affect that growth rate and how costs are distributed among different social groups. In industrialized countries, opposition to environmental policies frequently centers on their estimated costs, which means that those doing benefit–cost analyses of these programs are well advised to get the cost estimates right. In this chapter we will first take up some general considerations about costs, then look at some specific issues and examples of cost estimation.

The Cost Perspective: General Issues

Cost analysis can be done on many levels. At its simplest, it focuses on the costs to a single community or firm of an environmental regulation or of a single environmental project, such as a wastewater treatment plant, incinerator, or beach restoration project. The reason for calling these the simplest is that they usually proceed by costing out a definite engineering specification that has clear boundaries and for which the "rest of the world" can rightly assume to be constant.

At the next level we have costs to an industry, or perhaps to a region, of meeting environmental regulations or of adopting certain technologies. Here it is no longer possible to rely on simple engineering assumptions; we must do things such as predict with reasonable accuracy how groups of polluting firms will respond to changes in laws on emissions or how they will respond to changes in recycling regulations. Problems will arise because not all firms will be alike—some small, some large, some old, some new, and so on—and each of them will usually have multiple possibilities for reacting to regulations.

At a still higher level, our concern may be with the costs to an entire economy of achieving stated environmental goals. Estimating costs at the national level calls for an entirely different approach. Here everything is connected to everything else; when pollution-control regulations are imposed, adjustments will reverberate throughout the economy. Tracing them out requires **macroeconomic data** and usually fairly sophisticated aggregate models. After taking a look at several general issues in cost estimation, we will deal with the subject at these different levels.

The With/Without Principle

There is an important principle that has to be kept in mind in this work. In doing a benefit–cost analysis of how firms will respond to new laws, we want to use the **with/without** principle and not the **before/after** principle. We want to estimate the differences in costs that polluters would have with the new law, *compared to what their costs would have been in the absence of the law.* This is not the same as the difference between their new costs and what their costs used to be before the law. Consider the following illustrative numbers that apply to a manufacturing firm for which a pollution-control regulation has been proposed:

Estimated production costs:

Before the regulation:	$100
In the future without the regulation:	$120
In the future with the regulation:	$150

It would be a mistake to conclude that the added costs of the pollution-control regulation will be $50 (future costs with the regulation minus costs before the law). This is an application of the before/after principle and does not accurately reflect the true costs of the law. This is so because in the absence of any new law, production costs are expected to increase (e.g., because of increased fuel costs unrelated to environmental regulations). Thus, the true cost of the regulation is found by applying the with/without principle. Here, these costs are $30 (costs in the future with the regulation minus future costs without the regulation). Of course this makes the whole job of cost estimation harder because we want to know not historical costs of a firm or an industry but what its future costs would be if it were to continue operating without the new environmental laws.

The with/without scenario calls for **baseline analysis,** the estimation of what future cost levels could be expected to be in the absence of the regulation. What makes baseline analysis so difficult is that future technical change (better procedures, better equipment, etc.) will lower costs, and it is normally very hard to predict with accuracy how fast this technical change will take place.

A Word on Social Costs

In Chapter 3 we made a distinction between private and social costs. Social costs are all the costs stemming from an action, and are equal to private costs plus external costs. When a power plant produces electricity and air pollution, taking steps to reduce air pollution involves both a reduction in social costs, here the damages from air pollution, and increased production costs as a result of adopting and operating pollution-control technology. In effect, power production without pollution-control requirements amounts to a public subsidy to power producers, and a gain in social welfare is possible by adopting pollution-control policy.

There are many other examples of public subsidies leading to distorted output levels, which could be ameliorated by appropriate public policies.

Consider, for example, **coastal zone flood insurance** in the United States. Commercial insurance for property constructed in the coastal zone would normally have such high premiums, because of the expected losses from floods, that few coastal homeowners could afford it. The U.S. government, and sometimes state governments, will often subsidize coastal zone insurance so that people building in these areas can get insurance at substantially less than commercial rates. The effects of this have been to reduce the private monetary costs of building and maintaining houses in the coastal zone; thus, substantial development has occurred there, with attendant environmental impacts. A reduction in these public subsidies to coastal homeowners not only would work to reduce these environmental impacts but also would lead to an increase in national income. Of course, coastal homeowners would suffer losses.

There are many other examples such as this. **Agricultural subsidies** in many developed countries have provided the incentive to develop intensive, chemical-based production methods, which have resulted both in increased agricultural output and in the nonpoint-source water and air pollution to which these methods lead. Reducing these agricultural subsidies would increase national income and reduce the environmental impacts, though of course some farmers would be worse off.

The Distribution of Costs

The overall social costs of environmental regulations are important in assessing their cost-effectiveness. Beyond this, however, a major factor behind many policy controversies is how these total costs are **distributed** among different groups in society. Environmental regulations initially may lead to increased production costs in the industry to which the regulation applies, as firms undertake the pollution-control steps required by the regulations. But changes will not be confined to this one industry. As firms alter production technology, input mixes, and other aspects of their operations, their **prices** are likely to change, for both outputs and inputs. So some, or perhaps all, of the consequences of the regulation will be shifted to consumers and input-supplying firms. Employees of the regulated firms will be impacted when production rates increase or decrease in the affected industries. Very often there will be important **regional** differences in these impacts, because often industries are more concentrated in certain regions than in others. It is important, then, to be concerned not only with total costs, but also with how these costs are distributed.

Concepts of Cost

Opportunity Costs

In economics the most fundamental concept of costs is **opportunity costs.** The opportunity cost of using resources[1] in a certain way is the highest value these resources would have produced had they not been used in the manner under consideration. If resources are used to produce cars, they can't be used to produce something else. If resources are used to enforce air-pollution regulations, they can't be used to implement land-use regulations. It is the forgone values of these alternative uses that constitute the opportunity costs of pursuing a particular course of action.

Costs are incurred by all types of firms, industries, agencies, and other groups. From the perspective of a private firm, the opportunity cost of producing a good or service is what it could have produced if it had chosen a different output. We must differentiate **private costs** from **social opportunity costs.** The latter represent the costs to society of using resources in a particular way, meaning all costs, no matter to whom they accrue. We discussed earlier how social costs include private costs, but also include **external costs**, in the form of pollution damage costs incurred by third parties, whenever they exist.[2]

Sometimes items that a private group might consider a cost (e.g., a tax) are not a cost from the standpoint of society. Sometimes items that particular decision makers do not consider as costs really do have social costs. Suppose a community is contemplating building a bicycle path to relieve congestion and air pollution downtown. Its primary concern is what the town will have to pay to build the path. Suppose it will take $1 million to build it, but 50 percent of this will come from the state or federal government. From the town's perspective, the cost of the bike path will be a half million dollars, but from the standpoint of society the full opportunity costs of the path are $1 million.

When most people think of cost they usually think of money expenditure. Often the monetary cost of something is a good measure of its opportunity costs, but frequently it is not. Suppose the bike path is going to be put on an old railroad right-of-way that has absolutely no alternative use, and suppose the town must pay the railroad $100,000 for this right-of-way. This money is definitely an expenditure the town must make, but it is not truly a part of the

---

[1] Remember that *resources* is a word that can have two meanings: It can be a short way of saying *natural resources* or a general reference analogous to the word *inputs*. Here we are using it in the second sense.

[2] See Chapter 4.

opportunity costs of building the path because society gives up nothing in devoting the old right-of-way to the new use.

We must also distinguish between opportunity costs and **transfer payments.** The latter are monetary amounts that flow from one person or group to another without affecting actual resource commitments or true opportunity costs. In Chapter 12 we discuss pollution taxes (sometimes call "charges"). This is where polluters are charged for whatever quantities of emissions they produce. In evaluating the social costs of this type of program, we would include any real costs that polluters incur to reduce their emissions. But the monetary charges they pay to the administering government agency are actually transfer payments going from one group (the polluting firms) to another (the beneficiaries of the tax payments).

Environmental Costs

It may seem paradoxical to think that environmental protection control programs might have environmental costs, but this is in fact the case. Most specific emissions-reduction programs are media based; that is, they are aimed at reducing emissions into one particular environmental medium such as air or water. So when emissions into one medium are reduced, they may increase into another. Reducing untreated domestic waste outflow into rivers or coastal oceans leaves quantities of solid waste that must then be disposed of, perhaps through land spreading or incineration. Reducing airborne sulfur dioxide (SO_2) emissions from power plants by stack-gas scrubbing also leaves a highly concentrated sludge that must be disposed of in some way. Incinerating domestic solid waste creates airborne emissions.

Media switches are not the only source of environmental impacts stemming from environmental improvement programs. There can be direct effects—for example, sediment runoff from construction sites for new treatment plants or sewer lines. There also can be unforeseen impacts when firms or consumers adjust to new programs. Gasoline producers eliminated lead in their product, but because consumers still insisted on high-powered performance they added other compounds, which ended up having environmental impacts in their own right. With the beginning of community programs to charge consumers for solid waste disposal, some have been faced with substantial increases in "midnight dumping," that is, illegal dumping along the sides of roads or in remote areas.

Some of the potential environmental impacts from these public projects or programs can be **mitigated;** that is, steps can be taken to reduce or avoid them. More enforcement resources can help control illegal dumping, extra steps can be taken to reduce construction-site impacts, special techniques may be available to reduce incinerator residuals, and so on. These mitigation costs must be included as part of the total costs of any project or program. Beyond this, any remaining environmental costs must be set against the overall reduction in environmental damages to which the program is primarily aimed.

Enforcement Costs

Environmental regulations are not self-enforcing. Resources must be devoted to monitoring the behavior of firms, agencies, and individuals subject to the regulations and to sanctioning violators. Public environmental facilities, such as wastewater treatment plants and incinerators, must be monitored to be sure they are being operated correctly.

There is an important application of the opportunity idea in the enforcement phenomenon. Many environmental laws are enforced by agencies whose enforcement budgets are not strictly tailored to the enforcement responsibilities they are given. Thus, budgets can be stable, or even declining, at the same time that new environmental laws are passed. Enforcing the new laws may require shifting agency resources away from the enforcement of other laws. In this case the opportunity costs of new enforcement must include the lower levels of compliance in areas that now are subject to less enforcement.

Costs of Single Facilities

Perhaps the easiest type of cost analysis to visualize is that for a single, engineered project of some type. There are many types of environmental quality programs that involve publicly supported construction of physical facilities (although the analysis would be the same whatever the ownership), such as public wastewater treatment plants, of which hundreds of millions of dollars' worth have been built over the last few decades. Other examples include flood control projects, solid-waste handling facilities, hazardous-waste incinerators, beach-restoration projects, public parks, wildlife refuges, and so on.

Facility-type projects such as these are individualized and substantially unique, although of course they have similar objectives and use technology that is similar to that used for many other projects. To estimate their costs, primary reliance is placed on engineering and technical specifications, developed largely through experience with similar types of facilities. The data of Table 8.1 show costs for a representative 200 megawatt land-based wind turbine power plant. These are based on survey and engineering data obtained by the National Renewable Energy Laboratory, a unit within the U.S. Department of Energy. Naturally these types of costs will vary depending on the location and topography of the plant site, as well as other factors. The rated capacity of the plant would be 200 megawatts, but how much power it actually produces during a year would of course depend on wind velocity and duration.

The table shows capital costs, the up-front costs of procuring and installing the turbines, along with the costs of connecting them to the grid. These are shown in total, and in annualized form. The latter are the capital costs allocated to one year's operation and depend on assumptions about the discount rate and years of life. The annual operation and maintenance costs are also shown.

In Table 8.1, estimated environmental costs have not been included. Costs of this type that have been identified in other studies include:

- Costs of wildlife disruption, especially birds
- Noise pollution
- Degradation of scenic values

TABLE 8.1   Typical Costs of a 105 Turbine, 200 Megawatt Wind Energy Plant

	Total ($1,000)	Annual ($1,000)
Capital Costs		
Site preparation	10,500	
Turbines	238,000	
Assembly	21,000	
Electrical infrastructure	31,000	
Finance	10,500	
Contingency	21,000	
Other	18,000	
Decommissioning	(not estimated)	
Total	350,000	28,000*
Annual Costs		
Operations		2,800
Maintenance		5,600
Land lease		1,600
Total		10,000
Environmental Costs	(not estimated)	
Capital costs per installed kw $1,750		

*Based on an interest rate of 5 percent and a life of 20 years.

Source: C. Moné et al, *2013 Cost of Wind Energy Review,* National Renewable Energy Laboratory, Technical Report NREL/TP-5000-63267, 2013.

These costs clearly will vary greatly from one site to another, and will be difficult to measure with convincing accuracy, especially as they are not directly observable in market transactions. We will discuss possible estimation methods in the next chapter.

With the exception of unmitigated environmental costs, these cost items are all expenditure figures, and only close inspection can tell if they represent true social opportunity costs. Suppose, for example, that in the construction phase numerous local unemployed people are hired. Although the construction costs include their wages, their opportunity costs would be zero because society had to give up nothing when they went to work on the plant. It might be that the land on which the plant is to be placed is town land that is to be donated. In this case there will be no specific cost entry for land, but there will be an opportunity cost related to the value the land could have had in its next best use. Suppose that the construction firm is able to get subsidized loans from local banks (i.e., borrow money at lower-than-market rates). Then the true opportunity costs of construction will be higher than the monetary costs indicated. This also goes for any operating costs that could potentially qualify for renewable energy subsidies. There are no specific rules for making these adjustments; only a knowledge of the specific situations can reveal when it is important enough to make them and where sufficient data are available to do the job.

Costs of a Local Regulation

Environmental regulations are frequently enacted at the local level and have an impact on local firms. In fact, in the political economy of pollution control, it is often the fear of these local impacts that deters communities from enacting the regulations. Fears of lost payrolls and the secondary losses to other firms from shrinking local markets loom large at the local level; from a national perspective the opportunity costs are less severe.

Suppose in a particular small town there is a large apple orchard that provides substantial local employment. Suppose further that presently the orchard managers use relatively large applications of chemicals to control apple pests and diseases, and that the chemical runoff from this activity threatens local water supplies. Assume the community enacts an ordinance requiring the orchard to practice **integrated pest management** (IPM), a lower level of chemical use coupled with other means to compensate for this reduction. Assume further, for purposes of illustration, that the IPM practices increase the costs of raising apples in this orchard.[3] What are the social costs of this regulation?

If the orchard raises and sells the same number of apples it previously did, the true social opportunity costs of the regulation are the increased production costs. If local consumers are willing to pay somewhat higher prices for locally grown apples, some of this cost gets passed on to these consumers. Suppose, however, that competitive conditions make it impossible for the orchard to sell its apples for any higher price than pertained before. In this case the higher production costs must be reflected in lower incomes of the apple orchard owners themselves, or perhaps of the orchard workers, if they will accept lower wages.

Suppose the orchard was just breaking even before the local IPM ordinance, and that the statute leads to such cost increases that production is substantially curtailed; in fact, assume for purposes of argument that the orchard goes out of business. Clearly there will be local costs: lost payrolls of orchard workers, lost income to the local orchard owners, lost income to local merchants because their markets shrink. But these lost incomes are not likely to be social opportunity costs in their entirety, unless the workers become permanently unemployed. Assuming other employment is available and they transfer to other job opportunities, their new incomes will offset, at least partly, the lost incomes they were earning previously. There may be certain valid opportunity costs in the form of adjustment costs, as workers and owners have to move to new places of employment.

What about the value of the apples no longer produced in this orchard? If we assume that there are many other orchards in neighboring towns and other regions to take up the slack with essentially no cost increases, then this lost production is offset by others, consumer prices are stable, and the social opportunity costs of this marginal rearrangement of apple production are basically nil.

To summarize, when we are dealing with a single local ordinance affecting one firm and the economy is at or near full employment, ensuing resource

---

[3] In fact, various authorities and scientific studies suggest that some IPM practices can actually lower costs relative to chemical-intensive growing techniques.

adjustments ensure that social opportunity costs are small, limited to the costs of actually carrying out the adjustments. From the standpoint of the affected community, of course, costs will seem high, because of lost local incomes brought about by the increased apple production costs.

Costs of Regulating an Industry

These conclusions do not follow when we impose an environmental regulation on an entire industry. Higher production costs for the industry are true social opportunity costs because they require added resources that could have been used elsewhere. But in dealing with whole industries, we cannot make the assumption, as we did with the one apple orchard, that its production could easily be picked up by the others.

Consider first the standard approach to estimating increased industry production costs, which is to measure the **added expenditures** that an industry would have to make to come into compliance with an environmental regulation. Cost estimation in this case requires the analyst to predict how polluters will respond to environmental regulations and then to estimate the costs of this response. If the regulation is very specific, requiring, for example, that manufacturing firms install a certain piece of pollution-control equipment or that farmers adopt certain cultivation practices to avoid soil runoff, the cost estimation may be fairly straightforward. But if the regulation leaves the polluters considerable latitude in making their response, it may be hard to predict exactly what they will do, and therefore what their costs will be.

Suppose, for example, several pulp mills are required to reduce their emissions by some percentage, and that we (a public agency) wish to estimate the impact of this on the production costs of the firms in the industry. In effect, we want to estimate the aggregate marginal abatement cost function for this group of firms. To do this with reasonable accuracy requires enough knowledge about the pulp business to be able to predict how the firms will respond, what treatment techniques they will use, how they might change their internal production processes, and so on. Or suppose we wanted to estimate the costs among farmers of a ban on a certain type of pest control chemical. In this case the analysis would want to identify the alternatives that farmers had available to replace this chemical, what impacts this would have on yields, how much additional labor and other inputs they would use, and so on.

An Example

The Clean Air Act requires that the EPA set emission standards for significant sources air pollutants. Wood burning heaters are significant sources of particulate matter, one of the most damaging air pollutants. In 2015, the EPA set standards for newly designed wood heaters. In setting the standards, based on a concept called "best system of emission reduction" (BSER) technology,[4] they

---

[4] Formerly known as "best demonstrated technology" (BDT).

are required to look at the costs the firms in the industry would likely experience in developing them. A common way to do this is to estimate the costs that a single firm in the industry would encounter, and then expand this to the entire industry.

Table 8.2 shows some of their results. In this case, since new devices are expected to be required, substantial upfront research and development (R&D) costs are required. There are also significant costs for testing and for EPA certification. There are five different types of wood heaters, and costs are expected to vary for each. The top part of the table shows data for wood stoves. The comparable data for other types are not shown. In the bottom part of the table, total costs per manufacturer are shown for each type; these are then expanded to the industry, as also shown in the table.

Note that these costs are incomplete in at least one sense. In regulatory programs of any type, public enforcement resources are required in order to get large-scale compliance by the regulated firms. Table 8.2 contains nothing about these costs, but in a full social benefit–cost analysis, they obviously would have to be included.

Sources of Cost Data

Where does one get the cost data necessary to construct these representative firms? Many of the basic data are generated through **cost surveys** of existing firms. In effect, questionnaires are sent out to these firms asking them to supply information on number of employees, processes used, costs of energy and materials, and so on. With a sufficiently detailed questionnaire and a reasonably

TABLE 8.2   Cost Estimates for Developing New Wood Burning Heaters to Meet Stricter Particulate Emission Rates

Development Costs for "Best System of Emission Reduction" ($)		
R&D Engineering Costs		
Prototype design	$32,250	
Tooling	33,475	
Other	10,000	
Total		*$136,475*
EPA testing, certification	19,400	
Total		*155,875*
Annualized Capital Cost (6 yrs., 7%)		*32,702*
Total Costs for All Wood Burning Stoves ($)		
	Typical Manufacturer	**All Manufacturers**
Wood stoves	$88,968	$3,020,000
Single burn heaters	352,506	870,000
Pellet stoves	51,179	1,520,000
Forced-air furnace	2,986,523	15,360,000
Hydronic system	828,513	24,880,000
Total		*45,660,000*

Source: USEPA, *Regulatory Impact Analysis for Residential Wood Heater Final Report,* EPA-452/R-15-001, Feb. 2015, pp. 5–8 to 5–10.

high response rate by firms, researchers hope to get a good idea of basic cost conditions in the industry and how they might be affected by environmental regulations.

One problem with cost surveys is that they are usually better at getting information on past cost data than on future costs under new regulations. Firms can probably report past cost data with more reliability than they can estimate future costs of meeting environmental constraints. Historical data may not be a good guide to the future, especially because environmental regulations almost by definition confront firms with novel situations. In these cases it is common to supplement survey data with technical engineering data that can be better adapted to costing out the new techniques and procedures that firms may adopt.

The "representative firm" approach, although dictated by the large number of firms in an industry, has its own problems, especially when those firms are substantially heterogeneous among themselves. In following this procedure, for example, the EPA runs into the problem of whether costs of the real plants in the industry, each of which is to some degree unique, can be accurately represented by a composite cost estimate. In this case *accurately* means close enough that individual firms will not be inclined to take the agency to court on grounds that their own unique cost situations are misrepresented by the figures for the "representative" firm. Many court battles have been fought over this issue.

Misrepresentation of Costs

Because the regulated firms themselves are the source of much cost data used to develop the regulations, there is clearly a question of whether these firms will supply accurate data. By overstating the costs of reaching certain reductions in emissions, firms may hope to convince agencies to promulgate weaker regulations than they would if the agencies had an accurate idea of costs. It is a very common sight in public hearings on establishing emission-control regulations to see firms making vigorous claims that the regulations will be unduly costly for them to meet. There is evidence that many of these claims have been exaggerated in the past. This issue will come up numerous times when we examine the incentives surrounding different types of environmental policies. In effect, regulated firms have private information about their costs that regulating agencies often don't have.

Actual Versus Minimum Pollution-Control Costs

The costs shown in Table 8.2 show the estimated costs of the plywood veneer sector meeting the environmental standards imposed by law. There is an important question of whether these costs are the *least* costs necessary to achieve the emission reductions sought in the law. This is an important point because, as we saw in Chapter 5, the efficient level of emissions or ambient quality is defined by the trade-off of emission abatement costs and environmental damages. If abatement costs used to define the efficient level are higher than they need to be, the point so defined will be only a **pseudo-efficient** outcome.

When there is a single facility involved, we must rely on engineering judgment to ensure that the technical proposal represents the least costly way of achieving the objectives. When what is involved is an entire industry, both technical and economic factors come into play. As discussed earlier, in order for the overall costs of a given emission reduction to be achieved at minimum cost, the equimarginal principle has to be fulfilled. Frequently, environmental regulations work against this by dictating that different sources adopt essentially the same levels of emission reductions or install the same general types of pollution-control technology. As will be seen in later chapters, many environmental laws are based on administratively specified operating decisions that firms are required to make. These decisions may not lead, or allow, firms to achieve emission abatement at least cost. Thus, industry costs such as those depicted in Table 8.2 may not represent minimum abatement costs.

There is no easy way out of this dilemma. If one is called on to do a benefit–cost analysis of a particular environmental regulation, one presumably is committed to evaluating the regulation as given. In cases such as this it would no doubt be good policy for the analyst to point out that there are less costly ways of achieving the benefits.

The Effect of Output Adjustments on Costs

The increase in abatement expenditures may not be an accurate measure of opportunity costs when an entire industry is involved. This is because **market adjustments** are likely to alter the role and performance of the industry in the wider economy. For example, when the costs of a competitive industry increase, the price of its output increases, normally causing a reduction in quantity demanded. This is pictured in Figure 8.1, which shows supply and demand curves for two industries. For convenience, the supply curves have been drawn horizontally, representing marginal production costs that do not vary with output. Consider first panel (a). The initial supply function is C_1, so the initial quantity produced is q_1. The pollution-control law causes production costs to rise, represented by a shift upward in supply from curve C_1 to C_2. Suppose we calculate the increased cost of producing the initial rate of output. This would be an amount equal to the area $(a + b + c)$. The comparable cost in panel (b) is $(d + e + f)$. This approach to measuring costs, however, will overstate the true cost increase because when costs and prices go up, quantity demanded and output will decline.

How much output declines is a matter of the steepness of the demand curve. In panel (a), output declines only from q_1 to q_2, but in panel (b), with the flatter demand curve, output will decline from r_1 to r_2, a much larger amount. The correct measure of the cost to society is $(a + b)$ in panel (a) and $(d + e)$ in panel (b). Note that the original approach to cost estimation, calculating the increased cost of current output, is a much better approximation to the true burden on society in panel (a) than in panel (b). This is because the output adjustment is much larger in the latter. The lesson here is that if increased expenditures are to be taken as true opportunity costs, they must be calculated taking into account price and output adjustments that occur in the industries affected by the environmental regulations.

FIGURE 8.1 **Output Adjustments in Industries Subject to Pollution-Control Regulations**

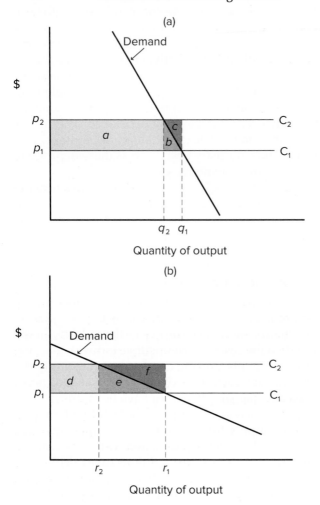

Figure 8.1 also can illustrate something about the distribution of pollution-control costs. Firms in the affected industries bear these costs in the beginning, but the final burden depends on how the cost increase is passed forward to consumers or backward to workers and stockholders. Note that in both panels (a) and (b) the market prices of the goods increased by the amount of the cost increase, but the response is quite different. In panel (a) consumers continue buying close to what they did before; little adjustment is called for in terms of output shrinkage in the industry. Thus, workers and shareholders in this industry will be little affected, in relative terms. In panel (b) the same price increase leads to a large drop in output. Consumers have good substitutes to which they can switch when the price of this output goes up; in effect, they can escape the

full burden of the price increase. The industry adjustment, however, is large. Resources, particularly workers, will have to flow out of the industry and try to find employment elsewhere. If they can, the costs may be only temporary adjustment costs; if not, the costs will be much longer run.

Long-Run Technical Change and Pollution-Control Costs

In the short run, firms must make whatever adjustments they can within the constraints of available technology and operating procedures. In the long run, however, costs can change because these technologies and procedures can be altered. Scientific and engineering **research and development** yield new and better (less costly) ways of controlling emissions. Some are straightforward, such as a new way of handling and treating residuals; some are more profound, such as a change in the basic technology of production so that fewer residuals are produced in the first place. When firms are subject to emission reduction requirements, they have an incentive to engage in R&D to find better emissions abatement technology. There is some evidence that in reality this may draw resources away from output-increasing R&D efforts, thereby affecting the firm's ability to reduce costs in the long run. There is also evidence, however, that environmental regulations have led to unanticipated, marketable products or processes stemming from their research. Some studies have even shown that after investing in pollution-control R&D, some firms have reduced their long-run production costs. In cases such as this, the short-run cost increases arising from pollution-control regulations are not accurate estimates of the long-run opportunity costs of these regulations.

Critical to the success of any effort to innovate in pollution-control technology is the economic health of the **envirotech industry.** This is the industry consisting of firms producing goods and services that are used by other firms to reduce their emissions and environmental impacts. It also contains firms that engage in environmental cleanup, such as the cleanup of past hazardous-waste dump sites. A healthy envirotech industry is one that produces a brisk supply of new pollution-control technology and practices. The growth of this industry over time will have a lot to do with how fast marginal abatement costs come down in the future (see Exhibit 8.1).

Costs at the National Level

We finally come to the most aggregative level for which cost studies are normally pursued, the level of the **national economy.** The usual question of interest is the extent of the macroeconomic cost burden of the environmental regulations a country imposes, or might be planning to impose, in a given period of time. Sometimes interest centers on the totality of the regulations put in place. Sometimes the focus is on specific regulations that will nevertheless have a broad impact on a national economy, such as a program of carbon dioxide (CO_2) emissions reduction.

The Environmental Industry

EXHIBIT 8.1

The U.S. environmental industry had total revenues of over $316 billion in 2010 and employed more than 1.6 million people. These are substantially higher than the comparable numbers of 1990, as the following data indicate. More than half of the industry actually comprises services, whereas the rest are technology and equipment based. The early growth of the industry was based on cleaning up the sins of the past, or controlling emissions from outdated facilities. Growth in the future will depend more on developments in pollution prevention.

Environmental Industry—Revenues and Employment, by Industry Segment: 1980 to 2010
[59.0 represents $59,000,000,000. Covers approximately 59,000 private and public companies engaged in environmental activities.]

Industry Segment	Revenue (bil. dol.)			Employment (1,000)		
	1990	2002	2010	1990	2002	2010
Industry total	152.3	221.3	316.3	1,223.8	1,510.0	1,657.3
Analytical services[1]	1.5	1.3	1.8	18.0	15.0	19.2
Wastewater treatment works[2]	19.8	30.2	46.9	88.8	123.7	178.9
Solid-waste management[3]	26.1	42.7	52.4	205.5	284.4	271.2
Hazardous-waste management[4]	6.3	4.7	8.7	53.9	38.6	42.0
Remediation/industrial services	11.1	11.1	12.2	133.3	105.9	101.0
Consulting and engineering	12.5	18.7	26.2	147.1	193.7	242.0
Water equipment and chemicals	13.5	20.8	27.2	92.7	135.3	159.3
Instrument manufacturing	2.0	3.9	5.5	18.0	30.9	37.5
Air-pollution control equipment[5]	13.1	18.6	14.9	96.4	126.0	95.6
Waste-management equipment[6]	8.7	9.9	11.1	69.6	74.1	73.7
Process and prevention technology	0.4	1.4	1.9	9.3	30.9	26.4
Water utilities[7]	19.8	32.3	42.1	98.5	139.1	167.2
Resource recovery[8]	13.1	14.1	25.2	142.9	110.1	91.5
Clean energy systems and power[9]	4.3	11.5	40.1	49.9	102.3	150.9

[1] Covers environmental laboratory testing and services.

[2] Mostly revenues collected by municipal entities.

[3] Covers such activities as collection, transportation, transfer stations, disposal, landfill ownership, and management for solid waste.

[4] Transportation and disposal of hazardous, medical, and nuclear waste.

[5] Includes stationary and mobile sources.

[6] Includes vehicles, containers, liners, processing, and remediation equipment.

[7] Revenues generated from the sale of water.

[8] Revenues generated from the sale of recovered metals, paper, plastic, and so on.

[9] Includes solar, wind, geothermal, and conservation devices.

Source: Environmental Business International, Inc., San Diego, CA, *Environmental Business Journal*, monthly (copyright) (as published in *Statistical Abstract of the United States: 1999*, p. 251, 2003, and 2012, p. 232).

There are basically two ways of approaching this question: **bottom up** and **top down.** The bottom-up approach looks at expenditures made throughout the economy for pollution-control purposes. Firms in the economy are subject to a number of pollution-control regulations. In response they install and operate a wide variety of technological means to reduce emissions. These expenditures detract from other outputs (assuming full employment) because of the input diversion. Economy-wide surveys can be done to estimate the size of these pollution-control expenditures. Some results are shown in Table 8.3, which presents pollution abatement costs (PAC) as a proportion of gross domestic product (GDP) for a number of economies around 2007. These ranged from a low of 0.5 percent in Australia to a high of 2.0 percent in Austria.

In the long run, numbers such as these may not give an entirely accurate picture of how pollution controls are affecting the national economy. More information would be useful about how PACs impact various sectors of the economy, as well as different firms within the same industry sector. It is sometimes asserted that environmental regulations affect smaller firms disproportionately more than large firms. Some recent research suggests this is not the case, but rather that large firms spend more on pollution control than do small firms.[5] In addition, expenditures for plant, equipment, labor, and other inputs for reducing emissions can affect other economic sectors not directly covered by environmental regulations, and macroeconomic interactions of this type need

TABLE 8.3   Pollution-Control Expenditures (PACs) as a Percentage of Gross Domestic Product (GDP), Selected Organization for Economic Cooperation and Development (OECD) Countries, Latest Available Year

Country	PAC as Percentage of GDP
Australia	0.5
Austria	2.0
Canada	1.2
Denmark	1.8
France	1.3
Germany	1.6
Japan	1.4
Mexico	0.7
Sweden	1.1
Turkey	1.1
United Kingdom	0.6
United States	1.6

Source: Organization for Economic Cooperation and Development, "Pollution Abatement and Control Expenditure in OECD Countries," ENV/EPO/SE (2007), Paris, March 6, 2007.

[5] Randy Becker, Carl Pasurka Jr. and Ronald J. Shadbegian, *Do Environmental Regulation Disproportionately Affect Small Businesses? Evidence form the Pollution Abatement Costs and Expenditure Survey*, Center for Economic Studies, U.S. Census Bureau, CES12-25R, August 2013.

to be accounted for to get the complete picture. An industry subject to environmental controls, and trying to lower its emissions, puts increasing demand on the pollution-control industry, which expands output and puts increasing demands on other sectors, for example, the construction sector, which respond by increasing output.

The long-run economic change—growth or decline—is a matter of the accumulation of capital: human capital and inanimate capital. It also depends on technical change, getting larger amounts of output from a given quantity of inputs. So an important question is how environmental laws will affect the accumulation of capital and the rate of technical innovation. Diverting inputs from conventional sectors to pollution-control activities may lower the rate of capital accumulation in those conventional sectors. This may be expected to reduce the rate of growth of productivity (output per unit of input) in the production of conventional output and thus slow overall growth rates. The impacts on the rate of technical innovation in the economy are perhaps more ambiguous, as mentioned previously. If attempts to innovate in pollution control reduce the efforts to do so in other sectors, the impact on future growth could be negative; however, efforts to reduce emissions might have a positive impact on the overall rate of technical innovation, which would have a positive impact. More research is needed on this question.

The standard way to proceed in working out these relationships is through a top-down analysis using **macroeconomic modeling.** The basic question is whether, and how much, pollution-control expenditures have resulted in a lowering of national economic performance. To explore this, mathematical models are constructed using the various macroeconomic variables of interest, such as total output, perhaps broken down into several economic subsectors: employment, capital investment, prices, pollution-control costs, and so on. The models are first run using historical data, which show how various underlying factors have contributed to the overall rate of growth in the economy. Then they are rerun under the assumption that the pollution-control expenditures were in fact not made. This comes out with new results in terms of aggregate output growth, employment, and so on, which can be compared with the first run. The differences are attributed to the pollution-control expenditures.

Future Costs and Technological Change

Many of the big controversies in environmental policy involve differences of opinion about what future pollution-control costs are likely to be, especially the future cost consequences of today's decisions. A good example of this is the cost of CO_2 emission reduction to reduce the effects of global warming. In the United States, much of the stated opposition to undertaking vigorous reductions in CO_2 stems from a concern that the future costs of doing so will be too high. Others say that the costs need not be high if the most effective policy approaches are used.

If the time horizon is short, future costs will depend on the adoption by polluters of currently available technologies. These technologies may be reasonably well known (e.g., catalytic converters in cars), in which case it will not be too hard to estimate what these new pollution-control costs will be. Much of the earlier discussion in this chapter is based on this perspective.

But when the relevant time horizon is longer, say 10 years or more (as it surely is with global warming), it is no longer easy to know what technological changes will occur, when they will be available for widespread adoption, and what impact they will have on pollution-control costs. Much discussion and research have been directed at the idea of a large-scale changeover to a hydrogen fuel system in cars and trucks, for example. But it is not easy to see when that might arrive and what its impacts may be, or whether other technologies may be more appropriate and feasible. In the long run, in other words, estimating future costs is likely to be very difficult.

One of the important aspects of this is how research, development, and adoption of new pollution-control technologies respond to environmental policies and regulations. This is a topic we will encounter a number of times in the next section dealing with the different types of pollution-control policies.

Summary

In this chapter we reviewed some of the ways that costs are estimated in benefit–cost studies. We began with a discussion of the fundamental concept of opportunity costs, differentiating this from the notion of cost as expenditure. We then looked at cost estimation as it applies to different levels of economic activity. The first was a cost analysis of a single facility, as represented by the estimated costs of a wastewater treatment facility. We then considered the costs of an environmental regulation undertaken by a single community, distinguishing between costs to the community and opportunity costs to the whole society.

We then shifted focus to cost estimation for an entire industry, giving special attention to the difference between short-run and long-run costs and the problem of achieving minimum costs. We finally expanded our perspective to the national economy as a whole, where cost means the loss in value of marketed output resulting from environmental regulations.

Questions for Further Discussion

1. Over the last two years, emission abatement costs in industry X have been about $1 million per year. A new regulation will lead to abatement costs of $1.8 million per year. Does this mean that the regulation will cause increased abatement costs of $800,000 per year? Explain.
2. In order to protect the quality of its nearby water resources, a community places a restriction on any housing development closer than 100 feet to a wetland. How might you estimate the social costs of this regulation?

3. "The costs of achieving emission reductions in the future will depend greatly on the types of policies used to reduce emissions today." Explain.

4. A tax on gasoline is proposed in order to raise money for the pollution-control activities of several public agencies. The tax will be 10¢ per gallon, and last year 10.3 million gallons of gasoline were used by motorists (this is strictly an illustrative number). Does this mean that we can anticipate $1,030,000 in revenues from this tax? Explain and use a graph to answer this question.

5. Most industries are composed of firms that, though perhaps producing roughly the same thing, are very different; some are large and some small; some are profitable and others not; some are located in one part of the country and some in others; some perhaps have undertaken a certain amount of voluntary emissions reductions and some have not; and so on. How does this complicate the job of estimating the total social costs of pollution-control regulations?

For additional readings and Web sites pertaining to the material in this chapter, see **www.mhhe.com/field7e.**

Section 4

Environmental Policy Analysis

The public policy problem arises when there is a discrepancy between the actual level of environmental quality and the preferred level. How can this state of affairs be changed? Something has to be done to change the way people behave on both the production and consumption sides of the system. The available public policy approaches for doing this are as follows:

Decentralized policies
    Liability laws
    Changes in property rights
    Voluntary action
    Command-and-control policies
    Standards
Market-based policies
    Taxes and subsidies
    Transferable discharge permits

In the chapters of this section we discuss each of these policy approaches, but before that we must address briefly a prior question: What criteria are appropriate to evaluate alternative policies and identify the one best suited to any particular environmental problem? We consider a number of these criteria in the next chapter, then analyze in depth the specific policy approaches just listed.

Chapter 9

Criteria for Evaluating Environmental Policies

There are many different types of environmental policies. Each type antici-pates that administrators and polluters will respond in particular ways. Each type has specific characteristics that make it more likely to succeed in some circumstances and not in others. When we evaluate the effectiveness and appropriateness of a policy for addressing a given problem in environmen-tal pollution control, it is important to have clearly in mind a set of **policy evaluation criteria.**[1] The criteria to be used in later chapters to discuss specific environmental policies are the following:

- Efficiency
- Cost-effectiveness
- Fairness
- Enforceability
- Flexibility
- Incentives for technological innovations
- Moral Considerations

Efficiency

A state of affairs is efficient if it is one that produces for society a maximum of net benefits. Note that we have said "society." Efficiency is sometimes miscon-strued to mean the maximum of somebody's net income. Although efficiency does not rule that out, it involves substantially more than this; it involves the maximum of net benefits, considering everybody in the society.

---

[1] Another way of describing the content of this chapter is as a discussion of "instrument choices." "Instrument" is a term often used to describe a specific type of action plan in an environmental law or regulation. We will use "instrument" as synonymous with "policy."

Efficiency in the case of pollution control implies a balance between abatement costs and damages. An efficient policy is one that moves us to, or near, the point (either of emissions or of ambient quality) where marginal abatement costs and marginal damages are equal.

One way of thinking about environmental policies is along a continuum from **centralized** to **decentralized.** A centralized policy requires that some controlling administrative agency be responsible for determining what is to be done. To achieve efficiency in a centralized policy, the regulatory agency in charge must have knowledge of the relevant marginal abatement cost and marginal damage functions, then take steps to move the situation to the point where they are equal.

A decentralized policy gets results from the interaction of many individual decision makers, each of whom is essentially making his or her own assessment of the situation. In a decentralized approach, the interactions of the individuals involved serve to reveal the relevant information about marginal abatement costs and marginal damages and to adjust the situation toward the point where they are equal.

Cost-Effectiveness

It is often the case that environmental damages cannot be measured accurately. This sometimes makes it useful to employ **cost-effectiveness** as a primary policy criterion. A policy is cost-effective if it produces the maximum environmental improvement possible for the resources being expended or, equivalently, it achieves a given amount of environmental improvement at the least possible cost. For a policy to be efficient it must be cost-effective, but not necessarily vice versa. A policy might be cost-effective even if it were aimed at the wrong target. Suppose the objective is to clean up New York harbor, regardless of what the benefits are. We would still be interested in finding policies that did the job cost-effectively; however, for a policy to be socially efficient, it must not only be cost-effective, but also balance costs with benefits. To be efficient, the harbor-cleaning project must balance marginal benefits with marginal cleanup costs.

The capability of a policy to achieve cost-effective emission reductions (i.e., yield the maximum improvement for the resources spent) is also important for another reason. If programs are not cost-effective, the policymakers and administrators will be making decisions using an aggregate abatement cost function that is higher than it needs to be, leading them to set less restrictive targets in terms of desired amounts of emission reductions. This is shown in Figure 9.1, for a case of sulfur dioxide (SO_2) emissions. With a *cost-ineffective* policy, the perceived marginal abatement cost is the higher one, labeled MAC_1; whereas with a cost-effective approach, marginal abatement costs would be MAC_2. Thus, with the MD function as shown, the emissions level a_1 appears to be the efficient level of pollution, whereas with a cost-effective program, the efficient level would be a_2. The real problem with having costs higher than they need

FIGURE 9.1 Mistaking the Efficient Emissions Level When Abatement Technologies Are Not Cost-Effective

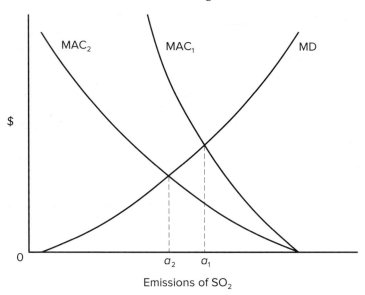

to be is that society will be inclined to set its objectives too low in terms of the amount of emission reduction sought.

Efficiency and cost-effectiveness are important because although preserving environmental resources is critically important, it is only one of the many desirable things that people seek. Advocates are usually convinced that their objectives are automatically worth the cost, but success depends on persuading large numbers of other people that environmental policies are efficiently designed. Thus, the resources devoted to environmental quality improvement ought to be spent in ways that will have the greatest impact. This is especially important in less developed economies, where people have fewer resources to put in environmental programs and can ill-afford policies that are not cost-effective and efficient. Cost-effectiveness also becomes an important issue in industrialized countries during times of recession or economic stagnation.

Cost-effectiveness (and efficiency, as cost-effectiveness is part of efficiency) clearly involves pollution-control costs in a major way. But accurate information about pollution-control costs is for the most part **private information** in a market system. Public policymakers typically do not have totally accurate information about the pollution-control costs that firms and industries face in the real world. What we have here is what economists call **asymmetric information**; polluters have better information about the costs of different pollution-control technologies than do public policymakers. As we shall see, different types of pollution-control policies create different levels of incentives for polluters to achieve cost-effective pollution control by making full use of their own private information regarding the costs of alternative pollution-control technologies.

Fairness

Fairness, or **equity**, is another important criterion for evaluating environmental policy (or any policy, for that matter). Equity is, first and foremost, a matter of morality and the concerns about how the benefits and costs of environmental improvements ought to be distributed among members of society. Fairness is also important from the standpoint of policy effectiveness, because policies may not be supported as enthusiastically in the political arena if they are thought to be inequitable. Having said this, however, it has to be recognized that there is no agreement on how much weight should be put on the two objectives: efficiency and distribution. Consider the following hypothetical numbers, which might relate, for example, to the costs and benefits of several alternative approaches to air-pollution control in a given region.

Program	Total Costs	Total Benefits	Net Benefits	Distribution of Net Benefits	
				Group X	Group Y
A	50	100	50	25	25
B	50	100	50	30	20
C	50	140	90	20	70
D	50	140	90	40	50

The first three columns show total costs, total benefits, and net benefits, respectively. Suppose Group X and Group Y refer to a low-income group and a high-income group, respectively. Programs A and B have the same net benefits, but these are distributed more progressively in B than in A, i.e., Group X (low-income) receives more of the net benefits than Group Y. We might agree that B is preferable to A because it has the same net benefits and "better" distributional effects. But compare Programs B and C. The net benefits of Program C are much higher than in B. Unfortunately, they are not distributed as progressively as those of B; in fact, they are distributed more toward high-income people (70 vs. 20). How should we choose between B and C? Some might argue that B is best, for equity reasons; others might argue for C on overall efficiency grounds.

Now compare Programs B and D. In this case, D has the advantage in overall efficiency (net benefits are 90), although, as in the case of C, more of the net benefits go to high-income people (50 vs. 40). Here we also see that low-income people would be better off in absolute terms, although not relatively, with D than with B. On these grounds, D might be preferred.

Suppose, on the other hand, that Group X and Group Y refer to people in two different regions of the country. Now we see that there is an issue of **interregional equity**. If we knew, for example, that the Group Y region was where the problem originated that is being addressed by these possible programs, C and D might definitely be regarded as inequitable, because most of the net benefits go to this region.

Equity considerations also loom large in the making of international environmental policy. As we will discuss later in chapters on global and international environmental problems, countries at different stages of development have different views on how the burdens of international pollution-control programs should be distributed. These views are driven by considerations of what seems fair in the light of the wide economic disparities around the globe.

The Idea of "Social"

We have talked about efficiency, equity, and other criteria somewhat in the abstract. It has to be kept in mind that when we talk about such concepts in "social efficiency," we must have some particular "society" in mind. If we are discussing global issues, the reference is presumably to the entire global society. But most environmental policy discussions and controversies take place at a lower level, especially national units or, increasingly, subnational regions. In the United States, the individual states are playing a growing role in environmental policy, as major federal initiatives slowed. What is socially efficient from the perspective of a single state may not be from a national viewpoint because, for example, a state may not take account of externalities running to other states. When evaluating different environmental regulations and programs, one has to keep in mind the perspective from which this evaluation is done.

Environmental Justice

Equity considerations are behind what has recently become prominent as the movement for **environmental justice**. The concern is that racial minorities and low-income people are disproportionately exposed to environmental contaminants, both those outside the home such as air and water pollution and those within the home and workplace such as lead. The primary concern has been largely about exposure to the pollutants coming from hazardous-waste sites. The question is whether hazardous-waste sites are disproportionately located in areas where there are relatively large populations of low-income people and people of color and, if that is so, what to do about it from a policy perspective. We will take up these matters at greater length in Chapter 16.

Enforceability

There perhaps is a natural tendency among people to think that enacting a law automatically leads to the rectification of the problem to which it is addressed. Among some in the environmental community, this tendency is depressingly strong. But anybody with even a cursory understanding of public policy knows this is not true. Regulations have to be **enforced**. Enforcement takes time and resources, just like any other activity, and because public budgets are always limited, the requirements of enforcement have to be balanced with those of other

The Importance of Enforcement   EXHIBIT 9.1

Following are excerpts from a General Accounting Office (GAO) report on EPA efforts to enforce regulations on the export of electronic waste.

U.S. hazardous waste regulations have not deterred exports of potentially hazardous used electronics, primarily for the following reasons:

- *Existing EPA regulations focus only on CRTs [cathode-ray tubes].* Other exported used electronics flow virtually unrestricted, even to countries where they can be mismanaged, in large part because relevant U.S. hazardous waste regulations assess only how products will react in unlined U.S. landfills.

- *Companies easily circumvent EPA's CRT rule.* Posing as foreign buyers of broken CRTs in Hong Kong, India, Pakistan, and other countries, GAO found 43 U.S. companies that expressed willingness to export such CRTs. Some of the companies, including ones that publicly tout their exemplary environmental practices, were willing to export CRTs in apparent violation of the CRT rule. GAO provided EPA with the names of these companies at EPA's request.

- *EPA's enforcement is lacking.* Since the CRT rule took effect in January 2007, Hong Kong officials intercepted and returned to U.S. ports 26 containers of illegally exported CRTs. EPA has since penalized one violator, and then only long after the shipment was identified by GOA. EPA officials acknowledged CRT rule compliance problems but said that given the rule's relative newness, they were focusing on educating the regulated community. This explanation, however, is undermined by GAO's observation of the apparent willingness by many companies to violate the rule, even by those aware of it. Finally, EPA has done little to ascertain the extent of non-compliance, and EPA officials told us that they have neither plans nor a timetable to develop an enforcement program.

Source: U.S. General Accounting Office Electronic Waste, GAO-08-1166T, Washington, D.C., Sept. 17, 2008.

---

public functions.[2] The importance of the issues can be appreciated by looking at reports of Environmental protection Agency (EPA) enforcement problems, one of which is summarized in Exhibit 9.1. All of this means that policy enforceability is an important criterion for judging particular policies.

There are two main steps in enforcement: **monitoring** and **sanctioning**. Monitoring refers to measuring the performance of polluters in comparison to whatever requirements are set out in the relevant law. The objective of enforcement is to get people to comply with an applicable law. Thus, some amount of monitoring is normally essential; the only policy for which this does not hold is that of moral suasion. Monitoring polluting behavior is far more complicated than,

---

[2] It is also clear that enforcement is a political football. Public officials can increase or decrease enforcement activity to match their positions on how stringent environmental regulations ought to be.

say, keeping track of the temperature. Nature doesn't really care, and so it won't willfully try to outwit and confound the monitoring process. Polluters, however, can often find ways of frustrating the monitoring process. The more sophisticated and complicated that process, the easier it may be for polluters to find ways of evading it. In recent years, great strides have been made in developing monitoring technology, particularly for large sources of airborne and waterborne pollutants.

Sanctioning refers to the task of bringing to justice those whom monitoring has shown to be in violation of the law. This may sound like a simple step; if violators are found, we simply take them to court and levy the penalties specified in the relevant law, but things are much more complicated than this. Court cases take time and energy and resources. With many laws and many more violators, the burden on the legal system of trying to bring all violators to justice may be overwhelming. In many cases the data underlying the sanctions will be imperfect, leading to challenges and costly conflicts. To create a demonstration effect it may be desirable for authorities to sanction only a few of the most egregious violations, but this opens up the problem of trying to determine just which violators to single out. Very often authorities try to achieve voluntary compliance and encourage violators to remedy the situation without penalty.

There is a paradox built into the sanctioning process. One might think that the greater the potential sanctions—higher fines, long jail terms for violators, and so on—the more the law would deter violators. But the other side of the coin is that the higher the penalties, the more reluctant courts may be to apply them. The threat to close down violators, or even to levy stiff financial penalties, can in turn threaten the economic livelihoods of large numbers of people. Courts are usually reluctant to throw a large number of people out of work, and so may opt for less drastic penalties than allowed by the law. So the sanctioning process can become much more complicated than the simple model implies.

Flexibility

A valuable characteristic of any policy or instrument is that it be sufficiently flexible to be adapted to changing circumstances. Most environmental regulations are put in place in accordance with what is known about the situation to which they are applied, for example, the known or estimated benefits and costs of the case. When these change, for example, new estimates of benefits and/or costs become available, the policies ought to be altered. In the real world of policy institutions and political strength, policies that meet stringent efficiency criteria may be less effective in the long run than policies that may be less efficient but easier to adapt to new circumstances.

It has recently been argued, for example, that the command-and-control provisions of the Clean Air Act, though somewhat inefficient if looked at in the short run, have been substantially more efficient in the long run.[3] This is

---

[3] Dallas Burtraw, *The Institutional Blind Spot in Environmental Economics*, Resources for the Future, Discussion paper 12–41, August 2012.

because it contains an array of provisions that permit its frequent adjustment and adaptation to new circumstances. A cap-and-trade plan, for example, may be efficient at first, but not over time if the overall cap cannot be readily adjusted as underlying conditions change.

Incentives for Technological Innovations

In our studies of environmental policy, much of the focus normally gets put on the performance of public officials because they appear to be the source of that policy. What needs to be kept clearly in mind, however, is that it is private parties, firms, and consumers whose decisions actually determine the range and extent of environmental impacts,[4] and the incentives facing these private parties determine how and where these impacts will be reduced. Thus, a critically important criterion that must be used to evaluate any environmental policy is whether that policy provides a strong **incentive** for individuals and groups to find **new, innovative ways of reducing their impacts** on the ambient environment. Does the policy place all the initiative and burden on public agencies, or does it provide incentives for private parties to devote their energies and creativities to finding new ways of reducing environmental impacts?

It is easy to miss the importance of this by concentrating on particular abatement cost and damage functions in the standard analysis. These show the efficient level of emissions with current technology, but over the longer run it is important that we try to shift the functions with new technology. It is especially important to try to shift downward the marginal abatement cost function, to make it cheaper to secure reductions in emissions, because this will justify higher levels of environmental quality. Technological change, flowing from programs of research and development (R&D), shifts the marginal abatement cost function downward. So do education and training, which allow people to work and solve problems more efficiently. So ultimately we want to know whether, and how much, a particular environmental policy contains incentives for polluters to seek better ways of reducing pollution. The greater these incentives, the better the policy, at least by this one criterion. As we shall see, a major criticism of much of historic environmental policy has been that it does not create strong incentives of this type to find improved solutions.

The development and widespread adoption of new pollution-control technology is a complex socioeconomic process. It involves resources being devoted to invention and development, patent and copyright laws, decisions about adoption by existing and new sources, as well as by firms that supply portions of necessary infrastructure for the new technologies. Inventions, and the ideas giving rise to them, are in the nature of public goods, and we saw earlier that private markets will normally undersupply public goods—which means that the rate of technological change in pollution control may be too slow in the absence of the public policy to promote it.

---

[4] However, many serious cases of environmental destruction have been caused by public agencies.

A major factor here is the incentive effect produced by stringent pollution-control regulations. It is hard to suppose, for example, that society will get enough effort devoted to technical change to reduce the cost of carbon dioxide (CO_2) emission reductions if there is essentially no public policy requiring that these emissions be reduced. In some cases policymakers may utilize **technology-forcing** regulations—that is, regulations that will require polluters to find innovative technology in order to meet pollution-control targets with reasonable cost.

A major factor in technological innovation is the status of the **envirotech industry**. As shown in the last chapter,[5] this industry consists of a wide variety of firms that produce new technology and operating procedures for use by polluting firms to help reduce their emissions more cost-effectively. The health and vigor of the envirotech industry, therefore, is of paramount importance for long-run improvements in technology. The economic health of this industry is directly related to the nature and stringency of environmental regulations.

Materials Balance Issues

Remembering back to Chapter 2, we need to remind ourselves of the **materials-balance** aspects of pollution control. Given a certain quantity of residuals, if the flow going into one environmental medium (e.g., the water) is reduced, the flow going into the others (air and/or land) must increase. Thus, one important dimension of a pollution-control policy is how well it addresses these potential **cross-media transfer** problems. The first thing is to be able to recognize cases where important problems of this nature might be encountered. The next thing is to shape the policies so as to reduce their potential impact. This might be done, for example, by simply proscribing certain actions or, if enough information is available, by specifying acceptable trade-offs across technologies and environmental media—that is, by allowing only transfers that substantially reduce total damages from a given quantity of residuals.

Moral Considerations

We earlier discussed questions of income distribution and the impacts of different environmental policies on people with different levels of wealth. These are ethical issues on which different people will have varied opinions, but they are important to discuss when deciding on alternative public policies. But moral considerations extend beyond these distributional questions. The innate feelings that people have about what is right and wrong undoubtedly affect the way they look at different environmental policies. These have to be weighed in the balance along with the more technical criteria discussed previously.

---

[5] See Exhibit 8.1.

Take, for example, the question of choosing between effluent taxes and effluent subsidies. Both are economic-incentive-type policies, and both might have roughly the same effect in given cases of pollution control. From the standpoint of effectiveness, one might argue that subsidies would be better. Polluters might very well respond quicker and with greater willingness to a subsidy program than to one that is likely to cost them a lot of money. Strictly from the standpoint of getting the environment cleaned up as soon as possible, subsidies might be the most effective; however, this may run counter to the ethical notion that people who are causing a problem ought not to be "rewarded" for stopping, which is how subsidies are sometimes viewed.

Some people would take this idea further, arguing that because we should regard polluting behavior as essentially immoral to begin with, we should adopt policies that tend to recognize it as such.[6] By this criterion, policies that declare outright that certain types of polluting behavior are illegal are to be preferred to policies that do not. Another idea grounded in morality is that those who cause a problem ought to bear the major burden of alleviating it. We see this, for example, in discussions of global environmental issues. The industrial nations, especially the most economically developed among them, are largely responsible for the atmospheric buildup of CO_2 and the deterioration of the protective ozone layer. Many people take the view that these countries ought to bear the major burden in rectifying the situation.

Government Failure

In Chapter 4, we discussed the idea of market failure, a situation where, because of externalities of one type or another, unregulated markets may not yield efficient and equitable results. This is especially true in the case of pollution because of the public-good nature of environmental quality. This leads, in turn, to the conclusion that public policy is called for to rectify the situation.

It is important to recognize another type of failure, however, that makes the outcome of public policy somewhat problematic. This is called **government failure**, which refers to systematic tendencies and incentives within legislatures and regulating agencies that work against the attainment of efficient and equitable public policy.

If public action were always undertaken by reasonable people seeking rationally to advance the public interest, we could perhaps be confident that these public policies were consistently making the pollution problem better. But this unfortunately doesn't fit reality. The policy process is a political phenomena as well as a problem-solving one. As such, policy outcomes are also affected by the vagaries of the political struggle, by the continuous attempts to accumulate and wield influence, and by simple grandstanding and political theatrics. What comes out of this process may not resemble anything like informed, rational

---

[6] Frank Ackerman and Lisa Heinzerling, *Priceless: On Knowing the Price of Everything and the Value of Nothing*, The New Press, New York, 2004.

public policy that advances the welfare of society. This is not a justification for doing nothing; rather, it is a reason for making sure that environmental policies and regulations have clearly stated objectives, well-designed means, and transparent ways of assessing results.

Summary

The purpose of this chapter is to review a number of criteria that may be useful in evaluating environmental policies in different circumstances. These criteria are

- Efficiency
- Cost-effectiveness
- Fairness
- Enforceability
- Flexibility
- Incentives for technological innovations
- Moral considerations

With these criteria at hand, it is now time to launch into discussions of the various types of environmental policies. We will begin with several traditional decentralized approaches, following this with a look at the use of standards, a centralized approach that has been the most frequently used historically. Finally, we will look at what are called incentive-based types of policies.

Questions for Further Discussion

1. "Efficiency implies cost-effectiveness, but cost-effectiveness does not imply efficiency." Explain this statement.
2. Environmental policy is sometimes criticized for being a white, middle-class preoccupation. How might you interpret this position, using the concepts presented in this chapter?
3. Do you think that the impacts of the program to control automobile pollution are progressively or regressively distributed? How about the program to ensure the quality of public water supply systems?
4. Is there ever a justification for adopting an environmental regulation that cannot be, or will not be, enforced?
5. Catalytic converters are required on all new cars to reduce tailpipe emissions. Explain how this technology could have a beneficial impact in the short run but a less beneficial impact in the long run.

For additional readings and Web sites pertaining to the material in this chapter, see **www.mhhe.com/field7e**.

Chapter 10

Decentralized Policies: Liability Laws, Property Rights, Voluntary Action

By **"decentralized"** policies we mean policies that essentially allow the individuals involved in a case of environmental pollution to work it out themselves. Think back to the previous example of water quality in a lake. Suppose there are several industrial plants around the lake. One is a food-processing plant, and the water of the lake is an important input in its operation. The other is an industrial operation that uses the lake for waste disposal. How is it possible to balance the pollution damage suffered by the first firm with the abatement costs of the second? A decentralized approach to finding the efficient level of ambient water quality in the lake is simply to let the two plants work it out between themselves. They might do this either through informal negotiations or through more formal interaction in a local court of law. Decentralized approaches can have several real advantages over other types of public policy:

- Because the parties involved are the ones producing and suffering the environmental externalities, they have strong incentives to seek out solutions to the environmental problems.

- The people involved may be the ones with the best knowledge of damages and abatement costs; therefore, they may be best able to find the right balance among them, that is, to find efficient solutions.

Liability Laws

Almost everybody has an intuitive notion of **liability** and **compensation.** To be liable for some behavior is to be held responsible for whatever untoward consequences result from that behavior. Compensation requires that those causing the damage compensate those damaged in amounts appropriate to the extent of the injury.

One approach to environmental issues, therefore, is to rely on liability laws. This would work simply by making polluters liable for the damages they cause. The purpose of this is not simply to compensate people after they have been injured, although that is important. The real purpose is to get would-be polluters to make careful decisions. Knowing that they will be held liable for environmental damages in effect **internalizes** what would otherwise be ignored **external effects.**

The Principle

Consider Figure 10.1. It's the familiar model of environmental pollution showing marginal abatement costs and marginal damages, both related to the rate at which some production residual is emitted.[1] Suppose that the actual emission rate is initially at e_1, substantially above the efficient rate e^*. Suppose also that there is a new law requiring polluters to compensate those damaged in an amount equal to the damages caused. The effect of the law is to internalize the environmental damages that were external before the law. They now become costs that polluters will have to pay and therefore will want to take into account when deciding on their emission rate. At e_1, the total damages, and hence the amount of the compensation payment, would be a monetary amount equal to the area $(b + c + d)$.

This polluter could reduce its compensation payments by reducing emissions. As it does that, of course, its marginal abatement costs increase. But as

FIGURE 10.1   **Policy Options: Liability and Property Rights Approaches**

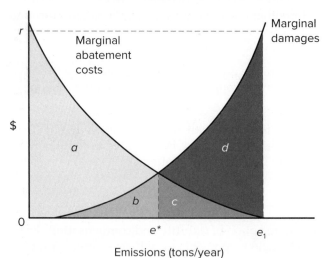

long as the marginal abatement costs are less than marginal damages, it would have an incentive to move to the left—that is, to reduce its rate of emissions. In theory, then, a liability system could automatically lead this polluter to emission level e^*. We say "automatically" because it would not require any centralized control authorities to intervene and mandate emission reductions. It requires, rather, a system of liability laws that would permit those damaged by pollution to be compensated for damages suffered.

Theoretically, this approach appears to address the incentive question—getting people to take into account the environmental damages they may cause—as well as the question of compensating those who are damaged. It may appear to solve the problem of determining just where e^* is along the emission axis. But whether this is actually true or not depends on the legal process through which the amount of liability and compensation is established. In the United States and other countries with similar legal traditions, this might be established through common law processes. Alternatively, it might be the result of statutory enactments by legislators.

Common Law

Common law systems rely on court proceedings in which plaintiffs and defendants meet to make claims and counterclaims, and in which juries are often called on to decide questions of fact and amounts of compensation. Judgments normally are based on precedent established from similar cases in the past. Common law cases usually involve actions of one private party, the polluter, that damage another private party. They may also involve cases, under the **public trust doctrine** of public or private actions, that damage **publicly held resources** (e.g., a fresh- or saltwater fishery in public waters).

In common law countries such as the United States (with the exception of the state of Louisiana), Canada (with the exception of Quebec), and the United Kingdom, doctrines of liability have developed through the evolution of court decisions. The law now recognizes **strict liability,** which holds polluters responsible for damages regardless of circumstances, and **negligence,** which holds them responsible only if they do not take appropriate steps to avoid the damage. A firm handling hazardous materials might be held strictly liable for damages done by these wastes. Thus, any damages that resulted, regardless of how careful the firm had been in handling the waste, would require compensation. On the other hand, negligence would hold it responsible only if it failed to take appropriate steps to ensure that the materials did not escape into the surrounding environment. As an example, British Petroleum (BP) was found negligent in the Deep Water Horizon oil rig explosion in 2010.

Another distinction is between **joint and several** and **nonjoint** liability. In the former, one party can be held liable for all of the damages stemming from a collective act of pollution; for example, one party may have to come up with the entire cleanup costs of a site to which it and many others contributed. In nonjoint liability, a party will be held liable only for its portion of the total.

The critical factors in a liability system are where the burden of proof lies and what standards have to be met in order to establish that proof. In the

United States, those who believe they may have been injured by pollution must file an action within a specified time period, typically two or three years, and then in court must establish a direct causal link between the pollution and the damage. This involves two major steps:

1. Showing that the polluting material at issue was in fact the cause of the damage, and
2. Showing that the polluting material did in fact come from the specific defendant who appears in court.

Both steps are difficult because the standards of proof required by the courts may be more than current science can supply. Most chemicals, for example, are implicated in increased disease only on a **probabilistic basis;** that is, exposure to the substance involves an increased probability of disease, not certainty. Even though we know that smoking causes lung cancer, for example, this causal link remains probabilistic; an increased number of people will get lung cancer if they smoke, but we can't tell exactly which ones. In Woburn, Massachusetts, contamination of well water was estimated by some epidemiologists to have probably caused 6 of the 12 excess cases of leukemia in the town. But under traditional standards of proof, a plaintiff could not conclusively prove that a *specific* cancer was caused by the water contamination. In other words, without being able to show explicitly how the polluting material operated in a particular body to produce cancer, the plaintiff cannot meet the standard of proof histori-cally required in U.S. courts.[2]

The other link in the causal chain is to show that the material to which one was exposed came from a particular source. This won't be difficult in some cases; the oil on the Louisiana shoreline definitely came from the Deepwater Horizon oil rig explosion, the hazy atmosphere over the Grand Canyon defi-nitely comes from the power plant, and so on. But in many cases this direct linkage is unknown. For an urban dweller in New York or Los Angeles, which specific industrial plant produced the sulfur dioxide (SO_2) molecules that a particular person may have breathed? For the people living in towns of the Connecticut Valley, which specific tobacco farms were responsible for the chemicals that showed up in their water supply? Without being able to trace a polluting substance to specific defendants, those who have been damaged by it may be unable to obtain compensation.

An important problem with using common law to address environmental damage is that economics and the law may use different criteria for identify-ing who is damaged from pollution. Under standard principles of economics, a person is "damaged" if he or she would be willing to pay to have the pollution reduced. On these grounds, for example, a person in New York could claim to be damaged by the Exxon *Valdez* oil spill even though he or she was never in Alaska.

---

[2] In some cases the law recognizes the special characteristics of pollution-caused damage. For example, statutes of limitation are being changed to count from the time the disease first becomes apparent, in recognition of the fact that many pollution-caused diseases may not show up for many years after exposure. Some courts are allowing statistical cause-and-effect linkages.

But legal doctrine requires that people have legal **standing** to proceed with a lawsuit. This requires normally that they show a close nexus between the degraded environment and their physical health and welfare. Thus, a person in New York may genuinely be worse off because of an Alaskan oil spill, in the economic sense, but lack legal standing to proceed with a case in court.

Another major point to make about liability systems can best be understood by introducing the concept of **transactions costs.** In general terms, transactions costs are the costs of reaching and enforcing agreements. The concept was first introduced in economics to apply to the costs that buyers and sellers encounter in making a successful transaction: costs of searching out information, costs of bargaining over terms, and costs of making sure an agreement is actually carried out. But the transactions costs also apply to liability systems where plaintiffs and defendants are competing in a court of law to determine the question of liability and the appropriate amounts of compensation. In this case, transactions costs are all the legal costs associated with gathering evidence, presenting a case, challenging opponents, awarding and collecting damages, and so on.

If the case is relatively simple, with one party on each side and a reasonably clear case of damage, the liability system may function, with a minimum of transactions costs, to give something approaching the efficient level of emissions. In the case of the two small factories on a small lake, the two can go to court and argue about the economic values to each of them of using the lake for their purposes. Because these values are comparable, it presumably would not be too difficult for a judge to determine the extent of the damages that the one firm is inflicting on the other. But transactions costs in many cases are likely to be very high. Complicated scientific questions often are involved, and judges and juries may find it virtually impossible to sort them out clearly (see Exhibit 10.1). And there may be many, many more than two parties involved, making it very difficult to agree on comprehensive solutions. In the case of the Deep Water Horizon oil rig explosion, for example, probably tens of thousands of people regarded themselves as having been directly damaged, hundreds of lawyers represented all the different sides, and numerous environmental groups, government organizations, and business groups were involved.

To summarize: liability laws and the incentive they create can help to lead to efficient pollution levels when

- Relatively few people are involved,
- Causal linkages are clear, and
- Damages are easy to measure.

Statutory Law

Another way to institute a system of liability for pollution is to include the appropriate provisions within statutory pollution-control laws. Numerous countries, individually and in international agreements, have sought to use this means to address the problem of maritime oil spills. One particularity of oil tanker spills is that it is very difficult to monitor the behavior of the polluters in this case. It is an episodic emission, so there is no continuous flow to measure, and spill

Common Law Courts and Questions of Science

EXHIBIT **10.1**

The citizens of Woburn, Massachusetts, thought they had found the cause of the excess cases of childhood leukemia in the town: the industrial chemicals that had contaminated their water groundwater supplies. Furthermore, they believed they had found the culprit, or at least two of them: manufacturing companies that had been in operation near the town and had engaged in questionable, probably illegal, disposal methods for their used chemicals.

So they sued in state court, alleging that the companies had improperly dumped their chemicals, that these chemicals had then migrated to the town's water supply, and that the contaminated water led to the deaths of the children. The case proceeded to a jury trial, and this is where things became complicated.

For a plaintiff to win a common law case, it's necessary to show clearly who committed the action and how this action affected the people claiming damage. The folks of Woburn thought the connection was clear, and wanted the jury simply to find for the plaintiff or the defendant.

But the judge thought that the case, as it proceeded, would require much more data: who dumped what, when, and how; definitive information on when the material reached the town wells; and what damage it might have caused. Epidemiologists could provide probabilistic answers to the last question, though this was subject to challenge by the companies. But the process by which the water might have gotten contaminated was much more complicated. The plaintiffs tried to keep it simple; the defendants sought to open up new possibilities and uncertainties. Eventually, it came down to a series of very complex technical questions on which the jury was asked to render judgment. At one point the judge said: "My God, to ask them a question like that: You're talking to plain folks, you know. You've got to cast these in some form of language that is not hedged around with reservations and clauses and subclauses and commas and all that."[1]

In fact, these questions were basically unanswerable by juries composed of ordinary people. "Science could not determine the moment when these chemicals had arrived at the wells with the sort of precision Judge Skinner was demanding of the jurors. The judge was, in effect, asking the jurors to create a fiction that would in the end stand for truth. Or, if they found themselves unable to do that, to end the case by saying they couldn't answer the questions based on the evidence. If these questions really were necessary to a just resolution of the case, then perhaps the case was one that the judicial system was not equipped to handle."

[1] **Source of quotes:** Jonathan Harr, *A Civil Action*, New York: Random House Vintage, 1996, pp. 368, 369.

probabilities depend on many practices (navigation, tanker maintenance, etc.) that are difficult for public authorities to monitor continuously. When polluter behavior is difficult to monitor, liability provisions may give them an incentive to undertake the appropriate steps to reduce the probability of accidents. The most recent such U.S. law is the Oil Pollution Act of 1990. This details the acts for which compensation is required and how the amounts will be determined. It also has terms requiring companies, prior to operations, to provide financial assurances showing that they will be able to meet payments if conditions require. In addition to national laws, several international agreements have been directed at specifying the liability requirements of companies whose tankers release, accidentally or not, large quantities of oil into the ocean.

Worker's compensation laws normally allow compensation for damages to individuals from workplace exposure to pollutants, such as toxic chemicals and excessive noise. The Radiation Exposure Compensation Act of 1990 provides for compensation to individuals damaged by radiation from nuclear weapons testing or working in uranium mines.

Another major law that incorporates liability provisions is the **Comprehensive Environmental Response, Compensation and Liability Act** of 1980 (CERCLA). In effect, it holds polluters liable for two types of costs: cleanup costs at certain legacy dump sites in which companies may have disposed of toxic materials in the past, and compensation for damages to public resources stemming from intentional or accidental releases of hazardous materials into the environment. In the former, the amount of compensation is related to the costs of cleanup, which may not be associated very closely with the amounts of damages actually caused. In the latter, compensation is more closely connected to damages, and major controversy surrounds how to measure these damages in particular cases. We will study CERCLA in greater detail in Chapter 16.

How well these types of statutory liability laws work in providing the correct incentive for polluters depends heavily on the formulas specified for determining the exact amount of the liability. The laws can provide the correct incentives only if the compensatory payments required from each polluter approach the actual amounts of damage they cause.

Property Rights

In the previous section we discussed the case of a small lake that one firm used for waste disposal and another for a water supply. On deeper thought, we are led to a more fundamental question: Which one of the firms is really causing damage and which firm is the one suffering damages? This may sound counterintuitive because you might naturally think that the waste-disposing firm is of course the one causing the damage. But we might argue just as well that the presence of the food-processing firm inflicts damages on the waste-disposing firm because its presence makes it necessary for the latter to take special efforts to control its emissions. (Assume for purposes of argument that there are no other people, such as homeowners or recreators, using the lake.) The problem may come about simply because it is not clear who has the initial right to use the services of the lake—that is, who effectively owns the **property rights** to the lake. When a resource has no owner, nobody has a very strong incentive to see to it that it is not overly exploited or degraded in quality.

Private property rights are, of course, the dominant institutional arrangement in most developed economies of the West. Developing countries also are moving in that direction, as are even the former socialist countries. So we are familiar with the operation of that institutional system when it comes to person-made assets such as machines, buildings, and consumer goods. Private property in land is also a familiar arrangement. If somebody owns a piece of land, he or she has an incentive to see to it that the land is managed in ways that maximize its value. If somebody comes along and threatens to dump something onto the land, the owner may call upon the law to prevent it if he or she wants to. By this diagnosis, the problem of the misuse of many environmental assets comes about because of imperfectly specified property rights in those assets.

The Principle

Consider again the case of the lake and the two firms. Apparently, there are two choices for vesting ownership of the lake. It could be owned either by the polluting firm or by the firm using it for a water supply. How does this choice affect the level of pollution in the lake? Would it not lead to zero emissions if owned by one firm and uncontrolled emissions if owned by the other? Not necessarily, if owners and nonowners are allowed to negotiate. Of course, this is the very essence of a property rights system. The owner decides how the asset is to be used and may stop any unauthorized use, but also may negotiate with anybody else who wants access to that asset.

Look again at Figure 10.1. Suppose the marginal damage function refers to all the damages suffered by the brewery—call this Firm A. Assume the marginal abatement cost curve applies to the firm emitting effluent into the lake—call this one Firm B. We have to make some assumption about who owns the lake, Firm A or Firm B. We will see that, *theoretically,* the same quantity of emissions will result in either case, provided that the two firms can come together and strike a bargain about how the lake is to be used.

In the first case, suppose that Firm B owns the lake. For the moment we need not worry about how this came about, only that this is the way it is. Firm B may use the lake any way it wishes. Suppose that emissions initially are at e_1. Firm B is initially devoting no resources at all to emissions abatement. But is this where matters will remain? At this point marginal damages are r, whereas marginal abatement costs are nil. The straightforward thing for Firm A to do is to offer Firm B some amount of money to reduce its effluent stream; for the first ton any amount agreed on between 0 and r would make both parties better off. In fact, they could continue to bargain over the marginal unit as long as marginal damages exceeded marginal abatement costs. Firm B would be better off by reducing its emissions for any payment in excess of its marginal abatement costs, whereas any payment less than the marginal damages would make Firm A better off. In this way, bargaining between the owners of the lake (here Firm B) and the people who are damaged by pollution would result in a reduction in effluent to e^*, the point at which marginal abatement costs and marginal damages are equal.

Suppose, on the other hand, that ownership of the lake is vested in Firm A, the firm that is damaged by pollution. In this case we might assume that the owners would allow no infringement of their property, that is, the emission level would be zero or close to it. Is this where it would remain? Not if, again, owners and others may negotiate. In this second case, Firm B would have to buy permission from Firm A to place its wastes in the lake. Any price for this lower-than-marginal abatement costs but higher-than-marginal damages would make both parties better off. And so, by a similar process of bargaining with payments now going in the opposite direction, the emissions level into the lake would be adjusted from the low level where it started toward the efficient level e^*. At this point any further adjustment would stop because marginal abatement costs, the maximum the polluters would pay for the right to emit one more ton of effluent, are equal to marginal damages, the minimum Firm A would take in order to allow Firm B to emit this added ton.

So, as we have seen in this little example, if property rights over the environmental asset are clearly defined, and bargaining among owners and prospective users is allowed, the efficient level of effluent will result irrespective of who was initially given the property right. In fact, this is a famous theorem, called the Coase theorem, after the economist who invented it.[3]

The wider implication is that by defining private property rights (not necessarily individual property rights because private *groups* of people could have these rights), we can establish the conditions under which decentralized bargaining can produce efficient levels of environmental quality. This has some appeal. The good part of it is that the people doing the bargaining may know more about the relative values involved—abatement costs and damages—than anybody else, so there is some hope that the true efficiency point will be attained. Also, because it would be a decentralized system, we would not need to have some central bureaucratic organization making decisions that are based mostly on political considerations instead of the true economic values involved. Ideas like this have led some people to recommend widespread conversion of natural and environmental resources to private ownership as a means of achieving their efficient use.

Rules and Conditions

How well is this property rights approach likely to work in practice? In order for a property rights approach to work right—that is, to give us something approaching the efficient level of environmental pollution—essentially three main conditions have to be met:

1. Property rights must be well defined, enforceable, and transferable.
2. There must be a reasonably efficient and competitive system that allows interested parties to come together and negotiate about how these environmental property rights will be used.
3. There must be a complete set of markets so that private owners may capture all social values associated with the use of an environmental asset.

If Firm A cannot keep Firm B from doing whatever the latter wishes, of course, a property rights approach will not work. In other words, owners must be physically and legally able to stop others from encroaching on their property.

---

[3] Ronald H. Coase, "The Problem of Social Cost," *Journal of Law and Economics,* 3, October 1960, pp. 1–44.

Owners must be able to sell their property to any would-be buyer. This is especially important in environmental assets. If owners cannot sell the property, this will weaken their incentives to preserve its long-run productivity. This is because any use that does draw down its long-run environmental productivity cannot be punished through the reduced market value of the asset. Many economists have argued that this is a particularly strong problem in developing countries; because ownership rights in these settings are often "attenuated" (i.e., they do not have all the required characteristics specified earlier), people do not have strong incentives to see that long-run productivity is maintained.

Problems with Property Rights to Internalize Externalities

In some cases property rights might be used creatively to advance the preservation of natural and environmental resources. Exhibit 10.2 discusses one of these: the protection of forests in places where their destruction is a major threat. But in modern cases of environmental pollution control, there are real problems in using property rights to internalize externalities.

Transactions Costs

We saw previously that the efficient use of the lake depended on negotiations and agreement between the two interested firms. Negotiating costs, together with the costs of policing the agreement, could be expected to be fairly modest. What we are referring to here is **transactions costs,** the idea that we introduced in the preceding section. In the simple lake case, transactions costs would probably be low enough that the firms would be able to negotiate on the efficient level of emissions. But suppose Firm A, the firm using the lake as a water supply source, is replaced with a community of 50,000 people who use it not only for a water supply, but also for recreational purposes. Now the negotiations must take place between a single polluting firm on one side and 50,000 people, or their representatives, on the other side. For each of these individuals the value of improved water quality is small relative to the value to the firm of polluting the lake. Moreover, the level of water quality in the lake is a public good for these individuals. This seriously increases the transactions costs of negotiating an agreement among different users.

To make matters worse, suppose that instead of one polluting firm there are 1,000 polluting firms, together with a few thousand homeowners who are not yet hooked into the public sewer system and so are using septic tanks on the shores of the lake. Here the possibilities of vesting the ownership of the lake in one person, and expecting negotiations between that person and prospective users to find the efficient levels of use, essentially vanish.

Public Goods

A factor that exacerbates transactions cost problems is that environmental quality improvements are **public goods.** So we could expect **free riding,**

Payments for Environment Services (PES)

EXHIBIT 10.2

A farmer owns a tract of land that developers would like to buy and convert into a large commercial development. A forest owner could gain by selling the timber from his land and converting it to agricultural fields. In each case the land currently has ecological value because it provides services such as habitat for diversity, flood control, and carbon sequestration. Markets for environmental services have increased and owners are able to realize their value and have an incentive to preserve them. Key types are carbon sequestration, biodiversity or watershed protection, and landscape protection.

One role for public authorities in this situation might be to enhance the demand side for such a market. This could be done by offering to pay the landowners an amount equal to the wider ecological value of the land, provided these ecological values were not impaired by the landholders' use of the land.

Around the world this type of program has come to be called **payment for environmental services.** Governments or other organizations identify critical ecosystem assets and pay landowners amounts large enough to ensure their preservation. Of course there are lots of problems that have to be solved for this type of property rights approach to work effectively:

- How ecological services are to be measured accurately
- How to make sure that ecological services are actually preserved
- How to ensure that political considerations don't enter the decisions to preserve ecosystem values.

especially when the number of affected individuals is large. In negotiating with polluters over the ambient quality levels to be achieved, some, perhaps many, potential beneficiaries could be expected to keep their true preference hidden in order to escape their fair share of the cost of pollution control. When public goods are involved, decentralized approaches such as property rights systems will not bring about efficient outcomes.

Absence of Markets

For private property institutions to ensure that an environmental asset is put to its best use, the process also must work in such a way that the owner is able to capture the full social value of the resource in that use. Suppose you own a small island in the Florida Keys. There are two possible uses: develop a resort hotel or devote it to a wildlife refuge. If you build the hotel, you get a direct flow of monetary wealth because the tourism market is well developed in that part of the world and you can expect customers to find your hotel and pay the going rate for your services. But there is no comparable "market" for wildlife refuge services. The value of the island as refuge may well be much higher than its value as resort, in terms of the actual aggregate willingness to pay of all the people in the country and the world. But there is no good way for them to be able to express that value; there is no ready market such as the one in the tourism market where they in effect can bid against the tourists who would visit the island. You might think that a **nature conservancy** could buy up the island if its value as refuge really is higher than its value as hotel. But nature conservancies run on the basis of voluntary contributions, and islands and other lands are in effect public goods. [4] We saw earlier that when public goods are involved, voluntary contributions to make something available are likely to be a lot less than its true value because of **free-riding behavior.** The upshot is that, while you as an owner could certainly expect to reap the full monetary value of the island as resort, you would not be able to realize its full social value if you held it as a preserve.

Or consider again the case above with the lake on which are located the chemical company and the brewery. Suppose there was a unique fish species in the lake that was of no value to either company, but of high value to society at large. In this case assigning exclusive property rights to either of the companies would not be an effective way of protecting the fish.

In recent years, policymakers, especially those in developing countries, have sought to develop an innovative property rights plan to preserve important ecosystem resources. It's called **payment for environmental services** and is discussed in Exhibit 10.2.

Markets for Green Goods

Once property rights are established, might new private markets be formed that could move the economy toward improved environmental quality? Among the citizenry at large, there is steadily growing concern about the impacts of environmental pollution. This represents an opportunity for private entrepreneurs to make available goods and services that are produced in more environmentally benign ways. Consider Figure 10.2 (a), for example. It shows a demand function by consumers for green power or renewable energy, that is, electricity generated in a way that produces less air pollutants than standard fossil-based technologies. This function is labeled D_1 in the figure. If the technological options available to produce green power (solar, wind, etc.) give a supply function of S_1, we could expect private markets to come into being and produce about q_1 units of clean power, at a price of p_1. If better technology is made available, the clean energy supply function might shift to S_2, increasing the amount of clean energy sold on the market to q_2 and lowering its price to p_2.[5]

The significance for this can be seen in Figure 10.2 (b), which shows the demand for fossil-based power. The lowering price in the green power market serves to shift back the demand curve for fossil power, because these two goods

---

[4] The Nature Conservancy is a national group that seeks to protect sensitive resources from damage by buying them outright. Founded in 1951, they have helped to protect more than 15 million acres of ecologically sensitive land in the United States; some has been transferred to other public and private conservation groups; the rest still belongs to the Nature Conservancy. Many individual states also have conservancy groups.

[5] The economic parameter of prime importance here is the *price elasticity of demand*, defined as the percentage change in quantity demanded of something produced by a 1 percent change in its price. The bigger this elasticity (in a negative sense, as p and q are moving in opposite directions), the bigger the quantity increase that would result from a price drop such as that from p_1 to p_2 in the diagram.

FIGURE 10.2   **Private Markets for a "Green Good"**

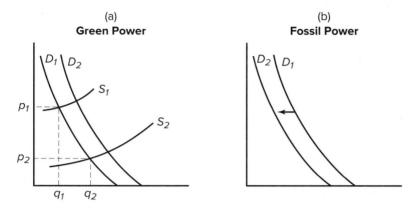

are substitutes for one another. In other words, the growth in a voluntary green power sector would lead to a shift back in the demand for dirty power.

How much might we expect private markets of this type to come into being and lead to reduced pollution? Clearly some will develop, because we can actually see growing markets in green power, organic food, recycled paper, and so on. Will they be able to provide the socially efficient amount of pollution reduction? Not likely. When I buy green power, I am conferring benefits not only on myself, but also on others whose air is made cleaner as a result. My purchase, in other words, produces a public good, and we have seen that private markets, left to themselves, will undersupply public goods. So although this means can move us part of the way toward efficient pollution reduction, it most assuredly cannot do the whole job.

Voluntary Action

By **voluntary action** we mean cases where individuals (including individual firms) engage in pollution-control behavior in the absence of any formal, legal obligation to do so. One might think that in this market-driven, competitive world, voluntary pollution control would be quite scarce, but this may not be true. There are many who feel that programs based on voluntary restraint can be used quite effectively. Table 10.1 is a partial list of voluntary programs that have been used in the United States. There are various social forces that presumably must be in operation for these programs to be effective. One of these is **moral suasion**; another is **informal community pressure.**

Moral Suasion

A classic case of moral suasion is the Smokey Bear and Woodsy Owl effort of the National Forest Service, a publicity campaign aimed at getting people to be more sensitive about littering in the woods and about avoiding things

TABLE 10.1 Examples of Voluntary Pollution Reduction Programs (VPRPs) in the United States

Program Type	Examples
Public programs aimed at individuals and based mostly on **moral suasion**	"Give a hoot, don't pollute"; "Pitch-in"; community recycling programs
Environmental Protection Agency (EPA) programs that encourage, but do not require, environmentally friendly process changes	**Green Lights**—encourage firms to adopt energy-efficient lighting technologies to reduce electricity consumption
	Design for the Environment (DfE)—encourage firms to meet "DfE" green labeling standards
Statutory or voluntary programs that provide information about the environmental performance of polluters	**Toxic Release Inventory**—make available toxic release data for public to use in programs of **informal pressure** or to design regulations
Voluntary programs of information release	**Energy Star Program**—publicize names of firms that adopt energy efficiency plans
	Drift Reduction Technology (DRT)—gives 1 to 4 stars for labeling for safer pesticide spray products that reduce pesticide drift
Programs undertaken unilaterally by polluters without the participation of public agencies	**Responsible Care**—program of the American Chemical Association to foster safe development and handling of chemicals
	ISO14001—voluntary international standards for environmental management systems
	LEED certification—certification from the Leadership in Energy and Environmental Design for buildings with green design and operation practices

Source: Keith Brouhle, Charles Griffiths, and Ann Wolverton, *The Use of Voluntary Approaches for Environmental Policy Making in the U.S.*, U.S. EPA, National Center for Environmental Economics, Working Paper #04-05, May 2005.

that would raise the risk of forest fires. Although there are fines and penalties for doing these things, the campaign was not based on threats of penalties as much as it was on appealing to people's sense of civic morality. "Reuse, Reduce, Recycle" campaigns are essentially the same type of approach.

In the early days of recycling, communities often mounted voluntary efforts, where appeals were made on the basis of civic virtue. In some cases these efforts were successful; in others they fell flat. Today there are many mandatory recycling programs, although it is true that they still must rely heavily on moral suasion to get high rates of compliance. Other situations clearly exist where appeals to civic morality may be effective public policy. This is especially the case with "emissions" such as litter, where violators are normally scattered throughout a population in a way that makes it impractical to monitor them and detect violations as they occur.

The good thing about moral suasion is that it may have widespread spillover effects. Whereas an effluent tax on a single type of effluent will have no impact on emissions of other types of waste products, appeals to civic virtue for one problem may produce side effects on other situations.

Of course, not all people are equally responsible from an ethical standpoint. Some people will respond to moral arguments; others will not. The burden of this policy will fall, therefore, on the part of the population that is morally more sensitive; those who respond less to moral arguments will be free riding on the others, enjoying the benefits of others' moral restraint but escaping their rightful share of the burden. Some electric companies issue neighborhood use reports which compare electricity consumption by one household to electricity use by neighbors within a geographic area.

It is easy to be cynical about moral suasion as a tool for environmental improvement. In this era of increasing internet connectedness and social media and heightened environmental destruction, tough-minded policymakers are naturally drawn toward environmental policies that have more teeth in them. This would probably be a mistake. It perhaps is true that we cannot rely very heavily on moral suasion to produce, for example, a significant reduction in air pollution in the Los Angeles basin or substantial drops in the use of groundwater-contaminating farm chemicals. But in our search for new, effective public policy devices to address specific pollution problems, we perhaps underestimate the contribution of the overall climate of public morality and civic virtue. A strong climate in this sense makes it possible to institute new policies and makes it easier to administer and enforce them. From which we can also deduce the importance of politicians and policymakers doing things that replenish this moral climate rather than erode it.

Informal Community Pressure

Another means through which some voluntary programs work is through **informal pressure** on polluters to reduce their emissions. It is informal because it is not exercised through statutory or legal means, and it is pressure because it attempts to inflict costs on those who are responsible for excessive pollution. The costs are in terms of such things as loss of reputation, the loss of local markets (perhaps going so far as to involve boycotts), or a loss of public reputation leading to declines in the stock values of firms that are publicly owned. The pressure is exercised through activities of local citizens groups, grass roots campaigns, internet, demonstrations, discussions with polluters, and so on. See Exhibit 10.3.

A major factor in voluntary actions of this type is the **information** that is available about polluters' emissions. If good data are lacking on the quantity and quality of emissions from particular sources, it will be difficult to mobilize public concern and focus it on the responsible parties. This is one of the motivations behind the U.S. Toxic Release Inventory, a program established under

A Case of Informal Economic Pressure
EXHIBIT **10.3**

Antipollution groups have long sought means of inflicting economic pressure on polluters. Attempts to boycott the products of polluting firms have been minimally successful. Disinvestment in the stock of polluting firms has been encouraged, also with modest success. Another tack that has been tried recently is to convince banks to reduce the credit they normally make available to polluting firms. Mountain-top coal mining in some eastern states has left a trail of denuded landscape and polluted water courses in many areas. Firms engaged in the practice often use short-term loans to finance these operations. Environmental groups have convinced some of the lending banks to cut back on these loans, thereby increasing the costs, and reducing the profitability of mountain-top mining.

Source: For more information, see Andrew Ross Sorkin, "A New Tack in the War on Mining Mountains," *New York Times,* March 10, 2015, p. B1.

the **Emergency Planning and Community Right to Know Act** (1986) and the **Pollution Prevention Act** (1990), whereby polluters are required to report their toxic emissions, which are then published in such a way that communities can identify emissions that directly affect them. The 2014 federal hydrological fracturing rules established Frac Focus, an industry listing of chemicals and liquids used for fracking. Sometimes called "sunshine laws" because they shed light on and disclose information available to the public, this public disclosure approach is being pursued also in other countries.

Summary

In this chapter we began the exploration of different types of public policies that might be used to combat environmental pollution. The chapter discussed two main decentralized types of approaches to environmental quality improvement. The first was to rely on liability rules, which require polluters to compensate those they have damaged. In theory, the threat of liability can lead potential polluters to internalize what would ordinarily be external costs. By weighing relative compensation and abatement costs, polluters would be brought to efficient emission levels. Although liability doctrines may work well in simple cases of pollution where few people are involved and cause-and-effect linkages are clear, they are unlikely to work reliably in the large-scale, technically complicated environmental problems of contemporary societies.

The second major approach we discussed was reliance on the institution of private property rights. Looked at from this perspective, environmental externalities are problems only because ownership of environmental assets is often not clearly defined. By establishing clear property rights, owners and others who would like to use environmental assets for various purposes can negotiate agreements that balance the relative costs of different alternatives. Thus, negotiations among parties theoretically could bring about efficient emission rates. But problems of transactions costs, especially related to the public goods aspects of environmental quality, and lack of markets for environmental services work against relying primarily on traditional property rights institutions in environmental quality issues. We will see in a subsequent chapter, however, that some new types of property rights approaches may hold greater promise.

Finally, we mentioned the idea of moral suasion, which may be useful when it is impossible to measure the emissions stemming from particular sources. The problem of moral free riding was discussed, as was the problem of public disclosure as a means of encouraging ethical behavior in environmental matters.

Questions for Further Discussion

1. It would seem that neighbors could easily negotiate among themselves to settle problems of local externalities such as noise and unsightly land uses. Yet most communities control these problems with local laws and regulations. Why?
2. Suppose courts changed rules regarding burden of proof, requiring polluters to show that their emissions are harmless, rather than pollutees to show that they have been harmed. What impact might this have?
3. Suppose a community weighed each resident's solid-waste disposal when it was picked up and published the individual totals each year in the local newspaper. Do you think this would lead to a reduction in the total quantity of solid waste disposed of in the community? If they were published monthly?
4. For what types of pollution problems is voluntary action likely to be the most effective policy approach?
5. Accidents with trucks carrying hazardous wastes are fairly common. Suppose regulators enact a rule requiring that the perpetrators of such an accident be liable for a sum equal to the average damages of all such accidents in the industry. Would this lead trucking companies to take the socially efficient amount of precaution against such accidents?

For additional readings and Web sites pertaining to the material in this chapter, see **www.mhhe.com/field7e**.

Chapter 11

Command-and-Control Strategies: The Case of Standards

A **command-and-control (CAC)** approach to public policy is one where, in order to bring about behavior thought to be socially desirable, political authorities simply mandate the behavior in law, then use whatever enforcement machinery—courts, police, fines, and so on—that is necessary to get people to obey the law. In the case of environmental policy, the command-and-control approach consists of relying on **standards** of various types to bring about improvements in environmental quality. In general, a standard is simply a mandated level of performance that is enforced in law. For example, a maximum level of a toxic, such as ppm (parts per million) of arsenic in drinking water. A speed limit is a classic type of standard; it sets maximum rates that drivers may legally travel. An emission standard is a maximum rate of emissions that is legally allowed. The spirit of a standard is, if you want people not to do something, simply pass a law that makes it illegal, then send out the authorities to enforce the law.

Figure 11.1 is our familiar graph showing marginal abatement costs and marginal damages related to the rate at which some production residual is emitted into the environment. Suppose that initially the actual level of effluent is at e_1, a rate substantially above the efficient rate of e^*. To achieve e^* the authorities set an emission standard at that level; e^* becomes a mandated upper limit for the emissions of this firm. The standard is then enforced by sending out whatever enforcement authorities are necessary to measure and detect any possible violations. If infractions are found, the source is fined or subject to some other penalty. If the firm reduces emissions in accordance with the standard, it will be incurring an amount equivalent to area a per year in total abatement costs. These total abatement costs are the **compliance costs** of meeting the standard.

Standards are popular for a number of reasons. They appear to be simple and direct. They apparently set clearly specified targets. They appeal, therefore,

FIGURE 11.1   **Emission Standards**

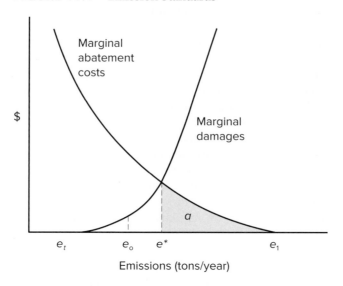

Emissions (tons/year)

to the sense that everybody has of wanting to come directly to grips with environmental pollution and get it reduced. Standards also appear to be congenial to our ethical sense that pollution is bad and ought to be declared illegal. The legal system is geared to operate by defining and stopping illegal behavior, and the standards approach conforms to this mind-set.

We will see, however, that the standards approach is a lot more complex than might first appear. Standards appear to offer a method to take away the freedom of sources to pollute, replacing it with mandated changes in behavior. In fact, a very practical reason for the popularity of standards is that they may permit far more flexibility in enforcement than might be apparent. What appears to be the directness and unambiguousness of standards becomes a lot more problematic when we look below the surface.

Types of Standards

There are three main types of environmental standards: *ambient, emission,* and *technology.*

Ambient Standards

Ambient environmental quality refers to the qualitative dimensions of the surrounding environment; it could be the ambient quality of the air over a particular city or the ambient quality of the water in a particular river. So an **ambient standard** is a never-exceed level for some pollutant in the ambient environment. For example, an ambient standard for dissolved oxygen in a particular river may be set at 3 parts per million (ppm), meaning that this is the lowest level of dissolved oxygen that is to be allowed in the river. Ambient standards cannot be enforced directly, of course. What can be enforced are the various emissions that lead to ambient quality levels. To ensure that dissolved oxygen never falls below 3 ppm in the river, we must know how the emissions of the various sources on the river contribute to changes in this measure, then introduce some means of controlling these sources.

Ambient standards are normally expressed in terms of average concentration levels over some period of time. For example, the current national primary ambient air quality standard for carbon monoxide (CO) is 9 ppm based on an 8-hour averaging time and 35 ppm based on a 1-hour averaging time. Neither can be exceeded more than once per year. The reason for taking averages is to recognize that there are seasonal and daily variations in meteorological conditions, as well as in the emissions that produce variations in ambient quality. Averaging means that short-term ambient quality levels may be worse than the standard, so long as this does not persist for too long and it is balanced by periods when the air quality is better than the standard.

Emission Standards

Emission standards are never-exceed levels applied directly to the quantities of emissions coming from pollution sources. Emission (or effluent) standards are normally expressed in terms of quantity of material per some unit of time—for example, grams per minute or tons per week. Continuous emissions streams may be subject to standards on "instantaneous" rates of flow: for example, upper limits on the quantity of residuals flow per minute or on the average residuals flow over some time period. These are sometimes called "performance standards."

It is important to keep in mind the distinction between ambient standards and emission standards. Setting emission standards at a certain level does not necessarily entail meeting a set of ambient standards. Between emissions and ambient quality stands nature, in particular the meteorological and hydrological phenomena that link the two.

Research to study the linkage between emission levels and ambient quality levels is an important part of environmental science. The environment usually transports the emissions from point of discharge to other locations, often diluting and dispersing them along the way. Chemical processes occur in all environmental media that often change the physical character of the pollutant. In some cases this may render the emitted substance more benign. Organic wastes put in rivers and streams will normally be subject to natural degradation processes, which will break them down into constituent elements. Thus, the ambient quality of the water at various points downstream depends on the quantity of emissions as well as the hydrology of the river: its rate of flow, temperature, natural reaeration conditions, and so on.

The link between emissions and ambient quality also can be vitally affected by human decisions. A classic case is automobiles. As part of the mobile-source air pollution program, emission standards have been set for new cars in terms of emissions per mile of operation. But because there is no effective way of controlling either the number of cars on the roads or the total number of miles each is driven, the aggregate quantity of pollutants in the air, and thus, ambient air quality, is not directly controlled.

Emission standards can be set on a wide variety of different bases. For example:

1. Emission rate (e.g., pounds per hour).
2. Emission concentration (e.g., parts per million of biochemical oxygen demand, or BOD, in wastewater).
3. Total quantity of residuals (rate of discharge times concentration times duration).
4. Residuals produced per unit of output (e.g., SO_2 emissions per kilowatt-hour of electricity produced).
5. Residuals content per unit of input (e.g., SO_2 emissions per ton of coal burned in power generation).
6. Percentage removal of pollutant (e.g., 60 percent removal of waste material before discharge).

In the language of regulation, emission standards are a type of **performance standard** because they refer to end results that are meant to be achieved by the polluters that are regulated. There are many other types of performance standards: for example, workplace standards set in terms of maximum numbers of accidents or levels of risk to which workers are exposed. A requirement that farmers reduce their use of a particular pesticide below some level is also a performance standard, as is a highway speed limit.

Technology Standards

There are numerous standards that don't actually specify some end result, but rather the technologies, techniques, or practices that potential polluters must adopt. We lump these together under the heading of technology standards. The requirement that cars be equipped with catalytic converters or seat belts is a technology standard. If all electric utilities were required to install stack-gas scrubbers to reduce SO_2 emissions,[1] these would be, in effect, technology standards because a particular type of technology is being specified by central authorities. This type of standard also includes what are often called design standards or engineering standards. There are also a variety of product standards specifying characteristics that goods must have and input standards that require potential polluters to use inputs meeting specific conditions.

At the edges, the difference between a performance standard and a technology standard may become blurred. The basic point of differentiation is that a performance standard, such as an emission standard, sets a constraint on some performance criterion and then allows people to choose the best means of achieving it. A technology standard actually dictates certain decisions and techniques to be used, such as particular equipment or operating practices to be used by polluters. For illustrative purposes, Exhibit 11.1 shows some typical standards,

---

[1] A scrubber is a device that treats the exhaust gas stream so as to remove a substantial proportion of the target substance from that stream. The recovered material then must be disposed of elsewhere.

Standards Applicable to Snowmobiles [1]

EXHIBIT 11.1

Snowmobiling is a major wintertime activity in the United States. Historically, snowmobiles were built with two-stroke engines, the same kind of engine that has been used to power lawn mowers and outboard motors. In a two-stroke engine, fuel enters the combustion chamber at the same time that exhaust gases are expelled from it. As a result, as much as one-third of the fuel passes through the engine without being combusted. This causes poor fuel economy and high levels of emissions, particularly hydrocarbons and carbon monoxide. In 1 hour, a typical snowmobile emits as much hydrocarbon as a 2001 model automobile emits in 24,300 miles of driving. Snowmobiles also emit as much carbon monoxide in an hour as a 2001 model auto does in 1,520 miles of driving. They are also very noisy. In the last two decades, there has been a political struggle over emission standards applicable to snowmobiles. Another aspect of the fight has been over efforts to control the entrance of snowmobiles into national parks, especially Yellowstone National Park. The tabulation shows standards adopted by the EPA after extensive review, mediation, and court battles, as the snowmobile industry regards them as too restrictive, and environmental groups regard them as not restrictive enough.

Emission Standards Applicable to New Snowmobiles	Carbon Monoxide g/kw-hr	Hydrocarbons g/kw-hr
Before 2006	397	150
2006/2007	275	100
2010	275	75
2012	200	75
Yellowstone 2003	120	15
Yellowstone 2015–2016	90	15

Yellowstone Entry Standards	Number of Snowmobiles Allowed (vehicles/day)
Clinton 2003	0
Bush	950
2011–2012 season	318
2015–2016 season	480[2]

Noise Standards for Yellowstone	Decibels
Yellowstone 2015–2016 season	67 dBA @ 35 mph

[1] Snowcoaches, another type of oversnow vehicle (OSV), have another set of specific emissions and noise standards.
[2] Limited to 48 transportation events with up to 10 snowmobiles per event.

Sources: Department of the Interior, National Park Service, *Special Regulations; Area of the National Park System; Yellowstone National Park; Winter Use,* Final Rule Federal Register 78(205), October 23, 2013, pp. 63069–63093. National Park System Yellowstone, *Oversnow Vehicle (OSV) Noise Emissions Testing,* 2015–16 update, **http://www.nps.gov/yell/learn /management/osvtest.htm.**

applicable in this case to snowmobiles. The carbon monoxide, hydrocarbon, and noise limits are emission standards; the limit on snowmobiles entering Yellowstone National Park can be thought of as a technology standard, as it restricts the use of certain machines in this setting.

Standards Used in Combination

In most actual pollution-control programs, different types of standards are used in combination. National air pollution-control policy contains all three, as we will see in Chapter 15. In the Total Maximum Daily Load program for water pollution control, authorities establish ambient standards for water quality, emission standards to reduce incoming pollution loads, and technology standards in the form of **best management practices.** We will encounter this program in Chapter 14.

The Economics of Standards

It would seem to be a simple and straightforward thing to achieve better environmental quality by applying standards of various types. Standards appear to give regulators a degree of positive control to get pollution reduced, but standards turn out to be more complicated than they first appear. The discussion in the rest of this chapter will focus on the efficiency and cost-effectiveness of standards, as well as the problem of enforcement.

Setting the Level of the Standard

Perhaps the first perplexing problem is where to set the standard. We saw in the case of the decentralized approaches to pollution control—liability laws and property rights regimes—that there was, at least, the theoretical possibility that the interactions of people involved would lead to efficient outcomes. But with standards we obviously can't presume this; standards are established through some sort of authoritative political/administrative process that may be affected by all kinds of considerations.

The most fundamental question is whether, in setting standards, authorities should take into account only damages or both damages and abatement costs. Look again at Figure 11.1, particularly at the marginal damage function. One approach in standard setting has been to try to set ambient or emission standards by reference only to the damage function. Thus, one looks at the damage function to find significant points that might suggest themselves.

A principle used in some environmental laws has been to set the standard at a "zero-risk" level: that is, at the level that would protect everyone, no matter how sensitive, from damage. This would imply setting emission standards at the **threshold** level, labeled e_t in Figure 11.1. This concept is fine as long as there is a threshold. Recent work by toxicologists and other scientists, however, seems to indicate that there may be no threshold for many environmental pollutants, that in fact marginal damage functions are positive right from the origin. In fact, if we followed a zero-risk approach, we would have to set all standards at zero.

This may be appropriate for some substances, certain highly toxic chemicals, for example, but it would be essentially impossible to achieve for all pollutants.

The standard might instead be set at a level that accepts a "reasonably small" amount of damages, for example, e_0, the point where the marginal damage function begins to increase very rapidly. Here again, however, we would be setting the standard without regard to abatement costs. A different logic might suggest that in setting the standard, damages ought to be balanced with abatement costs. This would put us squarely within the logic used in discussing the notion of economic efficiency and, in this way, lead us to set the standard at e^*, the efficient emission level.

Note that there is, in effect, a certain amount of "balancing" going on when standards are set on the basis of an average over some time period. In this case short-run periods, when ambient quality is relatively low, are considered acceptable as long as they do not last "too" long. A judgment is being made, in effect, that it is not necessary to install enough abatement technology to hold ambient quality within the standard under all conceivable natural conditions. In other words, an implicit trade-off is being made between the damages that will result from the temporary deterioration of ambient quality below the standard and the high costs that would be necessary to keep ambient quality within the standard under all conditions.

Uniformity of Standards

A very practical problem in standard setting is whether it should be applied uniformly to all situations or varied according to circumstances. This can be illustrated by using the problem of the spatial uniformity of standards. The ambient air quality standards in the United States, for example, are essentially national. The problem with this is that regions may differ greatly in terms of the factors affecting damage and abatement cost relationships, so that one set of standards, uniformly applied across these local variations, may have serious efficiency implications.

Consider Figure 11.2. It shows two marginal damage functions, one of which (labeled MD_u) is assumed to characterize an urban area, whereas the other (labeled MD_r) applies to a rural area. MD_u lies above MD_r because there are many more people living in the urban area, so the same quantity of emissions will affect the health of more people there than in the rural region. Assume that marginal abatement costs (labeled MAC) are the same in the two regions. Because the marginal damages are much higher in the urban than in the rural area, the efficient ambient level of benzene is much lower in the former than in the latter region; the efficient level is e_r in the rural region and e_u in the urban area. Thus, a single, uniform standard cannot be efficient simultaneously in the two regions. If it is set at e_u, it will be overly stringent for the rural area, and if it is set at e_r, it will not be tight enough for the urban region. The only way to avoid this would be to set different standards in the two areas. Of course, this confronts us with one of the great policy trade-offs: the more a policy is tailored so that it applies to different and heterogeneous situations, the more efficient it will be in terms of its impacts, but also the more costly it will be in terms of

FIGURE 11.2 **Regional Variation in Efficiency Levels**

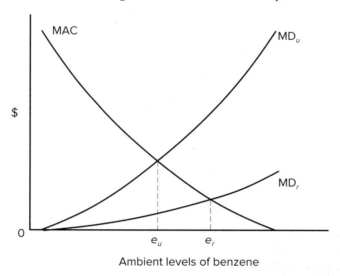

Ambient levels of benzene

getting the information needed to set the diverse standards and enforcing them once they have been established.

The curves in Figure 11.2 could be used to represent other heterogeneous situations as well as differences in geographical regions. For example, MD_u might represent marginal damages in a particular region under some meteorological conditions such as high humidity, or in one season of the year, whereas MD_r could represent the marginal damage function for the same area but under different meteorological conditions, like windy conditions, or at a different time of year. Now a single standard, enforced throughout the year, cannot be efficient at all points in time; if it is efficient at one time, it will not be at the other.[2]

Standards and the Equimarginal Principle

Having discussed the issue of setting the standard at the efficient level of emissions, we need to remember that the efficient level itself is defined by the minimum marginal abatement cost function. This means that where there are multiple emissions sources producing the same effluent,[3] the **equimarginal principle** must hold. The principle states that in order to get the greatest reductions in total emissions for a given total abatement cost, the different sources of emissions must be controlled in such a way that they have the same marginal abatement costs. This means that different sources of a pollutant would normally be controlled to different degrees, depending on the shape of the marginal abatement cost curve at each source. A major problem with standards is that there is almost always an overwhelming tendency for authorities to apply

[2] Uniformity is an issue in other environmental cases; for example, California water restriction set at 25% for all except agriculture.
[3] That is, in cases of "uniformly mixed" emissions.

FIGURE 11.3 **Marginal Abatement Costs for Two Sources**

Emission Level (tons/ month)	Marginal Abatement Costs ($)	
	A	B
20	0.00	0.00
19	1.00	2.10
18	2.10	4.60
17	3.30	9.40
16	4.60	19.30
15	6.00	32.50
14	7.60	54.90
13	9.40	82.90
12	11.50	116.90
11	13.90	156.90
10	16.50	204.90
9	19.30	264.90
8	22.30	332.90
7	25.50	406.90
6	28.90	487.00
5	32.50	577.00
4	36.30	677.20
3	40.50	787.20
2	44.90	907.20
1	49.70	1,037.20
0	54.90	1,187.20

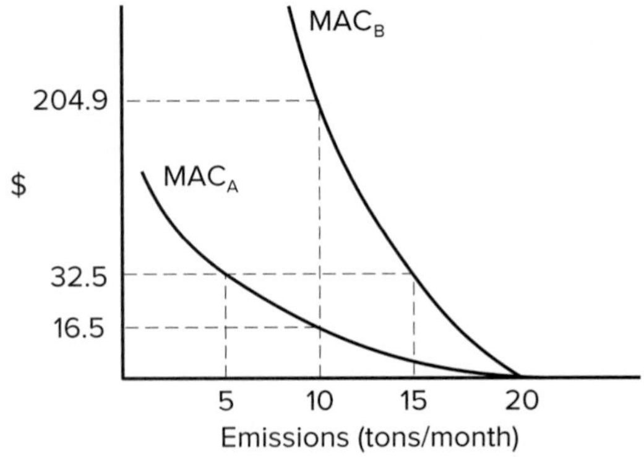

the same standards to all sources. It makes their regulatory lives much simpler, and it gives the impression of being fair to everyone because all are apparently being treated alike. But identical standards will be cost-effective only in the unlikely event that all polluters have the same marginal abatement costs.

Consider Figure 11.3, showing the marginal abatement cost relationships for two different sources, each emitting the same waste material. Note that the marginal abatement cost functions differ; for Firm A they increase much less rapidly as emissions are reduced than they do for Firm B. Why the difference? They may be producing different outputs with different technologies. One firm might be older than the other, and older technology may be less flexible, making it more costly to reduce emissions than at the plant with the newer equipment. One plant may be designed to use a different type of raw material input than the other. This, in fact, mirrors the situation in the real world. Normally one can expect considerable heterogeneity in abatement costs among groups of firms even though they are emitting the same type of residual.

TABLE 11.1   Illustrative Values for Polluters Shown in Figure 11.3

	Firm A	Firm B	Total
Beginning Solution			
Emissions (tons)	20	20	40
Marginal abatement costs	$0	$0	$0
Total abatement costs	$0	$0	$0
Equiproportionate Reduction			
Emissions (tons)	10	10	20
Marginal abatement costs	$16.50	$204.90	
Total abatement costs	$75.90	$684.40	$760.30
Equimarginal Reduction			
Emissions (tons)	5	15	30
Marginal abatement costs	$32.50	$32.50	
Total abatement costs	$204.40	$67.90	$272.30

The essential numbers are summarized in Table 11.1. Uncontrolled emissions are 20 for each firm, and control costs, marginal and total, are zero.

Under an equiproportionate rule, [4] each firm would cut back by 50 percent, to 10 tons each. Marginal control costs are then unequal, $16.50 for A and $204.90 for B. Total pollution control costs are $75.90 for A and $684.40 for B, for a total of $760.30.[5]

With equimarginal cutbacks, A goes to 5 tons and B to 15 tons. Pollution control costs total $272.30 for this situation. Compliance costs for a cutback that satisfies the equimarginal criterion are only about 36 percent of compliance costs in an equiproportionate reduction.

To summarize: Standards are usually designed to be applied uniformly across emission sources. This practice is almost inherent in the basic philosophy of the standards approach, and to many people this strikes them as an equitable way to proceed. But if marginal abatement costs in the real world vary across sources, as they usually do, the equal-standards approach will produce less reduction in total emissions for the total compliance costs of the program than would be achieved with an approach that satisfied the equimarginal principle. The greater the differences in marginal abatement costs among sources, the worse will be the performance of the equal-standards approach. We will see in the chapters ahead that this difference can be very large indeed.

Could command-and-control-type standards be set in accordance with the equimarginal principle? Unless the applicable law required some sort of

---

[4] An equiproportionate cutback is one that reduces each source by the same percentage of its original emissions. In the example in the text, the 10-ton cutback for each source was equal in absolute terms and also equiproportionate, as each source was assumed to be initially at an emission level of 20 tons per month.

[5] Note total abatement costs in Table 11.1 are the sum of MAC from Figure 11.3.

Firm A: 1.00 + 2.10 + 3.30 + 4.60 + 6 + 7.60 + 9.40 + 11.50 + 13.90 + 16.50 = $75.90

Firm B: 2.10 + 4.60 + 9.40 + 19.30 + 32.50+ 54.90 + 82.90 + 116.90 + 156.90 + 204.90 = $684.40

equiproportional cutback, there may be nothing to stop the authorities from setting different standards for the individual sources. To get an overall reduction to 20 tons/month in the previous example, they could require Source A to reduce to 5 tons/month and Source B to cut back to 15 tons/month. The difficult part of this, however, is that to accomplish this, the authorities must know what the marginal abatement costs are for the different sources. This point needs to be stressed. For almost any real-world pollution problem, there will normally be multiple sources. For a public agency to set individual standards in accordance with the equimarginal principle, *it would have to know the marginal abatement cost relationship for each of these sources.* We talked in Chapter 9 about the problem of asymmetric information. Polluters normally have a substantial amount of **private information** about pollution-control costs. These costs will usually vary among sources, so for the regulators to establish cost-effective pollution-control regulations, they will have to find some way to obtain this information. The primary source of data would have to be the polluters themselves, and there is no reason to believe they would willingly share this information. In fact, if they realize, as they certainly would, that the information would be used to establish individual source standards, they would have every incentive to provide the administering agency with data showing that their marginal abatement costs rise very steeply with emission reductions. Thus, there are real problems with authorities attempting to establish source-specific emission standards. *Nevertheless,* a considerable amount of this is done informally, through the interactions of local pollution control authorities, charged with enforcing common standards, and local sources, each of which is in somewhat different circumstances. We will come back to this later when we discuss issues of enforcement.

Standards and Incentives

An important issue for any policy is whether it creates incentives for sources to reduce emissions to efficient levels and in cost-effective ways. The command-and-control approach based on standards is seriously deficient in this regard. A basic problem is that standards are all or nothing; either they are being met or they are not. If they are being met, there is no incentive to do better than the standard, even though the costs of further emission reductions may be quite modest. By the same token, the incentives are to meet the standards, even though the last few units of emission reduction may be much more costly than the damages reduced.

It is easy to deal with the case of technology standards. Here, the incentives to find cheaper ways (considering all costs) of reducing emissions are effectively zero. If control authorities dictate in detail the specific technology and practices that polluters may legally use to reduce emissions, there are no rewards to finding better approaches.

Now consider emission standards. Figure 11.4 shows marginal abatement costs of a firm in two situations: MAC_1 refers to such costs before a given technological improvement; MAC_2 is the marginal abatement cost curve the

FIGURE 11.4   **Cost Savings from Technological Change: The Case of Standards**

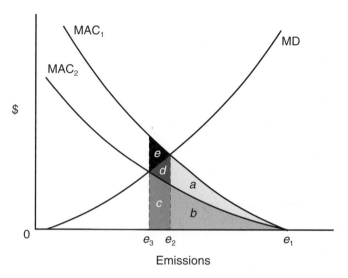

firm could expect to have after investing some large amount of resources in an research and development (R&D) effort to develop better treatment or re-cycling technology. Without any pollution-control program at all, there is ab-solutely no incentive to spend the money on the R&D. But suppose the firm is now faced with having to meet emission standards of e_2 tons/year. With the original marginal abatement costs the total annual cost of compliance for this firm is $(a + b)$ per year. If the R&D program is successful and MAC_1 reduces to MAC_2, compliance costs would be only b/year. The difference, a/year, is the amount by which compliance costs would be reduced and represents, in fact, the incentive for engaging in the R&D effort. We will see in the next chap-ter that this is a weaker effect than is provided by economic-incentive types of programs. Nevertheless, it is an incentive, which is more than we could say for technology standards.

To understand fully the incentive effects of standards, one has to look closely at the details. Figure 11.4 depicts a standard applied to total emissions. His-torically, most standards have been applied to emissions **per unit of input or output** of industrial firms. For electric utilities, an emission standard per unit of fuel burned is a standard per unit of input. There are important incentive implications of setting standards this way. Consider the following expression, showing how total emissions from an industrial operation are related to under-lying performance factors:

$$\frac{\text{Total}}{\text{emissions}} = \frac{\text{Total}}{\text{output}} \times \frac{\text{Inputs used for}}{\text{unit of output}} \times \frac{\text{Emissions per}}{\text{unit of input}}$$

Suppose authorities apply an input standard to, for example, coal-burning power plants. The standard could be expressed in terms of maximum amounts of SO_2 emissions allowed per ton of coal burned. This is a standard applied to the last term of the equation, and so the power plant will presumably reduce its emissions per unit of input to the level of the standard. But there are two other ways of reducing total emissions, as depicted in the first two terms to the right of the equals sign. One is to reduce total output through, for example, encouraging consumers to conserve electricity. The other is to reduce the amount of coal needed per unit of electricity generated, in other words, for the plant(s) to increase **fuel efficiency.** But the plants will have no incentive to reduce emissions in these last two ways because the standard has been written in terms only of the last factor in the expression.

In recent years, regulators have been moving more toward **output-based standards,** that is, standards expressed in terms of allowable emissions per unit of output.[6] If you multiply together the last two terms of the expression, you get **emissions per unit of output.** If you now place a standard on this factor, note that polluters can reduce it in two ways: by reducing inputs per unit of output and by reducing emissions per unit of input. The incentives of the polluters have been broadened. So in the case of a power plant, an output-based standard would involve both incentives: to reduce emissions per unit of coal burned (perhaps by switching to low-sulfur coal) and to become more fuel efficient (perhaps by upgrading the boilers of the plant).

Political-Economic Aspects of Standards

The theory of standards is that they are established by regulatory authorities, then responded to by polluters. In fact, this process can lead to patterns of political give-and-take between the parties that will substantially affect the outcome. Suppose that the authorities are making every effort to set the standard at something approaching the efficient level of emissions. In Figure 11.4, e_2 is their view of the efficient level before the technical change. But the new technology lowers the marginal abatement cost curve, and we know from Chapter 5 that this will reduce the efficient level of emissions. Suppose the authorities estimate that, given their view of marginal damages, the new technology shifts the efficient emission level to e_3 in Figure 11.4, and that they now change the standard to reflect this. Now the firm's compliance cost will be $(b + c)$ per year. The difference is now $(a - c)$. So the firm's cost savings will be substantially less than when the standard was unchanged; in fact, compliance costs may actually be higher than before the R&D program. In other words, the firm could suppose that because of the way regulators may tighten the standards, they would be worse off with the new technology than with the old methods. The standard-setting procedure in this case has completely undermined the incentive to produce new pollution-control technology. This is a case of what might be called **perverse incentives.** A perverse incentive is one that actually works against the objectives of the regulation.

---

[6] Automobile emission standards have always been in terms of output, for example, grams of pollutant per mile driven. We will talk about this in Chapter 15.

In this case, standard setting can work against long-run improvements in pollution-control technology.[7]

If emission standards create incentives for technological change, is it not desirable to establish very stringent standards so as to increase that incentive? This is another place where political considerations come into play. If, in Figure 11.4, the standard is set at e_3 right at the beginning, this would mean cost savings of $(a + d + e)$ with the new technology rather than just a as it would be with the standard set at e_2. This type of approach goes under the heading of **technology forcing.** The principle of technology forcing is to set standards that are unrealistic with today's technology in the hope that it will motivate the pollution-control industry to invent ways of meeting the standard at reasonable cost.

But stricter standards also create another incentive: the incentive for polluters to seek relief from public authorities by delaying the date when they become applicable. In an open political system, firms may take some of the resources that might have gone for pollution-control R&D and devote them instead to influencing political authorities to delay the onset of strict standards. The stricter and more near-term the standards, the more of this activity there is likely to be. Thus, technology forcing is another one of those strategies where the effectiveness of moderate amounts does not imply that more will be even more effective.

It needs to be remembered also that to a significant extent new R&D for pollution control is carried out by a pollution-control industry rather than the polluting industries themselves. Thus, to draw conclusions about the incentives of pollution-control policy for technological change means to predict how these policies will contribute to the growth and productivity of the pollution-control industry. Technology standards are stultifying on these grounds because they substantially drain off the incentives for entrepreneurs in the pollution-control industry to develop new ideas. Emission standards are better in this respect, as we have seen. The evidence for this is the fact that representatives of the pollution-control industry usually take the side politically of stricter environmental standards; in fact, they see the fortunes of their industry tied almost directly to the degree of stringency in the emissions standards set by public authorities.

The Economics of Enforcement

All pollution-control programs (perhaps with the exception of voluntary programs, mentioned in the last chapter) require enforcement. Much of the ongoing political conflict over environmental regulations involves questions of enforcement, with one side often saying that it is too harsh, the other side maintaining that it isn't harsh enough. In this section we deal briefly with some economic

---

[7] There is another perverse incentive lurking in equiproportionate reductions. If polluters realize that they will be subject to an equiproportionate cutback in the future, it is better for them to increase their base now by increasing their emissions. When the cutback is imposed, they will be able to emit higher amounts than they would have had they not inflated their base.

FIGURE 11.5 The Economics of Enforcement

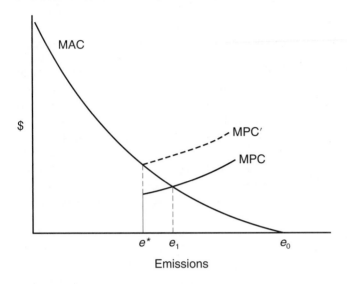

issues related to enforcement, discussing these particularly in their relation to enforcing standards. In later chapters we will discuss enforcement issues related to other types of policy instruments.

Enforcing Emission Standards

There are two primary dimensions of enforcement, monitoring and sanctioning. Consider Figure 11.5. This shows a marginal abatement cost function (MAC) representing as usual the marginal costs to the firm of reducing emissions. But on the other side, instead of a marginal damage function as in the standard model, there is a **marginal penalty function.** The line marked MPC represents the expected penalties that firms can be expected to face for violating an emission standard. Penalties arise when firms are detected to be exceeding their emission standard and when fines or other penalties are levied as a result. Suppose a standard is set at e^*. Perhaps this was established by comparing abatement costs with damages, or perhaps on some other criterion. What is relevant here is the way firms will actually be motivated to reduce their emissions.[8] MPC is zero below e^*; the firm is only penalized for emissions in excess of the standard, and the shape of the MPC curve shows how penalties would increase as the size of the violation increases.

If current emissions are at e_0, the firm will clearly reduce them because marginal abatement costs at this point are well below the marginal penalty costs currently in effect. But it will stop reducing emissions at e_1, because to go lower

---

[8] In the last chapter we discussed liability rules as a way of controlling emissions. In penalty function terms, liability rules turn the marginal damage function into an MPC curve, because they would make firms responsible for paying for the damages their emissions produce.

than this would require higher abatement costs than it would save in terms of reduced penalties. Unless something changes, therefore, the firm's emissions will end up at e_1, and the amount of noncompliance will be $e^* - e_1$.

The only way to reduce noncompliance is to raise the penalty function. Basically, there are two ways of doing this: raise monitoring activities so as to be better able to detect noncompliance, or raise fines for those who have been detected as noncompliant. Of course, authorities could do both and, if they did so enough, the penalty function could be raised to something like the dotted line labeled MPC′, which would then ensure a noncompliance rate of zero.

This analysis shows several things. It shows the basic result that there is a trade-off in enforcement; to get higher levels of compliance authorities will normally have to devote more resources to enforcement. There may be some trade-off also between monitoring and fines. The MPC curve of Figure 11.5 can be raised or lowered by changes in either one of these enforcement elements.

We should also note that monitoring in this case requires measuring, or estimating, the quantities of emissions, because the MPC function is essentially expressed in terms of deviations of actual emissions from the emission levels set in the standard. This deviation could apply to hourly, daily, or annual quantities. Over the years, there have been major advances in monitoring technology. In the early days of rigorous pollution control, much of the enforcement effort depended on **self-monitoring,** where sources themselves kept the books on emissions flows over time. This permitted the agencies to visit firms periodically to audit the records at each source. Agencies could also make random checks to measure emissions. The rate of auditing and random visits could be varied according to agency budgets. More recently, technologies have been developed for undertaking **continuous measurement** and electronic reporting (via the Internet, for example) of emissions in some cases. The future will undoubtedly also see new developments in **remote monitoring technology.**

The other main factor behind the MPC function of Figure 11.5 is the size of the fines or other sanctions (e.g., jail terms). Most pollution-control statutes contain provisions on the size of the fine (or jail term) that may be levied against violators if and when they are caught and found guilty. In many cases, fines have been set too low, lower than the abatement costs required to meet the standards. In these situations firms can actually save money by dragging their feet on compliance. With low sanctions like this, enforcement is therefore likely to be much more difficult and costly than if sanctions are higher. Sources faced with the possibility of having to pay substantially higher fines would presumably have a stronger incentive to come into compliance.

It needs to be kept in mind also that sanctioning ordinarily involves using the court system to pursue legal action. The functioning of courts may put some limits on what enforcing agencies may do. For example, if monetary fines or other penalties expressed in the law are very high, courts may be reluctant to hold sources in rigorous noncompliance because of the economic dislocation this may produce.

Enforcing Technology Standards

Technology standards require that sources adopt and operate approved technical means of pollution control. In this case an important distinction is between **initial compliance** and **continued compliance.** Initial compliance is where a polluter charged with meeting a particular technology standard installs the appropriate equipment. To monitor initial compliance it is necessary to have inspectors visit the site, check to see that the equipment is installed, and make sure it will operate in accordance with the conditions of the standard. Having ascertained this, the administering agency can then give the firm the necessary operating permit, but this does not ensure that the equipment will continue to be operated in the future in accordance with the terms of the permit. It may deteriorate through normal use, it may not be maintained properly, future operating personnel may not be properly trained, and so on. Without some amount of monitoring, therefore, there is no assurance that the source will continue to be in compliance. But here, again, the administering agency has great flexibility in setting up a monitoring program. It can vary from very infrequent visits to randomly selected sites all the way up to permanent observers stationed at each source.

The Enforcing Agency

When enforcement costs are included in the analysis, the question arises of whether standards should be set, at least in part, with enforcement costs in mind. Stricter standards may involve larger enforcement costs because they require larger operating changes on the part of sources. Less strict standards may be achievable with fewer enforcement resources for the opposite reason. Public environmental agencies are usually faced with budget stringencies. In some cases, greater overall reductions in emissions may be obtained by using less strict standards that can be easily enforced than by stricter standards involving higher enforcement costs.

One very common feature of environmental standards is that they are usually set and enforced by different groups of people. Standards often are set by national authorities; enforcement is usually done by local authorities. For example, the air quality standards established under the Clean Air Act are set at the federal level, but enforcement is mostly carried out by state-level agencies. This has a number of important implications. One is that standards often are set without much thought to costs of enforcement; it is more or less assumed that local authorities will find the necessary enforcement resources. Of course, this is not the case in practice. With limited enforcement budgets, local authorities may react to new programs by reducing resources devoted to other programs. Another implication is that, in practice, environmental policies incorporating standards end up having a lot more flexibility than might at first appear. Laws written at national levels are specific and apparently applicable everywhere. But at the local level, "where the rubber meets the road," as they say, it's a matter of local pollution-control authorities applying the law to local sources, and in this process there can be a great deal of informal give-and-take between the authorities and local plant managers, with participation by local environmental groups as well. A cynic, or a political realist, might conclude that standards approaches are favored because of the very fact that in the real world of tight public agency budgets, they permit partial or incomplete compliance. One of the advantages (some might say disadvantages) of policies using standards is that they permit flexibility in enforcement.

Summary

The most popular approach to environmental pollution control historically has been the setting of standards. This has been called the command-and-control approach because it consists of public authorities announcing certain limits on polluters, then enforcing these limits with appropriate enforcement institutions. We specified three primary types of standards: ambient, emission, and technology. Initial discussion centered on the level at which standards should be set and the regional uniformity of standards.

A leading problem with standard setting is the question of cost-effectiveness and the equimarginal principle. In most standards programs, the administrative bias is to apply the same standards to all sources of a particular pollutant. But pollution control can be cost-effective only when marginal abatement costs are equalized across sources. When marginal abatement costs differ among sources, as they almost always do, uniform standards cannot be cost-effective. In practice, differences among sources in their marginal abatement costs often are recognized informally by local administrators in applying a uniform national standard.

We dealt at length also with the question of the long-run impact of standards through their effects on the incentives to look for better ways of reducing emissions. Technology standards completely undermine these incentives. Emission standards do create positive incentives for R&D in pollution control, although we will see that these are weaker than those of economic-incentive types of pollution-control policies, the subject of the next two chapters. Finally, we discussed the all-important question of enforcement.

Questions for Further Discussion

1. Environmental protection programs are frequently designed to require all polluters to cut back emissions by a certain percentage. What are the perverse incentives built into this type of program?

2. If emission standards are ruled out because of, for example, the impossibility of measuring emissions (as in nonpoint-source emissions), what alternative types of standards might be used instead?

3. In Figure 11.2, show the social cost of setting a uniform national standard, applicable to both rural and urban areas (to do this, you can assume that the national standard is set at either e_u or e_r).

4. Consider the example of Figure 11.3. Suppose we define as *fair* a cutback in which the two sources have the same total costs. Would an equiproportionate reduction be fair in this sense? A reduction meeting the equimarginal principle? Is this a reasonable definition of *fair*?

5. It is sometimes suggested that the most equitable way to resolve issues in international trade agreements would be for all countries to adopt the same emission standards. What are the pros and cons of this from an economic standpoint?

For additional readings and Web sites pertaining to the material in this chapter, see **www.mhhe.com/field7e.**

Chapter 12

Incentive-Based Strategies: Emission Charges and Subsidies

In the last chapter we discussed some of the advantages and disadvantages of using a standards approach to pollution control. Although standards seemingly offer direct control of polluting activities, in many applications they have serious drawbacks by virtue of their tendency to treat all sources alike even though they may be very different, and to lock in certain technologies. A major problem is that they typically are unable to take advantage of the private information that polluters have about means and procedures they could use to reduce pollution. **Incentive-based** (IB) environmental policies are designed to rectify these drawbacks. IB plans work by having public authorities first set overall objectives and rules, and then leaving firms enough latitude that their normal commercial incentives will lead to the adoption of cost-effective pollution-control procedures and technologies.

There are basically two types of incentive policies:

1. **Charges (taxes) and subsidies,** and
2. **Market-based systems.**

Both require centralized policy initiative to get started but rely on flexible firm responses to attain efficient pollution control. In the first, firms are given latitude to respond however they wish to what is essentially a new price for using the services of the environment. The second is designed to work more or less automatically through the interactions among polluters themselves or between polluters and interested parties. In recent years many countries, including the United States, have introduced market-based systems, specifically **transferable discharge permits**. In Europe, many countries have relied upon environmental charges to motivate emission reductions, as well as raise public revenues. Exhibit 12.1 notes some of the plans adopted in

Environmental Taxes in Europe   EXHIBIT 12.1

Charge or Tax	Description
French aircraft noise charges	TNSA (Tax sur les nuisances sonore aériennes) charged at 11 busiest airports, based on maximum take-off weight, certified noise performance, and time of day
Czech Republic air pollution charges	Charges on power plants, covering SO_2, NO_x, particulate matter, and VOCs (excluding methane)
Plastic bag tax in Ireland	Charges on all plastic bags (biodegradable or not) except bags used for fresh meat and fruits
Pesticide tax in Norway	Tax on pesticides based on their components, a registration fee, a fee to fund efficiency and residue trials, and risk to environment and human health
Landfill tax in U.K.	Tax has two rates: a local rate on less polluting wastes (e.g., rocks and soils) and a higher rate for everything else
Water taxes in Denmark	Consisting of a water supply tax and a waste tax based on discharge of nitrogen, phosphorus, and organic matter
Swedish carbon tax	The first country to introduce a tax on CO_2 emissions, offset by a reduction in personal income taxes
Energy tax in the Netherlands	A "downstream" tax applying to energy products used for heating and electricity generation in households and small and intermediate-sized businesses
Natural resource tax in Latvia	Covers extraction of natural resources, waste disposal, hazardous goods, and air and water emissions

Source: Institute for European Environmental Policy, *Environmental Tax Reform in Europe: Opportunities for the Future*, Annexes to Final Report, Brussels, May 2014.

Europe. In this chapter we examine the economics of emission charges and subsidies. In the next chapter we will consider the technique of transferable discharge permits.

Environmental economists have long favored the idea of incorporating IB policies more thoroughly into environmental policies. These can serve to put more teeth into environmental policies in many cases and substantially improve the cost-effectiveness of these policies. They are especially important to consider for the difficult task of reducing emissions of greenhouse gases (GHG). But keep in mind something said before: No single type of policy is likely to be the best in all circumstances. IB policies are no exception. They have strengths and they have weaknesses. The strengths are sufficiently strong to encourage greater reliance on them in many circumstances. But there are many types of environmental problems where they may not be as useful as other approaches.

Emission Charges or Taxes[1]

Firms pollute because they do not take into account the social damage their actions cause. Thus, the most straightforward approach to controlling emissions is for authorities to charge a price for these emissions. This can be done in two ways: by charging for each unit of emissions or by giving a subsidy for each unit of emissions that the source cuts back.

We deal first with **emission charges,** sometimes also called **"emission taxes."** In a charge system polluters are told: "You may discharge any amount of residuals you wish, but your emissions will be measured and you will be required to pay a certain charge for every unit (e.g., ton) of effluent you discharge."[2] For example, one of the first emission charges proposed in the United States was in 1970, when President Nixon recommended a tax of 15 cents per pound on sulfur emissions from large power plants. It was never adopted. When an emission charge is put into effect, firms responsible for emissions must essentially pay for the services of the environment—transportation, dilution, chemical decomposition, and so on—just as they must pay for all other inputs used in their operations. And just as they have always had an incentive to conserve on scarce labor and other conventional production inputs, they will now have an incentive to conserve on their use of environmental services. How do they do this? Any way they wish (within reason). This may sound flippant but in fact it represents the main advantage of this technique. By leaving polluters free to determine how best to reduce emissions, this type of policy attempts to harness their own energy and creativity and their desire to minimize costs, to find the least-cost way of reducing emissions. It could be any combination of treatment, internal process changes, changes in inputs, recycling, shifts to less polluting outputs, and so on. The essence of the charge approach is to provide an incentive for the polluters themselves to find the best way to reduce emissions, rather than having a central authority determine how it should be done. And in so doing, they will have a strong incentive to use the private information they have about the pollution-control costs of alternative technologies.

The Economics of an Emission Tax

The essential mechanics of an emission charge are depicted in Figure 12.1. The numbers refer to a single source of a particular pollutant. The top panel shows the analysis numerically, while the bottom shows essentially the same information graphically. The tax has been set at $120/ton/month. The second column in the top panel shows the firm's marginal abatement costs and the third column

---

[1] Terminology varies in this subject. Some people prefer to talk of emission **charges,** others prefer emissions **taxes.** For our purposes, charges and taxes are synonymous and are used interchangeably.

[2] The idea of taxing "bads" was first put forth by A.C. Pigou in his *Economic of Welfare* (London, Macmillan, 1920). Thus, Pigouvian taxes are taxes meant to achieve changes in the behavior of, in this case, polluters, in contrast to standard taxes, whose purpose is primarily to raise public revenues.

FIGURE 12.1 An Emissions Charge

Emissions (tons/month)	Marginal Abatement Cost	Total Abatement Cost	Total Tax Bill at $120/Ton	Total Costs
10	0	0	1,200	1,200
9	15	15	1,080	1,095
8	30	45	960	1,005
7	50	95	840	935
6	70	165	720	885
5	95	260	600	860
4	120	375	480	855
3	150	525	360	885
2	185	710	240	950
1	230	940	120	1,060
0	290	1,230	0	1,230

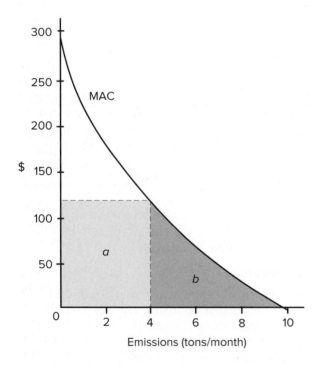

shows total abatement costs. The last two columns show the total monthly tax bill the firm would pay at different emission levels, and the total cost, consisting of the sum of abatement costs and the tax bill. We see that the minimum total cost of $855 occurs at an emission rate of 4 tons/month. Let's pursue the logic of this by considering marginal abatement costs. Suppose the firm is initially emitting 10 tons/month. If it does not reduce emissions, the firm's tax, or payment for using the environment, is $1,200. The firm has an incentive to reduce emissions.

If it were to cut emissions to 9 tons, it would cost $15 in abatement costs, but it would save $120 in total tax bill, clearly a good move because total costs drop to $1,095. Following this logic, it could improve its bottom line by continuing to reduce emissions as long as the tax rate is above marginal abatement costs. The rule for the firm to follow is thus: Reduce emissions until marginal abatement costs are equal to the charge on emissions. This is shown diagrammatically in the bottom part of Figure 12.1. With a continuous marginal abatement cost function, it's possible to talk about fractions of tons of emissions, something we could not do in the upper panel. So the graph is drawn to agree with the integer values above; that is, the charge of $120 leads the firm to reduce emissions to exactly 4 tons/month.

After the firm has reduced its emissions to 4 tons/month, its total (monthly) tax bill will be $480. Its monthly abatement costs will be $375. Graphically, total abatement costs correspond to the area under the marginal abatement cost function, labeled *b* in the figure. The total tax bill is equal to emissions times the tax rate, or the rectangle labeled *a*. Under a charge system of this type, a firm's total cost equals its abatement costs plus the tax payments to the taxing authority.

Why wouldn't the firm simply disregard the charge, continue to pollute as it has been doing, and just pass the charge on to consumers in the form of higher prices? If the firm stayed at 10 tons of emissions, its total outlay would be $1,200/month, consisting entirely of tax payment. This is much higher than the $855 it can achieve by cutting back to 4 tons/month. The assumption in an emissions charge program is that **competitive pressures** will lead firms to do whatever they can to minimize their costs. Thus, when there is competition in the industry subject to the emission tax, it will lead firms to reduce emissions in response to the tax. By the same token, however, we must recognize that if competition is weak, firms may not respond in this way. Electric power plants, for example, are usually operated by regulated monopolies subject to oversight by public utility commissions. They may not respond to charges on sulfur dioxide (SO_2) emissions in the same way as firms that operate in more competitive economic climates.

For competitive firms, the amount of the response will depend on several factors. The higher the charge, the greater the reduction, and vice versa. In the example of Figure 12.1, a tax of $50/ton/month would have led the source to reduce emissions only to 7 tons/month, whereas one of $180 would have produced a cutback to 2 tons/month; that is, the firm would select an emissions quantity closest to where MAC equals the charge. Also, the steeper the marginal abatement cost function, the less emissions will be reduced in response to a tax. We will come back to this later.

Compare the charge approach with an emission standard. With the tax the firm's total outlay is $855. Suppose that, instead, the authorities had relied on an emission standard to get the firm to reduce emissions to 4 tons/month. In that case, the firm's total outlay would be only the $375 of abatement costs. Thus, the charge system ends up costing the firm more than the standards approach. With a standard, the firm has the same total abatement costs as in the charge system, but it is still essentially getting the services of the environment free, whereas with a charge system it has to pay for those services. But although polluting firms would thus prefer standards to emission charges, there are good reasons, as we will see, why society would often prefer taxes over standards.

The Level of the Charge

In competitive situations, higher charges will bring about greater reductions in emissions, but just how high should the charge be set? If we know the marginal damage function, the answer presumably would be to set the charge so as to produce the efficient level of emissions, as in Figure 12.2. At a tax rate of t^*, emissions are e^*, and marginal damages equal marginal abatement costs. The firm's total costs of emission control are divided into two types: total abatement costs (compliance costs) of e and total tax payments of $(a + b + c + d)$. The former are the costs of whatever techniques the firm has chosen to reduce emissions from e_0 to e^*, whereas the latter are tax payments to the control agency covering the charge on the remaining emissions. From the standpoint of the firm, of course, these are both real costs that will have to be covered out of revenues. From the standpoint of *society*, however, the tax payments are different from the abatement costs. Whereas the latter involve real resources and therefore real social costs, the emission charges are actually **transfer payments,** payments made by the firms (ultimately by people who buy the firms' output) to the public sector and eventually to those in society who are benefited by the resulting public expenditures. When a firm considers its costs, it will include both abatement costs and tax payments.

FIGURE 12.2 **An Efficient Emission Charge**

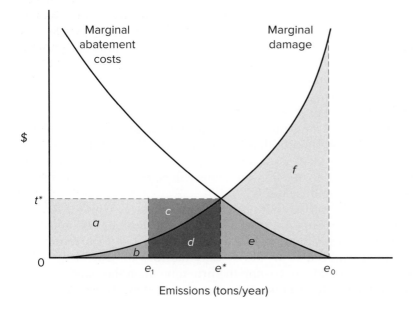

Emissions (tons/year)

The reduction of emissions from e_0 to e^* has eliminated damages of $(e + f)$. Remaining damages are $(b + d)$, an amount less than the firm pays in taxes. This underscores the idea that the emission charge is based on the right to use environmental resources, not on the notion of compensation. But a "flat tax" like this (one tax rate for all emissions) has been criticized because it would often lead to situations where the total tax payments of firms would substantially exceed remaining damages. A way around this is to institute a **two-part emission charge.** We allow some initial quantity of emission to go untaxed, applying the charge only to emissions in excess of this threshold. For example, in Figure 12.2 we might allow the firm e_1 units of emissions free of tax and apply the tax rate of t^* to anything over this. In this way the firm would still have the incentive to reduce emissions to e^*, but its total tax payments would be only $(c + d)$. Total abatement costs, and total damages caused by the e^* units of emissions, would still be the same.

How might the charge be set if regulators did not know the marginal damage function? Emissions are connected to ambient quality; the lower the emissions, the lower the ambient concentration of the pollutant, in general. So one strategy might be to set a tax and then watch carefully to see what this did in terms of improving ambient quality levels. We would have to wait long enough to give firms time to respond to the tax. If ambient quality does not improve as much as desired, increase the charge; if ambient quality improves more than is thought appropriate, lower the charge. This is a successive approximation process of finding the correct long-run emissions charge. It is not at all clear whether this approach would be practicable in the real world. In responding to a charge, polluters would invest in a variety of pollution-control devices and practices, many of which would have relatively high up-front costs. This investment process could be substantially upset if, shortly afterward, the authorities shift to a new tax rate. Any agency trying to use this method to find the efficient charge rate would undoubtedly find itself embroiled in a brisk political battle. Rather than planning to make successive adjustments in the tax rate, there would be a strong incentive for policymakers to determine the correct rate at the beginning. This would put a premium on prior study to get some idea of the shapes of the aggregate abatement and damage cost curves.

Emission Charges and Cost-Effectiveness

Perhaps the strongest case for a policy of effluent charges is to be made on grounds of their effects in controlling multiple sources of emissions in a way that satisfies the **equimarginal principle.** If the same tax rate is applied to different sources with different marginal abatement cost functions, and each source reduces its emissions until its marginal abatement costs equal the tax, then marginal abatement costs will automatically be equalized across all the sources.

This is depicted in Figure 12.3.[3] We assume here that there are two sources of a particular type of emission, labeled Source A and Source B. Also assume that

---

[3] We have seen a graph like this several times before, for example, in Figures 11.3 and 5.5.

FIGURE 12.3 Emission Charges and the Equimarginal Rule

Emission Level (tons/month)	Marginal Abatement Costs ($)	
	Source A	Source B
20	0.0	0.0
19	1.0	2.1
18	2.1	4.6
17	3.3	9.4
16	4.6	19.3
15	6.0	32.5
14	7.6	54.9
13	9.4	82.9
12	11.5	116.9
11	13.9	156.9
10	16.5	204.9
9	19.3	264.9
8	22.3	332.9
7	25.5	406.9
6	28.9	487.0
5	32.5	577.0
4	36.3	677.2
3	40.5	787.2
2	44.9	907.2
1	49.7	1,037.2
0	54.9	1,187.2

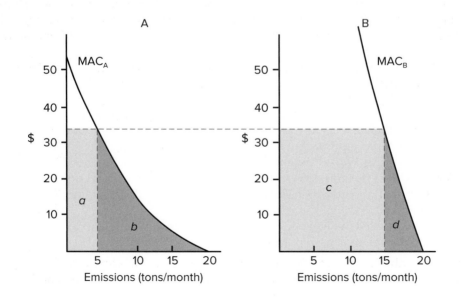

these emissions, after they leave the respective sources, are uniformly mixed together, so that the emissions of the two plants are equally damaging in the downstream, or downwind, impact area. The marginal abatement costs for the two sources are the same as those we used in the last chapter. They are shown in graphical form at the bottom of Figure 12.3. The marginal abatement costs of Source A increase much less rapidly with reductions in emissions than do those of Source B. In the real world, differences like this are normally related to the fact that the firms are using different production technologies. They may be producing different outputs (e.g., a pulp mill and a food-canning firm), or they may be plants in the same industry but using different production techniques (e.g., coal-fired and oil-fired electric power plants). According to the graphs, the production technology used by Source B makes emission reduction more costly than it is at Source A. If we impose an effluent charge of $33/ton on each source, the operators of Source A will reduce their emissions to 5 tons/month; those at Source B will cut back to 15 tons/month (dealing only with integer values). After these reductions, the two sources will have the same marginal abatement costs. The total reduction has been 20 tons per month, which the effluent charge has automatically distributed between the two firms in accordance with the equimarginal principle.

Note very carefully that the emission tax has led Source A to reduce its emissions by 75 percent, whereas Source B has reduced its emissions by only 25 percent. The emissions tax leads to larger proportionate emission reductions from firms with lower marginal abatement costs. Conversely, firms having steeper marginal abatement costs will reduce emissions less, in proportionate terms. Suppose that instead of the charge the authorities had instituted a **proportionate** cutback on the grounds that "everybody should be treated alike"; therefore, they require each source to reduce emissions by 50 percent. Our two sources in Figure 12.3 both reduce emissions to 10 tons/month. At this point their marginal abatement costs would be different. Furthermore, we can calculate total abatement costs by remembering that total cost is the sum of marginal costs. Thus, for example, for Source A the total costs of 10 tons of emissions would be $(1.0 + 2.1 + \ldots + 16.5) = \$75.90$.

The following tabulation compares the compliance costs of the equiproportionate reduction and the effluent charge with equimarginal rules.

	Total Compliance Costs ($/month)	
	Equiproportionate Reduction	**Effluent Charge with Equimarginal Rules**
Source A	75.90	204.40
Source B	684.40	67.90
Total	760.30	272.30

Note how much the totals differ. The total compliance cost of an equiproportionate cutback is about 2.8 times the total cost of an emission tax. The simple reason is that the equiproportionate cutback violates the equimarginal principle;

it requires the same proportionate cutback regardless of the height and shape of a firm's marginal abatement costs. The difference in total costs between these two approaches is quite large with these illustrative numbers. We will see in later chapters that in the real world of pollution control these differences are often much larger. The extra amount spent to treat all firms with the same proportionate percentage could have been used to further reduce pollution.

The higher the tax rate, the more emissions will be reduced. In fact, if the tax rate were increased to something over $55/ton, Firm A would stop emitting this residual entirely. The marginal abatement cost function for Firm B increases so rapidly, however, that an extremely high charge (more than $1,187/ton) would be required to get this source to reduce emissions to zero. A single effluent charge, when applied to several firms, will induce a greater reduction by firms whose marginal abatement costs increase less rapidly with emission reductions than from firms whose marginal abatement costs increase more rapidly. Because the firms are paying the same tax rate, they will have different total abatement costs and different tax bills. In Figure 12.3, the total abatement costs are equal to area *b* for Source A and area *d* for Source B. On the other hand, the monthly tax bill sent to Source A would be only *a*, compared to a bill of *c* sent to Source B. Thus, the less steeply the marginal abatement cost of a firm increases, the larger that firm's emission reduction will be and the smaller its tax bill.

It needs to be emphasized that the efficiency results of the emission charge approach (i.e., that it satisfies the equimarginal principle) are achievable *even though the administering agency knows nothing about the marginal abatement costs of any of the sources.* This is in clear contrast with the standards approach, where the public agency has to know exactly what these marginal abatement costs are for each firm in order to have a fully efficient program. In a charge approach the only requirement is that firms pay the same tax rate and that they are cost minimizers. After each one has adjusted its emissions in accordance with its marginal abatement costs (which we can expect them to know themselves), they will all be emitting at the appropriate rates to satisfy the equimarginal principle.

Emission Taxes and Nonuniform Emissions

So far the discussion has proceeded under the assumption that the emissions of all sources are uniformly mixed together; that is, the emissions from one source have the same marginal impact on ambient quality levels as those from other sources. In the real world this is usually not the case. Very often the situation is something like, although of course more complicated than, that depicted in Figure 12.4. Here there are two sources. Source A, however, is about twice as far away from the center of population as Source B. This means that emissions from Source A do not produce as much damage in the urban area as emissions from Source B. If the two sources are emitting some material into a river that flows toward the city, the emissions of Source A have a longer time in the water to be broken down and rendered less harmful than do the emissions from Source B. Or if it is an air pollution problem, Source A is much farther upwind than Source B, so there is more time for its emissions to be spread

FIGURE 12.4   Nonuniform Emissions

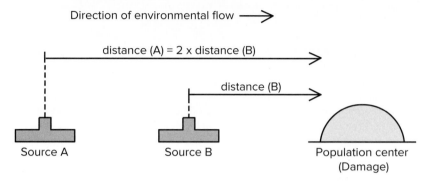

out and diluted than there is for the emissions from Source B. There could be other reasons than location differences for the different impacts; for example, they may emit residuals at different times of the year when wind patterns are different. Studying the location problem will allow us to examine the general problem of nonuniform emissions.

In this case a single emission charge applied to both sources would not be fully efficient. A single charge addresses only the problem of differences in marginal abatement costs, not differences in damages caused by the emissions from different sources. In Figure 12.4, a one-unit reduction in emissions from Plant B would improve environmental quality (reduce damages) in the urban area more than a one-unit reduction in emissions from Plant A, and this fact must be taken into account in setting emission charge rates. Suppose emission reductions at Source B are twice as effective at reducing damages as reductions in emissions at Source A. This means, in effect, that the effluent tax paid by Source B must be twice as high as the effluent charge paid by Source A.[4] Thus, after adjustment to these tax levels the marginal abatement cost of Source B would be twice the marginal abatement cost of Source A. But the damage reduction *per dollar spent in reducing emissions* would be equalized across the two sources.

The logic of the preceding discussion would seem to imply the conclusion that in these cases we would have to charge different emission charges to each source. To do this, we would have to know the relative importance of the emissions from each source in affecting ambient quality. Exhibit 12.2 discusses some results showing that for several important air pollutants, damages were

---

[4] The technical concept here is called a "transfer coefficient." A transfer coefficient is a number that tells how the emissions from any particular source affect ambient quality at some other point. In the previous example, suppose 1 ton of SO_2 emitted by B would increase SO_2 concentration over the urban area by 0.1 ppm. Then a ton emitted from Source A would increase the ambient concentration by 0.05 (assuming an effect that is strictly proportional to distance). If the transfer coefficient for Source B is 1, that for Source A is 0.5, so the tax at A has to be half the tax at B. More generally, if the transfer coefficient at A is t_1, and that of B is t_2, then the tax at A should be t_1/t_2 times the tax at B.

Emissions from Different Sources Can Produce Very Different Damages

EXHIBIT 12.2

Different sources with the same type and quantity of emissions may be very different in terms of the damages they cause. Two economists estimated source-specific damages from emissions of major pollutants from power plants in the United States. They used a large-scale model that tracks the consequences of emission through air quality changes, exposure levels, dose-response information, and the valuation of resulting health impacts on affected populations. Some results are shown in the following table. Results are in the form of "trading ratios," which is the number of tons of pollutant emitted from the power-plant stack that causes the same amount of damage as would 1 ton emitted at ground level at the same site. The results shown are for fine particulate matter ($PM_{2.5}$) and sulfur dioxide (SO_2). The top four power plants are near urban areas and the bottom four are in rural locations.

For the urban power plants, note the differences for the Con Edison plant in New York: it would take 11 tons of $PM_{2.5}$ emitted from the stack to produce the same damage as 1 ton emitted at ground level. For SO_2 it would take 8 tons coming out of the stack to generate the same damages as 1 ground-level ton. For the rural plants, the results are very different; here the stack and ground-level emissions produce the same levels of damage.

What these results show is that there can be very substantial differences between sources in terms of damages produced by the same pollutant.

Ground Source (city, state)	Power Plant (firm, facility)	Stack Height (feet)	Trading Ratios $PM_{2.5}$	Trading Ratios SO_2
New York, NY	Con Edison, 74th Street station	495	11:1	8:1
Washington, D.C.	Potomac Power Resources	400	23:1	8:1
Atlanta, GA	Georgia Power Co.	835	19:1	5:1
Houston, TX	Texas Genco, Inc. W.A. Parish	600	17:1	10:1
Grant Country, WV	Dominion, Mount Storm Station	740	1:1	1:1
Rosebud County, MT	PPL Montana, Colstrip Steam Elec	690	1:1	1:1

The trading ratio is the number of tons emitted from the stack of a power plant that would cause the same damage as 1 ton from a ground source at the same site.

Source: Nicholas A. Muller and Robert Mendelsohn, "Efficient Pollution Regulation: Getting the Prices Right," *American Economic Review*, 99(5), 2009, pp. 1714–1739.

substantially different among sources. The best response here might be to institute what is called a **zoned emission charge.** Here the administering agency would divide a territory into separate zones; the actual number of zones would depend on the circumstances of the case. Within each zone the agency would charge the same emission charge to all sources, whereas it would charge different charges in different zones.

FIGURE 12.5   **Zoned Emissions Charge**

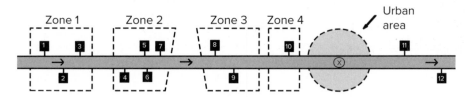

Key: ■   Emission sources
       ⊗   Water-quality monitoring station

Naturally, the zones would be identified by grouping together sources whose emissions have similar effects on ambient quality levels. Figure 12.5, for example, shows the schematic of a river with a dozen different sources of emissions and one urban area where water quality is measured and water quality targets are established. The 10 upstream sources are strung along the river at increasing distances from the urban area. Thus, each has a different impact on measured water quality at the monitoring station, and a fully cost-effective program of emissions reductions would have to account for this fact *in addition to* their different marginal abatement costs. But it would be administratively very costly to apply a different emissions charge to each source. We might, in this case, fall back on a zoned emission charge.

We first define different zones along the river, then apply the same tax to all sources within the same zone, but different taxes to sources in different zones. Each zone would contain sources whose emissions have roughly the same impact on measured water quality. In Figure 12.5, for example, four upstream zones along the river are sketched out. The three sources in Zone 1 would pay the same charge, as would the four sources in Zone 2, and so on. Sources 11 and 12 are downstream from the urban area and may not get taxed at all. Of course, this is a simplified diagram to show the basic idea; in the real world, there would also very likely be downstream damages. By using a zone system, we can achieve a certain amount of administrative simplification while recognizing differences in the locations of different groups of sources.

Emissions Charges and Uncertainty

Pollution-control policies have to be carried out in a world of **uncertainty.** Administrative agencies often do not know exactly what emissions are being produced by each source or exactly what the human and ecosystem impacts are. Another source of uncertainty is the shape of the marginal abatement cost curve of the sources subject to control; these may be known reasonably well by the polluters themselves, but administrators usually will be very unsure of how high they are, how steep they are, how much they differ from source to source, and so on. It is one of the advantages of emissions charges that they can bring about cost-effective results even within that state of uncertainty.

FIGURE 12.6 Emission Charges, Uncertainty, and Tax Revenues

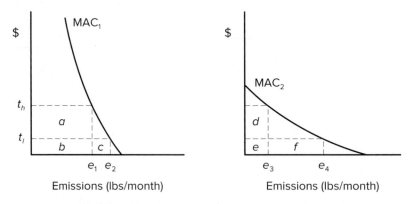

Nevertheless, when administrators set taxes at certain levels, they normally will be uncertain about how much emission reduction will ensue, for that depends on how sources respond to the tax. This is one of the drawbacks of emission charges. It may be difficult to predict accurately how much total emissions will decrease because exact knowledge of marginal abatement costs is often lacking. Observe Figure 12.6. It shows two different marginal abatement cost functions, a steep one (MAC_1) and one that is much less steep (MAC_2). Consider MAC_1. If the tax were set at the relatively high rate of t_h, this source would reduce emissions to e_1, whereas if it were set at the low rate of t_l, it would adjust emissions to e_2. These two emission rates are relatively close together. In other words, whether the tax is high or low, the emissions rate of this source would not vary much; we could count on having an emissions rate of something in the vicinity of e_1 and e_2.

But for the firm with the less steep marginal abatement costs (MAC_2), things are much more unstable. If the tax were set low, it would change emissions to e_4, whereas with a high tax emissions would go all the way down to e_3. In other words, for given changes in the tax rate, this firm would respond with much larger changes in emission rates than would the source with the steeper MAC curve.

The upshot of this discussion is that if most firms in a particular pollution problem have relatively flat MAC functions, regulators may have trouble finding the charge rate that will give us just the amount of reduction in total emissions we want. Because they don't know exactly where the MAC functions really are, they don't know exactly how high to set the tax. If they set it a little high or a little low, these firms will respond with large changes in their emissions. This is one of the main reasons administrators opt for standards: they seem to offer a definite control on quantities of emissions produced. In the next chapter, we will discuss an incentive approach that addresses this problem.

Emission Charges and Tax Revenues

Another important aspect of emission charges is that they lead to **tax revenues** accruing to the government. Carrying this line of thought further has suggested to many people that society could benefit by replacing certain existing taxes with emission taxes. Many countries tax employment, for example. When firms hire workers, they must pay employment taxes to cover such things as the public costs of unemployment insurance and social security payments. But employment taxes lead to reduced levels of employment because, in effect, they make hiring workers more expensive. A government, therefore, might reduce its employment taxes and increase emission taxes in such a way as to keep its total tax revenue the same. This action has come to be known as the **double-dividend hypothesis.** This refers to the fact that society would gain both from the emissions taxes (through reduced emission damage) and from reduced employment tax (through increased employment).

But predicting the revenue impacts of emission taxes may be difficult. Suppose, in Figure 12.6, an emission tax was increased from t_l to t_h. If the aggregate marginal abatement costs of the affected firm is MAC_1, total tax revenue will increase from $(b + c)$ to $(a + b)$. But if the marginal abatement cost is actually MAC_2, raising the emission tax will cause tax revenues to decrease from $(e + f)$ to $(d + e)$. This is because in the case of MAC_2 the tax increase leads to a large decrease in emissions, while in the case of MAC_1 it does not. Thus, if the tax authorities don't know much about the shape and location of the relevant marginal abatement, they may be in for some major surprises in terms of changes in tax revenues.

Research on the double-dividend idea has also brought out another important factor. This is the potential impact of increased prices of the goods and services produced by the sectors subject to emission taxes. This can have a direct negative effect on the welfare of consumers of these goods and services. It can also have an indirect effect working through changes in the labor market.[5]

Emission Charges and the Incentives to Innovate

In a dynamic world, it is critical that environmental policies encourage technological change in pollution control. One of the main advantages of emission charges is that they provide strong incentives for this. This is shown in Figure 12.7, which shows two marginal abatement cost curves for a single firm. MAC_1 represents the current condition. It shows the costs the firm would experience in cutting back its emissions with the particular technology it currently uses. MAC_2, on the other hand, refers to abatement costs that the firm would experience after engaging in a relatively expensive research and development (R&D) program to develop a new method of reducing emissions. Assume the firm has a reasonably good idea of what the results of the R&D will be, although of course nothing is ever a sure thing. We can use it to measure the strength of the incentives for this firm to put money into the R&D program.

---

[5] See Don Fullerton and Gilbert E. Metcalf, "Environmental Taxes and the Double-Dividend Hypothesis: Did You Really Expect Something for Nothing?" *Chicago-Kent Law Review*, 73(1), 1998, pp. 221–256.

FIGURE 12.7 **Emission Charges and the Incentive for R&D**

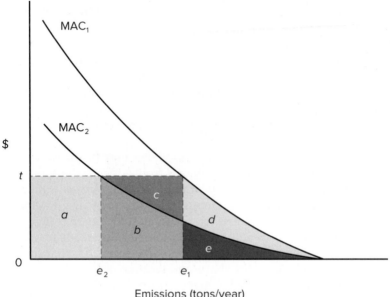

Suppose the firm is subject to an effluent tax of t/ton of emissions. Initially it will reduce emissions to e_1; at this point its total pollution-related costs will consist of $(d + e)$ worth of abatement costs and a tax bill of $(a + b + c)$. If it can lower its marginal abatement cost curve to MAC_2 through the R&D activities, it would then reduce its emissions to e_2. At this point it would pay $(b + e)$ in abatement costs and a in taxes. The reduction in total costs has been $(c + d)$. If the firm had instead been faced with an emissions standard of e_1, its cost savings with the new technology would have been only d, as we saw in the last chapter. Also, as we saw in the last chapter, if public authorities shift the standard to e_2 when the new technology becomes available (giving the same emissions reduction as the tax would have), the firm could actually experience an *increase* in costs because of its R&D efforts.

Thus, under a policy of emission charges:

• A firm's R&D efforts will lead to a bigger reduction in its pollution control-related costs (abatement costs plus tax payments) than under a standards approach.

• A firm would automatically reduce its emissions as it found ways to shift its marginal abatement cost function downward, whereas under the standard no such automatic process would result.

• Polluters must pay for emissions as well as for abatement costs, whereas with standards they only need to pay abatement costs.

• Potential cost savings from new pollution-control techniques are much larger under the charge program.

Emission Charges and Enforcement Costs

Charges pose a different type of **enforcement** problem than standards. Any charge system requires accurate information on the item to be taxed. If emissions are to be taxed, they must be measurable at reasonable cost. This means that residuals flowing from a source must be concentrated in a small enough number of identifiable streams that monitoring is possible. This rules out most nonpoint-source emissions because they are spread thinly over a wide area in a way that makes them impossible to measure. It would normally be impossible to tax the pollutants in city street runoff because the diffuse nature of the "emissions" makes them impossible to measure. This also may rule out certain toxic chemical emissions, which, in addition to being nonpoint source, often involve such small quantities that their flow rates are difficult to measure.

With emission charges the taxing authorities would be sending a tax bill to the polluting firms at the end of each month or year, based on their total quantity of emissions during that period. So the agency would require information on cumulative emissions from each source. This is more involved than just information on rate of discharge because cumulative discharge is rate times duration. There are several ways of getting this information. Perhaps the most ideal would be to have permanent monitoring equipment that measures emissions continuously over the time period in question. Lacking such technology, one could fall back on periodic checking of the rate of emissions, with an estimate of the duration based on normal business considerations or perhaps self-reporting by firms. Alternatively, engineering studies might be carried out to determine prospective emission quantities under specified conditions of operation, inputs used, and so on.

It is probably fair to say that the **monitoring requirements** of an emissions charge policy are more stringent than those for the typical standards program. Polluters, of course, have incentives to find ways, legal and otherwise, to get their tax bills reduced. One way to do this is to influence the monitoring process enough so that reported emissions are smaller. Once they do get their tax bills, recipients will have every incentive to contest them if they appear to be based on uncertain data or have other technical weaknesses. The lack of high-quality monitoring and reporting procedures has undoubtedly contributed to the unpopularity of effluent charge policies for environmental quality control.

Other Types of Charges

So far we have discussed only one type of charge, an effluent or emissions tax. Because it is the emission of residuals that leads directly to environmental pollution, charges on emissions presumably have the greatest leverage in terms of altering the incentives of polluters. But it is often impossible or impractical to levy charges directly on emissions. In cases where we can't measure and monitor emissions at reasonable cost, charges, if they are to be used, would obviously have to be applied to something else. A good case of this is the problem of water pollution from fertilizer runoff in agriculture. It is impossible to tax the pounds of nitrogen in the runoff because it is a nonpoint-source pollutant and thus not directly measurable. The same problem applies to agricultural pesticides. What may be feasible instead is to put charges on these materials as they are bought by farmers—that is, say, a charge per ton of fertilizer or per 100 pounds of pesticide purchased. The charge is to reflect the fact that a certain proportion of these materials ends up in nearby streams and lakes. Because they are paying higher prices for these items, farmers would have the incentive to use them in smaller quantities. Higher prices also create an incentive to use the fertilizer in ways that involve less wastage, for example, by reducing the amounts that run off.

Placing a charge on something other than emissions is usually a "second-best" course of action made necessary because direct emissions can't be closely monitored. In cases such as this we have to watch out for distortions that can come about as people respond to the charge, distortions that can substantially alleviate the effects of the tax or can sometimes make related problems worse. We mentioned in Chapter 1 the move by many U.S. communities to tax household trash. One technique is to sell stickers to the residents and require that each bag of trash has a sticker on it. The rate of tax is determined by the price of the stickers, and it is relatively easy to monitor and enforce the system through the curbside pickup operations. But the per-bag tax will produce an incentive to pack more into each bag, so the reduction in total quantity of trash may be less than the reduction in the number of bags collected.

On Carbon Taxes

We have now realized that reducing global emissions of GHGs is a critically important activity to pursue. An obvious idea would be to tax emissions of GHGs, especially carbon dioxide. CO_2 emissions result whenever fossil fuels, that is, fuels containing carbon, are burned to produce energy. A CO_2 emission tax could be placed directly on emissions, assuming they could be accurately measured.

Another approach is to place a tax on fuel used, since this is strictly proportional to carbon dioxide released.

- The **carbon footprint** of an item (a physical good, or a service) is the total emissions of GHGs occurring in the production and consumption of the item, usually expressed in equivalent tons of CO_2 (one ton of CO_2 is equivalent to 0.27 tons of carbon).

This tax could fall on commercial establishments. Perhaps a better approach would be to levy a tax "upstream," where fossil fuels are first extracted. The tax would then filter through the system, affecting more heavily the prices of those goods and services that have large carbon footprints and less heavily on prices of those with low or negligible footprints, as is depicted in Figure 12.8.

Distributional Impacts of Emission Charges

There are two primary impacts of emission charges on the distribution of income and wealth:

1. Impacts on prices and output of goods and services affected by the charges, and
2. Effects from the expenditure of tax funds generated by the charges.

FIGURE 12.8 **A Tax on Carbon**

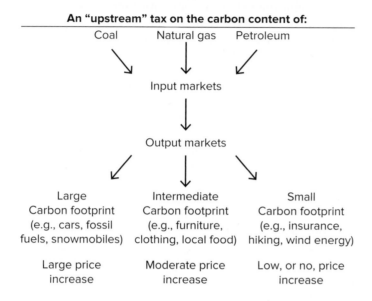

Businesses subject to a charge will experience an increase in costs because of both the abatement costs and the tax payments. From the firm's standpoint, these constitute increases in production cost, which the firm will presumably pass on to consumers just as with any cost of production. Whether and how much the firm can do this depends on competitive conditions and the conditions of demand. If the charge is applied to a single firm or small group of firms within a competitive industry, it will not be able to push its price up above the industry price, and so will have to absorb the cost increase. In this case the impacts will be felt entirely by owners of the firm and the people who work there. Many firms fear, or pretend to fear, being in precisely this situation and base their public objections to taxes on this outcome. If the charge is applied to an entire industry, prices will go up and consumers will bear part of the burden. How much prices go up depends on demand conditions.[6] For taxes applied directly to consumer goods, such as gasoline or heating oil, market prices would respond according to the supply and demand characteristics of the markets.

Price increases often are thought of as regressive because, for any given item, an increase in its price would affect poor people proportionately more than higher-income people. For something that both poor and well-off people consume, such as electricity, this conclusion is straightforward. For price increases in goods consumed disproportionately by more well-to-do people (e.g., airline travel), however, the burden would be mostly on them.[7]

---

[6] This was discussed in greater detail in Chapter 8.

[7] Sterner, Thomas, *Fuel Taxes and the Poor: The Distributional Effects of Gasoline Taxation and Their Implications for Climate Policy*, London, Routledge, 2011.

The burden on workers is tied closely to what happens to the rate of output of the affected firms. Here again, the extent of the output effect depends on competitive conditions and the nature of the demand for the good. If the emission tax program is applied to a single firm in a competitive industry or if the demand for the output of an industry is very responsive to price, output adjustments will be relatively large and workers could be displaced. The long-run burden is then a matter of whether good alternative sources of employment are available.

Although burdens because of price and output changes may be real, we have to remember that, on the other side, the charge program is creating substantial benefits in the form of reduced environmental damages. To know how a program affects any particular group, we would have to account also for how these benefits are distributed.

Effluent charges also could involve substantial sums going from consumers of the goods produced by the taxed industry to the beneficiaries, whomever they may be, of the funds collected by the taxing authorities. These funds could be used for any number of purposes; how they are used would determine their impacts. They might, for example, be distributed to lower-income people to offset the effects of price increases. They even might be returned in part to the firms paying the effluent taxes. This is done in some European countries to help finance the purchase of pollution-control technology. As long as the return payments do not make the marginal emissions tax rate effectively lower, the incentive effects of the charge are not affected. Alternatively, they might be used to pay for other environmental initiatives in places where direct public action is called for. They even might be used to reduce overall budget deficits, with benefits flowing to general taxpayers.

Abatement Subsidies

An emission charge works by placing a price on the environmental asset into which emissions are occurring. Essentially, the same incentive effects would result if, instead of a charge, we instituted a **subsidy** on emission reductions. Here a public authority would pay a polluter a certain amount per ton of emissions for every ton it reduced, starting from some benchmark level. The subsidy acts as a reward for reducing emissions. More formally, it acts as an **opportunity cost;** when a polluter chooses to emit a unit of effluent, it is in effect forgoing the subsidy payment it could have had if it had chosen to withhold that unit of effluent instead. Table 12.1, using the same numbers as in the preceding discussion on emission charges, shows how this works in principle. The firm's base level is set at its current emissions rate: 10 tons/month. It receives $120 per ton for every ton it cuts back from this base. The fourth column shows its total subsidy revenues, and the last column shows total subsidies minus total abatement costs. This net revenue peaks at 4 tons/month, the same emissions level the firm would choose with the $120 tax. In other words, the incentive for the firm is the same as for the tax.

TABLE 12.1   **An Abatement Subsidy**

Emissions (tons/month)	Marginal Abatement Cost	Total Abatement Cost	Total Subsidy at $120/Ton	Total Subsidy Minus Total Abatement Costs
10	0	0	0	0
9	15	15	120	105
8	30	45	240	195
7	50	95	360	265
6	70	165	480	315
5	95	260	600	340
4	120	375	720	345
3	150	525	840	315
2	185	710	960	250
1	230	940	1,080	140
0	290	1,230	1,200	−30

Although an abatement subsidy like this would have the same incentive for each individual source, total emissions may actually increase. To understand why, note the difference in the financial position of this firm when it emits 4 tons of pollutant under the two programs: With the tax it has total costs of $855 (see Figure 12.1), whereas with the subsidy it has a total *revenue* of $345. Thus, the financial position of the firm is much different. In effect, it will be earning higher profits after the imposition of the subsidy, and this can have the effect of making this industry more attractive for potential new firms. There is the possibility, in other words, of having the emissions per firm go down while the number of firms in the industry increases, and therefore total emissions increase. This feature is a major drawback of simple subsidies like this.

Although subsidies linked directly to emission reductions have never become particularly popular, governments around the world have frequently resorted to many other types of subsidies to further the goals of pollution reduction. A few of these are listed in Exhibit 12.3.

Deposit-Refund Systems

One place where subsidies may be more practical is in deposit-refund systems. A deposit-refund system is essentially the combination of a tax and a subsidy. For example, a subsidy (the refund) is paid to consumers when they return an item to a designated collection point. The purpose of the subsidy is to provide the incentive for people to refrain from disposing of these items in environmentally damaging ways. The funds for paying the subsidy are raised by levying taxes (the deposit) on these items when they are purchased. In this case, the purpose of the tax is not necessarily so much to get people to reduce the consumption of the item, but to raise money to pay the subsidy. The tax is called a deposit and the subsidy a refund, but the principle is clear.

Deposit-refund systems are particularly well suited to situations where a product is widely dispersed when purchased and used, and where disposal is

Types of Environmentally Related Subsidies

EXHIBIT 12.3

Subsidies in the Form of	Example(s)
Tax benefits	Tax exemptions for pollution-control equipment or recycling equipment Exemptions of ethanol-blended gas from federal taxes
Reduced environmental fines	Reductions in normal fines if firms undertake extensive pollution-control plans
Public grants to encourage environmental programs	EPA grants to communities to fund "brownfields" programs[1]
	Grants to farmers to adopt conservation practices
	Grants to businesses or communities to establish recycling programs
Development rights purchase programs	Public purchases of agricultural development rights to maintain land in agriculture or open space
Public support of environmental market development	Public rules on procurement of products made from recycled materials
	Cash payments for people who turn in old, high-emitting automobiles
Cost-sharing grants	Grants made to localities to cover a portion of the cost of building wastewater treatment facilities

[1]Brownfields are contaminated industrial sites that pose relatively low risks, but may be avoided by private developers because of potential liability problems.

difficult or impossible for authorities to monitor. In the United States, a number of individual states[8] have enacted deposit-refund systems for beverage containers, both to reduce litter and to encourage recycling. This approach also has been widely used in Europe. But many other products could be handled effectively with this type of system.

Germany instituted a deposit-refund on waste lubricating oil. Each year very large quantities of waste oil are disposed of improperly, putting many air, water, and land resources under threat. In the German system, new lubricating oil

[8] As of 2015 these were California, Connecticut, Hawaii, Iowa, Maine, Massachusetts, Michigan, New York, Oregon, and Vermont, plus Guam.

is subject to a tax (a deposit), the proceeds of which go into a special fund. This fund is then used to subsidize (the refund side) a waste oil recovery and reprocessing system. The terms of the subsidy are set so as to encourage competition in the recovery/reprocessing system and to provide an incentive for users to reduce the extent to which oil is contaminated during use.

In Sweden and Norway, deposit-refund systems have been instituted for cars. New-car buyers pay a deposit at the time of purchase, which will be refunded when and if the car is turned over to an authorized junk dealer. Experience with these systems shows that success depends on more than just the size of the deposit-refund. For example, it is essential that the collection system be designed to be reasonably convenient for consumers.

Other items for which deposit-refund systems might be appropriate are consumer products containing hazardous substances, such as batteries containing cadmium, and car batteries.[9] Automobile tires also might be handled this way. The deposit-refund system also might be adaptable to conventional industrial pollutants. For example, users of fossil fuels might pay deposits on the quantities of sulfur contained in the fuels they purchase; they would then get refunds on the sulfur recovered from the exhaust gas. Thus, they would lose their deposit only on the sulfur that went up the stacks.

Summary

Emission charges attack the pollution problem at its source, by putting a price on something that has been free and, therefore, overused. The main advantage of emission charges is their efficiency aspects: if all sources are subject to the same charge, they will adjust their emission rates so that the equimarginal rule is satisfied. Administrators do not have to know the individual source marginal abatement cost functions for this to happen; it is enough that firms are faced with the charge and then left free to make their own adjustments. A second major advantage of emission charges is that they produce a strong incentive to innovate, to discover cheaper ways of reducing emissions.

The apparent indirect character of emission charges may tend to work against their acceptance by policymakers. Standards have the appearance of placing direct control on the thing that is at issue, namely, emissions. Emission charges, on the other hand, place no direct restrictions on emissions but rely on the self-interested behavior of firms to adjust their own emission rates in response to the tax. This may make some policymakers uneasy because firms apparently are still allowed to control their own emission rates. It may seem paradoxical that this "indirect" character of effluent taxes can sometimes provide a stronger inducement to emission reductions than seemingly more direct approaches.

But emission charges require effective monitoring. They cannot be enforced simply by checking to see if sources have installed certain types of pollution-control equipment. If emission charges are to have the appropriate incentive effects, they must be based closely on *cumulative emissions*.

[9] As of 2015, 13 U.S. states had deposit-refund systems for car batteries.

An advantage of emission charges is that they provide a source of revenue for public authorities. Many have recommended that tax systems be changed to rely less on taxes that have distorting economic effects and more on emissions charges. Efforts to combat global climate change have led many to recommend carbon taxes; these have become quite popular in Europe.

Emissions subsidies would have the same incentive effect on individual polluters, but they could lead to increases in total emission levels. One place where subsidies have been used effectively is in deposit-refund systems, which are essentially tax and subsidy systems in combination.

Questions for Further Discussion

1. How might an emission charge program be designed to reduce automobile emissions?
2. Explain how emission charges solve the equimarginal problem.
3. Opponents of emission tax policies sometimes assert that they are simply a way of letting firms buy the right to pollute. Is this a reasonable criticism?
4. When emission charges are put into effect, who ultimately ends up paying for them? Is this fair?
5. Emission charges are sometimes seen as creating a "double burden": Firms must pay the costs of reducing emissions and also pay the government for polluting discharges. How might a charge system be designed to reduce this double burden?
6. Refer to Figure 12.1. Suppose the emissions tax is $95/ton/month. Find the efficient level of emissions for the firm. Explain why the firm would not reduce its emissions to 1 ton/month.

For additional readings and Web sites pertaining to the material in this chapter, see **www.mhhe.com/field7e.**

13

Incentive-Based Strategies: Market Trading Systems

An effluent charge requires that some central public authority establish a charge rate, monitor the performance of each polluter, and then collect the tax bills. It is essentially an interaction between polluters and public authorities in which we might expect the same type of adversarial relationship we get in any tax system. In this chapter we take a look at a policy approach that, while incorporating economic incentives, is designed to work in a more decentralized fashion. Rather than leaving everything to a centralized public agency, it works through decentralized market interactions in which polluters may buy and sell emission permits, and pollution is controlled by linking emissions with the number of permits held.

These programs have proliferated in recent years. The most well known in the United States is the sulfur dioxide (SO_2) trading scheme introduced as part of the Clean Air Act of 1990. A nitrous oxide (NO_x) trading plan was started among a group of eastern states in 1999. California has started several programs within its own borders. The countries of the European Union have recently inaugurated a multicountry trading plan to reduce carbon dioxide (CO_2) emissions.

General Principles

We can distinguish three types of trading systems for achieving more efficient pollution control:

- Offset trading
- Emission rate trading
- Cap-and-trade (CAP)

Offset trading initially came about to address a very practical problem: how to limit environmental pollution but still be able to accommodate economic growth. Under the original Clean Air Act of 1970, situations evolved (especially in Southern California) where all existing firms were subject to regulatory emission standards, but the air quality in the region was nevertheless still below standard. How to allow the growth of new firms, but avoid making air pollution worse? The answer was to allow new firms to pay existing firms to reduce their emissions below standard so as to offset the added emissions of the new firms. Trades of this type, since it involved transactions between two firms subject to regulatory control, were sometimes called **credit trading.** But offset-type trading can also occur between any two, or more, entities, whether or not they are under regulatory control. For example, if the selling firm is not under regulatory limits, they may be able to reduce their emissions below the level that would exist if an agreement was not reached, and sell the resulting offset to another entity that wishes to offset its emissions, either because it is required to, or it voluntarily choses to. One of the most well-known examples of offset trading is the Clean Development Mechanism under the Kyoto Protocol to reduce greenhouse gases. We will encounter this in Chapter 18.

Emission rate trading takes place in terms of the rate that a pollutant constitutes in total output. For example, a greenhouse gas emission rate might be defined in terms of tons of CO_2 per 1,000 megawatt hours of power production. After a base rate is set, either voluntarily or through regulation, trading would take place between sources. Sources that are willing and able to reduce their emission rate below the base would sell allowances to sources that want to continue to operate at a rate higher than the base. We will discuss this in more detail later in this chapter.

Cap-and-trade programs work a little differently. The first step in a CAP program is to make a centralized decision (by a regulatory agency or some other collective entity) on the aggregate quantity of emissions to be allowed. Permits are then written in accordance with this quantity. These permits are then distributed among the sources responsible for the emissions. Some formula must be used to determine how many permits each source will receive; we will come back to this problem later. Assuming that the total number of permits is less than current total emissions, some or all emitters will receive fewer permits than their current emissions.

Cap-and-Trade

Suppose, for example, that a CAP program has been instituted to reduce the amount of sulfur emitted by a group of power plants. Current total emissions are, say, 150,000 tons of sulfur per year, and policymakers have decided that this must be reduced to 100,000 tons per year. Let's focus on the situation of one of the power plants, which is depicted in Figure 13.1. We suppose it is emitting 5,000 tons of sulfur currently. Under the program, the plant

FIGURE 13.1   **Individual Firm Choices Under a Cap-and-Trade Program**

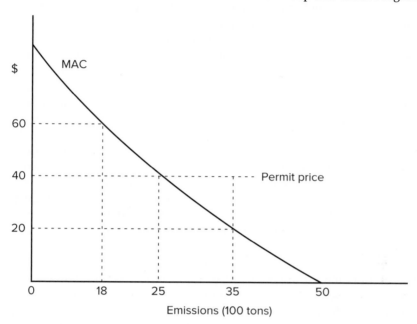

is initially given 2,500 discharge permits. The plant manager now has three choices:

1. Reduce the emissions to the level covered by the number of permits the plant was initially awarded.
2. Buy additional permits and emit at levels higher than the original award level (e.g., buy 1,000 permits to add to its 2,500 initial distribution, so its emissions would now be 3,500 tons/year).
3. Reduce emissions below the level of the original award, then sell the permits it doesn't need (e.g., reduce emissions to 1,800 tons/year and sell 1,000 permits).

Note that whether the firm is a buyer or seller of permits depends on the relationship of the price of permits and their marginal abatement costs at the emission level corresponding to their initial permit holding.

1. If the original award is 1,800 permits, the firm's marginal abatement costs would be $60/ton; with a permit price of $40, it can improve its situation by buying 700 permits and increasing its emissions to 2,500 tons.
2. If its original allocation is 3,500 permits, its marginal abatement costs would be lower than the permit price; it can improve its situation by selling 1,000 permits and reducing its emission to 2,500 tons.

Now think of a situation involving an industry where there are a large number of firms and each one is emitting a pollutant we wish to control with a cap-and-trade program. An overall level of aggregate emissions is set by the authorities, and transferable permits are allocated to each firm according to some formula. Marginal abatement costs can be expected to differ among firms, based on different production and pollution-control technologies available to each. Some sources will be potential buyers of permits (MAC > permit price), and some firms will be potential sellers (MAC < permit price). There are **gains from trade** to be had by the sources, by buying and selling permits, in effect rearranging the total number of permits (which has been fixed by the authorities) among the plants.

It is important to note, now, that each firm will be in a situation analogous to the one depicted in Figure 13.1. By buying or selling permits, they move to a situation where marginal abatement costs are equal to the price of permits. Assuming there is a single overall market for permits, and therefore a single market price for them, this means that the trading of permits among the firms will result in a cost-effective reduction in total emission, because each firm will end up equating its marginal abatement costs to the single permit price. Cost-effectiveness in cap-and-trade programs requires that that there be a single market for permits, where suppliers and demanders may interact openly and where knowledge of transactions prices is publicly available to all participants. The normal forces of competition would then bring about a single price for permits. The permits would in general flow from sources with relatively low marginal abatement costs to those with high marginal abatement costs.

A permit market is depicted in Figure 13.2. The demand for permits is simply the aggregate marginal abatement cost functions of all the firms participating in the market. The supply of permits is the quantity in the cap as initially established by public authorities; the supply curve is vertical at that quantity.

FIGURE 13.2   The Market for Discharge Permits

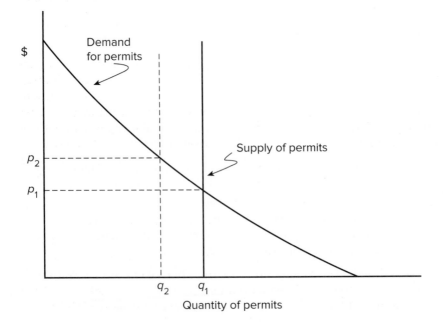

As in any competitive market, the price of permits is determined by the interaction of supply and demand. If the cap is set at q_1 in Figure 13.2, the price of permits will settle at p_1. A more restrictive cap, such as q_2, would give a higher permit price, the case at p_2.

It's important to understand that the permit price in a CAP program is what provides the incentive for emission reductions by participating firms. In this sense it is analogous to the emission tax as discussed in Chapter 12. But note that the two approaches proceed differently. With a cap-and-trade program, a quantity restriction (the cap) is set, and a permit price results as firms adjust their emission levels. In an emission charge program, authorities first set the tax level, and firms adjust their emission levels, leading to a change in the quantity of aggregate emissions.

In recent years, the idea of transferable discharge permits has become quite popular among some environmental policy advocates, as well as among policymakers themselves. Table 13.1 lists a few now in effect. Some of the largest programs have to do with air pollution. On the water pollution-control side there has been a proliferation of programs for particular water bodies.

Unlike effluent charge approaches, which basically make people pay for something they were once getting for free, CAP programs begin by creating and distributing a new type of right. These rights will have a market value as long as the total number of permits created is limited. From a political standpoint, it is perhaps easier for people to agree on a pollution-control policy that begins by distributing valuable new rights than by notifying people they will be subject to a new tax. Of course, like any pollution-control policy, CAP programs have their own set of problems that must be overcome if they are going to work effectively. What looks in theory like a neat way of using market forces to achieve efficient pollution reduction must be adapted to the complexities of the real world.

The Initial Rights Allocation

The success of the CAP approach in controlling pollution depends critically on limiting the number of rights in circulation; this is the "cap." Because individual polluters will no doubt want as many as they can get in the first distribution, the very first step of the program is one of potentially great controversy: what formula to use to make the original distribution of emission rights. Almost any rule will appear to have some inequities. For example, they might be distributed equally among all existing sources of a particular effluent. But this would encounter the problem that firms vary a lot in size. Some pulp mills are larger than others, for example, and the average size of pulp mills, in terms of value of output, may be different from the average size of, say, soda bottling plants. So giving each polluter the same number of permits may not be fair.

Permits might be allocated in accordance with the existing emissions of a source. For example, each source might get permits amounting to 50 percent of its current emissions. This may sound equitable, but, in fact, it has built-in incentive difficulties. A rule like this does not recognize the fact that some firms already may have worked hard to reduce their emissions. One easily could

TABLE 13.1 Selected Trading Programs Existing in 2015

Program	Item Traded
1990 Clean Air Act	Tons of SO_2 emissions from power plants
Southern California Reclaim	Tons of SO_2 and NO_x from large industrial sources
California Trading Program	Tons of greenhouse gases
New Zealand Trading Program	Tons of greenhouse gases
Kyoto Protocol Clean Development Mechanism	Tons of greenhouse gases from projects in developing countries
European Trading Scheme	Tons of greenhouse gases from large power, industrial, and cement plants
Regional Greenhouse Gas Initiative	Tons of greenhouse gases from large plants in northeastern and mid-Atlantic United States
Renewable Energy Certificates (in states where renewable energy portfolio standards exist)	Certificates for each 1,000 kWh of renewable energy produced
Illinois Emission Reduction Market System	Tons of volatile organic compounds emitted from large sources in eight Illinois counties
China Trading Program	Tons of CO_2 emissions
Long Island Sound Nitrogen Trading Program	Pounds of waterborne nitrogen emissions from wastewater treatment plants
Chesapeake Bay Agreement	Pounds of waterborne nutrients (nitrogen and phosphorus)
San Francisco Bay Offset Program	Kilograms of waterborne mercury emissions
Ohio Wetlands Mitigation Program	Acres of restored, enhanced, or preserved wetlands

argue that those firms that, out of a good conscience or for any reason, have already invested in emission reduction should not now be penalized, in effect, by receiving emission permits in proportion to these lower emission levels.[1] This tends to reward firms that have dragged their feet in the past.[2] It could go even further. If polluters believe that permits will soon be allocated in this way,

[1] When we study (in Chapter 15) the Clean Air Act of 1990, we will see that this was the source of great conflict when the details of the SO_2 trading program were being hammered out.

[2] This is just another example of the perverse incentives built into any program that asks everybody to cut their consumption by x percent from their current rate. It favors those who have consumed at high rates in the past and hurts those who have tried hard to live frugally.

they may have the incentive to *increase* today's emission rate because this would give them a larger base for the initial allocation of permits.

Each allocation formula has its problems, and those setting the cap must find some workable compromise if the approach is to be widely accepted. Closely related to this issue is the question of whether the rights should be given away or perhaps sold or auctioned. In principle it doesn't matter as long as the permits get distributed fairly widely. Subsequent market transactions will redistribute them in accordance with the relative marginal abatement costs of polluters, whatever the original distribution may have been. But free distribution of permits will confer windfall gains on the recipients, the amount of which would depend on the market price of the permits. What a sale or auction would do is transfer some of the original value of the rights into the hands of the auctioning agency. This might be a good way for public agencies to raise funds for worthy projects, but it has to be recognized that a plan like this would create political objections. A hybrid system would be to distribute a certain number of permits free and then auction some number of additional permits. Or a small surcharge might be put on permits in the original distribution.

Establishing Trading Rules

For any market to work effectively, clear rules must exist governing who may trade and the trading procedures that must be followed. Furthermore, the rules should not be so burdensome that they make it impossible for market participants to gauge accurately the implications of buying or selling at specific prices. This implies a hands-off stance by public agencies after the initial distribution of the rights. Working against this is the normal tendency for environmental agencies to want to monitor the market closely and perhaps try to influence its performance. The supervising agency, for example, may want to have final right of approval over all trades, so as to be able to stop any trades it considers undesirable in some way. The problem with this is that it is likely to increase the uncertainty among potential traders, increase the general level of **transactions costs** in the market, and interfere with the efficient flow of permits. The general rule for the public agency should be to set simple and clear rules and then allow trading to proceed.

One basic rule that would have to be established is who may participate in the market. Is this to be limited to polluters, or may anyone trade? For example, may environmental advocacy groups buy permits and retire them as a way of reducing total emissions?

As emission trading has grown (the global market for carbon emission permits and offsets is currently almost $100 billion annually),[3] a substantial body of law, both statutory and common, has developed to clarify the legal aspects of the approach; for example, how it fits into standard laws regarding the definition and transfer of property rights, and what evidence is required in cases of contested permit ownership.

---

[3] David Freestone and Charlotte Streck, *Legal Aspects of Carbon Trading: Kyoto, Copenhagen, and Beyond,* Oxford University Press, Oxford, U.K., 2009.

Reducing the Number of Permits

In most CAP programs, the total number of permits and their initial distribution are established by a public agency such as the Environmental protection Agency (EPA). Then the sources are allowed to trade with one another, and perhaps with other groups that are not polluters. One question that presents itself is, how does the total number of permits get reduced over time? If the efficient level of emissions is going down because of technological change, how do authorities reduce the overall number of permits in circulation?

The most direct way is that in the initial distribution each permit is dated according to the year in which it may be used. Then each participating emitter would be issued a declining series of dated permits. In this way, the annual total permit holdings would decline according to the formula adopted in the overall program. Exhibit 13.1 depicts this for the California CAP for reducing greenhouse gas emissions.

Another way the total cap may be reduced over time is for organizations, or individuals, to enter the market, buy allowances, and retire them. The Adirondack Council, a private conservation group in New York, has purchased CO_2 emission permits in the Regional Greenhouse Gas Initiative of the Northeastern

---

The Carbon Market of California   EXHIBIT 13.1

In the absence of action on the federal level to combat climate change, some states have taken the initiative. One of these is the carbon cap-and-trade program initiated in 2012 in California. It has the overall objective of reducing California greenhouse gas emissions to 1990 levels by 2020. In the first phase, it applied to power plants and large industrial plants; as of 2015 it was extended to suppliers of fuel, such as gasoline, natural gas, diesel, and propane. Covered emissions included CO_2, plus other greenhouse gases such as methane, NOx, and hydrofluorocarbons, recorded in terms of their CO_2 equivalent values. The statewide emissions cap will decline by about 3 percent per year, so that by 2020 total emissions will reach the target level. Emission allowances were distributed free to initial participants; additional allowances were auctioned by the managing agency, the California Air Resources Board. Fuel suppliers added to the program in 2015 were required to purchase allowances covering the greenhouse gas content of the fuels they delivered. In early 2014, this allowance market was linked to a similar cap-and-trade market in Quebec, Canada. The emission allowances of the California program can be exchanged one for one with allowances in the Quebec program. Prices of allowances fluctuated greatly during the first year of the program, and then settled down to around $13 to $14 per ton of CO_2 equivalent in 2013; during 2014 they stabilized at $10 to $12 per ton.

For added information, see **www.arb.ca.gov /cc/capandtrade/capandtrade.htm**

See also: Katherine Hsia-Kiung and Erica Morehouse, *Carbon Market California, A Comprehensive Analysis of the Golden States Cap-and-Trade Program, Year Two, 2014,* Environmental Defense Fund, Washington, D.C., 2015.

FIGURE 13.3 **Nonuniform Emissions and CAP Programs**

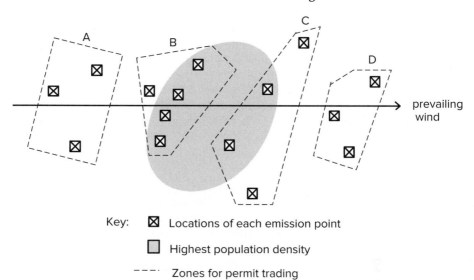

Key: ☒ Locations of each emission point

☐ Highest population density

- - - - Zones for permit trading

and Middle Atlantic States. The "Compensators" is a private group in Europe that purchases allowances on the European Trading program. For a number of years, the Clean Air Conservancy, a private group in the United States, bought SO_2, CO_2, and NO_x allowances in the programs of this country.

Nonuniform Emissions

Suppose we are trying to design a CAP program to control total airborne SO_2 emissions in a region where there are numerous different sources—power plants, industrial plants, and so on—scattered rather widely around the area. A schematic of this situation is depicted in Figure 13.3. All of the emission points are not equally situated relative to the prevailing wind or to the area of highest population density. Some sources are upwind, others are downwind, of the populated area. We assume they are not all equal in terms of marginal abatement costs, but neither are they equal in terms of the impact of their emissions on ambient SO_2 levels over the populated area. In technical terms, they have different **transfer coefficients** linking their own emissions with damages in the urban area.

Having distributed discharge permits, we now allow them to be traded. As long as the number of permits in circulation is held constant, we have effectively controlled total SO_2 emissions. But if we allow straight trading, unit for unit, of permits among all sources, the damage caused by that total could change. For example, if a downwind firm sold permits to an upwind firm, the total number of permits would remain the same but there would now be more emissions upwind of the population, and therefore more damage.[4]

The problem is similar to the one encountered under the effluent charge policy; in effect each firm is differently situated relative to the damage area, so the

[4] This is sometimes called the "hotspot" problem.

emissions of each will have a different impact on ambient quality in that area. If the program were simply to allow trading of permits among all sources on a one-for-one basis, it could easily come to pass that a firm or group of firms with higher transfer coefficients, whose emissions therefore have a greater impact on ambient quality, could accumulate larger numbers of permits.

One way to get around this might be to adjust the trading rules to take into account the impacts of individual sources. Suppose the emissions from Source A were twice as damaging as the emissions of Source B simply because of the location of the two sources. Then the administrators of the program might set a rule that if Source A is buying permits from Source B, it must buy two permits to get one. If this principle is extended to a situation with many sources, things can quickly get very complicated. Authorities would have to determine, for each source, how many permits would have to be purchased from each other source in order for the purchasing source to be credited with one new permit. If there were five sources, the agency would have to figure out only 10 such trading ratios, but if there were 20 different sources, it would have to estimate 190 of these ratios.[5] One way around this would be to use a zoned system, analogous to the zoned effluent charge we talked about earlier. Authorities would designate a series of zones, each of which would contain sources that were relatively similar in terms of their location and the impact of their emissions on ambient quality. Four such zones are shown in Figure 13.3. Authorities then could do one of two things: (1) allow trading by firms only with other firms in the same zone or (2) make adjustments for all trades across zone boundaries similar to the technique discussed previously. Thus, for example, if sources in Zone A were judged to have transfer coefficients twice the size, on average, as sources in Zone B, any trade between sources in these two zones would be adjusted by that same factor of two: Any firm in Zone A buying permits from any firm in Zone B would have to buy two permits in order to get credit for one new one; any source in Zone B would have to buy only half a permit from a firm in Zone A to get credit for one new permit.

CAPs and Problems of Competition

The question of allowing trading across zone boundaries or, on the contrary, restricting it to within zones has a much wider importance than might first appear. CAP programs work through a trading process in which buyers and sellers interact to transfer title to valuable rights. Markets work best when there is substantial **competition** among buyers and among sellers; they work significantly less well if there are so few buyers or sellers that competitive pressures are weak or absent. In cases where there are few traders, one of them, or perhaps a small group, may be able to exercise control over the market, colluding on prices, perhaps charging different prices to different people, using the control of discharge permits to gain economic control in its industry, and so on. From the standpoint of fostering competition, therefore, we would like to set our trading zones as widely as possible, to include large numbers of potential buyers and sellers.

---

[5] In general, if there were n sources, there would have to be $[n(n-1)]/2$ trading ratios established.

But this may work against the ecological facts. In many cases there may be meteorological or hydrological reasons for limiting the trading area to a relatively narrow geographical area. If the objective was to control airborne emissions affecting a particular city, for example, we would probably not want to allow firms located there to trade permits with firms in another city. Or if our concern is controlling emissions into a particular lake or river, we could not allow sources located there to trade permits with sources located on some entirely different body of water. Thus, for environmental reasons, it may well be desirable to have trading areas restricted, whereas for economic reasons we would want to have trading areas defined broadly. There is no magic rule to tell exactly how these two factors should be balanced in all cases. Authorities can only look at specific cases as they arise and weigh the particularities of the environmental features with the subtleties of the competitive conditions in the industries where trading will occur.

CAPs and Enforcement

The directly controlling aspect of a CAP program is that sources are constrained to keep their emissions at a level no greater than the total number of discharge permits in their possession. Thus, an administering agency would essentially have to keep track of two things: (1) the number of permits in the possession of each source and (2) the quantity of emissions from each source. Because the initial permit distribution will be well known, the agency must have some way of keeping track of permit transactions among market participants. Trades, in fact, could become complicated with multiple buyers and sellers and with different types of transactions, such as temporary rentals and long-term leases in addition to permanent transfers. Because permit buyers (or renters) would have a strong incentive to have their purchases revealed to the agency and because all purchases imply sellers, a system of self-reporting, coupled with modern means of information transfer, may be sufficient to provide reliable information on which sources have the permits.

As regards **monitoring,** the administrative agency must be able to monitor polluters to see whether emissions at each source exceed the number of permits it holds. If permits are expressed in terms of total emissions over some period of time, a means has to be available to measure cumulative emissions at each source. This is the same requirement as with an effluent charge. If there were reasonable certainty that emissions were fairly even throughout the year, authorities could get a check on cumulative emissions by making spot checks of instantaneous rates. For most industrial sources of pollution, however, there are considerable daily, weekly, or seasonal variations in emissions; therefore, more sophisticated monitoring would be required.

CAPs and the Incentive for R&D

One of our main criteria for judging an environmental policy is whether or not it creates strong incentives for firms to seek better ways of reducing emissions. Emission standards were weak in this regard, whereas emission charges were much stronger. CAP programs in this respect are identical to emissions charges,

FIGURE 13.4   **TDP and Technological Change**

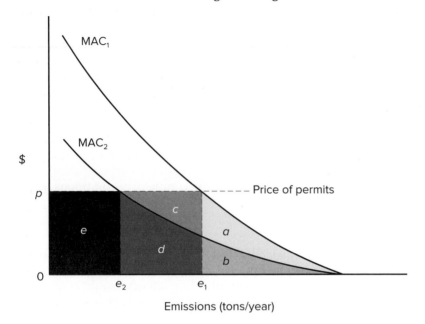

Emissions (tons/year)

at least in theory. Consider the firm in Figure 13.4. Suppose that at present the firm's marginal abatement cost function is MAC_1. Emission permits sell for p each, and let us assume that this price is not expected to change. The firm has adjusted its holdings so that it currently owns e_1 permits.[6] Its emissions are therefore e_1 and its total abatement costs are $(a + b)$. The incentive to do research and development (R&D) is to find a less costly way of controlling emissions, so the firm can cut emissions and sell the surplus permits. How much would it be worth to get marginal abatement costs shifted to MAC_2? With MAC_2, the firm would shift to an emissions level of e_2. Its total abatement costs here would be $(b + d)$, but it would be able to sell $(e_1 - e_2)$ permits for a revenue of $p(e_1 - e_2) = (c + d)$. The change in its position would thus be:

$$\text{Total abatement costs} \atop \text{with } MAC_1 \quad - \quad {\text{Total abatement costs} \atop \text{with } MAC_2} \quad - \quad {\text{Receipts from} \atop \text{CAP sale}}$$

or $(a + b) - (d + b) + (c + d)$, which equals $(a + c)$. Check this with the savings under an effluent charge (see Chapter 12). It is exactly the same. The market price of the permit has the same incentive as a pollution charge; by not reducing their emissions, firms are forgoing the increased revenues they could have obtained by selling some of their permits.

---

[6] These marginal abatement cost functions apply to a year; that is, they are the costs per year of changing emissions. The price p is therefore a one-year purchase (or sale) price—what it would cost to buy or sell a permit for just one year.

CAPs and Uncertainty

In the last chapter we discussed the use of emission charges to reduce pollution; you can think of that as a price-based system, because it starts with an emission charge, which leads to a reduction in the quantity of emissions. A CAP program can be thought of as a quantity-based system, because it starts with the setting of a quantitative limit on total emissions, which then produces a certain price for emission permits. We discussed how, when marginal abatement costs are certain, we couldn't be sure about how much of a reduction of emissions we would get from a given emission charge. With a CAP program the situation is the opposite: If emission control costs are uncertain, we can't be certain what price permits will trade for when the quantity of the cap is set at some particular level. If the cap is set too high, permit prices will be too low, weakening their incentive effect.[7] If the cap is set too low, permit prices could be very high, leading to economic disruption and volatile permit markets.[8]

This has led recently to the idea of a *safety valve* in CAP programs. This is an upper limit price that, if it is reached, would trigger an increase in the supply of permits. If permit prices reach this limit, firms would be able to buy additional permits from the governmental authorities operating the program. This effectively puts an upper limit on permit prices during periods when demand exceeds available supply in the permit market.

Offset Trading

Most emissions trading carried out in the absence of an authoritative cap comes under the heading of offset trading. Purchasers of offsets are entities who wish to compensate for their increase in emissions; sellers of offsets are entities who will reduce emissions in a quantity sufficient to compensate for the emissions of the buyers.

Offset demand may result from firms subject to legal limits on their activities. Many states now have statutory requirements that power companies generate some portion of their output from renewable sources (often called **renewable portfolio requirements**). It is acceptable, in most cases, that they are allowed to meet this requirement in part by buying renewable power offsets, usually from firms who build and operate new renewable power plants.

Offset markets may also be formed as a result of voluntarily accepted limits on emissions. For a number of years, the Chicago Climate Exchange provided this type of institution. Each voluntary participant agreed to a reduction in emissions of greenhouse gases, for example, perhaps by 5 or 10 percent. Individual participants who exceeded this reduction could sell the resulting credits to participants who were unable or unwilling to reduce emissions by the required amount. [9]

---

[7] This happened in the early stages of the European greenhouse gas program.

[8] This happened in the California Reclaim market in the 1990s.

[9] The Chicago Climate Exchange was merged into the Intercontinental Exchange in 2010.

Finally a substantial international market has developed in strictly voluntary offset trading. In these markets, emitters, looking to purchase offsets, seek to find suppliers of offsets who are willing to sell. These sellers agree to then reduce their own emissions. Another way to create emission offsets is to take steps that will naturally expand the carbon absorption of the environment, such as planting trees. In 2012, an estimated 101 million tons of carbon offsets were traded globally. The majority of these were traded directly between buyer and seller, the rest were transacted through a variety of exchanges. Almost 90 percent of these were bought by firms in the private sector, the rest chiefly by non-governmental organizations (NGOs). [10]

Transactions in offsets are somewhat different from transactions in physical goods. Offsets require emission reductions or altered technology by the offset suppliers. This creates the problem of validating that the changes have actually been made to supply the offset, that is, that a supplier has actually reduced their emissions. Exhibit 13.2 discusses this problem.

Emission Rate Trading

An example of emission rate trading is the system used to phase out of leaded gasoline in the United States.

In the 1950s, the practice of adding lead to fuel to augment its performance became common among gasoline refiners. As leaded gas became popular, the lead content of urban air began to show an alarming increase, and concern mounted over the resulting health effects. In addition, lead in gasoline interfered with catalytic converters, the technology of choice for reducing other emissions. The federal response was to establish a timetable for the elimination of lead in gasoline. The program included a **trading system** to help reduce the overall cost of a transition to lead-free gasoline. To decrease the lead content of gas but maintain normal octane ratings, refineries had to install new equipment and institute new operating procedures. But conversion costs differed among refineries, especially between large and small operations. Some could switch to lead-free gas quickly and at reasonably low cost, whereas for others conversion would take longer and be more costly. A lead trading program was introduced to allow more flexibility and lower costs in the conversion process.

Refineries were given (by the EPA) annual base rates for the amount of lead in the gas they produced. The rate declined over time, so all production of leaded gas was ended by 1988. Suppose, for example, the base rate for a given year was 1 g/gallon. If a refinery reduced its rate to, say, 0.5 g/gal for that year, and produced 100,000 gallons of gas in that year, it would have $100,000 \times 0.5 = 50,000$ of allowances (sometimes called lead credits) to sell to refineries which produced that year at a lead rate over the base level.

[10] Molly Peters-Stanley and Gloria Gonzalez, *Sharing the Stage, State of the Voluntary Carbon Markets 2014*, Report by Forest Trends' Ecosystem Marketplace, July 2014.

Carbon Offset Markets: Real or Greenwashing?

EXHIBIT 13.2

The market for carbon offsets has been growing rapidly. In 2007 about $54 million was spent on carbon offsets, which supposedly went to tree planting, solar energy, wind farms, and other means of reducing carbon dioxide emissions. This money was spent by people and corporations wanting to offset the increase in atmospheric carbon dioxide produced by their products or activities: buying and using a computer, taking a trip on an airplane, driving a new car, and so on.

Dell offers customers a chance to purchase carbon offsets to offset the carbon emissions created in producing its computers. Volkswagon is telling buyers that it will offset the carbon implications of purchasing one of its cars. General Electric and Bank of America will convert credit card awards points into carbon offsets. Pacific Gas and Electric in California gives customers a chance to purchase offsets to offset the carbon emissions stemming from their electricity consumption.

In all of these cases, the offsets are being produced not by these companies, but bought in a market that supposedly connects offset buyers with producers. The market consists of a growing number of firms, brokers, and others who specialize in offset transactions. Firms, and some nonprofits, such as Terra Pass, Carbonfund, and the Chicago Climate Exchange, are intermediaries between those who are supposedly producing carbon reductions, either through reducing emissions or increasing carbon sequestration, and corporations and individuals wanting to buy these reductions to offset their own emissions.

But the question is, how are buyers of offsets to know whether the producers of offsets are actually reducing atmospheric carbon as part of the deal? Is there any way of making sure that, at the end of the line, somebody is reducing carbon as a result of your buying some offsets?

The Federal Trade Commission (FTC), charged with consumer protection, has initiated steps to look into advertising claims made by suppliers of carbon offsets. It comes under the heading of green marketing, and is aimed at making sure that suppliers of carbon offsets (and also renewable energy certificates) can substantiate their claims that carbon is actually reduced after people buy offsets. It would like to make sure that people are not engaged in *greenwashing*, that is, selling carbon offsets without being able to substantiate that the offsets have led to real carbon reductions, which could be intentional, or simply mistaken because of lack of information.

The FTC has not accused anybody of actual wrongdoing, but recognizes that it is a market that depends on accurate information flowing through the long line between producers and consumers. If I buy a car and it doesn't work right, I can take it back. But if I buy some carbon offsets, it's almost impossible to know if carbon has actually been reduced somewhere. When Gaiam, a company that makes equipment for yoga, began selling offsets that were supplied through the Conservation Fund, a nonprofit organization, the general manager actually went to the tree-growing sites in Louisiana to verify that additional trees were in fact being grown.

Source: Based on Louise Story, "FTC Asks If Carbon-Offset Money Is Winding Up True Green," *New York Times*, January 9, 2008.

The lead market, which was national in scope, was widely used in the transition to low-lead gas. The EPA estimates that it probably saved several hundreds of millions of dollars in total transition costs. Its success has been chalked up to two main points:

- initial widespread agreement on the overall goal of phasing out leaded gas and
- the ease of monitoring the amount of lead in gas.

Although the lead trading program was a success in easing the lead "phase-down," getting lead out of gas was not achieved without compensating environmental costs. People wanted less lead, but they also still wanted high engine performance. Thus, the octane ratings of gasoline were to some extent maintained by substituting other compounds for lead.

Summary

Programs of transferable discharge permits have become popular. One of the first such programs was the SO_2 control CAP in the 1990 Clean Air Act Amendments. CAP programs for the control of greenhouse gas emissions have been initiated in Europe and in California. The spirit behind this approach, the transfer of emission rights from sources with low control costs to those with high costs, is also behind some recent developments in the control of nonpoint-source waterborne emissions; we will discuss these in the chapter on water pollution (see Chapter 14). There is the expectation that this approach could give us pollution control at a substantially lower cost than the current system of technology-based effluent standards, and also a sense that, politically, these programs would be more acceptable than emission charges.

But CAP programs come with their own set of problems. Most especially, CAP programs take some of the burden of pollution control out of the hands of engineers and place it under the operation of a market. How that market operates is obviously critical to whether this type of policy will work. There is a host of important factors: who gets the permits at the beginning, the strength of their incentives to minimize costs, the degree of competition in the market, the transaction rules set by the administering public agency, the ability to monitor and enforce compliance, and so on. Besides CAP programs, several other trading systems are common. Offset markets, both voluntary and regulatory, are widespread, particularly in efforts to reduce global greenhouse gas emissions. Emission rate trading systems have also been used, for example, in phasing out leaded gasoline.

Both transferable discharge systems and emission charge systems seek to take the burden and responsibility of making technical pollution-control decisions out of the hands of central administrators and put them into the hands of polluters themselves. They are not, we should stress, aimed at putting pollution-control *objectives* themselves into the hands of the polluters. It is not the market that is going to determine the most efficient level of pollution control for society. Rather, these systems are the means of enlisting the incentives of the polluters themselves in finding more effective ways of meeting the overall objective of reducing emissions.

Questions for Further Discussion

1. How might you design a transferable discharge permit system for solid waste? For phasing out of use a certain type of plastic? For phasing in a program for using recycled newsprint in newspapers?

2. Explain how a program of transferable discharge permits works to satisfy the equimarginal principle.

3. Following are the marginal abatement costs of two sources. They currently emit 10 tons each.

   a. What would the total abatement costs be for an equiproportional cutback to a total of 10 tons?

   b. Suppose we print up 10 transferable discharge permits, each of which entitles the holder to 1 ton of emissions. We distribute them equally to the two sources. What will the final emissions be for each of the two sources, and the total abatement costs after all adjustments have been made?

   c. Show that if the permits are originally distributed in a different way (say all to one source and none to the other), the final results will be the same in terms of total and individual emissions, but the distribution of the gains from trade will be different between the two sources.

	Marginal Abatement Costs	
Emissions (tons)	Source A	Source B
10	0	0
9	2	4
8	4	8
7	6	14
6	8	20
5	10	30
4	12	42
3	14	56
2	18	76
1	28	100
0	48	180

4. What are the pros and cons of letting *anybody* (banks, private citizens, environmental groups, government agencies, etc.) buy and sell transferable discharge permits, in addition to emission sources themselves?

5. Most of the carbon offsets traded globally are being bought by corporations, many of which are not currently subject to emission restrictions. Why do you think this is the case?

For additional readings and Web sites pertaining to the material in this chapter, see **www.mhhe.com/field7e.**

Section 5

Environmental Policy in the United States

Having looked at the principles of designing effective environmental policy, we now turn to an examination of actual policies. In fact, most of the remainder of the book consists of chapters about public policies that have been put in place to deal with environmental problems of various types. This section contains four chapters on U.S. environmental policies. There are three chapters on federal policy on problems of water, air, and hazardous materials. Then there is a chapter on environmental policies of the states. Each of these policy areas is extremely complex, with its own history, character, and vocabulary. The chapters aim to summarize the main elements of each policy area, utilizing the ideas discussed in the preceding chapters. Pollution-control policy is rife with acronyms. The appendix contains a list of acronyms used in the book.

Chapter 14

Federal Water Pollution–Control Policy

Water is biologically necessary for life, but, beyond this, water resources play a vital and pervasive role in the health and welfare of a modern economy. Water for direct human consumption is a small but critical part of the domestic system, which also includes water used in food preparation, cleaning, and sewage disposal. Water is an essential element in many industrial and commercial production processes, again both as an input and as a medium of waste disposal. Large amounts of water are used by farmers for irrigation, especially in the western United States. Also, water-based sports and recreation, both freshwater and saltwater, have become very popular.

The water resource system itself consists of a vast array of interconnected components, from the grandiose to the tiny. The surface-water system includes the huge main-stem rivers and Great Lakes, as well as the thousands of small neighborhood streams and ponds. Add to these the innumerable person-made components, from the mill ponds of the first industrial era to the vast reservoirs and canals of today. Swamps and wetlands abound, ranging from small local bogs to the huge Everglades in southern Florida. And then there is the vast, but unseen, system of groundwater aquifers, exceeding surface waters in terms of sheer quantity of water. Saltwater resources are also of vital importance. Marshes and coastal lowlands are critical for fish and wildlife resources; beaches and scenic coasts are important recreational resources; coastal waters provide transportation and pleasure boating services; and saltwater fisheries are a major source of food.

Efforts to protect these water resources have gone on for a long time but with increasing vigor in the last few decades. In this chapter we look at federal water pollution–control policy. Our objective is to review the main elements of that policy with the economic concepts developed in preceding chapters. We also look at some recent policy innovations that seek to make use of economic incentives to achieve improvements in water quality. Most states and localities also have active water pollution–control efforts, some of which are tied into the federal programs; we will consider some of these in a later chapter.

Types of Water Pollutants

There are many different types of waterborne pollutants. Within the policy arena it is common to differentiate the following categories:

Conventional pollutants: These represent some of the first water pollutants that were subject to control. They include biochemical oxygen-demanding (BOD) wastes, total suspended solids (TSS), bacteria, fecal coliform (FC), oil, grease, and pH.

Nonconventional pollutants: These include chemical oxygen demand (COD), total organic carbon (TOC), nitrogen, and phosphorous. Fertilizers, sewage, manure, and detergents are sources of these substances.

Toxic pollutants: These include 65 named (in the Clean Water Act) chemicals, consisting of natural and synthetic organic chemicals as well as metals discharged from industrial sources. From this list of chemicals, a list of "priority pollutants" is derived, for which testing and control programs are created.

Waterborne emissions include all the different types of discharges discussed in Chapter 2. **Point sources** include outfalls from industry and domestic wastewater treatment plants. **Nonpoint sources** include agricultural runoff of pesticides and fertilizers and the chemicals and oils that are flushed off urban streets by periodic rains. Many sources, especially point sources, have **continuous** emissions related to the rate of operation of the industrial plant or the domestic sewer system. There are also many **episodic emissions,** such as accidental releases of toxic materials, oil-tanker accidents, or occasional planned releases of industrial pollutants.

In Chapter 2 we also spoke of cumulative and noncumulative pollutants. In water pollution control, it is more common to speak of **persistent** and **degradable** pollutants. Degradable waterborne pollutants undergo a variety of biological, chemical, and physical processes that change their characteristics after emission. Especially important are the oxygen-using chemical processes that rely on the oxygen contained in receiving waters to degrade the wastes.[1] The reason for focusing on oxygen requirements is that oxygen plays a critical role in water quality. High levels of dissolved oxygen (DO) are usually associated with high-quality water, water that will support high-quality recreational uses and that can be used in domestic water-supply systems.

Because DO is used up in the degradation process, one way of measuring the quantity of waste emitted is through **biochemical oxygen demand,** or BOD, the amount of oxygen required to decompose the organic material under specified conditions of temperature and time.[2] A substantial proportion of the BOD

---

[1] Degradable wastes also include a variety of infectious bacterial agents that can cause such diseases as typhoid, cholera, and dysentery. Waste heat is also a degradable pollutant; it comes mostly from large-scale industrial processes that use water for cooling purposes.

[2] For example, 10 pounds of BOD10 is a quantity of material requiring 10 pounds of oxygen in order to be completely converted to its constituent elements during a period of 10 days and at a temperature of 20°C.

load introduced into the water resources of the country comes from municipal waste-treatment plants. Much of this consists of wastewater from treated domestic waste, which contains a variety of degradable organic compounds. Industrial sources also contribute large amounts of BOD wastes, some stemming from the sanitary facilities within the plants, but more importantly from the great variety of water-using steps in the production processes, such as cleaning, product formation, waste removal, and product transport.

When a BOD load is put into a river or body of water, it produces a temporary reduction in the DO level of that water as the oxygen is used to degrade the waste. But over time, through natural aeration processes, the DO content of the water will normally recover. The **DO "profile"** would thus look like Figure 14.1 (where the discharge point is marked x). This can be thought of as the average DO level at various distances downstream from the point at which a BOD load is introduced, or the DO level at various times after a BOD load has been introduced into a lake. This is called a DO "sag," and it illustrates the degradation process by which the water body is assimilating the BOD load. The important thing to see is that the DO reduction is reversible. It is also noncumulative—if the BOD source were stopped, the DO sag would shortly disappear.

Early water pollution–control efforts were centered on conventional pollutants such as BOD wastes, suspended solids, and so on, for which there are common water quality measures such as DO, turbidity, acidity, and coliform count. More recent programs also focus on **toxic pollutants.** Toxicity is often a matter of concentration; substances that are toxic at high concentrations may not be at low concentrations. This implies that the diluting ability of water is a valuable quality in addition to its capacity to transform degradable substances.

Persistent water pollutants are those that remain for a long period of time, either because they are nondegradable or because the rate of degradation is very slow. This category includes thousands of inorganic and organic chemicals. Industrial wastes contain many such persistent pollutants. Wastes from mining operations can contain various metals as well as acid-mine drainage.

FIGURE 14.1 Dissolved Oxygen Profile in Water After a BOD Load Has Been Introduced

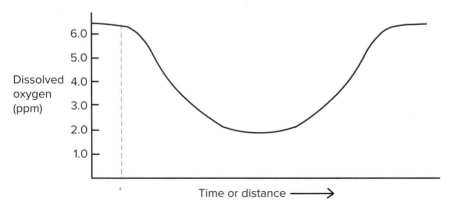

Agriculture is the source of pesticides, fertilizers, and soil runoff. The concept of "persistent" does not mean permanent in a technical sense; many chemicals, oils, and solvents break down but over a long period of time. In the process they pose a persistent threat. Radioactive waste is physically degradable over very long periods, but measured in terms of a human scale it is essentially a persistent pollutant. Viruses are also in this category.

Federal Policy: A Brief History

Prior to the 20th century, the only public policy initiatives taken toward water pollution control were at the state level. In the "sanitary awakening" of the mid-19th century, the public began to appreciate the importance of water quality for human health. Many states instituted public boards of health in response.[3] The first federal law of any note covering water pollution control was actually enacted at the very end of the 19th century (see Table 14.1). This was the **1899 Refuse Act** empowering the U.S. Army Corps of Engineers to grant permits to anyone desiring to put refuse of any kind into any navigable waterway. The primary objective of this act was to ensure navigation, not to control water pollution per se.

TABLE 14.1 Major Federal Legislation on Water Pollution Control

1899 Refuse Act
Required permit from the U.S. Army Corps of Engineers before refuse of any kind could be put into a navigable water. Primary purpose was to ensure navigability, but it had a brief, and not very successful, reincarnation in the 1960s as a water quality measure.
1948 Water Pollution Control Act (WPCA)
Federal government was authorized to conduct investigations, research, and surveys; however, no federal authority was established to enforce laws, set standards, or limit discharges. Authorized federal government to make loans to municipalities to construct sewage treatment facilities.
1956 WPCA Amendments
Authorized the states to establish criteria for determining desirable levels of water quality; introduced the idea of an "enforcement conference," sponsored by federal agencies to bring together state and local interests to develop enforcement plans. Authorized federal government to make grants for municipal waste-treatment facilities, with federal share up to 55 percent of construction costs.
1965 Water Quality Act
Required the states to develop *ambient quality* standards for interstate water bodies and implementation plans calling for effluent reductions from specific sources. State actions required federal approval, with a strengthened "enforcement conference" procedure.

(Continued)

[3] The first such agency was in Massachusetts in 1869.

TABLE 14.1   *(Continued)*

1972 WPCA Amendments
Provided for a federally mandated system of *technology-based effluent standards,* with federal enforcement through the granting of discharge permits. Phase I (starting in 1977) permits were based on "Best Practicable Technology" (BPT); Phase II (starting in 1983) permits were based on "best available technology" (BAT); states could ultimately take over the permitting process. Declared a goal of zero discharge to be attained by 1985. Made a large increase in the municipal treatment plant grant program, with federal share increased to 75 percent of construction costs. Mandated secondary treatment in municipal treatment plants.

1974 Safe Drinking Water Act
Requires the EPA to set maximum contaminant levels for drinking water; requires public authorities to protect, monitor, and test water supplies. Amended in 1986 and 1996.

1977 Clean Water Act
Established procedures for control of toxic effluent in addition to the conventional effluent on which previous acts had focused; sources were required to meet "best conventional technology" (BCT) for conventional pollutants and BAT for toxics, starting in 1984; increased authorization for treatment plant subsidies.

1981 Municipal Wastewater Treatment Construction Grant Amendments
Reduced federal share to 55 percent and substantially decreased the authorized funding level.

1987 Water Quality Act
Postponed some of the deadlines for adopting *technology-based effluent standards;* changed the waste-treatment subsidy program from federal grants to federal contributions to state revolving funds; requires states to develop and implement programs to control nonpoint sources of pollution.

Source: Allen V. Kneese and Charles L. Schultze, *Pollution, Prices and Public Policy,* Brookings Institution, Washington, D.C., 1973, p. 31; Tom H. Tietenberg, *Environmental and Natural Resource Economics,* 2nd ed., Scott Foresman, Glenview, IL, 1988, pp. 410–411; A. Myrick Freeman III, "Water Pollution Control," in Paul R. Portney (ed.), *Public Policies for Environmental Protection,* Resources for the Future, Washington, D.C., 1990, pp. 100–101; Claudia Copeland, *Clean Water Act: A Summary of the Law,* Congressional Research Service Report 7, 5700, RL30030, October 30, 2014.

Very little happened, thereafter, until after World War II. Then the Water Pollution Control Act of 1948 was enacted, which authorized federal authorities to assist the states in water pollution–control matters. Primary responsibility, however, was to remain at the state level. The 1948 act also authorized a program that over the years would become a major element of the federal effort: subsidies to municipalities to construct waste-treatment facilities. That act also sought to develop new enforcement institutions, so-called enforcement conferences, where federal, state, and local administrative authorities would come together and hammer out water pollution–control policies. In 1965 came the Water Quality Act, which, besides extending many provisions of past laws and refunding the municipal waste-treatment subsidy program, sought to encourage the states to develop **ambient standards** for water quality.

The early 1970s saw a rapid growth in the environmental movement and in environmental advocacy in Washington, D.C. There was at the time a feeling among environmental interest groups that past policy had not worked well enough and quickly enough to respond to growing pollution problems. The Environmental Protection Agency (EPA) had recently been formed (1970), and this gave environmental issues more visibility and greater political representation. One result was the 1972 Water Pollution Control Act Amendments. This act did several things: it set a goal of **zero discharges** to be accomplished within 13 years, and it substantially increased the amount of money for the municipal waste-treatment subsidy program. More important, however, it established a powerful, direct federal role in water pollution control.

The primary approach before then was an ambient-based one. States were supposed to establish ambient water quality standards, then translate these into specific emission reductions by the many firms and treatment plants contributing to the problem. The new approach was for federal authorities to set specific effluent standards for individual point sources of water pollutants. To enforce these standards the law reached all the way back to the 1899 Refuse Act, based on federally issued **discharge permits.** Each source of waterborne emissions would require a permit specifying the time, place, and maximum quantity of emissions. To provide the basis for these permits, the EPA would promulgate what are called **technology-based effluent standards** (TBESs) for all sources discharging wastes into the nation's waters. As we discuss in more detail later, these are essentially emission standards that are tied to particular types of pollution-control technology. Thus, the primary approach to water pollution control was changed from an ambient-based to a **technology-based system.** There is now a substantially completed system in place for establishing and enforcing TBESs for point sources.

The last major federal water pollution law was in 1987, which directed attention to **nonpoint sources.** In this case much of the initiative has been left to the states. A substantial focus of the program has been to encourage operators (especially farmers, whose operations account for a large part of nonpoint-source emissions) to adopt **best-management practices** (BMPs). A BMP is a federally approved (and often subsidized) procedure or technique whose adoption will reduce the runoff of NPS water pollutants. Agricultural BMPs might include, for example, changes in certain cultivation practices, construction of dikes or barriers, or planting of buffer zones around fields. Clearly this is strictly a technology-based approach to pollution control. The other major part of the Clean Water Act has been the program of **federal grants** to municipalities for the construction of **public wastewater treatment plants.** We will discuss this program later in the chapter.

Technology-Based Effluent Standards

The Clean Water Act (CWA) charges the EPA with establishing effluent standards for industrial facilities and publicly-owned treatment works (POTWs). To do this they establish technology-based effluent limitation guidelines, which identify the alternative pollution control technologies available to firms in each industry. These guidelines form the basis for identifying the appropriate emission standard. This whole process is called the effluent limitations guidelines and standards (ELGs).

A TBES, therefore, is an effluent standard set at the level of emissions that a source would produce if it were employing a particular type of abatement technology. Firms emitting waste materials or energy usually face a choice among different technologies and methods for reducing emissions. Different packages of technologies and operating procedures lead to different costs as well as a different level of emissions. To establish a TBES, the EPA studies the effluent abatement technologies and procedures available to a particular type of industrial operation. After having selected one technology from among the many available, it sets the emission standard at the level of emissions produced when that technology is used by firms in that industry.

It would require enormous effort to establish effluent standards for each and every individual source. Thus, the EPA sets standards for categories of polluting sources. For example, consider sugar-beet processing plants.[4] This is a process that uses a large amount of water for cleaning purposes; thus, the wastewater may contain large amounts of suspended solids and BOD wastes. Table 14.2 shows hypothetical costs and emissions performance of five different technology options for plants in this industry. Each technological option refers to a particular collection of treatment equipment, operating procedures, fuels, and so on, that the plants might adopt.

Clearly, lower levels of emissions can be obtained with greater costs; in fact, emissions into water bodies could be reduced to zero at a very high cost. To pick one set of emission levels for the standard requires that the EPA use some sort of criterion. The Water Pollution Control Act of 1972 states that the EPA

TABLE 14.2 Estimated Total Costs and Emissions from Sugar-Beet Plants Using Alternative Emission Abatement Technology

		Technological Option				
	No Control	**A**	**B**	**C**	**D**	**E**
Emissions (kg/kkg of raw product processed)						
BOD*	5.8	3.6	2.2	1.05	0.23	0.0
TSS†	10.2	5.7	2.5	1.02	0.30	0.0
Total costs ($ mil/year)	0.0	8.0	14.4	23.40	36.50	78.8

*Biochemical oxygen demand.
†Total suspended solids.

[4] Sugar-beet processing uses substantial quantities of water. Some is used simply to move the product around the plant, whereas some is used in actual processing. Hydrated lime is used as a purifying agent, which leaves a large amount of "lime mud" to dispose of. Emission control can be done with a variety of water recycling and recirculation processes, screening, settling, stabilization ponds, and land disposal.

should initially set emission standards on the basis of the **"best practicable technology"** (BPT) currently available to the firms. This was Phase I, to be achieved by 1977. Then, starting in 1983, firms would be subject to Phase II effluent standards, based on **"best available technology"** (BAT).

Thus, to set the Phase I emission standard for sugar-beet processing plants, EPA would have to determine which of the technologies displayed in the table represented the "best practicable" level of technology. Clearly, this is open to interpretation because the notion of "practicable" is not precise by any means. Suppose EPA decides that technology C, with an estimated cost of $23.4 million per year, represents the BPT for this type of processing industry. Then it would set emission standards at 1.05 kg/kkg for BOD waste and 1.02 kg/kkg for TSSs. All sugar-beet processing plants would then be subject to this emission standard. In Phase II EPA would be called on to select the "BAT" for this type of industry. BAT would appear to be a more stringent standard than BPT because it includes all technologies that are available, whether or not they are practicable. But the rules also specify that BAT has to be "economically achievable." On this basis, technology E in Table 14.2 might be regarded as the BAT for sugar-beet processing plants. On the other hand, some (especially those in the industry) might argue that such technology doesn't realistically exist, that it is too costly to be considered "available" in any economic sense, in which case the EPA might select D as the BAT.

Setting TBESs for an industry is obviously a time-consuming business. It requires large amounts of economic analysis and hinges on an agency judgment about what *available* and *practicable* mean when applied to pollution-control technology. It is also politically controversial, with industries ready to challenge in court when they feel the standards are too constraining.

In the 1977 Clean Water Act the criteria for selecting emission standards were changed. After 1984 sources were to meet standards based on **"best conventional technology"** (BCT). The notion of "conventional" technology is different, and weaker, than the idea of "available" technology; it presumably allows more weight to be put on the costs of installing and operating the technology.[5] In some cases the EPA has set BCT equal to BPT. The EPA also sets TBESs, called "pretreatment standards," for firms discharging wastes into public sewer systems. Their role is to reduce the burden on public wastewater treatment plants.

The original notion behind the 1972 act was that engineering studies by the EPA would identify preferred pollution-control technologies, and because emission standards would be based on these technologies, there would be few practical obstacles in the way of their timely adoption by firms. In fact, the very ambiguity of words like *practicable* and *conventional* means that a great amount of discretion and judgment must be used by people developing the standards.

---

[5]The ambiguities of using these criteria to choose specific technology options led the EPA at one time to establish a benchmark for BCT of $1.15 per pound of pollutant removed. Anything above this was considered too costly to be "conventional."

Efficiency and Cost-Effectiveness of TBESs

For a policy to be efficient, it must balance damages and control costs. The TBESs are designed, however, to be applied on a national basis. The same standards for, say, leather processing plants will be applied to all leather plants in the country, whether they are located on a river just upstream from a large urban area or on a river in some remote part of the country. Strict efficiency would call for different levels of pollution control for sources in different circumstances as regards the water resource on which they are located.

Cost-effectiveness, as we have discussed many times so far, is a question of whether society is getting the maximum effect, in terms of reduced emissions, for the money spent. The simple key to this question is whether the policy is designed so that when sources on a given water resource are in compliance they will have the same marginal abatement costs. There is nothing in the logic of the TBES process that moves water pollution sources in the direction of meeting the equimarginal condition. The procedure leads instead to the application of the same standards to all firms within each subcategory. For example, all sugar-beet processing plants in the country are subject to the same effluent standards. These will be cost-effective only if all individual plants in each category and on the same water resource have exactly the same marginal abatement costs. This is unlikely to be the case.

The EPA has designated around 600 subcategories of water-polluting industries, for each of which TBESs have been promulgated. But there are tens of thousands of individual industrial water pollution sources, so some of the subcategories must contain very large numbers of sources. There can be little doubt that the sources in most subcategories are heterogeneous in terms of the production technology they are using, so we would expect them to be heterogeneous in terms of their marginal emission abatement costs. But the questions are: how heterogeneous are they in practice, and therefore, how cost ineffective have they been in practice? It's impossible to examine the entire system to answer this, but studies have been done of particular river basins to compare the costs of the EPA technology-based approach to point-source control with least-cost means of attaining the same objectives. These use large-scale models of individual river basins, incorporating the different estimated marginal abatement costs of various sources of pollution, together with the main hydrological features of the basins' water resources. They compare the costs of water pollution-control programs in which all sources were treated alike to those where sources are controlled in accordance with relative marginal abatement costs.

Results of these studies show generally that costs of the actual CWA standards have been substantially more costly, often by a factor of two, than least cost systems. But we must bring other criteria into play. The analytical administrative and political costs of applying different standards to all sources in different locations would undoubtedly be very high. On these grounds, a reasonable second best may have been to apply similar standards across all firms in each industry.

Experience with TBESs

In assessing the actual experience with TBESs, an obvious question is, how much has the nation's water quality been improved as a result of the system?

This question is extremely complicated. The country's waters are very diverse, consisting of many different streams, rivers, lakes, estuaries, and aquifers, all variously situated with respect to both natural and human factors. It's reasonably easy to draw conclusions of a single, small water body, but very hard to do it for the entire system. Analysts in the EPA have undertaken a large-scale study to try to answer the question: What would the water quality of U.S. waters be at the present time if the Clean Water Act and its subsequent regulations had never been adopted?[6] Some of their first results are shown in Table 14.3. This refers to **conventional pollutants** in the nation's **rivers and streams.** The water quality characteristics of these water courses have been aggregated into recreational use categories: swimmable waters are those having high enough water quality to support this type of activity; they also will support the other two activities, fishing and boating. Fishable waters will support this together with boating, whereas boating waters will support only this activity and not the other two. The nonsupport category represents the lowest quality: waters that are so degraded they will support none of the recreational categories. The last three columns show the increases in mileage of rivers and streams that will support the given activities, first in terms of total mileage, then as a percent of the without–Clean Water Act provisions, and then as a percent of what would have occurred if it had been possible to reduce all point-source emissions to zero. Note that the CWA regulations have increased the number of

TABLE 14.3   Rivers and Streams (632,552 Miles) Supporting Recreational Uses: Comparison of With–Clean Water Act (CWA) and Without–Clean Water Act (CWA) Conditions in the Mid-1990s

Highest Use Supported	Without-CWA Conditions (miles)	With-CWA Conditions (miles)	Increase in Use Support		
			Miles	Percent Increase	Percent of Maximum Increase[a]
Swimmable	222,120	238,627	16,507	7.4	49.5
Fishable	399,999	424,712	24,713	6.2	57.8
Boatable	454,038	475,894	21,856	4.8	59.4
Nonsupport	178,514	156,658	−21,856	−12.2	59.4

[a]Analysts estimated the mileage of rivers and streams that would support the various uses if all point-source emissions had been reduced to zero.

Source: Mahesh Podar, *A Benefits Assessment of Water Pollution Control Programs Since 1972: Part 1, The Benefits of Point Source Controls for Conventional Pollutants in Rivers and Streams,* Final Report, U.S. Environmental Protection Agency, Office of Water, Office of Policy, Economics, and Innovation, Washington, D.C., January 2000.

[6] Note that this is a with/without question, not a before/after question. See the discussion of this issue in Chapter 8.

swimmable, fishable, and boatable miles by, respectively, 7.4 percent, 6.2 percent, and 4.8 percent over what they would have been without the CWA. Waters that will support none of these activities have decreased 12.2 percent. Although these percentages may seem quite modest, note that the increases are about 50 to 60 percent of what the increases would have been if all point-source emissions had been reduced to zero. In other words, the Clean Water Act, which has been primarily aimed at point sources, has moved us 50 to 60 percent of the way toward zero-discharge levels for point sources. This is a significant accomplishment. But it is apparent also that there are limits to the extent to which all watercourses could be restored to swimmable category solely through point-source control. We must also recognize that the results of Table 14.3 cover only part of the overall water quality problem. The results do not touch on water pollution in other parts of the water system, namely, ponds, lakes, coastal areas, estuaries, and underground aquifers. Further analysis will be needed to cover these resources.

TBESs and Incentives

The discussion in Chapter 12 showed that emission standards lead to weaker incentives to innovate in pollution control than economic-incentive types of policies. In the case of TBESs, incentives are made even weaker by linking the emission standards to particular control technologies. When polluters are faced with this type of technology-linked standard, compliance tends to become a matter of adopting the technology the authorities have used to set the standard. Because permanent emissions monitoring is quite costly, administering authorities can check compliance by making periodic inspections to ascertain whether sources are using approved emissions-control technology. To minimize the risk of being penalized for noncompliance, polluters have the incentive to adopt the particular technology that EPA used to establish the standard. The result is that although the TBESs are nominally just emission standards, they end up tending to dictate the particular effluent-control technologies chosen by firms. This substantially undermines the incentives to search for other, cheaper ways to meet the standards.

This is another important dimension of these incentive effects. Figure 14.2 shows an abbreviated sketch of a typical residuals and emissions loop. Residuals are generated in the production process, based on inputs used and the production technology in place. These residuals then move to what we

FIGURE 14.2   **End-of-the-Pipe Pollution Control Versus Pollution Prevention**

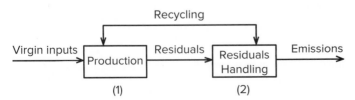

can call a residuals treatment phase, where some are perhaps converted into recyclable materials and some are converted in form and quantities, then these enter an emission stream that is introduced into the environment. The primary focus of the program of TBESs has been on technology in box (2), that is, on getting point sources to adopt new technological means of handling and testing residuals. This is known as an **end-of-the-pipe** program orientation, because it focuses only on the last step in the residuals/emissions process. It is clear, however, that emissions can be reduced in other ways as well. One is by developing better **recycling technology.** Another is to go back to the production process itself and introduce changes that lower the quantity of residuals that are produced. One way of doing this, for example, is to find ways of using fewer inputs in the production process. Another is to reduce the rate of output itself (as in, e.g., efforts to get consumers to conserve energy). As mentioned in Chapter 2, these efforts to reduce the residual stream have come to be called **pollution prevention.** By encouraging firms to concentrate on changing end-of-the-pipe technology, the regulatory program has weakened the incentives to take vigorous steps in the direction of pollution prevention.

TBESs and Enforcement

Effluent standards are enforced through a system of **discharge permits.** To discharge wastes into a river or body of water, a firm must have a permit issued through the relevant EPA-backed state permitting program. The permit specifies the allowable emissions the source may make and is subject to enforcement by state authorities. Given the enormous number of discharge points and the difficulties of monitoring emissions, enforcement becomes a critical program element. One response has been to distinguish between major and minor emitters, using criteria such as quantity, toxicity, conventional pollution load, and impact of emissions. In this way more enforcement resources can be devoted to the major sources, which account for the largest proportion of total emissions.

Lacking high-quality techniques for monitoring emissions, control authorities are forced back to some other means of ensuring compliance. When emission standards are tied to certain technologies, enforcing authorities can try to confirm compliance simply by checking to see if firms have put in place the criterion technology.[7] The problem here is that there is a difference between **initial compliance** and **continued compliance.** The fact that a firm has installed certain pollution-control equipment does not necessarily mean that this equipment will be operated efficiently in the years to come. If operating costs are substantial and if nobody is effectively monitoring emissions, the incentive will be to save on operating costs and let emissions increase.

---

[7] The word *simply* in this sentence may be misleading. Nothing is simple in the world of pollution control. Polluters have challenged virtually every part of the federal pollution-control program, including enforcement procedures. Thus, over the years, legal doctrine has developed regarding such things as the specific procedures for visiting sources to check for compliance.

Technology-based effluent standards have an aura of concreteness and directness. What better way to get pollution reduced than simply to require polluters to adopt certain types of pollution-control technology? But this engineering-based approach is far less effective than it appears. We have seen how, from an economic standpoint, it is likely to be seriously cost-*in* effective; for the money that is being devoted to pollution control under this system, substantially greater improvements in water quality could be achieved with other policy approaches. The apparent technological definiteness of the approach ("best practicable technology," "best available technology," etc.) is, in fact, far less effective in practice. The EPA is required to make countless engineering decisions in order to develop these standards. Not only is this very difficult for an administrating agency, but each of these decisions is a place where political interests can focus influence. The apparent concreteness of TBESs is also substantially undermined by the monitoring and enforcement problem. What looks like a straightforward technological fix becomes, in reality, a policy with a great deal of hidden flexibility.

The Municipal Wastewater Treatment Plant Subsidy Program

A large proportion of waterborne emissions into the nation's waterways comes not from private industries but from people themselves, especially from the public sewer systems of urbanized areas. Whereas in the case of industrial pollution, federal authorities adopted a policy of having polluters themselves pay for reducing emissions, the response toward public-sector pollution has been different. Here the major approach has been **federal subsidies** to construct treatment plants. The inspiration for this type of approach probably comes from two sources: the normal public works mentality of the Congress and the fact that it is better politics to "get tough" on industrial polluters than on cities, towns, and voters.

Treatment of domestic wastes uses both physical and biological processes and is fairly standardized. The different degrees of treatment are designated *primary, secondary,* and *tertiary,* according to the process used and the extent of treatment given to the wastes. Primary treatment is essentially a set of physical steps built around a basic sedimentation process; it can remove about 35 to 40 percent of the primary BOD waste in the original waste stream. Secondary treatment uses biological means (e.g., "activated sludge") to further treat the waste. Primary and secondary processes together can reduce BOD waste by between 85 and 90 percent. These processes, although quite effective in removing BOD load, are less so in handling plant nutrients such as nitrogen and phosphorus. So-called tertiary treatment, making use of a variety of chemical processes, can reduce waste loads even more. The sequence of primary, secondary, and tertiary processes is subject to increasing marginal abatement costs; the greater the reduction one wants in BOD waste or other pollutants in the waste stream, the higher the marginal cost of getting it.

The 1972 WPCA Amendments mandated that all municipal sewer systems have at least secondary treatment within 11 years. Congress authorized a program of federal subsidies to local municipalities to cover 75 percent of the costs of designing and constructing public wastewater treatment plants. Large sums were appropriated for the program. From 1960 to 1985, federal grants amounted to about $56 billion in real terms.[8] The figures in Table 14.4 seem to show the impact of the program. From 1960 to 1988, the percentage of public sewer systems discharging untreated waste declined from 63 percent to less than 1 percent, whereas the percentage having at least secondary treatment increased substantially.

From these numbers it is clear that great strides have been made in the last 30 years in community wastewater treatment. Although the federal program is the primary basis for this improvement, there are many ways in which it might have been improved. Any large subsidy program creates its own set of incentives; some may work toward the objectives of the program, whereas others may not. The federal program added large sums to the construction of POTWs; however, much of it simply displaced money that was being spent on this activity at the state and local levels. So although total capital spending for POTWs did in fact increase during the 1970s and 1980s, it did not increase by as much as it would appear if one looks strictly at the federal program.

Public subsidy programs are inevitably infused with political factors. From an efficiency standpoint, one would want to allocate the funds to municipalities where treatment plant construction would have the maximum impact on water quality improvement. The EPA has struggled to find a way of doing this in

TABLE 14.4 **Progress in Public Wastewater Treatment Facilities**

	1960	1970	1980	1996	2000	2008
Total U.S. population (millions)	180	203	224	264	270	284
Percentage served by waste-treatment systems	61	71	71	72	77	79
Percentage of served population with:						
No treatment	61	41	1	<1	N/A	N/A
Primary treatment only	33	N/A	31	9	N/A	N/A
At least secondary	4	N/A	68	91	97	97

Sources: 1960–1988: Council on Environmental Quality, *Environmental Quality,* 1990, p. 309, and previous issues; 1996: Environmental Protection Agency, *1996 Clean Water Needs Survey, Report to Congress,* U.S. EPA, Office of Water, September 1997, Appendix C; 2000: Environmental Protection Agency, *2012 Clean Water Needs Survey, Report to Congress,* U.S. EPA, Office of Wastewater Management, n.d., p. xix; 2012: Environmental Protection Agency, *Clean Watersheds Needs Survey 2008, Report to Congress Summary,* U.S. EPA Office of Wastewater Management, May 2010. (Figures rounded to the nearest whole number.)

---

[8] That is, adjusted for inflation; see the discussion of "real" versus "nominal" values in Chapter 6.

the face of overwhelming political pressures. Its approach has been to allocate grant funds on the basis of a "needs" survey. The needs survey was to take into account existing population, the pollution problem in different bodies of water, and the needs for preserving higher-quality water in these various bodies. The formula was open to interpretation and subject to judgment, especially political judgment. There have been strong pressures to allocate grant funds to states and municipalities more on the basis of their political significance than on water quality improvement criteria.

Federal subsidies for POTWs covered capital construction costs, but not operating costs. Thus, there was a built-in incentive to build plants with excess treatment capacity.[9] How much excess capacity this actually produced is open to question. Some amount is clearly rational to accommodate future population growth. At the time there was concern that municipalities would use the excess capacity to attract new industrial growth. One answer to this was to create a program of emission standards called **pretreatment standards**. These are standards applied to wastewater streams entering public sewer systems from private business sources. The objective is to get industrial polluters to undertake some treatment themselves before they put their wastes into the public sewer system.

Over the last three decades industrial pollution and the POTW program have become more closely interrelated. Prior to the 1970s most industrial polluters were **direct dischargers,** with emissions going directly into water bodies and subject to TBESs specified in the Clean Water Act. At the present time most industrial polluters are **indirect dischargers;** their emissions are sent to a POTW for treatment and are subject to the requirements of the pretreatment program. One thing that facilitated this shift is the "excess capacity" produced by the federally subsidized POTW program. In turn, most POTWs are charging unit-based disposal fees to the industrial sources using their facilities. These are somewhat akin to emission charges, and may be having the predicted effect—that is, providing an incentive for industrial polluters to search for ways of reducing their waterborne emissions.[10]

In the 1987 Water Quality Act, the treatment plant program was changed. States continue to receive federal grants, but states now must provide matching funds equal to 20 percent of the federal funds. The combined funds are used to establish **state revolving funds** (SRFs), which are used to make loans to communities to build wastewater treatment plants. The loans made from the funds are supposed to be largely paid back (this is why they are called "revolving funds"). This should substantially reshape local incentives because local groups will now be responsible for covering the actual costs of constructing

[9] "A community that expects to pay only 5 cents to 25 cents on the dollar will have fewer incentives to control plant costs than if they had to pay the entire investment." U.S. Congressional Budget Office, *Efficient Investments in Wastewater Treatment Plants,* Washington, D.C., 1985, p. 12.

[10] Winston Harrington, *Regulating Industrial Water Pollution in the United States,* Discussion Paper 03-03, Resources for the Future, Washington, D.C., April 2003.

their treatment plants. Although the SRF program was originally designed to expire in 1994, it has proven to be politically popular and has continued to receive federal funding.

The Safe Drinking Water Act (SDWA)

A similar SRF program has been established to help communities build drinking water treatment facilities. Approximately 90 percent of the population of the United States obtains its drinking water from public water supply systems. Although these are exclusively local and community organizations, public and private, the Safe Drinking Water Act of 1974 moved the federal government into the business of regulating these local systems.

The SDWA requires the EPA to set maximum contaminant levels (MCLs) for each recognized contaminant; currently about 100 contaminants have been identified. MCLs are, in effect, never-exceed levels, and determining where they should be is not easy. For each substance the EPA must set a maximum contaminant level goal (MCLG), "at a level at which no known anticipated adverse health effects occur and that allows for an adequate margin of safety."[11] For carcinogens and microbes the MCLGs must be set at zero. But to establish an enforceable MCL, the EPA is permitted to take into account the feasibility of achieving lower contaminant levels, considering the technologies available to do so and the costs involved.

In the 1996 amendments to the SDWA, some concern was expressed that feasible MCLs for large, better-financed systems might not be feasible for small communities where costs might loom larger and potential benefits smaller. Thus, language was put in the law allowing the EPA to establish standards based on a comparison of both the benefits and the costs of the standard.

Thus, in setting standards under the SDWA, the EPA can identify goals based solely on health impacts, but set enforceable standards at a less stringent level that is based on an analysis of both the benefits and costs of achieving them. In Chapter 5 we discussed this procedure under the general rubric of making trade-offs in pollution control. The approach also goes under the name *balancing* and is controversial in its application to environmental regulations. Environmental groups, in particular, are likely to look askance at balancing because they think it may give undue prominence to the costs of achieving pollution reduction. Others look on balancing as an essential part of achieving greater efficiency and cost-effectiveness in pollution-control programs. We shall discuss this at greater length in Chapter 16.

Economic changes, especially new technologies, have always presented society with new problems in controlling environmental pollution. This is certain to continue in the future. A recent example is the appearance of the technology

---

[11] Mary Tiemann, *Safe Drinking Water Act: Implementation and Issues,* Congressional Research Service, Report IB10118, August 20, 2003, p. 3.

Fracking and Groundwater Contamination

EXHIBIT **14.1**

In recent years a new technology has been deployed to extract natural gas from deep underground shale formations. It is called "hydraulic fracturing" or "fracking" for short. There exist a number of places in the country where large amounts of natural gas are held in a dispersed fashion in the small interstices of rock formations. Fracking involves drilling deep into these spots and then pumping at high pressures a combination of water and assorted chemicals. This produces the opening up of a number of large-scale fractures in the rock, which allow large volumes of the gas to migrate to the well head, where it can be drawn out.

Fracking has been touted because it appears to tap into a huge new energy source that was impossible to reach in the past, and because the combustion of natural gas produces substantially less carbon dioxide per BTU produced than from any other type of fossil fuel. The result has been that very large sums of money have flowed into the fracking industry. Operations have expanded rapidly, even though there are still lots of uncertainty about how much gas is really available through this means.

But there is an environmental downside to fracking, including the possibility of groundwater contamination, air pollution, the migration of chemicals to the surface, and the triggering of earth tremors from the underground rock disturbances.

In many parts of the United States, groundwater resources are critical as supplies for agricultural, industrial, and especially commercial and domestic uses. Groundwater aquifers are normally at much shallower depths than the very deep wells drilled for fracking. But water contamination can still result from wells that have to be driven through the aquifers. In fact, there have been reports of groundwater, and related surface water, contamination in many parts of the country as a result of fracking. These appear especially to be related to the chemical additives that operators use in the high-pressure water stream, as well as from methane that is released as a result of the drilling.

We appear to have a technology that addresses one of our problems, energy supply, but entails substantial risk on another front, the environment. Questions abound about how much the activity should be encouraged, what the real environmental risks are, how these risks can be reduced to acceptable levels, and what kind of public regulation should be pursued, and by whom.

called "fracking" for extracting deep underground natural gas, and the potential for groundwater contamination it produces. See Exhibit 14.1.

Coastal Water Pollution

Much of the effort to reduce water pollution focuses on inland freshwater bodies. Pollution of coastal waters is also a significant issue, as a large fraction of the U.S. population lives in close proximity to those waters, and because this resource is critical to the entire marine ecosystem. The full array

FIGURE 14.3   Volume and Number of Oil Spills for Incidents Above 100 Gallons
in U.S. Coastal Waters, 1973–2011

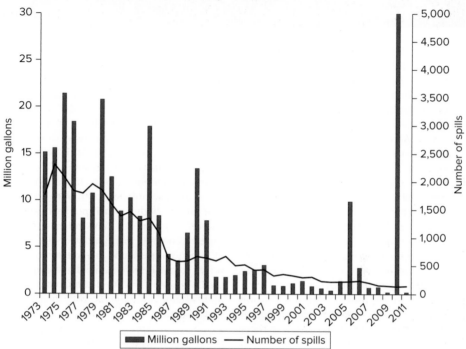

Sources: USCG, Office of Investigations and Compliance Analysis, *Polluting Incidents In and Around U.S. Waters A Spill/Release Compendium: 1969-2011*, Washington, D.C., December 2012.

Note: In 2010, the Deepwater Horizon oil spill reached 207 million gallons.

of point and NPSs is involved. One significant source, often revealed in dramatic ways by accidental releases, is oil spilled from tankers and barges that are transporting oil in coastal waters. Given the steady increase in oil imports into the United States, this will no doubt continue to require regulatory attention.

Ship and barge transportation in these waters has historically been regulated with a complex mix of state, federal, and international laws. Over the last 30 years, the number of significant spills and the quantity of oil released from these spills have dropped substantially, as Figure 14.3 shows.

The 1989 major oil spill in U.S. waters of the Exxon *Valdez* in Alaska led directly to the federal Oil Pollution Act of 1990. This law made comprehensive changes in the law through two means: expanding federal response authority and increasing spill liability. It also incorporated specific technology standards, such as requiring double-hulled tankers and a variety of performance requirements for operators.

Another oil-spill problem is water contamination stemming from accidents on off-shore oil drilling platforms. Exhibit 14.2 discusses this issue.

Incentives for Deterring Offshore Oil Spills

EXHIBIT **14.2**

Despite the notion of "peak oil" (that world production of petroleum has peaked and will gradually decline), modern economies will continue to use huge quantities of oil for many years to come. It is expected that an increasing proportion of petroleum will be extracted from offshore facilities. Offshore production facilities are subject to accidents and spills, especially in cases where safety mechanisms fail to deploy and well control is lost by workers on the platform. The danger of this has been known for a long time, and was recently underscored again in the *Deepwater Horizon* blowout. As offshore wells get ever deeper and more complex, this danger will increase.

How to give these companies a strong incentive to develop and deploy better accident containment technology? There are two parts to this:

1. Giving firms the financial incentive to act, and

2. Developing a more effective regulatory system.

The first of these can be pursued by having a liability arrangement whereby oil companies will be held liable for any damages caused by spills. The current liability system is complicated and appears to be ineffective in doing this. The second could be pursued in many ways. A regulatory system needs to make it possible for public officials to be able to determine whether adequate technology is in place. For example, a governance structure that includes either public-interest board members or an independent, expert panel and transparent disclosures of expenditures might provide some assurance that research and development (R&D) is adequately funded and containment technology keeps up with the latest drilling depths.

Source: Mark A. Cohen, Molly K. Macaulay, and Nathan Richardson, "The Next Battle: Containing Future Major Oil Spills, Resources for the Future," *Resources Magazine,* 177, Winter/Spring 2011, p. 46.

Recent Policy Innovations in Water Pollution Control

Nonpoint-Source Water Pollution Control

The EPA estimates that NPS emissions are responsible for more than 50 percent of water quality standards violations at the beginning of the 21st century. Major NPSs are agricultural runoff, urban street runoff, and activities related to land clearance and building construction. The fact that NPS emissions are diffuse and not concentrated into specific outfalls has made them very difficult to control. NPS pollutants are also normally weather related, which makes the runoff patterns more difficult to monitor.

Difficulties of control explain why NPS pollution has not been addressed as vigorously as point-source emissions, despite its importance. Early federal water quality laws directed state agencies to consider NPS pollution in their water quality programs, but did not require that specific steps be taken. The 1987 law gives it somewhat more prominence and authorizes federal money to subsidize local efforts to control NPS pollution. In fact, there is a major contrast between the national, uniform policy that has been followed to control point-source emissions and the policy for NPS pollution. In the latter case federal authorities have essentially thrown the problem into the hands of the states. Their reasoning is that "the application of uniform technological controls . . . is not appropriate for the management of NPSs. Site-specific decisions must consider the nature of the watershed, the nature of the water body, . . . and the range of management practices available to control NPS pollution."[12] So in this case there is recognition that a uniform national program is not appropriate.

Passing the major initiative to the states has led to a great variety of programs for NPS pollution control.[13] Traditional approaches such as emission standards are not common, because of the difficulties of measuring emissions with accuracy. This has pushed back the locus of control onto regulating activities and technologies that typically lead to NPS emissions. These are mostly what we have called **design standards.** These are standards that require certain techniques or practices to be used by sources whose activities lead to NPS emissions. Standards that rule out agricultural cultivation on steep, easily eroded land; standards specifying the design of urban storm sewers; and standards requiring homebuilders to take certain steps to control construction site runoff are types of design standards. The 1987 Water Quality Act, for example, establishes a program of federal subsidies for farmers to adopt **best management practices** to control agricultural pollution. Although design standards may be necessary in the case of NPS emissions, we should keep in mind the difficulties inherent in their use. They require administrative determination of what particular technologies and techniques will be allowed in different circumstances. These involve substantial amounts of pushing and shoving among regulators and polluters, and probably the weakening of individual incentives to find new and better ways of reducing emissions.

Another method of controlling NPS emissions is to tax those activities or materials that lead to the emissions, rather than the emissions themselves. Charges might be put on fertilizer used by farmers, for example, or on lawn chemicals used by suburban dwellers. The objective in this case is to induce a reduction in the use of materials that may ultimately end up in rivers, lakes, or groundwater aquifers.

Total Maximum Daily Load (TMDL) Program

The national system of TBESs has been criticized from its beginnings, especially by economists, for its relative inflexibility and cost ineffectiveness. A nationally mandated program based on the premise that all sources should be subject to the same standards is bound to make water quality improvements much

---

[12] U.S. Environmental Protection Agency, *Nonpoint Source Pollution in the U.S., Report to Congress,* Washington, D.C., 1984, pp. xiii–xiv.

[13] US EPA, State and Tribal Nonpoint Source Management Programs, 2015, **yosemite.epa.gov/R10 /ecocomm.nsf/Watershed+Collaboration/State+Tribal+NPS.**

more costly than they have to be. Furthermore, there has been a disconnect between the permit program and ambient water quality improvement goals. It is quite conceivable, for example, that all of the sources on a particular body of water, such as an estuary, could have adopted the legally mandated emission-control technologies, but for the water quality in the estuary to be substantially diminished. One way this could happen is through a growth in the number of sources as the economy expands; total emissions would increase even though each individual source had adopted the "best conventional technology." In recent years, therefore, federal water quality regulators have sought to reestablish an **ambient-based** orientation in water pollution control.

Although the 1972 Clean Water Act gave federal water pollution control a technology orientation, it also contained a section that in effect requires an ambient approach. In cases where the quality of water bodies is impaired, even after technology-based controls required by the law have been put in place, states are required to develop **total maximum daily loads** (TMDLs) for these waters; these TMDLs incorporate the following steps:

1. For individual bodies of water, the determination of the TMDL of individual pollutants that the water body can receive without violating ambient water quality standards set for that water body.
2. The identification of all the sources, both point source and nonpoint source, that contribute to the degraded water quality.
3. An allocation of the total daily load among the relevant sources located on the water body.

According to the law, the states are supposed to take the lead in establishing TMDLs, with backing from the EPA.[14] Because of budget limitations, and attention that was given to technology-based permit programs, little was done under the TMDL program in the first years of the Clean Water Act. Regulatory agencies are now grappling with the considerable problems this approach presents.

Establishing the TMDL may be the least controversial aspect of the program. To do this requires drawing a connection between total loadings and resulting water quality. In some cases this connection may be reasonably simple, whereas in others it will be complex. Exhibit 14.3 is an excerpt from the sediment TMDL for Los Peñasquitos Lagoon in San Diego, California. The problem here, as in most cases, in setting the total loading is that there is expected to be a very long time lag between reducing that loading and reduced material in the water, due to accumulations from the past. Thus, authorities must choose a total loading that yields improved water quality in a "reasonable" length of time.

No doubt the much harder job politically will be allocating the total loading among the various pollution sources. There is the standard public goods problem here, as each source will have the incentive to shift as much of the total control cost as possible onto other sources. An added problem is that in many cases NPS emissions, particularly those from agriculture, are the major contributing

---

[14] The EPA maintains a Web site that has information on all aspects of the TMDL program. See http://www.epa.gov/owow/tmdl/index.html.

Establishing the Sediment TMDL for Los Peñasquitos Lagoon, San Diego County, California

EXHIBIT 14.3

The purpose of a TMDL is to restore an impaired waterbody to water quality conditions under which applicable water quality standards can once again be attained. As required by CWA section 303(d), the Los Peñasquitos Lagoon was placed on the 1996 List of Water Quality Limited Segments due to sedimentation and siltation loads that exceeded water quality objectives. The beneficial uses that are most sensitive to increased sedimentation are estuarine habitat and preservation of biological habitats of special significance.

Conceptually, a TMDL is represented by the equation:

$$TMDL = \Sigma WLAs + \Sigma LAs + MOS$$

The waste load allocation (WLA) portion of this equation is the total loading assigned to point sources. The load allocation (LA) portion is the loading assigned to non-point sources. The margin of safety (MOS) is the portion of loading reserved to account for any uncertainty in the data and computational methodology. An implicit MOS was incorporated for this TMDL.

There are two broad categories of sediment sources to the Lagoon:

1. Watershed sources, and
2. The Pacific Ocean.

The watershed sources consist of all point and nonpoint sources of sediment in the watershed area draining to Los Peñasquitos Lagoon.

The point sources identified in the Los Peñasquitos watershed are Phase I MS4 copermittees (San Diego County and the cities of San Diego, Poway, and Del Mar), Phase II MS4s, Caltrans, and construction and industrial storm water permit holders.

The year 2000 estimated loads were solely the result of watershed runoff (land-use based) and stream bank erosion and no other types of point sources. The total sediment contribution for all responsible parties in the water shed is presented as the WLA.

As the primary point source to the Lagoon, a WLA of 2,580 tons/year was assigned to the responsible parties. A 67 percent sediment load reduction from the year 2000 load to the historical (mid-1970s) load is required of the responsible parties.

The responsible parties must develop a Load Reduction Plan that will establish a watershed-wide programmatic, adaptive management approach for implementation. The plan will include a detailed description of implementation actions, as identified and planned by the responsible parties, to meet the requirements of this TMDL. All responsible parties are responsible for reducing their sediment loads to the receiving waterbody or demonstrating that their discharges are not causing exceedances of the WLA.

Full implementation of the TMDL for sediment must be completed within 20 years from the effective date of the Basin Plan amendment. This timeline takes into consideration the planning needs of the responsible parties and other stakeholders to establish a Load Reduction Plan, time needed to address multiple impartments, and provides adequate time to measure temporal disparities between reductions in upland loading and the corresponding Lagoon water quality response.

Source: State Water Resources Control Board, *An Amendment to the Water Quality Plan for the San Diego Basin to Incorporate the Total Maximum Daily Load for Sediment in Los Peñasquitos Lagoon, San Diego, July 14, 2014*, California Regional Water Quality Control Board, June 2012

TABLE 14.5   TMDLs Approved by the EPA, 1996–2014

Year	Number of TMDLs Approved
1996	135
1998	402
2000	1,555
2002	2,742
2004	3,392
2006	4,204
2008	9,264
2010	2,572
2012	2,883
2014	3,338

Source: U.S EPA, *National Summary of Impaired Waters and TMDL Information,*
May 2015.

factor in water quality degradation. It has been much more difficult to develop effective regulatory programs for NPSs than it has for point sources, a problem that will only intensify with the TMDL program.

Despite these difficulties the states had made substantial progress in drawing up TMDLs for their polluted water bodies until 2008, when 9,050 were approved, as shown in Table 14.5. In the last few years TMDLs have been lower because of budget cuts and a notable shift toward more difficult TMDLs.

Emission Trading in Water Pollution Control

If total pollutant loads have been established for a body of water, and those loads have been allocated among the sources of emissions, it is only natural to think about **emission trading**. As we saw in Chapter 13, trading can often (but not always) offer substantial improvements over traditional approaches in terms of cost-effectiveness, leading to much greater pollution reduction per dollar of cost. In fact, water quality trading has been around for some time. In 1981 Wisconsin initiated a BOD trading program among sources on the Fox River.[15]

Water quality trading and offset programs are operating throughout the United States; some were established in the 1990s and continue today (Refer to Table 14.6). The EPA has encouraged states, interstate agencies, and tribes to devise trading plans for polluted water bodies in their jurisdictions, and has published guides to help in designing them.[16] Several environmental groups have begun to advocate well-designed water quality trading plans for addressing different parts of the water pollution–control problem.[17] Others have urged caution.

[15] Erhard F. Joeres and Martin H. David (eds.), *Buying a Better Environment: Cost Effective Regulation Through Permit Trading,* University of Wisconsin Press, Madison, WI, 1983, pp. 233–248.

[16] U.S. Environmental Protection Agency, *Water Quality Trading Toolkit for Permit Writers,* EPA-833-R-07-004, Washington, D.C., August 2007, **http://www.epa.gov/owow/watershed/trading/WQTToolkit.cfm.**

[17] The World Resources Institute has developed a model water quality trading plan that local groups might adapt to their needs. See **http://www.nutrientnet.org.**

Table 14.6—Active Water Quality Trading and Offset Programs

Location	Program Name	Program Type	Year	Pollution
Eastern U.S.				
• Connecticut	Long Island Sound Nitrogen Credit Exchange	Trading	2002	N
• Pennsylvania	Pennsylvania Nutrient Credit Trading	Trading	2010	N/P /sediment
• Delaware	Pinnacle Foods	Offset	1998	N/P
• Virginia	Chesapeake Bay Watershed Nutrient Credit Exchange	Trading	2011	N/P
• Maryland	Maryland Water Quality Trading	Trading	2008	N/P /sediment
• North Carolina	Tar-Pamlico Nutrient Trading	Trading	1990	N/P
	Neuse River Basin	Trading	2002	N
Central U.S.				
• Ohio	Great Miami River Watershed Trading Pilot	Trading	2006	N & P
	Alpine Cheese Company /Sugar Creek	Offset	2008	P
• Minnesota	Rahr Malting	Offset	1997	CBOD5
	Southern Minnesota Beet Sugar Cooperative	Offset	1999	P
	Minnesota River Basin Trading	Trading	2006	P
• Illinois	Piasa Creek Watershed Project	Offset	2001	Sediment
• Wisconsin	Red Cedar River Nutrient Trading Pilot	Offset	2007	P
Western U.S.				
• Colorado	Cherry Creek Reservoir Watershed Phosphorus Trading	Trading	1997	P
	Chatfield Reservoir Trading	Trading	1999	P
	Bear Creek	Offset	2001	P
• Oregon	Clean Water Services /Tualatin River	Offset	2005	BOD/NH4/ temperature
Foreign				
• Australia	South Creek Bubble Licensing	Trading	1996	N/P
	Hunter River Salinity Trading	Trading	2004	Salinity
• Canada	South Nation River Watershed Trading	Trading	2000	P

Notes: (N) nitrogen, (P) phosphorus, (BOD) Biochemical Oxygen Demand, (CBOD5) 5-day carbonaceous biochemical oxygen demand, (NH4) ammonia

Source: Karen Fisher-Vanden and Shelia Olmstead, *Moving Pollution Trading from Air to Water: Potential, Problems and Prognosis,* Journal of Economic Perspectives, 27(1), winter 2013, p. 151.

Nutrient Pollution Trading   EXHIBIT **14.4**

The Chesapeake Bay is a large, complex body of water, with many significant tributaries, and the recipient of huge volumes of water pollution from industrial, municipal and agricultural operations. A major feature of pollution control on the Bay is a nutrient trading system, established in 2005. The program initially featured trading among point sources, under an overall cap established in reference to the TMDL applied for portions of the Bay.

The trading system was subsequently expanded to include non-point sources, particularly urban storm-water and agricultural runoff. It allows offset trading, whereby sources may reduce their emissions to create offsets, which may then be traded. In this type of system regulators have to put in place very specific and practical requirements for creating offsets. Some of these are:

- Establishment of a baseline, an emission level that must be attained before further reductions would qualify as offsets.

- Additionality: no tradable credit may be generated for practices already in place, or reductions that would have occurred anyway without the trading program.

- Steps taken to create offsets must conform to "best management practices," as approved by the Chesapeake Bay Program.

- Any pollution reduction resulting from funding under a different program (e.g., support for agriculture) may not be used to create offsets.

- Absence of "leakages." Leakage is when reduction in emissions in one location, create the conditions for increased emissions at another location.

For further information, see Virginia Department of Environmental Quality, *Trading Nutrient Reductions from Nonpoint Source Best Management Practices in the Chesapeake Bay Watershed: Guidance for Agricultural Landowners and Your Potential Trading Partners*, Commonwealth of Virginia, Office of the Governor, January 2012.

It is clear that efficient water quality trading programs will have to be more geographically circumscribed than the typical air pollution trading system. Trading networks will be limited to sources discharging into particular water bodies, as the water quality issues of these individual bodies are hydrologically distinct from one another. In the proposed nutrient trading plan for the Chesapeake Bay, for example, trading is to be limited to within the sources of each of the major tributaries of the Bay. See Exhibit 14.4. Limitations of this type may lead to problems if the number of sources is small, because markets tend to work better when there are many potential participants.

There is also the problem of potential hotspots. Many water bodies (such as the Chesapeake just mentioned) have subsections that, though a part of the whole, nevertheless have somewhat distinct hydrologic systems. If sources in these types of areas are able to purchase additional emission permits from elsewhere, local water quality may be reduced even though overall water quality is not. The designers of water quality trading networks are attempting to address this issue by requiring that trading not lead to any localized diminishment in water quality as a result of trading.

Questions naturally arise about the suitability of trading for addressing NPS water pollution. Trading among individual sources implies that individual emissions can be monitored and measured. Conventional wisdom has been that nonpoint emissions are impossible to measure with accuracy. Thus, the stress is on using technological approaches such as voluntary or required adoption of **best management practices.** But in some cases individual emissions may be monitored, or estimated with sufficient accuracy, to allow trading. In the Central Valley of California, selenium discharges from agriculture have caused great damage to wildlife resources in the region. In this case circumstances are such that total and individual selenium runoff can be monitored, making it possible to implement an effective trading program for reducing this material.[18]

Summary

Current federal water pollution–control policy centers on the promulgation and enforcement of technology-based effluent standards (TBESs). These are emission standards stemming from the EPA's findings as to the "best available technology" or "best practicable technology" for specific industries. These technology-based standards, although appealing as "technological fixes," have a number of drawbacks. They are likely to give far less pollution control for the money spent than alternative approaches because they normally violate the equimarginal principle. They also have negative impacts through reducing the long-run incentives polluters might have to find better ways of controlling waterborne emissions. More recently, federal water pollution policy has shifted more toward an ambient-based approach, through the total maximum daily load (TMDL) system.

We also discussed the federal program of subsidies for municipal waste-treatment facilities. Over the last several decades the proportion of the U.S. population being served by advanced (secondary or tertiary) treatment facilities has been substantially increased.

One objective of a major revision of federal water pollution–control policy will be to try to find greater opportunities for using incentive-based strategies to combat water pollution. Most water pollution problems are local or regional, implying that the permit markets in water pollution control will have to operate with relatively small numbers of traders.

---

[18] Terry F. Young and Joe Karkoski, "Green Evolution: Are Economic Incentives the Next Step in Nonpoint Source Pollution Control?" *Water Policy,* 20, July 2000, pp. 151–173.

Questions for Further Discussion

1. Distinguish between a "technology-based" water pollution–control program and an "ambient-based" program.

2. In order to meet TMDL limits in a cost-effective manner, what is the appropriate role of the equimarginal principle? What about the economic efficiency principle?

3. Controlling the residuals from the production of bleached paper towels is about five times costlier than controlling the residuals from unbleached paper towels. Analyze this difference with our standard pollution-control model. What does it suggest in terms of public policy toward water pollution control?

4. What are likely to be the main problems in establishing cap-and-trade programs for water pollution control?

For additional readings and Web sites pertaining to the material in this chapter, see **www.mhhe.com/field7e.**

Chapter 15

Federal Air Pollution— Control Policy

As it travels through space, planet earth takes along with itself an enveloping, but relatively thin, layer of gases, without which it would be a cinder. That layer of atmospheric gases provides two critical services: direct life support for living organisms on the earth's surface and control over the radiation exchange between earth and space. Both of these services can be upset by human activity.

For human beings and other living organisms, the air is what water is for fish. Unless you wear a gas mask, there is no escaping what the air has to offer. The surface air (the troposphere) normally contains about 78 percent nitrogen, 21 percent oxygen, small amounts of other gases, and varying amounts of water vapor. It also may have many, many other things put there through special acts of nature and the activities of human beings. The upper layers of the earth's atmosphere (collectively called the stratosphere) contain only about 5 percent of the planet's air, but they have a critical role to play in making it habitable. Trace gases in the stratosphere, particularly ozone, filter out about 99 percent of incoming ultraviolet radiation, acting like a giant sun block, without which we would be exposed to damaging levels of radiation. Other trace gases in the stratosphere provide greenhouse services; they trap some of the infrared radiation that is reflected back from the earth's surface, warming it and making it more hospitable to living organisms. As we have recently found out, both of these vital phenomena can be disrupted by human activity.

Human disruptions of the atmosphere are not new; instances of local smoke pollution have occurred for centuries. But in the last 50 years, the potential severity of air-pollution problems has grown more acute, owing to the sheer scale of airborne residuals released and the exotic nature of some of the emitted substances. There are thousands of potential air pollutants: for example, oxides of carbon, nitrogen, and sulfur; volatile organic compounds (VOCs); suspended particulate matter; photochemical oxidants; radioactivity; heat; and noise. These pollutants cause a diverse set of damages. Perhaps the most important are human health impacts. Prolonged exposure to airborne substances can lead to lung cancer, bronchitis, emphysema, and asthma; accidental releases can have acute impacts. Air pollution also causes damage to plants, as in, for example, the destruction of forests and reduced crop yields stemming from acid deposition. Air pollution can lead to severe damage of exposed materials, such as the surface erosion and discoloration of stone and concrete work and the corrosion of metals. Stratospheric ozone depletion and enhanced global warming have significant implications for humans and the earth's ecosystem. Not all air pollution is outdoors; in fact, indoor air pollution is a critical problem in many homes, factories, mines, and farms.

Many airborne pollutants are emitted on a continuous basis. The sulfur dioxide (SO_2) emissions from power plants, for example, are continuously produced as long as the plants are in operation. For individual motor vehicles, emissions start and stop with their operation, although for an entire urban area, auto and truck emissions vary continuously throughout the days and seasons according to the rhythms of economic activity. Episodic, especially accidental, emissions have been the cause of severe air-pollution incidents, for example, the numerous transportation-related accidents that occur in many countries. The links between emissions and ambient air quality levels can be complicated because of the complexities of meteorological phenomena. The best-known example of this is the creation of local weather conditions that trap air pollutants, sometimes for extended periods of time. The infamous "temperature inversions" over urban areas are well known.

Annual expenditures in the United States for air-pollution control have increased substantially since the early 1970s. Has this had an impact? Table 15.1 shows aggregate U.S. emissions for major air pollutants for several years between 1980 and 2013. These are divided into emissions from stationary sources and emissions from mobile sources. All of these emissions have declined over this time period. Sulfur dioxide emissions are largely from stationary sources, and these have decreased substantially over this time period. Nitrogen oxides (NOx), on the other hand, are largely from mobile sources; there have been sharp decreases in these emissions in the more recent years. The biggest success story has been with lead emissions; these have decreased dramatically from both mobile and stationary sources.

Emission data like these do not tell us directly whether pollution-control policies have been effective. To know this, one needs a with/without analysis: what emissions were compared to what they would have been if the policies had not been pursued. As it happens, the Environmental Protection Agency (EPA) was instructed to do such an analysis to assess the impacts of the Clean Air Act (CAA) Amendments of 1990. Table 15.2 shows a part of its results. For the major air pollutants, it shows actual 1990 emissions and projected 2020 emissions with and without the 1990 law. Note that if there had been no 1990 law, total emissions of most pollutants would have increased somewhat, while emissions of carbon monoxide (CO) actually would have decreased. This is attributable to both the impacts of previous policies as well as basic changes at work in the economy. Emissions with the 1990 program, however, are substantially lower, with the exception of those of particulate matter. From data like these, we can conclude that the public policies have led to substantial emission reductions and no doubt to improved ambient air quality. What needs

TABLE 15.1   National Emissions Estimates for Common Pollutants and their Precursors

	Millions of Tons per Year						
	1980	1985	1990	1995	2000	2005	2013
Carbon monoxide (CO)	178	170	144	120	102	81	59
Lead	0.074	0.023	0.005	0.004	0.002	0.001	0.001
Nitrogen oxides (NO_x)	27	26	25	25	22	20	13
Volatile organic compounds (VOC)	30	27	23	22	17	16	14
Particulate matter (PM)							
PM_{10}	6	4	3	3	3	4	3
$PM_{2.5}$	NA	NA	2	2	3	3	2
Sulfur dioxide (SO_2)	26	23	23	19	16	14	5
Totals	267	250	218	189	160	135	94

Notes:
1. For CO, NO_x, SO_2, and VOC emissions, fires are excluded because they are highly variable; for direct PM emissions, both fires and dust are excluded.
2. PM estimates do not include condensible PM.
3. The estimates for 2008 and beyond are based on the final version 3 of the 2009 NIE.
4. $PM_{2.5}$ emissions are not included when calculating the emissions totals because they are included in the PM_{10} emissions number.
5. EPA did not estimate $PM_{2.5}$ emissions prior to 1990.
6. The 1999 estimate for lead was used to represent 2000; the 2002 estimate for lead was used to represent 2005; and the 2008 estimate was used to represent 2013.
Source: U.S. Environmental Protection Agency, *Air Quality Trends,* 2015, **http://www.epa.gov/airtrends/aq trends.html.**

TABLE 15.2   Estimated Impacts of 1990 Clean Air Act (CAA)

		2020		
Pollutant	1990	Without CAA	With CAA	Reduction
Volatile organic compounds	25,790	31,228	13,704	17,584
Nitrogen oxides	25,917	31,740	10,092	21,647
Carbon monoxide	154,513	155,970	84,637	71,332
Sulfur dioxide	23,143	27,912	8,272	19,640
Particulate matter (PM_{10})	25,454	28,280	20,577	7,702
Particulate matter ($PM_{2.5}$)	5,527	6,368	5,297	1,072
Ammonia (NH_3)	3,656	4,787	4,587	200

Source: U.S. Environmental Protection Agency, "The Benefits and Costs of the Clean Air Act from 1990 to 2020," Final Report, March 2011.

to be asked, however, is whether the sums of money the nation has put into air-pollution control have bought as much improvement in air quality as they could have and should have. Let's look more closely at the policies themselves.

Federal Air Pollution–Control Laws: A Brief Sketch

The major federal air-pollution statutes of the last six decades are summarized in Table 15.3. There was little federal concern or statutory activity in air-pollution matters prior to the late 1960s; in this respect, it was similar to water pollution. Air pollution was regarded as primarily a local concern, to be dealt with under **local nuisance laws.** Federal activity was regarded as best directed at helping the states deal with growing air quality problems. In the 1967 Air Quality Act, the Department of Health, Education and Welfare was charged with establishing criteria through which ambient air quality standards could be set for six common air pollutants: SO_2, NO_x, ozone, particulate matter, CO, and lead. These became known as the **"criteria" pollutants,** and ambient standards for these six were to be set by the states. The CAA Amendments of 1970 represented an aggressive assertion of federal power into air-pollution matters. It established the basic contours of air-pollution policy that persist to the present: uniform national ambient air quality standards, a variety of technology-based emission standards (TBESs) for stationary sources, and stricter emission standards for automobiles.

In the CAA Amendments of 1977, federal legislators addressed some of the problems created by the uniform ambient standards of the 1970 act. Air quality was worse in some cities than others, and better in rural areas. There was widespread concern after the 1970 law that cities in areas with air quality already better than the national ambient standard could compete unfairly for new industrial development. New firms might be attracted to these areas by the promise of less strict emissions controls than firms would face in areas where air quality was already worse than the standards. The 1977 CAA amendments differentiated **PSD areas** (PSD stands for "prevention of significant deterioration") and **nonattainment areas.** Different technology-based effluent standards would apply to PSD regions than to nonattainment regions.[1]

After the 1977 act, there were no new federal air-pollution statutes until 1990. There were, however, some significant policy innovations that occurred during this period within the existing laws. A major innovation was the EPA's decision to allow emission trading among sources; to accommodate economic growth and efficient pollution control, emission reduction credits could be traded between firms as well as intra-firm.

The CAA Amendments of 1990 contain five main sections dealing with:

- motor vehicles and fuels
- acid rain

[1] The PSD regions were differentiated into three classes; see the detail in Table 15.3.

TABLE 15.3 Major Federal Air-Pollution Laws

Air Pollution Control Act (APCA) of 1955
Authorized the Secretary of Health, Education and Welfare (HEW) to spend up to $5 million a year to do research and to help the states in training and technical assistance on matters of air pollution. Extended in 1959 and 1962.
Motor Vehicle Exhaust Study Act of 1960
Directed the Secretary of HEW to do a study on "Motor Vehicles, Air Pollution and Health" within two years.
Clean Air Act (CAA) of 1963
Authorized federal grants to states to develop state and local air pollution–control programs; established a conference system to deal with problems of interstate air pollution; extended authorization for federal research on air pollution.
Motor Vehicle Air Pollution Control Act of 1965
Authorized the Secretary of HEW to set *emission standards* for new cars (but no deadline was established); dealt with international air pollution and called for more research.
CAA Extension of 1966
Extended the CAA of 1963 and added authority to make grants to states to support air pollution–control programs.
Air Quality Act (AQA) of 1967
Provided for additional grants to states to plan air pollution–control programs; provided for interstate air pollution–control agencies, expanded research on fuels and vehicles; required HEW to establish air quality regions of the country and publish air quality criteria and control technology reports for the common pollutants; required states to establish ambient air quality standards for the "criteria" pollutants and develop attainment programs; authorized HEW to give financial assistance to states to establish motor-vehicle inspection programs.
CAA Amendments of 1970
Established national ambient air quality standards (NAAQSs) for criteria pollutants; required the establishment of new-car emission standards along with certification programs; EPA was to establish emission standards for major toxic or hazardous pollutants; EPA to establish technology-based emission standards for all *new sources* (NSPS) of the common air pollutants; required state implementation plans (SIPs) to control existing stationary sources of air pollutants.
CAA Amendments of 1977
Established the goal of "prevention of serious deterioration" (PSD) in areas already cleaner than the national standards; established three classes of already clean areas:
Class I areas: no additional air quality deterioration permitted (includes national parks, etc.).

TABLE 15.3 *(Continued)*

CAA Amendments of 1977

Class II areas: some air quality deterioration to be permitted (includes most PSD regions).
Class III areas: air quality to be allowed to deteriorate to level of NAAQSs.

Established a technology standard "lowest achievable emission rate" (LAER) for new sources in nonattainment areas and "best available control technologies" (BACT) for new sources in PSD regions.

CAA Amendments of 1990

Established tougher tailpipe standards for new cars, with longer warranty period; mandated pilot program of "clean" cars in some cities, reformulated fuels in some cities, Phase II pumps at gas stations, and onboard fume canisters on cars; streamlined stationary-source permitting procedures; provided for reduction of 189 toxic airborne emissions through TBES ("maximum achievable control technology," MACT); provided for stricter local plans to reduce ozone, carbon monoxide, and particulates in the worst cities; outlined further rules for phasing out of CFCs; provided for a system of transferable discharge permits among power plants to reduce sulfur dioxide emissions.

Sources: Arthur C. Stern, "History of Air Pollution Legislation in the United States," *Journal of Air Pollution Control Association*, 32(1), January 1982, pp. 44–61; Paul R. Portney, "Air Pollution Policy," in Paul R. Portney (ed.), *Public Policies for Environmental Protection*, Resources for the Future, Washington, D.C., 1990, chap. 3; *EPA Journal*, January/February 1991, pp. 8–9.

- air toxics
- urban air quality, and
- stratospheric ozone problems

The continued problem of motor-vehicle pollution was addressed by a further tightening of new-car emission standards and expansion of state inspection and maintenance (I&M) programs. In addition, the law mandated many new technologies, such as reformulated fuel, fume-catching nozzles at gas stations, and the development of a generation of clean cars.

To combat the ecological effects of SO_2 emissions from power plants, the 1990 CAA introduced an innovation plan for a transferable discharge permit program. The law also attempts to deal more directly with **toxic air pollutants.** The 1990 act specifically lists 189 toxic materials that are to be controlled and requires that the EPA establish effluent standards to apply to sources emitting more than 10 tons/year of a single toxic or 25 tons/year of any combination of toxic compounds. The standard is to be the "maximum achievable control technology" (MACT), defined as technology based on the "best control technologies that have already been demonstrated" in the designated industrial categories.

Regarding criteria pollutants, the 1990 act seeks to recognize degrees of nonattainment in different metropolitan areas. The law specifies increasingly stringent control techniques for cities according to the degree of nonattainment achieved. These techniques are based primarily on the enforcement of technol-ogy-based effluent standards and the outright specification of technologies that must be adopted in the various regions.

Efforts to protect the earth's stratospheric ozone layer are a response to scien-tific results showing that this layer was being degraded by the release of certain chemicals in industrial and domestic use. The 1990 program was put in place to implement the country's responsibilities as part of the Montreal Protocol to phase out the use of ozone depleting chemicals.

Current federal air-pollution policies are long and complex, but they can be boiled down to the following:

- National ambient air quality standards for criteria pollutants, with pollution-control programs of varying stringency based on the severity of the air pol-lution in different regions.
- Command-and-control type emissions standards for stationary sources of criteria pollutants and hazardous pollutants, with differential stringency de-pending on age and location of source.
- State Implementation Plans (SIPs): plans developed by the individual states and approved by the EPA, showing how they will meet the ambient standard.
- Emission standards for new cars, with I&M programs in some states.
- A variety of new technology specifications for automobile pollution ("clean cars," reformulated fuel, on-board vapor-catching devices, etc.).
- Increasing efforts to utilize market trading mechanisms to reduce airborne emissions.
- Efforts to develop new initiatives and programs to control greenhouse gases (GHGs).

In the next few sections we look more closely at these major parts of the air-pollution control program (the discussion of the chlorofluorocarbon [CFC] phaseout and the Montreal Protocol is postponed until Chapter 19).

National Ambient Air Quality Standards

The 1970 CAA specifies a system of **national ambient air quality standards** (NAAQS) for criteria pollutants, to be applied uniformly across the coun-try. In Chapter 11 we discussed the question of uniformity in standards. Unless marginal damage and marginal abatement costs happen to be the same in all regions, uniform national standards will not be efficient. They will be overly stringent where marginal damages are relatively low and/or marginal abatement costs relatively high, or not stringent enough where marginal damages are relatively high and/or marginal abatement costs rela-tively low. In this case, however, the policy advantages of having the same standards across the country outweigh the efficiency aspects of differential standards.

The current standards for criteria pollutants are shown in Table 15.4. There are two levels of standards established in the CAA: primary and secondary. The legal criteria to be used by the EPA in establishing these are as follows:

- **Primary standards:** To be set at whatever level is required to protect the **public health,** with an "adequate margin of safety." The latter clause has been interpreted to require that the standards be set to protect the health of the more sensitive members of the population, such as children, asthmatics, and the elderly.

- **Secondary standards:** To be set at the level necessary to protect the **public welfare.** This has been interpreted to include such things as protection from decreased visibility and damage to crops, animals, vegetation, and buildings.

From an efficiency standpoint, ambient standards should presumably be set at a level where marginal benefits are roughly equal to marginal abatements costs. According to the strict reading of the law, the EPA may not take costs into account in setting the standards. But in effect costs do enter into the decision. The EPA itself has developed procedures for allowing costs to affect decisions, implicitly if not explicitly. (See Exhibit 15.1.) Any regulatory change, including setting ambient air quality standards, must be approved by the Office of Management and Budget in the executive branch, and this is supposedly achieved only if benefits exceed costs. In addition, state implementation plans may take costs into account in considering steps to be taken to achieve the standards, so that enforcement involves an implicit trade-off of marginal damages and marginal costs.

The standards as set imply that the damage functions associated with these criteria pollutants have **thresholds,** below which damages are minimal or

TABLE 15.4   National Primary and Secondary Ambient Air Quality Standards as of 2014

Pollutant	Primary/Secondary	Averaging Time	Level
Carbon monoxide	Primary	8 hours	9 ppm
		1 hour	35 ppm
Lead	Primary and secondary	Rolling 3-month average	0.15 µg/m^3
Nitrogen dioxide	Primary	1 hour	100 ppb
	Primary and secondary	Annual	53 ppb
Ozone	Primary and secondary	8 hours	0.075 ppm
Particle pollution, PM$_{2.5}$	Primary	Annual	12 µ/m^3
	Secondary	Annual	15 µ/m^3
	Primary and secondary	24 hours	150 µ/m^3
Particle pollution, PM$_{10}$	Primary and secondary	24 hours	150 µg/m^3
Sulfur dioxide	Primary	1 hour	75 ppb
	Secondary	3 hours	0.5 ppm

The Search for an "Intelligible Principle"

Setting Air Quality Standards Under the Clean Air Act

EXHIBIT 15.1

Under the CAA the U.S. Congress sets emission standards for cars. But to set ambient air pollution standards for the criteria pollutants, it gives the job to the EPA; in effect, it delegates to that agency the legal power to set and enforce these standards. So in the EPA the battles take place over where the standard should be set, with people on one side saying it shouldn't be too strict and people on the other saying it should be stricter. There appears to be no major agreed-upon procedure for setting the standard.

In 1999 the U.S. Court of Appeals for the District of Columbia made a novel decision: It found, at the legal request of the American Trucking Association, that Congress had engaged in an unconstitutional delegation of power to the EPA to set the standards for ozone and particulate matter. According to the U.S. Constitution, Congress is the only body that may legislate new federal statutes. Many years ago the Supreme Court decided that this power may be delegated to a regulating agency provided Congress provides that agency with an "intelligible principle" for making the decision. The trucking association and its allies asserted that the CAA contains no such intelligible principle, hence the EPA's standard-setting was effectively illegal.

Of course, the CAA does contain language containing the criteria that EPA is supposed to follow in setting the standards: It is supposed to set standards "requisite to protect the public health" with "an adequate margin of safety." There is no mention of cost here (i.e., it doesn't say something like "tighten the standards until the added costs exceed the added benefits"), and in fact the Appeals Court concurred that cost factors could not legally be considered by the EPA.

So what "intelligible principle" is the EPA supposed to follow? Numerous people have suggested alternative approaches:

1. Significant tightening: tighten the standard until there is no significant improvement that could be gained by further improvement.

2. Knee-of-the-curve: tighten the standard until there is a significant drop-off in added benefits from further tightening.

3. De minimis rule: tighten the standard until further tightening would produce benefits that are too small to worry about.

But do these qualify as "intelligible principles"? It would seem that whatever rule the EPA should choose, it's always going to be faced with the question of whether it would be worth it to tighten the standards a little more; in other words, will the benefits of tightening the standard exceed the cost?

Despite the fact that the CAA does not contain explicit language of this kind, the U.S. Supreme Court reversed the decision of the Appeals Court, saying in effect that the EPA had, in fact, developed over the years procedures for intelligent interpretation and implementation of the health-related criterion contained in the CAA. In effect it has taken the general criteria as expressed in the law and evolved procedures for setting standards in a reasonably intelligent way. Of course, that does not necessarily satisfy the combatants in the policy process, who still fight over where the standards should be set.

nonexistent. When the standards were set, relatively little was known about the damage functions. Even today we are unsure if these thresholds exist. Recent results suggest that they may not, that in fact damages may occur even at very low levels of these pollutants. But the costs of achieving zero levels of these pollutants would be enormous.

Stationary-Source Control

A strictly ambient-based approach to air pollution control would take the ambient standards as given, and then determine the specific steps needed to attain them. The 1972 CCA involved a change to a technology-based system. It gave the EPA the authority and responsibility to establish emission standards that would, in effect, specify the technologies that polluters would have to install and operate to reduce emissions.

Technology-Based Effluent Standards

Emissions standards are never-exceed levels for the emissions of various pollutants coming from industrial sources. In theory, an emission level could be established while leaving the polluter free to figure out the best way (presumably the cheapest way) to achieve the standard. But that is not the way the 1970 CAA was written. The relevant language in the act is the following:

> The term "standard of performance" means a standard for emissions of air pollution which reflects the degree of emission limitation achievable through the application of the best system of emission reduction which (taking into account the cost of achieving such reduction and any nonair quality health and environmental impact and energy requirements) the Administrator determines has been adequately demonstrated.

This is indeed an emission standard, but it is tied to technology. In other words, the standard has to "reflect" the control achievable through a system that is in some sense the "best" one available. In this case the criterion seems to be technology that has been "adequately demonstrated." In other cases the EPA was instructed to set emission standards based on other criteria, as we will discuss below.

What initially might have sounded like a straightforward emissions standard (lower your emissions to the standard level using whatever means you want) in practice turned into a technology standard; the EPA identified acceptable technologies and provided incentives for firms to adopt these particular technologies. Firms treated these EPA-designated technologies as technology standards primarily because of monitoring difficulties and the need to assume compliance.

Differentiated Control

The 1970 CAA reinforced the tradition in pollution-control programs of treating certain types of sources differently in terms of pollution-control requirements.

The standards differ between existing and new sources and between nonattainment and PSD regions as shown in Table 15.5. Distinctions between existing

TABLE 15.5   **Technology-Based Effluent Standards (TBESs) for Control of Large Stationary Sources of Air Pollutants**

Nonattainment Regions	
Existing sources:	RACT: reasonably available control technology
New sources:	LAER: lowest achievable emission rate
Prevention of Significant Deterioration (PSD) Regions	
Existing sources:	None
New sources:	BACT: best available control technology

and new sources are a prominent feature in environmental control programs. New sources, or existing sources that are modified in some major way, are usually held to stricter standards than existing, established sources. In the air quality program, new sources in nonattainment areas are subject to a LAER (lowest achievable emission rate) standard,[2] which is meant to be more restrictive than the RACT (reasonably available control technology) standard applied to existing sources in those areas. In PSD regions, new sources are held to standards based on BACT (best available control technology), whereas existing sources are, in effect, not subject to any standard.

The case for holding new sources to stricter standards (a **new-source bias**) than those applied to existing sources is usually made on the basis of cost; it normally costs more to retrofit existing plants with pollution-control equipment than to incorporate the equipment into new plants when they are being built. In effect, the argument is that the marginal abatement costs of existing plants are normally higher than those of new plants, so cost-effectiveness justifies more restrictive emission standards for the former than for the latter. To a large extent, this is probably an economic argument being used to justify a course of action that is politically expedient. It is easier to put stricter limits on new sources than on existing ones because, by definition, the former will have less political clout than the latter. And existing firms may not be so opposed to applying stricter controls that make it relatively costly for new competitors to get into business. From an administrative standpoint, a new-source bias is also easy to understand. In any given year, there are many times more existing sources than there are new or modified sources, so more administrative resources may be concentrated on the latter. A focus on new sources also implies a gradualist approach because it means that stricter standards will gradually spread through the various industries as old capital is replaced with new.

But the price paid for holding new sources to stricter standards may be high. The problem is that a new-source bias creates incentives to hold on to existing

---

[2] LAER is defined as the lowest emission rate specified in any state implementation plan, whether or not any source is currently achieving that rate.

plants because they will be subject to less strict environmental standards than new or modernized plants. So in trying to ease the transition to lower pollution levels through a new-source bias, the regulations may inadvertently slow up the rate of adoption of pollution-abatement technology. A fierce battle has gone on through the years over how regulators define a "new" versus an "existing" plant. One of the results of this is that many urban regions of the United States continue to suffer from substantial air-pollution problems many years after the beginning of the federal program.

Virtually all of the observations we made about technology-based effluent standards in water-pollution control are also applicable to air pollution–control policy. It is an approach that tends to put the initiative and responsibility for pollution control in the hands of administrative agencies rather than the polluters themselves. Too much of the energy and creativity of polluting firms is devoted to finding ways of avoiding compliance rather than devising better means of controlling emissions. The incentives for research and development (R&D) to develop new techniques of pollution control or to reach back into the production process to reduce residuals in the first place are weakened. But most important, TBESs have the effect of encouraging uniform compliance measures among sources. In a world where marginal abatement costs differ substantially across sources, this cannot be a cost-effective policy.

Cost-Effectiveness of the TBES Approach

Numerous studies have been done by environmental economists to estimate excess costs of the command-and-control (CAC) approach to air-pollution control inherent in technology-based effluent standards. These studies involve complex models that incorporate economic factors, such as control costs at each source, with emission and meteorological factors that show how ambient air quality is affected by various patterns of emissions.

The results of these models show that actual programs involving TBESs were four to six times more costly than they would have been had they been designed to be cost-effective. The problem with this is not just that society is paying much more than is necessary to get the improvements in air quality, although this is certainly a serious shortcoming. The real problem is that because the actual control programs are so much more costly than they need be, the apparent aggregate marginal abatement cost function is much higher than it need be, and therefore we are probably settling for smaller improvements in ambient quality than might be achieved if control programs were fully cost-effective.

We need to be mindful, however, of the idea that efficiency is not the only criterion on which pollution-control policies should be evaluated. Another is flexibility, or adaptability, and on this criterion, technology-based effluent standards may be more effective. Since they depend on substantial regulator discretion, adjustments can be made in concepts, definitions, monitoring, enforcement, and other dimensions to adapt to new circumstances without triggering acrimonious political battles.

New Directions in Stationary-Source Control: Emission Trading

While the central regulatory mechanism of the Clean Air Act continues to be command-and-control standards, a number of emission trading plans have been implemented. In Chapter 13 we referred to the emission reduction credit trading that was initiated under the CAA so that economic growth could be accommodated in nonattainment areas.

More recently, a number of complete **cap-and-trade (CAP)** programs have been put in place to address some of the nation's most significant air-pollution problems:

- Pollution-control authorities in Southern California began the Regional Clean Air Incentive Market (RECLAIM) in 1993. It applies to emissions of NO_x and SO_2. Each of about 300 sources received a declining balance of dated emission permits (called RECLAIM trading credits). As of 2003, total NO_x and SO_2 emissions were reduced by 71 percent and 60 percent, respectively, from their 1994 levels.[3]

- CAP for Mercury. Mercury is a highly toxic pollutant, and about half of total U.S. emissions come from power plants. The EPA put forth a proposal for a CAP plan to reduce mercury emissions. However, in the end, the EPA chose to use standard MACT effluent standards to combat this pollutant.

- Beginning in 1999, 13 northeastern U.S. states/regions began a CAP program to control emissions of NO_x.[4] By interstate agreement, the total NO_x emissions for the group are allocated among the states, then each state allocates its total emissions as tradable permits among sources in the state. Trading among sources, which are mostly electric utilities and large industrial boilers, may be both intra- and interstate. This program was later expanded to include 10 midwestern states. It is expected to be superseded by new programs being developed to address problems of interstate pollution.

- Many individual states are establishing CAP programs to deal with air-pollution problems within their borders. One of these, for example, is the market for volatile organic material (VOM) emissions in northeastern Illinois. The purpose of this market is to allow Chicago to achieve attainment of the NAAQS ozone standard in a cost-effective way. Major sources of VOM emissions are assigned baseline emission levels on the basis of their historical VOM emissions during recent years. They are then allocated transferable discharge permits (called allotment trading units, ATUs, in this program) equal to 88 percent of their baseline levels. Each ATU corresponds to 200 pounds of VOM per ozone season (May 1 to September 30) and is tradable in keeping with the fundamental principles of CAP programs.[5]

---

[3] For more information, consult **http://www.aqmd.gov.**

[4] These are the states of the Ozone Transport Committee, a group set up to determine how best to reduce ozone pollution in the Northeast. The original group includes the states Connecticut, Delaware, Maine, Maryland, Massachusetts, New Hampshire, New Jersey, New York, Pennsylvania, Rhode Island, and Vermont; the northern counties of Virginia; and the District of Columbia.

[5] Additional information on this market is available at **http://www.epa.illinois.gov/topics /air-quality/planning-reporting/erms/index.html.**

The CAP Program for Reducing SO$_2$ Emissions

Emissions of SO$_2$ from power plants are a major source of acid precipitation, especially in the northeastern United States and eastern Canada. To reduce the ecological damages of these emissions, the 1990 CAA amendments included a cap-and-trade program to reduce emissions by 40 percent from 1990 levels.

The program was introduced in two phases. Phase I ran from 1995 to 2000 and involved 110 electric power plants located in 21 eastern and midwestern states. Phase II began in 2000 and includes about 1,000 power plants throughout the country. The EPA allocated to each plant a **time profile of discharge permits.**[6] Each permit is for a particular year and can be used either in that year or in any subsequent year (in other words, a permit dated for one year can be banked and used in a later program year).

In Phase I (1995–2000), sources were allocated permits at the rate of 2.5 pounds of SO$_2$ per million British thermal units (BTUs), multiplied by their average annual fuel consumed from 1985 to 1987. In Phase II, the allocation was based on 1.2 pounds of SO$_2$ per million BTUs. The EPA held back a number of permits, some to be sold in annual auctions, and some to be distributed on the basis of various incentive criteria.

Emission permits are **tradable.** Managers of an individual plant may do one of the three things. They may simply hold on to the permits they were originally allocated and reduce their sulfur emissions to or below that level.[7] They can reduce their emissions below their permit holdings and sell the surplus permits. Or they can maintain their emissions to something more than their initial permit holdings and buy extra permits to cover the overage. Thus, market participants—buyers and sellers—consist of these utility plants adjusting their permit holdings to match their emission rates, as well as other participants who may buy and sell permits. Other utilities that might wish to expand their electricity output, but are held in check by SO$_2$ emission limitations, may buy additional permits, as may new plants starting operations after the program is put into effect. The law also allows permits to be traded and held by private citizens, brokers, speculators, environmental groups, other types of business enterprises, and so on.

The Role of the EPA

The role of the EPA is to keep track of permit trades so that it knows at all times how many emission permits are held by each plant. It also must monitor emissions to ensure that no plant emits more than it is entitled to by the number of permits it holds. The law specifies that each source is to install and maintain continuous monitoring devices. Emissions and permit data are collected via the Internet.

In 1980, total SO$_2$ emission from phase I and phase II sources were 17.3 million tons. In 2012, total emissions from these plants were 3.3 million tons.

---

[6] In other words, a source might be given a profile such as 5,000 permits applying to emissions in 1996; 4,900 permits for 1997; 4,800 permits for 1998; 4,700 permits for 1999; 4,600 permits for 1999; and 4,500 permits for 2000 and every subsequent year. This allows for a gradual reduction in the overall level of SO$_2$ emissions. In this program permits are called "allowances."

[7] They might reduce emissions below their permit holdings in order to have a reserve of surplus permits on hand for future contingencies.

FIGURE 15.1   SO₂ Permit Prices, 1997 to 2015

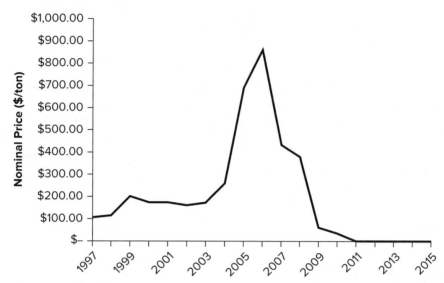

Source: U.S. Environmental Protection Agency, Allowance Markets, March 2015, **www.epa.gov/airmarkets/participants /allowance/index.html.**

Using this as the only criterion, the programs over succeeded, reducing emissions by approximately 80 percent in this period.

A substantial national market developed in SO₂ permits. In the early years prices were fairly stable around $160 per ton (see Figure 15.1). When it appeared around 2005 that the CAP would be tightened by the EPA, permit prices spiked to about $860 per ton. But in 2010, further actions by the EPA and the courts to limit emissions of specific upwind states, thereby putting substantial constraints on interstate trading, have effectively reduced the demand for permits.

Another factor reducing the demand for permits was the deregulation of the railroads, which reduced the costs of transporting low-sulfur coal from the west to power plants in the east. As a result SO₂ permit prices have fallen to near zero, and the SO₂ program has been effectively superseded by other policy initiatives. The EPA has concluded, however, that the program had very substantial net benefits. The costs of reducing SO₂ emissions were less than had been anticipated and the benefits were higher, because lowering emissions produced not only the expected ecological benefits, but also great health benefits through the ancillary reduction in particulate matter.

Interstate Air Pollution

The main thrust of stationary-source air-pollution control in the United States has been on intrastate pollution. States have been required to control sources within their boundaries in order to meet the ambient air quality standards in their states. Authorities have only recently started to come to grips with the fact that in many states, air quality is critically affected by emissions in other, upwind states. This was recognized in the CAA of 1972, which included a provision authorizing the

EPA to control emissions in one state if they ". . . contribute significantly to non-attainment in . . . any other state . . . ," of the ambient air quality standards.

In 2005 the EPA put forth a proposed program covering SO_2 and NO_x emissions from power plants in 28 eastern states. These emissions contribute to the nonattainment in downwind states, especially of the standards for ozone and particulate matter. This proposal, called the "Clean Air Interstate Rule" (CAIR), involved the establishment of state-level emission caps, with CAP programs that would have allowed both intrastate and interstate trading.[8,9] That plan was rejected by a federal court, on the grounds that trading could possibly lead to an increase in nonattainment in some locations because, by chance, permit buyers might have been concentrated in certain upwind states. This is the "hotspot" problem, discussed in Chapter 13.

In 2010 the EPA proposed a revised plan, again with state-level emission caps on SO_2 and NO_x, but with some limits on interstate trading of emission allowances. Since the SO_2 and NO_x CAP programs permit interstate trading, the status of these programs will be greatly affected by the final resolution of interstate pollution control, which has not yet been determined.

Another major factor affecting these SO_2 and NO_x markets in the future will be the statutory and regulatory steps that are eventually taken to control GHGs, especially carbon dioxide (CO_2).

Controlling Greenhouse Gas Emissions

The need to control GHG emissions to ameliorate global climate change has become widely accepted in the United States and around the world. The first major attempt to do this in the United States was a proposal for a national CAP program for carbon emissions. But CAP programs have been demonized by some of those who previously supported them. Thus the U.S. Congress was unable to come to agreement on its design and push it to enactment. Subsequently, the Supreme Court ruled that new legislation was not in fact necessary, and that the EPA had the power under the CAA, to regulate GHG emissions, even though they were not explicitly mentioned in that law.

This put the initiative back in the White House, which in 2014 proposed a new plan for control of GHG's from power plants. The essence of the program is to set specific state-level targets for power plant emissions, then essentially leave it up to the states, alone or in combination, to achieve the targets. The goals for each state depended on the following state-level characteristics:

- The prospects of improving fuel efficiency at power plants
- The extent to which natural gas could be substituted for coal
- The prospects for expanding renewable energy forms
- The prospects of achieving demand-side energy efficiencies.

---

[8] For information, see http://www.epa.gov/airmarkets/progsregs/nox/sip.html.

[9] For information about these programs, which are promulgated under the EPA's Clean Air Interstate Rule, see http://www.epa.gov/airmarkets/progsregs/cair/index.html.

The state goals are in terms of target emission rates, that is, lbs. CO_2/kwh, but may be converted to GHG quantity limits by multiplying by total electricity output. We have learned in the book that emission trading can substantially reduce the costs of meeting emission control targets. Opportunities are large in this plan to work together in regional groupings to establish trading networks. This program is politically controversial. Thus the extent to which it will be fully, or even partially, implemented will depend on the vagaries of the ongoing political struggle in Washington. We will address mobile-source GHG emissions in the next section.

Mobile-Source Air-Pollution Control

The other major part of the federal air quality program is control of mobile-source emissions. Although there are thousands of stationary sources of air pollution, there are many millions of mobile sources. Furthermore, the political fundamentals of mobile-source control are totally different from those of stationary-source emissions. It is often good politics to be seen chastising the polluting behavior of the businesses, especially corporations, responsible for stationary sources. It is quite different to take an aggressive stance against the millions of people whose cars cause the pollution but who also vote. So the spirit of the mobile-source program has been to reduce emissions, but in a way that avoids placing an obvious burden on individual drivers.

To examine the mobile-source program, it will help to set the stage. The total quantity of mobile-source emissions in a given period can be expressed in the following way:

$$\text{Total quantity of emissions} = \text{Number of vehicles} \times \text{Average miles traveled} \times \text{Emissions per mile}$$

If we were devising a cost-effective way of reducing the total quantity of emissions, we would want to balance the three factors on the right side of this equation according to the **equimarginal principle.** In fact, the federal mobile-source pollution-control program has focused almost completely on the last of these factors. And a major reason air pollution is still a serious problem in many regions is that although car makers have been quite successful in producing cars with ever-smaller emissions per mile, the first two factors in the equation have continued to grow along with economic and demographic growth.

The federal mobile-source pollution-control program consists of the following major elements:

- At the manufacturing level, a "new-car certification" program that essentially sets emission standards on new cars, together with a warranty program that is meant to ensure the continued emissions performance of automobiles after they have left the plant.
- At the state level, I&M programs aimed at ensuring that the emissions performance of automobiles does not deteriorate as they are used.
- In nonattainment areas, a variety of technological specifications dealing with vehicles, fuels, and other components of the transportation system.

New-Car Emission Standards

The main emissions from mobile sources are hydrocarbons (sometimes called volatile organic compounds or VOCs), NO_x, CO, and particulate matter. Lead used to be a major mobile-source pollutant but, since the advent of lead-free gas, this is no longer the case. The first two of these (VOCs and NO_x) are smog precursors; that is, after they are emitted, they react with sunlight and among themselves to form the smog and elevated ozone levels that characterize so many urban areas.

The primary federal approach to controlling mobile-source emissions was set in the 1970 CAA. It consists of a **new-car certification program**—essentially a program of mandated emission standards on new cars. Manufacturers are required to certify that the emissions of new cars do not violate the legally mandated standards. Violations may lead to a variety of penalties, up to and including shutting down the assembly lines that produce the offending vehicles. Table 15.6 shows the emission standards established in federal laws over the last several decades. The first row shows emissions for a typical car of around 1970, based on average performance and gas mileage data. Subsequent rows show more recent standards. The last row shows standards as they are expected to come into effect in future model years.

It is clear that current and prospective future emissions are very small relative to earlier years. It must be remembered that these apply to new vehicles (cars and light trucks), so that how widespread and how soon they become in actuality depends on how fast the vehicle fleet is replaced as people trade in old cars and replace them with new ones. The "fleet turnover ratio" (new car sales in a year divided by total cars registered) is affected by many factors, most notably by the state of the economy. In the 2008–09 recession, for example, it fell to very low levels but has since recovered.

These reductions in tailpipe standards have been controversial. Critics, especially automobile companies, maintained that they were unrealistic when they were enacted. But advocates held that unrealistic standards were useful

TABLE 15.6   **Automobile and Light Trucks Emission Standards, Past and Future**

	VOCs	CO	NO_x	PM	HCHO
	Grams per Mile				
Uncontrolled emissions	8.7	87.0	3.5		
1974	3.0	28.0	3.1	n/a	n/a
1990	0.41	3.4	1.0	n/a	n/a
2009	0.09	4.2	0.07	0.01	0.18
2017[†]	NMOG* 0.086	2.1		0.003	0.004
2022[†]	NMOG* 0.056			0.003	

VOCs: volatile organic compounds, now called nonmethane organic gas; CO: carbon monoxide; NO_x: nitrogen oxides; PM: particulate matter; HCHO: formaldehyde.
[†] Standards as they would apply beginning with these model years.
*As of 2002 VOCs (volatile organic compounds) and NO_x (nitrogen oxides) have been combined into a single form: NMOG (non-methane organic gas).

because they provided the incentive for car companies to search for new control technologies. This approach goes under the name of **technology forcing**. Technology forcing is one of those things, of which there are many others, that are good in moderation but perhaps counterproductive if used in excess. The very stringent emission standards written into the 1970 clean-air legislation were in fact not met; rather, they were postponed and not finally achieved until the early 1980s. We do not know whether more realistically timed emission standards might have led the automobile companies to spend more money on research and less on political efforts to get the standards postponed.

Although the emission standards have been progressively lowered through time, this trend actually overstates the reduction in emissions performance by cars in actual operation. The problem is that emissions performance of cars progressively deteriorates as the cars age and accumulate mileage. The federal program attempts to attack this problem in two ways. First it required pollution-control equipment on automobiles to be long-lived enough to ensure that emissions standards will continue to be met for a given number of miles (the "warranty" program). It will increase from 120,000 miles to 140,00 miles in 2017. In addition, it mandated that states with severe air-pollution problems initiate **inspection and maintenance** (I&M) programs, whereby individual cars can be checked for emissions. Owners whose cars exceed emission standards can then be held liable for repairs to bring them into compliance.

Direct Controls in the 1990 Clean Air Act

Despite the apparent progress in lowering new-car emissions over the years, many urban areas of the country continue to exceed ambient standards. One reason is that the number of cars and the total mileage driven continue to increase unrelentingly, as the following tabulation shows:

Year	Total Miles Driven (billions)
1970	1,120
1980	1,520
1990	3,147
2000	2,747
2010	2,967
2014	3,038

Source: U.S. Federal Highway Administration, as reported in Federal Reserve Bank of St. Louis, *Economic Research: Moving 12-Month Total Vehicle Miles Driven*, 2014.

The 1990 CAA, besides tightening emission standards, also incorporated many federally mandated technology standards that are supposed to allow nonattainment areas to move toward attainment even without any direct controls on the overall number of cars. These standards include:

- "Reformulated" fuels, the use of oxygenated fuels at certain times of the year. At the federal level this requirement was ended in 2007, but it remains in certain areas, such as California.

- "Renewable" fuels, in particular a requirement that ethanol be added to gasoline produced in the United States to reduce fuel imports.
- Development of "clean" cars, for example, a program to research hydrogen fuel-cell cars.
- A requirement that the sulfur content of fuel be reduced, since lower sulfur content makes it easier to achieve reduced pollutant emissions.

The mobile-source parts of the 1990 law are a veritable jungle of technological specifications and requirements. In this it carries on the historic command-and-control tradition of pollution-control policy. It is an ongoing arena of great conflicts over detailed technical specifications and regulations in which economic and political incentives are thoroughly intertwined and opaque to the outsider.

One evolutionary development, however, is the gradual increase in trading opportunities. Most standards, such as tailpipe emission standards, are subject to phase-in schedules. To reduce the cost of phase-ins (but not increase the length of time), various flexibility mechanisms are allowed, such as trading offsets from early compliance, offsetting some higher-emitting vehicles with extra clean ones, and an "… averaging, banking, and trading program that allows refineries and importers to spread out their investments through an early credit program and rely on ongoing nationwide averaging to meeting the standard."[10]

Clean Cars

The mobile-source pollution-control program is a classic example of a technology approach to a problem that is largely behavioral. It has focused almost completely on developing **clean cars.** If emissions per mile can be lowered enough, according to this line of thought, then total emissions will be reduced even if the total number of cars and total miles driven keep on increasing.

California has been leading the charge in this respect. As part of the 1990 CAA, that state mandated that as of 1998, car companies would have to sell a certain number of zero-emission vehicles (ZEVs) in California. This date has now been pushed back because of difficulties in developing electric vehicles (EVs) that have power and endurance performance that customers will find attractive. In 2012 their new "Advanced Clean Cars" program introduced, among other things, the requirement that 15 percent of the cars produced and offered for sale in California must be zero-emission vehicles.

Meanwhile, attention has shifted to low-, but not zero-, emission vehicles. The hybrid technology, used for a long time in diesel-electric locomotives, has now been embraced by auto makers. Around the country, policymakers have put in place various subsidies to make these technologies more attractive to consumers.

[10] Richard K. Lattanzio and J.E. McCarthy, "*Tier 3 Motor Vehicle Emission and Fuel Standards,* Congressional Research Service," Report R43497, Washington, D.C., 2014, p. 4.

Mobile-Source Standards and Climate Change

When national mobile-source emission control was first adopted in the 1970s, and even in the 1990 CAA Amendments, the focus was on the standard types of vehicle emissions, particularly NO_x and hydrocarbons. More recently, of course, global climate change has become a major issue, and policy questions abound in trying to do something about it. Many countries around the world have imposed GHG restrictions on vehicles, sometimes directly, usually through fuel economy measures, as the data in Table 15.7 show. In the United States the main federal policy response has been to resurrect interest in the 1970s Corporate Average Fuel Economy (CAFE) law. The law was enacted with the primary objective of reducing petroleum imports into the country. The reasoning now is that tightening the CAFE standards will be an effective way of addressing the greenhouse problem, through reducing a major source of CO_2 emissions.

Table 15.8 shows these standards for selected years, 1978 to 2025. It also shows GHG standards in terms of grams of CO_2e per mile, which commenced in 2012. CAFE standards are set by the National Highway Traffic Safety Administration in the Department of Transportation, while GHG standards are set by the EPA. They are not the same because there are some ways of reducing vehicle GHG emissions in addition to increasing fuel economy, for example, improving vehicle air conditioning systems.

TABLE 15.7   Vehicle GHG Restrictions in Selected Countries

Country or Region	Target Year	Standard Type	Unadjusted Fleet Target
EU	2015 2021	CO_2	130 gCO_2/km 95 gCO_2/km
China	2015 2020 (proposed)	Fuel consumption	6.9 L/100 km 5 L/km
U.S.	2016 2025	Fuel economy/GHG	36.2 mpg or 225 gCO_2/mi 56.2 mpg or 143 gCO_2/mi
Canada	2016 2025 (proposed)	GHG	217 gCO_2/mi NA
Japan	2015 2020	Fuel economy	16.8 km/L 20.3 km/L
Brazil	2017	Fuel economy	1.82 MJ/km
India	2016 2021	CO_2	130 g/km 113 g/km
South Korea	2015	Fuel economy/GHG	17 km/L or 140 gCO_2/km
Mexico	2016	Fuel economy/GHG	39.3 mpg or 140 g/km

gCO_2/km: grams of carbon dioxide per kilometer; gCO_2/mi: grams of carbon dioxide per mile; g/km: grams per kilometer; km/L: kilometer per liter; L/100 km: liters per 100 kilometers; MJ/km: mega joules/kilometer; mpg: miles per gallon

Source: The International Council on Clean Transportation, *Global Comparison of Passenger Car and Light-commercial Vehicle Fuel Economy/GHG Emission Standards*, February 2014.

TABLE 15.8   U.S. CAFE and GHG Standards for Automobiles,
Selected Years, 1978–2005

Year	Mileage Standard (mpg)	GHG Standard (g CO_2e/m)
1978	18.0	None
1983	26.0	None
1985	27.5	None
1987	26.0	None
1990	27.5	None
2010	27.5	None
2011	30.2	None
2012	33.2	261
2013	34.4	253
2016	38.2	225
2019	42.5	182
2022	48.2	164
2025	55.3	143

Source: National Highway Traffic Safety Administration, *Summary of Fuel Economy Performance,*
Washington, D.C., April 2011.

U.S. Environmental Protection Agency, *EPA and NHTSA Set Standards to Reduce Greenhouse Gases
and Improve Fuel Economy for Model Years 2017–2025 Cars and Light Trucks,* Office of Transportation
and Air Quality, EPA-420-F-12-051, August 2012.

As can be noted, CAFE standards were tightened in the late 1980s, then left
unchanged for about 20 years. They have been tightened again starting in 2010,
with plans for substantial further tightening over the next 20 years. GHG standards are also expected to be tightened over this period. Whether these future
schedules are actually met depends on political developments in the United
States.

Economic Issues

The CAFE and mobile GHG programs are essentially a continuation of the focus
on technology-based solutions to mobile-source emissions, in which improvements are sought through a series of technological fixes.

Of course a major part or the policy struggle has focused on differing estimates of long-run benefits and costs of these tightened standards. To estimate
these one has to predict the future mix of vehicles that will ultimately be built,
purchased, and used by consumers. In the last two decades, for example, the
mix has swung strongly toward light trucks and away from cars. In addition,
the procedure for setting CAFE standards was changed in 2011. Before this all
cars were held to the same standard; as of that year, different types of cars, in
terms of size, are given different standards. The complexities these introduce

into estimating future benefits and costs have made it difficult to come to any agreement about future benefits and costs.

In addition, little attention has been directed at behavioral factors associated with the fully mobile lifestyle, such as multiple-car families, dispersed living patterns, and long-distance voyaging. The basic fact is that mobile-source emissions are linked not only to the technical characteristics of cars and fuel systems, but also to the millions of decisions that individuals make about where, when, and how to travel.

A behavioral factor that comes into play is the "rebound effect." A car that has better mileage means that the cost per mile of overcoming distance has gone down. One expects this to lead to the average consumer driving longer distances, thus exacerbating the "total miles driven" phenomenon.

Other things equal, buying cars with better mileage will cost more than a car with lower mileage. The purchase involves an investment, in the sense that there is usually an upfront cost that is recovered over a period of years through reduced energy consumption. Studies have shown that there is often a general hesitancy on the part of consumers to make these investments, even though engineering-type studies show that substantial savings in energy costs would result. This is sometimes called the **energy-efficiency gap**.

What is it about consumer behavior that leads to this phenomenon? Why aren't consumers willing to buy more fuel-efficient vehicles when it appears that in the long run, and not too long at that, they would save more money than they cost? Some possible answers to the conundrum are the following[11]:

1. Consumers may use higher discount rates than we believe they do for the future savings in energy costs.
2. Although technical data seem to show potential for future cost savings, consumers may be responding to the uncertainty inherent in making any decision about the future; they may hold back until these uncertainties are resolved.
3. Consumers may lack convenient access to credit (liquidity) required for up front purchases of energy-efficient goods, including fuel-efficient cars.
4. New work in psychology and economics, called **behavioral economics**, has documented many cases where consumers do not necessarily behave as fully informed, rational, decision makers. Rather, consumers may be normally subject to biased beliefs, inattention, and self-control issues that lead them to make decisions that appear to be suboptimal in the classic sense.

Some of these factors imply a need for incentive-based policies that impact people's decisions about automobile use. One approach that has been suggested is to levy a significantly higher tax on gasoline. With gasoline more expensive, motorists would have the incentive to think more about their driving

---

[11] For further discussion, see Kenneth Gillingham and Karen Palmer, *Bridging the Energy Efficiency Gap, Policy Insights from Economic Theory and Empirical Evidence*, Resources for the Future, Discussion Paper DP13-02-REV, October 2013; Virginia McConnell, *The New CAFE Standards: Are They Enough on Their Own*, Resources for the Future, Discussion Paper 13-14, May 2013.

habits, organize their driving more coherently, reduce total miles traveled, shift to more fuel-efficient vehicles, use mass transit to a greater extent, and so on. The effects of the higher fuel price would filter throughout the transportation system and lead people to shift their behavior in places where the marginal costs of doing so are lowest, much as they did in the energy "crisis" of the 1970s. Gasoline taxes also might help reduce traffic congestion in some cases. Taxes on gas have historically been levied at the state level. This might make it possible to adapt the tax to the level of air pollution in the region, but it also complicates the policy from a political point of view.

Another suggestion is to place a charge directly on vehicle emissions. As part of the state I&M programs, inspectors could record each year the total mileage that a vehicle had been driven. This total mileage could be multiplied by the emissions per mile, also measured at the time of inspection, to yield an estimate of total emissions in the preceding year. A charge could then be levied on these emissions. Unlike a fuel tax, which would have no direct incentive for drivers to worry about emissions, a charge on emissions would create an incentive to look at all the ways of lowering them, including reducing total miles driven, driving low-polluting vehicles, and so on. One attractive aspect of this approach is that the charge could be varied among regions to match the severity of regional air quality problems. Frequency of paying such an emission tax would need examination so that people's change in driving behavior could be closely reinforced by a change in the emissions tax.

Summary

The federal effort to control airborne emissions has had several main elements. National ambient air quality standards have been established not on the basis of efficiency considerations as we have discussed them, but "to protect the public health," with an "adequate margin of safety," irrespective of the costs. In fact, the essential trade-offs between costs and benefits were left for administrators to work out behind the scenes. A distinction is made between nonattainment areas, where ambient standards are not met, and PSD regions, where they are. To meet the ambient standards, primary reliance in the case of stationary sources is placed on technology-based emission standards. These TBESs are based on a number of different concepts, such as lowest achievable emission rate (LAER) for new sources in nonattainment areas and maximum achievable control technology (MACT) for hazardous emissions. Most economic studies of these TBESs in air pollution control show that for the total amount of money spent on pollution control, they achieve only a fraction of the emission reduction that a fully cost-effective program would attain.

The 1990 Clean Air Act contained an innovative national program of transferable emission permits, in this case applied to SO_2 emissions from large power plants. Emission permits were allocated to existing power plants; these permits could then be traded. The objective is to achieve a roughly 50 percent reduction in total SO_2 emissions in a cost-effective way. The market in SO_2 permits has been heavily impacted by programs to combat interstate pollution. Other trading programs are being developed to achieve efficient reductions in GHG emissions.

Mobile-source emission reductions have been sought almost entirely through establishing emission standards for new cars, and then trying to ensure that emissions do not increase as the cars are being used. The 1990 CAA attempted to mandate a number of technological changes, such as reformulated fuel and low-polluting vehicles. Less attention has been given to the important behavioral problems of reducing total vehicle miles in urban areas with seriously degraded air quality.

Questions for Further Discussion

1. Discuss the importance of the question of whether air-pollution damage functions have thresholds for establishing ambient air quality standards.
2. Suppose that engineers invented an accurate and reliable means of monitoring and measuring the emissions from individual automobiles throughout the year. What possibilities would this open up for new types of mobile-source emission control programs?
3. The federal mobile-source air-pollution program means that new cars sold in rural regions meet the same emissions standards as cars sold in urban areas. Because there are fewer cars in rural areas, this means that air quality will be a lot better there than in the cities. Is this efficient? Is it equitable?
4. What are the advantages and disadvantages of a "new-source" bias in stationary-source air-pollution control? Consider especially its impacts on the incentives of the operators of existing sources.
5. If people ordinarily will invest in items that save money in the long run, why is the CAFE program necessary at all?

For additional readings and Web sites pertaining to the material in this chapter, see **www.mhhe.com/field7e.**

Chapter 16

Federal Policy on Toxic and Hazardous Substances

Within the general domain of environmental analysis and policy there is a class of pollutants that have come to be called "toxic" substances and "hazardous" materials. Although all pollutants are damaging to some extent, these have been singled out for their special short- or long-run potency. Most are chemicals, the person-made organic and inorganic compounds that are now ubiquitous throughout all industrialized economies, and even widespread in developing countries. From virtually nothing in 1950, the field has grown in exponential fashion, and today chemicals and chemical products have permeated into every corner of the world economy. In product improvements, new materials, food safety, health innovations, and many other dimensions, chemicals have enriched the lives of almost everyone. There is, however, a downside. A large number of these substances may cause human and ecosystem damages, certainly from exposure to concentrated doses, but also from long-run exposure to the trace amounts that show up virtually everywhere in workplaces, consumer products, and the environment.

The call to arms on chemicals in the environment was made by Rachel Carson in her book *Silent Spring* published in 1962. She documented the ecosystem damage caused by the popular pesticide DDT, which was subsequently banned in the United States in 1972 and in Europe in 1986. Other events have multiplied concern. Health damages to workers exposed to chemicals in the workplace, such as vinyl chloride and certain potent agricultural chemicals, have occurred with disconcerting frequency. In 1978, in the celebrated case of Love Canal, people found chemicals oozing into their houses built on top of an abandoned hazardous-waste disposal site. Accidental releases of chemicals have become a growing problem, from the legendary spills like that in Bhopal, India (1984) to more recent ones such as that at Elk River in Charleston, West Virginia (2014), and to innumerable smaller airborne and waterborne accidents.[1] There is rising

---

[1] An appreciation for the ongoing seriousness of this problem can be gained by looking at the Web site of the National Response Center, **http://www.nrc.uscg.mil.**

concern about the damages from long-term exposure to chemical residues in food, clothing, and other consumer products.

A primary concern is the impact of chemicals on human health. Health damages from accidental releases and workplace exposure are relatively easy to identify. Those from long-run exposure to trace amounts of chemicals in water, air, and soil are much harder to measure. Ecosystem damages are also important. Accidental waterborne chemical releases have wreaked havoc among fish and other organisms in enclosed bodies of water. Agricultural and industrial runoff has substantially damaged many rivers and estuaries around the world.

Hazardous and toxic materials have characteristics that present unique problems for monitoring and control.

1. They are **ubiquitous** in the modern economy; each year sees the development of new chemicals. This makes it difficult even knowing what substances are being used and in what quantities. It accounts for the fact that much public policy has been directed at simply getting better information about quantities of hazardous and toxic materials at various places in the system.

2. With the thousands of substances in use, each with different chemical and physical properties, it is extremely difficult to be fully informed about the **levels of danger** that each one poses to humans and other parts of the ecosystem.

3. In many cases, the quantities used are **relatively small,** as are the quantities that end up as effluent. This substantially increases monitoring problems. It also makes it easier for users to carry out surreptitious disposal. It is easy to see the plume of smoke coming out of the stack of an industrial plant; it is harder to track the much smaller quantities of chemicals used in production.

4. The damages caused by exposure to hazardous materials often can take many years, even decades, to show up. And whenever there is a **long time gap** between cause and effect, there is a tendency to downgrade the overall seriousness of the problem.

In the next few sections we consider some of the major economic issues in the management of these materials. The policy world governing these materials is a jungle. There are numerous major and minor laws at the federal level, each applying to a piece of the total picture. Many federal agencies are involved, with territories staked out and objectives pursued in ways that are often inconsistent. Then there are public agencies at state and local levels that are actively pursuing efforts to come to grips with these types of pollutants. And all of this is within a setting where thousands of different substances are in use, hundreds more are introduced each year, massive uncertainties exist about the human and nonhuman effects of most of them, and public concerns flare up and die down in unpredictable ways.

To help sort out these complexities we have organized the following discussion under three groupings:

1. laws governing the use of chemicals in industrial and agricultural production processes and in consumer goods,

2. laws governing airborne and waterborne emissions of toxic materials, and

3. laws governing the handling, treatment, and disposal of hazardous wastes.

We will deal in each section with some of the important economic issues these laws, and their implementation, present.[2]

Economic Issues in Laws Governing Chemicals in Production and Consumer Products

At issue here is the management of chemicals in consumer products and in the workplace, with the objective of ensuring that these products and workplaces are "reasonably" safe. **Household and work environments** are not, properly speaking, parts of the *natural* environment and, in these cases, the relations of consumers to producers, and of workers to firm owners, are played out directly through markets. Nevertheless, environmental concerns have to some extent reached out to subsume certain elements of the private environment as well as the world of nature properly speaking, so we follow that lead here. Homeowners exposed to formaldehyde leaking from insulation or a worker exposed to asbestos fibers in the workplace are subject to the same kinds of actual and potential damages as are individuals exposed to toxic emissions coming from a neighborhood factory.

Issues of workplace safety and consumer product safety have been around for a long time. In the early years of the Industrial Revolution, the rush to produce often led to unsafe working conditions. It also led to inadvertent, and sometimes intentional, product adulteration. The rise of the chemical economy in the later 20th century has substantially complicated these relationships and has led to a number of federal laws, the most important of which are indicated in Table 16.1.

The "Balancing" Issue

Perhaps the most important question in the use of chemicals is the criterion for determining acceptable levels of exposure or protection. What principle should regulating agencies follow in setting exposure standards—for example, in setting the benzene or cotton dust standards in workplaces or the formaldehyde regulations for building materials, or the acceptable application levels of a weed killer? In discussing our general model of environmental pollution

---

[2] For good discussions of toxic and hazardous substance laws, see Miriam V. Gold and Jean Warshaw, *The Toxic Substances Control Act,* Matthew Bender Publishing, 2014; Linda-Jo Schierow, *The Toxic Substances Control Act (TSCA): A Summary of the Act and Its Major Requirements,* Congressional Research Service, 7-5700, July 29, 2011.

TABLE 16.1   Federal Laws Dealing with Chemicals in Production
and Consumer Products

Statute	Responsible Agency	Coverage
Federal Insecticide, Fungicide, and Rodenticide Act (1972)	EPA	Requires that all pesticides be registered with the EPA
Food, Drug, and Cosmetic Act (1938)	FDA	Basic coverage of food, drugs, and cosmetics
Food additives amendment	FDA	Food additives
Color additives amendments	FDA	Color additives
New drug amendments	FDA	Drugs
New animal drug amendments	FDA	Animal drugs and feed additives
Medical device amendments	FDA	Medical devices
Section 346(a) of the Food, Drug, and Cosmetic Act	EPA	Establishes tolerances for pesticide residues in human food and animal feeds
Federal Hazardous Substances Act (1960)	CPSC	"Toxic" household products (equivalent to consumer products)
Consumer Product Safety Act (1972)	CPSC	Dangerous consumer products
Poison Prevention Packaging Act (1970)	CPSC	Packaging of dangerous children's products
Lead-Based Paint Poison Prevention Act (1991)	CPSC	Use of lead paint in federally assisted housing
Federal Meat Inspection Act (1907)	USDA	Food, feed, and color additives and pesticide residues in meat and poultry products
Poultry Products Inspection Act (1957)	USDA	Poultry products
Egg Products Inspection Act (1970)	USDA	Egg products
Federal Mine Safety and Health Act (1977)	MSHA	Coal mines or other mines
Toxic Substances Control Act (1976)	EPA	Requires premanufacture evaluation of all new chemicals (other than food, food additives, drugs, pesticides, alcohol, tobacco); allows the EPA to regulate existing chemical hazards
Occupational Safety and Health Act (1970)	OSHA	Establishes permissible exposure levels to chemicals in the workplace
Food Quality Protection Act of 1996	EPA	Sets maximum levels of pesticides in food

Note: EPA = Environmental Protection Agency; FDA = Food and Drug Administration; OSHA = Occupational Safety and Health Administration; CPSC = Consumer Product Safety Commission; USDA = United States Department of Agriculture; MSHA = Mine Safety and Health Administration.

FIGURE 16.1 Cost–Benefit Balancing in Regulating Exposure to a Chemical

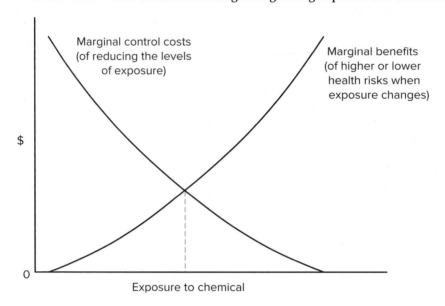

control in Chapter 5, we developed the idea of the efficient level of environmental pollution as being a trade-off between control costs and damages. Applying the same logic to the case of chemicals means that in setting chemical exposure levels, society would try to determine the point where the benefits of reducing health or other risks are just balanced by the costs of decreasing the production and use of the chemical. This trade-off is pictured in Figure 16.1.

The Toxic Substances Control Act (TSCA) mandates the regulation of chemicals that pose an "unreasonable risk of injury to human health or the environment." In addition, in setting regulations the Environmental Protection Agency (EPA) is required to take into account "…the reasonably ascertainable economic consequences of the rule, after considering the effect on the national economy, small business, technological innovation, and public health."

The provision, which is similar to those in the Federal Insecticide, Fungicide and Rodenticide Act (FIFRA) and the Food, Drug and Cosmetic Act (FDCA), though not in OHSA,[3] mandates a balancing, or benefit–cost, approach to decisions about the use of chemicals.

Many objections have been made to a balancing approach in managing chemicals: that scientific results are often too weak to show benefits and costs clearly; that matters of life and death are moral issues and ought to be treated as such; that it's the job of politicians, not economists, to determine the values that society ought to put on different outcomes; and so on. There is not the space to deal with all the issues here. They are basically the same questions that arose in our previous discussions of the concept of the efficient level of emissions, or ambient quality.

---

[3] The standard under FIFRA is "unreasonable risk to human health," and under FDCA is "reasonable certainty of no harm."

There is no question that the data and analytical requirements of a balancing approach are high.[4] This approach requires good dose–response information, exposure data, and estimates of the benefits of reducing risks to workers and consumers. Additionally, it requires accurate estimators of economic costs of reducing the use of particular chemicals. In the nature of the case, chemical damages, especially those associated with health impacts, are likely to be much more difficult to estimate than are the costs of reducing the chemical's use. They are normally probabilistic and uncertain, calling for special studies and data analysis, and dependent on attitudes toward risk, which are anything but straightforward. Under the circumstances, costs may be accorded greater weight in decisions, essentially biasing outcomes away from decisions to regulate. An illustration is the conflict over the impact of pesticides on honeybees as discussed in Exhibit 16.1.

Differentiated Control: "Old" versus "New"

The discussion of water- and air-pollution policy, especially the latter, showed that the major laws have differentiated between "old" sources and "new" sources, regulating the latter more stringently than the former. We also discussed some of the problems this leads to. In toxics control the same thing exists, especially under TSCA. This act differentiates between existing chemicals and new chemicals and, in effect, sets more stringent testing requirements for the latter. The same is true of FIFRA. This may provide an incentive for chemical producers and users to hold on to older, more toxic chemicals, rather than develop replacements that are less toxic but that would have to go through more rigorous testing.

On the other hand, this incentive may not be particularly strong if the regulatory requirements for new chemicals—for example, testing their degree of toxicity—are not particularly rigorous. The EPA has sought to examine the chemicals that were grandfathered in by FIFRA and TSCA, to determine whether they meet the safety criteria of the laws. While short-term toxicities may be relatively easy to determine, the number of chemicals for which we have good data on the effects of long-term exposure is quite small. But not entirely absent.

Between 1975 and 1989, for example, the EPA reviewed 19 cancer-causing pesticides widely used in raising agricultural crops. Of the 245 registered food uses permitted with this group of pesticides, 96 were canceled as a result of the EPA review. According to the researchers who studied this EPA experience, "balancing" considerations played an important role in these decisions.[5] Not exclusively, however. The decisions were made partly in response to political activity ("lobbying") by environmental groups on one side and industry groups on the other.

---

[4] In a famous court case, the EPA worked for two years to detail the benefits and costs that would have supported their decision to require the phasing out of asbestos; the work was rejected by the courts for being incomplete.

[5] Maureen L. Cropper, William N. Evans, and Paul R. Portney, "An Analysis of EPA Pesticide Regulation," *Resources*, 102, Winter 1991, pp. 7–10.

Honeybees and Neonicotinoids

EXHIBIT **16.1**

Honeybees are a critical element in the production of many agricultural crops for the pollination services they provide and the honey they produce. In the last decade, however, honeybee numbers have been in decline. One causal factor for this is thought to be the use of pesticides on agricultural and horticultural crops. One major point of debate is whether a widely used class of insecticides, called neonicotinoids (neonics for short) damages honeybees as they go about their work. These chemicals were introduced in the 1990s, and gained wide acceptance because they are less toxic to mammals. Producers of neonics have claimed that damages to honeybees are minimal compared to the benefit that would have to be given up if they were banned. But evidence of damage led the European Union to ban the chemical on a number of agricultural crops. Recently the EU decided to revisit the ban. The United States EPA is doing the same thing. More recent research appears to provide more definitive results showing the damage these chemicals do to honeybees. But differences of opinion still exist, over the effects of pesticides, and even over whether the number of honeybee colonies is increasing or decreasing. This demonstrates the great difficulty of regulators weighing benefits and costs and settling on the most appropriate course of action.

Source: *Wall Street Journal, May 27, 2015.*

On Testing Chemicals and the Burden of Proof

For the thousands of chemicals that existed at the time TSCA was enacted, testing has been contentious and slow. This is because of the issues related to the **burden of proof**.

Burden of proof refers to the question of which party has the responsibility of providing information sufficient to decide the issue of a chemical's safety. In the decision of whether or not to regulate a chemical, the burden could be on the EPA, to show it is dangerous; or on the chemical company, to show that it is not dangerous. Since testing is expensive, the placement of the burden of proof is not an insignificant issue.

TSCA permits the EPA to require information from producers about the safety of particular chemicals. But for this request to be legal according to the wording of the law, the EPA must find that the chemical in question may present an unreasonable risk to human health or the environment. This has put the EPA in a "catch 22" dilemma: to obtain safety data from the companies it has the burden of proof to show that the chemical may be dangerous. This procedure for finding that an existing chemical must be tested has been a substantial administrative hurdle for the EPA, with the result that progress in testing existing chemicals (i.e., chemicals already in use when TSCA was enacted) has been slow.

Chemical testing procedures have improved over the last several decades. The future no doubt will see further changes, and we may hope that at some point we will develop cheap, effective ways of testing a chemical for toxicity to humans. In the meantime, it has to be recognized that there is still a lot of uncertainty surrounding the average estimate of risk arising from using a particular chemical, and this has to be taken into account in making balancing decisions about its use.

Uniform Standards

The problem of toxic materials in the workplace and in consumer products has been addressed largely by establishing standards of various types. This brings up several important issues. One is the issue of whether the standards should be **uniform.** Another is the issue of how **markets** ordinarily function to take account of risks present in workplaces and consumer products. We can illustrate these with a discussion of workplace standards of the type that would be established by the Occupational Safety and Health Administration (OSHA).

Consider Figure 16.2. It applies to a case of workplace exposure where workers are faced with the risk of accidental exposure to a chemical used in production. The horizontal axis shows the level of risk, starting at zero and increasing to the right. Higher risks are associated with increasing marginal damages, through the health effects of exposure to the chemical. There are two MC curves, each showing the marginal control costs of reducing

FIGURE 16.2 **Management of Workplace Exposure**

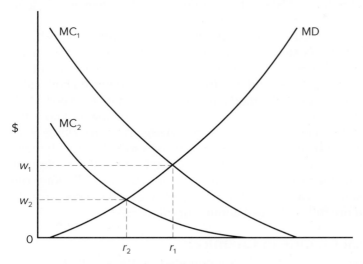

Risks of workplace exposure

workplace risk. Risk can be reduced through a variety of means: introducing safety equipment, rearranging the workplace, policing safety procedures, and so on. But the costs of achieving reductions in risk vary from one situation to another. Because of different production technologies, workplaces differ, and the marginal costs of decreasing exposure risk also differ. Figure 16.2 shows two such marginal cost curves: MC_1 and MC_2. The former lies well above the latter because we assume it represents a technology that is inherently riskier than the other; that is, it is one where the marginal costs of reducing risk are relatively high.

Suppose a common standard for workplace exposure were set at r_1. In other words, a standard was established saying that all workplaces had to be arranged so that exposure risks were no higher than r_1. This standard is efficient for the workplace whose marginal control costs are MC_1. But it is not restrictive enough for the other one. Because of lower marginal control costs, the efficient level of risk for the latter is r_2. Enforcing a weaker standard in that workplace implies substantial efficiency loss.

There is a wider issue here. Note that if workplace exposure were managed efficiently in the two workplaces, marginal damages would be higher in one than in the other. For the riskier workplace, marginal damages would be w_1, whereas for the less risky workplace they would be w_2. We might expect, if the labor market works smoothly, that wages in Firm 1 would be higher than those in Firm 2; the higher wages would be necessary to attract workers into the riskier work situation of Firm 1. In other words, the normal working of the labor market may function in such a way as to produce higher wages in riskier situations. Then workers contemplating employment would face an array of wages and risks, and each could choose the combination that most closely matched his or her own preferences. Moreover, this also would produce an incentive for firms to find ways of reducing risks in the workplace because they would gain through the savings in wages this would produce.

If the labor market worked smoothly like this, there would perhaps be no need for public efforts to set standards. To some extent it does, but there are always ways of making it work better. For the labor market to work smoothly, it must be reasonably **competitive** and, to be competitive, people on both sides of the market must have reasonably good alternatives. Often they do not. More important, competitive labor markets require that all participants know the risks involved in different job situations. This **knowledge** is often lacking. Very often workers are not fully aware of the chemical risks to which they are exposed, either because they do not know what chemicals are in the workplace, or more likely because they lack knowledge of the effects, especially long-run effects, of these substances. This suggests a strong role for public action to see to it that workers are more fully informed about workplace risks.

On Technological Change in Chemicals

The problem of chemical regulation is compounded by the fact that to regulate one substance, we need more than just information on the risks and benefits of that one material. If a chemical is banned, either altogether or in particular uses, the full impact depends on what other substance might be used as a **replacement.** Thus, to assess a particular substance we have to know not only its own characteristics, but also what products would replace it if it were controlled, and what the full characteristics of these substitutes are. The possibility exists that a substitute chemical could have a greater negative impact than the one being considered for prohibition.

This very much implies that testing will continue to be impacted by rapid change in chemical substances. Recently (see Exhibit 16.2) the ideas of

---

Nanomaterials: The Challenge of New Technology   EXHIBIT 16.2

Recent years have seen the rapid growth of a new materials technology, called nanotechnology (NT). It involves the production and use of materials using nanoparticles, which are extremely small particles, generally less than 100 nanometers in diameter (a nanometer is a billionth of a meter; a human hair is roughly 80,000 nanometers in diameter). These materials have turned out to be very useful in many products; it is also possible that they have a significant downside. Nanomaterials can behave very differently than similar materials with conventional particle size. They may therefore present unique environmental effects and unforeseen health effects in humans.

Are the risks of nanomaterials being investigated and adequately taken into account in the development of this new technology? History has shown that the potential external costs of new technologies may be substantially overlooked in decentralized profit-motivated market systems. This is especially true when these costs are little understood scientifically, are long run, and are hard to monitor and measure. A decentralized market system is, in this case, unlikely to be able to find the right balance between public risks and private rewards.

There are essentially three ways that we could proceed in terms of public policy:

1. Have a complete prohibition of these materials until much more is known about them and their potential effects on humans or other parts of the environment. This is an application of the "precautionary principle" for new technology.

2. Adapt current policy to address the unique problems inherent in NT. For example, the Clean Air Act directs the EPA to regulate emissions of fine particulate matter, defined as material less than 2.5 microns in diameter. This could perhaps be extended to particles of smaller size, though this would have to be adapted to the fact that nanomaterials may not have the same relation between dose and response that we currently understand for conventional materials.

3. Develop an all-new policy and regulatory regime specific to NT and its unique characteristics. Although this may seem like the best approach for a technology that is very different from what we have now, it also may be the most difficult to do politically.

For a substantial discussion of these issues, see Robert Falkner and Nico Jaspers, "Regulating Nanotechnology: Risk, Uncertainty and the Global Governance Gap," *Global Environmental Politics,* 12(1), February 2012, pp. 30–55.

nanotechnology have led to new materials and the prospects of many more. These are substances composed of extremely small particles (a nanometer is one billionth of a meter) that may have unknown, and perhaps negative, impacts on humans and nonhuman organisms. The existing laws applying to chemicals may be ill-equipped to deal with new materials such as these, because they do not put a high enough burden of proof on their originators that they are reasonably safe. The continued development of new technology and materials will ensure that these issues and problems will continue to be with us.

Globalization and Chemicals

The chemicals industry has developed, as most industries have, under the influence of the forces of globalization. The huge chemical industries in Europe and the United States, and the growing industry in China, have been accompanied by ever increasing quantities of chemicals entering international trade. This implies that the way chemicals are managed in one country, especially as regards testing and safety issues, will be substantially impacted by chemicals policy developments elsewhere.

The use of some of the most hazardous chemicals is restricted on an international basis under the Stockholm Convention on Persistent Organic Pollutants (POPs), which was adopted in 2001 by UNEP and includes 152 country signatories as of 2013. The conditions of the agreement are that each nation will prohibit and/or take legal and administrative action necessary to eliminate high-risk POPs and devise a plan for their disposal, while also reducing or minimizing the impact of all future chemicals that could be used in the same capacity. The idea is to minimize the impact on the environment and health risks. Of the top 12 most toxic pesticides or chemicals, called the "dirty dozen," that had been listed when the convention was formed, ten have been eliminated while the remaining two are restricted in use.

The EU adopted in 2006 a more aggressive program for regulating chemicals in its member countries. It is based on a registration system (similar to FIFRA in the United States) and involves, among other things, more rigorous protocols for determining chemical safety. Its acronym is REACH (Registration, Evaluation, Authorisation and Restriction of Chemicals) and allows the administering agency to designate "substances of high concern" and require producers to carry out risk studies. In effect it puts the burden of proof on chemical producers and importers, rather than on the regulating agencies.[6]

Another decision concept widely used in Europe, which impacts the way benefits and costs are evaluated, is the **precautionary principle.** It is intended to introduce greater caution into public decisions in cases where there could be substantial future costs (damages) that are currently unknown. It stems

---

[6] For added information, see Jerry H. Yen, *Chemical Regulation in the European Union (EU): Registration, Evaluation, and Authorization of Chemicals,* Congressional Research Service, 7-5700, RS22673, October 2013.

from well-known cases of many countries where the introduction of a product or material that had substantial up-front benefits turned out in the end to have some very high costs that were not foreseen. Asbestos is an example, as are chlorofluorocarbons (CFCs). The precautionary principle essentially states that if there is a perceptible threat of serious and/or irreversible damage in undertaking some action, these future costs should not be overlooked or discounted simply because they are scientifically uncertain. In a sense, the principle emphasizes the burden-of-proof issue in environmental decision making: Should the burden of demonstrating that a new product or practice is safe be put on those who introduce it, or on those who might question its safety?

The Economics of Pest Resistance

When a pesticide is used repeatedly, the organisms toward which it is directed are subject to selection pressure, such that they will tend to evolve resistance toward the pesticide. Genes that would confer resistance to a pesticide normally occur at very low frequencies among members of that species, because they are not important to its survival. Once a pesticide is applied, however, individuals possessing the resistance gene will survive, while those not possessing that gene will be killed off. Thus, the gene conferring resistance will increase in frequency among individuals in the population. Eventually, if pesticide use is kept up, the resistance gene may become so common that it seriously reduces the overall effectiveness of the pesticide.

In the language we introduced in Chapter 4, susceptibility (the opposite of resistance) is a public good. Were any pesticide user to reduce its application, a benefit, in terms of extending the effectiveness of the pesticide, is conferred not only on that one operator, but also on everyone else who is using that material. Under normal market conditions, we saw that public goods will be underprovided. The implication here is that pesticide users, each making their own individual decisions, will overuse the pesticide and contribute to the target pest becoming resistant.[7]

As Exhibit 16.3 discusses, effective policy requires joint action on the part of pesticide users, in this case joint action among them to keep the gene conferring resistance from becoming dominant in the target pest population.

Economic Issues in Federal Policy on Toxics in Water and Air Emissions

Toxic emissions come in a great variety of forms, from small airborne releases of cleaning fluid from dry cleaning establishments to large-scale releases of toxics from substantial industrial plants. Also included are the concentrated accidental

---

[7] Exactly the same phenomenon occurs in the overprescription of antibiotics to treat human illnesses.

Pesticides and the Evolution of Resistant Bugs

EXHIBIT **16.3**

Insect pests account for hundreds of millions of dollars of losses each year in agricultural crops. Pesticides can help to reduce these losses. But high levels of pesticide use, besides causing damage of the traditional sort, can lead to pest resistance, thereby increasing losses and producing incentives for even higher pesticide applications.

Pests evolve resistance because in any insect population the susceptibility to a particular pesticide will vary among individual bugs. The pesticide tends to kill off the highly susceptible ones and leave those that are less susceptible. Over time the latter grow in proportion until a whole pest population can become essentially resistant.

This goes for pesticides applied in the traditional way as well as for newer types. Some species of corn, cotton, soybeans, and other crops have been engineered to express a protein of *Bacillus thuringiensis* (Bt), a soil microbe that can kill caterpillars and some other insect pests. But the concern is that Bt-resistant insects will evolve just as they have with traditional chemicals (the first instances of pesticide resistance were noted almost a century ago in 1914).

In recent years weed control in agriculture has encountered the same problem: weeds have started to show resistance to the very popular herbicide called "Roundup." What to do about this problem? It's important to understand that this is a resource conservation problem, the "resource" here being the susceptibility of a pest to the pesticide. Steps taken to conserve this resource are actually supplying a public good, and therefore will be "undersupplied" if it's left up to individual farmers with standard commercial incentives. Round-up can now be purchased in a less concentrated formula by consumers for home gardens; this increases the potential for future resistance to grow.

Possible public policy steps include:

1. Standard integrated pest management practices: reduced spraying, cultural practices, crop rotation, and so on.

2. Alternate different insecticide classes so insects will be less likely to gain resistance to a single pesticide that is used repeatedly.

3. In the case of Bt crops, get farmers to plant a certain proportion of their fields with non-Bt crops. In the United States, the EPA has required seed companies to ensure that farmers do this; similar regulations have been imposed in Canada. The objective here is to allow for interbreeding between pests that may have developed resistance to Bt and pests that remain susceptible to Bt but feed on the non-Bt crop. Crop "refuges" of this type can be required by law, or can be encouraged through a variety of incentive-type programs.

releases that have helped in the past to spur public concern about toxics in the environment. Not all toxics are chemicals; some, like heavy metals (mercury, cadmium, etc.), are by-products of various industrial and mining operations.

When emissions-control policies at the national level were first being hammered out, the main focus was on the management of conventional airborne and waterborne pollutants. For air this meant the criteria pollutants—sulfur

TABLE 16.2   The Four Primary Pollution Control Statutes
as They Affect Toxic Emissions

Statute	Coverage
Clean Air Act (amended 1970, 1977, 1990)	Establishes technology-based effluent standards for 189 named toxics, based on "maximum achievable control technology"
Emergency Planning and Community Right to Know Act (1986)	Establishes the Toxic Release Inventory
Clean Water Act (amended 1972, 1977)	Establishes technology-based effluent standards for 125 chemicals, based on "best available technology"
Safe Drinking Water Act (1974, amended 1986, 1996)	Requires the EPA to set "maximum contaminant levels" for 189 named substances

Sources: Michael Shapiro, "Toxic Substances Policy," in Paul R. Portney (ed.), *Public Policies for Environmental Protection*, Resources for the Future, Washington, D.C., 1990, pp. 198–199. Original sources: Toxic Substances Strategy Committee, *Toxic Chemicals and Public Protection*, Washington, D.C., 1980; and Council of Environmental Quality, *Environmental Quality—1982*, Washington, D.C., 1982.

dioxide (SO_2), carbon monoxide (CO), ozone (O_3), nitrous oxide (NO_x), total suspended particulates, and lead—and for water it meant biochemically oxygen-demanding (BOD) waste, suspended solids, coliform count, and so on. Even in these early days, however, it was known that there was a potentially serious class of toxic emissions stemming from industrial production operations, as well as from household sources. But the difficulties with even enumerating all of the possible substances involved, and of knowing what impacts each might have, essentially led to putting off coming to grips with the problem. In addition, the control of conventional pollutants has been effective to some extent in also controlling toxics, as they are often closely associated. The main laws governing toxic emissions are shown in Table 16.2.

Instrument Choice

The primary regulatory approach to regulating toxic emissions has been the use of technology-based effluent standards. Under the Clean Water Act, sources are supposed to adopt the "best available technology" (BAT) for the toxic materials listed in the act. Under the Clean Air Act, the criterion is "maximum achievable control technology" (MACT) for 189 specific toxic materials listed in the act. As we have mentioned,[8] a standard such as this has to be made operational through additional specification. The EPA defines MACT in the following way:

> For existing sources: The average emissions performance of the 12 percent of best-performing (in terms of emissions, in terms either of percentage reduction or of concentration limit) sources in the same industry.

[8] See Chapters 14 and 15.

For new sources: Emissions equal to the emissions performance of the best-performing source in the same industry.

These MACT specifications are actually minimum reductions (called in the argot of the air toxics program the MACT floor). The MACT standard may be set more restrictively if this is deemed necessary.

The EPA had issued MACT standards for well over 100 air toxics. Not without great controversy, of course, as Exhibit 16.4 depicts for the case of mercury.

Hazardous Waste Reduction

The early laws on hazardous waste were aimed at managing the flow of hazardous emissions coming from firms in order to reduce potential impacts, especially on human health. In this respect the method mirrored the approach taken with conventional pollutants. But toxic emissions are more difficult to manage. Smaller quantities make them much more difficult to monitor, even though in many cases, small quantities can be quite damaging. This has led policymakers to attack the toxics problems by "moving back up the line," that is, by trying to reduce the amounts of material that are in need of disposal. This can be done in two ways: (1) by recycling residuals back into the production process and (2) by shifting technologies and operations so that the amount of residuals actually generated by firms is reduced. We call these methods **waste reduction**.[9]

The thought behind waste reduction is that by changing production processes and adopting new technologies and operating procedures, firms can substantially reduce the quantities of hazardous waste they produce per unit of final product. For example, a firm might find a new way to operate a materials cleaning process to get the same effect but with less cleaning solvent. Or a firm might shift from using a process requiring a toxic material to one involving a nontoxic substance. Or an end product might be redesigned in a way that permits its fabrication using smaller quantities of hazardous materials. Waste reduction is obviously very complicated and firm-specific. Different processes lend themselves to different waste reduction procedures, and the costs of achieving significant waste reduction in one situation will be very different from the costs of other cases. This is a setting where it is essentially impossible to achieve efficient controls by having a regulatory agency dictate particular technology choices for firms using toxic substances. The technical aspects of production processes and the situation of each firm are too heterogeneous for this approach. Instead, more effective means need to be found that will give firms themselves strong incentives to reduce toxic emissions in cost-effective ways.

How to give firms the appropriate incentives for waste reduction? Certain recent changes in hazardous-waste disposal laws have moved in this direction.

---

[9] Some people prefer to distinguish between "waste reduction" and "recycling" as separate processes, but these are lumped together here.

Sparring over MACT for Mercury

EXHIBIT **16.4**

To control toxic airborne releases, the Clean Air Act (CAA) directs the EPA to establish minimum technology-based emission standards according to the criterion of maximum achievable control technology (MACT). The agency has defined MACT as the emissions attained by the average of the 12 percent of best-performing sources. This may sound straightforward, but it isn't, as is illustrated by the case of mercury. Mercury is an important toxic, and about 85 percent of airborne mercury emissions in the United States comes from large coal-fired power plants. Mercury is one of the specific toxics, identified in the 1990 CAA, for which the EPA was to proceed expeditiously to develop emission standards. After spending much of the 1990s studying the situation, the EPA issued a 1998 report: *Study of Hazardous Air Pollutants from Electric Utility Steam Generating Units,* Final Report to Congress, but put off specifying explicit MACT standards for the future.

The result of this was a lawsuit brought by environmental groups, which produced a settlement agreement by which the EPA promised, among other things, to issue a "regulatory finding" by 2000; and a final regulation by December 15, 2004. The regulatory finding was duly issued in December 2000, stating that power plant mercury emissions were sufficiently damaging to warrant regulation. Over the next few years some vigorous sparring took place over how stringent the EPA would make the MACT standards. On one side were environmental groups, which wanted a standard giving up to a 90 percent reduction in mercury emissions from the source. They cited in particular the presence of emerging new and cheaper technologies for controlling mercury emissions, the adoption of which would be encouraged with strict standards. On the other side were utility companies, which wanted far less, citing issues of cost and scientific uncertainty. The EPA's advisory committee looking at the issue recommended the larger cutbacks. The Bush administration leaned strongly toward less restrictive standards.

On December 15, 2003, the EPA issued a proposed rule specifying new MACT standards, but also giving states an option to control power plant mercury with cap-and-trade programs. On March 16, 2004, the EPA published a supplemental statement proposing that mercury emissions be controlled uniquely through cap-and-trade programs, thus essentially sidestepping the whole MACT apparatus in this case.

In 2008 the D.C. Circuit Court of Appeals vacated the proposed EPA Mercury plan. In 2012 the EPA proposed a new rule, based on BACT standards. In April 2015 the court upheld the new mercury emission plan.

With waste disposal more costly, firms will be motivated to search for better ways of reducing the quantities of waste requiring disposal. A major flaw in this approach, however, is that the vast majority of hazardous waste is not subject to disposal regulations because it never leaves the premises of the firms where it is used. We will come back to this later.

To what extent might we rely on **liability and compensation laws** to provide the necessary incentives? We discussed the issue of liability conceptually in Chapter 10. By requiring polluters to compensate those whom they have damaged, these costs can become internalized, which would lead firms to take them into account in making their decisions. This could also operate through an insurance market if premiums for hazardous-waste damage policies could be set so as to reflect accurately the risks of damage associated with a firm's hazardous-waste actions. The real problem is whether enough is known about risks to be able to rely on an efficient insurance market and compensation system. Although there are thousands of chemicals in use, we have very little hard information on exactly how much damage they may cause to humans; most of the dose–response information we have comes from studies on animals, especially mice. Under the circumstances, there is not enough information about risks and damages to be able to establish consistent compensation awards or insurance premium rates that reflect true risks.

Several possibilities exist for using incentive mechanisms to control toxic or hazardous substances:

- Apply **emission charges** to toxics: Taxing emissions would provide a strong incentive for firms to dispose of toxics illegally, which would usually be difficult to detect because of the relatively small volumes involved. The biggest problem here is accurate emissions monitoring. The widespread **dispersion** of these materials throughout the economic sector, together with the fact that many are emitted in nonpoint modes, makes widespread monitoring very difficult. Taxes on waste disposal, however, may be somewhat more feasible, as will be discussed later.
- Levy a **tax on the feedstocks**: Apply a tax on the inputs used to manufacture chemicals, as these would be fewer in number and easier to measure than the chemicals themselves once they have moved into production channels.
- Institute **deposit-refund systems** for chemicals: Firms would pay a deposit along with the purchase price when the chemicals were bought. They could recover that deposit, or a portion of it, by documenting a reduction of emissions, that is, the recovery of the chemical from the normal waste stream.
- Increase transparency about release of toxic materials: One way that incentives for waste reduction have been created in recent years is through making **information** more widely available about the presence and release of toxic materials.

One reason hazardous wastes have been hard to manage is that with the relatively small quantities often involved, and with most disposal taking place in the same location where the materials were used, it has been difficult for the public to get accurate information on the quantities and qualities of hazardous materials present in the immediate area. This has been addressed in the Emergency Planning and Community Right-to-Know Act of 1986, which requires facilities with 10 or more employees that manufacture, process, or use chemicals in quantities above some threshold level to report their chemical emissions to the EPA and state authorities. These are compiled and published periodically in the EPA's Toxic Release Inventory (TRI).[10] Communities can then find out what hazardous materials are being used and discharged in their areas. The negative publicity of this revelation has motivated many firms to seek ways of reducing their use of hazardous materials. The law is a fairly blunt tool, however; it provides no guidance on what actual damages may be coming from the hazardous-materials releases and, in some cases, real damages and public concern may not be closely connected.

The Management of Hazardous Wastes

The control of airborne and waterborne toxic residuals does not address the major issue of the large quantities of hazardous materials that are left over after production (and recycling) is completed, and which must then be disposed of. This is the problem of **hazardous wastes.** Hazardous waste consists of a diverse set of materials. In liquid form there are waste oils, solvents, and liquids containing metals, acids, PCBs, and so on. There are hazardous wastes in solid form, such as metals dust, polyvinyls, and polyethylene materials. There are many materials between liquid and solid, called sludges, such as sulfur sludge; heavy metal, solvent, and cyanide sludges; and dye and paint sludges. Then there are a variety of mixed substances such as pesticides, explosives, lab wastes, and the like. In legal terms, the EPA and various state environmental agencies have power to define what is considered a hazardous waste; in past years, the definitional net they have thrown over the full physical list of substances has left out some significant materials (e.g., waste oil).

Hazardous-waste generation is not spread evenly over the United States. The largest quantities of hazardous waste are produced in Texas, Ohio, California, Illinois, Louisiana, New Jersey, Michigan, and Tennessee. At the other end of the scale, Vermont, the Dakotas, Hawaii, Alaska, Maine, and Nevada produce relatively small amounts of hazardous waste.

Table 16.3 shows the results of an EPA survey to find out how hazardous wastes were being disposed of in 2005. The greatest proportion was disposed of in injection wells, that is, deep wells driven into underground geologic formations (salt caverns and aquifers). From an industry standpoint, this method is relatively cheap and flexible. About 10 percent of hazardous waste generated is subject to some type of recovery (recycling) operation, and about 9 percent is burned, roughly half of which is done to produce useful heat. Although these numbers do not show it directly, about 80 percent of all hazardous waste

---

[10] The EPA makes TRI available at **http://www2.epa.gov/toxics-release-inventory-tri-program**, where visitors can easily access TRI data for their local areas. The webpage has data on criteria air pollutants, ambient concentrations of some hazardous chemicals, and hazardous-waste sites, organized so that users can see the data for their local regions.

TABLE 16.3 Hazardous-Waste Quantities Managed in 2011, by Major Technology Used

Technology	Tons Managed (1,000)	Percent of Total
Recovery operations		
Fuel blending	652	1.6
Metals recovery	1,039	2.6
Solvents recovery	255	0.6
Other recovery	185	0.4
Land disposal		
Deep well/underground injection	22,852	58.6
Landfill/surface impoundment	1,291	3.3
Other disposal	4,241	10.9
Thermal treatment		
Energy recovery	1,563	4.0
Incineration	1,009	2.5
Other		
Sludge treatment	395	1.0
Aqueous organic treatment	2,848	7.2
Aqueous inorganic treatment	703	1.8
Other	1,991	5.1

Source: U.S. Environmental Protection Agency, *National Biennial RCRA Hazardous Waste Report: Based on 2011 Data,* Washington, D.C., 2013, pp. 2–5, **http://www.epa.gov/wastes/inforesources/data/br11/national11.pdf.**

generated in the United States is disposed of on-site, that is, at the site of the industrial plant where it was manufactured and/or used. Only 20 percent was transported to off-site disposal facilities.

The two major pathways leading to damage are through accidental releases and releases stemming from improper handling, either at the site of use or at waste-disposal facilities. Accidents have led to severe and obvious damages, to humans and to other parts of the ecosystem.[11] It has been less easy to document the damages coming from long-run exposure to small amounts of hazardous wastes. Ecosystems in the vicinity of industrial waste dumps are sometimes visibly affected. Human health effects have been harder to show, particularly when what is at issue is long-run exposure to small quantities of hazardous materials. Much more epidemiological and laboratory work remains to be done.

Federal policy has been directed at two types of problems: (1) developing a system to manage the storage, transportation, and disposal of current hazardous wastes, and (2) cleaning up land disposal sites where large quantities of hazardous wastes were dumped in years past. The major laws addressing these problems are shown in Table 16.4.

---

[11] In Chapter 7 we discussed efforts to develop techniques to estimate ecosystem damages arising from hazardous-waste releases.

TABLE 16.4 **Basic Laws Dealing with Handling, Storage, Treatment, and Disposal of Hazardous Wastes**

Statute	Responsible Agency	Coverage
Resource Conservation and Recovery Act (1976)	EPA	Defines hazardous wastes and sets standards for landfills; establishes a manifest system
Maritime Protection, Research, and Sanctuaries Act (1972)	EPA	Ocean dumping
Comprehensive Environmental Response, Compensation, and Liability Act (1980)	EPA	"Superfund"; sets procedures for cleaning up hazardous-waste sites, and establishes a liability program for damages to natural resources
Hazardous Materials Transportation Act (1975)	DOT	Transportation of toxic substances generally
Federal Railroad Safety Act (1970)	DOT	Railroad safety
Ports and Waterways Safety Act (1972)	DOT	Shipment of toxic materials by water
Dangerous Cargo Act (1871)	DOT	Shipment of toxic materials by water
Nuclear Waste Policy Act of 1982 (amended 1987)	DOE	Requires DOE to find and develop a repository for high-level nuclear waste
Low-Level Radioactive Waste Policy Act of 1980 (amended 1985)	States	Encourages states to enter into compacts to establish landfill sites for low-level radioactive waste
National Defense Authorization Acts	DOD DOE	Allocate funds to DOD for cleaning up military bases, and to DOE for cleaning up nuclear weapons sites

Note: EPA = Environmental Protection Agency; DOT = Department of Transportation; DOE = Department of Energy; DOD = Department of Defense.

Sources: Michael Shapiro, "Toxic Substances Policy," in Paul R. Portney (ed.), *Public Policies for Environmental Protection*, Resources for the Future, Washington, D.C., 1990, pp. 198–199. Original sources: Toxic Substances Strategy Committee, *Toxic Chemicals and Public Protection*, Washington, D.C., 1980; and Council of Environmental Quality, *Environmental Quality—1982*, Washington, D.C., 1982.

Economic Issues in Handling Current Hazardous Waste

The primary policy here is the Resource Conservation and Recovery Act (RCRA) of 1976. RCRA does essentially four things:

1. **Defines hazardous waste.**
2. Creates a **manifest system**, essentially a paper trail, so that material can be tracked through the system from production to disposal.

3. Requires the EPA to set **standards** for treatment, storage, and disposal facilities.
4. Directs the EPA to establish a **permit system** for approval of RCRA landfills and incinerators.

RCRA is largely a command-and-control system, requiring the EPA to set technical and managerial requirements for handling hazardous waste.[12]

Incentive-Based Possibilities

There may be useful programs that could be installed to reshape the incentives relating to using and disposing of hazardous materials. Taxes on hazardous wastes, levied at the place where they are generated or where they are disposed of, are a feasible way of providing the incentive for reducing the quantities produced, as well as directing the flow of wastes toward various channels. These have come to be called **waste-end taxes**. The monitoring problem is much less a factor than with toxic emissions because wastes are often in bulk form that lends itself to quantitative measurement. In fact, a tax of $2.13/ton of hazardous waste was at one time charged at approved disposal sites as part of the RCRA program, but this has been abandoned. Many states have established waste-end charges for sites within their jurisdictions. Charges of this type would stimulate industry efforts at waste reduction. They also would lead to increases in the prices of products that produce substantial quantities of waste in their manufacture. They have one unfortunate effect, however, in that they also will create an incentive to dispose of hazardous materials surreptitiously.

A major problem with many hazardous wastes is that they are in quantities that are difficult to monitor. This will continue to be the case even with the manifest system. Any kind of tax placed on hazardous material creates an incentive for disposers to conceal material discharged, perhaps by disposing of it on-site, into a public sewer system, or in some unapproved landfill. One way of turning these incentives around is to offer a subsidy for hazardous materials disposed of in approved ways. This, of course, would require a source of funds. A possibility would be to institute **deposit-refund** systems for hazardous materials. Firms would pay a deposit per unit of hazardous chemical at the time of purchase from a chemical supplier. They would then be paid a refund on materials when they were properly disposed of.[13]

One area in which RCRA incorporates some incentive-based provisions is in making hazardous-waste handlers and operators liable for certain costs associated with their operations. Thus, operators of hazardous-waste landfills are liable for closure, cleanup, and restoration costs associated with the sites.

---

[12] RCRA also contains requirements for nonhazardous-waste landfills, particularly those handling municipal solid waste (MSW), essentially trash from households and public agencies. This material can contain significant amounts of hazardous waste, for example, used electronic devices.

[13] For more on this idea, see Clifford S. Russell, "Economic Incentives in the Management of Hazardous Wastes," *Columbia Journal of Environmental Law*, Vol. 13, Spring 1988, pp. 257–274; Jason R. Bent, "An Incentive-Based Approach to Regulating Workplace Chemicals," *Ohio State Law Journal*, 73(6), 2012, pp. 1391–1455.

RCRA also holds owners and operators of underground storage tanks responsible for cleanup costs in the event that they leak, which many do.

As we have discussed earlier,[14] liability requirements are, at least in principle, effective ways of getting polluters to take potential environmental costs into account in their decision making. If they know they will be held liable for certain environmental costs, they will balance this prospect with their costs of taking actions to reduce the risk, thus arriving at an "efficient" outcome. The actual outcome may be somewhat different, however. Liability provisions in these laws set up a complex game between regulators and private firms that are motivated to find ways of reducing their exposure to the provisions. One aspect of this is that firms can shield themselves from liability by going out of business or declaring bankruptcy. For small firms (e.g., an operator of a gas station) faced with large liability costs, this may be an attractive alternative. To counter this, many environmental statutes combine liability provisions with **financial assurance rules**. These are requirements that owners and operators demonstrate financial resources sufficient to cover their potential environmental liabilities. The full impact of these rules is unclear. In some cases (e.g., leaking underground storage tanks), states have set up financial funds to help operators and owners meet these obligations, thus potentially weakening some of their impacts on incentives.

Environmental Justice

All environmental issues involve **distributional** questions, having to do with which particular individuals or groups from among the whole population bear the costs and experience the benefits of environmental programs. **Environmental justice** is the term used to describe the search for programs that are equitable to the less advantaged members of society. Much of the environmental justice focus has been on the location of hazardous-waste sites in relation to communities in which there are relatively large numbers of low-income residents and people of color. This issue gained prominence in the early 1980s, largely as the result of efforts to site a large hazardous-waste dump in Warren County, South Carolina, a county with a predominantly African-American population. A 1987 study sponsored by the United Church of Christ came to the conclusion that "in communities where two or more hazardous waste sites were located, or where one of the nation's largest landfills was located, the percentage of the population composed of minorities was, on average, more than three times that of communities without such facilities."

Since this first study, many others have been carried out to assess the relationship between the locations of hazardous-waste sites and the demographic characteristics of the surrounding population. Results have not always been consistent because of different data sets used (e.g., whether data from countries, census tracks, or zip code area are used) and the time periods covered. But the preponderance of evidence to date does indicate that RCRA sites tend to be located in areas where there are relatively large numbers of low-income

---

[14] See Chapter 10.

and minority populations. Having established this pattern, the next question is, why has it occurred? There are essentially two ways this could have occurred:

1. The siting process itself has worked against people of color and poor people. This could be either because of rank discrimination, in which undesirable activities are foisted onto certain people, or because in the political process surrounding these siting decisions, certain people lack the political influence necessary to ward off these facilities.
2. The dynamics of the land and housing market may lead to this type of pattern, even though the original siting decisions were not discriminatory. If these facilities make local neighborhoods less desirable, the better-off people may be motivated to move out. Furthermore, if the facility works so as to depress land prices, it could make housing there more attractive to low-income families. This could also happen if racial or income discrimination in general relegates certain people to less desirable neighborhoods.

Recent research suggests that both of these factors are at work, though at specific sites one factor may be substantially more important than the other.[15] It is clear that policymakers need to look carefully at the siting decision process to make it more democratic and remove its discriminatory features. It's also clear that economists need to learn much more about how the land and property markets function so that we can identify situations where certain people will end up being unfairly exposed to environmental risks.

Radioactive Wastes

Radioactive wastes are governed by a separate set of statutes. There are two types of radioactive wastes: **high-level wastes** (HLWs) and **low-level wastes** (LLWs). HLW is made up primarily of spent fuel from nuclear power plants and wastes from government nuclear processing facilities. LLW comes from a variety of industrial and medical processes that utilize small amounts of radioactive material, and includes the material itself together with all manner of items that have become contaminated in normal production operations.

The primary problem in HLW is to find a secure, *permanent* storage site, because the rate of radioactive decay is so slow that these wastes will be lethal essentially forever by human standards. The Nuclear Waste Policy Act of 1982 requires the Department of Energy (DOE) to find and develop a permanent underground depository for nuclear HLW. This has proved to be an immensely complicated task and one full of political conflict. The effort is funded

---

[15] See, for example, Vicki Been, "Unpopular Neighbors: Are Dumps and Landfills Sited Equitably?" in Wallace E. Oates (ed.), *The RFF Reader in Environmental and Resource Management,* Resources for the Future, Washington, D.C., 1999, pp. 191–196; David Schlosberg, "Defining Environmental Justice: Theories, Movements, and Nature," *Ethics in International Affairs,* 22(3), 2008, pp. 335–338; H. Spencer Banzhaf, *The Political Economy of Environmental Justice,* Stanford University Press, Redwood City, CA, 2012.

by a tax of one-tenth of a cent per kilowatt-hour of electricity generated at all nuclear power plants. The standards for storage have been set by the EPA, in terms of the maximum allowable rate of release of radionuclides from the repository for the next 10,000 years! It is difficult, if not essentially impossible, to identify underground geological formations that are sure to be secure for the next 10,000 years. It is even more difficult to convince people living near candidate sites that no damage will come their way and that this is the best use of a portion of their landscape. Thus, the projected year of opening for the depository has been continuously set back, and now, 2012, appears to be off in the indefinite future.

Low-level radioactive wastes are disposed of for the most part in approved landfills. Prior to 1980, there were three landfill sites in the United States accepting low-level radioactive waste. These were in South Carolina, Washington, and Nevada. With the volume of these wastes climbing rapidly, these states began to raise objections to being the only recipients. But there were negative incentives for other states to open their own sites, because of their fear (via the interstate commerce clause) that they would be forced to accept LLW from other states. The first result was a 1980 federal law, the Low-Level Radioactive Waste Policy Act of 1980, which encouraged states to enter into interstate compacts to open sites that would accept all the waste from states in each compact. Very little happened over the next few years, however, because groups of states could not come to an agreement on these compacts. The law was therefore amended in 1985 to provide greater incentives for groups of states to enter into compacts to develop and operate LLW landfills. The primary incentive was a rapidly increasing surcharge per cubic foot of LLW that the sites in South Carolina, Washington, and Nevada would be authorized to charge. As of 2014, however, the 10 compacts that have formed have yet to identify new locations for LLW storage sites.[16]

Economic Issues in Handling Legacy Hazardous-Waste Sites

The main law governing legacy hazardous-waste sites is the Comprehensive Environmental Response, Compensation, and Liability Act (CERCLA) of 1980. The law has come to be called Superfund, perhaps in reference to the massive sums of money involved. CERCLA was enacted in response to heightened public fears about the health impacts of past, and often forgotten, hazardous-waste disposal sites. In some cases, as in the notorious Love Canal incident, people were exposed directly to hazardous materials that

---

[16] The incentive for entering into interstate compacts was that by law they could then exclude waste from noncompact states. The compact system has not developed as Congress envisioned, and the full legal ramifications of the approach are still not settled. See Richard Benjamin and Jeffrey Wagner, "Reconsidering the Law and Economics of the Low-Level Radioactive Waste Management," *Environmental Economics and Policy Studies,* 8(1), December 2006, pp. 33–53.

migrated through the soil; in other cases, the fear was, and is, of groundwater contamination from these old dump sites.

The law established:

1. **A financial fund** derived from taxes on petroleum and chemical feedstocks, a corporate environmental tax, and payments made by those responsible for past dumping. The fund is used to carry out site investigations and cleanup actions. The legal authority for the taxes expired in 1995, so now the fund is supported entirely by payments from responsible parties.

2. A method for selecting sites for cleanup actions. This is called the **National Contingency Plan** (NCP) and specifies procedures for identifying and investigating sites, determining cleanup plans, and deciding on who will pay for it. Part of the procedure involves a state–federal effort to create the list of sites that are in greatest need of action; this is called the **National Priorities List** (NPL), and it involves a hazard-ranking system taking into account the types and quantities of hazardous materials at the site and the possibility of human exposure.

3. Authority for the EPA to clean up sites itself or to identify responsible private parties to clean up the sites.

4. A **liability provision** for natural resources damage. Besides cleanup liability, CERCLA has a provision for holding responsible parties liable for damages to natural resources stemming from spilled or released toxic materials. Thus, if a chemical is accidentally released into a river, the people causing the spill can be held liable for the damages this causes; or if an old landfill leaks toxic compounds, responsible parties may be held liable not only for cleaning up the site but also for damages to surrounding groundwater resources.

Financing Hazardous-Waste-Site Cleanups

From its beginning to the end of the 1990s, the EPA spent over $20 billion on Superfund activities. Private parties have also expended substantial sums over the years to fulfill the objectives of the act. Similar magnitudes may be necessary to "finish" the job as it was initially envisaged. The activity levels under Superfund were substantially reduced under the Bush administration, so there is much uncertainty about how fast existing sites will be cleaned up and new sites will be added to the NPL.

Progress under Superfund has entailed a continuing battle between the EPA and the private firms that are responsible for the sites. In the lexicon of this work, the latter are called potentially responsible parties (PRPs). The courts have ruled that PRPs may be held to a standard of strict, joint, and several liability in Superfund clean ups. Strict liability means that they are liable even though their actions were at the time legal. Joint and several means that when more than one firm has dumped hazardous wastes into the site, the EPA may nevertheless sue and recover total cleanup costs from just one of the responsible parties. So, for example, a company that has dumped only a small portion of the wastes into a site can nevertheless be held responsible for the total cleanup costs at the site. The effect of this is to provide an incentive for this one firm to identify and recover costs from other parties that were responsible for dumping at the site. But there are disadvantages as well. Firms may be reluctant to come forward voluntarily to enter cleanup agreements if they feel they could get stuck with a substantial amount of the total costs of the cleanup. Firms will also be very reluctant to acquire land that may be contaminated if they think this will expose them to liability. These and other problems have made the law highly contentious and litigious, with firms spending enormous amounts of money suing one another, the EPA, municipalities, states, insurance companies, and so on.

There have been many suggestions over the years for changing the way legacy hazardous-waste-site cleanup is funded. Some have suggested, for example, the establishment of **trust funds**, from mandatory or voluntary contributions, to be devoted to the task.

How Clean Is Clean?

Superfund activity has produced a continuing debate over how thorough the cleanup should be at any particular site. Should all sites be restored to pristine condition? Should cleanup actions be undertaken in the light of how the site is likely to be used in the future? Criteria as to how to clean up sites have largely been established with the objective of making each site totally risk free under the worst possible future development scenario. Thus, at many sites very costly cleanup techniques have been used in cases where the risk of damage to humans is relatively low. An economic analysis of 150 randomly selected Superfund sites concludes that the expected number of cancer cases averted at each cleanup site is less than 0.1 and that the cost per cancer case averted was on average greater than $100 million.[17] What this indicates is that perhaps a more explicit benefit–cost approach might be able to adapt cleanup techniques at each site more closely to the benefits to be expected in terms of human exposures. This would allow more sites to be cleaned up with a consequent increase in overall human protection, given the total amount of money that is spent on the program.

Brownfields

As of the end of 2014, there were 1,322 Superfund sites listed on the NPL. Cleanups at 1,123 sites have been completed. One can argue, therefore, that despite its inefficiencies, the Superfund program has made a real dent in the number of sites needing attention. The EPA also has identified over 10,000 other sites where light to moderate contamination is suspected or has been confirmed. Superfund, as it was originally developed, does not address these many sites that are contaminated to a lesser degree. Substantial portions of these additional sites are within urban and suburban areas and have potential for industrial or commercial redevelopment.

There may be important incentive problems associated with these sites. Developers may avoid them in favor of sites in pristine environments in order to avoid the possibility of being made legally responsible for cleaning them

---

[17] James T. Hamilton and W. Kip Viscusi, "How Costly Is 'Clean'? An Analysis of the Benefits and Costs of Superfund Site Remediations," *Journal of Policy Analysis and Management*, 18(1), Winter 1999, pp. 2–27.

up. This possibility has led the EPA, and many of the states, to develop special programs dealing with these types of sites, which are called **brownfields**. The programs consist of efforts to relax potential liability problems at the sites, and funding assistance to assess and ameliorate contamination problems at the sites.

Natural Resource Damages

Besides providing a program for cleaning up legacy hazardous-waste sites, CERCLA also contains a provision making polluters **liable for damages to public resources** stemming from their activities. This has been used primarily against those responsible for accidental releases of oil and toxic chemicals. Exhibit 16.5 describes a recent natural resource damage settlement in Massachusetts. The Oil Pollution Act, approved after the Exxon *Valdez* accident

---

Companies Agree to $4.25 Million Natural Resource Damages Settlement at Industri-plex Superfund Site, Woburn, Massachusetts   EXHIBIT **16.5**

Two companies have agreed to pay $4.25 million to federal and state natural resource trustees to resolve claims for natural resource damages connected with the Industri-plex Superfund site located in Woburn, Massachusetts, the Department of Justice announced.

Operations at the Superfund site from the 1850s to the 1960s contaminated the Aberjona River, as well as associated wetlands and the Mystic Lakes, with arsenic, chromium, and other hazardous substances. Under CERCLA, parties that have disposed of hazardous substances at a site are liable for damages for injury to, destruction of, or loss of natural resources, including the reasonable costs of assessing such injury, destruction or loss. In this case, the Wildlife Service, and the National Oceanic and Atmospheric Administration, as well as the state natural resource trustee, the Massachusetts Executive Office of Energy and Environmental Affairs, determined that the hazardous substances disposed of by the settling defendants or their predecessors

had degraded wetland, river, and lake habitat used by a variety of wildlife, which includes fish, turtles, amphibians and migratory birds, such as great blue herons, black ducks, and kingfishers.

In settlement of the trustees' natural resource damages claims, the defendants have agreed to pay $4.25 million. Of this amount, $3,812,127 will be used by the trustees to implement natural resource restoration projects to compensate for injury caused by the hazardous substances disposed of at the site. The trustees have not determined which particular projects will be implemented, but examples of potential projects include the creation of new wetlands and the restoration, enhancement, or protection of existing wetlands. The remaining amount of the settlement figure, $437,873, will reimburse federal and state trustees for damages assessment costs.

Source: Department of Justice, Office of Public Affairs, *Justice News*, May 12, 2012, **http://www.justice.gov/opa/pr.**

in Alaska, also has provisions for assessing natural damages and identifying reasonable parties. An early study of 46 cases listed the following:[18]

- 15 sites where decades of industrial activities were accompanied by releases of a variety of hazardous substances into rivers, harbors, marshlands, and other wetlands, as well as one case of disposal to the ocean.
- 11 sites where mines and associated waste piles contaminated surface waters and groundwater with acid drainage and leachate containing heavy metals.
- 9 cases where vessels ran aground; in 3 of them oil was the cargo that spilled, in 3 others the ships' own fuel spilled, and in the other 3 incidents the ships ran onto coral reefs causing damage to the reef.
- 4 oil pipeline ruptures.
- 2 cases where retaining walls ruptured, allowing gypsum slurry to be released into a bayou in one case, and sewage into a river in the other.
- 2 incidents where train derailments resulted in a spill of diesel fuel and a spill of chemicals.
- 2 oil well accidents that released oil and other liquids into bayous.
- 1 case where containers of a toxic chemical were lost overboard in rough seas.

The biggest issue in NRD cases is how to measure the damages. Part of these damages consists of the costs of restoring the resource to its original condition. The other, and probably harder, part is to estimate the actual damages that the release inflicted on people, either in the vicinity or elsewhere. Environmental economics has provided a tool, **contingent valuation** (CV), for doing this.[19] Controversies over the techniques used in CV analysis, and the answers it has given in particular cases, have continued.

Cleaning Up After the Cold War

During the **cold war,** the development and production of nuclear weapons took place at a large number of sites around the United States. The stress at that time was on military needs, not potential environmental damage. Weapons production stopped about a decade ago, after about 50 years of activity. There are more than 100 sites across the country where massively contaminated soil, water, structures, and equipment pose serious health threats to nearby people and ecosystems. The Office of Environmental Management (OEM) within the U.S. DOE has estimated that cleaning up these sites could cost as much as $200 billion. This is probably a substantial underestimate.[20] There are many serious questions that need to be addressed, having to do with which sites to clean up, how the clean ups should proceed, who should carry them out, and so forth.

---

[18] See Mark Reisch, "Superfund and Natural Resource Damages," Congressional Research Report RS20772, Washington, D.C., January 8, 2001, p. 2.

[19] See Chapter 7.

[20] For a good discussion of this problem, see Katherine N. Probst and Adam I. Lowe, *Cleaning Up the Nuclear Weapons Complex: Does Anybody Care?* Resources for the Future, Center for Risk Management, Washington, D.C., January 2000.

Summary

The coming of the chemical society has led to new sources of environmental damage and opened up new requirements for managing toxic and hazardous materials. At the federal level, numerous major laws deal with toxic and hazardous substances, and numerous federal agencies are responsible for their administration. For the most part the laws incorporate a variety of command-and-control measures to identify and monitor the use of toxic materials in workplaces and consumer products, to control toxic emissions from production, and to manage the complex process of disposing of hazardous materials. The most important laws are TSCA, FIFRA, FDCA, and OSHA.

Important points exist where the management of toxics could be substantially improved. One of these is to improve the procedures for "balancing" the costs and benefits of using chemicals in particular products and processes. We also discussed the new emphasis on waste reduction, that is, changes in production systems that lead to lower quantities of hazardous-waste requiring disposal. Finally, we discussed the federal laws governing the handling and disposal of hazardous waste, the cleaning up of past dump sites, and radioactive waste.

Questions for Further Discussion

1. Handlers of hazardous wastes, that is, firms that accept hazardous materials and transport them for disposal, sometimes dispose of the materials illegally or in unapproved landfills. How might a deposit-refund system be designed to provide incentives to dispose of hazardous materials in approved ways?

2. "The EPA has estimated that the chemical residues on a certain food most likely contribute to 14 excess deaths in the U.S. population each year. Thus, if use of the chemical is banned we can expect the number of excess deaths to decrease by this number." Comment.

3. What are the advantages and disadvantages of using the doctrine of strict, joint, and several liability for Superfund sites?

4. What are the two primary alternative explanations for the demographic patterns found in the vicinity of many hazardous-waste dump sites?

5. In conducting a "balancing" analysis for a particular chemical or pesticide, what role is played by people's attitudes toward risk?

6. In what way does TSCA put the burden of proof for a chemical's safety on the EPA?

For additional readings and Web sites pertaining to the material in this chapter, see **www.mhhe.com/field7e**.

Chapter 17

State and Local Environmental Issues

In the 1950s and 1960s there was no strong federal presence in U.S. environmental policy; what initiative there was lay mostly at the state level. In the 1970s this changed dramatically, as strong federal laws were written that essentially shifted the policy center of gravity toward Washington. But in more recent years nonfederal involvement in environmental policy issues has grown rapidly. The current trend in Washington is to push many policy problems back to the states for action.

States and communities are playing three primary roles:

1. Contributing to federal laws; most federal policies permit, require, or encourage some type of contributing state action, especially in enforcement. About three quarters of the environmental enforcement actions undertaken in the United States are carried out by the states. States generate more than 90 percent of the data that feed federal environmental data bases. Refer to Table 17.1.
2. Adopting companion policies that express the particular environmental values, goals, or circumstances of individual states; these have often been a source of innovative policy ideas.
3. Dealing with certain major issues that have been left for the most part to the states.

There is substantial diversity among the states in terms of their environmental problems and policy responses, as is suggested by the expenditure data of Table 17.1. Air pollution is much more severe in some states than others. Hazardous-waste releases, although occurring in every state, are nevertheless concentrated in certain ones, particularly Texas and Louisiana. Florida has special water quality problems because of the Everglades and because of its reliance on groundwater. Coastal states have special problems in managing their coastal resources. Mining regulation is a particular problem for some states, as is agricultural runoff in others. Given these great variations, equal state expenditures on environmental programs do not necessarily imply equal concern about environmental quality or equal achievements in pollution control.

TABLE 17.1   Percentage of Federal Data Collected by States
in Six National Systems

System	Type of Data in System	% Data Collected by States
Aerometric Information Retrieval System/Air Facility System (AIRS/AFS)	Air pollution B stationary sources	99
Aerometric Information Retrieval System/Air Quality System (AIRS/AQS)	Air pollution B ambient sources	99
Safe Drinking Water Information System (SDWIS)	Drinking water	99
Permit Compliance System (PCS)	Wastewater discharge	83
Storage and Retrieval Data Warehouse (STORET)	Waterway quality	90
Biennial Reporting System (BRS)	Hazardous waste	92

Source: Environmental Council of the States, 2015, **http://www.ecos.org/section/states/data.**

We will not try to survey the environmental policies pursued in each one. The first section of the chapter will deal with some general issues in **environmental federalism.** After this we take up a major environmental issue that has been left to the states: municipal solid waste.

Environmental Federalism

Environmental federalism refers to the question of whether, and to what extent, environmental regulations ought to be established at the national level, or decentralized for independent actions of the individual states. There are several dimensions to this question.

Constitutional Issues

The U.S. Constitution governs the division of powers between the federal government and the states. In cases where valid (i.e., constitutional) environmental laws have been enacted at the federal level, these normally **preempt** state action. Thus, for example, federal laws to control coastal tanker traffic so as to reduce the threat of oil spills will usually preempt any state actions aimed at the same result. In cases where the federal government has not acted, states may do so provided they do not exceed constitutional limits. The most important of these is that states may not pass laws that discriminate against interstate commerce. In environmental matters, this has been held to bar states from passing laws restricting the importation of solid waste from other states. But virtually all state environmental actions will have some impact on interstate commerce, so the federal courts have become the arena for ongoing controversy about the legitimacy of state environmental actions.

One such action is California's attempt to set carbon dioxide (CO_2) emission standards on cars sold in that state. The only practicable way of doing this at the present time is to require cars that get substantially better mileage, as CO_2 emissions per mile are directly related to fuel use per mile. But Congress has preempted the setting of automobile mileage standards, in the CAFE program enacted in 1975. This program was discussed in Chapter 15.

Efficiency Issues

Economic efficiency in environmental regulation is, as we have discussed many times, a matter of finding the appropriate balance between environmental damages and abatement costs. Will this balance be realizable more closely with a national system of pollution control, or a decentralized one? Consider a simple case, one in which the emissions from sources in each state produce damages only within that state. This is an extreme assumption; it means that no individual in any other state will be affected in any way by the level of emissions in any one state. This would appear to call for a completely decentralized determination of environmental regulations; each state would set its own standards and enjoy its own level of environmental quality.

Now consider a different case at the other end of the spectrum. Suppose the emissions from each state are uniformly mixed with those of all others in such a way that the emissions from any state affect everybody, in state and out of state, to the same extent as emissions from any other state. In this case we would have an efficiency argument for a purely centralized regulatory regime. No state has control over its own environmental quality. All emissions spill over and affect all other states. A centrally determined emission standard applicable to all states would presumably be efficient.

There are some pollutants that meet these two cases: perhaps municipal solid waste (MSW) for the first one and CO_2 emissions for the second. But many pollutants fall between these cases: interstate air pollution, for example. In this case the appropriate degree of decentralization is somewhere between none and complete. In the United States, for example, it might call for environmental regulations to be established at the regional level. In fact, the mixed case has been addressed largely by states taking active roles in coordinating and managing federally initiated programs.

Virtually all federal programs have provisions for substantial state and local participation. Federal water-pollution law (incorporating technology-based effluent standards) works through a **permitting system;** sources must obtain permits for waterborne emissions and are supposed to operate in accordance with the terms specified in the permits. For the most part, it is the states that actually operate the permit system, though there are a few (e.g., Idaho, New Mexico, New Hampshire, and Massachusetts) where federal authorities are still responsible. Federal water law also requires the states to establish ambient water quality standards in the various bodies of water within their boundaries. Traditionally these standards have been expressed in terms of the functions that particular water quality levels would allow; for example, standards for fishable/swimmable water and standards for drinkable water. In recent laws, states also have been given the responsibility of setting ambient standards for waterborne toxics.

States have many responsibilities in controlling air pollution. A major activity is the design and operation of State Implementation Plans (SIPs). These are plans of action through which national ambient air quality standards are to be reached in current nonattainment regions. The states have permitting authority to achieve these SIPs. The 1990 Clean Air Act Amendments allows them to operate **fee systems** for these permits, similar to the water program. Permit fees may be charged, *and these may be based on emission levels;* but fees are only supposed to be high enough to cover the costs of running the permit program. They may not be used, in other words, as full incentive-changing emission charges such as those we discussed in previous chapters. In recent years, this type of "dedicated funding" system is being increasingly relied upon by states to fund their environmental programs. Rather than fund these efforts from general state revenues, they are turning to using sources in particular programs—permit fees, fines, trust funds, and so on—to get the money to run these programs. Examples include dedicating the money collected through wastewater discharge fees to other types of water-pollution control projects. In times of economic hardship, these dedicated funds sometimes are "raided" to cover budget shortfalls.

States also may regulate hazardous wastes, but, according to the Resource Conservation and Recovery Act (RCRA), the state regulations must be at least as strict as applicable federal regulations. Many states have done this in various areas: definition of hazardous wastes, standards for incinerators, requirements for the manifest system, location requirements for hazardous-waste disposal sites, insurance requirements for hazardous-waste facility operators, and so on. State hazardous-waste regulations are almost exclusively performance and technology standards. New Jersey's laws on incinerating hazardous wastes, for example, specify such details as minimum operating temperatures allowed and staffing requirements. Arkansas mandates the disposal method for different types of hazardous wastes. California statutes specify detailed design standards for hazardous-waste landfills that are more stringent than federal standards. Many states have enacted their own Superfund laws to supplement the federal law. Many of these are designed in the image of the **Comprehensive Environmental Response, Compensation, and Liability Act** (CERCLA), with a response fund, a site priority list, and various action criteria.[1] States also have taken varying degrees of responsibility for actions at some of the National Priorities List (NPL) sites.

Race to the Bottom?

States usually feel that they are in competition among themselves to attract business growth and provide jobs for growing populations. This has led to a fear among some that states will try to use lax environmental standards to attract this economic activity, in which case we would see them progressively

---

[1] Environmental Law Institute, *An Analysis of State Superfund Programs 50-State Study*, 2001, Update November 2002.

lowering their environmental standards in a competitive **race to the bottom** in terms of environmental regulations. Although it is possible theoretically to explain the conditions that would lead to such a race, most empirical evidence to date suggests that such a race has not happened. In fact, if anything, there has been a race to the top, fueled perhaps by the concerns of states for having quality living conditions to attract economic activity.[2]

Policy Innovations at the State Level

During the last few decades, the states have been the source of some innovative environmental policy initiatives. This is especially true of California, which has been the source of several policy initiatives that have later spread to other states and the federal level. Chief among these has been mobile-source pollution control. The Los Angeles area was the first in the nation to experience smog, and the California response in the early 1960s was to require technological improvements in cars to reduce emissions. Since that time, vehicles sold in California have had to meet more stringent state emission standards. The standards have not been legally preempted by federal emission limits, and in recent years some other states have adopted the California standards as a way of dealing with increasingly severe urban air pollution. The new federal standards, discussed in Chapter 15, will bring federal and California standards in harmony.

California has been a pioneer in the use of tradable emission permits to control airborne emissions. The South Coast Air Quality Management District, a regional organization whose objective is to manage air-pollution reductions in the Los Angeles basin, is now trying to develop a cap-and-trade program covering greenhouse gas emissions in that region.

Many other environmental programs that have become law at the federal level were initially developed by one or more of the states. The pesticide DDT was first banned by Wisconsin; this later became a national effort. The Federal Strip Mining Control and Reclamation Act of 1977 was substantially modeled after the Pennsylvania strip mining reclamation law. The federal Toxics Release Inventory (TRI) program is an idea that originated with programs in New Jersey and Maryland.

Municipal Solid Waste

In the rest of this chapter we deal in some detail with several important environmental problems that traditionally have been left to states and localities. The first of these is **solid waste**, the disposal of which has emerged as a leading problem in many cities and towns across the country. Landfilling, for a long time the preferred disposal method for urban solid waste, has come up hard against rising land shortages in many places, leading some localities to ship their solid wastes long distances for disposal. In addition, rising fears of

---

[2] Wallace E. Oates, *A Reconsideration of Environmental Federalism*, Discussion Paper 01-54, Resources for the Future, Washington, D.C., November 2001.

groundwater contamination from landfills and of air pollutants from incineration have turned what once was a disposal activity to which nobody gave a second thought into a prime environmental concern.

The Nature of the Problem

The **municipal solid waste** stream is actually a trickle at the end of a long and very large flow of materials used in the U.S. economy. The Environmental Protection Agency (EPA) estimates that the total quantity of materials of all types generated per person per day is about 254 pounds. Most of this is industrial waste. Municipal solid waste consists of trash or garbage from homes, businesses, and institutions. In 2013 there were an estimated 4.4 pounds per person per day of MSW generated in the country. This was up from 2.7 pounds in 1960 (see Table 17.2). Slightly over half of this MSW was disposed of in landfills in 2013, down from about 80 percent in 1980. Over the last 50 years, the amount of MSW that is recycled has increased, from 6.3 percent in 1960 to 34 percent in 2013, with a doubling since 1990. These are aggregate numbers, which hide substantial variation among states and communities in the country. The MSW problem is not equally acute everywhere. In localities with large populations and/or constrained landfill space, the problem is one of immediate concern; in areas with the opposite characteristics, it is much less so.

Technical Options for Reducing MSW

We define the following terms: TM is total materials used, by a firm or industry or economy, in a period of time; VM is virgin materials used; and RM is recycled materials used. Then it must be true that for any time period:

$$TM = VM + RM.$$

Materials-balance considerations[3] tell us that all materials inputs taken into an economic system must eventually end up back in the environment in some

TABLE 17.2   Municipal Solid Waste, Selected Data

	1960	1970	1980	1990	2000	2010	2013
Total quantity generated (mil. tons)	88.1	121.0	151.6	196.9	238.3	249.9	254.1
Quantity generated per capita (lbs./person/day)	2.7	3.3	3.7	4.3	4.6	4.4	4.4
Disposal, percent of total:							
Landfill	63.0	72.6	81.4	66.7	54.7	54.2	52.8
Combustion	30.6	20.7	9.0	16.2	16.2	11.7	12.9
Recycled	6.3	6.6	9.6	17.2	29.1	34.1	34.3

Source: U.S. Environmental Protection Agency, *Municipal Solid Waste Generation, Recycling and Disposal in the United States: Facts and Figures for 2012, Washington, D.C., February 2014,* **http://www.epa.gov/wastes/nonhaz/municipal/pubs /msw_2012_rev_factsheet.pdf**; U.S. EPA, *Advancing Sustainable Materials Management: Facts and Figures 2013,* Washington, D.C., EPA530-R-15-002, June 2015, **http://www3.epa.gov/epawaste/nonhaz/municipal/pubs/2013_advncng_smm_rpt.pdf**.

[3] See Chapter 2.

fashion. The form may change, as when solid materials are burned to yield energy and waste products. The time span can differ; some materials do not lend themselves to reuse and so are discarded almost immediately, whereas others can be recycled, perhaps many times. But recycling can never be perfect because of conversion losses, waste in consumption, and so on. This means we should focus on the quantity of virgin materials used. Rearranging the above expression gives:

$$VM = TM - RM, \quad \text{or} \quad = TM\,(1-r)$$

where r is the **rate of reuse**, or RM/TM. There are essentially two ways to reduce the use of virgin materials: (1) reduce the overall quantity of materials (TM), and/or (2) increase the reuse rate, r— or, in other words, increase waste reduction and recycling.

Total materials use can be reduced in two ways: by reducing the rate of economic activity or by reducing the **materials intensity** of that activity. By "materials intensity" we mean the quantity of materials used per unit of production or consumption. And this in turn can be done in two ways:

(1) by rearranging the composition of output and consumption away from products that use relatively large amounts of materials and toward those that use less (e.g., a shift away from tangible goods toward services) and

(2) by decreasing the materials intensity of particular products (e.g., reducing the amount of packaging material in consumer electronics or food products, or increase in online payments).

The other alternative is **recycling**. This means reaching into the waste stream to extract materials that may be reused. Some may be reused directly, as when consumers reuse clothing. Consignment shops are healthy businesses in many communities; some used cloth can be redirected to building insulation. The separation, transportation, and reprocessing technologies that are available critically affect the costs of recycled materials, and thus their ability to displace virgin materials.

Current Policy

The present policy picture is very complicated, as you would expect from the nature of the physical problem, the large number of materials involved, and the thousands of municipalities, small and large, searching for solutions. Table 17.3 lists some of the various measures that are, or have been, pursued in various states. For the most part these focus on some facet of recycling. When MSW first became an issue, it was regarded primarily as a disposal issue—people were taking to the landfill materials and products that could be recycled. Thus, the initial response of most communities was to think about materials recovery and recycling. **Voluntary recycling programs** began in the 1970s (the first was in Oregon). In some communities recycling has become mandatory for items that are recyclable. Recent figures show that about 35 percent of MSW is currently recycled. As Table 17.4 shows, the recycling rate for different materials varies from a high of 64 percent for paper to a low of 5 percent for food wastes. Of the material discarded, about 80 percent is landfilled and most of the remainder is incinerated.

TABLE 17.3   MSW Reduction and Recycling Actions Undertaken in States and Communities

Product bans: plastic nondegradable plastic bags, plastic-coated paper, polystyrene containers, disposable diapers, plastic six-pack rings, cans containing both plastic and metal, plastic bag purchases by state or local agencies.

Returnable disposal fees: fee on newsprint that is returned for recycling, returnable deposits on tires and car batteries.

Taxes on virgin materials content.

Consumer fees on MSW: fees per bag or bin of unsorted MSW.

Prohibitions on landfilling certain products, such as yard clippings, metal, and tires.

Bottle deposits.

Mandatory recycled content of purchased material by public agencies.

Voluntary or mandatory material separation and curbside recycling.

Recycled or recyclable labels on products.

Technical assistance for recycling programs.

Grants and loans to municipalities for recycling programs.

Public construction of waste separation and reprocessing plants.

Public construction of waste-to-energy plants: combustion with energy recovery.

Tax credits and exemptions for recycling equipment and other investments by private businesses.

Food waste composting requirements for large restaurants, schools, grocery stores, etc.

TABLE 17.4   Municipal Solid Waste Generated and Recovered in the United States, 2013

	Waste Generated (million tons)	Materials Recovered (percent of generation)
Paper	68.6	64
Yard waste	34.2	60
Plastics	32.5	9
Metals	23.1	34
Wood	15.8	16
Food waste	37.1	5
Glass	11.5	27
Other	31.3	15
Total	254.1	34

Source: U.S. Environmental Protection Agency, *Municipal Solid Waste Generation, Recycling and Disposal in the United States: Facts and Figures for 2012*, Washington, D.C., February 2014, **http://www.epa.gov/wastes/nonhaz/municipal/pubs /msw_2012_rev_factsheet.pdf;** U.S. EPA, *Advancing Sustainable Materials Management: Facts and Figures 2013*, Washington, D.C., June 2015, **http://www3.epa.gov/epawaste/nonhaz/municipal/pubs/2013_advncng_smm_rpt.pdf**.

The Economics of Recycling

The complete materials recycling loop is actually a complex process involving a number of stages and interconnections. A schematic outline of this loop is depicted in Figure 17.1. It shows the primary actors at each stage and how the flow

FIGURE 17.1   **Recycling Consists of a Number of Markets Linking Generators and Users**

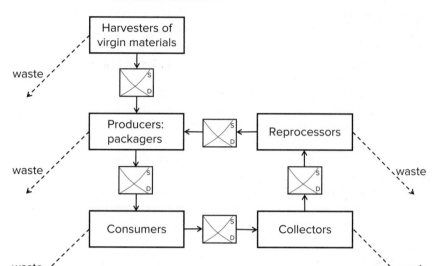

of materials goes from one stage to the next. At each stage there is also some material disposal, depicted by the dashed arrows. The connections among actors at each stage are worked out through markets; these markets are depicted by small supply/demand figures between each stage of the recycling loop.

The size and composition of the material flows are determined by the many decisions made by the demanders and suppliers in these markets. Producers and packagers design products and the materials used for them; they make decisions on the total quantities of materials used and the amounts of virgin and recycled feedstocks they will use. Consumers choose products that contain different types and amounts of material; they also decide how to dispose of the various materials after the products have been "consumed." There is a stage consisting of collectors: firms that collect, transport, and sort material and make it available to materials reprocessors. The latter, in turn, convert the various materials of the solid-waste stream into materials that may be reused by producers/packagers, thus closing the loop.

Solid waste is a problem because of pricing difficulties in the various markets around the loop. For example,

- The harvesting of virgin materials leads to a variety of economic costs. In most cases these costs are external to the harvesting firms, making the prices of virgin materials too low from the standpoint of social efficiency.
- Because of low prices for virgin materials, it is difficult for entrepreneurs to be competitive in supplying materials pulled from the waste stream and reprocessed into reusable forms.

- Discarded solid waste involves environmental costs that ought to be reflected in prices paid by consumers facing different disposal options. Pay-as-you-throw (PAYT) systems are common and give incentives for recycling as a waste-disposal method for households. By increasing recycling the household has less trash and incurs less PAYT fees. Some communities even penalize households that include recyclable materials in their trash, even though the household can pay-to-throw. When solid waste-disposal services are paid through flat fees levied to cover the cost of collection and disposal, there is no incentive, other than moral obligation, for consumers to be concerned about the amounts of solid waste they discard. Also, there is no incentive to reduce the excess packaging materials that accompany their purchases; for example, electing to use cloth, reusable shopping bags rather than one-use plastic shopping bags.
- For the past several decades the approach to recycling has placed the responsibility of sorting of recyclable materials on the consumer. A system called **Single Stream Recycling** shifts this responsibility and thus the cost from the consumer to the waste-management facility. Single Stream Recycling is a system whereby a variety of recyclable items can be collected together in a single container, hauled off site, and later sorted at the sorting facility. Such a system increases convenience at the point of recycling, and thereby the incentive to recycle, because consumers don't have to decide among mixed paper (newspapers, copy paper, junk mail, etc.) or containers (bottles, cans, certain types of plastics, etc.) or trash, the decision rule is simplified to trash or recycle.

Producer Use of Recycled Material

Let us take a closer look at the top-most market in Figure 17.1, the market in which producers of goods and services use various amounts and types of material. This market is modeled in Figure 17.2. The demand curve applies to a firm or industry; it shows the quantity demanded of a particular type of material in a given period, such as a year. There are two sources of this material: virgin and recycled. We assume that this firm or industry is small relative to the total use of this material; thus, it can obtain virgin material in whatever quantity it wishes at a constant price. This price is marked p_v and is shown as a horizontal line intersecting the demand curve at a quantity level q_0. But this material also may be obtained from recycled sources. Here, however, the procurement cost picture is more complicated. Reaching into the waste stream for recycled materials involves a number of special costs—of collection, separation, transportation, reprocessing, and so on. We assume that these costs increase with the amount of recycled material used. The supply curve of recycled material to this firm or industry is therefore an increasing function such as S_1 or S_2. These two supply curves refer to situations with different recycling technology. For S_1, costs go up relatively rapidly; S_2 increases much less rapidly. Consider for the moment the recycled material supply curve labeled S_1. If this is the one faced by this firm or industry, it will end up using q_1 of recycled materials. In other words, the producer will use recycled materials up to the point where its cost is equal to the price of virgin materials. Because the total materials use is q_0, the difference $(q_0 - q_1)$ consists of virgin materials.

The reuse ratio, the proportion of total materials coming from recycled feed-stock, is q_1/q_0. This ratio can be increased in three ways: increase q_1 while holding q_0 constant, decrease q_0 while holding q_1 constant, or both. Most community efforts at recycling are aimed at the first of these. For example, public curbside sorting and collection programs are ultimately aimed at making the supply of recycled material more abundant and, hence, less costly to producers. In terms of the model of Figure 17.2, these programs have aimed at shifting the recycled supply curve downward, say, from S_1 to S_2. If this is done, recycled materials use increases to q_2, the recycling rate increases to q_2/q_0, and use of virgin materials drops to $(q_0 - q_2)$.

Another way of increasing the recycling ratio is to reduce the demand for materials in general while holding constant the use of recycled materials. Diagrammatically this means shifting the whole materials demand curve back. This might be done, for example, by finding ways of producing output using fewer materials. It also might simply happen as consumers shift away from materials-intensive products. Finally, there is one way of simultaneously reducing total materials used and increasing recycled materials: Increase the price of virgin materials. If, in Figure 17.2, we lift the virgin materials price to, say, p_2 through a tax, this will lead to a move both up the recycling supply curve and up the materials demand curve. This means an increase in the quantity of recycled materials and a decrease in the quantity demanded of materials in total. Raising the price on virgin materials with a tax thus has a double effect on the reuse ratio, because it works at both ends of the problem.

FIGURE 17.2   Use of Recycled Materials in Production

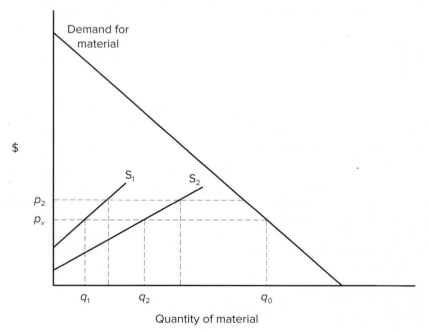

We can use this simple model to examine proposals for **recycled-content standards** in materials-using industries. Early enthusiasm for community recycling efforts led to situations in which the amounts of collected material outstripped technical ability to turn it into useful raw material, and in the absence of demand, large quantities of sorted and collected material actually ended up in landfills. Thus, policy efforts have turned toward trying to increase the strength of demand for the recycled material. Numerous states have thought to try this by introducing minimum-content standards for materials-using production processes. Minimum-content standards require that all materials-using products manufactured or sold within a given state contain some specified percentage of recycled material.

We have talked many times of the cost-ineffectiveness of uniform standards in the face of heterogeneous emissions withholding costs. In the case of uniform content standards for materials, the same principle applies, but here the important factor is heterogeneity across materials-using firms in terms of the costs of obtaining and using recycled materials. For a truly cost-effective approach to the problem, we would want to achieve equality across industries and materials in terms of **marginal recycling costs.** What this implies is having higher rates of recycled materials use by industries whose recycling costs are relatively low and lower rates for industries with relatively high recycling costs. One way to achieve this is to apply a tax on virgin materials. As mentioned previously, a tax of, say, $p_2 - p_v$ per unit of virgin materials, charged to all firms, would lead each to increase its recycling ratio in a way that satisfied the equimarginal principle. A transferable permit system in the recycling market is a possibility but not one that has been adopted.

In the real world, of course, things are a lot more complicated than they appear in this simple model. For example, one underlying assumption built into Figure 17.2 is that recycled material and virgin material are physically interchangeable. This is hardly ever true in practice. Although newspaper can be produced largely from recycled newspaper, some virgin newsprint is usually necessary to achieve minimum quality levels. The same is true of many recycled metals. It is also true that the recycling market, like any economic market, is very dynamic, whereas the model displayed in Figure 17.2 is essentially static; that is, it is limited to events happening in a single time period.

Consumer Recycling Decisions

Let us now take a look at the second and third markets depicted in Figure 17.1, where consumers purchase goods and services and make decisions about solid-waste disposal. Consumers can be expected to purchase products based on their private net benefits: benefits minus purchase price minus disposal costs. Historically most private disposal costs have been small, so getting rid of containers, packaging, and so forth has not been a big issue for consumers. But with landfills filling up, and environmental contamination looming as a problem in many places, there is an added social cost of disposal. In effect, the full social costs of disposal are now the private costs just mentioned, plus the environmental damage costs that may be caused by the disposal of products.

These damage costs are external costs, a concept that we have discussed at length in this book.

With trash, one way to reduce these environmental damages is for consumers to extract certain items from their waste stream and make them available for recycling. Many years ago, private markets existed in recycled materials. More recently communities have moved heavily into recycling, in which consumers are asked to separate recyclable material from trash and make it available for collection. If recycling is voluntary, the incentive for this comes either from public exhortation or from the "warm glow" effect. Substantially greater recycling effort can normally be induced by putting a charge, per bag or per can, on material that is thrown away rather than recycled. This charge is an example of an emissions tax, where "emissions" in this case refer to material discarded rather than recycled. See the discussion of "unit pricing" in Chapter 1. These may be accompanied by regulations that prohibit certain items from going to landfills that may risk substantial damage to the environment, for example, florescent light bulbs and oil-based paints.

To avoid consumer disposal of certain recyclable items, a number of states have instituted deposit-refund programs. Charging a deposit on these items provides funds that can be used to offer refunds for their return to designated locations. If the deposit refund is high enough, it provides the incentive for the consumer to keep these items, or at least a substantial proportion of them, out of the waste stream.

Producer Take-Back Programs

Take-back programs create a greater direct incentive for front-end improvements in product design as compared to situations where the consumer assumes total responsibility for recycling. Incentives enhance the recyclability of materials in end-of-life electronics and reuse. Take-back programs are useful by-products of selling in reusable packaging; those containing energy value after their useful life, such as power tools and batteries; those containing useful components, such as printer cartridges and computers; and those becoming obsolete quickly, such as electronics and appliances. A variety of companies have voluntary take-back programs. Ford Motor Company's Core Recovery Program seeks to refurbish or recycle fuel injectors, wiper motors, headlights, underbody shields, battery trays, and carpets, for example. Plastic car bumpers are melted and reformed into plastic taillight housings and new bumpers. Take-back programs tend to be concentrated in the technology sector. A number of communities and states have started mandatory take-back programs, for such items as car batteries and paint. Attempts to start mandatory U.S. federal programs have not been successful.

The European Commission adopted a mandatory directive on Waste from Electrical and Electronic Equipment (WEEE) that delegates the responsibility to the producer to manage the electronic product throughout its product life cycle. The producer is required to assume the physical and financial responsibility, including the cost of the disposal of e-waste, with consumers being able to return their equipment free of charge. See Exhibit 17.1.

Waste from Electrical and Electronic Equipment (WEEE)

EXHIBIT 17.1

The European WEEE Directive, established in 2003, promotes sustainable production and consumption of electrical and electronics equipment and the reuse, recycling, and recovery of WEEE. Further, the Directive restricts the use of certain hazardous materials used in electronic products. Collection schemes enable consumers to return e-waste free of charge.

However by 2012, only about one-third of WEEE was being collected and appropriately treated, while illegal trade of e-waste across European borders continued. A revised WEEE Directive was adopted, effective in 2014, to reduce producer administrative burdens and set mandatory collection targets for each European Union member state equal to 65 percent of the average weight of electrical and electronic equipment placed on the market over a two-year period. Member states with high consumption of electrical and electronic products have higher targets; those states with lower consumption have lower targets.

Although the United States has no federal regulations for e-waste, about 22 states have enacted their own laws governing its disposal with the intent of keeping heavy metals and toxic substances out of landfills. All laws, except California and Utah, use a Producer Responsibility approach where manufacturers must pay for recycling. Often a registration fee is assessed on manufacturers to help pay for state program administration costs. The National Center for Electronics Recycling provides a state-by-state list of these regulations.

The product categories include: large and small household appliances, information technology and telecommunications equipment, lighting equipment, electrical and electronic tools, toys, leisure and sports equipment, medical devices, monitoring and controlling instruments, photovoltaic panels, and automatic dispensers.

Source: European Commission Environment, *Directive 2012/19/EU on WEEE FAQs,* Center for Recycling, April 2014, **http://www.ecyclingresource.org.**

Local Environmental Regulations

In this chapter we have focused on local programs for the management of household solid waste. Many communities also have enacted regulations dealing with other environmental issues, for example:

- Protection of wetlands (no building in or near wetlands)
- Protection of scenic values (no building on ridge lines)
- Water quality (no road salt near streams or ponds)
- Noise pollution (no loud parties on weekends)

These regulations (often called ordinances) come under the exercise of the **police power,** which confers on communities the constitutional right to enact environmental (and other) regulations, provided they are reasonable, clearly related to public welfare, and are not arbitrary, or discriminatory. In effect, we have, at the community level, the same regulatory problem that is posed by our standard economic model of pollution control: how to balance the benefits of public regulation with their costs.

From the standpoint of public health, there may be little difficulty barring development in sensitive wetlands, on the grounds that these are linked into the hydrological systems on which many people depend for water supply. But when public health is not so directly involved, things can be much less clear. Suppose there is a particular farm in a community and that over time the people of the community have come to value the scenic qualities of that land. Clearly the land has environmental (scenic) value, but may the town pass a regulation saying that it may not be developed because of the scenic value? In doing this, the town is essentially putting on the farm the entire burden of providing these scenic values.

In issues of this type, much of the outcome depends on the impacts of environmental regulations on land values. One of the most contested issues in using local land-use controls for environmental protection purposes is the **takings** problem. The Fifth Amendment to the U.S. Constitution contains the following language: "No person shall be . . . deprived of life, liberty, or property, without due process of law; nor shall private property be taken for a public use, without just compensation." This authorizes the government to "take" private property, but only if it is for a public purpose and only if the owners receive just compensation. Land may be taken physically (e.g., for a public park, or highway) under **eminent domain**, and the main question will revolve around how much the compensation should be.

When a community passes land-use regulations—for example, to protect water quality or scenic views—the issue is not a physical taking, but whether the regulations substantially reduce the value of the affected property, constituting what is known as a **regulatory taking**. If it does, then compensation is due to the affected landowners. The regulatory takings issue hangs over the community exercise of the police power for environmental purposes. If affected individuals must be compensated for regulations, it makes these regulations, in effect, more costly for the community.

The Increasing Role of the States

At the beginning of the 21st century, continued political stasis at the federal level have worked against new national pollution control statutes. One result of this is to shift more initiatives to the states, many of which have developed notable analytical and administrative competencies in environmental matters. Of course California has long been in the forefront of this effort. But states' actions are now more widespread, both to grapple with problems that are unique to particular states (such as coastal pollution in Rhode Island), and to address issues of national significance on which the U.S. Congress is unable to act.

State-level programs are paramount for controlling non point source water pollution, now considered the largest remaining source of water quality impairments.

Regulations to control mercury, emissions, especially from power plants, have been in contention for well over a decade at the federal level. So a number of states have sought to enact mercury regulations on their own initiative. [4]

In the absence of federal action to upgrade national procedures for approving chemicals, some states have tried to install their own programs for testing and approving chemicals often patterned after the new European program designed around the precautionary principle. [5]

Steps to address greenhouse gas emissions, a global phenomenon, have been undertaken by the states, either singly (California's carbon trading program) or in groups (the Regional Greenhouse Gas Initiative of the Northeastern States).

Even new initiatives at the federal level are recognizing the greater capabilities of the states. Recent efforts to shape a national program on greenhouse gas control have leaned heavily on the ability of individual states to design cost-effective pollution-control programs for sources within their boundaries.

Summary

In recent years, state and local efforts have become more important in environmental policy matters. As greater attention shifts to problems of enforcing environmental policies and regulations, state-level efforts in this respect have become more critical. States also have served as the source of innovation in many areas of environmental policies, spurring federal efforts and trying out new ideas in the control of emissions. The leading role of California in fostering more aggressive air-pollution control is especially notable.

States and localities have had the primary responsibility for solid-waste management, land-use controls, and the protection of groundwater resources. Community efforts at recycling are a major part of the effort to address solid-waste issues. We saw how recycling decisions depend on complex incentive situations facing consumers in their buying and disposal decisions and producers whose demands for recycled materials may lead them to reach into the solid-waste stream for sources of raw materials. Producer take-back programs push responsibility for reducing MSW up the supply chain. Communities are also active in enacting environmental regulations, which have to be shaped in accordance with constitutional limits on the police power.

---

[4] Howard A. Learner, "Restraining Federal Preemption when there is an 'Emerging Consensus' of State Environmental Laws and Policies," *Northwestern University Law Review,* 102(2), 2008, pp. 649–663.

[5] *State Chemical Laws: Trends and Profiles,* National Pollution Prevention Roundtable, April 2003, **www.p2.org/wp_content/uploads/2013-state-toxics-policy-profiles-report-2.pdf.**

Questions for Further Discussion

1. What are the implications for cost-effective recycling programs of regulations that establish the same recycling ratios for all sectors of the economy?

2. How might a system of transferable permits be designed to achieve an aggregate recycling target cost-effectively?

3. Another way of increasing the use of recycled material by industry is to subsidize its purchase of materials taken from the waste stream. How would you analyze this in terms of Figure 17.2?

4. What are the factors, both economic and environmental, that make a problem more properly a local issue rather than a state issue?

5. Investigate the rules for recycling and solid waste disposal for a local community with which you are familiar. What are the incentives that increase the rate of reuse (r)?

For additional readings and Web sites pertaining to the material in this chapter, see **www.mhhe.com/field7e.**

Section 6

Global Environmental Issues

In the last four chapters we have dealt with economic issues of domestic U.S. pollution control. It is now time to turn to international issues. The prospects for the 21st century are for the world to continue to shrink and nations to become increasingly interconnected. These interactions will grow in environmental matters. Regional and global problems will demand greater levels of cooperation and more effective international institutions.

We turn first, in Chapter 18, to environmental issues that are global in scale. Of course the most critical of these is global climate change arising from modern industrial economies. Coming to grips with climate change is going to require effective international agreements, so this is the subject of Chapter 19. Next we turn to the phenomenon called globalization, environmental issues arising from the growing interdependence among economies of the world. Finally, the last chapter discusses some economic aspects of environmental issues facing countries of the world that are putting a strong emphasis on economic development.

Chapter 18

The Global Environment

People all around the world are struggling to come to grips with local environmental problems and improve their immediate surroundings. But over the last few decades, people also have had to broaden their outlooks to recognize that there is a **global environment** that is critical to human welfare. Moreover, the scale of human activities has become so widespread and intense that it has begun to have an impact on this global environment in significant ways.

For all of history, one of the ways humans have reacted to local environmental destruction is migration. But at the planetary level this option is not available. There is no escape if we inadvertently make our planet less habitable.

Complementing the daunting physical facts are the sobering political/economic facts that have made it very difficult for the world's nations to act collectively. There is a race on between the accumulating scientific data that scientists, still with great uncertainty, are straining to interpret and the growing efforts to develop international institutions and perspectives that will make concerted action possible.

Global Climate Change

The Physical Problem

Clearly the most important global problem facing us today is the possibility that, because of our current behavior, we are rendering the planet substantially less habitable, for humans as well as other members of the biosphere. This sometimes goes under the name of "climate change," or the global "greenhouse" effect. The principle of a greenhouse is that the enclosing glass or plastic allows the passage of incoming sunlight, but traps a portion of the reflected infrared radiation, which warms the interior of the greenhouse above the outside temperature. Greenhouse gases (GHGs) in the earth's atmosphere play a similar role; they serve to raise the temperature of the earth's surface and make it habitable. With no GHGs at all, the surface of the earth would be about 30°C cooler than it is today, making human life impossible.

Under preindustrial conditions, trace amounts of GHGs were in global balance. They were given off by decaying plant and animal materials and absorbed by forests and oceans. Into this rough balance came human beings and one of their greatest cultural accomplishments: the Industrial Revolution. That event was basically a revolution in energy use, involving a vast increase in the extraction of energy from fossil fuels—first coal and later petroleum and natural gas. Combustion of fossil fuels, together with deforestation and a few other activities, has led to vast increases in emissions (see Exhibit 18.1) and to an increase in the carbon dioxide (CO_2) content of the atmosphere by about 40 percent from the beginning of the Industrial Revolution. In the last three decades alone, it has increased 15 percent, and many scientists predict an approximate doubling by the middle of the 21st century. Although CO_2 is the most important **greenhouse gas**, it is not the only one. Another is methane, which is in fact 22 times more potent as a GHG than CO_2. Analysis of ice cores shows that over the last 800,000 years atmospheric concentrations of methane have never exceeded 750 parts per billion. Today it is about 1,800 parts per billion. The main GHGs, their approximate proportionate contribution to global warming, and their major sources are shown in Table 18.1.

Accompanying this buildup of GHGs has been a rise in mean surface temperatures around the globe. Study of temperature records, the composition of long-lived glaciers, and other sources shows that the earth has warmed about

The Quick Story   EXHIBIT **18.1**

The data below show very quickly the nature of the problem in global climate change. They show emissions of CO_2, the main GHG, for a few selected countries and for the global total, at points over the last 22 years. Key observations are:

- For the total, a modest increase in the last decade of the 20th century, then a 36 percent jump over the next 12 years.
- Some evidence that emission increases have been contained in the United States and Europe (though the recession is probably responsible for a substantial part of this).
- A massive increase in China in the last decade.

- Emissions in India almost doubled over the last 12 years, though from a low base.

Emissions of CO_2 (billion tons)

	1990	2000	2012
Global Total	22.70	25.40	34.50
United States	4.99	5.87	5.19
European Union (15 countries)	3.33	3.33	3.00
China	2.51	3.56	9.86
India	0.66	1.06	1.97

Source: Netherlands Environmental Assessment Agency, *Trends in Global CO_2 Emissions*, 2013 Report, pp. 16–17.

TABLE 18.1   Major Greenhouse Gases

Gas	Percent of Total
Carbon dioxide (CO_2)	
Fossil fuel use	57
Deforestation, decay of biomass	17
Other	3
Methane (CH_4), agriculture, landfills, termites	14
Nitrous oxide (N_2O)	
Fertilizer, industry, waste incineration	8
Other (ozone-depleting chemicals, carbon monoxide, etc.)	1

0.5°C (1°F) over the past 100 years. Some scientific models predict that over the next century temperatures could rise 1.5°C to 4.5°C. The rate of heating is put at about 0.5°C per decade. This may not sound like a very rapid change, but historical studies have shown that in past episodes of warming and cooling, during which agricultural societies of the time suffered major dislocations, climate change occurred at a rate of only about 0.05°C per decade. Today's rate of change, in other words, is expected to be very much faster than those faced by humans in the past.

Global warming is expected to bring about a general rise in sea level because of the expansion of sea water, the melting of glaciers, and perhaps eventually the breaking up of polar ice sheets. Although this will be a general rise, it will have different local impacts on tidal and current patterns. Changes in meteorological patterns also will vary widely among regions. In the northern hemisphere, polar regions will warm faster than equatorial zones; on the continental landmasses, the centers will become drier than the peripheries, and so on. Our ability to predict these changes will improve as the global climate models of atmospheric scientists are better developed.

Human and Ecosystem Impacts

Although this is a problem of the global environment, its impacts on humans and the ecosystem will vary greatly from one country and region to another. A sea-level rise would have devastating impacts in certain societies, such as those of the Pacific islands or those concentrated in low river deltas. Impacts will be relatively less in countries where development may be redirected toward interior regions. The drowning of coastal wetlands throughout the world could have important impacts on fisheries, and thus on societies that rely heavily on marine resources. Another potential impact of great importance is the increased acidification of the oceans caused by higher levels of atmospheric CO_2, which reacts with water to create carbonic acid. There will be very substantial impacts on ecosystems and individual species of plants and animals, not just because of the amount of change but also because the rate of change will be fast by evolutionary standards. In ice ages of the past, weather changes have happened slowly enough to allow species of plants and animals to migrate and survive.

The rapid pace of change expected in the greenhouse phenomenon may be too quick for many organisms to adjust to changing habitats. It also will put a severe strain on species that occupy narrow ecological niches because relatively small changes in weather patterns can destroy the habitats on which they depend.

Some of the biggest impacts on humans will be through the effects of changed climate patterns on **agriculture and forestry.** Here the story gets very complicated, not only because weather patterns will be differently affected throughout the world, but also because crops, and the systems of cultivation adopted by farmers, vary a lot in terms of their ability to withstand changes in temperature and water availability. It is generally thought that the agricultural impacts of atmospheric warming will hit developing nations harder than developed countries. It is expected that African nations will bear the greatest impact. Some studies concluded that agriculture could be adapted to future climate changes through crop development and technical changes. But others cast some doubt on the ability of many developing countries to do this because many of their crops are already closer to the limits of tolerance for warmer temperatures. Research on the impacts of the greenhouse effect will challenge scientists for many years to come.

Scientific Uncertainties and Human Choice

Although there are yet a few skeptical political voices, all respectable scientific judgment is that human produced global climate change is occurring, and will get worse, if nothing is done about it. How much worse? Scientists of the IPCC have settled on consensus views about future climate consequences, in particular, on probabilities of future global surface mean temperatures. One such conclusion, for example, is that the probability that the temperature increase will exceed 4.5°C lies between 5 and 17 percent. A more recent estimate by leading climate experts is that this probability is about 23 percent. One can conclude from these that there is a rather large probability of very large, even catastrophic, temperature increases.

In Chapter 6 we introduced a few concepts to help in analyzing situations involving risk, in particular, the concept of risk aversion in cases involving small probabilities of very large losses. There is uncertainty about the extent of global warming in the future, but the potential negative consequences are so great that it behooves us to be risk averse. In plain terms: better to be safe than sorry. All of this suggest strongly that significant steps must be undertaken today to reduce the probability of serious global warming in the future.

In a sense there are two fundamental choices for this problem: **mitigation** and/or **adaptation.**[1] Mitigation refers to taking steps today to reduce GHG emissions so as to delay or reduce global temperature increases. Adaptation refers to the efforts of future generations to adjust in ways that will substantially reduce the negative impacts of these temperature increases.

---

[1] The policy issues surrounding the climate-change phenomenon have been, and are being, much researched and discussed and written about. A good place to start for exploring them is the Energy and Climate program of Resources for the Future (http:/www.rff.org).

Technical Responses to the Greenhouse Effect

It needs to be recognized, however, that there are many things that could be done to mitigate CO_2 emissions, and that these come at different costs. It is very important, therefore, to keep the concept of **cost-effectiveness** clearly in mind when developing contemporary mitigation steps. The primary means of reducing the warming lies in reducing the output of GHG and/or augmenting the GHG-absorbing capacity of the natural world. Because CO_2 is the main GHG, we focus on the issue of reducing global CO_2 emissions.

To get an overall view of the current world production rate of CO_2 and how it may be altered, consider the following equation (GDP is gross domestic product):

	Total CO_2 Emissions (mil tons CO_2)	$=$ Population (millions)	$\times$ $\dfrac{\text{GDP}}{\text{Person}}$ (1,000)	$\times$ $\dfrac{\text{Energy}}{\text{GDP}}$ (tons oil equiv.)	$\times$ $\dfrac{CO_2}{\text{Energy}}$ (tons CO_2)
World	35,917	6,361.9	8.2	0.255	2.70
U.S.	6,870	293.7	36.4	0.254	2.53
India	1,603	1,079.7	2.9	0.245	2.09
Rates of Change					
World	1.7	1.7	1.0	−0.6	−0.4
U.S.	3.7	0.9	3.8	−1.0	0.0
India	4.5	2.0	1.2	1.2	0.1

The quantity of CO_2 emissions depends on the interaction of four factors. The first is **population**. Other things remaining equal, larger populations will use more energy and therefore emit larger amounts of CO_2. The second term is **GDP per capita**, a measure of the domestic output of goods and services per person. We normally associate increases in this factor with economic growth.

Neither population nor per capita GDP can be considered likely candidates for reducing CO_2 emissions in the short run. Deliberate population control measures are unlikely to be effective, and no country is likely to be willing to reduce its rate of economic development. In the long run, however, the interaction of these two factors will be important, as history seems to show that lower population growth rates can be achieved by substantial improvements in economic welfare.

This means that significant near-term CO_2 reductions will have to come from the last two terms in the expression. The third factor is what we mean by **energy efficiency**, the amount of energy used per dollar (or per euro or rupee or cedi) of output. The key here is to move toward technologies of production, distribution, and consumption that require relatively smaller quantities of energy. The last term is **CO_2 produced per unit of energy used**. Because different energy forms have markedly different CO_2 outputs per unit, reductions in CO_2 can be achieved by switching to less-CO_2-intensive fuels. The move toward **renewable energy** also comes into play here.

The table under the equation shows these four factors for 2000 and how they have been changing in recent years.[2] The first row shows the annual growth rate in global CO_2 output, which is the sum of the global growth rates of the factors comprising the formula. Note that, worldwide, although energy efficiency and CO_2 intensity are declining, these are being more than offset by high growth rates in population and GDP per capita. But growth rates in the underlying factors differ a great deal among countries. The table shows data for India and the United States for illustrative purposes. In India, increases in all factors, especially population, have contributed to a very rapid rate of growth in CO_2 emissions. In the United States, lower population growth rates, together with increases in energy efficiency (decreases in energy per GDP) have moderated the growth rate of CO_2 emissions. It is differences among countries in these contributing factors that complicate the adoption of effective worldwide agreements to limit CO_2 emissions.

Reducing Domestic GHG Emissions

Effective global action to combat global warming will require individual countries to undertake steps to reduce their GHG emissions. The question is: How should this be undertaken? In the short run, say over the next 20 years or so, the emphasis will be on getting increases in fuel conservation and efficiency, switching to low-carbon fuels, and reducing the use and emissions of chemicals with high greenhouse impacts. From a policy perspective, perhaps the first thing to note is that there is no single source we could call on to get drastic reductions in GHG production. Instead, changes need to be made across the spectrum of stationary- and mobile-source emissions, from households, industries, transport sector, and agriculture. These needed changes are both technological—for example, a switch to more fuel-efficient equipment and low-carbon fuels—and behavioral—for example, a change in driving habits and the adoption of less energy-intensive lifestyles.

The big question is, how much is it going to cost to reduce GHG emissions significantly? And the answer to this is: It depends on how it is done. Given the long histories of command-and-control policies in the United States and other countries, many are likely to be attracted to technology or emission standards. This has been the tradition in the United States (as well as most other countries), so first efforts here have been directed at subsidizing, or requiring, technology options. This includes, for example, biofuel and renewable energy mandates, and performance requirements for vehicles in the Corporate Average Fuel Economy (café) program. As we have discussed many times in this book, mandated technology and performance standards are highly unlikely to be cost-effective, meaning that going this route to combat global warming will be much more costly to society than the alternatives.

---

[2] These data are from the World Resources Institute, *Climate Analysis Indicators Tool (CAIT 2.0)*, **http://cait2.wri.org.**

TABLE 18.2 Cost-Effectiveness of Alternative Means of Reducing CO_2, United States, 2030

Means	Costs per Ton of CO_2 Equivalent ($)
Coal-fired power plants, carbon capture storage	55
Afforestation of pasture land	15
Nuclear power	10
Residential efficiency	47
Fuel economy, light trucks	−70
Fuel economy, cars	−80
Active forest management	20
Commercial buildings, combined heat and power	−35
Onshore wind	28

Source: McKinsey and Company, "Reducing Greenhouse Gas Emissions: How Much at What Cost," December 2007.

This is because there are really substantial differences among technical options in terms of GHG control costs. Table 18.2 shows some cost-effectiveness results obtained from a large study by the analysts at McKinsey and Company. The first thing to note is that there are substantial differences in costs among the different means of reducing GHGs. In fact some of them are estimated to have a negative cost; these are approaches that would pay for themselves without even considering GHG removal, primarily through savings in energy costs. Those with positive costs are in the range of $15 to $50 per ton. Considering that the total quantity of GHG emissions in the United States today is about 7 billion tons per year, one can get a rough idea of the costs of decreasing these emissions by a substantial fraction. These are also marginal costs; that is, they are costs of reducing GHG emissions starting with where we are today. If we ever succeed in moving to a much more energy-efficient economy, the costs of making further reductions in GHG emissions will no doubt increase, probably a lot.

Some cost figures that stand out are the low estimates for afforestation, as essentially an add-on to the current conservation reserve program, and the high costs of GHG removal through CO_2 capture and storage. Afforestation is not an emission reduction method, but an attempt to augment the CO_2-absorbing capacity of the earth's ecosystem. Afforestation looks like a good buy for CO_2 removal, but the other side of the coin is that because of the relatively small numbers of acres involved, the total amount of CO_2 that could be removed through this means in the United States is relatively modest. Note also the low (in fact negative) costs of achieving greater fuel efficiency for cars and trucks. The potential for cost-effective GHG reduction through these means is tremendous.

This list includes only technology options, and does not include the thousands of behavioral changes that would effectively reduce GHGs. This includes driving slower, driving shorter distances, shifting away from meat consumption, reducing air-conditioning use, and so on. In fact, it is in altering the behavior of consumers, producers, and technology innovators and adopters that cost-effective GHG reductions will be achieved. To include the effects of these behavioral changes, it is important to consider the costs of policies and not just the costs of technologies.

Incentive-Based Approaches for Reducing Greenhouse Gas Emissions

When there are substantial differences among sources and technologies in terms of the costs of reducing GHG emissions, the use of incentive-based policies can get a substantially bigger bang for the buck than traditional command-and-control policies. In the United States, and many other countries, therefore, analysts and policymakers have started to look closely at the two major types of incentive-based approaches: cap-and-trade plans and emission taxes or charges. Countries of the European Union (EU) have recently instituted a large, intercountry cap-and-trade (CAP) program targeting CO_2 emissions; this is described in Exhibit 18.2.

Details of the European Trading Scheme   EXHIBIT **18.2**

The European Trading Scheme (ETS) began in 2005. The aggregate European-wide cap consisted of a collection of national caps, as specified by the individual countries themselves in their national allocation plans. They applied only to CO_2. The total number of allowances originally distributed exceeded actual emissions in the six industrial sectors included (electricity and heat production, oil refineries, coke ovens, metal ore and steel operations, cement kilns, glass and ceramic producers, and pulp and paper mills). Over the next few years allowance prices dropped from a peak of 30€ per ton to almost zero.

The second phase of the program ran from 2005 to 2012. While initial allowance allocations were given away free, a small quantity were now auctioned. Allowance prices at first recovered, but then collapsed again under the influence of the worldwide recession of those years. Controversy arose over extending the system to other sectors, especially airlines. Fines for noncompliance were increased, from 40€ per ton in the first phase, to 100€ per ton in the second phase. Limited amounts of allowance banking were allowed.

Phase III runs from 2013 to 2020. The concern that free allowance allocation was leading to windfall profits led to an increase reliance on allowance auctions; in electricity production it is anticipated that 100 percent of the allowances will be auctioned. Phase III also will involve a shift away from individual country caps, to an overall European cap set by the European Union. Continued weakness in allowance prices has led authorities to "back load" the allowance allocation procedure, meaning to push back the allocation of 900 million allowances until 2019-2020. Authorities also established a "market stability reserve" essentially a central bank for allowances, to reduce the over allocation problem.

Source: Sidney M. Field, *Carbon-Trading in the Air: Why Europe Should Clamp Down on International Aviation Emissions,* unpublished paper, 2015. See also: Pew Center on Global Climate Change, *The European Union Emissions Trading Scheme: Insights and Opportunities,* accessed September 2015, **http://www.c2es .org/docUploads/EU-ETS%20White%20 Paper.pdf.**

In that agreement, the EU collectively agreed to reduce its CO_2 emissions to a level 7 percent below its 1990 emissions. Individual country goals vary around this, depending on their own circumstances. In their national plans, each country is to allocate a portion of its total cutback requirement to the firms of four sectors: energy, iron and steel, minerals (cement, glass), and pulp and paper. These firms may then trade emission allowances among themselves and with sources in other EU countries.

Experience with existing CAP programs, such as the sulfur dioxide (SO_2) emission reduction program, have convinced many that this type of program should be extended to GHG reductions. Others have suggested that a carbon tax, or a tax on CO_2 emissions, would be the best approach. Several proposals have been made to Congress for such a tax, or charge. One would introduce a charge of $15 per ton of carbon, applied at the point of production or importation of fuels, and increasing through time to reflect the fact that the problem of global warming will get worse through time. There are also proposals that the carbon charge be combined with income tax rebates so that the net effect on people's real incomes will be minimal.[3]

As discussed in Chapters 12 and 13, cap-and-trade is a quantity-based plan, in which a quantitative limit is placed on emissions and prices are established on emission permit markets. The use of emission taxes is a price-based policy, where a monetary fee on emissions is set and the quantity of emissions is adjusted as polluters react to that fee.

International Efforts in Global Warming

But the greenhouse effect is in fact a global problem, requiring concerted and coordinated action by the countries of the world. Joint action by groups of countries is not easy to get in this time of strong nationalistic attitudes. In addition, countries find themselves in markedly different conditions in terms of their economic states and GHG-producing industrial production. What formula might be followed in assigning individual responsibilities? Consider the following possibilities:

- Equiproportionate reduction in emissions.
- Ability to pay: base emission reductions/transfer payments on current income levels.
- Polluter pays principle: base emission reductions on current or past contributions to the problem.
- Equal per capita emissions: base emission reductions on the principle that everyone is "entitled" to the same level of use of the global environment.

---

[3] See, for example, Gilbert E. Metcalf, *A Proposal for a U.S. Carbon Tax Swap, An Equitable Tax Reform to Address Global Climate Change*. The Hamilton Project, Discussion Paper 2007–12, The Brookings Institution, Washington, D.C., October 2007.

Table 18.3 shows some relevant data for a number of countries, selected and shown to demonstrate the diversity that exists among countries of the world.

Any plan for global action will impact these countries differently, and will imply different criteria for distributing the responsibility among them. If we seek reductions simply of total emissions, the largest reduction would come from the United States, followed by China, India, and France. If control is based on emissions per capita, the largest reductions would come from the United States, then France, China, and India. If reductions were based on energy efficiency, the largest would be sought from China and India because, although their emissions per capita are low, incomes are even lower, giving them relatively high numbers for emissions per dollar of GDP. Finally, if reductions are based on percentage of world total, the order would be the United States, followed by China, India, and France.

The Kyoto Protocol

The focal point for international reductions in GHG emissions has been the **Kyoto Protocol,** an agreement negotiated under the auspices of the United Nations in 1997.[4] It covered six GHGs and established emission reduction targets that countries were obligated to reach by the years 2008 to 2012. The targets were in terms of aggregate anthropogenic CO_2-equivalent emissions, expressed as a percentage of 1990 emissions in the various countries. The agreements contained commitments from 39 countries and one country group, the European Union. These are primarily European countries and the former communist countries of Eastern Europe, together with the United States, Canada, Russia, and Japan.

TABLE 18.3 Greenhouse Gas Emissions Data for Selected Countries, 2012

	Population (1,000)	GDP per Capita ($1,000)	Total Emissions (MtCO₂e)[1]	Emissions per Capita	Emissions per ($1,000 GDP)	Emissions % of Total
			→ tons ←			
U.S.	314,112	51.5	6,235	19.8	0.44	13.9
France	65,639	40.9	457	6.9	0.19	1.0
China	1,350,695	6.2	10,976	8.1	2.43	24.5
India	1,236,590	1.5	3,014	2.4	2.2	6.8
World	7,089,269	10.4	44,816	6.3	0.79	—

[1] Million tons CO_2 equivalent.

Source: World Resources Institute, CAIT, **http://cait.wri/.org;** The World Bank Group, 2015, **www.data.worldbank.org /indicators.**

[4] The Kyoto Protocol is a furtherance of the United Nations Framework Convention on Climate Change, which was completed in 1992.

The Kyoto Protocol came into force on February 16, 2005, after being ratified by the requisite number of countries. The agreement required relatively large cutbacks of GHGs by countries of the developed world, but none by developing countries, such as India and China. Exhibit 18.3 shows relevant GHG emission data for the 14 largest emitting signatory countries, and for the total of all countries participating in the Kyoto Protocol (the so-called "Annex B" countries). Overall emissions in 2009 were below the Kyoto targets, but there is a question as to how much of this is attributable to the protocol. Large reductions occurred in Russia and Eastern Europe, mainly because of the general economic contractions in these countries. Many of the other countries experienced economic recessions in the 2000s and 2010s, contributing to the decline. But some efforts, especially in Europe, have had an impact, and in general we may conclude that the protocol has helped to keep the issue on the "front burner" of policy battles around the world.

The agreement included **flexibility mechanisms** that would presumably help countries meet their cutback targets with a lower overall cost. Flexibility approaches include the following:

- International emission trading: Annex B countries could alter their GHG cutback responsibilities by buying or selling emission quantities among themselves.[5] Thus, one country could cut emissions by more than that is required, and sell the excess to another country, which may then cut back by a smaller amount.

- Joint implementation: Annex B countries could undertake joint projects (e.g., a reforestation project in the United States partly funded by another country) and transfer emission allowances on the basis of the projects.

- Clean development mechanism: Annex B countries could finance emission reductions in non–Annex B countries and gain credits toward their GHG cutback responsibilities.

The trading possibilities inherent in these flexibility mechanisms have encouraged the growth of a substantial private sector whose firms specialize in promoting and carrying out these trades.[6]

The Kyoto Protocol was the first effort internationally to address GHG control. Few expected it to make much of a dent in the overall global problem. Its deficiencies have been widely discussed:

- It set quantitative limits on GHG emissions without regard to any specific objective in terms of atmospheric carbon content or future increase in global temperatures.
- It did not involve in any significant way of participation of the countries of the developing world, several of which are becoming major GHG emitters.

---

[5] Annex B countries are those that have committed to some cutback in GHG emissions.

[6] Simply search under "emissions trading" to find the names and business objectives of many of these firms.

The Kyoto Protocol for Limiting Greenhouse Gas Emissions   EXHIBIT 18.3

At a conference held in December 1997 in Kyoto, Japan, the parties to the United Nations Framework Convention on Climate Change agreed to a historic protocol to reduce emissions of GHGs into the earth's atmosphere toward the objective of forestalling the phenomenon of global warming.

Key aspects of the protocol included emission reduction targets for the 38 signatories and timetables for reaching them. The specific limits varied from country to country, as indicated. For most of the industrial countries, the reductions were about 8 percent (7 percent for the United States).

	Emissions (millions TnCO$_2$ equivalent)		
	Base Year	Kyoto Target	2012
Australia	423	457	543
Canada	599	563	699
France	567	521	496
Germany	1,226	1,128	939
Italy	520	478	460
Japan	1,272	1,196	1,343
Netherlands	213	196	192
Poland	564	530	399
Romania	262	241	119
Russian Fed	2,990	2,990	2,295
Spain	287	264	340
Ukraine	925	925	401
U.K.	776	714	586
U.S.	6,103	5,676	6,488
Total of Annex B countries	18,266.3	17,304.3	16,497.3

Source: United Nations Framework Convention on Climate Change, *National greenhouse gas inventory data for the period 1990 – 2012*, November 2014, **http://unfccc.int/resource/docs/2014/sbi /eng/20.pdf.**

- It paid insufficient attention to implementation and enforcement.
- It focused entirely on short-term goals without sufficient consideration of the long-term needs of the global atmosphere and its management.

A New Global Greenhouse Climate Agreement

Many ideas have been put forward for an international plan that will follow the lapsed Kyoto Protocol.[7] Although the exact form of any future agreement

---

[7] For a good discussion of these ideas, see Joseph E. Aldy and Robert N. Stavins (eds.), *Architectures for Agreement, Addressing Global Climate Change in the Post Kyoto World*, Cambridge University Press, Cambridge, U.K., 2007.

is in doubt, the criteria that ought to govern an agreement are reasonably straightforward:

1. The quantitative targets of GHG reductions that should be aimed for, in the short and long runs. Experience with the targets established under the Kyoto Protocol has led to the idea that new negotiations should start by having countries individually commit to quantitative targets.

2. The benefits and costs of achieving these targets, with particular emphasis on having policies and procedures that are cost-effective.

3. Equity concerns in terms of how the burden of emission reductions should be distributed among rich and poor countries.

4. Flexibility concerns in terms of the ability to shift plans in the face of new scientific information, and to change the terms of participation by countries within and outside the agreement.

To these should be added a whole set of considerations dealing with the political and institutional aspects of an agreement, and its implementation. There is widespread acceptance, at least among economists, that for a new GHG treaty to be efficient and cost-effective, it must incorporate incentive-based techniques.

Some have suggested that there be designed a system of transferable GHG emission permits at the international level. Countries would be assigned quantitative targets, much as in the current agreement. Sources within each country would then be given transferable permits, which could be traded within or across country borders, similar to the current European Trading Scheme (ETS). Besides striving for cost-effectiveness, a program of this type could address questions of international equity. The current belief is that it will cost developing countries less, relative to their current wealth, to reduce CO_2 emissions than developed economies. Thus, the direction of transfers would go in general from more developed countries to less developed countries. On top of this, developing countries might be given proportionately larger numbers of permits in the initial distribution. In buying these extra permits, developed nations would be transferring extra amounts of wealth to the developing countries, which they could use to switch to low-carbon development paths.

Whether this type of system could be designed to include all of the major GHG-emitting countries is an open question. One idea could be to first develop a series of regional CAP programs, as in the ETS and the Regional Greenhouse Gas Market of the northeastern United States. Once these markets are functioning smoothly they could be tied together by allowing inter-program trading.

There are also many advocates of an international program of carbon taxes. Levied upstream, at points of fuel production, these taxes would filter through economies and shift prices of goods and services according to their contribution to global warming. Many individual countries, especially those of Europe, have instituted carbon taxes in recent years.[8]

Whether any significant international effort can be mounted to establish a worldwide carbon tax is highly problematic. A tax high enough to produce significant coordinated CO_2 reductions would be especially burdensome in developing countries. Support might be encouraged if the proceeds of the tax could be shared among countries so as to reduce the overall impact on poorer nations. Another suggestion to increase the political palatability of a global carbon tax is to start it off at a relatively low level, with some delay by developing nations (analogous to the Montreal Protocol), and gradually increase it over time.

In international agreements, real questions come up about monitoring and enforcing. Self-monitoring by the individual countries is likely to be the only practical solution to this issue because it is unlikely that countries would willingly permit international monitoring efforts. The United Nations lacks executive power to enforce international environmental agreements. The International Court of Justice (ICJ) acts chiefly as a place for discussing disputes and lacks mechanisms to enforce rulings. This leaves enforcement up to a combination of moral pressure and whatever unilateral actions states might take, such as trade sanctions. Enforcing a tax might be easier to enforce than a CAP program, because a tax can be implemented as a carbon tax on energy producers or importers, whereas a CAP program requires that the quantities of emissions of all sources, and their permit trades, be monitored and reported.

An important factor not mentioned so far is the costs to the various countries of doing nothing: that is, simply adapting to global warming. These costs are likely to place limits on the extent to which any particular country will readily accept CO_2 emission reduction requirements, as no country is likely to want to spend more in control costs than the cost of accommodating to the change. For cooler countries in higher latitudes, with relatively little critical shoreline, adaptation costs may be fairly "modest." Countries in the opposite situation will have very high costs of adapting to higher temperatures and rising sea levels. Countries differ also in terms of agricultural adaptability, the ability to shift crops, crop varieties, cultivation methods, and so on, to maintain production in the face of climate changes. So countries are likely to have very different perceptions about how they will be affected by global warming. The obstacles to an effective international agreement on GHG reduction are many, and the need for creative treaty diplomacy is great.

---

[8] See Jenny Summer, Lori Bird, and Hilary Smith, *Carbon Taxes: A Review of Experience and Policy Design Considerations*, National Renewable Energy Laboratory, Technical Report NREL/TP-6A2-47312, December 2009.

Estimating the Social Cost of Carbon

In Chapter 6 we discussed briefly the concept of **regulatory impact analysis**. For the past 30 years, this type of analysis has been required when federal agencies introduce new regulations, or change existing ones. Essentially the requirement is to estimate the benefits and costs of the regulations, with the presumption that any proposed regulation would not go forward unless **net benefits** were positive. Among the regulations that the contemporary EPA is required to promulgate are those having the objective of reducing future GHGs. Thus it must have some notion of what it is worth to reduce future GHGs by a given amount. The term for this is the **social cost of carbon** (SCC). It is a marginal value: a monetary estimate of the global external (i.e., non-market) costs of one CO_2-equivalent ton of future GHGs.

It's obvious that estimating the value is fraught with difficulties. It requires estimating the long-run future costs of all the impacts expected to occur: more frequent and intense storms, sea-level rise, higher production costs, human health effects, and so on. And these impacts must be expressed in a common metric; usually this is in dollars of reduced future GDP. So estimating the SCC involves dealing with all the uncertainties of climate change, both the uncertainties of scientists who are trying to understand the physical effects and natural and social scientists trying to predict impacts on humans and other elements of the biosphere.

In 2010 a federal working group brought together the results from a large number of climate/economy simulation models used to predict future impacts. The resulting numbers are shown in Table 18.4. The estimates are shown by year and using three different discount rates. For example, one form of carbon emitted in 2015 will result in a stream of damages into the future; when the stream is discounted at a rate of 5 percent then its present value is $12.00. With lower discount rates, the estimated present values of damages are higher. Remember that these numbers are averages of the various simulation runs of all the studies. The estimates go up with time because emissions in later years are assumed to cause greater damages in economies that are already stressed by climate change up to that date.

The last columns shed light on the possibility of extreme outcomes. For example, for 2015 emissions, 95 percent of the studies evaluated showed estimated damages of $116 per ton or less. In other words, 5 percent of the studies predicted more extreme outcomes, that is, damages in excess of $116 per ton.

We have mentioned that the estimates may be useful in guiding regulatory decisions by the EPA. Another is a guide to setting carbon taxes. Recall that a carbon tax of, say, $14 per ton would provide emitters of CO_2 (and CO_2 equivalent), an incentive to abate emissions up to the point where marginal abatement costs are $14 per ton. Since $14 is the SCC, emissions at that point would be at the socially efficient level.

There is at least one dimension of this result that is problematic. It is that the SCC as shown in Table 18.4 are global damage costs, while national policies of

TABLE 18.4   Social Cost of CO_2, 2015–2050* (in 2011 Dollars)

Year	Discount Rate and Statistic			
	5%	3%	2.5%	3%
	Average	Average	Average	95th percentile
2015	$12	$39	$61	$116
2020	13	46	68	137
2025	15	50	74	153
2030	17	55	80	170
2035	20	60	85	187
2040	22	65	92	204
2045	26	70	98	220
2050	28	76	104	235

*The SCC values are dollar-year and emissions-year specific.

Source: U.S. EPA, *SCC Fact Sheet*, Interagency Working Group on Social Cost of Carbon, Nov 2013, **www.epa.gov /climatechange/downloads/EPAactivities.**

carbon taxes, if they are to be politically acceptable, may have to be based on estimates of nation-specific damages.

Biological Diversity

Another problem that we have begun to appreciate in recent years is the worldwide reduction in diversity among the elements of the biological system. This can be discussed at several levels: diversity in the stock of genetic material, species diversity, or diversity among ecosystems. The long-run health of the whole system requires that there be diversity among its parts. Biological uniformity produces inflexibility and weakened ability to respond to new circumstances; diversity gives a system the means to adapt to change.

The human population cannot maintain itself without cultivating certain species of animals and plants. But the continued vigor of this relationship actually depends also on the stock of wild species. This dependence can manifest itself in a variety of ways. About 25 to 50 percent of the **prescription drugs** in the developed societies are derived from plants. Diseases are not static; they evolve in response to efforts made to eradicate them. Thus, wild species of plants constitute a vital source of raw material needed for future medicines. Wild species are also critical for **agriculture.** Through traditional plant and animal breeding, and even more through modern methods of **biotechnology,** genetic material and the qualities they entail may be transferred from wild species into cultivated ones. For example, a species of wild maize resistant to an important crop virus was discovered in a remote corner of Mexico. When transferred to species of domestic corn, this characteristic substantially enhanced the agricultural value of that crop.

The stock of species at any particular time is a result of two processes: the random mutations that create new species of organisms and the forces that determine rates of extinction among existing species. Scientists currently are uncertain about even an estimate for the number of millions of extant species on earth. Approximately 1.5 million have been described. When a species goes extinct, we lose forever whatever valuable qualities that organism may have had. The normal, long-run rate of species extinction has been estimated at about 100 extinctions per million species per year. Thus, this is the normal rate at which the information contained in the species stock vanishes. At several times in the geological past, the rate of extinctions has been very much higher. One of these times was the period, millions of years ago, during which the dinosaurs died off. Another is today. But while the earlier period was the result of natural causes, today's rapid destruction of the stock of species is due primarily to the actions of human beings.

Some species go extinct because they are **overexploited**. But the vast majority is under pressure because of **habitat destruction.** This comes primarily from commercial pressures to exploit other features of the land: logging off the trees for timber or wood, converting the land to agricultural uses, clearing the land for urban expansion, and so on. This has been a particular problem in many developing countries, which contain a disproportionately large share of the world's wild species, but which are also under great pressure to pursue modern economic development.

The information contained in the global stock of genetic capital has consistently been **undervalued**. This is partly because we do not know what is there or what portions of it may turn out to be important in the future. It is also because, almost by definition, it is impossible to know the value of the genes in a species that has gone extinct; we cannot miss something we never realized we had. But primarily the undervaluation of the stock of wild germ plasm is a function of the **institutions** governing the management of wild species. Whereas the market values of conventional products ensure that their production will be pursued with vigor, there are normally no comparable market values for the information contained in the wild gene pool.

In the United States, the Endangered Species Act (ESA) of 1973 was enacted to help preserve individual species. When a species is listed as either "endangered" or "threatened," steps may be undertaken toward its preservation. This includes prohibitions on the "taking" (killing or wounding) of any individual of that species, and a requirement that actions authorized or funded by any federal agency not put in jeopardy the continued existence of the species. This **ESA type of approach** is pursued also in a number of other federal animal protection statutes (e.g., the Bald Eagle Protection Act of 1940, the Marine Mammal Protection Act of 1972, and the Salmon and Steelhead Conservation and Enhancement Act of 1980). Each state also has its own endangered species laws. Although these laws have had some success in preserving individual species, they are relatively ineffective at preserving diversity, which is not a matter of a single species but of a relationship among a large number of species.

The effective maintenance of biodiversity depends on the **maintenance of habitats** in amounts big enough that species may preserve themselves in complex biological equilibria. This involves first identifying valuable habitats and then protecting them from development pressures that are incompatible with preserving the resident species. In the United States, a large network of reserved lands has been preserved in the public domain, national parks, wilderness areas, wildlife refuges, and the like. The fact of the matter is, however, that the world's primary areas of genetic and species abundance and diversity are in developing countries in Central and South America, Africa, and Southeast Asia.[9]

Efforts have been made in some of these countries, sometimes vigorously and sometimes not, to protect areas of high biological value by putting them into some sort of **protected status**—sanctuaries, reserves, parks, and so on. But here the situation is usually much more complicated by high-population pressures. People who are struggling to get enough resources to achieve some degree of economic security may feel that something called biological diversity is not particularly relevant. Land reservation for species preservation is essentially a zoning approach, and it suffers the same fundamental flaw of that policy: it does not reshape the **underlying incentives** that are leading to population pressure on the habitats.

One suggestion that has been made to change this is to create a more complete **system of property rights** over genetic resources. At the present time, property rights are recognized for special breeder stock, genetically modified organisms, and newly developed medicines. This provides a strong incentive for research on new drugs and the development of improved crops. But this incentive does not extend backward to the protection of wild gene plasm, especially in developing countries. Thus, the suggestion is to clarify property rights in wild species and let countries themselves exercise these property rights in world markets for genetic information. By allowing them to sell the rights to parts of the genetic stock, countries would have a way of realizing the values inherent in these stocks and would therefore be motivated to devote more effort and resources to their protection. Such Research Collaborative Agreements (RCA) give countries stronger incentives to inventory and describe species that are still unknown.

In fact, events may be moving in this direction already. A contract was recently signed between Merck and Company, a U.S. pharmaceutical firm, and the Instituto Nacional de Biodiversidad of Costa Rica. The contract calls for an up-front payment of $1 million, plus royalties on discoveries of commercial value, while the Costa Rican agency will undertake steps to catalog and preserve biological resources in that country. The American Cancer Institute has negotiated contracts with Zimbabwe, Madagascar, and the Philippines

[9] The countries especially recognized for biological diversity are Mexico, Colombia, Brazil, Madagascar, South Africa, Ecuador, Venezuela, and Indonesia.

for access to genetic resources in these countries. A British firm named Biotics is functioning as a broker between potential suppliers and buyers of genetic resources.[10]

In some places of the world, a market has developed for the services of endangered species in the form of **ecotourism**. Conservation by landowners and others creates value in the sense that people are willing to pay the landowner for opportunities to observe or photograph species in their preserved natural habitat. Ecuador manages the Galapagos Islands for this benefit.

Especially important is how this type of approach would filter down to affect individuals who are actually using the land. It is highly doubtful if substantial amounts of land could be put off limits to any type of development if **population pressure** continues high. So attention needs to be directed also at developing modes of commercial agriculture that are compatible with genetic and species preservation. Production based on retaining natural habitat requires two things: that cultivators have secure property rights and that there be strong markets for the types of "crops" produced in this kind of system.

Summary

In recent years we have seen the rise of truly global environmental problems, especially those dealing with the disruption of the global atmosphere. In these cases it is as if all the nations of the world were homeowners living around a small lake, each one dependent on the lake for water supply, but each one also using the lake for waste disposal.

The greatest problem facing the global community is climate change, stemming from atmospheric buildup of CO_2 and other "greenhouse gases" that are affecting the earth's radiation balance and leading to an increase in mean global temperatures. Substantial impacts are expected on weather patterns around the globe. These are expected to disrupt agricultural operations in significant ways. A rise in the sea level will have profound impacts on coastal communities. A substantial attack on the phenomenon will require cutting back on the use of fossil fuels. Virtually all countries are dependent to a greater or lesser extent on fossil fuels to power their economies. Thus, we must emphasize cost-effective policies to improve energy efficiency and to switch to fuels that emit less CO_2. As part of this effort, much attention has been given to estimating the social cost of carbon. The Kyoto Protocol was the first major international effort to reduce GHGs. New efforts are underway to structure a more effective agreement.

The destruction of biological diversity is a subtler global problem, but it may be just as costly in the long run. Dealing with this problem will require greater efforts to preserve habitat and develop agriculture that is compatible with species preservation. Effective action will mean doing something about the incentives that currently lead to species destruction.

---

[10] R. David Simpson and Roger A. Sedjo, "Contracts for Transferring Rights to Indigenous Genetic Resources," *Resources*, 109, Fall 1992, Resources for the Future, Washington, D.C., pp. 1–5.

Questions for Further Discussion

1. Many countries are adopting a "wait-and-see" strategy toward CO_2 emissions and atmospheric warming. What would a rational "wait-and-see" strategy look like?

2. In the absence of a worldwide agreement to reduce CO_2 through a carbon tax, how effective might it be if just one country, or a small number of countries, instituted a tax unilaterally?

3. Rather than placing a tax on fuels or the carbon content of fuels, taxes might be put on fuel-using items, such as "gas-guzzling" cars, less efficient appliances, or houses with poor insulation. Which type of tax would be more efficient?

4. Global warming is predicted to affect countries differently, which is one reason it is difficult to get all countries to agree on a global CO_2 treaty. Do you think it will be easier to get agreement *after* the results start showing up in different countries?

5. How many different formulas can you think of for allocating a reduction in global CO_2 among the nations of the world? Compare and contrast these in terms of efficiency and equity. Consider the equiproportionate and equimarginal principles, population, income, etc.

For additional readings and Web sites pertaining to the material in this chapter, see **www.mhhe.com/field7e.**

Chapter 19

International Environmental Agreements

In the last chapter we discussed several global environmental issues. As countries continue to grow, more and more environmental problems will spill beyond national borders—not just these global cases, but also a rising number of environmental externalities inflicted by people in one country on those of another. So while environmental policies continue to evolve within individual countries, there will be a growing need to develop **multicountry** attacks on environmental problems.[1] In this chapter we take a look at some of the economic issues involved in the creation of **international environmental agreements**.[2]

International environmental policy has a distinctly different character from national policies. The most salient difference is that on the international level the available enforcement mechanisms are much weaker than at the national level. Within any country, authoritative regulatory authorities can be called upon to enforce whatever laws are passed, although this does not imply by any means that all environmental laws will be adequately enforced. But on the international level enforcement authorities do not exist. Thus, environmental policy at this level consists essentially of international agreements among sovereign states, where each country pledges to follow certain specified courses of action

---

[1] The international scope of many environmental problems was first highlighted by the 1972 United Nations Conference on the Human Environment (the "Stockholm Conference" or first "earth summit"), which led to the United Nations Environment Program (UNEP) and the "earth summits" of Rio de Janeiro in 1992, Johannesburg in 2002, and Rio+20 in 2012 in Canada.

[2] In writing this chapter we have relied heavily on Scott Barrett, *Environment and Statecraft: The Strategy of Environmental Treaty-Making*, Oxford University Press, Oxford, U.K., 2003. See also his book *Why Cooperate? The Incentive to Supply Global Public Goods*, Oxford University Press, Oxford, U.K., 2007.

regarding emissions reductions or other steps for environmental protection. Enforcement then has to be carried out either through voluntary means such as moral suasion, or else through retaliation by whatever pressure a country or group of countries may be able to exert on recalcitrant countries. Sometimes environmental agreements are incorporated into international trade agreements, so that relaxation of restrictions on the trade of goods and services becomes linked to environmental regulations. For example, regulations pertaining to emissions of vehicles that are used for transport across the Mexican and United States and Canadian borders are part of the North American Free Trade Agreement (NAFTA). Trades restrictions are also part of the Montreal Protocol for reducing ozone-depleting substances.

In this chapter we review some of the main features of international environmental agreements, focusing especially on the incentive situations facing countries that are considering an agreement. The discussion begins with a brief descriptive section that shows the great variety of international environmental agreements that have been concluded to date. It then moves to cases that involve just two countries, followed by the case of multiple-country agreements. The chapter ends with a discussion of an issue that will become increasingly important as national economies continue to grow: the environmental quality implications of **international trade**.

General Issues

The history of international agreements on natural resource matters goes back many centuries, to the time when countries sought to agree on navigation rules to cover ocean passages. In the 20th century, international treaties proliferated as a result of the rapidly expanding list of environmental problems involving multiple countries. Now in the 21st century, climate change dominates treaty negotiations. Table 19.1 shows a partial list of **current multilateral agreements** pertaining to natural and environmental resources. The number of countries involved varies from 3 to 161.

Numerous treaties have been concluded on marine pollution, beginning with oil-pollution agreements and later extending to more general pollution-control measures. Although much attention has been given recently to the issue of protecting the resources of biological diversity, the first international treaties on flora and fauna were actually made decades ago. Now there are many such treaties, including the important 1973 convention on international trade in endangered species (CITES).

International agreements come in several forms:

- A **convention** is an agreement in which countries define a problem and jointly commit to addressing it, but without specifying exactly the concrete steps that will be undertaken to meet its objectives.
- A **protocol** is an agreement that attempts to fill in some of the details of a convention: what specific actions and signatories will undertake, what institutions will be established to implement the agreement, and so on.

TABLE 19.1 Selected International Environmental Agreements

Name of Agreement	Date of Adoption	Date of Entry into Force	Number of Signatories
Marine Pollution			
International Convention for the Prevention of Pollution of the Sea by Oil (as amended 11/4/62 and 10/21/69)	1954	1958	69
Agreement for Cooperation in Dealing with Pollution of the North Sea by Oil	1969	1969	8
International Convention on Civil Liability for Oil Pollution Damage (as amended)	1969	1975	64
International Convention Relating to Intervention on the High Seas in Cases of Oil Pollution Casualties	1969	1975	75
Convention on the Prevention of Marine Pollution by Dumping of Wastes and Other Matter ("London Dumping")	1972	1975	82
International Convention for the Prevention of Pollution from Ships, 1973	1973	1983	113
Convention on the Prevention of Marine Pollution from Land-Based Sources	1974	1978	13
Convention for the Protection of the Mediterranean Sea Against Pollution	1976	1978	21
International Rivers			
Protocol Concerning the Constitution of an International Commission for the Protection of the Mosel Against Pollution	1961	1962	3
Agreement Concerning the International Commission for the Protection of the Rhine Against Pollution	1963	1965	6
Convention on the Protection of the Rhine Against Chemical Pollution	1976	1979	6
Convention Creating the Niger Basin Authority and Protocol Relating to the Development Fund of the Niger Basin	1980	1982	9
Flora and Fauna			
European Treaty on the Conservation of Birds Useful to Agriculture	1902	1905	10
Convention Relative to the Preservation of Fauna and Flora in Their Natural State	1933	1936	10
Convention of Nature Protection and Wildlife Preservation in the Western Hemisphere	1940	1942	22

TABLE 19.1   *(Continued)*

Name of Agreement	Date of Adoption	Date of Entry into Force	Number of Signatories
Flora and Fauna			
International Convention for the Regulation of Whaling (as amended)	1946	1948	40
International Convention for the Protection of Birds	1950	1963	15
International Plant Protection Convention	1951	1952	111
International Convention for the High Seas Fisheries of the North Pacific Ocean (as amended)	1952	1953	3
Convention on Fishing and Conservation of the Living Resources of the High Seas	1958	1966	57
International Convention for the Protection of New Varieties of Plants (as amended)	1961	1968	46
Convention on the African Migratory Locust	1962	1963	16
African Convention on the Conservation of Nature and Natural Resources	1968	1969	43
European Convention for the Protection of Animals During International Transport	1968	1971	20
Benelux Convention on the Hunting and Protection of Birds (as amended)	1970	1972	3
Convention on Wetlands of International Importance Especially as Waterfowl Habitat	1971	1975	124
Convention for Conservation of Antarctic Seals	1972	1978	12
Convention on International Trade in Endangered Species of Wild Fauna and Flora	1973	1975	155
Agreement on Conservation of Polar Bears	1973	1976	5
Convention on Conservation of Nature in the South Pacific	1976	1990	6
Convention on Migratory Species	1979	1983	75
Convention on Biological Diversity	1992	1993	178
Nuclear			
Convention on Third Party Liability in the Field of Nuclear Energy (as amended)	1960	1968	16
Vienna Convention of Civil Liability for Nuclear Damage	1963	1977	35

(Continued)

TABLE 19.1 *(Continued)*

Name of Agreement	Date of Adoption	Date of Entry into Force	Number of Signatories
Nuclear			
Treaty Banning Nuclear Weapon Tests in the Atmosphere, in Outer Space and Under Water	1963	1963	117
Treaty on the Prohibition of the Emplacement of Nuclear Weapons and Other Weapons of Mass Destruction on the Sea-Bed and the Ocean Floor and in the Subsoil Thereof	1971	1972	79
Convention on Early Notification of a Nuclear Accident	1986	1986	97
Air Pollution			
Convention on Long-Range Transboundary Air Pollution	1979	1983	49
Protocol to the 1979 Convention on Long-Range Transboundary Air Pollution on Long-Term Financing of the Co operative Programme for Monitoring and Evaluation of the Long-Range Transmission of Air Pollutants in Europe (EMEP)	1984	1988	38
Protocol to the 1979 Convention on Long-Range Transboundary Air Pollution on the Reduction of Sulphur Emissions or Their Transboundary Fluxes by at Least 30 Percent	1985	1987	22
Protocol to the 1979 Convention on Long-Range Transboundary Air Pollution Concerning the Control of Emissions of Nitrogen Oxides or Their Transboundary Fluxes	1988	1991	29
Vienna Convention for the Protection of the Ozone Layer	1985	1988	176
Montreal Protocol on Substances that Deplete the Ozone Layer	1987	1989	175
Kyoto Protocol to the United Nations Framework Convention on Climate Change	1999	2005	140
ASEAN Agreement on Transboundary Haze Pollution	2002	2003	8
Miscellaneous			
The Antarctic Treaty	1959	1961	44
European Convention on the Protection of the Archaeological Heritage	1969	1970	25

TABLE 19.1   *(Continued)*

Name of Agreement	Date of Adoption	Date of Entry into Force	Number of Signatories
Miscellaneous			
Ramsar Convention on Wetlands	1971	1975	124
Convention on the Prohibition of the Development, Production and Stockpiling or Bacteriological (Biological) and Toxin Weapons, and on Their Destruction	1972	1975	145
Convention Concerning the Protection of the World Cultural and Natural Heritage	1972	1975	98
Treaty for Amazonian Cooperation	1978	1980	8
Convention on the Conservation of Antarctic Marine Living Resources	1980	1982	21
Convention Concerning Occupational Safety and Health and the Working Environment	1981	1983	34
United Nations Convention on the Law of the Sea	1982	—	161
Convention of the Regulation of Antarctic Mineral Resource Activities	1988	—	17
Basel Convention on the Control of the Transboundary Movements of Hazardous Wastes and Their Disposal	1989	1992	142
Stockholm Convention on Persistent Organic Pollutants	2001	2004	176

Source: United Nations Environment Programme, *Register of International Treaties and Other Agreements in the Field of the Environment*, December 2005.

- A **treaty** is a fully developed agreement specifying problems, actions to be undertaken by signatories, steps to be taken under implementation and enforcement, and so on.

A **bilateral agreement** is one entered into by two countries to manage a particular resource. For example, the China-Australia Migratory Bird Agreement and the Columbia River Treaty between the United States and Canada.

Multilateral agreements, as the name implies, are agreements among groups of countries with the objective of managing an important resource. This includes **regional agreements**, which are groups of propinquitous countries whose concerns focus on a resource of local interest.

A standard international agreement will contain provisions specifying the actions to be undertaken by each signatory country, as well as numerous institutional and logistical matters, such as what kind of governing agency is to be established, how its work is to be funded, what information is to be shared, and so on.

Many of the multilateral treaties are actually regional in scope. This includes, for example, the treaties concerning water- and air-pollution control among the countries of Europe. The United Nations has sponsored a number of regional agreements involving countries bordering particular seas (Mediterranean Sea, Red Sea, southeastern Pacific Ocean, western African coastal waters, Caribbean Sea, etc.). Besides the multilateral treaties there are hundreds of bilateral treaties, addressing the environmental problems of just two countries. The United States and Canada have concluded a number of bilateral agreements, including agreements dealing with acid rain and with the management of the Great Lakes. The United States and Mexico also have worked out several environmental agreements dealing with hazardous waste shipments, the use of the Colorado and Rio Grande rivers, and other matters. The European Commission on Environment oversees agreements among the member countries of the EU.

The Economics of International Agreements

When international agreements are being negotiated, the focus is usually on political issues. This is natural, as what is going on are complex negotiations among sovereign states. But underlying the political interactions—national sovereignty, political assertiveness, creative diplomacy, and so on—lie many bedrock economic factors that affect the **perceived benefits and costs** accruing to the different participants and the incentives they have for entering into environmental agreements. In the next few sections we discuss some of these issues.

Bilateral Agreements

First consider the case of just two countries—call them Country A and Country B. B is downwind from A, so sulfur dioxide (SO_2) emissions from A contribute to acid rain both at home and in B. In B, SO_2 emissions contribute to acid rain only in that country; because of prevailing wind patterns, there is no reciprocal acid rain externality inflicted by B upon A.[3] This situation is pictured in Figure 19.1. It shows the marginal abatement costs in A (MAC_A) and the marginal damage functions associated with the emissions of that country. Marginal damages arising in A itself are shown as MD_A, whereas MD_T are aggregate marginal damages for both A and B. The marginal damages in B from A's emissions, in other words, are ($MD_T - MD_A$). If A were managing its emissions without regard to the externalities produced in B, it would regard point e_1 as the efficient level of emissions.

But for emissions in A to be internationally efficient, it is necessary to take into account the effects on B. The **"globally efficient"** level of emissions is e_2. The added attainment cost in A to achieve this further reduction in emissions is an amount equal to the area ($d + f$). But this is more than offset by a reduction in damages totaling ($c + d + f$), of which f represents damage reduction in A, whereas ($d + c$) is damage reduction in B.

We saw in Chapter 10 that negotiations between polluters and those damaged can result in efficient emission levels, given that property rights are clearly defined and that transactions costs are minimal. On the international level, direct

---

[3] This situation is characteristic of prevailing wind patterns that sweep across North America, and Europe, from west to east.

FIGURE 19.1 **Bilateral Transboundary Pollution and the Economics of Reaching an Agreement**

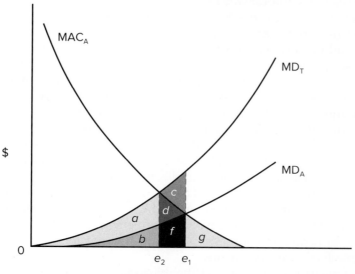

Emissions of country A

negotiations between private parties involved are essentially ruled out, because under international law private citizens of one country do not have the right to sue private citizens in another country. Instead, negotiations must be carried out among political authorities of the two countries. This is where diplomacy comes in because, in the example given previously, the reduction in A's emissions from e_1 to e_2 involves negative net benefits *in that country*—added costs of $(d + f)$ and reduced damages of only f. So, in effect, authorities would be asking people in Country A to make a sacrifice to benefit people in another country. This kind of thing happens all the time within individual countries. But across countries the institutions of policy are weaker, depending essentially on diplomatic skills and whatever international sanctioning can be carried out through moral, economic, or political means.

According to the precedents in international law, cases like this are supposed to be covered by a **polluter pays principle** (PPP). The *Trail Smelter* case of 1935 is an important source of that precedent. Trail Smelter was a metal refinery in British Columbia whose SO_2 discharges damaged farm crops across the border in the United States. The tribunal finding in favor of the farmers stated that under the principles of international law, "no State has the right to use or permit the use of its territory in such a manner as to cause injury by fumes in or to the territory of another."[4] This declaration was embodied in the Declaration of the

[4] Quoted in William A. Nitze, "Acid-Rain: A United States Perspective," in Daniel Barstow Magraw (ed.), *International Law and Pollution*, University of Pennsylvania Press, Philadelphia, 1991, p. 346.

1972 United Nations Conference on the Human Environment (the first "earth summit"), which covered all types of transboundary pollution. Most international agreements seek to incorporate the PPP.

But because international agreements are voluntary, it may be supposed that individual countries will never sign any agreement that makes them worse off. In other words, all prospective signatories must regard the agreement as leaving them at least as well off as they would be without it. In our example, this means that the two countries may have to shift partially to a **"victim pays principle"** (VPP). The net loss to A in going from e_1 to e_2 would have to be compensated by Country B. Country A has added abatement costs of $(d + f)$ in going from e_1 to e_2, but it also experiences added benefits (reduced damages) of f, so its extra costs are equal to d. Because B's damage reduction totals $(c + d)$, it could compensate A for these costs and still be ahead by an amount equal to c.

It is not straightforward politically for countries to make payments of this sort (sometimes called **side payments**) as part of an environmental agreement. They sometimes do occur, however. For example, the convention on controlling chlorine pollution in the Rhine River involved payments from downstream countries to sources in upstream countries. Numerous treaties for allocating water rights have involved direct payments.

Rather than direct payments, countries may be able to arrange side payments by shaping their normal trade agreements. Countries that are trying to reach environmental agreements will usually be involved in normal commercial interactions. Side payments can thus be arranged by altering some of these trade interactions. Hilary Sigman has shown that the greater the interaction among countries in terms of trade, the lower the pollution levels in shared rivers.[5] This presumably happens because countries that have a lot of mutual trade have more leverage over one another to conclude formal or informal environmental agreements.[6]

Multilateral Agreements

Consider now a situation where a number of countries contribute to an environmental problem that affects all of them. Examples are acid rain pollution stemming from SO_2 emissions, pollution of a regional sea by riparian countries, stratospheric ozone depletion through emissions of chlorofluorocarbons (CFCs), and the greenhouse effect stemming from CO_2 emissions. In these cases the damages suffered by each country are related to the level of total emissions, present and probably past, of all the countries. From an economic standpoint there are both **efficiency** and **equity** issues in these types of international agreements. There is the basic efficiency question of balancing overall benefits and costs. For

---

[5] Hilary Sigman, "Does Trade Promote Environmental Coordination? Pollution in International Rivers," *Contributions in Economic Analysis and Policy*, Vol. 3, Issue 2, Article 2, 2004.

[6] In addition, John Krutilla's early study of the Columbia River Treaty between the United States and Canada shows that the distribution of costs in the treaty was primarily related to the desire of the United States to stimulate economic development in Canada. See John V. Krutilla, *The Columbia River Treaty: A Study of the Economics of International River Basin Development*, Johns Hopkins Press, Baltimore, MD, 1968.

most international agreements, especially the truly global ones, there are enormous difficulties in estimating total global benefits with any accuracy. The impacts are too massive, and there are extraordinarily difficult problems of trying to compare benefits across countries that are in very different economic circumstances. So on the benefit side we usually settle for an enumeration of the physical impacts of various environmental changes and some idea of how these impacts might be distributed among countries. This means that most of the emphasis is likely to be placed on abatement costs and their distribution.

There are two major issues related to cost: (1) what methods to adopt in various countries to meet the performance required by the agreements and (2) how to share the overall costs among the participating countries. Of course, the questions are related because cost-effective measures undertaken by signatory countries can substantially reduce the costs of the overall program that must be shared. The importance of cost distribution arises because these global emission control agreements supply **global public goods**. The benefits accruing to any particular country from, say, a 20 percent cut in CO_2 will be the same no matter where, and by whom, the CO_2 is reduced.[7] Thus, each country has some incentive to get other countries to bear as much of the total global abatement costs as they can. The incentive difficulties are very similar to those we discussed when introducing the concept of **public goods** in Chapter 4. They can be illustrated with a simple numerical example.

Suppose a country (call it "Country A") is trying to decide whether to invest $10 billion in reducing CO_2 emissions. These emissions contribute to a global problem of temperature increases. Suppose that the proposed action is part of a multilateral effort by countries all around the world to reduce global emissions by getting each country to reduce its emissions. There are three interesting situations that might occur. The following tabulation shows the benefits and costs to Country A in each of these cases:

Situation	Costs	Benefits	Net Benefits
1. All countries agree to reduce emissions.	10	20	10
2. No agreement is reached.	0	−5	−5
3. All other countries agree to reduce emissions, but Country A does not.	0	19	19

If all countries follow the agreement, Country A devotes $10 billion to control costs and then experiences, for example, $20 billion in benefits. The net benefits to Country A in this case are $10 billion.

If there is no agreement, however, Country A has no control costs. But it now experiences negative benefits, in the form of environmental costs, of $5 billion. Its net benefits in this case are therefore $5 billion. It would seem rational for Country A to be part of the global agreement.

[7] This does not mean that the benefits will be the same for all countries—we know this is not true because of the way the global meteorological system works—only that the effects on any particular country are invariant to the source of the reduction.

But there is a third possible situation. Country A may try to take advantage of an agreement entered into by all the other countries. It could do so by staying out of the agreement and experiencing zero control costs. Its benefits would then appear to be $19 billion (a billion less than if it were to join the agreement because it won't be cutting back its own emissions), so its net benefit would be $19 billion. It can gain with an agreement, but it could gain even more by staying out of the agreement put together by the other countries. In this case it is **free riding** on the control efforts of the others.

The problem is, if one country perceives that it could better its circumstances by trying to free ride, other countries can have the same perception. But in that case there would be no agreement. Situation C can arise when a country joins an agreement at an international level, but domestic regulations or legislation prevent the private firms in that country from adopting the treaty's protocols.

The Distribution of Costs

The control costs that a country experiences can be affected in three ways:

1. In the choices it makes about reducing its own emissions, for example, through strict command-and-control measures or through greater reliance on incentive-based policies. This factor is important whether or not a country is part of a large multilateral agreement.
2. Through the choice of the rules chosen in an international agreement as to how overall emission reductions will be distributed among countries.
3. Through payments made by some countries to others as part of an international agreement to help offset costs in the recipient countries. These are transfer payments, sometimes called, in the jargon of economics, **side payments**.

Side payments can take many forms. In the Montreal Protocol dealing with global CFC reductions, discussed later in this chapter, the advanced economies agreed to help the developing countries through **technology transfer**, a process whereby the recipient countries are aided financially and technically to adapt and adopt technologies produced in the developed countries for reducing CFC use.

Bargaining Issues

Numerical examples such as those used in the last section are useful to depict the incentives facing individual countries that might be considering an international environmental agreement. But it's impossible to use them to predict the results of such agreements because international negotiations on environmental treaties are only one dimension of the full set of international interactions among countries. How an individual country behaves in bargaining over, for example, a treaty reducing CO_2 emissions depends not only on the merits of that particular problem but also on the whole gamut of international relationships in which it is involved. If it is involved simultaneously in negotiations on other matters, it may be more concerned with the total outcome and be willing to compromise in some areas in return for concessions in others. In addition, when countries are involved in many negotiations, they may be concerned particularly with shoring up their reputations as **hard bargainers**, which may lead them to behave in certain cases in ways that look to be inconsistent with their self-interest. The outcomes of treaty negotiations depend on context and the **strategic possibilities** that the times have made available, which is another reason we use the simple examples of the previous section for depicting the underlying economic logic of international agreements and not for actually predicting events.

Cost-Effectiveness in Multinational Agreements

The previous discussion was couched in terms of an international agreement to secure certain emission reductions from each of the participating countries. This is the way most international agreements are shaped; there is a strong bias toward treating each country in the same way by applying the same reduction goals to each.

We have discussed the efficiency aspects of this approach many times. The main problem is that it does not take advantage of differences in marginal abatement costs among sources, meaning countries in this case. To accomplish this would require larger cutbacks from nations with relatively low marginal abatement costs and less reduction from those with higher costs. But these non-uniform reductions appear to run counter to the principle of treating everybody alike. Suppose each of two countries would benefit the same amount from cutbacks in emissions, but have different marginal abatement cost functions. These are pictured in Figure 19.2. The marginal abatement costs of Country A rise much more steeply than those of Country B. Current emissions are 100 from Country A and 80 from Country B. An agreement requiring a uniform 50 percent reduction would put A at 40 and B at 50. But the costs of achieving

FIGURE 19.2   **Cost-Effectiveness in International Agreements**

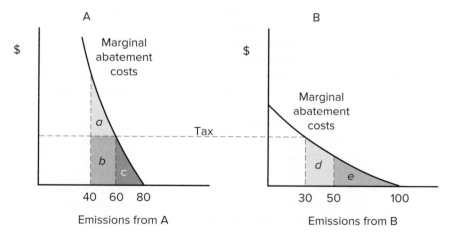

this would be much higher for A $(a + b + c)$ than for B $(d + e)$. Country A might very well fail to agree with uniform reductions when there would be such a large discrepancy in total abatement costs. If it were desired nonetheless to specify a treaty in terms of specific cutbacks from each, they could perhaps be set so that the total abatement costs of each country were the same (assuming each country had reliable information about the other country's abatement costs), but this would violate the uniform emission reduction principle, and it would not be cost-effective.

When abatement costs differ among countries, in other words, it will be difficult to achieve cost-effectiveness if there is strong allegiance to the same type of equiproportionate rule.

So, although incorporating country differences in abatement abilities increases the economic efficiency of a treaty, negotiating those differences takes more time and, thus, increases the costs of the negotiation process. One possible way of doing this might be to institute a global **transferable discharge permit** (TDP) system, whereby the number of permits given out in the initial distribution met some equiproportionate reduction principle, with trading then moving the distribution of permits toward one that more nearly satisfied the equimarginal rule. Whether this is even remotely feasible in today's international political climate is highly doubtful.

A Multilateral Success Story: The Montreal Protocol

One outstanding success in achieving a meaningful multilateral agreement is the 1987 Montreal Protocol on Substances that Deplete the Ozone Layer.

The Physical Problem

At sea level, ozone is a pollutant produced when emissions of hydrocarbons and nitrogen oxides interact in the presence of sunlight. Various health problems and agricultural crop damages have been traced to elevated levels of surface ozone. But most of the ozone in the earth's atmosphere is located in the stratosphere, a zone extending from about 10 km to about 50 km in altitude. This stratospheric ozone is critical in maintaining the earth's radiation balance. The atmosphere surrounding the earth essentially acts as a filter for incoming electromagnetic radiation. The atmospheric gas responsible for this is ozone, which blocks a large percentage of incoming low-wavelength, or ultraviolet, radiation.

Significant ozone reduction has been found throughout the entire stratosphere, although depletion is concentrated over Antarctica, that is, the hole in the ozone. Ozone disappearance is linked to a variety of manufactured chemicals, which, released at ground level, slowly migrated up to higher altitudes. The culprits are substances called **halocarbons**, chemicals composed of carbon atoms in combination with atoms of chlorine, fluorine, iodine, and bromine. The primary halocarbons are called **chlorofluorocarbons**, which have molecules consisting of combinations of carbon, fluorine, and chlorine atoms. Carbon tetrachloride and methyl chloroform also are implicated in ozone destruction.

CFCs were developed in the 1930s as a replacement for the refrigerants in use at the time. Unlike those they replaced, CFCs are extremely stable, nontoxic, and inert relative to the electrical and mechanical machinery in which they are used. Thus, their use spread quickly as refrigerants and also as propellants for aerosols (hair sprays, deodorants, insecticides), industrial agents for making polyurethane and polystyrene foams, and industrial cleaning agents and solvents. Halons are widely used as fire suppressors. When these substances were introduced, attention was exclusively focused on their benefits; there was no evidence that they could have long-run impacts on the atmosphere. But the very stable nature of these gases allows them to migrate very slowly in the atmosphere. After surface release, they drift up through the troposphere into the stratosphere, where they begin a long process of ozone destruction.

Current research indicates that there are two main sources of damage to humans: **health impacts** and **agricultural crop losses**. Health damages are related to the increased incidence of skin cancers and eye disease. The dose–response relationships developed by the Environmental Protection Agency (EPA) indicate that for each 1 percent increase in UV_B radiation, basal-cell and squamous-cell cancer cases would increase by 1 percent and 2 percent, respectively, while melanoma skin cancers would increase by less than 1 percent and cataracts by about 0.2 percent.[8] Increased UV_B radiation also can be expected to increase food production costs because of the physical damages it produces in growing plants. Damages also are expected in other parts of the earth's physical ecosystem.

International Response

The potential seriousness of the ozone-depletion problem has concentrated people's minds and led to some relatively vigorous policy responses. Initially several countries took **unilateral actions**. In 1978, the United States and several other countries (Canada, Sweden, Norway, Denmark) banned CFCs in aerosol cans, but not as a refrigerant. In the 1980s, the continued scientific evidence of ozone depletion led to international action. Under the auspices of the United Nations, 24 nations signed in 1987 the *Montreal Protocol on Substances That Deplete the Ozone Layer*. The agreement committed these nations to phase out the production and consumption of ozone-depleting substances. In some cases the phaseout periods were preceded by a consumption freeze. Soon after the original agreement was signed, it became clear that the problem was getting worse, partly because some large CFC-producing countries had not signed the original agreement. Thus, in subsequent amendments countries agreed to phase out the production of CFCs completely by the year 2000, to add carbon tetrachloride and methyl chloroform to the list, and to introduce a longer-run schedule for phasing out hydrochlorofluorcarbons (HCFCs). Additional countries signed

---

[8] U.S. Environmental Protection Agency, *Regulatory Impact Analysis: Protection of Stratospheric Ozone,* Vol. II, Appendix E, Washington, D.C., 1987, pp. E3–E4.

TABLE 19.2 Phaseout Schedules Contained in the Montreal Protocol and Subsequent Amendments

Substance	Developed Countries Consumption Freeze	Developed Countries Phaseout	Developing Countries Consumption Freeze	Developing Countries Phaseout
Chlorofluorocarbons (CFCs)	1 July 1989	1 January 1996	1 July 1999	1 January 2010
Halons	—	1 January 1994	1 January 2002	1 January 2010
Other fully halogenated CFCs	—	1 January 1996	—	1 January 2010
Carbon tetrachloride	—	1 January 1996	—	1 January 2010
Methyl chloroform	1 January 1993	1 January 1996	1 January 2003	1 January 2015
Hydrochlorofluorocarbons (HCFCs)	1 January 1996	1 January 2030	1 January 2016	1 January 2040
Methyl bromide	1 January 1995	1 January 2005	1 January 2002	1 January 2015

Source: United Nations Development Program, *Montreal Protocol*, http://www.undp.org/seed/eap/Montreal/Montreal .htm.

the agreement in subsequent years, so that by 2012 the agreement had been ratified by 197 countries, including India and China.

Table 19.2 shows the consumption freeze and phaseout schedules for the main ozone-depleting substances covered in the agreement. One of its important features is that it treats developed and developing countries differently: the latter have delayed phaseout schedules relative to the former, in deference to their needs to foster economic growth.

The Montreal Protocol has been a success in many ways:

- It has found wide agreement among nations of the world.
- It very effectively focused attention on the burgeoning body of scientific evidence of ozone depletion, using it to motivate political agreement.
- It created conditions where both developed and developing countries could find agreement.
- Currently, it provides a model for future international agreements.

The protocol deals essentially with a restricted set of substances. In all producing countries, the CFC-producing industry is composed of a few large chemical companies. So international policy has been driven not only by scientific results, but also by international competition in this industry.

As of the 25th anniversary (2007), the Montreal Protocol appears to have been very successful and is on a path to continue well into the 21st century. The overall abundance of ozone depleting substances continues to decline.[9] Scientists are predicting that the ozone hole will be substantially diminished by 2070. Note the very long time lag between policy steps and rectification of the problem.

[9] WMO (World Meteorological Organization), *Scientific Assessment of Ozone Depletion: 2014*, Global Ozone Research and Monitoring Project-Report No. 55, 416 pp., Geneva, Switzerland, 2014.

The Economics of CFC Controls

In economic terms, the problem here was similar to the phasing out of leaded gasoline. The objective was reasonably clear and widely shared; the basic problem was how to bring it about in different countries. In advanced economies, the main focus has been put on developing **substitute chemicals** that will perform the same tasks as CFCs—as refrigerants, cleaning agents, and so on—but have little or no ozone-depleting impact. Among the developed countries a major factor driving the agreement and its amendments was the **cost of developing these substitutes**, together with the costs of changeover from the old to the new chemicals. Some substances may be simply "drop-in" substitutes, whereas others will require getting rid of old capital equipment (refrigerators, air conditioners, etc.) and installing new equipment.

The main provisions of the Montreal Protocol are the following:

- Requirements for individual countries to **phase out** the production and consumption of designated substances.
- A **multilateral fund** into which industrialized countries could contribute funds that would be used to help developing countries achieve the control measures specified in the agreement.
- A provision for **trade restrictions**, banning trade between signatories and nonsignatories in designated ozone-depleting chemicals. It also bans trade in products containing these substances, such as refrigerators and air conditioners.

The latter two provisions help explain why the protocol, originally signed by only a handful of countries, has now been acceded to by almost all the countries of the world.

To meet the conditions of the protocol, all CFC-producing countries had to phase out their production levels. The policy enacted in the United States was to create declining production quotas for each of the firms producing CFCs, quotas that would eventually reach zero. To reap the benefits of the differential costs of reducing CFC output, these production quotas were made transferable, similar to the transferable quota program that was used in the phasing out of leaded gasoline.

A major problem with setting production ceilings in this way was that it could lead to unwarranted increases in profits for current manufacturers of CFCs. In effect it gave firms in the industry, which may have been operating as rivals, a way of acting like monopolists. Figure 19.3 illustrates this with a simple market model. It shows a typical downward-sloping demand curve for CFCs, together with a flat marginal cost curve. Left to itself, competitive forces would lead to a production level of q_1 and a price that equals marginal production costs. But if public authorities limit production to q_2, the price will increase to p_2, which is substantially above production costs. Thus, an amount equal to area a becomes potential **excess profits** earned in the industry because of the output restrictions.

To tighten CFC controls and phase out CFCs faster, the United States adopted a tax on the production of CFCs. In theory, a tax equal to $(p_2 - p_1)$ would transfer

FIGURE 19.3 **Government-Imposed Production Limitations Lead to Monopoly Profits**

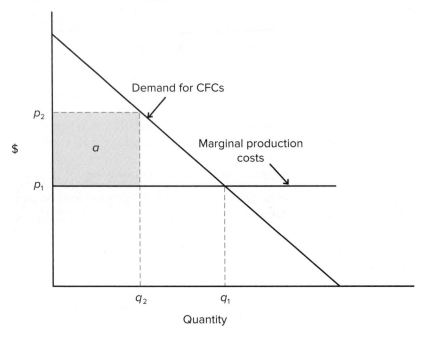

all of the excess profits to the public. The funds then could be used for any number of purposes, perhaps put into general revenues or used specifically to help the CFC conversion process.

The system that was adopted established a base tax rate, then set different taxes on the various ozone-depleting chemicals according to the formula:

$$\text{Tax rate} = \text{Base rate} \times \text{Ozone-depleting potential}^{10}$$

The base rate was originally set at $1.37 per pound but has since been increased. The rate in 2012 was $13.00 per pound.

The 1990 Clean Air Act Amendments contained a number of other parts on ozone depletion. They established a phaseout program for HCFCs, with production to be eliminated by 2030. They established a national recycling program for CFCs used in refrigerators and air conditioners, and they introduced prohibitions on the venting of CFCs from equipment currently containing these substances.

In an earlier chapter we talked about how lead trading was used to reduce the overall cost of switching to no-lead gas. The Montreal Protocol contains the same type of approach for switching out of the production of substances

---

[10] The ozone-depleting potential (ODP) of a substance is a number showing its relative ability to destroy atmospheric ozone. CFC-11 has an ODP of 1.0, and other substances range upward and downward from this.

controlled by the agreement. This is the trading of **emission reduction credits** among countries. Thus, if a country failed to meet its required production cutback because of the needs of "industrial rationalization," it was supposed to offset the excess emissions by getting comparable reductions in other countries.

Although phasing out the production of some material might sound like a simple task, this is not really true. CFCs are produced throughout the world, so enforcement runs into important international complications. Reducing the production of virgin CFCs also has been made more difficult by the need to capture and recycle the existing stock of CFCs in use. On problems of implementation, see Exhibit 19.1.

Rehabilitating the Ozone Layer   EXHIBIT **19.1**

To meet the conditions of the Montreal Protocol, countries have had to find ways of stopping people from using a chemical that has become widely used throughout the economy. The huge, modern air-conditioning industry, among others, has been built on CFCs, the wonder class of chemicals that was developed in the 1930s. There are several substantial problems in phasing out CFC use. One of these is simply enforcing a ban on the material. Smuggling can become a problem, as users attempt to procure supplies through clandestine channels. Legal provisions put in place for handling the chemical have to be monitored and enforced. Country performance has to be assessed and judgments made about possible compliance.

A second issue is the substitutions that are developed to replace CFCs. Industry has substituted large amount of HCFCs (hydrofluorocarbons: molecules containing hydrogen in addition to carbon, chlorine, and fluorine) for the earlier CFCs. These have substantially less impact on ozone depletion, but they are still potent greenhouse gases, as were CFCs. Thus in 2007 the Montreal Protocol was amended to include HCFCs, and a phaseout schedule was adopted for this class of chemicals.

In response to the HCFC phaseout, and the continued strong worldwide growth in demand for refrigeration and air conditioning, there is now a major switch occurring toward HFCs (hydrofluorocarbons: molecules that contain only one or few fluorine atoms). This will reduce stratospheric chlorine even more; however, HFCs are very strong global warming chemicals.

So now the emphasis has shifted to finding substitutes for HFCs. Numerous countries have proposed that the Montreal Protocol be expanded to include an HFC phaseout. The Environmental Protection Agency (EPA) has a program to identify technical substitutes for HFCs that would be relevant to all countries around the globe.[a]

This cascade of chemical substitutions and phaseouts shows the difficulties of controlling the use of chemicals that are under strong commercial demand but have important environmental impacts.

[a] See U.S. Environmental Protection Agency, *Recent International Developments in Saving the Ozone Layer*, October 14, 2011, **http://www.epa.gov/ozone/intpol/mpagreement.html**.

Summary

With environmental issues becoming more international in scope and significance, there will be increasing interest among countries to address these issues with international agreements. International agreements are much more problematic than domestic policies because enforcement is much weaker on the international level. International externalities are essentially of two types. In the first, one country's pollution causes damage in another country. Here the problem of who pays (polluter or victim) when agreements are negotiated is of primary relevance. In the second, each country's emissions affect all countries, including the home country itself. Here the basic problem is how to get individual countries to forgo attempts to free ride on the control efforts of others. The strength of the incentive to free ride depends on a country's perceived benefits and costs of an international agreement, together with whatever "side payments," money subsidies, technology transfers, and so on, are part of the agreement.

One successful multilateral agreement has been the Montreal Protocol. Depletion of the earth's protective ozone layer has been a result of the widespread use of chlorofluorocarbons (CFCs) for refrigerants, solvents, and other uses. What once were regarded as miracle chemicals now have turned out to be life threatening. The increased ultraviolet radiation that use of CFCs produces at the earth's surface will increase skin cancers and eye cataracts and have a substantial impact on agricultural production. Chemical companies have had success in developing substitutes for CFCs. This greatly facilitated the signing of the Montreal Protocol, an international agreement among most of the nations of the world that is leading to a phaseout of the production and consumption of CFCs over the next few decades. One of the factors contributing to the success of the Montreal Protocol is that developing countries were given more time for the phaseout than developed countries.

Questions for Further Discussion

1. Following are illustrative numbers indicating benefits and costs to Country A of taking specific actions on an international treaty to reduce CO_2 emissions. The choice is either to adhere to the CO_2 emissions cutbacks called for by the treaty or to disregard the treaty.

	Costs	Benefits	Net Benefits
All countries adhere to treaty	10	20	10
No countries adhere to treaty	0	−5	−5
Other countries adhere to treaty, Country A does not	0	19	19

What is the incentive for Country A to free ride on the abatement efforts of other countries? If all countries become free riders, what is the result?

2. We talked about "side payments" given to countries to lower the costs to them of joining international environmental agreements. What types of side payments might be effective?

3. What is free-riding in the context of international agreements and what might be some ways of overcoming it?

4. "International environmental agreements are very much shaped by the fact that enforcement on the international level is difficult, if not impossible." Discuss.

5. When CFCs were first introduced 50 years ago, their benefits were obvious, and nobody appreciated the long-run impacts they might have. How do we guard ourselves against unforeseen long-run effects such as this?

For additional readings and Web sites pertaining to the material in this chapter, see **www.mhhe.com/field7e**.

Chapter 20

Globalization

Few economic stories have caught the public attention and imagination more in recent years than the phenomenon called **globalization**. Globalization appears to involve inexorable, worldwide forces that are producing fundamental changes in the way people live. Proponents point out the advantages of globalization and the positive impacts it can have on the welfare of people in diverse circumstances around the world. Critics stress the economic and social threats to which many people will be exposed as globalization rolls onward in apparently ever strengthening waves.

Our subject in this chapter will be the environmental implications of globalization. We will first look at the kinds of changes that globalization entails, then discuss a number of ways in which globalization and environmental issues appear to be closely interwoven.

Dimensions of Globalization

First let us be clear about what globalization actually is. Globalization has a number of dimensions:

- Increasing trade among nations: Over the last 60 years, the annual growth rate of total economic activity in the world has been about 3.5 percent; the annual growth rate in total global exports has been about 6.2 percent. In other words, international trade has grown about twice as fast as overall economic growth. Economies are becoming increasingly interconnected through trade.

- A part of the trend is interconnectedness of financial markets; money and other financial assets can be, and are, moved about the world very rapidly. The flows are large, and they can be volatile, moving into and out of a country so fast that they can destabilize economies, especially those that are relatively small by international standards.

- Globalization also involves movements of people: Every year millions of people in the world move from one country to another (and there is even more moving around within countries). The movement is response to many things, but a primary factor is economic migration, where people move from one country to another in search of better economic prospects. Demographic factors (e.g., differentiated fertility rates) are also important here.

In addition to these very direct and obvious impacts of globalization, there are others that perhaps are less obvious:

- Changes in economic institutions: Globalization is often thought to involve a general predisposition for shifting economic activity toward private sector and market-oriented institutions. This has been stressed especially in the developing world, where substantial fractions of the economies have been run by state-owned and/or operated firms. On the other hand, a huge impetus to global trade has been the ascendency of China, which has encouraged the growth of **managed trade**, using large public, or combination public/ private enterprises.

- Significant realignments in political power: Many observers feel that globalization will have important local political impacts, especially shifting political power away from national governments and toward international bodies. Two types of institutions are singled out: multinational companies and international policy bodies. By opening up their economies to the full forces of international commerce, nations may give large international companies (the multinationals) greater power over domestic economic policy, at the expense of local authorities. This would not necessarily be bad if these multinational companies had the interest of the local citizenry at heart, but they very often do not. Globalization may also shift political power toward large international agencies such as the World Bank, the International Monetary Fund (IMF), and the World Trade Organization (WTO).

- Greater inequalities in income and wealth: A major point of contention on globalization is whether it is leading to greater levels of **economic inequality** among and within countries. Critics say it does; others say it doesn't. In fact, the distribution of income and wealth and its connection with trade and economic development have been much studied. While there have been small changes in the worldwide distribution of wealth over the last 50 years, these are nowhere near the extreme changes that took place in the first half of the 19th century, when some countries were embracing the industrial revolution aggressively.

- Cultural and economic homogenization: The term cultural homogenization is sometimes taken to imply an increased attachment to the "cultural products" of the developed world, especially American products. Likewise, economic homogenization usually refers to a situation in which people strive to achieve a material standard of living characteristic of the developed world as opposed to the local, subsistence-based economies of much of the developing world.

On Sorting Out Cause and Effect

As the above comments suggest, while globalization is obviously a major force in the world, the extent and direction of its impacts are matters of great controversy. In sorting out the causes and effects of these events, it is important to guard against several modes of thought. One is to attribute everything that happens to globalization. The problem with this is that there are many other profound changes taking place around the world: political, social, religious, and so on. These developments are important drivers of world events in their own right. For example, we have seen a profound demographic revolution in the last 50 years; for every world citizen at the beginning of this time there are now 2.5 people. Much of the turmoil and conflict around the world can be attributed to this population explosion. Some have argued that integration of world economies may have had the effect of actually ameliorating the impacts of this phenomenon.

In analyzing the impacts of globalization, we must also guard against drawing general conclusions based on anecdotal evidence. It is abundantly clear that globalization does not benefit everyone. But looking at the circumstances of individual components may not be a reliable way to draw conclusions about overall trends. For example, reading a story about a highly polluting company relocating to a developing country doesn't necessarily mean that low-income countries are becoming havens for polluting firms headquartered elsewhere. To find out whether this incident is part of a larger trend we have to look at all the data in a comprehensive way.

But it is important also to keep in mind the opposite tendency: looking only at averages without breaking these down to examine subgroups of populations. The movement of averages (e.g., rising average income levels) can sometimes mask the fact that important subgroups of a population are moving in the opposite direction. A drop in the average levels of urban air pollution, for example, doesn't necessarily mean that air pollution in each and every urban area has been reduced.

Trade and the Environment

What are the interactions, or connections, between trade and the environment? The most direct question that could be asked is: does trade, in and of itself, involve higher environmental costs?

As we have discussed throughout the book, environmental damages in production and consumption are the result of externalities and public goods. If, in a producing country, the production of a tradable good is also producing environmental damage of one type or another, increased export demand will clearly result in increased environmental damage.

History, and experience, is replete with instances in which added production for export has added to the burden of environmental damage. China's export-driven growth can be taken as a macro example of this. But micro cases are also common, as Exhibit 20.1 illustrates.

The Plundering of Nauru   EXHIBIT 20.1

Nauru is a tiny (8-square mile) speck of an island in the western Pacific, home historically to about 10,000 people, but since reduced by the depredation of colonialism and WWII to about 600 souls. In the early 1900s, a valuable deposit of phosphate was discovered on the island. One might think that this would have been a great boon to the people of Nauru, whose livelihoods had been sorely constrained by the natural limits of the island. The extraction and export of phosphate should have been a source of rising incomes and improved welfare. It was not, however.

For many years extraction and export were controlled by colonial powers, chiefly, Australia. Net incomes (revenues minus costs) were chiefly to these powers, not to the local people. Most importantly, scant attention was given to the consequences of the extraction operation.

The people of Nauru achieved independence in 1968, by which time two-thirds of the phosphate was gone. Phosphate continued to be extracted and exported, now under local control, and several funds were set up to rehabilitate the land and provide for social services. But money distributed to the local population was not wisely spent. In effect the incomes from the resource extraction were squandered, so today Nauru is sinking back into impoverishment, this time with a natural resource base that has been seriously degraded.

Nauru is clearly a case where an open economy and world trade did not lead to sustainable economic growth.

For more information, see *Paradise Well and Truly Lost, Economist,* December 22, 2001; Naazneen H. Barma, K. Kaiser, T. Minh, and L. Viñuela, *Rents to Riches? The Political Economy of Natural Resource-Led Development.* Washington, DC: The World Bank, 2012.

One could argue effectively that in cases like this it is not the trade that leads to environmental costs, but the lack of effective pollution-control technology and institutions by the trading countries. If there is sufficient control over detrimental externalities in the affected countries, added trade will not create added environmental costs. This essentially means that it is a question of the political economy of the environmental policy within exporting countries.

Free Trade Versus Environmental Trade Restrictions

Over the last four decades or so, the countries of the world have made special efforts to foster free and unhindered trade. This has been done in the name of improved economic welfare. **Free trade** allows countries to prosper by giving them expanded markets for things on which they have a comparative advantage in production and gives them greater opportunities to procure goods for which they have a comparative disadvantage. The prosperity of many countries, both developed and developing, depends critically on international trade. The problem is whether the emphasis on moving toward free trade may make it more difficult for countries to protect the environmental resources that they value.

The main international institution governing trade is the World Trade Organization.[1] Its purpose is to set out a list of rules and procedures to be followed by nations in their international trade relationships. It is especially aimed at reducing the barriers to trade, to get nations to refrain from putting tariffs and quotas on imports or subsidies on exports, and in general to move toward conditions of free trade among the world's nations, almost all of which are members of the WTO. One section of the WTO agreement also outlaws what are called nontariff barriers such as excessive inspection requirements, excessive product specifications, and the like. But there is a very broad list of conditions that are exceptions to WTO rules; one is that governments are allowed to set restrictions in order to achieve the "protection of human, animal or plant life or health," and the "conserving of natural resources."

Consider the analysis of Figure 20.1. It shows the behavior of producers and consumers of a product in a particular country that also relies upon imports for a large part of its supply. The demand curve (D) is domestic demand for the product, whereas S is the domestic supply curve, that is, the supply curve of domestic producers. Without imports, price and quantity would settle at the intersection of these two curves. But let us introduce an import supply

FIGURE 20.1   **Effects of Environmental Regulations on Domestic Production and Imports**

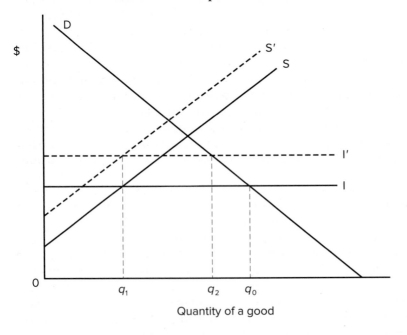

[1] WTO is the successor to the General Agreement on Tariffs and Trade (GATT), which came into being in the 1940s as an international effort to foster an increase in world trade.

curve, labeled I. This supply curve is actually horizontal because we assume that a relatively large amount of this item is produced in the world, so this importing country could import larger or smaller quantities without affecting the world price. With the addition of imports, this country now ends up with a total consumption at q_0. Domestic production, meanwhile, is q_1. The difference, $(q_0 - q_1)$, is imported. With imports, the domestic price is also equal to the world price.

WTO rules allow governments to set import restrictions on products that have direct health implications, as long as it is done in a nondiscriminatory way. Suppose the good in question is automobiles, the use of which causes air pollution. Setting tight emission standards increases the production costs for automobiles and therefore their prices. The importing country may require imported cars to meet strict emission standards, which would have the effect of lifting the import supply curve to I'. This is nondiscriminatory as long as domestic producers are held to the same standards, in effect shifting the domestic supply curve up to S'. The result of this is first to lower the total quantity of cars purchased by people in this country, from q_0 to q_2. Second, assuming that the emission standards increase the costs of domestic supply as much as they do imports, the pollution control applied to both domestically produced cars and imports will leave domestic production unchanged but reduce imports, from $(q_0 - q_1)$ to $(q_2 - q_1)$.

In this case the purpose of the strict emission standards was to protect human health. When it is not a matter of human health but, say, one of environmental aesthetics, the case may be less clear. In recent years Denmark placed a ban on the use of nonrefillable drink containers. This was presumably done in the name of reducing litter. It also proceeded to ban the importation of nonrefillable containers from neighboring European countries. These countries objected, saying that the ban was really just a way of protecting Danish drink producers from competition. But in this case the European court ruled in favor of Denmark.

Things become decidedly less clear when it is not the consumption of a good that causes pollution but its production. Suppose that a country produces a product and in the process also causes a certain amount of air pollution. Suppose further that it adopts an air-pollution program to curb emissions from this industry. Suppose even further that the item is produced in other countries and imported, but that the countries from which it is imported do not undertake any type of pollution-control efforts. The producers of the importing country are now at somewhat of a cost disadvantage because they have to operate under environmental constraints and their competitors don't. Can this country legally (i.e., within the WTO rules) put a tariff on the importation of this item to equalize the cost burden? One might argue that this would tend to protect people in other producing countries who are exposed to air pollution from the firms making this item, but WTO rules presumably allow countries to take action only to protect their own citizens, not those in other countries. And a tariff against the good may have no impact on lessening air pollution in other countries; the only way that could be done would be through explicit pollution-control programs in those countries, and there is certainly no way for the first country to enforce such programs.

The interrelationship of environmental issues and trade problems has recently raised the possibility that environmental standards will be co-opted by those whose interest is primarily to protect themselves against international competition. It is a familiar sight to see representatives of some industry that feel threatened by producers in other countries appealing to political authorities for a tariff or some other barrier against imports. Environmental factors now may give them added ammunition. If they can plausibly argue that the foreign competitors are causing damage to environmental resources, they may be better able to justify the trade barrier. The key is whether the environmental impacts of foreign producers are legitimately a concern of the importing country. In one case, the United States barred imports of tuna from Mexico that had been caught using methods that cause excessive mortality among dolphins. The question that needs to be sorted out is whether Americans really do have a substantial willingness to pay for protecting dolphins, wherever they may be, or whether this was just being used as an excuse by U.S. tuna companies to shield themselves from foreign competition.

Globalization and a "Race to the Bottom"

Opponents of globalization sometimes paint a bleak picture about the impact it might have on environmental regulations throughout the world. The supposed scenario goes something like this: trade and finance liberalization increases international commerce and the flow of investment among countries. More people around the world, in both developed and developing countries, become dependent on international markets for their livelihoods and prosperity. In an increasingly competitive world economy, countries and regions look for ways of boosting the competitiveness of their local businesses. This means trying to find ways of lowering the costs of production and distribution. Governments are pressured to relax environmental regulations so that firms can avoid costly pollution-control measures. Countries that have had higher environmental standards have to lower them to keep their businesses from fleeing to countries with the lower standards. Pollution levels surge as countries engage in competitive lowering of their environmental standards in order to give their own firms an advantage in international markets.

The phrase sometimes used to describe this phenomenon is **race to the bottom**, a progressive weakening of environmental standards brought on by the need to be competitive in an increasingly integrated world economy.

Is this concern well founded? Are we actually seeing a general race to the bottom in environmental regulations as a result of globalization? There has been a lot of close analysis of this question in the last decade or so, and the clear answer is: no. Around the world we see general improvements in environmental quality and increasingly stringent environmental regulations. There has been many an anecdote that globalization critics can point to in apparent support of their argument. But anecdotes do not make trends, and the trends are clearly in the other direction. Most integrated economies grow faster, and the higher incomes and wealth this produces lead societies to pursue more stringent standards, not weaker ones.

Studies have been done to assess the correlation across countries between their income levels and the stringency of their air pollution–control regulations.[2] That correlation is clearly positive—higher incomes are associated with higher standards, not lower ones. Many other studies have found corroborating evidence: the race-to-the-bottom hypothesis, as a generalized phenomenon, is false. If the diagnosis is wrong, so is the implied prescription: that countries should either restrict trade, or all agree to adopt the same set of environmental standards governing their industries.

But let us not be overly glib about this relationship. Environmental pollution from industrial firms are externalities, impacts that take place away from perpetrators, downstream or downwind. Getting polluters to do something about these effects doesn't just happen automatically as a country's economy grows. It requires also the development of legal structures and the growth of politically active groups who will raise the necessary questions and work for their resolution. These laws and groups are more likely to materialize in situations where the economic welfare of people is improving.

The Pollution-Haven Issue

Closely allied to the race-to-the-bottom idea is the pollution-haven hypothesis. A major part of globalization is the international fluidity of capital. Financial capital can flow easily and rapidly among most countries, often with destabilizing effects. Investment capital is also globally mobile, as firms in one country can invest in new or existing firms in others. Thus many have expressed fears that heavily polluting firms in countries of the developed world, rather than undertaking the costs of lowering their emissions, would pick up and relocate to countries where effective environmental standards are less restrictive. Countries with lower standards would thus tend to attract firms with relative large emissions; they would become, in other words, **pollution havens**.

Is there any credence in the pollution-haven hypothesis? Is there evidence that this process is underway? There is no question that there is some amount of truth in the pollution-haven hypothesis. An example is the ship-breaking industry. Every year hundreds of very large, old, oceangoing tankers and freighters are dismantled; the separated parts and materials are then recycled.

---

[2] Dasgupta S, A. Mody, S. Roy, and D. Wheeler, *Environmental Regulation and Development: A Cross Country Empirical Analysis*, World Bank Policy Research Department Working Paper No. 1448, March 1995.

This activity is currently concentrated in coastal enclaves located in several developing countries, India and Bangladesh, in particular. One of the attractions of these locations is that there are no effective environmental regulations governing the activity; to this extent it is pollution-haven story. Beyond this, however, it is largely a story of low labor costs; the work is extremely labor intensive and supplies of low-wage labor are abundant in these locations. This highlights the main problem with trying to determine the validity of the pollution-haven thesis; while weaker environmental regulations are clearly a plus if you are trying to decide where to locate a dirty industrial enterprise, other factors, especially labor and transportation costs, are also primary criteria.

The behavior of multinational firms in developing countries is also an issue. Suppose a large manufacturing firm in a developed country is moving to a developing country. Suppose further that environmental standards in the two countries differ. They are quite strict in the firm's home country and much less so in the adopted country, either because the standards themselves are weaker or because they are badly enforced or both. Which standards should the firm follow in its new home? There are two extreme points of view on this. One is that the company should seek to adopt the local practices with respect to acceptable emission controls and emissions. This means recognition of local laws, as well as "normal" behavior vis-á-vis the local authorities who enforce these laws. The other is that the firm should continue to follow the stricter pollution-control practices of its original country, with the same technology and practices that would have governed its operations had it not moved. But there is also an intermediate ground. A company may, for example, move toward local standards, but operate with progressive attitude; that is, it could obey local rules even though they may not be energetically enforced or showcase new pollution-control methods that local firms might be persuaded to adopt, and so on.

Trade and Carbon

Globalization implies increased trade, which involves large quantities of goods and services entering international transport. Transport requires the expenditure of fossil fuels. From which it may be concluded that more trade will increase the **carbon footprint** of global output. This conclusion follows, however, only if there is no substantial difference between exporting and importing countries in terms of the carbon footprints of their respective production technologies. It does not follow if the technology of the exporting country is less carbon intensive than that of the importing country. The difficulties of knowing this a priori is illustrated by the example in Exhibit 20.2. This also shows the difficulty of trying to estimate, with reasonable accuracy, the carbon footprints of the tens of millions of items, both goods and services, entering international, or even national, commerce.

Carbon Footprints — EXHIBIT 20.2

The complexity of measuring embodied carbon is illustrated in Blanke's (2006) life-cycle analysis of apples, which compares the primary energy consumed for both imported and home-grown apples in the Rhein-Ruhr area in Germany in the month of April. The primary energy to produce home-grown apples included energy for five months of cold storage, compared to the energy requirements of transporting apples from New Zealand (28 days transport) or South Africa (14 days transport). The increased energy required to import fresh fruit from overseas was partially offset by the energy needed for cold storage of domestic apples. But in order to *fully* offset the differences in embodied carbon for fruit imports from South Africa or New Zealand, home-grown apples had to be stored locally for nine or 18 months, respectively, that is, in the latter case beyond the next harvest. As such, in this case, the embodied carbon differential between local and imported goods changed with the month of the year and the age of the local produce.

Source: Kejun, Jiang, Aaron Cosbey and Deborah Murphy: *Embodied Carbon in Traded Goods*, International Institute for Sustainable Development, Winnipeg, Manitoba, June 2008.

Regional Trade Agreements

The WTO agreement is worldwide in scope, meant to address trade-related issues among all the countries of the world. There also have been many bilateral or regional trade agreements among smaller groups of countries, and these have had, and will continue to have, important environmental implications. Two major agreements now being negotiated by the United States are the Transatlantic Trade and Investment Partnership, and the Trans-Pacific Partnership. Agreements of this type are controversial, because the general desire for increased trade opportunities sometimes conflicts with other goals. Environmental factors play an important role. Most countries have public regulations to protect the environment, though not all are vigorously enforced. It is important that the enthusiasm for more trade opportunities not be used to weaken current environmental regulations or the need to tighten these regulations as conditions change.

From the standpoint of the United States and its neighbors, an important trade agreement is the North American Free Trade Agreement, NAFTA (1994). This is an agreement negotiated among the United States, Canada, and Mexico primarily to reduce tariffs and other barriers to trade among the three countries by expanding markets for the goods and services they produce, or might produce in the future. Environmental concerns played an important role in the NAFTA negotiations. There were, and still are, substantial differences of opinion about how NAFTA has impacted environmental quality in the participating countries. The specific concerns related to NAFTA are:

- Increased pollution in the countries, especially Mexico, because of increased economic activity accompanied by pollution-control regulations that are too lax, or are not sufficiently enforced.

- Increased cross-border pollution as a result of the economic stimulus NAFTA apparently gives to the Maquiladora program. This Maquiladora program allows firms in Mexico to import production supplies and equipment duty free if the resulting output is exported. Although there are few limits on where these firms may locate in Mexico, in practice they have concentrated near the Mexico/U.S. border.

- Pressure for reduced environmental standards, particularly in the United States and Canada, so firms in those countries can better compete in a liberalized trade environment. This is the familiar "race-to-the-bottom" argument.

It is not easy to find unambiguous and definitive information on the environmental effects of NAFTA. The political combat surrounding NAFTA is ongoing, so information tends to be presented to support particular political positions rather than to provide objective analysis of the situation. It is also true that environmental issues, though important, are not the main points of contention in the NAFTA conflict; the main issue is the effect on wages and employment on both sides of the U.S./Mexico border.

The common perspective at the time of the NAFTA negotiations, especially among U.S. environmental interests, was that environmental regulations in Mexico were substantially weaker than in the other two countries. While laws might be on the books, there was a serious problem with enforcement. This would have several effects, according to NAFTA critics. It means that increased economic activity in Mexico would have large environmental impacts. Not only would there be increased pressure on Mexican wildlife, forests, and energy resources, but the added air and water pollution would be significant. This is a familiar argument; for any given regulatory regime, more economic activity implies more pollution. But the way to attack this is by tightening regulations, not by suppressing economic activity. Having said this, one should not underestimate the difficulty of doing this. An enormous amount of political energy and activity will be needed to introduce effective environmental regulations into a situation where polluters have been operating without them, and where there may be many poor people. Moreover, the perception of weaker environmental restrictions in Mexico fuels the concern that American and Canadian firms relocate to Mexico in search of a pollution haven.

As regards the Maquiladora program, there has been a substantial industrial growth of this type in the borderlands area of Mexico. Initially a large part of this was in the clothing industry, while more recently the largest components are chemicals, electronics assembly firms, and automotive producers. Also, Mexican agricultural production, particularly fruits and vegetables often associated with intense pesticide use, has expanded, with increased exports to Canada and the United States. Much of this growth occurred before NAFTA. There is no doubt that the growth of Maquiladora firms has led to more pollution in the border area, but whether it is more or less in proportion to non-Maquiladora industry in Mexico is still an open question. The other unanswered question is whether NAFTA had indeed led to higher Maquiladora growth, or whether the latter was caused by other non-NAFTA events.

Environmental Trade Restrictions

In some cases international environmental agreements involve trade agreements.

Montreal Protocol

As part of the international effort to reduce ozone-depleting chemicals, the Montreal Protocol prohibits exports of controlled substances (basically CFCs) from any signatory nation to any state not a party to the protocol. Furthermore, signatory countries may not import any controlled substance from any nonsignatory state. The purpose of these trade regulations is to ensure that production of CFCs and other ozone-depleting chemicals does not simply migrate to nonsigning countries.

London Guidelines on Chemicals

As we have discussed many times throughout this book, one major obstacle to controlling environmental pollutants is lack of information—information on pollutant emissions, damages, control costs, and so on. On the international level the problem is even more severe than it is domestically because of the different ways countries have approached pollution-control problems and the vastly different information requirements and availabilities among them. In 1989, 74 countries agreed to adopt the London Guidelines for the Exchange of Information on Chemicals in International Trade, under the auspices of the United Nations Environment Program (UNEP). The guidelines require that any country banning or severely restricting a particular chemical notify all other countries of its actions, so that the latter can assess the risks and take whatever action they deem appropriate. The guidelines also encourage "technology transfer," stating that states with more advanced chemical testing and management technology should share their experience with countries in need of approved systems.

Basel Convention on Transboundary Movements of Hazardous Wastes

This agreement, enforced in 1992, is aimed at the issue of international trade in hazardous wastes. It does not prohibit this trade but does put requirements on it, especially information requirements. It puts an obligation on countries to prohibit any export of hazardous wastes unless appropriate authorities in the receiving country have consented in writing to the import and unless it has assurances that the waste will be properly disposed of. It also has provisions on notification, cooperation on liability matters, transmission of essential information, and so on.

Convention on International Trade in Endangered Species of Wild Fauna and Flora

Roughly 35,000 species of animals and plants, whether they are traded as live specimens, leather accessories or herbs, are protected under the international

Convention on International Trade in Endangered Species of Wild Flora and Fauna (CITES). CITES came into force in 1975; now 180 countries are parties to CITES. Under it, each country establishes its own permit system to control the movement of wildlife exports and imports, and must designate a management body to handle the permit system and a scientific body to determine whether trade is likely to be detrimental to the survival of the species. Species are separated into three classes:

Class I. Species threatened with extinction, in which commercial trade is banned and noncommercial trade regulated;

Class II. Species that may become threatened if trade is not held to levels consistent with biological processes, for which commercial trade is allowed with conditions; and

Class III. Species that are protected in at least one country and international cooperation is appropriate, for which trade requires permits.

The endangered species trade is considered by many to be a qualified success, although much more remains to be done, especially in improving national permit processes. There are some simple lessons to be derived from considering this type of trade restriction, which we will pursue by looking at an international supply-and-demand model of an endangered species. The same conclusions can apply to other cases, such as export restrictions on logs to protect rain forests. Consider the market model of Figure 20.2. This shows the world, or aggregate, supply and

FIGURE 20.2 **Effects of Trade Policy on the International Market in an Endangered Species**

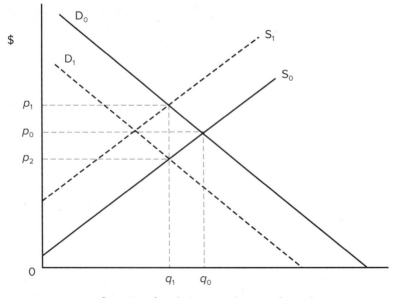

Quantity of trade in an endangered species

export demand conditions for a species of wildlife. The supply function is based on the costs of hunting, transporting, processing, recordkeeping, and so on, necessary to bring the wildlife to the point of export. It is an aggregate supply function made up of the supply function of the various countries in which that species grows. The demand function shows the quantities that the export market will take at alternative prices. The intersection of the two functions shows the market price and quantity of this type of wildlife that will be traded in a year's time.

Two types of trade constraints could be used to reduce the quantity of this species moving in international trade: export controls and import controls. Each will reduce the quantity traded, but they will have very different impacts on price. Export controls work by essentially making exporting more costly, which has the effect in Figure 20.2 of shifting the supply function upward from supply curve S_0 to supply curve S_1. The result of this is a reduction in quantity traded, in this case to q_1. The amount that quantity falls depends on the extent to which the supply curve shifts up and also on the slope of the demand function; the steeper this slope, the less will quantity contract. But this approach to trade reduction also leads to an increase in price, from the original price p_0 to p_1. This price increase could have several impacts, depending essentially on property rights. Imagine a case where the endangered species is subject to private ownership, either by individuals or by small, well-defined groups. Perhaps the habitat of the species is under private ownership, for example. The higher price for the species now becomes a signal for its owners to be more concerned about its safety and welfare because, in this circumstance, efforts at conservation will have a direct market payoff.

The added price will have the opposite effect, however, when property rights in the endangered species are ill-defined or completely absent, which is the usual case. Most of the habitats for the world's endangered species are common property, in the sense that either everybody has the right to enter and harvest the animal or plant, or that, as in public parks, authorities are unable to keep people from taking the species "illegally." We saw, in Chapter 4, the problem to which common-property resources are prone: because other users cannot be kept out, nobody has an incentive to conserve the resource. It's either use it or lose it to some other harvester. The increased price for the endangered species in this case will work against conservation. It will encourage higher rates of extraction, higher rates of poaching on common-property habitats, and thus higher pressure on the endangered species.

Controlling imports, however, drives the price downward. Import controls have the effect of reducing the demand for the imported species. In Figure 20.2 this leads to a backward shift in demand, from D_0 to D_1. This has been drawn so as to give the same quantity reduction as before. But in this case the price drops to p_2. The effect of this price decrease is to decrease the incentives discussed in the previous paragraphs. In particular, where endangered species are subject to common-property exploitation, the lower price would lead to reduced pressure to harvest and less rapid population decline. Something of this sort has happened recently as a result of an international ban on ivory imports. The ban has led to a substantial drop in the world price of ivory, which has reduced the pressure of poachers on the elephant in many parts of Africa.

Summary

Globalization is the increased integration of national economies around the world, involving greater international flows of goods and services, financial assets, and people. It may also lead to significant institutional change and altered power relations. There are important questions about the interaction of trade and the natural environment. If national environmental regulations are unchanged, increased trade will lead to greater environmental damages. This has led in many cases to calls for trade restrictions to protect environmental values. Trade also opens up the opportunities for strategic behavior among countries, such as the potential "race-to-the-bottom" and the "pollution-haven" phenomena. In the context of potential climate change, increased trade may increase the carbon footprint of the global economy. The contemporary efforts to foster regional trade agreements have led to conflicts over their possible environmental impacts, and some established environmental agreements incorporate trade limits.

Questions for Further Discussion

1. Suppose Country A imports a product from Country B, and that Country B lacks environmental laws governing the production of the item. Under what conditions might Country A be justified in putting a tariff on the imported item?

2. If all countries adopted the same emission standards in similar industries, would this tend to equalize production costs and put each country on the same footing with respect to environmental matters?

3. Which of the many aspects of globalization do you think will have the greatest long-run impact on environmental quality around the world?

4. In the early 1990s, the United States attempted to put restrictions on the importation of tuna from Mexico because Mexican fishers used methods that destroyed relatively large numbers of dolphin when catching the tuna. These fishing methods are illegal for U.S. tuna fishers. Is this trade restriction efficient? Is it equitable?

5. How might globalization and the growth of multinational corporations in the envirotech industry be a positive force for environmental protection in the countries of the world?

6. Why has trade policy been effective in protecting some endangered species and not others?

7. What do we mean by "race to the bottom" in environmental regulation? As countries discuss climate change mitigation options, how does race-to-the-bottom relate to establishing CO_2 emissions or GHG reductions among countries?

For additional readings and Web sites pertaining to the material in this chapter, see **www.mhhe.com/field7e.**

Chapter 21

Economic Development and the Environment

There was a time, several decades ago, when problems of environmental quality were widely regarded as being unique to developed, industrial economies. Industrial development was associated with air and water pollution, overreliance on chemicals, visual blight, and so on. Developing countries, however, were thought to have fewer environmental problems because their preindustrial technology was more environmentally benign, and because they had not yet committed themselves to a materialistic style of life, with the negative trade-offs many believe that this implies.

Ideas have changed, however. For one thing, it has become clear that massive environmental degradation has occurred in the developing world. Rural areas have seen large-scale soil erosion and water quality deterioration, deforestation, and declining soil productivity. Urban areas have experienced seriously diminished air and water quality. Furthermore, this environmental deterioration in developing countries is not just a matter of aesthetics or quality of life, but rather a more serious issue involving the diminishment of economic productivity and the acceleration of social dislocation. In addition, developing countries obviously wish to put a strong priority on **economic growth;** thus, the interaction between this growth and the quality of the environment is of paramount importance.

In this chapter we explore the interrelationship of economic development and the environment among the nonindustrialized countries of the world. In keeping with the distinction made in Chapter 2, we approach it on two levels: the positive and the normative. From the positive standpoint, the problem is to understand how development and environmental degradation are reciprocally related and what factors account for this interrelationship. From a normative standpoint, the problem is to deal with questions about the types of public policies that are the most appropriate for countries of the developing world.

It is common to distinguish between **economic growth** and **economic development.** There is a simple, as well as a more complicated, way of distinguishing between these concepts. In simple terms, growth refers to increases in the **aggregate level of output,** whereas development means increases in **per capita output**. Thus, a country could grow, but not develop, if its population growth exceeded its rate of economic growth. The more complicated way is to say that economic growth refers to increases in economic activity without any underlying change in the fundamental economic structure and institutions of a country, whereas development also includes a wider set of technological, institutional, and social transformations. Changes in such things as education, health, population, transportation infrastructure, and legal institutions are all part of the development process. This should alert us to the fact that when talking about environmental issues in developing countries, we will usually be talking about situations where the social and technological milieu can be very different from that in industrialized countries. At the same time it implies that in environmental policy matters, a wider set of choices may be available because of the more thoroughgoing institutional transformations taking place in many developing countries. Furthermore, policy instruments deemed best for the developed world may not be for developing countries because of differences between them in political, economic, and cultural factors.

In speaking of these issues, we tend to divide the world into just two parts: developed and developing.[1] Of course, any brief classification such as this is an enormous oversimplification of the real world. At the very least we should think not of a simple categorization such as this but of a continuum, running from the poorest to the richest, or along any other dimension of interest. The countries of the world are spread along that continuum, although not necessarily evenly. It's also true that **national aggregates** can tend to obscure some important development problems within particular countries. Many countries that look reasonably good on the basis of national macrodata have pockets of poverty and underdevelopment that would be sufficient to put these regions in the less developed ranks if national political boundaries were drawn differently.

Environmental Degradation in Developing Economies

Many people in the developed world have been brought to a realization of the existence of environmental problems in the developing world through recent global concerns, such as climate change and the rapid pace of species extinction.

A disproportionately high number of the world's endangered species are residents of developing countries, so efforts to preserve the habitats of these species have brought people to focus on the development–environment

---

[1] Other terms sometimes used are industrial, newly-industrialized countries, and less developed countries.

linkages in nonindustrialized countries. Similarly, the developed world's concern about global warming has heightened concern about deforestation because forests act to absorb atmospheric carbon dioxide (CO_2). In many developing countries the harvesting of fuel wood and timber and the conversion of forested lands to agricultural uses have led to high rates of deforestation. Thus, large-scale deforestation has the potential to worsen the global greenhouse effect.

But from the standpoint of the developing countries themselves, their worst environmental problems are probably the water and air pollution they suffer, especially in their expanding urban areas. In the developed world, the chemical treatment of water supplies, together with the treatment of wastewater, has largely neutralized the water system as a source of widespread human disease; continued water-pollution control is justified on recreational and aesthetic grounds. This is not the case in many developing countries, where water pollution is still responsible for vast amounts of disease and death. Lack of treatment facilities leads to widespread exposure to disease-bearing human wastes. In places where there has been an expansion of industry, mining, and the use of agricultural chemicals, rivers have become contaminated with toxic chemicals and with heavy metals. Seepage of hazardous materials from industrial sites and waste dumps is increasingly threatening the groundwater resources toward which many countries are turning as surface waters become more heavily contaminated.

The World Bank made the following assessments:

- 5 to 6 million people die each year in developing countries due to waterborne diseases and air pollution.
- Economic costs of environmental degradation have been estimated at 4 to 8 percent of gross domestic product (GDP) per year in many developing countries.
- Climate change threatens to further undermine long-term development and the ability of many poor people to escape poverty.[2]

In many countries auto and truck emissions lead to serious damages from airborne pollution. Indoor air pollution is also a more serious problem than in developed countries, owing to the continued heavy reliance on biomass fuels for cooking and heating with poor ventilation.

Another important phenomenon is **urbanization**. In the United States about 80 percent of the population lives in urban and suburban areas. In Asia and Africa this percentage is about 54, but this has been increasing rapidly in recent decades and is expected to continue in the future. It is also true that no country has ever achieved substantial economic growth without large-scale urbanization; in most countries rapid industrialization has been accompanied by huge environmental problems.

---

[2] See Skoufias, Emmanuel, Mariano Rabassa and Sergio Olivieri, *The Poverty Impacts of Climate Change: A Review of the Evidence,* **http://documents.worldbank.org/curated/en/2011/04/14004825.**

Economic Growth and the Environment

Whereas the concern about environmental problems has been of more recent origin, issues related to economic growth in the less developed world have been uppermost for many years; indeed, historically they have been a defining focus of this group of countries. This emphasis on economic development will continue as they strive to close the economic gap with the developed economies. What needs to be examined, therefore, is the relationship between economic development and environmental quality.

A Static View

Probably the most frequently mentioned viewpoint on these matters is that developing countries simply cannot afford high levels of environmental quality. According to this view, the situation of these countries, in comparison to developed economies, can be pictured by the production possibilities curves (PPCs) of Figure 21.1. **Marketed output** refers to the conventional types of goods and services produced and distributed through economic markets. The PPC labeled A is for a typical developed country, while B refers to a developing nation. Because of past resource exploitation, or population pressures, or less sophisticated technology, B lies entirely within A. Thus, to achieve higher levels of marketed income, which it must if it is to develop, it must be willing to put up with lower levels of environmental quality. For example, for the developing country to reach a level of marketed output of c_1,

FIGURE 21.1 **Production Possibilities Curves of Developed and Developing Countries**

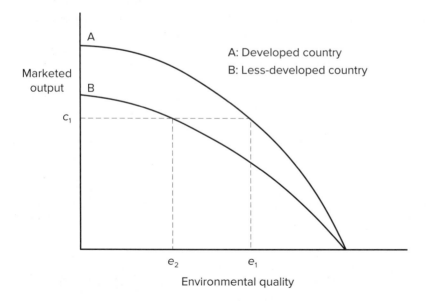

it must **trade off** environmental quality back to the level e_2. The developed country, because of the factors mentioned previously, can have c_1 of marketed output with a much higher level of environmental quality—e_1 instead of only e_2. As one economist put it:

> The poorer countries of the world confront tragic choices. They cannot afford drinking water standards as high as those the industrial countries are accustomed to. They cannot afford to close their pristine areas to polluting industries that would introduce technical know how and productive capital and that would earn urgently needed foreign exchange. They cannot afford to bar mining companies from their unexploited regions. Nor can they afford to impose antipollution requirements on these companies that are as strict and expensive as those in richer industrial countries. They should always realize that environmental protection measures are financed out of the stomachs of their own people; the multinationals cannot be made to pay for them.[3]

Developing countries, according to this view, cannot afford the high levels of environmental quality sought in the developed world because this would mean lower monetary incomes and a lessened capacity to support their populations.

There is another side to this argument, however. The PPC approach sees marketed output and environmental quality as **substitutes**, with more effort devoted to reducing environmental impacts leading to lower monetary incomes. But in the developing world there are clear cases where environmental quality and measured GDP are **complementary**. Most developing countries depend proportionately more on primary industries than do developed ones. For example, they usually have a greater proportion of their population involved in agriculture. Thus, degradation of environmental resources has the potential for being more highly destructive of productive assets in developing countries. In industrial countries, environmental quality issues hinge primarily on matters of human health and the aesthetic quality of the environment. Furthermore, technological developments have **decoupled,** to a considerable extent, the resource-using sector from the rest of the economy. In developing countries, however, environmental issues are related to human health and productivity and also to the degradation of the future productivity of the natural resource base on which many people are directly dependent. Conversely, improvement in environmental quality, particularly land, can yield greater agricultural productivity. According to this argument, the environment and the economy are not so much substitutes as they are complements.

Sustainability

But these are essentially static arguments, and the essence of economic development is long-run change. So the relevant question is: How is long-run economic development likely to affect environmental quality? The normal expectation is that development would shift the production possibility curve of Figure 21.1 outward.

---

[3] Robert Dorfman, "An Economist's View of Natural Resources and Environmental Problems," in Robert Repetto (ed.), *The Global Possible,* Yale University Press, New Haven, CT, 1985, pp. 67–76.

As economies change, becoming less tied to natural resources, and as less-polluting technologies are adopted, this outward shift would improve the potential trade-offs between marketed output and environmental quality. Developing countries could then devote more resources to improving environmental quality.

Sometimes the opposite has happened, however; the short-run effort to increase or maintain marketed incomes, in effect, tended to shift the PPC curve to the left and worsen the available choices. This has occurred when the search for short-run economic growth has led to **irreversible** reductions in the productivity of some part of a country's environmental assets. Here we are defining **environmental assets** very broadly, to include such things as soil fertility and forestry resources along with urban air and water pollution. The concept that has become widely used to talk of this phenomenon is **sustainability**. A practice is sustainable if it does not reduce the long-run productivity of the natural resource assets on which a country's income and development depend.[4]

Sustainability is fundamentally a matter of **renewable** resources. When **nonrenewable** resources are used, they automatically become unavailable to future generations. The rule to follow here is to use them at the correct rate—neither too fast nor too slow—and to see to it that the natural wealth that they represent is converted into long-lived human-made wealth as they are used. Thus, for example, the mineral resources of many developing countries must be converted to long-term productive capital, both private and public, if they are to contribute to the long-run economic development of the extracting country. By productive capital we mean not only physical capital (roads, factories, etc.), but also human capital (education, skills) and what we might call institutional capital (an efficient legal system, effective public agencies, etc.).

Long-Run Relationships

In the late 2000s, many developing countries experienced substantial growth slowdowns. As of the beginning of the next decade, however, many countries are recovering; growth rates of 3 to 6 percent a year are often considered healthy targets by economists. In addition, growth rates in sub-Saharan Africa, which for several decades have been stagnant for the most part, have in recent years started to be much more buoyant. With long-run growth rates of this type, what impacts can be expected on environmental quality in these countries? If all technological factors were to stay the same over this period, environmental impacts and damages would increase along with this economic growth. But these factors are unlikely to remain constant. Economic development brings with it many changes. The most obvious is an increase in per capita incomes, and, as people's income goes up, so does their willingness to sacrifice for improved environmental quality. Developing economies usually also experience a variety of structural

---

[4] The concept of "sustainability" received its major impetus in the influential report put out by the World Commission on Environment and Development: *Our Common Future,* Oxford University Press, Oxford, England, 1987. This report is popularly called "The Brundtland Report" because the Commission, created by the United Nations in 1983, was headed by Prime Minister Gro Harlem Brundtland of Norway.

changes, often in the direction of replacing relatively high-polluting industries with those that pollute less.

Studies have been done to investigate the relationship between various environmental quality indices and the income levels attained in different countries. The objective is to see if, as income levels change, there are systematic changes also in environmental quality variables. Several of the leading results are shown in Figure 21.2. These are based on "cross-section" analyses of income levels and environmental quality. This involves looking at the environmental characteristics of a large number of countries, with widely varying income levels, and then using statistical methods to discover the underlying relationships, if

FIGURE 21.2   **Environmental Indicators in Relation to Country Income Levels**

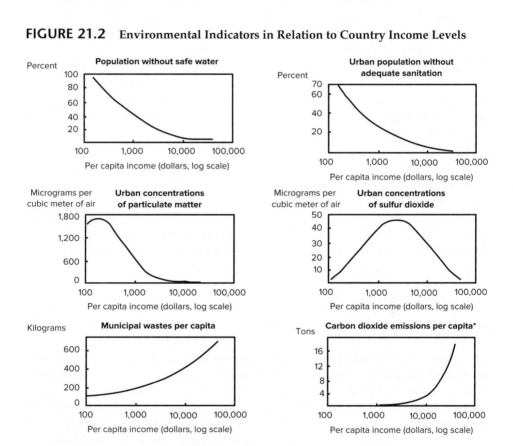

*Emissions are from fossil fuels.

Note: Estimates are based on cross-country analysis of data from the 1980s. For another update, see Daniel Esty and Michael Porter, "Ranking National Environmental Regulation and Performance: A Leading Indicator of Future Competitiveness?" *The Global Competitiveness Report*, Michael Perry and Jeffrey Sachs, eds., Oxford University Press, 2001.

Sources: World Bank, *World Development Report 1992, Development and the Environment*, Oxford University Press for the World Bank, New York, 1992, p. 11, based on a paper by Nemat Shafik and Sushenjit Bandyopadhyay, "Economic Growth and Environmental Quality: Time Series and Cross-Section Evidence"; Gene Grossman and Alan B. Kreuger, "Environmental Impacts of a North American Free Trade Agreement," Discussion Paper No. 158, Woodrow Wilson School, Princeton University, 1991.

indeed there are any. In fact, studies show clear relationships between income levels and a variety of environmental quality indices. In Figure 21.2, note that there are essentially three types of relationships:

1. Those showing steady declines as incomes increase: This applies to access to safe water and sanitation facilities, which countries can presumably more easily afford as incomes rise, but which also are normal goods in the sense that as incomes increase people are willing to pay larger amounts for them.
2. Those that first increase but then decrease with income: This applies to ambient amounts of particulates and sulfur dioxide (SO_2). This pattern is probably due to the fact that in its early stages industrial development leads to greater air pollution, whereas with continued development there is a shift in industry type toward cleaner industries, as well as a rising public demand in more well-to-do countries for pollution control.
3. Those showing a steady increase with income gains: This applies to municipal solid wastes and CO_2 emissions per capita. The first is a reflection of the growth in material standards of living as incomes increase, whereas the second results from the increasing demand for fossil-based energy that normally accompanies development.

These relationships as pictured are not inevitable. They can be taken as general tendencies, which may be different in particular countries, depending on **technology choices** adopted as well as the **preferences** of their citizens. It points out that for many environmental problems, the situation is likely to get better as development occurs; indeed, economic development may be seen as a way of combating these problems, which is why continued efforts need to be directed at encouraging equitable growth and open political processes in the developing world.

Environmental Policy Choices in Developing Countries

Although it may be true that development can help to alleviate some environmental problems, there is nothing automatic about this; appropriate public policies are still called for. This is especially true for those factors, such as CO_2 emissions and solid waste, that get worse with development. Most discussions of the strengths and weaknesses of alternative policies have been directed toward developed countries. There is an important question about how much the lessons learned in this context apply also to developing countries. Although the environmental problems are in principle the same, involving externalities, common-property resources, public goods, and so on, the sociopolitical situations are markedly different from those in most developed countries.

Benefit–Cost Analysis

The basis of effective policy is in the analysis of the benefits and costs of different courses of action. Much more than in developed countries, damages in developing countries affect economic productivity through impacts on human health, soil fertility, resource depletion, and the like. In addition, with relatively low incomes and high importance given to matters of economic development, it is important to understand, and place in priority, the various steps that might be taken to achieve environmental improvement. Thus, there is a critical need to be able to assess the benefits and costs of alternative environmental policies and regulations in countries of the developing world.

There are several important issues regarding the use of standard techniques of **benefit–cost** analysis in developing countries. One is the emphasis on willingness to pay as a measure of the benefits of pollution reduction. Willingness to pay reflects not only tastes and preferences, but also ability to pay. In many developing economies, poverty is widespread, so a standard **willingness-to-pay** (WTP) approach to valuing environmental damages may yield only modest estimates of these damages. In the face of extensive poverty, WTP estimates may be quite small despite what look to be high rates of environmental degradation. Thus, if WTP approaches are used, they must be used with frank recognition that the **distribution of income** is heavily skewed, and value judgments are called for making decisions on environmental quality programs. This argues also for putting more emphasis on **lost productivity**, particularly in the **long run**, in assessing the damages of environmental degradation.

Another special difficulty in applying benefit–cost analysis of environmental programs to developing countries is **discounting**. In developed economies, discounting is a relatively benign procedure that helps make choices among programs with different time profiles of benefits and costs. But in developing countries the focus is more on long-run development, and here the role of discounting is less clear. It's often asserted that people in developing countries, especially those with lower incomes, discount the future very highly, preferring to emphasize actions that will pay off in the short run because of their immediate need for income.[5] Thus, environmental improvement programs, if they deliver the bulk of their benefits only in the long run, may take lower priority than economic development projects that pay off more quickly. High rates of discount also can lead people to overlook negative environmental impacts that occur far off into the future. This becomes a matter of **intergenerational equity**, which is fairness between generations. The present value of even severe long-run environmental damage can be quite low when it is evaluated with a positive discount rate.[6] For some people these arguments imply using a

---

[5] Recall that lower discount rates put greater weight on long-run future costs and benefits, while higher discounts rates put greater weight on near-term costs and benefits.

[6] We are not talking here about unpredictable consequences; rather, those that are predictable but far into the future. When chlorofluorocarbons (CFCs) were introduced as refrigerants in the early 20th century, nobody predicted the impacts they would have on the global atmosphere. Likewise, nobody foresaw the negative effects of the pesticide DDT. At the time these substances were introduced, science was not well enough advanced to have predicted these outcomes. There is a difference, however, between consequences that are not predictable and those that are predictable but far enough in the future to be neglected in today's decision making.

very low, perhaps even zero, discount rate in evaluating environmental and developmental projects in developing countries. But this would make it impossible to coordinate public policies and development projects with decisions being made in the private sector and would treat a dollar of net benefits 10 years from now as equivalent to a dollar of net benefits today. It is perhaps better to utilize a normal discount rate in evaluating programs, and augment the typical benefit–cost study in developing countries with an analysis of the impacts of the program on long-run **sustainability** and intergenerational equity.[7]

Valuation Issues

Valuation, as we discussed in Chapter 7, refers to analyses that attempt to measure the relative worth of environmental improvements of various kinds. Indirect studies utilize secondary data (house prices, travel distances, wage rates, etc.), whereas direct studies, such as contingent valuation, use survey data generated specifically for the analyses.

The original impetus to develop and apply valuation techniques came from the developed economies, but recent years have seen its increasing application in the developing world. Some recent studies include the following:

- Estimating the value of water quality improvements in Sri Lanka and a similar one about the Ganges River.[8]
- Valuation of forest ecosystem benefits in Nepal.[9]
- Valuing the proximity of urban amenities such as clean water and open space in India.[10]
- Valuing the local impact of mine dust and radon in South Africa.[11]
- Estimating the benefits of maintaining beachfront quality in Thailand.[12]

[7] David Pearce, Edward Barbier, and Anil Markandya, *Sustainable Development, Economics and Environment in the Third World*, Edward Elgar Publishing, Aldershot, England, 1990.

[8] W.R. Rohitha, "Evaluating Gains from De-eutrophication of the Dutch Canal in Sri Lanka," in A.K. Enamul Hague, M.N. Murty and Pina Shyamsundar (eds.), *Environmental Valuation in South Asia*, Cambridge University Press, 2011, pp. 99–113; Ekin Birol and Sukanya Das, *Valuing the Environment in Developing Countries*, International Food Policy Research Institute, Discussion Paper 01043, December 2010.

[9] Rajesh K. Rai and Helen Scarborough, "Nonmarket Valuation in Developing Countries: Incorporating Labour Contributions in Environmental Benefits Estimates," *The Australian Journal of Agricultural and Resource Economics*, 28 August 2014, online version.

[10] Pradeep Chaudhry, M.P. Sharma, G. Singh and Arun Bansal, "Valuation of Urban Environmental Amenities in Developing Countries: A Case Study from Chandigarh, India," *Global Journal of Science Frontier Research*, 13(2), September 2013.

[11] Robert A. Simons, et al., "Use of Contingent Valuation Analysis in a Developing Country: Market Perceptions of Contamination on Johannesburg's Mine Dumps," *International Real Estate Review*, 11(2), 2008, pp. 75–104.

[12] Colin Cushman, Barry C. Field, Tom Stevens, and Dan Lass, "External Costs from Increased Island Visitation: Results from the Southern Thai Islands," *Tourism Economics*, Vol. 10, June 2004, pp. 220–240.

Reducing Environmental Disincentives

Environmental policy is usually regarded as requiring activist intervention to remedy the problems of uncontrolled externalities, the undersupply of public environmental goods, and so on. But many times environmental improvements can be had by **altering current policies** that have negative environmental impacts. In many cases these policies have been put in place in the belief that they will spur economic growth. But their impact is to create **distortions** in local economies that lead both to lower growth rates and to environmental degradation.

A good example of this is the practice many governments have of subsidizing pesticide use by farmers. In many cases these subsidies were undertaken in the belief that they would spur farmers to adopt new crop varieties and intensive methods of cultivation. But the subsidies often continue well after their usefulness in this regard has ceased. The result of these subsidies is predictable: the overuse of agricultural chemicals and the damages that result. These include heavy pesticide exposure of farm workers, contamination of nearby surface- and groundwater resources, and the rapid development of immunity by target pests. In recent years, numerous developing countries have sought to reduce their pesticide subsidies in the light of the impacts they have had.

Other agricultural subsidies, for example, on irrigation water and fertilizer, have similar effects. Much attention also has focused on overly rapid rates of deforestation in developing countries. In many cases this happens because of government policies. Policies that underprice the value of timber concessions offered to logging companies increase the incentive to harvest timber at a high rate. Uncontrolled private access to communal forest resources reduces the incentive to conserve timber stocks. Misguided public road building can open up large areas to timber harvesting. In some cases land grants to individuals cannot become permanent unless and until the land is cleared and put into agricultural production, which obviously creates the incentive to get rid of the trees as soon as possible. The result of these policies is timber harvest that is higher than it should be, and pursued in places it should not be, with the resulting impacts in soil loss, polluted water, reduction in the global CO_2 sink, and so on.

We should not think, however, that distorting public policies with negative environmental impacts are features solely of the developing world. In fact, the developed world also has many such policies. In the United States, agricultural price supports coupled with land-use restrictions have led to excessive rates of pesticide use in certain crops. Publicly subsidized flood insurance has led people to develop shoreline property that might best be left undisturbed.

Institutional Policy: Property Rights

Economic development usually implies wide-ranging economic and political transformations. An important part of this is developing modern economic institutions that can provide the appropriate incentive structures to shape the decisions that will lead toward development. Inappropriate property rights institutions often have been singled out for having environmentally destructive consequences. Thus, one major avenue for policy to protect environmental resources is to alter property rights institutions.

In a study of resource depletion in Ethiopia, the author lists a series of stages through which a portion of the rural economy had evolved.[13]

Stage 1: Because of population pressure, the average harvest of fuel wood begins to exceed the average rate of wood production.

Stage 2: Farmers begin to use straw and dung for fuel; thus, less of these are available for maintaining soil fertility.

Stage 3: Almost all tree cover is removed, all dung is sold for cash, and wheat yields begin a serious decline.

Stage 4: Soil erosion becomes dramatic because of reduced tree cover and declining fertility.

Stage 5: There is a total collapse of fertility; farmers abandon their land, swelling urban populations.

The basic question is: Why did this sequence of stages take place? It might be more instructive to ask this the opposite way: Why didn't something like the following scenario happen? Fuel wood harvest increases because of increasing demand, and this increases the price of fuel wood because of increased scarcity. Farmers see the increasing incomes to be made by growing and selling fuel wood, so they devote portions of their land to growing fuel wood and act to conserve the remaining supplies in the face of its increasing value. Finally, a substantial fuel wood harvest and market appear, with a considerable proportion of the land devoted to fuel wood production. Why, in other words, did the rising market price of fuel wood lead to wiping out the forest? Why did the farmers not act to make themselves better off by conserving and even increasing the production of an increasingly valuable resource?

One part of the answer is property rights. Most of the forested land was not owned by individuals or small groups, but was essentially an open-access resource. Anyone who wanted to harvest wood from these lands had the right to do so. In Chapter 4 we examined a simple model of an open-access resource showing that individuals making decisions on the basis of benefits and costs to themselves will overlook **common-property externalities** they inflict on others. A resource of this type often will be overexploited. Viewed from another angle, when there is open access to a resource, the incentive that any individual might have to reduce the rate of use and conserve the resource is totally undermined. If someone reduces his or her harvest, others will simply take what has been left. Open-access resources promote a "use-it-or-lose-it" situation.

Thus, one of the root causes of the deforestation, which began the whole unraveling process in the example, was an institutional one, a property rights system that created incentives for wiping out the resource even though rising scarcity was making it socially desirable to conserve it. This problem has occurred with great regularity in developing countries, especially with land

[13] Kenneth J. Newcombe, "An Economic Justification for Rural Afforestation: The Case of Ethiopia," in Gunter Schramm and Jeremy J. Warford (eds.), *Environmental Management and Economic Development*, Johns Hopkins Press for the World Bank, Baltimore, MD, 1989, pp. 117–138.

and forest resources. The most straightforward response would seem to be to change the property rights system so that the normal incentives for conservation can operate. This means instituting a system of individual or small-group property rights.

We have to keep in mind that like any single policy recommendation, this one is no panacea for all of the environmental problems of developing countries. It will work in some situations and not in others. Overuse of resources, such as the deforestation mentioned previously, can occur on "private" lands if the owners cannot effectively defend their boundaries and keep out would-be encroachers. This means, among other things, that there have to be effective and equitable **legal institutions** to settle land-use conflicts. Establishing private property rights in developing countries also means facing the **demographic realities**. In places with great population pressure, private property rights would hardly be feasible if that cut off a substantial proportion of the population from resources needed in order to subsist. Even in places without noticeable population pressure, essentially the same problem could occur if the property rights are distributed inequitably in the first place.

There are many other dimensions to the property rights issue. It is a topic of great controversy, and the debate is often carried out in overly simplistic terms. It is clear, however, that widely ranging resource and environmental problems in developing countries have been made much worse by ill-defined property rights and the open-access externalities to which these give rise. In those situations, innovations in property rights institutions can be extremely effective.

Population Policy as Environmental Policy

Many people feel that the only effective way to control environmental destruction in developing countries is to control the **number of people** in those countries. In the simplest possible terms, the total impact of a group of people on its environmental resources can be expressed in the following way:

$$\text{Total environmental impact} = \text{Environmental impact per person} \times \text{Number of people}$$

It is clear that total environmental impact can increase as a result of increases in either or both of these factors. The contrary is also true: Decreases in total impact can result from decreases in either or both of the factors. More complicated scenarios are possible: Changes in technology, economic structure, and so on, that lower the per capita environmental impacts in a country can be more than offset by population increases. But both factors are involved. Population declines or declines in the rate of population increase may be very helpful, but they are not sufficient in themselves to ensure a reduction in aggregate environmental degradation.

The world population is generally expected to increase from the current 7.4 to 10 billion over the next half century. It's expected that about two-thirds of this increase will occur in countries of the developing world. Whether the increase is at the high end of this range or substantially lower depends in large part on the long-run behavior of **fertility rates** in these developing countries.[14] Although fertility rates in developing countries are sometimes very high, many have started to decline in recent years. To some extent this is a reflection of rising incomes, because increasing incomes are almost always associated with lowered fertility rates. Other important causal factors are a reduction in infant mortality, increased availability of family planning services, and (especially) increases in educational opportunities for women. Continued emphasis on these factors is in the best interest of people in the developing world, not solely for environmental reasons, but also to reduce poverty directly and to make it easier to institute developmental changes.

However, although reductions in population growth rates can certainly help to reduce the overall impacts any group of people has on its environmental resources, it is no substitute for undertaking environmental policies in their own right. For one thing, diminished population growth rates do not necessarily automatically imply diminished environmental damages. Even with comparatively lower populations, for example, it is anticipated that developing countries will experience marked increases in **urbanization** in the next half century and probably beyond. Unless confronted directly, this will lead to more severe air and water pollution in these burgeoning urban areas. As another example, decreases in agricultural populations may not be accompanied by reduced resource damages if, simultaneously, a shift to chemical agriculture occurs without proper safeguards against water pollution and increased pest resistance. In other words, although population policies may facilitate reduced environmental damages, they are no substitute for direct environmental policy itself.

Instrument Choice in Developing Countries

We come, therefore, to the important question of the types of environmental policies that are most appropriate for developing economies. We have stated several times, in the context of developed economies, that no single policy approach will be the best for all environmental problems: certain problems call for one approach; others call for something else. And many situations call for combinations of policies. The same is true of developing countries. But beyond this, it needs to be asked if anything characterizing the developing world might cause policymakers to rely more heavily on one type of policy than another. The main argument in developed economies is the choice between **command-and-control** and **incentive-based** policies. Is this also relevant to the setting of developing countries?

One especially relevant factor is that developing countries can ill afford, given the resource requirements of economic development, to devote more resources to environmental quality improvement than is necessary. This is an argument for making sure that the pollution-control policies adopted are **cost-effective,** and this in turn is an argument in favor of incentive policies. We have

---

[14] The fertility rate is the average number of children born per woman over her lifetime; a rate of 2.0 implies zero population growth. Some developed countries have fertility rates of less than 2.0. In the developing world although fertility rates are falling, they range from 1.6 in Thailand to 7.6 in Niger.

seen repeatedly throughout this book that incentive-type policies, in situations where monitoring emissions is possible and where materials-balance problems are addressed, can be expected to be substantially more cost-effective than command-and-control strategies. They make it possible to take advantage of different abatement costs across sources and also provide long-run incentives for firms to search for cheaper ways of reducing emissions.

To date many other countries have been following in the early footsteps of the developed economies; that is, they have relied primarily on command-and-control policies. There are some exceptions. Emission charge plans have been instituted in Colombia, China, Malaysia, and the Philippines. A tradable permit system has been initiated by authorities in Chile to address air pollution in Santiago.[15] Singapore led the world in 1975 with congesting pricing by instituting a program to charge drivers for using urban roads during heavily congested peak-use times of the day. Since then, the program has moved from a flat fee to a charge per 10 seconds of road use and expanded the geographic area to which the rates are applied. Substantial improvements in air quality have resulted.[16]

Nevertheless, command and control is still the dominant trend in environmental policy in most developing countries. This may be the result of relatively weak policy institutions. It is a common observation that the capacities and performance of public regulatory agencies are relatively weak in many third-world countries. This problem, of course, is not unique to them; administrative deficiencies in developed countries account for part of the large gap between the laws and their enforcement. But most observers agree that this is a particularly thorny problem for developing countries. It is not solely a matter of professionalism and lack of political clout. It is also very generally true in the developed world that public concern and activist political participation by private environmental interest groups are often weak.

For some observers, this institutional and political weakness implies that developing countries ought to move away from command-and-control measures toward economic-incentive policies. For others, who perhaps are impressed that developed countries themselves are only beginning to place greater reliance on incentive measures, these institutional shortcomings imply that environmental regulations in developing countries are best kept relatively simple and direct: in other words, simple command-and-control strategies through uniform standards. The Brundtland Commission itself concluded that in developing countries, "regulations imposing uniform performance standards are essential to ensure that industry makes the investments necessary to reduce pollution."[17]

[15] For information on these programs, see David B. Wheeler, *Greening Industry: New Roles for Communities, Markets, and Governments*, Oxford University Press for the World Bank, New York, 2000; Jessica Coria and T. Sterner, *Tradable Permits in Developing Countries: Evidence from Air Pollution in Santiago, Chile*, Resources for the Future Discussion Paper No. 08-51, December 2008.

[16] Danish Architecture Centre, *Singapore: the World's First Digital Congestion Charging System*, January 2014, online at **http://www.dac.dk/en/dac-cities/sustainable-cities/all-cases/transport/singapore-the-worlds-first-digital-congestion-charging-system**.

[17] World Commission on Environment and Development, *Our Common Future*, Oxford University Press, New York, 1987, p. 220.

Perhaps a partial resolution of this question rests on recognizing that the category "developing countries" actually includes a wide range of experience. At one end of the spectrum are countries that are still almost totally agricultural, substantially uniform technologically, and with only the beginnings of a modern economic sector. At the other end of the spectrum are countries that have developed relatively large industrial, financial, and transportation sectors; important economic links to the rest of the world; and, most important, comparatively sophisticated political institutions. In the former countries, simple command-and-control approaches are likely to be best—a prohibition on a certain pesticide, for example, or limits on a certain irrigation practice. These may be enforced without sophisticated monitoring, and technical uniformity among producers means that these steps will be reasonably cost-effective. But in more advanced developing countries, incentive-based policies have much more to recommend them. Here the necessary political institutions may have been put in place, technological complexity makes it much more difficult to achieve acceptable levels of cost-effectiveness with command-and-control approaches, and strong long-run incentives for continued technical innovation in pollution control are of paramount importance. Exhibit 21.1 discusses a policy initiative to develop incentive-based approaches, in the form of payments (subsidies) for providing environmental services, which have become popular in many developing economies.

The Role of the Developed Countries

Developing countries are struggling with a wide array of economic, political, and social problems that stand in the way of lasting economic modernization. To graft environmental concerns onto the process puts an added burden on everyone in these countries, whatever their position. The developed countries have an important role to play in helping to make this transition, not just for humanitarian reasons but also because many environmental problems are becoming increasingly international in scope. As these countries catch up to the developed economies, their technical choices and emission-control efforts will have a direct bearing on important global problems, such as CO_2 emissions and the global greenhouse effect, toxic chemical releases, nuclear radiation emissions, and so on.

Technology Transfer

By *technology transfer* we refer to the transfer, from developed to developing countries, of technologies and skills that can provide the impetus for economic development with lower environmental impacts than could be attained without the transfer. The focus is on the transfer of knowledge that citizens of developing countries themselves can adapt to their own needs and styles of operation. **Technology transfer** is an important concept in economic development. But it has taken on new urgency in light of the growing awareness of the scale of environmental problems faced by developing countries. Technology transfer means making technology available to countries so that their pace of economic development can be increased; this will have a positive impact on the demand for

Conditional Cash Transfers and Payments for Environmental Services

EXHIBIT 21.1

In the last several decades, two innovative policies have emerged in countries of the developing world in an attempt to guide decisions toward environmental and social goods. These can both be thought of as incentive-based policies, because they try to give individual decision makers monetary incentives for adopting certain behaviors. **Conditional cash transfers** (CCTs) offer cash payments conditional on recipients engaging in socially productive activities, such as keeping kids in school or maintaining routine health care visits. **Payment for environmental services** (PES) are monetary payments given to people who engage in environmental conservation activities such as maintaining an area in forest cover or refraining from cultivating steeply sloped lands.

PES programs have become very common in the developing world. Most are small-scale projects. They work, at least in principle, by identifying farmers or other landowners who might be expected to convert ecological land, then offering them payments, cash or otherwise, to refrain from that action. Of course it is based theoretically on the notion that land conversion often produces external costs, in the form of, for example, downstream siltation or flooding, habitat loss, or atmospheric carbon release. Payments are justified by these avoided external costs.

PES programs are being touted because they are likely to be:

- Institutionally simpler;
- More cost-effective in delivering benefits to buyers;
- More effective in generating economic growth among suppliers by improving cash flow, diversifying income sources, and reducing income variance; and
- New sources of finance for conservation.

There have been thousands of PES programs initiated in the last decade. Proponents are confident that they have had a substantial positive impact on natural resource and environmental conservation. But little has been done to evaluate the programs in a rigorous way. One issue has been the question of "additionality," simply the question of whether in many cases landowners are being compensated for actions they might have undertaken anyway, even without the program.

Nevertheless, PES programs are a good example of an incentive-based approach to environmental conservation. Over time they are likely to become more popular, and with luck and perseverance, more fully evaluated in terms of the way they should be planned and implemented to maximize their effectiveness.

Source: Pattanayak, Subhrendu K, Sven Wunder and Paul J. Ferraro, "Show Me the Money: Do Payments Supply Environmental Services in Developing Countries?" *Review of Environmental Economics and Policy*, 2010, Vol. 4, No. 2, pp. 254–274.

improved environmental quality, as discussed earlier. Transfer of environmental technology has the objective of reducing the environmental impacts of economic development, below what would occur otherwise, and perhaps below what has occurred historically in the developed world. It has become evident that if the rest of the world goes through the same high-pollution course of development as the developed countries have done, the drain on world resources will be enormous and the impact on the global environment potentially disastrous.

Concrete provisions for the transfer of technology have been written into some **international environmental treaties**. The 1989 Basel Convention on Hazardous Waste obligates the signatories to provide technical assistance to developing countries in the implementation of the treaty. The 1990 amendments to the Montreal Protocol on protection of the ozone layer has a requirement that developed countries make available to developing countries, on reasonable terms, new reduced-CFC technology; it also establishes a fund to help developing countries meet the requirements for reduced emissions.[18] The Nordic Environment Finance Corporation provides help for environmentally sound investment in Eastern and Central Europe. The Global Environment Fund Management Corporation (GEF Management Corp) is an effort to raise money from institutional investors in the United States with the backing of the Overseas Private Investment Corporation (OPIC), a U.S. government agency. The objectives of the GEF include investing in such activities as clean technology, sustainable forestry and agriculture, waste management systems, and energy efficiency technologies.

Technology transfer has two important parts. The first is the initial development of new technologies and procedures. These are a product of innovation in industries searching for ways of reducing emissions and in the pollution-control industry itself. Thus, one element in technology transfer is the provision of incentives for a brisk level of innovation in the originating countries. This implies pollution-control policies that provide these incentives, about which we have said a lot in earlier chapters. In particular, we have discussed the positive incentives for innovation provided by economic-incentive types of policies and the negative effects provided by technology-based standards.

The second element of environmental technology transfer is getting the ideas, technical means, and necessary training effectively into the receiving countries. The word *effectively* is important because history is full of cases in which transferred techniques have failed to work as anticipated. It is much more than just moving a machine from one location to another; a tremendous array of problems must be worked out to bridge the informational, cultural, commercial, and political gaps that separate people in different countries. At the end of the process, which normally will involve many different business, trade, political, and environmental groups, the objective is to transfer technology that is compatible with local skills and labor availabilities. See Exhibit 21.2.

Most environmental technologies in the developed world have been developed by firms in the private sector. In the United States, the **envirotech sector** consists of thousands of large and small firms in all phases of environmental activity. Getting technology and practices transferred and

---

[18] Chapter 19 contains a discussion of international environmental treaties in general, including the specific provisions of the Montreal Protocol.

Barriers to Technology Transfer Between Countries

EXHIBIT 21.2

The barriers to technology transfer of transport options between countries can be categorized into technological, financial, institutional, informational, and social. These should be seen along with generic barriers. In the transport sector, an overriding barrier that requires emphasis is the lack of an enabling business environment for both technology supplier and technology recipient countries to promote technology transfer. Industrialized countries, which are mostly technology suppliers, can institute economic and fiscal measures and regulations with the necessary compliance regimes that can stimulate the private sector to transfer transport technologies. Technology recipients, which are mostly developing countries, need to create the enabling environment that is receptive to transport technologies. Lack of a suitable enabling environment is particularly absent in low-income and capital-constrained countries. In general, technology recipient countries need to build an effective business environment to attract involvement of the private sector, which is now increasing its role in transport technology flows, especially in transport infrastructure.

An important technical barrier to technology inflows to any country is lack of the necessary manufacturing capabilities, especially in technology recipient countries. Additionally, a lack of companies to undertake subcontracting, as may be required by large transport companies, and the absence of suitable facilities for training and R&D can create serious problems for technology development and transfer. An important financial barrier is access to capital, because most of the transport options are very expensive and involve long lead times such as building or modifying highways and bridges. These activities may involve significant capital outlay and many institutions with different interests. Harmonizing and optimizing these interests can prove to be challenging. Also, implementing some nonmotorized measures such as wider use of cycling can be expensive, because of the need for dedicated lanes and other support infrastructure, which would be a barrier for many countries. Lack of compliance and arbitration institutions can be a barrier for effective private sector participation. Lack of knowledge of the existence and development of environmentally friendly transport options, including their weaknesses and benefits, will be a major barrier in adopting them. This is common among technology recipients. Differences in social and cultural systems among countries can be a barrier, because some transport options are sensitive to these differences. Adopting cycling may require certain lifestyle change as well as some other nonmotorized systems. Similarly, adoption of recently smaller and more fuel-efficient cars that are being manufactured by many of the major manufacturers may not be acceptable to many countries because of their transport needs. Political will by respective governments for technology transfer is needed and so can be a major obstacle if absent.

Source: Bert Metz et al. (ed.), "Methodological and Technological Issues in Technology Transfer," *Special Report of the Intergovernmental Panel on Climate Change*, Cambridge University Press, Cambridge, U.K., 2000, Chapter 8.

adopted in the developing world, therefore, involves creating effective connections between these firms and the responsible public and private agencies of the developing world.

Technology transfer must be looked at in the light of recent concerns about **globalization**. This concept has come to mean a lot of different things, one of which is the quality of the commercial contacts between multinational firms (and firms of the developed world) and people in the developing world. At issue is whether envirotech firms with potential technology treat this as an opportunity simply for short-run profit maximization, or whether they make sure that technology is adapted to the long-run needs and capabilities of people in developing nations.

Environmental Values in International Development Banks

Some of the most egregious cases of environmental damage in developing countries actually have stemmed from projects initiated and funded by international aid organizations, whose objectives are primarily to help these countries develop economically. A well-publicized example is the project funded partly by the World Bank to build roads and encourage colonization in the northwestern part of Brazil. The building of the roads attracted many more migrants into the area than was anticipated, "making already underfunded public agencies even less capable of controlling large-scale deforestation."[19] Many international donors have leaned toward the big project: dams, power stations, infrastructure, and so on. These often have been pursued in ways that were not sensitive to environmental impacts because the donors, together with governments in recipient countries, have been so focused on spurring economic growth.

What this problem calls for is a more complete adoption of the general benefit–cost approach, interpreted broadly to mean the accounting for, and comparison of, all benefits and costs, whether or not they can be monetized in a formal framework. In particular, more attention must be given to working out the environmental impacts of these development projects. Now many international lending organizations take the environmental issues of developing countries more seriously. The World Bank, along with other regional multilateral development banks, requires complete environmental assessments for all projects and takes these into account in making lending decisions. Because the United States insists on taking the leading role in the World Bank, there are pressures for other countries and country groups to form new development banks, which would be responsive to their own international aims and objectives. China has worked to form the Asian Infrastructure Investment Bank to focus on infrastructure rather than poverty. Although there will be attention paid to environmental assessments, it remains to be seen if environmental

[19] World Bank, World Development Report 1992, *Development and Environment,* Oxford University Press, New York, 1992, p. 80.

considerations play a strong role in decisions by these new international institutions.

Summary

Environmental problems in developing countries have become increasingly critical in the last few decades. While the appearance of global issues has helped people to see that all countries are inextricably linked in the global environment, more attention also has been directed at traditional air- and water-pollution problems of developing countries. The issue of long-run sustainability of the natural resource and environmental assets of these countries has become a policy focus point.

Analysis of past trends shows that development tends to make some environmental problems worse and others better. Some phenomena, such as SO_2 pollution, seem to get worse as countries initially begin to develop rapidly and then improve as development leads to higher per capita incomes.

Policy institutions in developing countries historically have been relatively weak, but this is changing. Most environmental policy in these countries has followed the lead of the developed world, in terms of being based on command-and-control principles. Some have suggested that developing countries should emphasize incentive-based policies so as to achieve higher levels of cost-effectiveness. Population control has frequently been recommended as a means of lessening environmental impacts. Although lower rates of population growth may facilitate environmental improvements, they are not sufficient for attaining improvements in environmental quality.

Finally, the developed world can play a substantial role in helping countries develop without large-scale environmental destruction. The primary mechanism for this is through technology transfer, understood broadly to include the transfer of skills and technological capabilities that are culturally sound and not solely the transfer of capital goods.

Questions for Further Discussion

1. What is the relationship between economic growth, population growth, and environmental quality in developing countries?

2. Environmental pollution is, for the most part, reversible, in the sense that it can be decreased if the appropriate steps are taken. What are the pros and cons, therefore, of using sustainability as a criterion for evaluating environmental policies?

3. When a multinational business firm from the developed world opens operations in a developing nation, should it be held to the environmental standards of its country of origin or to those of the country in which it is operating?

4. Suppose we introduce a new criterion, "administrative feasibility," for evaluating environmental policies in developing countries. How might this affect choices among different types of policies?

5. Refer to Figure 21.1. How would a technology transfer from country A to country B alter the PPC?

For additional readings and Web sites pertaining to the material in this chapter, see **www.mhhe.com/field7e.**

Appendix

Abbreviations and Acronyms Used in the Book

APCA	Air Pollution Control Act
AQA	Air Quality Act
ATU	Allotment trading unit
BACT	Best available control technology
BAT	Best available technology
BCT	Best conventional technology
BMP	Best management practice
BOD	Biochemical oxygen demand
BPT	Best practicable technology
Btu	British thermal unit
CAA	Clean Air Act
CAC	Command and control
CAFE	Corporate average fuel economy
CAIR	Clean Air Interstate Rule
CAP	Cap and trade
CARB	California Air Resources Board
CCR	Coal combustion residues
CERCLA	Comprehensive Environmental Response, Compensation and Liability Act
CFC	Chlorofluorocarbon
CH$_4$	Methane
CITES	Convention on International Trade in Endangered Species of Wild Fauna and Flora
CO	Carbon monoxide
CO$_2$	Carbon dioxide
CO$_2$e	Carbon dioxide equivalent
COD	Chemical oxygen demand
COI	Cost of illness
CPSA	Consumer Products Safety Act
CPSC	Consumer Products Safety Commission
CRE	Credit trading program
CV	Contingent valuation

CWA	Clean Water Act
DO	Dissolved oxygen
DOD	Department of Defense
DOE	Department of Energy
DOI	Department of the Interior
DOT	Department of Transportation
EIA	Environmental impact analysis
EPA	Environmental Protection Agency
ESA	Endangered Species Act
ETS	European Trading Scheme
EU	European Union
EV	Electric vehicle
FC	Fecal coliform
FDA	Food and Drug Administration
FTC	Federal Trade Commission
FDCA	Food, Drug and Cosmetic Act
FIFRA	Federal Insecticide, Fungicide and Rodenticide Act
GATT	General Agreement on Tariffs and Trade
GDP	Gross domestic product
GEF	Global Environmental Fund
GHG	Greenhouse gas
HCHO	Formaldehyde
HEW	Health, Education & Welfare Administration
HCFC	Hydro chlorofluorocarbon
HLW	High-level wastes
I&M	Inspection and maintenance
IB	Incentive based
ICJ	International Court of Justice
IMF	International Monetary Fund
IPCC	Intergovernmental Panel on Climate Change
IPM	Integrated pest management
kwh	kilowatt hour
LA	Load allocation
LAER	Lowest achievable emission rate
LLW	Low-level wastes
MAC	Marginal abatement cost
MACT	Maximum available (or achievable) control technology
MC	Marginal cost
MCL	Maximum containment level
MCLG	Maximum containment level goal
MD	Marginal damages
MEC	Marginal external costs
MOS	Margin of safety
MPC	Marginal private costs
mpg	miles per gallon
MSHA	Mine Safety and Health Administration

MSW	Municipal Solid Waste
MWTP	Marginal willingness to pay
NAAQS	National ambient air quality standards
NAFTA	North American Free Trade Agreement
NCP	National contingency plan
NEPA	National Environmental Policy Act
NGO	Non governmental agency
NMOG	Non methane organic gas
NOAA	National Oceanic and Atmospheric Administration
NOx	Nitrogen oxides
NPL	National priorities list
NPS	Nonpoint source
NSPS	New-source performance standards
O₃	Ozone
ODP	Ozone Depleting Potential
OECD	Organization for Economic Cooperation and Development
OEM	Office of Environmental Management
OPIC	Overseas private investment corporation
OSHA	Occupational Safety and Health Administration
PCBs	Polychlorinated biphenyls
PES	Payment for environmental services
PM 2.5	Particulate matter smaller than 2.5 micrometers in diameter
PM 10	Particulate matter smaller than 10 micrometers in diameter
POTW	Publicly owned treatment works
PPC	Production possibility curve
PPP	Polluter pays principle
PRP	Potentially responsible party
PS	Point source
PSD	Prevention of significant deterioration
R&D	Research and development
RACT	Reasonably available control technology
RCRA	Resource Conservation and Recovery Act
REACH	Registration, Evaluation, Authorisation and Restriction of Chemicals
RECLAIM	Regional Clean Air Incentive Market (of Southern California)
RFF	Resources for the Future
RIA	Regulatory impact analysis
RM	Recycled materials
RMP	Resources management plan
SCC	Social cost of carbon
SDWA	Safe Drinking Water Act
SIP	State implementation plan
SMSA	Standard metropolitan statistical area
SO₂	Sulfur dioxide
SRF	State Revolving Fund
TBES	Technology-based effluent standard

TDP	Transferable discharge permit
TM	Total materials
TMDL	Total maximum daily load
TOC	Total organic carbon
TRI	Toxics release inventory
TSCA	Toxic Substances Control Act
TSP	Total suspended particulates
TSS	Total suspended solids
UNEP	United Nations Environment Program
USDA	United States Department of Agriculture
VM	Virgin materials
VOCs	Volatile organic compounds
VOM	Volatile organic material
VPP	Victim Pays Principle
VSL	Value of a statistical life
WEEE	Waste from Electrical and Electronic Equipment
WHO	World Health Organization
WIP	Water implementation plan
WLA	Waste load allocation
WPCA	Water Pollution Control Act
WTO	World Trade Organization
WTP	Willingness to pay
ZEV	Zero-emission vehicle

Name Index

Subject Index

Pages number followed by e, f, n, t, indicate exhibits, figures, footnotes, tables respectively.

$$80 + \frac{10}{1+.10} + \frac{10}{1+.10} = \overset{9.09}{\underset{9.09}{}} \quad 98$$

$$50 + \frac{\overset{22.72}{25}}{1.10} + \frac{25}{1.00} \quad 95.44$$

$$60 + \frac{\overset{36.36}{40}}{1.10} + \frac{0}{1.10} \quad 96.36$$